# Dynamics of Organizational Change and Learning

# Dynamics of Organizational Change and Learning

*Edited by*

## Jaap J. Boonstra

*Sioo, Utrecht and University of Amsterdam,*
*Amsterdam, The Netherlands*

John Wiley & Sons, Ltd

*Other Wiley Editorial Offices*

John Wiley & Sons Inc., 111 River Street, Hoboken, NJ 07030, USA

Jossey-Bass, 989 Market Street, San Francisco, CA 94103-1741, USA

Wiley-VCH Verlag GmbH, Boschstr. 12, D-69469 Weinheim, Germany

John Wiley & Sons Australia Ltd, 33 Park Road, Milton, Queensland 4064, Australia

John Wiley & Sons (Asia) Pte Ltd, 2 Clementi Loop #02-01, Jin Xing Distripark, Singapore 129809

John Wiley & Sons Canada Ltd, 22 Worcester Road, Etobicoke, Ontario, Canada M9W 1L1

Wiley also publishes its books in a variety of electronic formats. Some content that appears
in print may not be available in electronic books.

*Library of Congress Cataloging-in-Publication Data*

Dynamics of organizational change and learning / edited by Jaap J. Boonstra.
     p.  cm.—(Wiley handbooks in the psychology of management in organizations)
   Includes bibliographical references and index.
   ISBN 0-471-87737-9 (Cloth : alk. paper)
   1. Organizational change.   2. Organizational learning.   3. Industrial management
I. Boonstra, J. J. (Jaap J.)   II. Series.

  HD58 .8 .D96   2004
  658 .4′06—dc22                        2003025488

*British Library Cataloguing in Publication Data*

A catalogue record for this book is available from the British Library

ISBN 0-471-87737-9

Typeset in 9.5/11.5pt Times by TechBooks, New Delhi, India
Printed and bound in Great Britain by TJ International Ltd, Padstow, Cornwall, UK
This book is printed on acid-free paper responsibly manufactured from sustainable forestry
in which at least two trees are planted for each one used for paper production.

# Contents

# About the Editor

**Jaap J. Boonstra,** *Sioo, Inter-university Centre for Organizational Change and Learning, Admiraal Helfrichlaan 1, 3527 KV Utrecht, The Netherlands*

Jaap Boonstra is a Professor of Organizational Change and Development in the Faculty of Social and Behavioural Sciences at the University of Amsterdam, The Netherlands. He is also Dean and Scientific Director of Sioo, Inter-university Centre for Organizational Change and Learning. Founded by the Dutch universities, Sioo has been the bridge between scientifically founded theory and the practice of organizational and change processes in the Netherlands since 1958. He is also a visiting professor in Esade Business School in Barcelona, Spain. He is a research fellow and member of the scientific staff of The Netherlands School of Communications Research and the Amsterdam School of Social Research.

After studying social and organizational psychology at Leiden University, The Netherlands, he obtained his doctorate with a thesis on integral organizational development and management of complex change processes. Previously, he was Associate Professor in organizational psychology at Leiden University, and has worked as a consultant, researcher, and managing partner at the Research Foundation for New Technology and Organizational Development.

He lectures on the management of change, strategic decision-making, power and politics in organizations, and organizational learning. He has conducted research into the social and organizational aspects of technological innovations, sustainable development and change of organizations, strategic decision-making, and innovation. His research interests focus on barriers to organizational change and innovation, power dynamics in organizational change, sustainable development of organizations, democratic governance, and societal development.

He has published over a hundred articles on technological and organizational innovation, management of organizational change, organizational learning, politics in organizations, strategic decision-making and fundamental change programmes in the service sector, and public administration in the *Academy of Management Review, Concepts and Transformations*, the *European Journal of Work and Organizational Psychology*, and *Applied Psychology: An International Review*. He is a member of the editorial board of several journals. Recently, he published a book on designing and developing organizations, and edited a special issue of the *European Journal of Work and Organizational Psychology* on power dynamics and organizational change.

# About the Contributors

**Chris Argyris,** *Harvard Business School, Organization Behavior Faculty, Soldiers Field, Boston, MA 02163, USA*

Chris Argyris was appointed as the James Bryant Conant Professor of Education and Organizational Behavior at Harvard University, Cambridge, MA. His present focus is on organizational learning, which is the subject of the Academy of Management Executive Award. Chris is the author of 33 books and monographs and over 400 articles. He has been awarded 11 honorary doctorates. The Chris Argyris Chair in Psychology has been established in his honour at Yale University. Other honours include the Academy of Management's Irwin Award, the Kurt Lewin Award, the American Psychological Association's Gold Medal Award for Life Achievement in the Application of Psychology, and several other 'lifetime achievement' awards. He has been elected a Fellow of the Academy of Management, the American Psychological Association, the National Academy of Human Resources, the Canadian School of Management, and the International Academy of Management.

**Ronald Beckett,** *The Reinvention Network, Level 2, 215–219 George St, Liverpool, NSW, Australia*

Ronald Beckett is managing director of The Reinvention Network and is professorial Fellow at the University of Wollongong in Australia, a Fellow of the Australian Institute of Management, and a Fellow of the Institute of Engineers, Australia. His current interest as the Foundation Director of a change agent network is in stimulating growth in small and medium-sized enterprises (SMEs) through learning, innovation, and collaboration. His career in industry spans more than 30 years of engineering research, executive management in the aerospace industry, and change management in communities of SMEs, with an ongoing focus on achieving beneficial business outcomes. He actively supports enhanced university–industry collaboration and is a board member of a number of organizations that encourage such engagement. He has authored or co-authored more than 30 conference papers or journal articles related to organizational learning, knowledge management, innovation management, and successful collaboration.

**Kilian Bennebroek Gravenhorst,** *University of Amsterdam, Faculty of Social and Behavioural Sciences, Department of Communication Science, Kloveniersburgwal 48, 1012 CX Amsterdam, The Netherlands*

Kilian Bennebroek Gravenhorst is an Associate Professor in the Communication and Organization Division of the Department of Communication Science at the University of Amsterdam, The Netherlands. He is also a member of the Netherlands School of Communications Research. His background is in Social Sciences and he studied Psychology at Leiden University. He obtained his doctorate in social sciences at the University of Amsterdam with a thesis on barriers to organizational change, on using survey feedback as an intervention. His fields of interest include change management, communication and organizational change, interventions, influence behaviour of change agents, organization research, and survey feedback. He has written on these topics for *Applied Psychology: An International Review* and the *European Journal of Work and Organizational Psychology*.

**Patricia Bradshaw,** *York University, Schulich School of Business, 4700 Keele Street, Toronto, Ontario, Canada, M3J 1P3*

Patricia Bradshaw is an Associate Professor of Organizational Behaviour at the Schulich School of Business at York University, Toronto, where she is currently Director of the MBA Program and Course Director of a core MBA course, 'Skills for Leadership and Governance'. Her research explores various aspects of power and organizational change through topic areas such as gender and feminist theory, governance, and the dynamics of political processes. Her current research is an exploration of diversity and power on non-profit boards and her consultancy work is primarily with non-profit organizations in the area of governance. She has published articles in the *European Journal of Work and Organizational Psychology*, *Organization Science*, and the *Journal of Applied Behavioral Science*.

**Marc Buelens,** *Vlerick Leuven Gent Management School, Competence Centre People and Organization, Bellevue 6, B-9050 Ghent, Belgium*

Marc Buelens is scientific partner at the Vlerick Leuven Gent Management School and Professor at the University of Ghent. After studying experimental psychology at the Katholieke Universiteit Leuven, he became a staff member of Vlerick's Business School at the University of Ghent. Between 1982 and 1987, he was Head of Training and Organization Development and Personnel Manager at Brasseries Artois, now called Interbrew, Belgium's largest brewery. In 1987, he became managing director and Dean of the Vlerick Leuven Gent Management School. In the course of his career, he has taught managerial and organizational behaviour, behavioural decision-making, and general management and organization at different universities.

**Colin Carnall,** *The University of Warwick, Strategic Management Group, Coventry, CV4 7AL, UK*

Colin Carnall is Professor of Management in the Strategic Management Group at the Warwick Business School at the University of Warwick, UK. He is Associate Dean for the Executive Development Programmes at Warwick. He is interested in strategic change and implementation, executive development programmes, intervention methods, and the design and deployment of integrated delivery systems. He has worked at Bradford Management Centre and held numerous non-executive appointments. He has published widely in the field of Strategic Change, most recently *The Management of Organizational Change* and *The Change Management Toolkit*.

**Stewart Clegg,** *University of Technology Sydney, School of Management, PO Box 123, Broadway, NSW 2007, Australia*

Stewart Clegg is Professor at the University of Technology, Sydney, and the University of Aston Business School, UK. He is also Director of ICAN (Innovative Collaborations, Alliances, and Networks), a key university research centre. He has held posts at the University of St Andrews, Scotland, the University of New England, and the University of Western Sydney, in all of which he was Professor and Head of Department, and at Griffith University, Brisbane, where he was a Reader. He has held visiting professorships at several universities in the UK, France, Denmark, Hong Kong, Brazil, Canada, and the United States. He has written extensively on power and organizations and his most recent books are *Trends in Japanese Management*, co-authored with Toyohiro Kono, and the eight-volume collection on *Central Currents in Organization Theory*. He publishes regularly in journals such as the *Academy of Management Education and Learning*, *Organization Studies*, *Human Relations*, and *Administrative Science Quarterly*.

**Thomas Cummings,** *University of Southern California, Marshall School of Business, Department of Management and Organization, Bridge Hall 306 B, Los Angeles, CA 90089-0808, USA*

Thomas Cummings is Professor and Chair of the Management and Organization Department at the Graduate School of Business Administration, University of Southern California. He is a senior affiliate of the renowned Center for Effective Organizations at USC, a centre in applied knowledge of strategic change, high-involvement organizations, team-based work, and innovative reward systems. During the past 30 years, he has been a senior consultant for numerous companies in managing strategic change. His consultancy work facilitates innovative organizations that emphasize self-managed teams, skill-based pay and gain-sharing, flat hierarchies, employee empowerment, and creative selection methods. He has written over 50 articles and 19 books, including the critically acclaimed *Self-Designing Organizations: Learning How to Create High Performance* and *Organization Development and Change*. He is Associate Editor of the *Journal of Organizational Behavior* and Program Chair and Vice-President-Elect of the Academy of Management.

**Léon de Caluwé,** *Twynstra, Management Consultants, PO Box 907, 3800 AX Amersfoort, The Netherlands*

Léon de Caluwé is Professor at the Vrije Universiteit in Amsterdam and senior partner with the Twynstra Group, management consultants. He works for all types of clients in government and industry. He specializes in change, conflict resolution, quality of cooperation, culture interventions, and organization development. He regularly works with gaming methods as an intervention for advanced learning. His research interests are change theory, intervention methods, and consultancy. He has published more than 80 articles and more than 15 books. In 2003, *Learning to Change: A Guide for Organizational Change Agents* was published in the USA. He has received several professional awards and is a board member of the Management Consultancy Division of the Academy of Management, editor of several scientific journals, and a lecturer in many postgraduate and master's programmes.

**Geert Devos,** *Vlerick Leuven Gent Management School, Competence Centre People and Organization, Bellevue 6, B-9050 Ghent, Belgium*

Geert Devos is Professor at Vlerick Leuven Gent Management School and is affiliated to the University of Ghent and the University of Antwerp. He lectures on organizational change and educational administration. He is a scientific adviser on educational research for the Flemish Ministry of Education. His research interests are educational management and the processes of organizational development and change. His recent publications include texts on assessment of organizational change, readiness to change, school-based self-evaluation, and decentralization in higher education.

**Klaus Doppler,** *Organisationsberatung und Verhaltensstraining Klaus Doppler, Ammergaustrasse 15, 81377 München, Germany*

Klaus Doppler is an independent consultant for organizational change and development. He facilitates organizational strategic change and development, and is involved in mergers and industrial collaborations. He also acts as a trainer for group dynamics and a coach in leadership development for all types of clients in both government and industry. He specializes in long-term change projects and management of change, leadership behaviour, group dynamics, and conflict management. He is a trained psychologist and obtained his doctorate at the University of Salzburg in Austria. He has published articles in *Organizationsentwicklung* and *Group Dynamics* and is a co-author of *Managing Corporate Change* (2000), *Unternehmenswandel gegen Widerstände: Change Management mit den Menschen* (2002), and *Der Change Manager* (2003).

**Merrelyn Emery,** *Fred Emery Institute, 20 Gatty Place Scullin, ACT 2614, Melbourne, Victoria, Australia*

Merrelyn Emery is Associate Professor in the Department of Applied Human Sciences at Concordia University, a 'Visitor' at the Centre for Continuing Education at the Australian National University, and a founding Director of the Fred Emery Institute, Melbourne. She has worked in several fields, including psychology and education research, and since 1970 has, with Fred Emery, helped to develop the theory and practice of Open Systems Theory (OST). She continues that work and teaches intensive workshops around the world on the history and 'state of the art' of OST. She has published several books and many articles. Her best-known books are *Participative Design for Participative Democracy* and *Searching: The Theory and Practice of Making Cultural Change.*

**Cynthia Hardy,** *University of Melbourne, Department of Management, Parkville 3010, Victoria, Australia*

Cynthia Hardy has been Professor of Management at the University of Melbourne since 1998. Her main research interests are the study of power and politics in organizations. Currently, her research focuses on organizational discourse theory and critical discourse analysis, and she is particularly interested in how power and politics in organizations take place within a larger discursive context. She recently published *Discourse Analysis: Investigating Processes of Social Construction* with Nelson Phillips, as well as co-editing a special issue of *Organization Studies* on organizational discourse and the Sage *Handbook of Organization Studies,* which won the 1997 George R. Terry Book Award at the Academy of Management. She has written over 60 journal articles and book chapters, and her work has appeared in many leading international journals, including the *Academy of Management Journal, Organization Studies,* the *Journal of Management Studies,* and *Organization Science.*

**Luc Hoebeke,** *Hoebeke, Staes & Partners, 22A Ruisbroekstraat, B-3360 Bierbeek, Belgium*

Luc Hoebeke is visiting Professor at the Business School of the University of Cape Town in South Africa and director of Hoebeke, Staes & Partners. He serves as a senior consultant to numerous international companies involved in strategic change and development. He is an associate member of the Faculty of Economics at the University of Amsterdam, and an associate member of the Faculty of Philosophy at the University of Leiden. He is also a visiting lecturer at Sioo, the Inter-university Centre for Organizational Change and Learning in The Netherlands. Previously, he was a partner and consultant at the International Institute for Organizational and Social Development. He has published articles in *The Journal of Applied Systems Analysis, Human Systems Management,* and the *Holland Management Review.* In 1994, his book *Making Work Systems Better* was published by Wiley.

**Dian Marie Hosking,** *University of Tilburg, PO Box 90153, 5000 LE Tilburg, The Netherlands*

Dian Marie Hosking is a Professor in the Department of Organizational Studies in the Social Sciences faculty of the University of Tilburg. Previously, she was at the University of Aston Business School, Birmingham, UK. She has been a visiting Professor at the University of St Gallen in Switzerland, President of the European

Association of Work and Organizational Psychology, and Chair of the British Psychological Society's Occupational Section. Her current interests include changing work methodologies, intercultural relations, and distributed organization, distributed leadership, and new information and communication technologies. She has published widely in the area of organizing processes, leadership, and collective conceptions of skill. Her recent journal articles have appeared in the *European Journal of Work and Organizational Psychology* and *Concepts and Transformation*. With Ian Morley, she published a book, *A Social Psychology of Organising: Persons, Processes and Context.*

**Alice Lam**, *Brunel University, School of Business and Management, West London, Uxbridge, UB8 3PH, UK*

Alice Lam is Professor of Human Resources and Organizational Behaviour at the School of Business and Management, Brunel University, UK. Her recent research focuses on the following three areas: organizational learning and innovation; comparative management and organization studies; and work and employment in a knowledge-based society. She is currently leading a research programme on 'Knowledge, Innovation, and Organisational Change' at BRESE, Brunel University. Her recent journal articles have been published in the *Journal of Management Studies*, the *International Social Science Journal*, and *Organization Studies*.

**Morten Levin,** *Department of Industrial Economics and Technology Management, the Norwegian University of Science and Technology (NTNU), N-7491 Trondheim, Norway*

Morten Levin is a Professor in the Department of Industrial Economics and Technology Management, at the Norwegian University of Science and Technology in Trondheim, Norway. Throughout his professional life, he has worked as an action researcher with particular focus on processes and structures of social change related to technology and organization. This action research has taken place in industrial contexts, in local communities, and in university teaching where he has developed and been in charge of PhD programmes in action research. He is the author of a number of books and articles, including *Introduction to Action Research: Social Research for Social Change, Researching Enterprise Development*, and *Change as Practice*. He serves on the editorial boards of *Systems Practice and Action Research, Action Research, The Handbook of Qualitative Inquiry*, and *The Handbook of Action Research*.

**Robert Quinn,** *University of Michigan Business School, 701 Tappan Street, Rm E2546, Ann Arbor, Michigan 48109, USA*

Robert Quinn is the Margaret Elliot Tracy Collegiate Professor of Business Administration, University of Michigan Business School, Michigan, USA. His general research interests focus on management, organization theory, organizational behaviour, and organizational change. His recent publications are *Positive Organizational Scholarship* (with Kim Cameron and Jane Dutton), *Letters to Garrett: Stories of Change, Power, and Possibility* (with Garrett Quinn), and *A Company of Leaders: Five Disciplines for Unleashing the Power in Your Workforce* (with Gretchen Spreitzer). He has published several articles in the *Journal of Applied Behavioral Science*, the *Journal of Human Resource Management*, and other international journals. He is a member of the editorial board of the *Journal of Organizational Behavior* and the *Journal of Management Inquiry*.

**Michael Russell,** *Mercer Delta Consulting, LLC, 1177 Avenue of the Americas, 38th floor, New York, NY 10036, USA*

Michael Russell is an associate at Mercer Delta Consulting, and specializes in organization architecture and the management of large-scale change. He is the editor of *Research Notes*, the firm's monthly internal survey of books and articles in the field. He has taught at the City University of New York and at Touro College.

**Alfons Sauquet**, *Esade Business School, Department of Human Resources Management, Av. Padralbes 60–62, E-08034 Barcelona, Spain*

Alfons Sauquet is Professor of Management at Esade Business School in Barcelona, Spain. Currently, he is Vice-Dean of the business school at this university. He is a member of the EUDOKMA (European Doctorate in Knowledge and Management) network. He has also chaired the Organizational Behaviour Group of the Community of European Schools (CEMS) where he is currently a member of the programme and quality committees. He currently chairs the Learning and Innovation domain of the European Academy for Business in Society (EABiS). His main fields of interest are team learning in relation to conflict and persuasion, the different forms of knowledge in practice and its relationship to degrees of expertise, the organizational and institutional frames for learning, and the learning and transformational dimension of social responsibility.

**Gerhard Smid,** *Sioo, Inter-university Centre for Organizational Change and Learning, Admiraal Helfrich-laan 1, 3527 KV Utrecht, The Netherlands*
Gerhard Smid is Research Director and Programme Manager at Sioo, Inter-university Centre for Organizational Change and Learning. His interests are learning and innovation in professional work and organization, design theory, and practice. His current research is on interdisciplinary collaboration, hybrid roles of professionals, and leadership and management of innovation ventures. He has published articles and books on innovation in trade unionism, in university management, on professionalization and learning, and on the design of learning environments. Some of his recent publications are 'Management consultants: carriers and developers of knowledge?' in *Comportamento Organizacional e Gestão* and 'Consultants' learning within academia' in *Studies in Continuing Education*.

**Roeland in 't Veld,** *NSOB, Netherlands School of Government, Lange Voorhout 46, 2514 EG Den Haag, The Netherlands*
Roeland in 't Veld is a Professor of Public Administration at Utrecht University and Professor in Organizational Science at the University of Amsterdam, The Netherlands. He is Dean of the (Graduate) Netherlands School of Government and serves in advisory positions for several ministers; moreover, he has held positions as an adviser for the World Bank, for the OECD, for the EC, and for the Council of Europe. He is also a member of the High Council and the Research Council of the European University Institute in Florence. He is chairman of the National Council for Spatial and Environmental Research and chairman of the Board of Directors of the Railways infra provider. He has published books on planning theory and on structuring higher education, and recently on theoretical foundations of steering theory.

**Hans Vermaak,** *Twynstra, Management Consultants, PO Box 907, 3800 AX Amersfoort, The Netherlands*
Hans Vermaak, MMC, is a senior partner with the Twynstra Group, management consultants. He has worked as a coach and a consultant for about 15 years. His principal area of consulting concerns change management in professional firms and institutions, including the service industry, the art world, NGOs, and educational institutions. A substantial part of his work takes place in an international context. He trains and coaches change agents and heads a knowledge centre on 'Change Management' for the Twynstra Group. He frequently lectures and publishes on subjects such as change, learning, coaching, and professionalism in Dutch and in English, and has received several publication awards. His publications include *In Search of Corporate Learning*, *The Archipelago of Learning*, and *Comparing Psychotherapists' and Change Agents' Approaches to Change*.

**Elise Walton,** *Mercer Delta Consulting, LLC, 1133 Avenue of the Americas, 43rd floor, New York, NY 10036, USA*
Anna Elise Walton is a Director of Mercer Delta Consulting in New York. As a consultant she specializes in strategy development, governance, change management, executive leadership, and executive teams. She works with international and professional firms on large-scale change efforts, such as identifying strategic opportunities for technology firms, restructuring organizations around strategic opportunities, designing governance systems, and culture integration during international mergers. Together with Nadler and Shaw, she published the book *Discontinuous Change*. With Michael Beer she has published articles on organizational change and development in the *American Psychologist* and the *Annual Review of Psychology*.

**Karl Weick,** *University of Michigan Business School, 701 Tappan Street, Ann Arbor, Michigan 48109, USA*
Karl Weick is Professor of Organizational Behavior and Psychology at the University of Michigan in the United States. He is widely regarded as one of the most influential thinkers of his generation in the field of organizational studies. He holds different professorships at several universities. His research interests focus on the effects of stress on thinking and imagination, the consequences of indeterminacy in social systems, high reliability organizations, management of professionals, and narrative rationality. He was elected a Fellow of the American Psychological Association, of the American Psychological Society, of the Academy of Management, and of the British Academy of Management. He received a lifetime achievement award from the Academy of Management. For his contribution to the field of organizational behaviour, the University of Michigan honoured him with the Rensis Likert Distinguished University Professor Chair in Organizational Behavior and Psychology. He has published seven books and more than 170 journal articles and book

chapters on organizations. His book *The Social Psychology of Organizing* is considered to be a classic in the field.

**André Wierdsma,** *University of Nyenrode, Straatweg 25, 3621 BG Breukelen, The Netherlands*

André Wierdsma is Professor in Organizing and Co-creating, and Programme Director for the Advanced Management Programme at Nyenrode University in the Netherlands. He is a visiting Professor in international executive and MBA programmes at CEIBS in China and SIMI in Denmark. Since 1978, he has been a faculty member at Nyenrode University and one of the founders of the Nyenrode Executive and Management Development Centre (EMDC). He is responsible for the design and execution of a wide variety of in-company learning programmes for international companies. He is the author of *Becoming a Learning Organization: Beyond the Learning Curve*. His latest book on organizational learning offers a perspective on organizing, changing, and learning based on continuous change.

**Gary Yukl,** *State University of New York, School of Business, Management Department, Albany, NY 12222, USA*

Gary Yukl is a Professor of Management at the State University of New York in Albany. His current research and teaching interests include leadership, power and influence, and management development. He has worked as a consultant with a variety of business and public sector organizations, and collaborates with Right Management/Manus Associates in Stamford, Connecticut, to design management development programmes. He is a Fellow of the Academy of Management, of the American Psychological Association, of the Society of Industrial-Organizational Psychology, and of the American Psychological Society. He has written 10 books, including *Leadership in Organizations*. He is also the author of many book chapters, invited reviews, and articles, including contributions to the *Handbook of Industrial-Organizational Psychology,* the *Annual Review of Psychology*, the *Journal of Applied Psychology*, the *Academy of Management Journal*, the *Journal of Social Psychology*, and the *European Journal of Work and Organization Psychology*.

# Series Preface

**Peter Herriot**
*The Empower Group*

The dictionary definition (Random House, 1987) of 'handbook' runs as follows:

- A book of instruction or guidance, as for an occupation; a manual
- A guidebook for travellers
- A reference book in a particular field
- A scholarly book on a particular subject, often consisting of separate essays or articles.

These definitions are placed in the historical order of their appearance in the language. So the earliest use of a handbook was as a set of instructions which members of particular occupations kept to hand, in order to be able to refer to them when they were at a loss as to how to tackle a problem at work. The most recent definition, by way of contrast, refers to a scholarly book consisting of separate essays or articles.

It is the modest ambition of the Wiley Handbooks in the Psychology of Management in Organizations to reverse the course of (linguistic) history! We want to get back to the idea of handbooks as resources to which members of occupations can refer in order to get help in addressing the problems which they face. The occupational members primarily involved here are work and organizational psychologists, human resource managers and professionals, and organizational managers in general. And the problems which they face are those which force themselves with ever greater urgency upon public and private sector organizations alike: issues such as how to manage employees' performance effectively; how to facilitate learning in organizations; how to benefit from a diversity of employees; and how to manage organizational change so that staff are engaged and supported.

Now the claim to provide something useful for professionals, rather than a set of scholarly articles, is a bold one. What is required if such a claim is to be justified? First, practising professionals need a clear theoretical basis from which to analyse the issues they face, and upon which to base their solutions. Practice without underpinning theory is merely applying what has worked in some situations to other ones without knowing why, and hoping that they will work there too. This is blind empiricism.

Theory without practice, on the other hand, is mere indulgence. It is indulgent because theories in applied science can never be properly tested except by application, that is, their attempted use in solving problems in the real world. A handbook in the original sense of the word will therefore contain elements of practice as well as statements of theory. The Wiley Handbooks in the Psychology of Management in Organizations seek to demonstrate by descriptions of case studies, methods of intervention, and instruments of assessment how theory may be applied in practice to address real organizational issues.

It is clear that Work and Organizational Psychology is a core discipline for addressing such issues as those listed above. For they are all issues which depend for their solution upon an understanding of individuals' behaviour at work, and of the likely effects of various organizational interventions upon the stakeholders involved. These latter include employees, customers, shareholders, suppliers, and the wider community (Hodgkinson & Herriot, 2001).

The success criterion for these handbooks, then, is a simple one: will professionals find them useful in their practice? If they also help in the development of apprentice professionals, for example by being used on training courses, then so much the better. The field of Work and Organizational Psychology is currently at risk from a failure to integrate theory and practice (Anderson et al., 2001). Theory and research often seem to practitioners to address issues of interest only to academics; practice appears to academics to lack careful empirical, let alone theoretical, underpinning. These handbooks will help to bridge this divide, and thereby justify the title of 'Handbook'.

What is clear is that if we psychologists fail to impact upon the urgent issues which currently crowd in upon organizations, then those who claim to address them better or faster than us will gain power and influence. This will happen even if the solutions which they provide offer little longer-term benefit to clients. The Wiley Handbooks in the Psychology of Management in Organizations provide a resource to help professionals serve their clients more effectively.

There is no more urgent issue today than the management of organizational change. This fourth handbook in the series, edited by Jaap Boonstra, will prove to be a milestone in the development of theory and practice in this area. Organizational change is so frequent that many of the contributing authors believe that it has become the norm. In other words, rather than change being the transition from one steady state to another, it is in fact the steady state itself!

In such a fluid situation, organizations have recently grasped at a series of structural and cultural changes. Yet considerable research shows that these programmes have very often failed to achieve their desired effects. The contributors to this volume point out that this is largely because the psychological aspects of organizational change have been downplayed relative to its economic and structural features. So how do psychologists recommend that change programmes should be designed? The answer is: it all depends. It depends on the context and purpose of change, but, more important, it depends on the underlying beliefs and values of those seeking to change. At stake are the futures of our organizations: so read on!

## REFERENCES

Anderson, N., Herriot, P. & Hodgkinson, G.P. (2001) The practitioner–researcher divide in Industrial, Work, and Organisational (IWO) Psychology: where are we now, and where do we go from here? *Journal of Occupational and Organisational Psychology*, **74**, 391–411.

Hodgkinson, G.P. & Herriot, P. (2002) The role of psychologists in enhancing organisational effectiveness. In I. Robertson, M. Callinan & D. Bartram (eds) *Organisational Effectiveness: The Role of Psychology*. Chichester: John Wiley & Sons, Ltd.

*The Random House Dictionary of the English Language* (2nd edn) (1987) New York: Random House.

# Preface

Realizing organizational change and innovation is a complex change process, and many organizations do not attain the desired outcomes. The progression of fundamental change is related to the management of the change process and the behaviour of groups and individuals in organizations. The ability to change and of innovation in organizations can be increased by paying dedicated attention to the management of change and the development of learning capacities of organizations and their members.

## AIMS OF THIS HANDBOOK

This handbook focuses on processes, problems, and successes of organizational change. The aim is to relate current knowledge of organizational change and learning and new perspectives from social constructionism and postmodern insights to the understanding of the dynamics of change and the progression of change and innovation in organizations and organizational networks.

Most textbooks on the management of change focus heavily on techniques and procedures for change in a prescriptive way. This relative emphasis on techniques passes over the complex and dynamic social processes which influence people and groups in organizations and ignores the behaviour of change agents in the dynamics in the change processes itself. Other textbooks give descriptions of effective change processes and try to formulate criteria for successful change, or develop a best way to realize change in organizations. These best ways of change, the explanations, and prescriptions, encourage managers to focus on uniformity, control, and planning in changing organizations and the behaviour of its members and this leads to failure rather than success in sustainable change. This handbook holds a critical position regarding the conventional wisdom of planned change.

*Dynamics of Organizational Change and Learning* is concerned with the dynamics of organizational change, the behaviour of individuals, and the social processes in groups and organizations. It offers a critique of the conventional wisdom of planned change. The particular concern of this book is with the dynamics of change, which means that complementary and competing insights are presented in overviews of theory and research. Implications of the theories and research for practice will be outlined, and methods and tools will be described in more detail. The use of theories and methods in specific situations will be discussed, giving helpful insights about choosing them in specific situations and in national and organizational contexts.

## READERSHIP OF THE HANDBOOK

This book is intended to serve as a source of knowledge and inspiration for organizational professionals, change managers, and academics who want to explore current knowledge on the dynamics of organizational change and learning, want to elaborate the theoretical insights in this field, and want to contribute to successful and sustainable change in organizations and organizational networks.

The book will be useful for consultants and applied psychologists in the field of organizational change and learning because it offers a comprehensive and contemporary overview of the field and combines theoretical insights with practical methods and solutions for changing human systems effectively.

For students and academics the book will be interesting because it focuses on the dynamics of change with a multiple perspective on change processes. The presentation of complementary and competing insights on theories of organizational change and learning invites the student to develop a personal and professional viewpoint in the field of organizational change and learning. Researchers and academics will find implications of the theories and ideas for research in practice.

Change managers and organizational professionals will be supported in their work by the description of theoretical insights provided here, and the implications of these theories in professional action. Useful perspectives on the application of intervention methods in specific situations are offered. Overall, the combination of multiple theories, implications for professional action, practical methods, and illustrative practices makes this book unique.

## STRUCTURE OF THE BOOK

This book starts with an overview of and introduction to the field of organizational change and learning. The central ideas are presented in five coherent Parts, each of four chapters. The chapters offer a comprehensive and critical overview of theories and methodologies, and a multiple perspective on processes of change. The book concludes with a reflection on theories, methodologies, and practices.

### INTRODUCTION

The Introduction provides an overall picture of the dynamics of organizational change and learning, and the contemporary challenges that face the discipline of organizational change management. The chapter deals with the question of why many change programmes fail, and what we can do about this. It starts by discussing the insights that can be derived from theories of organizational behaviour, planned change, and organizational development. New approaches to organizational change processes are elaborated. Dynamics in organizing, changing, and learning are looked upon as a source of renewal in the processes of self-organization and organizational sense-making. Descriptions of practice illustrate the theories in use. The chapter concludes with current topics that are relevant to the management of change and learning, and offers methodologies for developing practical and scientific knowledge.

### MANAGEMENT OF CHANGE AND LEARNING: FIVE COHERENT PARTS

In **Part I**, a framework of organizational change and development is presented. In this framework, the history and development of theories on organizational change and development are described, the implications of these theories are discussed, and a critical overview is given of widely used methods and tools.

**Part II** describes the art of designing and organizing processes of change. Here, an overview is given of parameters for the psychological management of change processes. Implications are discussed for initiating a change process and handling uncertainty. Also, the roles of people in changing organizations are analysed. Monitoring and feedback systems are described as part of the management of change.

In **Part III**, strategies and interventions for organizational change are discussed in depth. This means initiating change in an unpredictable world with an increase in complexity and multiplicity in organizational life. Well-known approaches of change management are contrasted with more critical and topical approaches on organizing, changing, and learning. Attention is given to sense-making and management of meaning. New principles, insights, and roles for managers, consultants, and participants in changing are presented.

**Part IV** presents new perspectives on power dynamics and resistance. Resistance and conflicts are seen as powerful forces to enable changes and developments in human systems. This Part highlights power dynamics, influence tactics, and barriers to change. After a critical reflection on the traditional and managerial use of power in managing change, and an analysis of the position of middle management, new experiences are presented to enable the mobilization of energy and creativity for change and to realize the involvement of middle management and employees in far-reaching change.

**Part V** focuses on learning and developing for sustainable change. A theoretical framework is given on individual and organizational learning and the dynamics of learning processes. The implications of these theoretical insights mean a departure from general training programmes and adopting lifetime learning by experience, reflection, and doing. Methods are presented for assessing learning conditions in the processes of change. This Part concludes with a discussion of the optimal level of conflict and discomfort in learning situations and the relationships between individual and organizational learning in dynamic change.

## RELATING THEORETICAL INSIGHTS, IMPLICATIONS, METHODS, AND CRITICAL REFLECTIONS

In every Part, the four chapters offer the existing state of the art on knowledge, methodological implications for approaching organizational change, change strategies and interventions, and a reflective and critical perspective on the issues which are raised in that specific Part:

- The *first chapter* in each Part presents historical and multiple overviews of theories and existing knowledge. In these chapters, results of practices and research are described and attention is given to actual debates in theory and practice.
- The *second chapter* focuses on theories in action, and sets out general implications of existing knowledge for practice. These chapters build methodological ground for the application of strategies and interventions.
- The *third chapter* offers a broad scale of change strategies, methodologies, and interventions. In case descriptions, the use of strategies and interventions are illustrated in practice.
- The *fourth chapter* in each Part is strongly evaluative, indicating which methods are likely to be most useful in which situation, and giving theoretical considerations and practical suggestions on the art of choosing specific interventions and methods. These final chapters are reflective and critical on the issues addressed in this handbook.

## WAYS OF READING, EXPLORING, AND REFLECTING

There are many ways to read this handbook. People interested in the state of the art in the field of organizational change and learning might focus on the first chapters of each Part. These first chapters offer a multiple perspective on existing knowledge and scientific debates. Professionals and practitioners looking for methodologies might pay attention to the second and third chapters, describing strategies and interventions for organizational change and learning. I would invite everyone to read the final chapters of each Part, because they present reflective and critical perspectives on organizational change and learning and question existing knowledge and practice.

By structuring the handbook in this way, the authors have attempted to stimulate a dynamic, useful, and reflective approach to organizational change and learning. We aim to stimulate reflection on our knowledge and practice, and hope to make a real contribution to new ways of viewing, thinking, and acting to realize sustainable changes in human systems.

# Acknowledgements

First, I would like to thank everyone who has helped in realizing this handbook. I am most grateful to all the authors who contributed to this book as they were productive, and willing to adjust their chapters to the other contributions. Together, we produced a coherent book on organizational change and learning, and realized our ambition to publish a book that is comprehensive, interesting, critical, and inspiring. I have had the good fortune to work with some of you in change practices, which was always enjoyable. Without doubt, all of you have inspired me in my thinking, acting, and reflecting as a scientist, and as practitioner by sharing your experiences and ideas.

I am indebted to Peter Herriot for his inspiration and patience; without him the project would never have started. I wish to thank Arienne van Staveren, who helped make this project possible. Without Rosemarie Boers, the project would never have been completed; she handled much of the administrative work associated with the book. My colleagues at the University of Amsterdam have supported me in many small ways. The Inter-university Centre for Organizational Change and Learning (Sioo) has provided continued support for this project over the years, without which I would never have been in a position to realize this book. Kilian Bennebroek Gravenhorst and Renate Werkman were magnificent, both as friends and colleagues. Working together in a small cottage on chapters stimulated me to compile and finish this book. My last acknowledgement is to the readers of this book. I will be pleased if this book helps you in understanding dynamics of change and learning, and stimulates your own professional reflecting and learning.

*Jaap Boonstra*
*Amsterdam*
*November 2003*

# Introduction

## Jaap Boonstra

*Sioo, Utrecht, and University of Amsterdam, Amsterdam, the Netherlands*

More than 70 per cent of the change programmes in organizations either stall prematurely or fail to achieve their intended result. Goals are not achieved, policies are not implemented, customers do not experience improvement in service and quality, and employees, supervisory staff, and middle management are confused by all the change efforts. In the USA, by far the majority of the attempts to redesign business processes turn out to be in vain (Bashein et al., 1994). The development of new strategies also runs aground in 75 per cent of cases (Beer et al., 1990). A study by Pettigrew (1987, 1988) in the UK showed that many change programmes, such as total quality management, business process redesign, and empowerment, are unsuccessful. A study of change processes in the Netherlands showed that more than 70 per cent of the change programmes lead to poor results (Boonstra, 2000).

Far-reaching organizational change programmes, such as strategic renewal, privatization, outsourcing, mergers, redesign of business processes, total quality management, and empowerment affect the patterns of collaboration at work and the relations between actors in and around the organization. People must learn to deal with these changes in their daily work. In many such change processes, social and behavioural scientists and practitioners try to guide the changes (Beer, 1980; Pettigrew et al., 1994).

This chapter asks why many change programmes stall and what we can do about it. The aim of this chapter is to provide an overall picture of the dynamics of organizational change and learning, and the contemporary challenges that face the discipline of organizational change management.

The srtucture of the chapter is as follows. In the beginning, it is argued that many explanations why change programmes fail concentrate too much on organizational and psychological aspects and entities, and pay too little attention to the change process itself. Next, the underlying reasons why change programmes stall are sought in the behaviour of different key players during the change processes and in the assumptions regarding organizational change on which the behaviour of these actors is based. Insights from planned change and organizational development are discussed, and change strategies are elaborated. Then, an alternative is outlined in which the dynamics in organizing and change are looked upon as a source of renewal in the processes of self-organization and organizational sense-making. Finally, attention turns to current topics that are relevant to the management of change and learning, and to methodologies for developing experience and knowledge of these topics.

## WHY ORGANIZATIONAL CHANGE IS DIFFICULT

Many of the explanations given why organizational change programmes fail pay insufficient attention to the complexity of change processes. Five points of view are described in which the stumbling blocks for change are explained as:

- inadequate policy-making and strategic management;
- existing organizational structures;
- power and politics in organizations;

*Dynamics of Organizational Change and Learning.* Edited by J.J. Boonstra.
© 2004 John Wiley & Sons, Ltd. ISBN 0-471-87737-9.

- organizational cultures;
- individual uncertainties and psychological resistance to change.

## POLICY-MAKING AND STRATEGIC MANAGEMENT

The policy-making and strategic management perspective seeks the reason for policy failure in problems with implementation or in lack of sufficient support for the policy measures. An almost classic theme in public administration is the way in which, during the implementation process, policy formulation requirements are merged with the constraints of the administrative organizations; these are often potentially contradictory. Here, it is noteworthy that theories of policy-making pay only limited attention to theories of organizational change and renewal. The content of the policy is often blamed for policy failure, as being inadequately developed, or giving too little direction, or being unfeasible. Organizations responsible for implementing the policy are unable to deal effectively with the policy as it is formulated.

In my opinion, this explanation is too limited. The failure of many policies is due just as much to the nature and organization of the policy-making process itself. According to Yanov (1996), objective information is rarely available during the policy-making process. The assessment of problems and the evaluation of solutions are subjective processes, where the standards and values of the parties involved differ. Furthermore, a problem changes in the course of time because it is related to other issues and changing opinions. For this reason, Hajer (1995) suggests a process approach. This means that the parties concerned reach agreements beforehand about how the decision-making process will be implemented. According to both these authors, a carefully formulated process of policy development generates content and support for change.

Within organizations, the strategy realized often differs significantly from the strategy intended. Mintzberg (1988) ascribes this to technical and political factors and the adjustment of the strategic policy by those implementing it. Beer et al. (1990) ascribe the failure to realize strategic policy to conflicting strategic priorities, ineffective top management, poor vertical communication, and insufficient interdisciplinary cooperation. They suggest a departure from the traditional command-and-control managerial style and propose that all members of the organization be involved in reaching decisions and coordinating activities. These positions point to the structural perspective of why organizational change is a difficult process.

## ORGANIZATIONAL STRUCTURES AND THE DIVISION OF LABOUR

The structural perspective suggests that existing technologies and the division of labour are the main reasons for the difficulties in bringing about organizational change. The classic hierarchical organization with a high degree of task specialization leads to a fragmentary view of the various functions within the organization and prevents a common perspective on why change is needed. This results in resorting to *ad hoc* solutions using tried and tested measures. In the past, many organizations have been successful in improving efficiency through task specialization and control of the labour process, which makes it difficult for them to operate under other organizing principles (Mintzberg, 1979). Organizational renewal provides a new perspective on organizing, but this new logic on organizing cannot be understood on the basis of the dominant logic. As a result, the change process founders because of incomprehension and fixed routines in technology and human behaviour.

Making the break from task specialization through redesign is offered as the source of solutions to the problems found in how organizations operate and introduce change. Examples are business process redesign and the sociotechnical design of work processes. To redesign successfully, considerable attention has been given in recent years to optimizing the design process, the steps required to do this, the role of the expert, and the leadership qualities of management. The perspective of power and discipline in organizations is linked to the structural perspective on the obstacles to change when the hierarchy and the division of labour are seen as mechanisms that produce power (Braverman, 1974), or when the division of labour is regarded as an outcome of power processes (Hardy & Clegg, 1996).

## POWER, POLITICS, AND DISCIPLINE

The perspective of power, politics, and discipline attributes the difficulty in realizing organizational change to the existing power relationships and the agencies, powers, and networks that want to maintain these relationships (Mintzberg, 1983). Different interest groups then concentrate on the preservation of their own interests, goals, and positions. Change casts doubt on stability and the institutionalization of power in structures, rules, relations, ideologies, and processes of meaning (Hardy & Clegg, 1996). Stability stems from the interests with previously made decisions concerning the strategy, the organization, and the balance of power. The existing task procedures and balance of power are assumed to be the reality. In addition, those who already possess power have the possibility of extending their power by supporting certain actions, appointing managerial and executive staff, and accumulating contacts which can be used in the future to gain more power and to influence the decision-making process (Greiner & Schein, 1988).

From this point of view, some propose the use of power by management and consultants in order to break through paralysing power structures. They look upon power as a system of authority, ideology, and expertise. I question this concept because such actions often lead to a struggle for power and divert energy from the change process. In the power perspective on change, a manager often tries to force the desired changes and secure their implementation. From their position at the top of the organization, managers present content-related solutions, adjust organizational structures, and guide the change process. The progress of the change process is controlled and adjusted using monitoring systems. This approach can lead to willingness to change if the members of the organization are convinced that the change is necessary and if they know nothing about alternative strategies for change. However, the exercise of power often stirs up opposition and leads to increasing resistance and problems in realizing the changes.

## ORGANIZATIONAL CULTURES

The cultural perspective attributes resistance to change to the prevailing standards and values within the organization. These limit the ability of people to choose between alternative behaviours and hence the ability of members of the organization to change (Schein, 1992; Cummings & Worley, 2001). This point of view is in agreement with the assumption that ideas, shared values, and perspectives of reality form the basis of organizations. Social relationships have their own structures and cultures, based on the rules, habits, institutions, consultation styles, language, communication, use of symbols, and definitions of reality that groups use as starting points for mutual interaction. In this perspective, managers have particular difficulty in changing their standards and values because they have come to see their own way of behaving as appropriate. Managers then act as the guardians of the organization (Schein, 1992).

Solutions to effect changes are sought in broad cultural programmes and training programmes for managers. The focus of such programmes is to discuss and provide insights into the existing standards and values, after which new behaviour patterns can be learned through training. The underlying idea is that the culture of an organization can be deliberately and systematically changed and that by changing cultural values and the perspectives of reality, the behaviour of people in the organization can also be indirectly affected. From the cultural perspective, the aim is often to actively involve individuals in the change process. Several forms of intervention have been proposed in recent years for this purpose, such as game simulations (de Caluwé & Vermaak, 2003), large-scale interventions (Bunker & Alban, 1997), and broad system interventions and conference methods (Weisbord, 1992; Jacobs, 1994). I distrust such interventions when they are used by people in power and their consultants to implement preconceived goals. Conferences and game simulations then become nothing but a way to ease in planned change.

## UNCERTAINTY AND RESISTANCE TO CHANGE

The individual psychological perspective attributes the problems encountered in change processes primarily to people's desire for certainty and stability (Heller, 2003). This point of view emphasizes fear of the unknown, a lack of confidence in other people, and the individual need for safety and stability. Changes in work procedures can lead to loss of identity, decreased work satisfaction, and uncertainty as to whether the new task can be carried out. The lack of a personal grasp of the events and negative experiences with previous changes can also lead to an attitude of indifference by those involved. Resistance to change by individuals and small groups has also been explained on the basis of theories of social categorization (Tajfel, 1982). Particularly in times of uncertainty, groups form and stereotyping occurs which quickly gives rise to misunderstanding and distrust between groups. This does not make the change process any easier.

Solutions to the difficulties encountered during change are looked for in methods for diagnosing and dealing with resistance. In order to make change processes acceptable, interventions have been developed at individual and group levels and more recently also at the organizational level (Bunker & Alban, 1997; French & Bell, 1998; Cummings & Worley, 2001). These interventions are intended to reduce uncertainty through teaching, by providing good communication about the change, and by involving people in the change. At the group level, the emphasis is on negotiating, conflict management, and counselling on how to work as a team (Mastenbroek, 2000). This point of view emphasizes more attention for interventions during the process in order to realize changes. I question the value of many of these interventions because they carry with them the inherent danger of manipulation and rarely contribute to lasting changes.

## PROCESSES OF ORGANIZATIONAL CHANGE

The perspectives described thus far use existing policy processes and organizational processes as starting points. Obstacles to change are sought in the nature of the policy-making process, the characteristics of the organization, the power processes, the organizational culture, or the resistance of groups and individuals. These perspectives can overlap and reinforce each other. In this way, a high degree of division of labour often leads to cultural differences between departments, attempts to hold on to positions, and tension between management and staff. This makes individuals uncertain, especially if the problems are not clearly defined and open to different interpretations.

It is noteworthy that many managers and consultants forget to look at themselves and their own behaviour when searching for the reasons for obstacles to organizational change. They often assume that the reason lies in the organizational context and approach the problems of change from an entity perspective. My perspective is that problems with change should be sought more in how the change process is approached than in the existing organizational context. This is a good reason for taking a deeper look at the management of the change process and examining the psychological management of change.

## THE MANAGEMENT OF CHANGE

From the management perspective, change is a process of guidance and adjustment aimed at achieving the goals for change. This perspective is linked to insights and theories on planned change and organizational development. The key to this approach is that businesses try to anticipate and take advantage of developments in their surroundings.

## PLANNED CHANGE

Planned change is seen as a conscious and deliberate effort to adapt and improve the operations of a human system through the utilization of scientific knowledge. It concerns how change is created, implemented, evaluated, and maintained (Bennis et al., 1979). In order to achieve adaptations and improvements, managers and consultants take a rational approach: they analyse the surroundings, formulate goals, develop a strategy, and then implement the change. This approach is based on the assumption that the organization is in a state of stable equilibrium and that the relationship between the organization and its surroundings must be kept in balance. If the surroundings change, then the organization must move from equilibrium state A to a new equilibrium state B in which the organization will again be able to fulfil the requirements of its surroundings. The change process can be planned and controlled by means of feedback mechanisms and interventions.

---

### CASE STUDY: PLANNED CHANGE IN THE INTRODUCTION OF THE EURO

All organizations in the 12 euro countries had to adapt their financial and information systems, and to be cash-compatible with the introduction of euro banknotes and coins. The problem was well known, as well as the solutions. Because many companies faced the same problem, the approach could be routine work and seen as a compliance-based exercise.

An international biscuit firm started the adaptive change project in 2000 for conversion to the euro. The firm is a major player in Western Europe and has several brands of biscuits and snacks in Holland, Belgium, the UK, France, Germany, Spain, and Portugal, with 16 production sites across Europe. With 9000 employees, its manufacturing capacity is 1.1 million tonnes of biscuit and snack products. The customers of the biscuit firm are mainly large wholesale and retail chains, mostly small and medium-sized enterprises. As this is mainly a business-to-business relationship, there are significant implications for the euro conversion project, such as the need for dual currency.

The company's overall euro project was directed by a steering group which focused on milestones, strategy, and progress. The steering group consisted of the Finance Director, the Marketing and Sales Director, an executive from the Information Systems Department, and an external senior consultant with experience in the adaptation of financial and information systems to the euro. The consultant worked for an international firm offering accountancy and consultancy services. This consultancy firm had developed a standardized programme for euro conversion with strictly described steps, procedures, and milestones. The steering group and the lower board accepted the recommendations of the external consultant to proceed with detailed planning and implementation of a project with the aim of switching over all systems and processes involved by September 2001 at the latest. All companies had to be cash-compatible by January 2002. The information systems were largely AS400-based and most European applications were run centrally from headquarters. The consultancy firm offered a technical conversion programme to convert the accounting and to deal with dual currency. The programme was supported by a project team of eight. The project leader had a very good record in technological change and accountancy and was assisted by four external consultants and three people from the Financial, IT, and Marketing and Sales Departments. The euro project team was primarily supported by work teams and national champions, creating a core team of some 120 people. National champions were responsible for the local planning and delivery of their own euro plans at the local board level. At the national level, support was provided by external consultants from the consultancy firm.

The project team produced detailed plans at the central and local levels. The first step was to analyse existing processes and systems and to test process changes. The second step focused on the development and implementation of plans to reach a point where all processes, accounting, internal trading, and reporting were carried out in euros. The third step was to give support to the operating units with a helpdesk through which the company could resolve queries on an as-needed basis. The fourth step was to be ready to adopt customer practices and prepare for a possible demand from customers and suppliers. It was also seen as important to manage customer expectations and processes, regarding the use of one currency for agreeing prices and using on invoices.

Nationally, more detailed plans were produced and all milestones were logged. The consultancy firm provided a set of one-off utility programmes to handle conversion to the euro.

The biscuit firm was adequately prepared for the conversion of national currencies to the euro. One critical success factor was sufficient resources, such as the budget, and the specialists in information systems and accountancy, computers, and technical systems. Other success factors were strict planning, commitment from the board for the plan and use of resources, establishment of a dedicated project structure with project champions, and external adviser support available on all levels.

Planned change is a relatively programmatic approach. This approach requires the ability to predict and control developments. To be able to predict developments, an eye must be kept on relationships between causes and effects over a long period of time. The desire to predict and reduce uncertainties accompanies an effort to gain control.

Planned change came about in a period when two idea systems in science opposed each other: the law of non-intervention, based on the doctrine of *laissez-faire*, and the law of radical intervention, with emphasis on conflict and class struggle (Burrell, 1996). This debate between no change and radical change also involved the methods employed in controlling and directing the forces of change. An important objective of planned change in this early period was to develop a method that used social technology self-consciously and experimentally to help solve the problems of people and societies. Another aim was to bridge the gap between a substantial body of theory of social action and a rich body of practice of social change in human systems, as well as to integrate the principles of theory and practice. The point was to develop new knowledge regarding changes in human systems and to test this in practice. The first publications had a broad orientation and covered a great range of topics, such as the use of scientific knowledge, the role of experts, change strategies, collaboration and conflict, change methodology and interventions, resistance to change, and ethical dilemmas of the change agent (Bennis et al., 1979). In the course of time, the approach was directed more and more at the development of an expert-driven methodology where change agents initiate and guide changes with the aid of social theories and behavioural knowledge.

In planned change, the changes are initiated, guided, and controlled by top management (Boonstra, 1997). Experts play an important role in problem analysis and in the guidance and implementation of changes. Steering groups and project teams support and execute the change project. The approach is solution-oriented and decision-making is mostly highly structured and formalized and greatly influenced by top management. Decisions are made based largely on economic and technical arguments. The method of change is based on formal models in order to reduce the complexity of the organization. Generally valid rules and uniform work procedures are adhered to. The change process usually has a linear structure with a clear beginning and end and with strict standards and planning. The approach often begins by setting abstract goals, and attention is given particularly to the desired output from the organization, the formal transformation process, and the information process coupled to it. Little attention is given to increasing the learning capacity within the organization. It is difficult to enlist the participation of the people in the organization because existing work procedures are consciously pushed aside. Powerful, coercive, and expert strategies are generally followed in planned change (Boonstra & Bennebroek Gravenhorst, 1998).

Examples of standard approaches to planned change are Business Process Redesign, Management by Objectives, Total Quality Management, Lean Production, ISO Certification, Team-based Organizations, Time-based Competition, Benchmarking, and the Balanced Scorecard. Many of these standard approaches ignore cultural aspects of change and invite resistance. Mostly, these programmes do not contribute to the performance of the organization or of the people working in the organization.

Planned change may be useful in stable and predictable situations where the problems are unambiguous. It is then a question of incremental and first-order change, in which familiar problems are solved in an existing context. Improvements are often logical adjustments to normal operations. First-order changes focus on the improvement of the added value in operations. In the context of behavioural science, this often means increased attention to human needs and values as well. Improvements can be realized through technical solutions and changes in the structure. The consultant plays the role of the expert who applies his or her knowledge in a goal-oriented way to bring about improvements. This is a useful approach in the case of readily definable problems that are not too complex and do not involve too many people. However, many changes do not satisfy these conditions. If planned change is, nevertheless, chosen in the case of complex problems in structure and culture, for example, then it is understandable that managers and consultants attribute the obstacles to change to rigid structures and cultures and to political behaviour. These are precisely the aspects that they have ignored in their approach.

I find it intriguing that planned change is the approach chosen in the majority of businesses, even though research and practice have shown that such an approach has problems in more than three-quarters of all cases (Boonstra, 1997, 2000). There must be thousands of plans lying in desk drawers that have never been implemented, or have had no effect on the real key processes in the organization. Planned change often leads to a cascade of change projects that tumble over each other because the previous changes have had too little effect, and starting a new project seemed the only thing to do. The result is confusion and uncertainty among the parties involved, lack of clarity as to the course of the organization, and decreased motivation. And if people in the organization, who are not involved with customers or their own work, then concentrate on carrying out the primary process and therefore block any change, they are accused of being resistant to change and are bombarded with implementation programmes. In this context, it is not surprising that some consultancy firms have come to see implementation as their profession. What they actually do is preserve the distinction between problems, solutions, and the activities of those involved.

## ORGANIZATIONAL DEVELOPMENT

Various authors have proposed a developmental approach in situations where the problems are vague, where there are several perspectives on the problems and solutions, and where the direction of change is not yet completely clear (Boonstra, 2000; Cummings & Worley, 2001). Organizational development is defined as a systematic process for applying behavioural science principles and practices in organizations to increase individual and organizational effectiveness (French & Bell, 1998: 1). In their view, the change process is initiated and supported by top management. They see an important role for consultants who support the change process by applying theories and methods from social and behavioural science. In Chapter 1 of this volume, Cummings states that organizational development applies behavioural-science knowledge and practices to help organizations change themselves to achieve greater effectiveness. It seeks to improve how organizations relate to their external environments and function internally to attain high performance and quality of work life.

Organizational development has emerged principally from the theory and practice of behavioural science, especially in the fields of social psychology and group dynamics, and work and organizational psychology. An important influence was the Research Center for Group Dynamics in the USA. This centre conducted research on group dynamics and change processes and applied behavioural science to the development of group training programmes in which participants learn from their own interactions with the evolving dynamics. It developed interventions at the interpersonal, group, and intergroup levels, such as team building, conflict handling, leadership, and survey feedback (Beer & Walton, 1987). Survey feedback is a kind of action research, and consists of data gathering from the client group, data feedback to the client group, data exploration and action planning by the client group, and actions to realize improvements. The development of theory and practice is stimulated by practitioners working in organizations following the principles and methodology of organizational development.

---

### CASE STUDY: ORGANIZATIONAL DEVELOPMENT AND TRANSITION IN FINANCIAL SERVICES

A newly appointed Chief Executive Officer of a national division of an international re-insurance company is uncertain about the future of his business. The organization is performing very well, is the market leader in re-insurance, and has a very good reputation for service and product innovation. Almost all the insurance companies in the national market are business partners of this re-insurance company. The company provides a full service concept, consisting of re-insurance, administration, medical assessments, product innovation, risk management, and investment banking and has a staff of 140.

Although his organization is performing very well, the CEO feels that it is not well prepared for the future. His own observations during the first months of his appointment indicate that management is not well developed, business processes are inefficient, and the organizational culture is patriarchal. He starts a process for organizational development with the help of an external consultant and members of his organization. He wants to improve his organization in a change process while it is still performing very well, and wants to make the transition to an innovative, flexible, and profitable organization based on self-managed teams and highly motivated people.

To support and coordinate the change process, a task force of seven is established, consisting of managers and employees. The task force is facilitated by an external adviser and reports directly to the board of directors.

The change process starts by studying documents and undertaking interviews to understand the history and market position of the organization, to get a feel for earlier processes of change and innovation, and to get an idea of the relationships between business strategy, management, business processes, the organizational culture, technological systems, and human resource management. After the orientation phase, a collaborative diagnosis takes place in which the management team, line managers, and all employees examine the situation of their organization. The diagnosis shows that problems are related to an unclear strategic mission, an inflexible structure and information systems, fragmented business processes, a limited degree of entrepreneurship in management, and lagging human resources management. Performance is still very good, thanks to the motivation of employees, a client-oriented culture, strong internal collaboration, and a huge level of experience and knowledge in the organization.

For each of the observed and shared problems, a general direction for improvement is worked out. Exploring new directions and solutions starts with a conference attended by almost all members of the organization. Subsequently, so-called theme groups are formed to discuss the proposed solutions. Among other things, this leads to profound change in the business processes, the technological systems, and the structure of the organization. The new organization is based on teamwork for specific business partners. During the change process, which took less than a year, the development of management and leadership was incorporated into the process, and a new strategy for human resources was developed. The performance of the organization thus became even stronger in respect to customer satisfaction, work satisfaction, and financial results.

Critical success factors in this change process were: understanding that customers and clients set higher standards for products and services; understanding that managers act as supporters and agents of the necessary changes; giving attention to changes in the style of management through specific support and training; ensuring participation of all organizational members in the change process; providing open communication to exchange ideas and information; openly consulting on solutions and alternatives; cooperating in the development of solutions; and providing feedback of information and achievements to further learning.

In general, a process of organizational development starts with an analysis by all parties concerned of problems and possible solutions. The changes are realized gradually, and the members of the organization are involved in all phases of the change process. Experts provide support by contributing their experience of change processes and by facilitating the change process. The procedures and methods are highly dependent on the course of the change process. A coordinating and guiding framework and guidance of the process by managers and process experts are often necessary to accomplish the changes.

The approach of organizational development is reasonably effective if the problem is to realize improvements within an existing context or if there are non-routine problems which require custom-made solutions. Attention is given to changes in structure, culture, and individual behaviour. The role of the change agent is that of a facilitator who, in the course of the change process, regularly tries to find solutions to the identified problems, together with the parties concerned, and who guides the implementation of the changes. These are frequently fundamental or second-order changes. Following a second-order change, the new state of affairs can have an entirely different nature from the old state of affairs. There is a transition to a known new state over a period of time. Second-order changes focus on renewal and innovation. Once the organization's leaders and change agents have assessed the existing needs and opportunities, they develop a more desirable future state. To achieve this new state, the old way of working must be set aside and the organization must pass through a period of transition when it is not yet out of the old and not yet fully in the new. During the course of the change process, the aspects that inhibit this transition are examined, and the change agents and consultants try to eliminate these obstacles by means of interventions. Often, the transition phase is managed by two parallel structures, one that oversees the ongoing operations and one that manages the changes. Over the years, a large number of intervention techniques have been developed from the behavioural sciences that may be used in organizational development. Methods have been developed for individual guidance and training, team development, conflict management, collaboration, changes in structure and culture, strategic change, problem-solving in organizational networks, search conferences to create new futures, and innovation.

Organizational development is also based to a great extent on the basic principles of planned change. In many cases, a phased structure is introduced and interventions are carried out in order to facilitate the change process. Because the course of a change process is often capricious and unpredictable, it is necessary to monitor the course of the process carefully and to intervene when necessary. Many practitioners base their work more or less implicitly on such a perspective on change, and formulate prerequisites for successful change on the basis of their experience. Although the developmental approach is indisputably effective in the realization of changes, there is a danger that the combination of a developmental approach with the provision of a framework for change may lead to a paternalistic approach that carries within it the danger of manipulation. The consultant then becomes a social engineer who directs the change process and seduces people to take part in the process.

## PLANNED CHANGE, ORGANIZATIONAL DEVELOPMENT, AND INTERACTIVE LEARNING

Many change processes in organizations encounter difficulties. The reasons for this are usually sought in the nature of the strategy, the structure of the organization, the balance of power, individual psychological factors, and the culture of the organization. It is noteworthy that the obstacles to change are usually sought in the existing organization, and that the problems connected with the change techniques themselves are seldom considered. In my opinion, it is precisely the approach to the change process that determines the success or failure of the changes (Boonstra & Vink, 1996). This means that a closer examination of the psychological management of change is highly appropriate.

Planned change may be suitable if one is faced with technical and instrumental aspects in which the problems and solutions are known. These are *first-order* improvements. Social and behavioural scientists try to achieve results with the aid of standard techniques. Using this procedure, it is understandable that the reasons for resistance to change are sought in the obstinacy of structure and culture, unclear strategies, or other aspects that are ignored in the change project.

When the changes to be made are far-reaching, the problems are not entirely unambiguous but still recognizable, and there is some idea as to the direction in which the solutions must be sought, then organizational development is a more successful approach than planned change. In organizational development, suitable solutions for shared problems are generally looked for, involving the members of the organization. In this process, the organization undergoes a transition from a stable situation A to a stable situation B. These are *second-order* changes in which the organization responds to the demands made by the environment. From this point of view, it is understandable that the problems encountered during change are connected with complexity and turbulence in the organization and its surroundings. Changes in the environment lead to instability and provide the motive to create a new equilibrium situation between the organization and the environment. To the extent that there is more turbulence and complexity in the environment, it becomes more difficult to maintain this equilibrium and the realization of change becomes problematic.

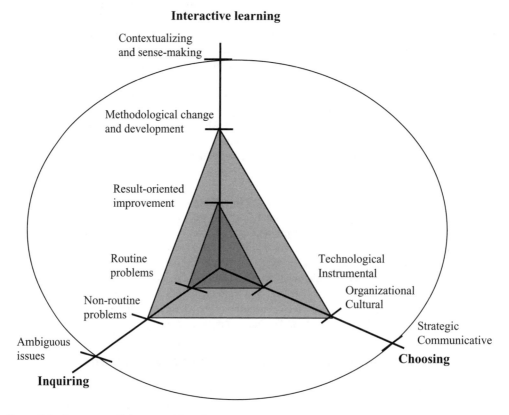

**FIGURE 0.1**  Processes of change and learning

   This argument is presented schematically in Figure 0.1. When the problems are known and the solutions are technical or instrumental, the most suitable approach is one of results-oriented implementation, indicated by the dark triangle. These are improvements within an existing context. Viewed from this triangle, the obstacles to improvement are sought mainly in the context outside of the triangle: the obstinacy of the structure and culture, unclear strategies, and inadequate methods for change. In the search for structural and cultural solutions, it is usually a question of tailor-made answers to known and definable problems and the choice often falls on methodical change. Now there is a great deal of knowledge about such changes, originating in the theory and practice of organizational development. These changes are represented in Figure 0.1 by the lighter triangle.

   It now becomes relevant to ask what it means for our looking, thinking, and acting when we have to deal with ambiguous questions and poorly defined problems, where situations are unstable, and interaction patterns are unpredictable. These are no longer improvement projects or change processes in organizations, but renewal processes involving actors from various organizations. These are *third-order* or transformational changes.

   Transformational change is the emergence of a totally new state of being out of the remains of the old state (Ackerman, 1986). New forms of organization arise because renewal processes are started on the way to an unknown future. Such third-order changes focus on value systems at the organizational and individual level. In my opinion, these are strategic communicative solutions in which the actors interact with one another, reconstruct the organizational principles, create new contexts, envision the future, and create a collective desire for change and learning. In Figure 0.1 this is represented by a circle. This perspective on change and renewal is based on the dynamic systems theory and social constructionism, and is supported by theories on organizational learning. This approach is discussed in general terms in the following section.

## PLAYING WITH DYNAMICS AND UNCERTAINTY

Both planned change and organizational development take the perspective of equilibrium and guidance as they move from a stable initial situation to a stable final situation. These are change processes in which an organization is first unfrozen, then changed, only to be refrozen again in the new situation. It can be questioned whether a striving for equilibrium and guidance is sufficient in a situation in which the environment is less predictable and the phenomena are entirely new.

   Organizations increasingly have to deal with complexity and dynamics in the processes of production, innovation, and creation. As a result of globalization and the developments in communications technology, the boundaries between organizations and their surroundings are becoming more flexible. There is an increasing amount of network organization and collaboration in logistic chains. In many business sectors, expansion is reaching the multinational level. This expansion is often accompanied by the need for decentralization and self-management at the local level. The distribution channels between businesses and customers are being changed by data networks and new means of communication. These developments lead to complex patterns of interaction between actors. Our Western society is evolving into a knowledge society; there is an increase in both knowledge and the exchange of knowledge. Knowledge is becoming more multidisciplinary, which adds to its complexity. The acquisition, development, and application of this knowledge bring about innovation and offer organizations possibilities for new products and services. Government organizations are faced with the question of how the knowledge of multiple actors can best be used in the development of policies. The increased interdependence between public and private organizations is blurring the boundaries between the marketplace and government, and leading to hybrid organizations that operate in a state of tension between the public and private sectors. International boundaries between states are also being blurred by international cooperation and regulation, and because social problems are manifesting themselves at the global level. The problems in these dynamic worlds of management and organization are becoming increasingly unstructured and ambiguous areas in which a great diversity of actors interact with each other and create new realities. As long ago as the 1960s, Emery and Trist characterized the dynamic environment as a 'turbulent field' (Emery & Trist, 1965). They believe that the dynamics are caused by interaction between actors in an environment that is constantly in motion. It is an environment in which the consequences of one's own actions are uncertain. According to Emery and Trist, the uncertainty that this creates can only be overcome if actors interact with each other, look for solid footing in collaboration, and define standards and values together.

## Organizational Dynamics

Since the observations of Emery and Trist, organizational systems theory has developed further into a dynamic systems theory, due to inputs from chaos theory and complexity theory, among others (Hoebeke, 1994; Checkland & Howell, 1998; Vennix, 1999; Stacey, 2003). Dynamic systems theory assumes that organization takes place in complex dynamic systems in which actors constantly interact with one another and give meaning to the events around them. Thus, they create a social construction of reality. Causal relationships between specific actions and their effects become blurred by the complexity of the interactions between actors both inside and outside the organization. In these interactions, the boundaries between organizations and their surroundings become less distinct. The system produces and creates its environment, but the opposite is just as true. The organization and the surroundings are complementary; they define each other. The unit of renewal is no longer the organization but consists of organizational networks in their surroundings. Various networks and actors interact with one another and thus form dynamic systems at the local, national, and global levels. These interactions can reinforce or weaken each other. Changes unfold in circular patterns of interaction between these complex systems of people, organizational networks, and environments (Checkland & Scholtes, 1995).

Organizations are always situated between equilibrium and disequilibrium. Unstable situations lead to creativity which gives shape to innovations. Movement develops in an open-ended evolutionary space without any known objectives. Because the direction and goal cannot be predicted, room is created for unforeseen processes, creativity, and new forms of organization. This may lead to uncertainty, disagreements, and conflict but it is precisely these contrasting points of view that contribute to creativity and renewal. Dynamic systems have the ability to take on new forms in response to changes. These forms are not prescribed by the surroundings but develop in the interactions between people in the organization and the surroundings. The actors are spontaneously active, organize themselves, and create new interactions in which renewal can flourish. In this concept, chaos and order are not opposites but parallel each other. Self-organization develops when stability and instability merge. Instability always leads ultimately to a stable situation if the actors have insight into the dynamics of the system and can intervene in the processes of interaction. This stability gives rest, but is nevertheless temporary because new developments and interaction patterns cannot be predicted and the complexity again increases. It is a bounded instability: periods of stability alternate with periods of instability.

The dynamics of organizational networks increases and makes room for renewal if the following occurs:

- Many actors with different points of view interact.
- There is a high degree of interaction between the actors and the differences are visible.
- Information and feedback circulate rapidly in the system.
- Feelings and assumptions regarding renewal can be discussed.
- There is an atmosphere of safety in which to express and manage uncertainties.
- Room is created for processes of self-organization.

Managers and the supervisors of change processes can start up a dynamic process by creating the conditions in which the actors can give their own interpretations to the points requiring attention shown above.

## SENSE-MAKING

From the perspective of dynamic systems theory, the renewal of organizations is linked to interactions and the exchange of viewpoints on organizing. According to Weick (1979, 1995), these interactions take place on the basis of the meanings that individuals give to social situations and the way in which they talk about them. The role of sense-making in social processes is one of the key themes in social constructionism. This perspective has received important input from social psychology (Weick, 1979, 1995; Gergen, 1982, 1999; Hosking & Morley, 1991; Bouwen, 1995). It suggests that people construct their own reality on the basis of what they experience. This subjective reality helps people to understand, explain, and predict what is going on. Sense-making is seen as a process involving the creation and reproduction of shared meanings (Weick, 1979). In this process, shared meanings that were formed previously may be destroyed and alternative or new meanings are created. New meanings can be achieved by exchanging points of view, reflecting critically on them, thoughtfully evaluating various viewpoints and the assumptions behind them, opening a dialogue to discover new perspectives, and acting to create new possibilities. It is assumed that, by means of dialogue, consensus can be reached about present states and desirable states in the future. The significance of dialogue in effecting change in social systems is attested to by Schein (1993). Genuine dialogue offers the possibility of the exchange of ideas and cross-influencing each other's attitudes and opinions. Dialogue presupposes multiple-voiced communication. Such a process allows the development of both a shared set of standards and values and a shared language to understand events that occur in the process of transformation. Understanding each other's points of view, interests, and convictions is a prerequisite for developing a common image of a desirable future.

The importance of communication is stressed by Hosking (1999). She advocates a relational approach, which allows social processes to be constructed in joint acts, and voices to be intermingled in communicative processes. Relational processes are seen as inherently political; there is always room for multiple voices and points of view. The expression of multiple voices improves knowledge, enriches perspectives, and stimulates development.

According to the theories of sense-making and social constructionism, the interaction between the actors takes place in the context of the constructs that were produced by earlier interactions. The production of constructs is made possible by what was produced earlier, but is at the same time limited by it. The common meanings or social constructs form a reality and cultural practice constructed by the actors which incorporate the common experiences that direct the course of action. The possibilities and boundaries of this manufactured context are not fixed. The multiple and pluralistic character of this makes it possible to exchange, discuss, and adjust the underlying meanings, and initiate processes of renewal in this way.

## INTERACTIVE LEARNING

The combination of dynamic systems theory and social constructionism brings us to the concept of *interactive learning*. In ambiguous situations, people become confused because these situations are difficult to understand, due to the unpredictability of interactions and feedback processes, and the multiple meanings and multiple voices of actors. This implies that meanings should be constructed socially in direct interaction with others, in dialogue that makes room for multiple voices.

## CASE STUDY: TRANSFORMATION AND INTERACTIVE LEARNING IN NEIGHBOURHOODS

A joint forum of 24 community associations in the city of Amsterdam was struggling with the question: 'What is the meaning and what is the usefulness of the community associations in the new century in relation to the city of Amsterdam and to their neighbourhood?' This ambiguous issue was grounded in the decentralization of governance and administration of the city into district councils.

The city councils were set up after World War II, when there was a housing backlog to be cleared away and the infrastructure had to be re-planned and re-built. The city council was centralized, driven by the need for political and economic reconstruction. To stimulate the reconstruction of the city, the city council formed and financed local community associations in the neighbourhoods. These community associations consisted of voluntary workers who had a close relationship with the citizens in the neighbourhood and participative decision-making in the community centre was an important basis for the realization of numerous activities. After the reconstruction and the programme of urban renewal, the municipal services increasingly worked with the community associations and kept in close touch with them, because the associations had a wealth of information about the neighbourhoods, which the municipal services needed for policy-making and did not themselves possess. At the end of the 1970s a start was made in the decentralization of the governance and administration of the city into district councils. The rationale behind this process was to narrow the gap between residents and the city council. The district councils organized their own civil services in the neighbourhoods as a way to narrow the gap between residents and administrations. Consequently, the contribution of the associations to democracy was seen as less relevant by the civil services, because they focused more on the ins and outs of the politics in the neighbourhood themselves.

In searching for new futures for community associations, data gathering and feedback gave more insight into their activities and functions. It turned out that the most important fields of activity were living conditions, housing, environment, safety, transport, employability, the position of minorities, and welfare. It was concluded that the community associations have an important role in securing amenities in the neighbourhood, and that they also have a role in pointing out problems in the neighbourhood to local politicians and in suggesting improvements. Most associations work in close relationship with the residents, and have a good feel for the problems and issues in the neighbourhood. The associations are, more than the local authorities, capable of bringing people together in order to know and understand problems in the neighbourhood, and to translate them into realistic action plans or programmatic development. Working from the perspective of the residents is seen as valuable and a way of taking action. Possibilities for new futures reside in the forms of participative democracy espoused by the associations, their knowledge of problems in the neighbourhood, the coordination of activities to contribute to the amenity, and the need to bridge the gap between citizens and councils. Based on dialogues, the participants formulated guidelines for their own future:

- collective problems, more than individual problems;
- initiating tasks, more than the implementation of tasks;
- knowledge based on experience, more than professional knowledge;
- interest of residents, more than the specific interest of volunteers;
- perspectives of residents, more than the perspectives of institutions;
- own identity and independence, more than cooperation with institutions;
- own objectives, more than objectives of the councils;
- critical attitude towards councils, more than facilitating tasks assigned by councils;
- participative democracy, more than representative democracy.

These guidelines were helpful in formulating policies, strategies, and action plans.

> The participants decided to work out their policies and action plans in their own neighbourhood, and to share their experiences which each other and with members of the councils. Almost all associations learned the necessity of making their policy, strategy, and action plans with volunteers and residents in the neighbourhood more explicit. Almost all participants initiated a process to elaborate policy, strategy, and action plans in their association, together with volunteers, members of the council, and residents. During these discussions the relationship between association and council developed positively in most cases. Members of the associations found common ground with the politicians and civil servants in the need for more attention to the amenity in the neighbourhoods. In most discussions, the tasks and action plans of the associations were seen as significant contributions to the issues of the amenity. The associations that did not want to discuss their policy with the councils were satisfied with their decision, and according to them they were able to fulfil their mission to criticize the council and the undemocratic structures in society more effectively.
>
> For a detailed description of this transformation process, see Boonstra and Van de Graaf (1999).

Based on dynamic systems theory and social constructionism, the principles of interactive learning are as follows:

- Understanding organizing as being feedback systems with positive and negative feedback that maintain or in some cases activate the present method of organizing. It is relevant here to recognize and discuss negative and positive feedback patterns, and to obtain insight into processes and actions that reinforce each other.
- Making room for self-organization in which people have freedom of action, and actors interact on the basis of different functions, backgrounds, hierarchical positions, and groups. Actors should make their own rules in a process of self-organization, and should have the courage to question and adjust these rules so that the underlying assumptions may also be understood and adjusted.
- Jointly charting, recognizing, and clarifying mutual relationships so that the dynamics become visible and the relationships themselves are involved in the renewal process. It is important to strive for transparency in interaction patterns because systems are ongoing, and to accept that engagement consists of temporary and loose coalitions.
- Making room for multiple constructs of reality by the actors in the interaction. Interactions and innovations should be understood in their local contexts because meanings are linked to the situations in which actors construct and use these images. It is desirable to create room for the exchange of knowledge, experiences, and insights, the interpretations of events, personal feelings and ambitions, and different points of view on future possibilities.
- Reflecting on the interrelationships between the actions, constructs, and contexts of actors. It is important that this should not result in an unambiguous and deterministic view of how the meaning should be understood. After all, the interrelationships are merely subjective descriptions that have been produced during interactions and can always be modified.
- Striving for a shared sense-making of events in which pluriformity is nevertheless preserved and as a result of which common perspectives on action can arise in which actors reconstruct their meanings and are actively engaged in interventions to create new futures.
- Finally, there must be room for interaction and reflection on personal actions and the underlying assumptions to make room for learning processes.

These principles of interactive learning have consequences for renewal and learning in dynamic environments. During renewal processes in organizational networks, acting, reflecting, and learning are inseparable. This is a process of experiential learning, or learning by doing in interaction with others. In 1984, Kolb published his model of experiential learning. The underlying idea is that learning takes place in a cyclical process in which concrete experiences are followed by the reflective observation of these experiences. These reflections are then analysed and incorporated into new concepts with the creation of abstract conceptualizations and generalizations. On this basis, one can choose to experiment actively with new behaviour, testing the implications of new concepts in new situations and forming new questions and new behaviour. This leads in turn to new experiences to reflect on. According to Kolb, learning is a never-ending process; we are capable of learning through acting and reflecting. Kolb's theory of experiential learning fits in with the ideas of Argyris and Schön (1978) on first-order and second-order learning.

In first-order learning, we learn from our mistakes by making ourselves aware of the effectiveness of rules of action, and then we adjust our actions accordingly. First-order learning applies to improving actions based on an acquired store of knowledge and experience.

Second-order learning pertains to reflecting, while acting through an interactive process of asking questions, testing, reflecting, and adjusting while acting. Second-order learning is initiated when surprises are encountered during routine actions, when the problem is not immediately clear and known solutions no longer work. First-order and second-order learning help in solving known problems and approaching definable issues. They contribute to professional and methodological actions in the case of first- and second-order changes in organizations. With third-order changes, where problems are ambiguous and renewal processes are initiated by interactions in organizational networks, learning and acting reach another level and go further than the existing concepts about the learning of individuals within organizations.

In third-order learning, according to Schön (1983), it is a matter of 'reflection-on-reflection-in-action'. This means reflecting on our own manner of thinking, acting, and learning, and the underlying assumptions on which they are based: the way in which we observe and interpret events, define problems, analyse and conceptualize, act, and interact. The point is to recognize and reconsider our own assumptions and patterns of action. In this context of learning, Schön speaks of reflective communication between the professional and the material. In processes of interactive learning, this material is formed by actors who interact and impart meaning. Reflections and sense-making then take place in the course of direct communication and interaction. This means that feedback processes are necessary for renewal, and that there is no unambiguous reality. Meanings are imparted and social realities are produced in the processes of continuing interaction. In these interactions, it is not only the actions that count but also the underlying interpretations of events, the hypotheses regarding positions, the ideas as to possibilities, and the assumptions on which these are based. In order to make the hypotheses and assumptions visible, it is important to allow feedback, to interact and to work with the differences. Differences in acting and thinking expose the processes of sense-making, reveal the underlying assumptions, and create possibilities for new assumptions and patterns of action. Cyclic processes of interaction and feedback arise in which people can learn at the first, second, and third levels and can renew their assumptions and action repertoires.

The heart of interactive learning is that feedback processes become visible, that there is room for processes of self-organization, that interactive processes between actors are initiated, that multiple voices are heard against a background of multiplicity and diversity, that meanings and assumptions become visible, that a shared sense-making comes through dialogue, that joint alternative actions are developed, and that processes of discovering, choosing, acting, reflecting, and learning are initiated.

## THEORY IN PRACTICE

I have just sketched a picture of the dynamics of organizing, changing, and learning, of balancing between stability and instability, of ambiguous questions and blurred boundaries, of actors who interact and thereby assign meaning and create possibilities. Many questions remain unanswered. Some of the relevant topics addressed in this book are formulated below:

1. The background of planned change and the knowledge and methodology which are available to contribute to first-order and second-order changes in organizations.

2. The background of organizational development and the knowledge and methodology which are available for second- and third-order changes in organizations.
3. The dynamics of renewal in organizations and organizational networks, the decision-making processes that either stimulate or inhibit this, and the political processes that can either initiate or stop the renewal.
4. The conditions under which people use power and exert influence in renewal processes, and are willing to combine their powers in order to develop a shared perspective and common alternatives for action through dialogue.
5. The interactive processes between actors in dynamic systems, how they act, impart meaning and reflect, and how this contributes to renewal and learning.
6. The development of defensive mechanisms from the perspective of systems dynamics which require appropriate explanatory models and behavioural practices from the fields of psychology, sociology, and political science.
7. The way in which professionals learn and act in confusing, ambiguous, and conflicting situations by reflecting simultaneously on the context, their actions, and their assumptions about reality.
8. The way in which we develop knowledge about organizing, renewal, and learning in dynamic social systems.

The reality of organizing, renewal, and learning is rather turbulent. It is a world of social systems in action, in which the relations between theory and practice play a role. The final question in this chapter I want to address is how we can know this reality and how this world can be understood and changed.

## ACADEMIC RESEARCH

In my opinion, traditional academic research is inadequate to generate knowledge about the dynamic reality of interactive learning. This research is guided by traditional values of objectivity in order to attain scientific purity. The investigator's task is to collect and interpret data, independent of the object, and to transform the results into a scientific theory. Naturally, the insights derived from this theory can ultimately be used by change managers and consultants who are engaged in renewal. This includes, for example, the application of generic knowledge about social behaviour and processes in human systems. Theoretical knowledge in such areas as human motivation, leadership, decision-making, the use of power, socialization, interpersonal communication, intergroup relations, conflict management, and learning processes is certainly useful. Knowledge in these fields can support the facilitation of change processes. The application of these theories in practice might even lead to testing the theory; however, their application seldom leads to any doubt regarding the theory or any new knowledge regarding real-life problems. My most important objection to this type of research is that it denies the relationships between the investigator and the empirical object. As put so succinctly by Van Beinum et al. (1996: 181): 'The object is also subject: it talks back.' In my opinion, the ambiguous and changeable world in which dynamic systems operate cannot be understood from the detached position of a pure observer. Academic research is too limited to be able to understand the dynamics of third-order changes.

## APPLIED RESEARCH

Applied research is also, in my opinion, inadequately equipped to generate new knowledge about dynamic social systems. Applied research can be helpful in developing methods for planned change. It is certainly useful in the development of knowledge and methods for first-order and second-order changes. It is less useful, however, for understanding and solving chaotic problems in ongoing contexts. After all, applied research has its roots in the model of technical rationality. The practice of change in this model consists of the instrumental or methodological application of scientific knowledge and techniques. The scientist develops knowledge and techniques that are applied by practitioners. The scientist develops these techniques independently of the object and strives for objective and cumulative knowledge. The practitioners have at their disposal tangible and reproducible techniques that have their basis in research. These techniques are variable and can be applied in accordance with the situation. Practitioners use their knowledge to decide which techniques are best to achieve the intended results. Their actions are then dedicated to the purposeful implementation of changes. In applied research, research and practice enter into a relationship in which the professional investigators supply the theoretical insights and applicable techniques, while professional practitioners supply the investigators with new problems and with assessments of the techniques in practice. Schön used the metaphor of the high land looking out over a swamp. On the high land, problems can be solved using tested theories and techniques. In the swampy lowlands, problems are muddled and messy, and there are limited capabilities for regulated approaches and technical solutions. According to Schön, it is ironic that problems in the high land become of less importance for human beings and society, although they might have a technical importance. The most realistic and fundamental problems emerge from the swamps. In this situation, the organizational professional is confronted with a choice. Would the professional and researcher rather stay on the solid ground of the high land to work on problems which are not really important for society, or is the professional and researcher prepared to go down into the swamps of crucial problems and to work on messy problems with non-regulated research?

Applied research assumes that the problems posed by practitioners can be understood and that, over a longer period of time, the goals will be consistent and more or less unambiguous. However, if we are dealing with dynamic systems, unfamiliar and ambiguous problems, and interactive processes between actors that are both renewing and learning, then this research model is insufficient, no matter how useful the model may be for more stable situations and for first- and second-order changes in organizations.

## REFLECTIVE ACTION RESEARCH

The reality of interactive learning consists of actors and experienced experts who must decide how to act. Through their actions, they develop knowledge in interaction with others. In dynamic systems, the researchers interact with the research subjects. In these interactions, the researchers are involved in sense-making and interpreting the reality which is subject to renewal due to their common actions. The relationship between the researchers and research subjects is based on equality, common engagement, and shared responsibility. They consult each other about choosing the starting points for the study, the context of the renewal, the underlying assumptions, and the methods to be used. These choices are made and can be adjusted during the interactions in the process of organizing, renewing, and learning. French and Bell (1998) use the term 'action research' in this context. I prefer the term 'reflective action research' because knowledge is generated in an interactive process in which the actors act, reflect on their actions, and pay attention to the way in which they are learning and generating new knowledge.

Reflective action research is directed at action, reflection, and the generation of knowledge (e.g. Reason & Bradbury, 2001). It is a question of understanding ambiguous problems, initiating processes of interaction, and searching jointly for alternative behaviours so that the problems can be managed. And the point of it all is to generate knowledge and develop theory on the processes of renewal and learning. I consider it unsatisfactory if the knowledge remains available only to the actors in the process itself. It must be possible to make acquired knowledge and learning experiences meaningful for others. All aspects of the renewal process are communicated, giving attention to the context of the study, the various voices that have made themselves heard, the conflicts and tensions that have arisen, and the perspectives and reflections of the actors on their actions and the underlying assumptions. This means that the theoretical assumptions and starting points are made explicit, as well as the tools and methodologies that were used (Burrell, 1996). In my opinion, publishing and presenting practices, insights, ideas, methodologies, and theories are an essential part of communicating, making things explicit, reflecting, and interacting with actors in the research process and with professional colleagues.

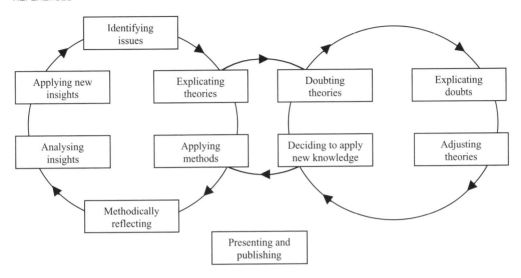

**FIGURE 0.2**   Reflective action research as a double loop

In their reflections on action research, Eden and Huxham (1996) state that the development of theories takes place in an incremental and cyclical process. In my view, this process comprises the following activities:

1. Identifying ambiguous issues.
2. Making starting points, contexts, and theoretical assumptions explicit.
3. Applying methods and insights when acting.
4. Methodically reflecting on the effects of the actions.
5. Analysing and conceptualizing new insights.
6. Making decisions to apply new insights when acting.

This first cycle is linked to a second cycle in a double loop which consists of:

1. Casting doubt on the earlier theoretical hypotheses and assumptions.
2. Making the doubts and the underlying reasons explicit.
3. Adjusting previous theoretical hypotheses and methods.
4. Making decisions to apply the new hypotheses.
5. Presenting and publishing experiences.

This process of reflective action research as a double loop is shown in Figure 0.2.

The knowledge and insights in this handbook are based largely on reflective action research. Theoretical knowledge has been tested and further developed in practice, methods have been used in practice, and the experience with these methods has been incorporated into a methodical approach to give shape to change processes and bring them to a successful conclusion.

## REFERENCES

Ackerman, L.S. (1986) Development, transition, or transformation: the question of change in organizations. *OD Practitioner*, **18**(4), 1–9.

Argyris, C. & Schön, D. (1978) *Organizational Learning*. Reading, MA: Addison-Wesley.

Bashein, M.L., Marcus, M.L. & Riley, P. (1994) Business process reengineering: preconditions for success and failure. *Information Systems Management*, **9**(2), 24–31.

Beer, M. (1980) *Organizational Change and Development: A Systems View*. Santa Monica, CA: Goodyear.

Beer, M., Eisenstat, R.A. & Spector, B. (1990) *The Critical Path to Corporate Renewal*. Boston: Harvard Business School Press.

Beer, M. & Walton, A.E. (1987) Organization change and development. *Annual Review of Psychology*, **38**, 339–367.

Bennis, W.G., Benne, K.D., Chin, R. & Corey K.E. (1979) *The Planning of Change* (3rd edn). New York: Holt, Rinehart & Winston.

Boonstra, J.J. (1997) Redesign, development and organizational learning. In J.J. Boonstra & K.M. Bennebroek Gravenhorst (eds) *Barriers to Organizational Change and Innovation* (pp. 7–30). Leuven: EAWOP.

Boonstra, J.J. (2000) Walking on water: dynamics of organizing, changing and learning [Lopen over water: over dynamiek van organiseren, vernieuwen en leren]. Inaugural lecture, 10 February 2000, Faculty of Social and Behavioural Science. University of Amsterdam, the Netherlands.

Boonstra, J.J. & Bennebroek Gravenhorst, K.M. (1998) Power dynamics and organizational change: a comparison of perspectives. *European Journal of Work and Organizational Psychology*, **7**(2), 97–120.

Boonstra, J.J. & Van de Graaf, H. (1999) The paradox of democracy in a cosmopolis. *Concepts and Transformations*, **4**(3), 423–448.

Boonstra, J.J. & Vink, M.J. (1996) Technological and organizational innovation: a dilemma of fundamental change and development. *European Journal of Work and Organizational Psychology*, **5**(3), 351–376.

Bouwen, R. (1995) Social construction of power relationships in workplace conflict episodes. In J.J. Boonstra (ed.) *Power Dynamics and Organizational Change*. Conference proceedings, Congress of European Association of Work and Organizational Psychology, 19–22 April, Hungary, pp. 23–31.

Braverman, H. (1974) *Labor and Monopoly Capital: The Degradation of Work in the Twentieth Century*. New York: Monthly Review Press.

Bunker, B.B. & Alban, B.T. (1997) *Large Group Interventions: Engaging the Whole System for Rapid Change*. San Francisco: Jossey-Bass.

Burrell, G. (1996) Normal science, paradigms, metaphors, discourses and genealogies of analysis. In S.R. Clegg, C. Hardy & W.R. Nord (eds) *Handbook of Organization Studies* (pp. 642–658). London: Sage.

Checkland, P. & Howell, S. (1998) *Information, Systems, and Information Systems: Making Sense of the Field*. Chichester: John Wiley & Sons, Ltd.

Checkland, P. & Scholtes, J. (1995) *Soft Systems Methodology in Action*. Chichester: John Wiley & Sons, Ltd.

Cummings, T.G. & Worley, C.G. (2001) *Organization Development and Change* (7th edn). Cincinnati, OH: Thompson, South Western College Publication.

De Caluwé, L. & Vermaak, H. (2003) *Learning to Change: A Guide for Organizational Change Agents*. Thousand Oaks, CA: Sage.

Eden, C. & Huxham, C. (1996) Action research and the study of organizations. In S.R. Clegg, C. Hardy & W.R. Nord (eds) *Handbook of Organization Studies* (pp. 526–542). London: Sage.

Emery, F.E. & Trist, E.L. (1965) The causal texture of organizational environment. *Human Relations*, **18**(1), 21–32.

French, W.L. & Bell, C.H. (1998) *Organization Development: Behavioral Science Interventions for Organizational Improvement* (6th edn). Englewood Cliffs, NJ: Prentice Hall.

Gergen, K.J. (1982) *Towards the Transformation of Social Knowledge*. New York: Springer.

Gergen, K.J. (1999) *An Invitation to Social Construction*. Thousand Oaks, CA: Sage.

Greiner, L.E. & Schein, V.E. (1988) *Power and Organization Development: Mobilizing Power to Implement Change*. Reading, MA: Addison-Wesley.

Hajer, M. (1995) *The Politics of Environmental Discourse: Ecological Modernization and the Policy Process*. Oxford: Oxford University Press.

Hardy, C. & Clegg, S.R. (1996) Some dare to call it power. In S.R. Clegg, C. Hardy & W.R. Nord (eds) *Handbook of Organization Studies* (pp. 622–641). London: Sage.

Heller, F. (2003) Participation and power: a critical assessment. *Applied Psychology, An International Review*, **52**(1), 160–173.

Hoebeke, L. (1994) *Making Work Systems Better*. Chichester: John Wiley & Sons, Ltd.

Hosking, D.M. (1999) Social construction as process: some new possibilities for research and development. *Concepts and Transformations*, **4**(2), 117–132.

Hosking, D.M. & Morley, I.E. (1991) *A Social Psychology of Organizing: People, Processes and Contexts*. New York: Harvester Wheatsheaf.

Jacobs, R.W. (1994) *Real Time Strategic Change*. San Francisco: Berrett-Koehler.

Kolb, D.A. (1984) *Experiential Learning*. Englewood Cliffs, NJ: Prentice Hall.

Mastenbroek, W.F.G. (2000) Organizational innovation as the management of interdependencies in networks. In R.T. Golembiewski (ed.) *Handbook of Organizational Consultation* (2nd edn) (pp. 725–733). New York: Marcel Dekker.

Mintzberg, H. (1979) *The Structuring of Organizations*. Englewood Cliffs, NJ: Prentice Hall.

Mintzberg, H. (1983) *Power in and around Organizations*. London: Prentice Hall.

Mintzberg, H. (1988) Opening up the definition of strategy. In J.B. Quinn, H. Mintzberg & R.M. James (eds) *The Strategy Process: Concepts, Contexts and Cases*. London: Prentice Hall.

Pettigrew, A.M. (1987) Context and action in the transformation of the firm. *Journal of Management Studies*, **24**(6), 649–670.

Pettigrew, A.M. (1988) *The Management of Strategic Change*. Oxford: Blackwell.

Pettigrew, A., Ferlie, E. & McKee, L. (1994) *Shaping Strategic Change: Making Change in Large Organizations*. London: Sage.

Reason, P. & Bradbury, H. (2001) *Handbook of Action Research: Participative Inquiry and Practice*. Thousand Oaks, CA: Sage.

Schein, E.H. (1992) *Organizational Culture and Leadership* (2nd edn). San Francisco: Jossey-Bass.

Schein, E.H. (1993) On dialogue, culture, and organizational learning. *Organizational Dynamics*, **22**(2), 40–51.

Schön, D.A. (1983) *The Reflective Practitioner: How Professionals Think in Action*. New York: Basic Books.

Stacey, R.D. (2003) *Strategic Management and Organizational Dynamics: The Challenge of Complexity* (4th edn). London: Pearsons.

Tajfel, H. (1982) Social psychology of intergroup relations. *Annual Review of Psychology*, **33**, 1–33.

Van Beinum, H.J.J., Faucheux, C. & Van der Vlist, R. (1996) Reflections on the epigenetic significance of action research. In S. Toulmin & B. Gustavsen (eds) *Beyond Theory: Changing Organizations through Participation*. Amsterdam: John Benjamins.

Vennix, J.A.M. (1999) *Group Model Building: Facilitation Team Learning Using System Dynamics*. Chichester: John Wiley & Sons, Ltd.

Weick, K.E. (1979) *The Social Psychology of Organizing*. Reading, MA: Addison-Wesley.

Weick, K.E. (1995) *Sensemaking in Organizations*. Thousand Oaks, CA: Sage.

Weisbord, M.R. (1992) *Discovering Common Ground*. San Francisco: Berrett-Koehler.

Yanov, D. (1996) *How Does a Policy Mean? Interpreting Policy and Organizational Actions*. Washington, DC: Georgetown University Press.

# Fundamentals and Practices in Organization Development

In Part I of this handbook, a framework of organizational change and development is presented. In this framework, the history and development of theories on organizational change and development are described, the implications of these theories are discussed, and a critical overview is given of widely used methods and tools. Helpful insights are given for choosing change strategies and intervention methods in specific situations and organizational contexts.

In Chapter 1, Thomas Cummings describes the roots of Organization Development (OD). OD is an evolving field of applied social science with an increasing diversity of concepts and applications. In more than 50 years, OD has evolved a complex and diverse body of knowledge. This expertise derives mainly from reflections by practitioners and action research. The enormous growth of new approaches and methods has broadened the scope of organization change and development. OD can be defined as a systems-wide process of applying behavioural-science knowledge to the planned change and development of policies, business strategies, design components, and processes that enable organizations to be effective. OD treats change as a process, not a discrete event. It involves an ongoing series of diagnostic, action-planning, implementation, and evaluation actions. It rests on a core set of psychological concepts that guide how it is conceptualized and applied. The focus of OD has expanded beyond social processes that occur mainly between individuals and between groups to include strategies and design components of the total organization. It draws on a variety of disciplines and concepts, including social processes, work designs, human relations, structuring of organizations and work processes, relations between organization and environment, and organization learning. The application of OD closely follows its historical roots and psychological foundations. According to Cummings, and many other scholars, the processes and activities used to initiate and carry out organizational change are deeply embedded in values of openness, trust, and collaboration among organization members; they are grounded in the belief that members should be actively involved in change. Action research and action learning are helpful because they serve as methods for action and change, and also produce new knowledge about organizations and change.

The implications of the theoretical and historical roots of OD are elaborated by Merrelyn Emery in Chapter 2. The choice of a theoretical framework has momentous implications for the management of change, particularly the psychological aspects of it, as nothing less than the very definition of a human being and human behaviour is at stake. Conceptual frameworks and assumption of human behaviour underlie the choice of methods, tools, and practices. In this chapter, Emery suggests examining the systems of ideas and the assumptions which lie behind change strategies and intervention methods, before applying them in practice. She elaborates on diagnosing organizational problems, with respect to human behaviour, human motivation, leadership, communication, organization design, relationships in interactions, and the strategy process. To redesign and change organizations effectively and with humility, change strategies and intervention methods must be carefully considered. Changing organizations in an unpredictable environment requires active adaptive change strategies, which are not top-down

*Dynamics of Organizational Change and Learning.* Edited by J.J. Boonstra.
© 2004 John Wiley & Sons, Ltd. ISBN 0-471-87737-9.

or expert-driven. From Emery's epistemological point of view, learning is essential to effective and sustainable change. For sustainable systematic change, all levels and functional areas must be involved in the same sort of processes, and everybody must learn what is involved in the change, conceptually, as well as methodologically. This chapter concludes with a searching description of action research and action learning. Action research and action learning could be enablers of sustainable change and learning in organizations.

In Chapter 3, Morten Levin conceptualizes organizational developmental processes. He presents strategies for managing participative change processes, and describes several intervention methods to effect sustainable change in organizations. Special attention is given to the role of change agents and professional outsiders. Participation is understood as the core value in OD. The driving force in participative change processes is experimentation and learning. From the core value of participation, local knowledge is utilized during change and implementation. The fundamental choice of participation generates new local insights and shared understanding through collective reflection and learning during the change process. In OD the change process is conceptualized as a continuous cycle of problem identification, experimentation, reflecting, and learning. External facilitators may participate in these change processes. In Levin's opinion, these facilitators play a role in promoting change that will increase the ability of members of the organization to enhance the learning abilities of the organization and its members. In fact, the outside facilitator must integrate with the insiders in a joint reflection and learning process. The phase of problem identification is obviously most difficult because insiders and outsiders do not know each other, and their world-views and values are probably very different, and there is no basis for mutual understanding, while open dialogue may not be developed. In this phase, it is crucial to find a common point of departure that is meaningful for all participants. Experimenting, reflecting, and learning could be initiated and stimulated through several change strategies and intervention methods. Attention is given to search conferences, dialoguing conferences, mutual gains bargaining, conventional meetings, and task forces. Choosing a suitable arena for collective reflection is crucial in OD. In this arena, problem-owners and outside facilitators share reflection and learning opportunities and give shape to transformative activities.

In the reflective chapter of this Part of the handbook, the effectiveness of change strategies and intervention methods is questioned. In Chapter 4, Marc Buelens and Geert Devos reflect on the effectiveness of change efforts, and underline the importance of understanding the context of a change process and deliberately choosing the most appropriate change strategy depending on this context. Change strategies are seen as the overall approach of the change process, and a pattern in a stream of decisions and activities, reflecting consistency of behaviour over time. These authors steer clear of general change theories that can be applied to all change efforts. The internal and external environments of organizations can be so different that a clear understanding of the specific situation is essential when choosing an appropriate change strategy. They discuss the central value of participation in OD. Although participation can be crucial in some change efforts, it could impede change in other environments. The change environment is described in terms of two general dimensions: power distance and uncertainty. In a context with high power distance and low uncertainty, a change strategy based on action planning seems most appropriate, with a top-down approach, strong leadership, and participation in the implementation process. Situations of low power distance demand the negotiation approach. In contexts of high uncertainty, a change strategy of information registration and experimentation is needed. Because organizational change is complex and diverse, there are many reasons for failure. Specific change failures are discussed in traditional environments, high-pressure environments, professional environments, and experimental environments. This chapter concludes with the proposition that effective integration of different change strategies adapted to the change environment will determine the success of change efforts.

# CHAPTER 1

# Organization Development and Change
## Foundations and Applications

**Thomas Cummings**
*University of Southern California, Los Angeles, USA*

Organization development (OD) applies behavioral-science knowledge and practices to help organizations change to achieve greater effectiveness. It seeks to improve how organizations relate to their external environments and function internally to attain high performance and high quality of work life. OD emphasizes change in organizations that is planned and implemented deliberately. It is both an applied field of social practice and a domain of scientific inquiry. Practitioners, such as managers, staff experts, and consultants, apply relevant knowledge and methods to organization change processes, while researchers study those processes to derive new knowledge that can subsequently be applied elsewhere. In practice, this distinction between application and knowledge generation is not straightforward as OD practitioners and researchers often work closely together to jointly apply knowledge and learn from those experiences (Lawler et al., 1985). Thus, OD is an 'action science' where knowledge is developed in the context of applying it and learning from the consequences (Argyris et al., 1985).

This chapter provides an overview of the theory and research underlying OD. First, OD is defined in the context of recent changes and developments in the field. Then, a brief history of OD is provided to show how the field has evolved. Next, the psychological foundations of OD are discussed, and, finally, how OD is applied in organizations is presented.

## DEFINITION OF OD

OD encompasses a diversity of concepts and methods for changing organizations. Although several definitions of OD have been presented (Beckhard, 1969; Bennis, 1969; French, 1969; Beer, 1980; Burke, 1982), the enormous growth of new approaches and techniques has blurred the boundaries of the field and made it increasingly difficult to describe. The following definition seeks to clarify emerging aspects of OD while drawing on previous definitions of the field: *organization development is a system-wide process of applying behavioral-science knowledge to the planned change and development of the strategies, design components, and processes that enable organizations to be effective.*

OD addresses an entire system, such as a team, department, or total organization. It also deals with relationships between a system and its environment as well as among the different features that comprise a system's design. This system-wide application follows from an open-systems approach to organizations (Thompson, 1967; Katz & Kahn, 1978; Cummings, 1980). Organizations are viewed as open systems with multiple levels and interrelated parts that exist in the context of a larger

*Dynamics of Organizational Change and Learning.* Edited by J.J. Boonstra.
© 2004 John Wiley & Sons, Ltd. ISBN 0-471-87737-9.

environment. Thus, change at one level of the organization—individual member, work team, or total organization—can affect other levels. Change in one part or design feature of the organization, such as a reward system, work design, or organization structure, can require supporting changes in other parts. Change in the organization's environment can necessitate change within the organization, and so on.

OD treats change as a process, not a discrete event or end state. Organization change involves an ongoing series of diagnostic, action planning, implementation, and evaluation actions. These activities overlap and feed back on each other, so that initial diagnosis informs action planning and implementation while evaluation guides subsequent diagnosis and modification of the changes. Consequently, this process is highly adaptive and changes as new information is encountered and new events are experienced.

Like most applied sciences, OD draws on a variety of disciplines and concepts to guide practice and research. Because organizations are complex social systems, OD uses ideas from several behavioral sciences, including anthropology, economics, political science, psychology, and sociology. At the micro-level of application, OD relies on knowledge about individuals and their relationships within organizations. This includes concepts having to do with motivation, communication, conflict, group dynamics, leadership, and work design. At the macro-level, OD applies knowledge of how organizations develop strategies, divide and coordinate labor, and relate to external forces. This includes ideas about corporate strategy, organization design, international relations, and strategic alliances. OD applies this broad knowledge base to diagnose how organizations function and to develop interventions for improving them. These applications, in turn, can result in new knowledge about processes of organization change and effects of particular interventions. Moreover, OD practice can produce 'generative' knowledge by creating entirely new forms of organizing and changing that current knowledge does not yet address or anticipate (Gergen, 1994).

OD involves both planned change and development of the organization itself (Cummings & Worley, 2001). Planned change includes processes and techniques for helping organizations implement particular changes. It is highly pragmatic and focuses on implementing changes that promote organization effectiveness. Development is concerned with improving organizations' capacity for problem-solving and improvement. The more developed an organization, the more able it is to solve its own problems and to implement change and improve itself. Thus, in addition to helping organizations implement specific changes (planned change), OD is concerned with transferring skills and knowledge to organizations so they are more able to manage change in the future (development). Consistent with this developmental perspective, OD places a strong value on human potential, participation in the workplace, and interpersonal relationships based on openness and trust.

OD focuses on changing and improving three key aspects of organizations: strategies, design components, and processes. Strategies have to do with how organizations use their resources to gain competitive advantage. This includes choices about the functions an organization will perform, the products or services it will provide, and the markets and customers it will serve. Design components include decisions about organization structure, work design, measurement systems, and human resources practices. Processes have to do with how organizations go about doing things and include how members relate to each other and their tasks and how different functions, such as communication and decision-making, are performed. OD seeks to bring congruence or fit among strategies, design components, and processes so they mutually guide and reinforce organizational behavior in a strategic direction.

Finally, OD focuses on improving organization effectiveness. This includes helping organizations achieve high performance, good quality of work life, and capacity for continued problem-solving and improvement. Effective organizations perform at high levels while meeting the needs of various stakeholders, including owners, customers, employees, suppliers, and government regulators. They have a high quality of work life that enables them to attract and retain talented members.

Effective organizations are able to solve their own problems while continually improving and renewing themselves.

## HISTORY OF OD

In a little over 50 years, OD has evolved a complex and diverse body of knowledge and practice. Because this expertise derives mainly from helping organizations change and improve themselves, the history of OD can be understood in terms of the kinds of changes that organizations have implemented over this time period. These include changes aimed at: (1) social processes; (2) work designs; (3) human resources; and (4) organization structures. Although these changes are interrelated, each represents a distinct background in the growth of OD.

### SOCIAL PROCESSES

The earliest applications of OD involved helping organizations improve social processes including relationships among members, communication, group decision-making, and leadership. These process changes started in the early 1950s and were largely in response to emerging social problems that organizations experienced as they became larger and more bureaucratic. During the first half of the twentieth century, organizations grew increasingly large with numerous departments, levels of management, and rules and procedures. Management was largely responsible for commanding and controlling the enterprise typically in an authoritarian or paternalistic manner. Over time, these organizational conditions generated a host of unintended social problems as members found it increasingly difficult to communicate both laterally and vertically, to resolve problems within and across groups, and to respond energetically to managerial directives.

OD's response to these social problems started in the late 1940s with the work of Kurt Lewin and his colleagues in laboratory training. It began with a training program for community leaders which included both cognitive learning about leadership as well as informal feedback about participant behavior (Bradford, 1967). Unexpectedly, the feedback aspect of the training was found to be a rich source of leadership expertise. This led to the development of laboratory training, commonly called a T-group, where a small, unstructured group of participants learn from their own interactions about group dynamics, leadership, interpersonal relations, and personal growth. T-groups expanded rapidly with the formation of the National Training Laboratories (part of the National Education Association) whose members increasingly applied these methods to helping organizations improve social processes (Argyris, 1964b; Marrow, 1967). In the 1950s, this included ground-breaking work by Douglas McGregor at Union Carbide, Herbert Shepard and Robert Blake at Esso Standard Oil, and McGregor and Richard Beckhard at General Mills (French, 1985). These early applications of T-group methods to business spawned the term 'organization development'. They led to an impressive array of interventions for improving social processes in organizations, such as team building (Patten, 1981; Dyer, 1987), process consultation (Schein, 1969, 1987, 1998), organization confrontation meeting (Beckhard, 1967), and, more recently, large-group interventions such as search conferences and open-space meetings (Bunker & Alban, 1997).

Early OD applications were also guided by work on action research and survey feedback. Action research started in the 1940s with applied studies by John Collier, Lewin and his colleagues, and William Whyte and Edith Hamilton (Collier, 1945; Lewin, 1946; Whyte & Hamilton, 1964). They showed that research could be used in the service of organization improvement if it was closely tied to action. Action research is highly collaborative, involving both OD practitioners and organization members; it is cyclical with initial research guiding action, and further research directing additional action, and so on. Action research has become a key process in applying OD to organizations, and will be discussed more thoroughly later in this chapter.

Survey feedback also started in the 1940s and has become a major component of most company-wide OD interventions. It involves systematically collecting survey data about the organization and feeding them back to members so they can discover sources of problems and devise relevant solutions. Based on the work of Rensis Likert, Floyd Mann, and their colleagues, survey feedback resulted in a variety of instruments for assessing member attitudes towards organizations (Seashore, 1987). It showed how feeding back that information to members can motivate and guide them to create meaningful change (Mann, 1962). This initial work in survey feedback also directed attention to how organizations were managed. It provided evidence that participative systems of management were more effective than traditional authoritative or benevolent systems (Likert, 1967). This encouraged the growth of participative management in organizations, which today has evolved into popular interventions for enhancing employee involvement or empowerment at the workplace (Lawler, 1986; Spreitzer, 1996).

## WORK DESIGNS

This branch of OD history involves designing work to make it more motivating and fulfilling. Traditionally, work was designed to promote technical rationality, resulting in jobs that were highly specified, fragmented, and repetitive. In the 1960s, the benefits of such work designs came more and more under question. Employees complained that work was boring and meaningless; they felt alienated from their jobs and the organizations that employed them. Organizations experienced growing problems with absenteeism, turnover, quality, and productivity. These problems spawned widespread calls for government, labor, and business to work jointly to improve the quality of the work life of the employees.

OD sought remedies for these problems in new work designs that were more geared to employee needs and aspirations than to traditional designs. These interventions were based on the work of Eric Trist and his colleagues in socio-technical systems and of Frederick Herzberg and his colleagues in job enrichment (Herzberg et al., 1959; Trist et al., 1963). The socio-technical approach, which originated in Europe and Scandinavia in the 1950s, structured work to better integrate technology and people. It resulted in work designs that enhance both productivity and employee satisfaction. Socio-technical systems also showed that when tasks are highly interdependent and require significant decision-making, teams comprised of multi-skilled members who can make relevant decisions are the most effective work design (Cummings & Srivastva, 1977). Today, such self-managed work teams are the cornerstone of work design in many organizations.

Like socio-technical systems, job enrichment aimed to make work more productive and humanly rewarding. It approached work redesign from a motivational perspective, showing how traditional jobs could be enriched to make them more motivating and satisfying. This required expanding jobs both horizontally and vertically by providing a greater variety of tasks to perform and greater amounts of discretion and decision-making. It also involved giving more direct feedback of results to job holders. Early success with job enrichment at such prominent companies as AT&T led to rapid diffusion of this OD intervention to work redesign in business, government, and the military (Ford, 1969).

## HUMAN RESOURCES

This background of OD involves integrating people into organizations so they join, remain, and produce at high levels. Concern for human resources has traditionally been associated with the personnel function in organizations. Starting in the 1970s, however, OD's interest in human resource practices grew rapidly. Many organizations faced serious global competition for the first time. They needed to produce at higher levels at lower costs. This placed heavy demands on human resources to achieve exceptional performance; however, organizations increasingly questioned whether their traditional human resource practices were up to the task. Answers to this question showed that many practices were not performance driven, particularly the way organizations rewarded employees. Because people generally do those things for which they are rewarded, rewards can play a powerful role in promoting performance. Unfortunately, many of the reward systems in use at the time were not linked closely to performance; employees were typically paid for a particular job level, time at work, or seniority.

Based on the work of Edward Lawler and his colleagues, OD examined how rewards affect organization performance (Lawler, 1981, 2000); this led to interventions aimed at making rewards more contingent on performance. One method that has grown in popularity over the past two decades is called 'gain sharing'. It involves paying organization members a bonus based on measurable gains in performance over some baseline standard. Gain sharing typically covers all members of a particular business unit and includes only performance measures that members can control. To achieve gains in performance, members are given the freedom to innovate and to discover more effective ways of working. They are encouraged to work together because their personal rewards are based on the performance of the total business unit. Another reward system intervention that has achieved widespread application is 'skill-based pay'. Traditionally, organizations pay members for the jobs they perform. Skill-based pay rewards members for the number of different jobs they can perform. This encourages members to learn new skills and to broaden their expertise. It creates a highly skilled, flexible workforce that is essential to high performance in today's rapidly changing environments.

## Organization Structures

The most recent applications of OD involve structuring organizations so they are better aligned with their strategy and environment. Such large-scale change has become more prevalent in the past two decades as organizations have increasingly faced complex, rapidly changing environments that often demand radical changes in how they compete and design themselves (Mohrman et al., 1989). To help organizations make these transformations, OD has expanded its focus to the total organization and its competitive environment. Drawing on a variety of perspectives in corporate strategy (Miles & Snow, 1978; Porter, 1980; Hamel & Prahalad, 1994; Grant, 1998), OD has created interventions for assessing an organization's competitive situation and making relevant changes in strategy if necessary. This typically includes a so-called 'SWOT analysis' where the organization's strengths and weakness are compared to opportunities and threats in its competitive environment. Then, a strategy is created to build on the strengths and to take advantage of the opportunities, while accounting for the weaknesses and threats.

OD has also generated applications for designing the various features of an organization so they promote and reinforce strategy. Based on a growing literature in organization design (Galbraith, 1977; Nadler et al., 1992; Galbraith & Lawler, 1993), OD has created new structures that fit better to today's situations than traditional bureaucratic designs. These include: 'high-involvement organizations' that push decision-making, information and knowledge, and rewards downward to the lowest levels of the organization (Lawler, 1986); 'boundaryless organizations' that seek to eliminate unnecessary borders between hierarchical levels, functional departments, and suppliers and customers (Ashkenas et al., 1995); and 'virtual organizations' that focus on the organization's core competence while outsourcing most other functions to other organizations who do them better (Davidow & Malone, 1992). All these structures are extremely lean and flexible; they enable organizations to respond rapidly to changing conditions.

Consistent with these new structures, OD has applied recent work on organization learning and knowledge management to organization change (Senge, 1990; Argyris & Schön, 1996; Davenport & Prusak, 1998). These interventions help organizations gain the capacity to continually learn from their actions and to make effective use of such knowledge. Such learning capability is essential if organizations are to continually change and renew themselves. It can provide strong competitive advantage in complex, changing environments (Teece, 1998).

# PSYCHOLOGICAL FOUNDATIONS OF OD

OD is an evolving field that draws on a diversity of theories. Its focus has expanded beyond social processes that occur mainly among individuals and within groups to include strategies and design components for the total organization. This evolution has added theoretical complexity to OD and made it increasingly difficult to define its conceptual boundaries and to develop a unified theory of changing and developing organizations. Despite this proliferation of knowledge, OD rests on a core set of psychological concepts that guide how it is conceptualized and applied. These psychological foundations have to do with: (1) the nature of human beings in organizations; (2) motivation that drives their behavior; (3) resistance of such behavior to change; and (4) groups as the focus of organization change.

## NATURE OF HUMAN BEINGS IN ORGANIZATIONS

All approaches to changing people and organizations include, either implicitly or explicitly, assumptions about the nature of human beings. These beliefs affect how people's behavior is explained, changed, and developed. OD draws heavily on humanistic psychology to understand behavior in organizations (Maslow, 1968; Rogers, 1972; Ellis, 1973). Often referred to as the 'third force' in psychology, humanistic psychology provides a more complex and positive view of human behavior than those offered by the other two dominant forces in the field: behaviorism which emphasizes environmental influences on behavior, and depth psychology which focuses on unconscious drives. Humanistic psychology calls attention to people's subjective experiences and the values, intentions, and perceptions that guide their choices about how to behave and interact with the environment. It proposes that people are inherently good and have a substantial capacity for self-determination, creativity, and psychological growth. Moreover, human beings are not only driven to gain things they lack, but also to seek opportunities to experience new things and to develop their full human potential. Although humanistic psychology has been criticized as more a value orientation than a rigorous science, there is growing evidence to support its views of human beings (Reason, 1988; Csikszentmihalyi, 1990; Wertz, 1995).

This positive view of human beings is deeply embedded in OD theory and practice. It guides how OD addresses a fundamental issue underlying all cooperative social action: How to integrate the personal interests and needs of individuals with the collective interests and needs of organizations? For OD, the answer lies in how well organizations enable members to develop towards psychological maturity which is essential if they are to achieve their full human potential (Argyris, 1962, 1964a). When organizations promote psychological maturity, members are likely to be self-controlling, to take responsibility for their actions, to have deeper, more stable interests, to take longer-term perspectives, and to be aware of how others see them. They are likely to expend psychological energy towards realizing their potential while meeting the challenges facing the organization. Thus, providing opportunities for members to behave maturely and to self-actualize benefits both the organization and its members. It integrates members' interests with those of the organization, providing mutual rewards for both.

Unfortunately, organizations are often structured and managed in ways that thwart members' psychological maturity and the positive behaviors that result from it. Pyramid or command-control structures, which have dominated organizations for much of the last century, seek to control and coordinate members through highly routine tasks, hierarchical lines of authority, centralized decision-making, and formal rules and procedures. Inherent in these structures are certain values and assumptions about organization members and how they should be managed (McGregor, 1960; Likert, 1961; Argyris, 1962, 1964a). Members are seen as lazy, self-centered, and resistant to change. Thus, management must actively motivate, direct, and control them. Such managerial practices make it almost axiomatic that members will behave immaturely and expend minimal energy on behalf of organizations. Because members are treated as immature adults, they are likely to behave accordingly, becoming apathetic, short-sighted, and irresponsible.

Pyramid structures also include assumptions about human relationships in organizations (Argyris, 1962). Relationships among members are expected to focus on organization goals and to be rational, logical, and formal. Emotions and informal relations are considered extraneous and ineffective. Because of these assumptions, interpersonal competence tends to be relatively low in most organizations. Members are often self-centered and ignore how their behaviors affect others; they suppress or deny interpersonal problems and the feelings underlying them. This reduces information sharing, risk taking, and trust among members. It results in conflicts and rigidity that impede the problem-solving capacity of organizations.

Given the prevalence of pyramidal structures and the management practices and interpersonal problems associated with them, OD focuses on helping organizations create conditions that promote members' psychological maturity and interpersonal competence. These, in turn, contribute to organization effectiveness. This humanistic perspective is evident in the values that underlie OD and the normative interventions that derive from them (Beckhard, 1969; Bennis, 1969). OD strongly values human development, democratic principles, and open inquiry. It seeks to develop organizations that encourage an open, problem-solving climate, trust, collaboration, and teamwork among members, and opportunities for members' self-control. OD interventions contribute to these ideals (Cummings & Worley, 2001). Human process interventions, such as process consultation, team building, and conflict resolution, increase members' interpersonal competence. Techno-structural interventions, such as job enrichment, self-managed teams, and employee involvement, enhance members' self-control. Human resource management interventions, such as performance management and career development, help members develop their full potential. Strategic interventions, such as culture change, organization transformation, and organization learning, help organizations change themselves from traditional pyramid structures to more organic forms that promote flexibility, innovation, and rapid response. The managerial values inherent in these new structures promote members' psychological maturity and interpersonal competence.

## MOTIVATION AND ORGANIZATIONAL BEHAVIOR

A key aspect of organization effectiveness is how well organizations motivate members to perform at high levels. OD draws mainly on three psychological theories to help organizations understand and improve motivation: (1) need theory; (2) job characteristics model; and (3) expectancy theory. Consistent with OD's humanistic roots, these approaches explain motivation in terms of members' psychological states, expectations, and values. They provide insights into individual differences among members and the kinds of organizational conditions that motivate behavior.

### Need theory

This approach explains motivation in terms of satisfying people's needs. It argues that motivation is energized and directed by unfulfilled needs. When a need is unsatisfied, it creates tension within people which, in turn, releases and directs energy toward satisfying the need. Although several need theories of motivation exist (McClelland, 1961; Alderfer, 1969), the one most closely associated with OD is based on the work of Maslow (1954), a pioneer of humanistic psychology. His model of motivation is based on a five-level hierarchy of human needs, starting at the bottom with physiological needs and progressing upward to safety, social needs, esteem, and self-actualization. It suggests that as each level of need becomes relatively satisfied, the next higher level of need emerges to energize and direct behavior, and so on up the hierarchy.

Although Maslow's need hierarchy has received limited empirical support, it is used widely in OD primarily because of its humanistic origins, intuitive appeal, and ease of understanding for organization members. When applied to organizations, the theory sensitizes managers to the full range of needs that can motivate members, particularly those needs at higher levels such as social needs, esteem, and self-actualization. It encourages them to consider more alternatives for motivating members than the traditional incentives of money and job security which mainly satisfy needs at the lower end of the hierarchy. This has led to a variety of OD interventions aimed at satisfying members' higher-level needs including job enrichment, self-managed teams, employee involvement, and career development. There is considerable evidence to suggest that when organizations provide opportunities for satisfying all levels of members' needs, they are more likely to attract and retain talented people who perform at high levels (Pfeffer, 1998).

## Job characteristics model

This theory of motivation focuses on the jobs that members perform. It is based on the work of Hackman and Oldham (1975, 1980), and examines jobs in terms of their motivating potential. The theory proposes that jobs affect members' motivation through their impact on three psychological states: (1) experienced meaningfulness of work; (2) experienced responsibility for the work; and (3) knowledge of results. The more that jobs are designed to enhance these states, the more motivating they will be, especially for people with strong growth needs.

Hackman and Oldham's approach has considerable empirical support (Fried & Ferris, 1987); it is used in OD to assess jobs and to redesign them if necessary. In many organizations, jobs are traditionally designed to maximize efficiency and control; they are highly specified, routine, and repetitive. Because such jobs have little motivating potential, OD has applied the job characteristics model to enrich them along a variety of dimensions. Designing jobs with high levels of skill variety, task identity, and task significance increases members' experienced meaningfulness of work. Providing members with greater autonomy over work methods and scheduling enhances their felt responsibility for work outcomes. Designing jobs that provide members with direct and clear feedback about performance increases members' knowledge of the actual results of their work activities. Together, these enriched features provide a strong motivational base for how jobs are designed and performed.

## Expectancy theory

This approach explains motivation in terms of choices that members make about how much effort they will expend on performing organizational tasks. Drawing on the work of Vroom and others (Vroom, 1964; Porter & Lawler, 1968), expectancy theory proposes that decisions about work effort are based on certain beliefs or expectations that members hold about the likely consequences of their efforts. People are likely to exert high levels of effort when they believe that it will result in good performance, that good performance will be rewarded, and that those rewards are personally valued. Moreover, the linkages between these beliefs and values are multiplicative, so that if one is low, overall motivation will be low. For example, if members do not believe that their effort will result in good performance, then motivation will be low even if they believe that good performance will result in valued rewards. Or, if members do not believe that good performance will result in valued rewards, then motivation will be low even if they believe that their efforts will result in good performance. Thus, to be highly motivated, members must strongly believe that their efforts will result in valued rewards.

Expectancy theory has a strong research base (Van Eerde & Thierry, 1996) and is increasingly used in OD to help organizations enhance member motivation. This is especially prevalent in reward system interventions that seek to obtain more motivational benefits from rewards by linking them more directly to members' performance and skill learning (Lawler, 1981, 2000). These variable or contingent reward practices, such as gain sharing and skill-based pay, help to strengthen members' beliefs that their efforts will lead to valuable rewards. To the extent that members value money, these reward systems are likely to encourage members to put forth high amounts of effort to perform (or learn) organization tasks (or skills).

## RESISTANCE TO CHANGE

All approaches to change must address a key issue inherent in organizations: why they are so stable and resistant to change. Knowing how to change organizations starts from understanding the conditions that promote the status quo or no change. OD has discovered a long list of causes for resistance to change, such as structural inertia, work habits, fear of the unknown, powerful interests, and members' security needs. It has also identified a variety of forces that promote organization change, such as competitive pressures, performance problems, workforce changes, and new technologies. The work of Lewin and his colleagues provides the underlying framework for explaining resistance to change (Lewin, 1947, 1951; Coch & French, 1948; Marrow, 1969). It shows how forces for resistance and change combine to create a status quo and how to change it effectively.

According to this approach, organization change is directed at processes, not things. The targets of change, such as performance levels and work methods, are the result of ongoing social processes occurring in organizations. For example, the level of a team's performance is the product of a myriad of behaviors, decisions, and interactions occurring among team members over time. Forces in the situation that drive and restrain change influence those social processes. In the team example, new work technologies might push for change while team performance norms might resist it. When these opposing forces are roughly equal, targets of change and the social processes underlying them are relatively stable and resistant to change, a condition called 'quasi-stationary equilibrium'. This stability is not static but dynamic, like a river flowing in a particular direction at a certain velocity. Driving and restraining forces, like the banks of a river, shape how social processes evolve over time. They affect the degree those processes are stable and hence resistant to change.

To change organizations, driving and restraining forces that affect the change target must first be identified and their strength assessed. Then, depending on the results of this analysis, the strength of these opposing forces can either be increased or decreased to achieve desired changes. Increasing driving forces or decreasing restraining forces may result in the same degree of change. The secondary effects of these two change strategies are likely to be quite different, however. Organization changes that result from increases in driving forces are likely to be accompanied by relatively high levels of tension as restraining forces rise to push back against the changes. Such tension can lead to higher aggressiveness and emotionality, and lower levels of commitment to change. The more effective change strategy is to reduce restraining forces, and thus let driving forces promote change while facing less resistance. This low-pressure method results in greater acceptance of the changes and more positive reactions to them. In the team performance example described above, improvements in performance are likely to be more successful if team performance norms (restraining force) are modified first and then new technologies (driving force) are introduced.

## GROUPS AS FOCUS OF CHANGE

Organization change involves, either directly or indirectly, changes in individual behavior. New structures, work methods, and performance goals, for example, all require adjustments in the way organization members behave. To change individual behavior, however, may require changes in the groups to which people belong. Drawing heavily on the field of group dynamics (Lewin, 1947; Cartwright & Zander, 1953, 1960), OD has long discovered that individual behavior is firmly grounded in groups. Whether groups emerge formally to perform organization tasks or informally to meet members' social needs, they can have powerful effects on members' behaviors, beliefs, and values. In organizations, for example, groups can influence members' performance levels, task methods, and work relationships. They can exert pressure on members to conform to norms governing group behavior. This can make changing individual behavior extremely difficult, as members are likely to resist organization changes that run counter to group norms and expectations. To overcome such resistance may require changing the group itself, thus making it the focus of change.

Initially referred to as 'participative management', this group approach to organization change is used extensively in OD. It includes getting members directly involved in understanding the need for change, developing appropriate changes, and implementing them. When members perceive the need for change, pressure for change is likely to arise from within the group (Kirkpartick, 1985). A key method for creating shared perceptions of the need for change is to engage members in analyzing their own situation. This can create ownership over the diagnosis and the conclusions drawn from it, therefore promoting a shared readiness for change among members (Burke, 1987). Similarly, member participation in developing organization changes can help to assure commitment to implementing them. When group members are involved in making decisions about what changes are most appropriate to their situation, their interests are likely to be taken into account in those changes. Consequently, members will be committed to subsequently implementing the changes because it is in their vested interest to do so (Cummings & Molloy, 1977). Moreover, such involvement can bring more diverse and local knowledge to decisions about change, thus improving their quality and practical relevance (Vroom & Jago, 1988).

## APPLICATION OF OD

How OD is applied in organizations closely follows its historical roots and psychological foundations. The processes and activities used to initiate and carry out organization change are deeply embedded in values of openness, trust, and collaboration among organization members; they are grounded in beliefs that members should be treated maturely and actively involved in change. Based on these fundamentals, applications of OD have evolved to meet the emerging demands of organizations and their environments. As shown in the history section of this chapter, OD interventions have grown larger and more complex; they have become more strategic, involving a greater array of stakeholders and organization design components. These changes are reflected in how OD is carried out and practiced in organizations today. To understand this evolution of OD practice requires knowledge of three general approaches to change: (1) Lewin's three steps; (2) action research; and (3) action learning.

### LEWIN'S THREE STEPS

This approach to organization change derives from the work of Lewin and his colleagues on how to overcome resistance to change and how to sustain change once it is made (Lewin, 1951). It starts from the premise that targets of change and the social processes underlying them are relatively stable when forces driving for change are roughly equal to forces resisting change. To change this status quo requires a three-step process: (1) 'unfreezing' the balance of forces that keep the change target stable; (2) 'moving' the change target to a new level or kind of behavior; and (3) 'refreezing' the balance of forces to reinforce the new behaviors and to keep them stable. This simple yet profound framework has guided OD practice for over half a century. It has led to numerous techniques for leading and managing change.

### Unfreezing

This step underscores the need to assess the present situation before change is contemplated. Referred to as a 'force field analysis', this diagnosis examines the driving and restraining forces in the change situation that maintain the status quo. It can reveal which forces are strongest (or weakest) and which are easiest (or hardest) to modify. Such information is essential for unfreezing the current situation and creating a readiness for change among organization members. For example, a force field analysis might discover that the key forces restraining change are members' lack of understanding about the need for change and strong group norms about task performance. Techniques to overcome these resistances, and thus to unfreeze the status quo, might include clearer and more direct communication about the rationale underlying the proposed changes and member participation in the change process itself.

## Moving

This stage involves intervening in the situation to change it. OD includes a variety of interventions for improving organizations. These change programs address organization issues having to do with human processes, strategic choices, human resource management, and work designs and structures (Cummings & Worley, 2001). To implement these changes effectively, OD has devised methods for creating a compelling vision of the desired changes (Collins & Porras, 1994), developing political support for them (Greiner & Schein, 1988), and managing the transition from the current to the desired situation (Beckhard & Harris, 1987).

## Refreezing

This final step involves making changes a permanent part of the organization's functioning. When this stage is ignored, organization changes rarely persist but regress to their previous stable state. Thus, refreezing calls for re-balancing the driving and restraining forces in the changed situation so it remains relatively stable. OD has discovered a variety of practices that can contribute to such permanence. Generally referred to as 'institutionalizing' change, these methods include: reinforcing organization changes by making rewards contingent on them; socializing existing members and newcomers into the beliefs, norms, and values underlying the changes; diffusing changes throughout the organization to provide a wider base of support for them; and sensing and calibrating the changes to detect deviations from desired changes and to take corrective actions (Goodman & Dean, 1982).

## ACTION RESEARCH

This approach to organization change shows that research can be practical; it can serve as an instrument for action and change. Action research applies scientific methods to help organizations identify problems, discover their underlying causes, and implement appropriate changes. It can also produce new knowledge about organizations and change that can be applied elsewhere. In addition to its problem-solving focus, action research is highly collaborative, involving both OD practitioners and organization members in the research and action process. Such participation gains members' input and commitment to the changes, thus increasing the chances that they will be implemented. It can also result in higher quality, more situation-relevant changes. Although several variants of action research have been developed (Lippitt et al., 1958; Shani & Pasmore, 1985; Argyris & Schön, 1989), applications to OD generally involve the following cyclical activities: (1) preliminary data gathering and diagnosis; (2) action planning; (3) implementation; and (4) assessment. In practice, these activities result in an iterative process where initial research informs action, and additional research informs further action, and so on.

## Preliminary data gathering and diagnosis

Action research typically starts with a pressing problem that organization members are motivated to resolve. Based on this presenting issue, preliminary data are gathered to determine whether the problem has been correctly identified and to diagnose its underlying causes. This initial research is generally informed by diagnostic models that show what features of the organization to examine and what data to collect to discover the source of organizational problems. OD practitioners use a plethora of diagnostic models to assess various aspects of organizations, from members' individual motivation to relationships between the organization and other organizations in its environment (Lawler et al., 1980). They use a variety of methods to collect diagnostic data, from informal interviews with a few people to formal surveys of the total organization (Nadler, 1977). When these data are collected and analyzed appropriately, they provide valid information about causes of organization problems.

## Action planning

Based on this preliminary research, participants develop action plans specifying what organization changes will be made and how they will be implemented. The choice and design of change interventions depend on a variety of factors having to do with the target of change and the change situation itself. In selecting a change target, participants can draw on a large diversity of OD interventions to improve various aspects and problems of organizations. Indeed, OD is known primarily for its interventions, such as team building, self-managed teams, and high-involvement organizations. The preliminary diagnosis guides which of those interventions are most relevant for the organization. Moreover, it helps participants choose interventions that are likely to succeed in their specific change situation. Researchers have identified key situational contingencies that can affect intervention success, such as individual differences among members and the nature of the organization's technology and competitive situation (Porras & Berg, 1978; Nicholas, 1982). Knowledge of these contingencies can help to assure that action plans fit well with the change situation.

## Implementation

Implementing action plans involves making changes that move the organization towards its desired future. Such change does not occur instantly but requires a transition period during which members learn how to enact the changes and make them work. OD has identified activities and structures that can facilitate this transition phase (Beckhard & Harris, 1987). These include specifying the change tasks that need to occur, temporally ordering them, and monitoring their progress. It also involves identifying key stakeholders whose commitment is needed for change to occur and gaining their support. In cases where change is large scale and involves several features and levels of the organization, special structures for managing the change process may need to be created. These structures mobilize resources for change, coordinate the changes, and account for progress. Members who have both the power to make change happen and the respect of key stakeholders lead them.

## Assessment

This final phase of action research involves gathering and analyzing data to determine the effects of the changes. Such information is used to decide whether the changes are having their intended results, and, if not, how they can be modified to be more effective. Assessment tends to occur at different stages of the change process both during implementation and after it is completed (Cummings & Worley, 2001). During implementation, evaluation provides timely feedback about whether the changes are being implemented as intended. Because organization change generally involves considerable learning and experimentation, such information is vital to members learning new behaviors and procedures needed to implement change. Assessment that occurs after implementation provides feedback about the overall impact of the organization changes. It helps members determine whether the changes should continue to be supported or whether other possible interventions should bc tried.

## Action Learning

Action learning has been variously referred to as 'participatory action research' (Greenwood et al., 1993), 'action inquiry' (Fisher & Tolbert, 1995), and 'self-designing organizations' (Mohrman & Cummings, 1989). It is a relatively new and still evolving form of planned change. Action learning moves beyond the problem-solving focus inherent in traditional applications of OD, and treats change as a continuous learning and transformation process. It responds to the enormous pressures for change facing organizations today (Vaill, 1989). They are experiencing competitive demands to perform more quickly and efficiently at lower cost and higher quality. They are being forced to adapt to turbulent environments where technological, economic, and cultural forces are changing rapidly and unpredictably. To respond to these forces, organizations are radically transforming themselves into leaner, more flexible structures capable of continuous adaptation and change. Such change involves considerable learning and innovation as members try new behaviors, structures, and processes, assess the results, make necessary adjustments, and so on. It also requires significant support and commitment from key stakeholders including managers, employees, and staff experts.

Action learning addresses these issues. It helps members acquire the skills and expertise to design their own innovations, to manage their own change processes, and, perhaps most important, to learn how to do these things more effectively and efficiently. It identifies key stakeholders and gets them actively involved in analyzing the organization and its environment, designing appropriate changes, and implementing them. It builds the capacity to change and to improve continually into the organization so it becomes part of normal functioning.

Action learning involves a number of interrelated actions that comprise an iterative learning process. As members move through these activities, they learn how to change and improve the organization, including their own work behaviors and interactions. This learning feeds into the next cycle of action learning and so on, thus enhancing members' capacity to change both the organization and themselves. Action learning general includes the following steps: (1) valuing; (2) diagnosing; (3) designing; and (4) implementing and assessing.

## Valuing

Action learning generally starts with clarifying the values that will guide the change process. Organization values influence members' behaviors and decision-making; they affect which innovations and changes are seen as good or bad. Because organization values are tacit and rarely questioned, they tend to perpetuate the status quo (Mohrman & Cummings, 1989). Thus, valuing seeks to make explicit the organization's values and to judge their relevance to competitive conditions. This may result in modifying or replacing certain values, or considering entirely new ones. Moreover, because stakeholders often have diverse interests, valuing attempts to uncover underlying value conflicts and to resolve them so they do not adversely affect subsequent design and implementation activities. Unless organization changes take into account the interests of different stakeholders, there is likely to be differential support and commitment for them.

OD practitioners have developed various methods for resolving value conflicts, including collaborating, compromising, and negotiating (Walton, 1987). The key objective is to achieve sufficient value agreement among stakeholders so they can proceed with changing the organization in a shared and committed direction. A common outcome of valuing is a 'vision statement' that explains the values that will guide organization change, including valued human and performance outcomes and valued organizational conditions for achieving them (Mohrman & Cummings, 1987; Collins & Porras, 1994). Although valuing occurs early in action learning, members may periodically reassess and modify the values as they continually move through the cycle of learning activities.

## Diagnosing

This phase of action learning involves assessing the organization against the values. This can reveal value gaps where the organization is not functioning or performing consistent with the values. Such inconsistencies direct the subsequent design of organization changes to close the gaps. Thus, action learning is aimed at continually assessing and improving the organization in a valued direction.

## Designing

This step involves developing specific organization changes to reduce value gaps and to move the organization in a valued direction. Depending on the diagnosis, members may determine that limited change is necessary and existing conditions only need to be fine tuned; or that more extensive change is needed requiring innovations that either imitate what other organizations are doing or that are entirely new and original. Thus, designing is not deterministic but involves considerable creativity and choice. Members explore new ways for organizing that are consistent with the values. They iterate back and forth between the values which serve as design guides and the designs themselves.

Designing typically results in organization changes that are minimally specified and flexible (Cummings & Srivastva, 1977). This enables members to adjust the changes to fit situational contingencies during implementation. It provides members with sufficient freedom to modify the changes as they learn how to enact them behaviorally and how to modify and improve them as the circumstances demand.

## Implementing and assessing

In this phase, members implement and assess organization changes. This involves learning by doing. Members take action to implement or modify the changes. They periodically assess whether the changes and implementation process are progressing as intended, and, if not, make plans to modify them. This feedback–adjustment process enables members to learn how to change the organization and themselves. It continues indefinitely as members learn how to improve the organization continuously.

Implementing and assessing can involve three levels of learning (Bateson, 1972; Argyris & Schön, 1996). At the most basic level, which is referred to as 'single-loop learning', members concentrate on getting the changes implemented in accordance with the values. They seek to reduce deviations from the changes' underlying values. This learning occurs continuously and involves considerable problem-solving and trial-and-error as members learn to move the organization closer to its values. Single-loop learning is involved in all approaches to organization change, including Lewin's three steps and action research. It enables members to implement planned changes as intended.

Action learning goes beyond these other approaches, however, to also include higher levels of learning. Called 'double-loop learning', the next level involves changing the values themselves. Members learn how to confront value inconsistencies and conflicts and modify values accordingly; they learn how to change values that may no longer support the organization's strategy and competitive situation. This level of learning occurs periodically and generally requires members to return to the valuing and designing phases. They may learn that the values set initially need to be modified and that renewed designing, implementing, and assessing activities need to occur.

At the highest level, action learning involves 'deutero learning', or learning how to learn. This is the most difficult yet important level of action learning. Because organization learning processes tend to be tacit and taken for granted, members are not accustomed to examining or questioning them. This can lead to repetition of learning mistakes and disorders. Thus, deutero learning is aimed at the learning process itself. Members examine values, organizational conditions, and behaviors that inhibit single- and double-loop learning; they design more effective learning processes. Members then engage in implementing and assessing the new learning behaviors. Over time, deutero learning enables members to enhance their capacity to learn, and thus become better at implementing changes and improving the organization.

## CONCLUSION

OD is an evolving field of applied social science with an increasing diversity of concepts and applications. From its traditional roots in small groups and social processes, OD has grown to include the total organization and work designs, human resources, and organization structures. This development closely parallels the changing needs of modern organizations. It moves beyond solving the unintended social problems inherent in large bureaucracies to helping organizations become leaner, more flexible, and more performance driven, so they can compete in today's complex, rapidly changing environments. To guide these applications, OD draws on a core set of psychological concepts. They include humanistic perspectives of human beings, resulting in organization changes that enhance members' maturity and interpersonal competence; motivation frameworks that promote changes satisfying a wide array of members' needs; process views of change that account for driving and restraining forces; groups as the focus of change, and the need for members to participate in developing and implementing change. These psychological foundations influence how OD is applied in organizations. They result in change processes that are cyclical and collaborative, and that closely tie research to action. Such change applications can help organizations address specific problems, or, more radically, help them learn how to continuously transform and renew themselves.

Because OD is an action science, it will continue to grow and evolve as it helps organizations change and improve. As organizations face new challenges, OD will create new methods and applications. It will draw on new concepts and approaches to guide future practice. OD's success will depend largely on how well those ideas and innovations account for the fact that organization change is essentially a social process requiring human beings to change their behavior. Continued attention to the psychological foundations of OD can help this occur.

## REFERENCES

Alderfer, C. (1969) An empirical test of a new theory of human needs. *Organizational Behavior and Human Performance*, May, 142–175.

Argyris, C. (1962) *Interpersonal Competence and Organizational Effectiveness*. Homewood, IL: Dorsey Press.

Argyris, C. (1964a) *Integrating the Individual and the Organization*. New York: John Wiley & Sons, Ltd.

Argyris, C. (1964b) T groups for organizational effectiveness. *Harvard Business Review*, **42**, 60–74.

Argyris, C., Putnam, R. & Smith, D. (1985) *Action Science: Concepts, Methods, and Skills for Research and Intervention*. San Francisco: Jossey-Bass.

Argyris, C. & Schön, D. (1989) Participatory action research and action science compared. *American Behavioral Scientist*, **9**, 612–623.

Argyris, C. & Schön, D. (1996) *Organizational Learning II: Theory, Method, and Practice*. Reading, MA: Addison-Wesley.

Ashkenas, R., Ulrich, D., Jick, T. & Kerr, S. (1995) *The Boundaryless Organization*. San Francisco: Jossey-Bass.

Bateson, G. (1972) *Steps to an Ecology of Mind*. New York: Ballantine Books.

Beckhard, R. (1967) The confrontation meeting. *Harvard Business Review*, **4**, 149–155.

Beckhard, R. (1969) *Organization Development: Strategies and Models*. Reading, MA: Addison-Wesley.

Beckhard, R. & Harris, R. (1987) *Organizational Transitions: Managing Complex Change*. Reading, MA: Addison-Wesley.

Beer, M. (1980) *Organization Change and Development: A Systems View*. Santa Monica, CA: Goodyear Publishing.

Bennis, W. (1969) *Organization Development: Its Nature, Origins, and Prospects*. Reading, MA: Addison-Wesley.

Bradford, L. (1967) Biography of an institution. *Journal of Applied Behavioral Science*, **3**, 127.

Bunker, B. & Alban, B. (1997) *Large Group Interventions*. San Francisco: Jossey-Bass.

Burke, W. (1982) *Organization Development: Principles and Practices*. Boston: Little Brown.

Burke, W. (1987) *Organization Development: A Normative View*. Reading, MA: Addison-Wesley.

Cartwright, D. & Zander, A. (eds) (1953) *Group Dynamics: Research and Theory*. Evanston, IL: Row, Peterson.

Cartwright, D. & Zander, A. (eds) (1960) *Group Dynamics: Research and Theory* (2nd edn). Evanston, IL: Harper & Row.

Coch, L. & French, J. (1948) Overcoming resistance to change. *Human Relations*, **1**, 512–532.

Collier, J. (1945) United States Indian Administration as a laboratory of ethnic relations. *Social Research*, **12**, 275–276.

Collins, J. & Porras, J. (1994) *Built to Last*. New York: Harper Business.

Csikszentmihalyi, M. (1990) *Flow: The Psychology of Optimal Experience*. New York: Harper & Row.

Cummings, T. (ed.) (1980) *Systems Theory for Organization Development*. Chichester: John Wiley & Sons, Ltd.

Cummings, T. & Molloy, E. (1977) *Improving Productivity and the Quality of Work Life*. New York: Praeger.

Cummings, T. & Srivastva, S. (1977) *Management of Work*. Kent, OH: Comparative Administration Research Institute, Kent State University.

Cummings, T. & Worley, C. (2001) *Organization Development and Change* (7th edn). Cincinnati, OH: South-Western College Publishing.

Davenport, T. & Prusak, L. (1998) *Working Knowledge: How Organizations Manage What They Know*. Boston: Harvard Business School Press.

Davidow, W. & Malone, M. (1992) *The Virtual Organization: Structuring and Revitalizing the Corporation of the 21st Century*. New York: Harper Business.

Dyer, W. (1987) *Team Building: Issues and Alternatives* (2nd edn). Reading, MA: Addison-Wesley.

Ellis, A. (1973) *Humanistic Psychology: The Rational-Emotive Approach*. New York: Julian Press.

Fisher, D. & Tolbert, W. (1995) *Personal and Organizational Transformations: The True Challenge of Continual Quality Improvement*. New York: McGraw-Hill.

Ford, R. (1969) *Motivation through the Work Itself*. New York: American Management Associations.

French, W. (1969) Organization development: objectives, assumptions, and strategies. *California Management Review*, **12**(2), 23–34.

French, W. (1985) The emergence and early history of organization development with reference to, influences upon, and interactions among some of the key actors. In D. Warrick (ed.) *Contemporary Organization Development: Current Thinking and Applications* (pp. 12–27). Glenview, IL: Scott, Foresman.

Fried, Y. & Ferris, G. (1987) The validity of the job characteristics model: a review and meta-analysis. *Personnel Psychology*, **Summer**, 287–322.

Galbraith, J. (1977) *Organization Design*. Reading, MA: Addison-Wesley.

Galbraith, J. & Lawler, E.E. III (eds) (1993) *Organizing for the Future: The New Logic for Managing Complex Organizations*. San Francisco: Jossey-Bass.

Gergen, K. (1994) *Toward Transformation in Social Knowledge* (2nd edn). London: Sage.

Goodman, P. & Dean, J. (1982) Creating long-term organizational change. In P. Goodman (ed.) *Change in Organizations* (pp. 226–279). San Francisco: Jossey-Bass.

Grant, R. (1998) *Contemporary Strategy Analysis* (3rd edn). Malden, MA: Blackwell.

Greenwood, D., Whyte, W. & Harkavy, I. (1993) Participatory action research as process and goal. *Human Relations*, **46**, 175–192.

Greiner, L. & Schein, V. (1988) *Power and Organization Development: Mobilizing Power to Implement Change*. Reading, MA: Addison-Wesley.

Hackman, J.R. & Oldham, G. (1975) Development of the job diagnostic survey. *Journal of Applied Psychology*, **60**, 159–170.

Hackman, J.R. & Oldham, G. (1980) *Work Redesign*. Reading, MA: Addison-Wesley.

Hamel, G. & Prahalad, C. (1994) *Competing for the Future*. Cambridge, MA: Harvard Business School Press.

Herzberg, F., Mausner, B. & Snyderman, B. (1959) *The Motivation to Work*. New York: John Wiley & Sons, Ltd.

Katz, D. & Kahn, R. (1978) *The Social Psychology of Organizing* (2nd edn). New York: John Wiley & Sons, Ltd.

Kirkpatrick, D. (ed.) (1985) *How to Manage Change Effectively*. San Francisco: Jossey-Bass.

Lawler, E.E. III (1981) *Pay and Organization Development*. Reading, MA: Addison-Wesley.

Lawler, E.E. III (1986) *High-Involvement Management*. San Francisco: Jossey-Bass.

Lawler, E.E. III (2000) *Rewarding Excellence: Pay Strategies for the New Economy*. San Francisco: Jossey-Bass.

Lawler, E.E. III, Mohrman, A. Jr, Mohrman, S., Ledford, G. Jr, Cummings, T. & Associates (eds) (1985) *Doing Research that is Useful for Theory and Practice*. San Francisco: Jossey-Bass.

Lawler, E.E. III, Nadler, D. & Camman, C. (eds) (1980) *Organizational Assessment*. New York: John Wiley & Sons, Ltd.

Lewin, K. (1946) Action research and minority problems. *Journal of Social Issues*, **2**, 34–46.

Lewin, K. (1947) Group decision and social change. In T. Newcomb & E. Hartley (eds) *Readings in Social Psychology* (pp. 197–211). New York: Holt, Rinehart & Winston.

Lewin, K. (1951) *Field Theory in Social Science: Selected Theoretical Papers*. Ed. D. Cartwright. New York: Harper & Row.

Likert, R. (1961) *New Patterns of Management*. New York: McGraw-Hill.

Likert, R. (1967) *The Human Organization*. New York: McGraw-Hill.

Lippitt, R., Watson, J. & Westley, B. (1958) *The Dynamics of Planned Change*. New York: Harcourt, Brace.

Mann, F. (1962) Studying and creating change. In W. Bennis, K. Benne & R. Chin (eds) *The Planning of Change: Readings in the Applied Behavioral Sciences* (pp. 605–615). New York: Holt, Rinehart & Winston.

Marrow, A. (1967) Events leading to the establishment of the National Training Laboratories. *Journal of Applied Behavioral Science*, **3**, 145–150.

Marrow, A. (1969) *The Practical Theorist: The Life and Work of Kurt Lewin*. New York: Basic Books.

Maslow, A. (1954) *Motivation and Personality*. New York: Harper & Brothers.

Maslow, A. (1968) *Toward a Psychology of Being* (2nd edn). Princeton, NJ: Van Nostrand.

McClelland, D. (1961) *The Achieving Society*. New York: Van Nostrand.

McGregor, D. (1960) *The Human Side of Enterprise*. New York: McGraw-Hill.

Miles, R. & Snow, C. (1978) *Organization Strategy, Structure, and Process*. New York: McGraw–Hill.

Mohrman, S. & Cummings, T. (1989) *Self-Designing Organizations: Learning How to Create High Performance*. Reading, MA: Addison-Wesley.

Mohrman, A., Mohrman, S., Ledford, G., Cummings, T. & Lawler, E.E. III (eds) (1989) *Large-Scale Organizational Change*. San Francisco: Jossey-Bass.

Nadler, D. (1977) *Feedback and Organization Development: Using Data-Based Methods*. Reading, MA: Addison-Wesley.

Nadler, D., Gerstein, M. & Shaw, R. (eds) (1992) *Organizational Architecture*. San Francisco: Jossey-Bass.

Nicholas, J. (1982) The comparative impact of organization development interventions on hard criteria measures. *Academy of Management Review*, **7**, 531–542.

Patten, T. (1981) *Organizational Development through Team Building*. New York: John Wiley & Sons, Ltd.

Pfeffer, J. (1998) *Putting People First*. Boston: Harvard Business School Press.

Porras, J. & Berg, P. (1978) The impact of organization development. *Academy of Management Review*, **3**, 249–266.

Porter, L. & Lawler, E.E. III (1968) *Managerial Attitudes and Performance*. Homewood, IL: Richard D. Irwin.

Porter, M. (1980) *Competitive Strategy*. New York: The Free Press.

Reason, P. (ed.) (1988) *Human Inquiry in Action: Developments in New Paradigm Research*. London: Sage.

Rogers, C. (1972) *On Becoming a Person*. Boston: Houghton Mifflin.

Schein, E. (1969) *Process Consultation: Its Role in Organization Development*. Reading, MA: Addison-Wesley.

Schein, E. (1987) *Process Consultation II: Lessons for Managers and Consultants*. Reading, MA: Addison-Wesley.

Schein, E. (1998) *Process Consultation Revisited*. Reading, MA: Addison-Wesley.

Seashore, S. (1987) Surveys in organizations. In J. Lorsch (ed.) *Handbook of Organizational Behavior*. Englewood Cliffs, NJ: Prentice Hall.

Senge, P. (1990) *The Fifth Discipline*. New York: Doubleday.

Shani, A. & Pasmore, W. (1985) Organization inquiry: towards a new paradigm of the action research process. In D. Warrick (ed.) *Contemporary Organization Development*. Glenview, IL: Scott, Foresman.

Spreitzer, G. (1996) Social structural characteristics of psychological empowerment. *Academy of Management Journal*, **39**, 483–505.

Teece, D. (1998) Capturing value from knowledge assets: the new economy, market for know-how, and intangible assets. *California Management Review*, **40**, 55–79.

Thompson, J. (1967) *Organizations in Action*. New York: McGraw-Hill.

Trist, E., Higgin, G., Murray, H. & Pollock, A. (1963) *Organizational Choice*. London: Tavistock.

Vaill, P. (1989) *Managing as a Performing Art: New Ideas for a World of Chaotic Change*. San Francisco: Jossey-Bass.

Van Eerde, W. & Thierry, H. (1996) Vrooms expectancy models and work-related criteria: a meta-analysis. *Journal of Applied Psychology*, **October**, 575–586.

Vroom, V. (1964) *Work and Motivation*. New York: John Wiley & Sons, Ltd.

Vroom, V. & Jago, A. (1988) *The New Leadership: Managing Participation in Organizations*. Englewood Cliffs, NJ: Prentice Hall.

Walton, R. (1987) *Managing Conflict: Interpersonal Dialogue and Third-Party Roles* (2nd edn). Reading, MA: Addison-Wesley.

Wertz, F. (ed.) (1995) *The Humanistic Movement: Recovering the Person in Psychology*. London: Gardner Press.

Whyte, W. & Hamilton, E. (1964) *Action Research for Management*. Homewood, IL: Irwin-Dorsey.

# CHAPTER 2

# Open Systems Theory
## Implications for Development and Learning

**Merrelyn Emery**
*Fred Emery Institute, Melbourne, Australia*

This chapter is written from the perspective of Open Systems Theory (OST) as it has developed from the early work of Fred Emery, Eric Trist, and their colleagues. The three-volume anthology of the Tavistock Institute gives some flavour of OST (Trist & Murray, 1990, 1993; Trist et al., 1997). The reasons for my preference for this conceptual framework will become obvious below. Choice of framework has momentous implications for the management of change, particularly the psychological aspects of it, as no less than the very definition of a human being and human behaviour is at stake in this field. Once we understand that this most basic level of consideration is involved, the choices presented by such matters as diagnosing organizational problems and addressing them become very stark indeed.

I argue here that the major reason for the high failure rate of change processes in organizations, as well as communities and other entities, lies not with the particulars of the methods and tools themselves but much deeper in social science. I believe it lies in the general failure of social science to come to grips with people and human behaviour. As the conceptualizations of people are inadequate, so too are the means devised from the conceptual base.

I would argue that concepts and conceptual frameworks are also tools. Assumptions also are essential tools as they provide the necessary economy we must all employ when we consider the diverse range of human behaviours. Assumptions underlie the choice of conceptual framework and the methods that flow from that choice. But today's social science landscape lies strewn with mutually exclusive assumptions and the tools they spawn. What is the basis for such opposing assumptions? Basically everything we use in social science is a means to an end, which raises the interesting question of how people are defining the end(s). Most method designers, hopefully, would aim for a conceptually based, orderly arrangement of meaningful steps to achieve their main aim.

In this chapter I will use the term 'social science' to cover all conceptual and applied work although I am aware that many practitioners do not see themselves as 'social scientists'. Perhaps they should? Science, including social science, is itself a process, something that human beings do (Chein, 1972: 304). As we have argued from Charles Peirce's concept of retroduction, everyone does research (Emery & Emery, 1997). Many who consider themselves part of the 'helping' professions could add to social science knowledge by realizing that their actions and effects can contribute to universal or general rather than merely particular or local knowledge (Gloster, 2000).

Social science has devised a range of methods and tools which claim to be tailor-made for the investigation of human and social issues and problems but this claim does not always stand up to scrutiny. 'Willy-nilly, in our conduct as scientists, we commit ourselves to philosophical, metaphysical, ontological, epistemological and axiological positions' (Chein, 1972: 301). As much as it would appear silly to adopt a philosophical or epistemological position without thinking about how it could be

*Dynamics of Organizational Change and Learning.* Edited by J.J. Boonstra.
© 2004 John Wiley & Sons, Ltd. ISBN 0-471-87737-9.

operationalized or even if it would work in practice, it also appears silly to rush into practice without examining the system of ideas and assumptions which lie behind it. And yet, when one does attempt such a methodological analysis, it can become readily apparent that the assumptions made about human behaviour simply do not fit with anything observable about our species and its diverse behaviours. Yet our 'first responsibility, one that transcends all others, is to our observables' (ibid.: 8). Chein, like many before and after him, expressed disquiet that a field concerned with human behaviour and social systems such as organizations has produced so little of lasting relevance to its subject matter. Chein says 'the failure must, then, become [an] occasion of searching self-examination' (ibid.: 4). I will show that as many methods employ assumptions at odds with the observables, such self-examination must be pretty rare.

## DIAGNOSING ORGANIZATIONAL PROBLEMS

Accurately diagnosing problems is of course the first step to solving them and it is here that the relationship of assumptions and observables can become acute. This applies no less to organizational problems than it does to the medical variety. Attempting to cure the wrong problem, or a problem that does not exist, can cause more trouble than accepting the status quo.

### Two Systems of Conceptual Tools

Our tools derive from accumulating knowledge, but there are two streams of knowledge based on two views of the nature of reality. Within each stream many different schools of thought have waxed and waned over the centuries but each school within a stream bears greater resemblance to others within that stream than it does to those in the second stream. The streams may be characterized as 'realism' and 'idealism' (Mead, 1932).

The idealism stream runs through philosophers such as Kant to the physicist Newton, to social scientists such as Thorndike, Freud, Hull, and Lewin. Lewin occupies a unique place in this schema as the diverse nature of his huge contribution spawned two separate interpretations of his work: open human systems and the human relations movement (Trist, 1985; Emery, M., 2000a). Realism runs through the philosopher Leibnitz to the physicists Maxwell, Faraday, and Wigner who explored electrical fields, and then to the polymath philosopher Charles S. Peirce. In the modern era of social science proper there are many, some referenced herein, who have made significant contributions to realism. Table 2.1 shows that realism and idealism contain quite different assumptions that lead to very different processes.

**TABLE 2.1** Assumptions from two systems of conceptual tools

| From Material Universals—Realism | From Abstract Universals—Idealism |
|---|---|
| Reality exists | Reality is a social construct |
| Human and social systems are open | Human and social systems are closed |
| People directly extract meaningful knowledge of their environments | People cannot know their environments, they are *tabulae rasae* and must be taught |
| People actively and purposefully shape their environments, physical and social | People are passive recipients of environmental forces, both physical and social |
| The sufficient conditions of behaviour are in 'system-in-environment' | The sufficient conditions of behaviour are within the organism or social unit |
| Units transact | Units interact |
| There are universal or species-wide laws governing human behaviour | There are no universal or species-wide laws governing human behaviour |

Those employing material universals accept 'as real physical bodies and their activities; the other nontangible formal qualities and logical and mathematical truths' (Chein, 1972: 146). Human knowledge develops from the identification and classification of particulars and these competing views of reality identify entirely different types of taxonomies. Cassirer and Lewin define them as the 'class concept and the series concept' which are also described as phenotypical (superficial appearances or similarities) and genotypical or 'genetic' (Lewin, 1931: 10–11). These classes or laws are called 'universals' and there appear to be only two basic forms of universal, known as material and abstract. Material universals describe a material or real world (Feibleman, 1946: 451) and derive from particular dynamic events. Realism uses a language based on serial genetic constructs or functional entities that have testable relations with other entities, including context (Cassirer, 1923). This language is very different from the everyday usage of nouns to express the generic nature of things. Identifying things as nouns out of context involves us in circular arguments as properties such as extroverted behaviours define an 'extrovert' and the 'fact' that a person is an 'extrovert' explains the extroverted behaviours.

Choice of material or abstract universals for social scientists is more fraught than for others as people deliberately create novel phenomena. Do the sufficient conditions of this behaviour lie purely within the person or in the person-in-environment? Realists choose person-in-environment because they perceive people transacting and coevolving with their environments. They behave very differently from inanimate things and from animals without consciousness. Therefore, realists make the assumption that human systems have boundaries open to environments. If boundaries are permeable, people must be able to learn from their environments. Also, you can observe people learning from their environments.

> [Realism] in all its forms, is the movement toward recovery of the sense of transaction. The schools of thinking based on self action and interaction assume that the sufficient conditions of behaviour are within the 'organism' or, in social determinism, in the (so-called) 'social organism'. With self action and interactionism the emphasis is on analysis: with transactionalism the emphasis is on synthesis. This is not the synthesis of metaphysics—it is [the synthesis of] systems. (Emery, F., undated)

Choice of realism leads to choice of unit as person- or system-in-environment in all their changing particulars. That choice yields an holistic social science. In the course of a day a person may behave quite differently in each setting in which they find themselves. A study of that person as a human being involves asking 'What is s/he doing, how and why?' It identifies what in a particular context has effects on that person and what changes in that person's behaviour can affect what changes in the context. Such a study identifies the universal in the particulars. Novelty or emergence is recognized as such and perceived to follow from transaction or coevolution.

Choice of an intra-individual or social unit taken context-free is handled by asking 'What is it?', 'What is its essence?' When the latter question is asked, problems of novelty or emergence can be handled only by reductionism or the postulation of other different entities. Hence we see the endless multiplication of specializations and taxonomies within social science and the search for smaller, determining units until we arrive at the absurdity of 'medieval genetic determinism' (Sapolsky, 2000: 12). 'The boundaries of genes are in fact no more clearly definable in the long term than those of individuals' (Rayner, 1997: 36). But we have lost the species as the subject matter long before we get to DNA. Specializations within social science have led us into innumerable varieties of people, in families, in management or worker roles, in sickness and in health.

Explaining novelty and human creativity is a critical choice point for material and abstract universals and, therefore, it is in social science that the choice becomes consequential for practice. The endless definitions of a 'human nature', a static generic concept, contrast starkly with Ackoff and Emery's (1972) serial genetic construct of a person as an open purposeful system, given in full below. These people 'also use conversation as preparation for concerted action (de Laguna, 1927) with a huge range of skills, motives, and affects (Tomkins, 1962).

> These people choose, change their minds and in all ways behave just like us. They appear to be an entirely different species from the impoverished creatures we tend to find in other varieties of social science. On the line of abstract universals we find people who are imprisoned within their skins or other static boundaries such as the life space (e.g. Lewin), who must be induced or taught to cooperate (e.g. the Human Relations school), who are passively subject to irresistible 'drives', instincts and forces (e.g. Freud), and those who, incapable of directly perceiving reality, are condemned to guessing it from reading their instrument panel (e.g. Maturana & Varela, 1980). We end up with two quite irreconcilable human portraits. (Emery, M., 2000b: 636–637)

Another of the implications of using abstract universals within social science is that specialization and fragmentation have led to the position where there is abrogation of responsibility for discovering laws governing human behaviour and, therefore, being able to identify species-specific behaviours. Gustavsen et al. (1996: 54) observed that the 1980s were a period of postmodernism that 'came to imply deconstruction and "downsizing" of many of the earlier efforts to create a "grand theory"— a theory identifying universal front lines in organization development'. This trend elevates cultural relativism to an art form and, in the process, loses opportunities inherent in, for example, the cross-cultural testing of concepts and methods. Everything becomes a discrete case study. 'The problems arising in organizations and workplaces share no essences. We see "family resemblances" in the good and bad points of organizations, but action research does not generate a theory of workplaces in general' (Toulmin, 1996: 214). Leaving aside the fact that 'essence' is a key concept in theories deriving from abstract universals, Toulmin's position is something more than a failure to see the wood for the trees. It virtually denies the possibility of the accretion of knowledge about organizations or people since because every organization is different, there can be only 'local theory'. This in turn leads to an educational failure since if there is no general species knowledge, then there is nothing of continuing value to pass on to others. It may also help account for a demarcation between those who see themselves as practitioners or 'facilitators' and those who class themselves as researchers. As we shall see below, while every organization is phenotypically different, they are certainly not genotypically different.

Each stream provides a system of internally consistent dimensions. An expression of one dimension of the set of transaction/interaction, open/closed, purposeful/not purposeful, and synthesis/analysis almost inevitably involves the author in the others (Emery, M., 2000b). They are systems of assumptions.

The two streams are captured by 'world hypotheses' which are systems of assumptions flowing from root metaphors, that is, they are hypotheses about how to approach the world. Contextualism assumes there is a whole changing over time, one that we can know by investigating a series of historic events within the changing context of the whole. It is the only world hypothesis that can deal with novelty and change (Pepper, 1942). The other three adequate hypotheses assume a closed and static system. The two most relevant today are 'mechanism', which assumes that everything is and works like a machine, and 'organicism', which is based on constant integration of data into wholes. Neither can encompass the notions of open purposeful systems, a social field or active adaptation. Mechanism assumes a closed, static mechanical universe inhabited by goal-seeking people (Ackoff & Emery, 1972) with fragmented sensory systems who are unable to extract meaningful information about their world. Organicism is currently manifesting itself as 'whole systems' (context-free). If we are dealing with organizational change, it becomes pretty obvious that only a conceptual framework that lies within the world hypothesis of contextualism will work.

But despite there being a reliable and known alternative, the allure of abstract universals remains strong within the social sciences. Bertalanffy's open system has spawned the burgeoning progeny of General Systems Theory (GST):

> In 1965 Trist and I provided a conceptual framework whereby systems could be related to empirical testable environments instead of to the abstract undifferentiated environments of Bertalanffy and Prigogine. It became fashionable to make references to our Type IV, 'turbulent' environment'. Otherwise the conceptual framework could be said to have met no felt need amongst system theorists. Ackoff and I made an attempt to provide a common language, and a common goal of seeking to understand purposive systems (1972). This was ignored. (Emery, F., undated)

The GST offspring have become part of the problem rather than the solution because they are simply variations on the other three world hypotheses while pretending to be different. In this class we can include the current variants of complexity and chaos theories which De Paoli (2000) recognizes as mechanistic, empiricist, and positivist. *The Economist* (2001: 79) claims that these variants are showing a 'new-found humility' but that is not really the point. While they remain wedded to abstract universals, they may well continue to make 'a big noise but cast little light'.

To illustrate the differences between these two approaches in diagnosing organizational problems I shall take four common examples of presenting symptoms as defined by the organization. These are expressed as (1) variants of strategic plan failed; (2) lack of employee motivation which also includes failure of employees to accept responsibility; (3) communication problems which include a subclass of personality conflicts; and (4) error rates. All four are highly interrelated and are also related to productivity, flexibility, and organizational viability, and futures in general. Notions of people and organization are inseparable as there is a potential organization any time two people meet. Organizations are fundamentally sets of structured relationships between people pursuing some purposes. Definitions of a person and human behaviour are, therefore, crucial to organizational analyses.

## DEFINITIONS OF PEOPLE AND HUMAN BEHAVIOUR

Following the historical material universal stream in Table 2.1, OST defines people as open, purposeful systems who 'can produce (1) the same functional type of outcome in different structural ways in the same structural environment and (2) can produce functionally different outcomes in the same and different structural environments'. They display will (Ackoff & Emery, 1972: 31). By constantly acting as active, responsible agents (Chein, 1972: 6), they change the environment. A belief that there is only passive adaptation, 'that life merely adapts to its environment' (Bond, 2000: 47), is not only conventional wisdom in the social sciences but also in science more generally. As Bond notes, this belief is changing. But not only do people constantly and purposefully change their physical environments, they actively and purposefully change their social field as they change their minds about what they value and why, and persuade others of their view. All this is directly observable and measurable (Emery & Emery, 1979; Alvarez & Emery, 2000).

The first basic premise underlying any purposeful behaviour is 'that things do exist and events do occur independently of our perceptions of them' (Chein, 1972: 51). If this first premise is rejected, the rejection itself does not exist, which leads to an absurdity. Using our criterion of everyday observation tells us that 'people live their lives in a real world and . . . their behavior never leaves the reality even when it most seems to be doing so' (ibid.: 145). This applies, for instance, when people are imagining and expecting events, characters and characteristics that are at the moment strictly unreal. 'Much of human endeavor . . . is concerned with controlling and shaping the future' (ibid.: 142) and organizational change involves a future referent. Chein continues the discussion by pointing out that the complete set of determinants of the future including organizational change includes what people will do as well as variables that exist within the bodies of individuals and within the environment. In other words, the outcomes are also a function of human motivation. For example, if an individual cannot envisage a particular, more desirable future state or specific set of outcomes, there will be little or no motivation to pursue that outcome. It will be classed as impossible and treated accordingly.

Methods that ignore purposefulness as the defining human characteristic are truly doomed to failure. The dismal track record of attempts at organizational change (see Introduction in this volume) is a testament to both our ingenuity at 'beating the system' whenever we choose, and to the fact that so many methods continue to implicitly deny our purposefulness. If employees don't want a method to succeed, it won't.

OST includes four other major characteristics of people. For development and mental health, people require a reasonable balance of autonomy, self-governance, homonomy, and interdependence with others (Angyal, 1965: 254). Autonomy without corresponding homonomy actually restricts and inhibits personal growth. Methods that isolate individuals and deny interdependence will have very different effects from those that build in or at least encourage it. Fortunately many popular methods today (Holman & Devane, 1999) are based on small and/or large groups but the current rash of applications of personal coaching could be an emergent and worrying trend back to individuation.

People also have the potential for ideal seeking. They can confront choices between purposes and choose outcomes called ideals that are endlessly approachable but unattainable (Emery, F., 1977: 69). The ideals spring from our capacity for potential directive correlation (Sommerhoff, 1969), to imagine and expect. Ideal seeking and autonomy–homonomy are linked through the genotypical organizational design principles discussed below. When structures are based on the first design principle, they encourage autonomy and cannot provide an environment for ideal seeking. Only structures based on the second principle provide this environment (Emery, F., 1977) and they encourage autonomy and homonomy simultaneously. Methods that fail to take the human capacity for imagination, expectations, and the ideals into account are not optimizing, let alone maximizing, their potential for change. When people collectively seek ideals, the ideals take precedence over their individual but different values, creating stability of direction. Ideals have also been shown to be motivators in their own right and the necessary and sufficient conditions for their elicitation are known (Emery, M., 1999). Clearly, if a method cannot elicit ideal seeking, it is missing a component that is vital for sustainable change.

Also, because we are physically adapted to our planet, we are able to directly extract meaningful information from physical and social environments (Gibson, 1966; Emery, F., 1980; Emery, M., 1999). Once we view people as ecological learners rather than *tabulae rasae* who need teaching about how their world works, a variety of methods that rest on the latter assumption come into doubt. We return to this characteristic below.

Last but not least, humans have consciousness. Any time we consider processes involving cultural evolution, individual learning, or system or organizational development, we immediately confront the complexities of human adaptation caused by consciousness. Chein (1972: 77, 95) defines behaviour as 'any spontaneous directed action' and from this basis derives his definition of consciousness as 'an awareness accompanied by an awareness of it'. Both Chein and Vygotsky conclude that that consciousness demands a hierarchical framework which is itself a system (Vygotsky, 1962: 92). This is inherent not only in Chein's derivation of consciousness from awareness and consciously motivated behaviours from behaviour, but also in Ackoff and Emery's (1972) hierarchy of goals, purposes, and ideals. People may function at quite different system levels. A full model of consciousness and its relation to adaptation has been developed in terms of actual and potential directive correlations (Emery, M., 1999: 70–95). This allows us to better explain phenomena associated with various methods and derive testable hypotheses to improve their efficacy.

This model shows among other things that the effectiveness of methods may be judged by the extent to which they induce upward changes in the system of motivated behaviours. If a method reliably demonstrates that it can induce the replacement of lower-order and more fragmented goals by higher-order conscious behaviours and motives, it can create an econiche for perceptual reconstruction or Lewin's original unfreezing–refreezing phenomenon (Lewin, 1943).

## The Last Strategic Plan Failed—Try Again?

There are several reasons why strategic plans fail. Here I address the most common one. Also common is lack of employee motivation to implement the plan which is discussed below.

Most strategic plans fail because they use a closed systems framework. Those charged with the responsibility of determining the strategic plan very carefully work out what the organization's strategic goals should be and how they should achieve them. Because they assume that their organization is closed, they plan in a social vacuum. They ignore influences or pressures from outside sources, the changing ideals, values, and expectations of the global community, those that supply, distribute, and consume. They forget they are also at the mercy of their employees who may or may not choose to implement their little bit of the plan.

For example, the reality is that consumers may decide that a particular product or service no longer fits their value system. During the 1960s and 1970s, consumers began to decide that they valued products that contributed to environmental sustainability. Phosphates disappeared out of detergents. Construction of nuclear power plants became astronomically expensive. Now genetically modified substances are being resisted around the world, reflecting the continuing public resistance to having change imposed upon them. These phenomena are neither random nor chaotic. They are demonstrations of a very orderly and lawful human process.

If one adopts the world hypothesis of contextualism and, therefore, a socio-ecological or open systems framework, people and organizations can be seen to exist in a social field, exactly as they exist within a physical or ecological environment.

An open system (Figure 2.1A) expresses the transaction of system and environment, all components of which are governed by laws (L) which are able to be known (Emery & Trist, 1972; Emery, F., 1977). The system (designated '1') acts upon the environment (designated '2'). This is the planning function ($L_{12}$). Environment acts upon the system and is known to us through the function of learning ($L_{21}$). $L_{11}$ and $L_{22}$ express the intrinsic nature of the system and environment respectively.

A system ($L_{11}$) is defined by its *system principle*, *unitas multiplex*, or construction principle (Anygal 1941: 259). This principle expresses the unique relationship between the entity and the environment, and governs the behaviour of the system and the arrangement of its parts. Organizations may or may not be systems.

The environment ($L_{22}$) is a social field consisting of the changing values, expectations, and ideals of the human systems within it. It is formally defined as the 'extended field of directive correlations: a social field within a shared natural environment' (Emery, F., 1977: 2) with a changing causal texture

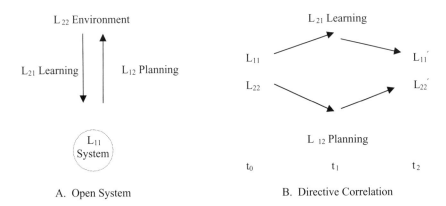

**Figure 2.1**   The models of open system and directive correlation

(Emery & Trist, 1965). This conceptualization provides a framework for cultural change and its fluctuating adaptivity.

Figure 2.1B also shows that the open systems model is based on the concept of directive correlation (Sommerhoff, 1969). The concept of *directive correlation* (DC) states that it is a necessary condition for the subsequent occurrence of a certain event or goal that two or more variables, at least environment and system, should at a given time be in exact correspondence for an adaptive relationship. Environment and system are then directively correlated with respect to the goal and the starting conditions, that is, they are correlated in terms of direction. They act to bring about the same future state of affairs from the same starting point. From the original condition at $t_0$ which consists of system and environment, both system and environment make changes at $t_1$, resulting in a new set of conditions consisting of a changed system and environment at $t_2$. In Figure 2.1B the changes shown are directively correlated and, therefore, adaptive. There are, of course, an infinite number of cases in which system and environment are not directively correlated and, therefore, are maladaptively related. The DC model expresses precisely when adaptation is or is not occurring over time.

Directive correlation not only encompasses what Holt (1915), Chein (1972), and Ackoff and Emery (1972) define as purposive behaviour, it also models coevolution rather than evolution. It can encompass the concepts of perception, cognition, memory, and motivation. Expressing these phenomena as directive correlations enables testable hypotheses (see Emery, M., 1999: 70–103).

When an organization is involved, the basic model in Figure 2.1 is elaborated by adding the level(s) of organization, or organizational system. Depending on the focus of the inquiry, an organization can be seen either as an entity or system in a social field or as a task environment for the people within it (Emery, M., 1999: 18–19). Using the DC model enables a full conceptualization of cultural change over time and that may be used both to explain and to plan long-term strategic changes, taking into account all levels of organization and environment (de Guerre, 2000).

As organizational change is a subclass of human adaptation, and making cultural change towards adaptation, it is critical to understand the changing nature of the social field with which organizations and people transact. This is given by the changing causal texture of the $L_{22}$ over time (Emery & Trist, 1965; Emery, F., 1977). The most long-lasting and adaptive $L_{22}$ option yet tried by the human race is called the Type II or 'clustered, placid' environment which lasted from our dim beginnings to about 1790. 'Placid' means stable value systems and the Type II was characterized by cooperative systems. The Industrial Revolution ushered in a totally new environment, known as the Type III or 'disturbed reactive' environment. The Type III was characterized by competition between large, virtually identical systems accompanied by the widespread introduction of hierarchical dominance into the West. Introducing this led to a suppression of group life with consequential societal maladaptions (Emery, F., 1977).

The Type III in the West was inevitably short-lived as, first, it conflicted with predispositions to the earlier Type II environment and, second, a series of events in the period 1945–53 ushered in the Type IV field. According to Fred Emery:

> I think I had been looking in the wrong places for what pushed us into turbulence. I was looking at what was new, big and growing in the old society. Now I think the answer lies quite elsewhere; in the demise of two silent assumptions that have provided the historical rationale for the persistence of the principle of 'hierarchical domination'; and done so even after the demise of 'the divine right of aristocracies' and the eternal threat of 'hell fire and brimstone'. (Emery, F., 1978: 12–13)

The two assumptions that have governed the subordination of individuals to their nation–states are:

- there is not enough to go around to support everyone at a decent level of living, and hence some centralized bodies or agreed practices must exist to ensure survival of the 'worthy' (the 'work ethic'). In its so-called socialist form, this was parodied as 'to each according to his contribution'.

- preservation of the nation–state as the prior requirement for having adequate centralized power to allocate; and hence all individual aspirations must be subordinated to the nation's requirement for waging war and to preserving and enhancing that power (patriotism). Together they enshrine a 'struggle for the survival of the fittest' and 'the indispensability of elites' (Emery, F., 1978: 13).

The extraordinary levels of production achieved during World War II destroyed the assumption that government control was required to guarantee the equitable distribution of scarce resources. They weren't scarce and we could produce more. The dropping of the A bombs on Japan, followed by the development of thermonuclear weapons and the MAD (mutually assured destruction) strategy of the cold war, were more than sufficient to convince the global population that the assumption that the state guaranteed their security was untrue. Both assumptions were discarded (Emery, F., 1978).

With these two assumptions gone, the old value systems that sprang from the acceptance of hierarchical domination also began to be rejected. People are still sorting out what they now value to replace the previous value set, and it is this process which creates the *relevant uncertainty* of the Type IV. This is its characteristic feature which is the consequence of us changing our minds as above. Since 1945 we have had *dynamic systems in a dynamic field* with an accompanying growth of maladaptions, particularly dissociation and superficiality (Emery, F., 1977). These maladaptions indicate a reluctance to engage with the structures left over from the Type III environment and we have obtained similar pictures of them from Australia and the USA (Emery & Emery, 1979; Alvarez & Emery, 2000).

It is important to understand the genesis of the Type IV because such understanding cuts through the confusion about what is really going on in the world today. Obviously, we have to be able to diagnose global social maladaptions as well as discrete organizational problems because if we cannot, what chance do we have of redesigning organizations in such ways that we can move towards adaptation rather than produce further maladaptions? I have also used the term 'unpredictable' rather than the commoner and original term 'turbulent' environment because we have learnt a lot about this environment since 1965. In particular, we saw that the name itself was causing problems of interpretation and understanding as the analogy is with aero- and hydro-dynamic systems rather than the intended psychological and social variety. 'Turbulent' lent an impression of mechanism to what is one of humanity's unique characteristics, our propensity to change our minds, a phenomenon far from mechanistic.

For a planning method, then, not to include an examination of the extended social field, extracting the learning from it and building that learning into the strategic plan for ongoing active adaptation mean that the method has denied its participants an opportunity to be genuinely active adaptive. Active adaptation within a social system is by definition a property of system–environment transaction. It is being in a constant state of purposeful change appropriate to the people, particularly their ideal seeking, and to a continuously changing environment. It encompasses the continuous learning and dynamism that are inherent to open systems. Once an organization has embarked on the implementation of an active adaptive plan, it returns at regular intervals to survey changes in the $L_{22}$ and adjust accordingly if necessary. Without active adaptation and coevolution with the environment, the organization is likely to be taken unawares when the next environmental discontinuity hits. Similarly, without an experience of examining the $L_{22}$, people will lack even the implicit knowledge of the laws operating within it that is gained from methods such as the search conference.

Some methods have gone half-way to examining the $L_{22}$. Many today include an examination of the 'business environment' but this is merely a narrow and usually a quite idiosyncratic slice of the $L_{22}$. While this may be an improvement on being environment-free, these methods cannot hope either to discover the major value shifts occurring globally or learn how to anticipate them. Additionally, because the organization will attempt to actively adapt to its business environment, it increases the relevant uncertainty in the $L_{22}$ and risks further maladaption. The search conference, the first of which was held in 1959 (Trist & Emery, 1960), distinguished itself from all previous methods of strategic planning in that the $L_{22}$ was addressed as a major component of the planning process. Other methods, particularly those adapted from the search conference, may incorporate an environmental scan based on the $L_{22}$ but treat it as a motivator or icebreaker. The serious implications of the scan are neglected as also is the emphasis on hard data and the hard work it takes to ensure that the strategic direction and system principle are actually adaptive.

## LACK OF MOTIVATION

If the assumption is made that the sufficient conditions for the unmotivated behaviour lie within the people or within their interaction, then the symptom can be cured by directly attempting to increase the motivation of each individual or by changing the nature of their interactions. The marketplace is full of 'motivational' techniques that their promoters claim will motivate the 'turned off' when professionally applied. Similarly, we do not lack for variety in the multitude of 'motivational' methods covered by the terms 'team building'.

If 'motivation' really does arise from or reside within an individual, it can be seen as a commodity to be moved from one person to another, hence the 'pep talk' delivered by one animated person to the unmotivated. However, the evidence says that the conditions for motivation lie in the transactions between the people and their social environment, and also particularly in the organizational case, in the nature of its genoptypical structure.

What is a motive? Chein (1972: 77, 23), who defines behaviour as 'any spontaneous directed action', argues that 'a behavior is a motive of the behaviors it includes'. A motive is an expression of purpose-fulness and hence drives such as hunger are not motives. People can choose not to eat when they are hungry. This is why Maslow's hierarchy of needs is an inaccurate portrayal of human behaviour. Even in extreme circumstances, people frequently choose to ignore basic needs in favour of 'higher' ones (Des Pres, 1976). Motivation involves perception, learning, memory, inference, meaning, and all the other psychological processes, and also

> involves transaction between subject and object, transaction that requires commerce with me-diating and intervening objects. In other words, it is in the very nature of motivation, and particularly of complex motivational structures that one should be concerned with the world in which behavior is taking place. (Chein, 1972: 85)

He sees it inevitable that we should be constantly scanning our environments and ourselves for infor-mation relevant to our purposes.

People live and work within organizational structures that function as task environments for them and these exist within the extended social field. There are, therefore, three sets of transactive relations. The relation between individuals and the field is often forgotten but it is required to explain the dynamic nature of life within organizational structures. People bring to any organization the ideals, values, and expectations derived from the whole of their life and their immersion within the field. They find there is either a congruence or a lack of it between these features of the field and those operationalized within the organization. When these ideals, values, and expectations are not met within the organization, an intensifying spiral of discontent is generated (Emery, M., 1999: 19). This was noted in the original study (Trist & Bamforth, 1951) which led to the development of open jointly optimized sociotechnical systems (Emery, F., 1959) and has been constantly documented since. The organization must be one which is appropriate for open purposeful systems and, when it becomes so, those who work within it negotiate to ensure that it begins to meet their ideals, values, and expectations.

How best to measure motivation? Motivation or, rather, its lack is immediately evident when one confronts any basic organizational statistics such as error or accident rates, productivity, machine downtime, or customer complaints. These are indirect measures but motivation can be more directly measured. Here we normally make a distinction between *extrinsic motivation*, which derives from such factors as money, and *intrinsic motivation*, which derives from the whole person-in-organization-in-social-field unit. It should be noted here that there is an asymmetric relationship between such extrinsic and intrinsic motivations. Financial increases do not necessarily motivate the intrinsically unmotivated but perceiving that one is unfairly compensated for one's work will quickly demotivate.

Intrinsic motivation, which is what makes people want to leap out of bed and do a great day's work, is measured by the psychological requirements for productive human activity, known for short as the 'six criteria'. These criteria are the intrinsic motivators, first published by Emery and Thorsrud (1969). The six criteria are:

1. Elbow Room, optimal autonomy in decision-making.
2. Continual Learning for which there must be:
   (a) some room to set goals;
   (b) receipt of accurate and timely feedback.
3. Variety.
4. Mutual Support and Respect, helping out and being helped out by others without request, respect for contribution rather than IQ, for example.
5. Meaningfulness which consists of:
   (a) doing something with social value;
   (b) seeing the whole product or service to which the individual contributes.
6. A desirable Future, not having a dead-end job.

The first three pertain to the individual who can have too little or too much and are measured from −5 to +5 where 0 is optimal. The second three pertain to the climate of the organization and of these you can never have too much. They are measured from 1–10. They have a long history and have been routinely measured in countless Participative Design Workshops since 1971 (Emery, M., 1993). They provide a highly reliable measure of intrinsic motivation and work equally well regardless of the purpose or nature of the organization, including universities (Emery, M., 2000c).

The six criteria are correlated with the genotypical organizational design principles (Emery, F., 1967; Emery & Emery, 1974). It is difficult to get good scores on the six criteria from structures based on the first design principle (below), even when management has gone out of its way to attend to all hygiene factors (Herzberg, 1987) and such efforts are appreciated. Hygiene factors and intrinsic motivators are independent. The nature of the relationship between design principles and the six criteria has held in every country and culture tried so far. They are very good examples of species or human laws.

The relations between people in an organization are governed by the two genotypical organizational design principles. The first design principle (DP1) is called 'redundancy of parts' because there are more parts (people) than are required to perform a task at any one given time. In DP1, responsibility for coordination and control is located at least one level above where the work, learning, or planning is being done. DP1 yields a supervisory or dominant hierarchy. Individuals have fragmented tasks and goals. The second (DP2) is called 'redundancy of functions' because more skills and functions are built into every person than that person can use at any one given point in time. In DP2, responsibility for coordination and control is located with the people performing the task. The self-managing group works to a comprehensive set of agreed and measurable goals. DP1 structures are hierarchies of personal dominance. DP2 structures are hierarchies of function where all change is negotiated.

The design principles underlie all organizational structures. Three examples should suffice. First, most of our governments are representative democracies, DP1 structures. Voters go to the polls and elect a government to which they pass responsibility for coordination and control for their futures. DP2 alternatives or participative democracies have existed and currently exist (Emery, F., 1976; Emery, F., 1998). Second, committees are DP1 structures where the chairperson holds responsibility for coordination and control of the work of the committee and its members. Their dynamics fully justify the joke about committees designing camels. Groups with a set of agreed goals can be substituted. Third, a conference is a temporary organizational structure and as such can be structured on either the first or second design principle. DP1 gives the conventional 'talking heads' variety where responsibility for coordination and control of the conference rests not with the audience, the learners, but with the sponsors, organizers, chairs, and speakers. The purest form of DP2 conference is the search conference (Emery, M., 1999). Given the diversity of organizations from multinationals to tiny voluntary organizations and families, I use the term 'members' rather than 'staff'.

There is a third form called '*laissez-faire*' which is the absence of a design principle and coherent structure. Its behavioural effects are similar to those of DP1 but more intense (Lippit & White, 1943). Unfortunately, we have many *laissez-faire* organizations today where the structure is DP1 on paper but generally ignored (de Guerre, 2000: 657–658).

These design principles have also been discovered independently by Riane Eisler (1995: 105) who calls the systems flowing from them 'androcracy' and 'gylany'. She also recognizes they are extremely powerful and affect most aspects of organizational life as well as male–female relationships. The design principles have relevance for each of the matters discussed below. Over time DP1 actively deskills and demotivates, DP2 skills and motivates (Emery & Emery, 1974). If an organization genuinely wants high levels of intrinsic motivation, it appears to have no choice but to change the design principle that underlies the structure. Many other organizational problems such as failure to follow the strategic plan are motivational. Usually only those who produced the plan bother with it. Genuine psychological ownership produces intrinsic motivation.

## COMMUNICATION PROBLEMS

Those who use a conceptual framework or make assumptions that flow from abstract universals will accept that communication problems are a legitimate concern and should be dealt with directly. They will say 'of course people and communication can be difficult, and as communication is a primary property of behaviour and organizational life, it is important to give people additional communication skills. Increasing these skills will overcome the problems and then the organization will work better.' This view fuels a huge training industry.

There are difficulties with this view. The first is that communication is not a primary property but a secondary one. 'It is and has always been a necessary condition for people to act socially. Not, however, a *sufficient* condition. Many situations can be observed where communication channels exist but are not used. In many situations communications can reduce social activity' (Emery & Emery, 1976: 147). The second is that both quantity and quality of communication are significantly influenced by the organizational structure. The third is that an increase in skills does not translate into improved communication unless the person is motivated to use the skills. As we have seen above, in DP1 structures people are less likely to enjoy optimal or satisfactory levels of the six criteria and, correspondingly, they will be less likely to be motivated to employ the communication skills they hold which are readily displayed in other settings.

Ackoff and Emery (1972: 142) define communication by stating that one purposeful system (B) communicates with another (A) when a message produced by B changes one or more of the parameters of A's purposeful state. The message may change the degree of A's familiarity with something by *informing*, it may change A's perception of the probable effectiveness of courses of action by *instructing*, or it may change the probability of an outcome by *enlightening* or producing understanding (Emery & Emery, 1976: 154).

'Both parties in communication must be purposeful. If we push a button to start a machine and the machine has no choice, communication has not taken place' (Ackoff & Emery, 1972: 142). In other words, the act of pushing the button has not produced change in a parameter of the state of 'mind' of the other and, therefore, the nature of the relationship is interaction, not transaction as above. When we consider communication within the whole system environment unit, we see that communication can be more broadly defined as the response functions which map a set of starting conditions of both the system and the environment for a behaviour to meet a purpose (Emery, M., 1999: 79). Because

**TABLE 2.2**   Formal reporting channels and task-mediated relations

| Steps removed from policy-maker | No. in DP1 | No. in DP2 |
|---|---|---|
| 1 step | 5 | 2 |
| 2 steps | 15 | 0 |
| 3 steps | 8 | 0 |
| Total of formal reporting channels | 28 | 2 |
| Task-mediated relations between peers, maximum. This is calculated for within groups. We could add 1 under DP2 for between peer groups | 0 | 136 |
| Paper-generating function* | 59 | 2 |

* *Note*: This table is adapted from Emery and Emery (1976: 166–171) where we stated that this was an estimate of the paper-generating function based on previous experience that it increased by the square of the distance from the bottom level. We multiplied number of steps by steps removed from the top.

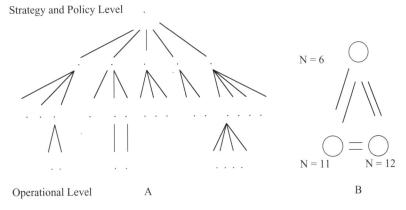

Strategy and Policy Level

N = 6

N = 11      N = 12

Operational Level            A                                    B

**FIGURE 2.2**   Structures of a small organization under the two genotypical design principles

all experiences and behaviour are coloured if not motivated by emotion or affect (Tomkins, 1962; Thatcher & John, 1977: 113), communication has the potential to be maladaptive as well as adaptive for individual, organization, and environment. This becomes important below when we consider the nature of communication in a structure that induces competition.

Looking first at the influence of design principle on quantity of communication, consider Figure 2.2A and B. Both A and B are charts of the same organization. All that has changed is the genotypical design principle, yielding in A, a typical 4-level DP1 structure. B shows the structure based on self-managing groups after the principle has been legally changed from DP1 to DP2. In fact, if this organization were to really redesign itself, it would quickly be found that a group of six people is far too many in such a small self-managing organization. There simply wouldn't be enough productive work to keep them occupied and in DP2 structures everybody does productive work and nothing but productive work.

Table 2.2. documents the differences in quantity of communication in the two structures shown in Figure 2.2. Even for this small organization, the quantity of communication is vastly different. Also while I continue to use the term 'formal reporting channel', it should be noted that relations between the strategy or policy-making level and the operational level in DP2 are vastly different from the asymmetrical relations between superior and subordinate found in DP1. The double lines in Figure 2.2B indicate that these relations are negotiations between peers. We now consider this qualitative aspect in more detail.

Within DP1 structures with their relations of personal dominance, communication has three charac-teristic features: asymmetry, egocentrism, and 'them and us', an adversarial characteristic. Asymmet-rical relations lack the reciprocity of sender and receiver that can be observed in a discussion between equals. There can be a total absence of discussion and a predominance of orders or instructions. Orders require reactions or responses, not conversation or negotiation. Asymmetry is a characteristic of the 'communication' between an operator and a machine and that it is reflected in person-to-person com-munication should come as no surprise. The principle is 'redundancy of parts'; the world hypothesis from which it derives is mechanism. The replaceable parts often refer to themselves as 'cogs in the machine'.

Egocentrism is expressed in statements such as 'I want this by Friday' and 'It should be done this way'. Use of 'I' versus 'we' was one of the most distinctive language differences between autocratic and democratic organizations (Lippitt & White, 1943). In DP1 structures whole tasks are split into one-person pieces with individual responsibility attached. The interests of individuals are, therefore, best served by looking out for themselves. They are not concerned to communicate information that could be of benefit to others, either laterally or up and down. Similarly, unless a received communication is of benefit, there is little concern to attend to it, let alone remember it. When we analyse a DP1 structure, we see that it is essentially competitive with all the dynamics that are associated with competition. This is illustrated by the simplest example of promotion which in DP1 structures is usually up the hierarchy. When the top position in Figure 2.2A becomes vacant, those below will be competing for that position. Communication patterns including remembering and forgetting reflect the competitive dynamics.

The competitive nature of the DP1 structure also explains the adversarial nature of bureaucratic communications. Each step in the communication chain represents a difference in status and, therefore, a difference in the interest of the parties towards the effects of the communication. Superiors want the truth if they know they can do something about it. If not, they would prefer not to know or they may request a report because simply requesting it makes them look good and responsible. Unfortunately, superiors frequently believe they do know what is going on in their organizations but have been suffering from distorted information or a severe lack of information. Failing to inform is a powerful way of waging organizational war vertically as well as horizontally. Inferiors may distort communications to make themselves look good or blameless, and make competitors look bad:

> A status gap between communicants is always a potential barrier to communication. It consti-tutes an inherently unstable medium: always ready to amplify or attenuate messages in ways that have nothing to do with a truthful correspondence of source events and message. (Emery & Emery, 1976: 152)

These three characteristics illustrate the dilemmas involved in placing a great mass of purposeful systems into a structure which by its nature forces them to act primarily as goal-seeking systems (Ackoff & Emery, 1972), able to choose only means to an end rather than being involved in choosing the ends. They get their revenge by exercising their purposefulness in exactly the way the structure demands. As it is inherently competitive, so they compete. But the ends they serve bear no relation to the organization's goals. Because the organization is not adaptive to the nature of the people within it, the communications serve their own adaptive needs. This may lose them a job in the long term if the organization fails. (This is not a speculative statement. Some of us know organizations that failed because of constant deliberate sabotage.)

Nor do these distortive effects operate only at the level of the individual. They also operate at the level of the group. Bion (1952, 1961) discovered that groups can make a set of three basic assumptions (bas) about their leadership. The bas are a totally different mode of operation from the 'creative working mode' which Bion referred to as W for task-oriented work. Calling them dependency, fight/flight, and pairing, Bion saw these bas as modes which preserve the life of the group. (For a discussion of the bifurcated form of pairing, see Emery, M., 1999: 127–132.) After nearly thirty years of working with the bas, we now know that they are structure-specific. They appear only when DP1 is operating. As implied by the statement above about the leadership of the group, Bion's patients knew that he was the boss. While Dr Bion remained in charge, his chances of creating a 'leaderless group' were low. In contrast, when people begin work in a DP2 structure, they immediately go into the creative working mode and stay there.

The bas create even more problems for team builders and communication skills developers. They also help explain the frequent lack of transfer effects from the training situation to the organization. Usually the trainers attempting to improve communications or teamwork find themselves in the same structural position as Bion. Their trainees are vulnerable to the bas. Many trainers believe that every group must go through the stages of 'forming, storming, norming, performing' (Tuckman, 1965). Some who work with groups will deliberately engineer these phenomena to speed up to the performance stage. But for many employees, this is the stuff of everyday life. They are also experts in it and if they don't feel like performing, they won't. Our experience shows that it is possible to go straight to performing (Emery, M., 1999: 132–133). The bas are far easier to prevent than to cure, by designing methods based on DP2 structures.

If the trainees adopt either of the most common bas, dependency or fight/flight, there will be little learning. 'Least learning occurs in dependency, more in fight/flight and more again in pairing' (Emery, M., 1999: 117, 134) but less than in the creative working mode. Add this to the motivational deficit, particularly when it is realized that they are being sent to fix their problems, and then wonder why they have poor 'listening skills'. 'Poor listening skills' is yet another mythical problem promulgated by the schools of self-action and interaction. Exactly the same people show no deficit in listening skills when they are enjoying a spirited discussion at the pub or are working together for their local voluntary organization. Listening is also subject to motivation and refraction.

## Error Rates

Because organizational structures are an econiche (Emery, M., 1999) and function as a communications medium, they not only distort or refract messages, they also affect other forms of errors including accidents. DP1 structures are inherently error-amplifying. Error rates are intimately related to communication failures and reflect the same sort of system failure. Errors seep in from the environment and are then subject to the refraction of the three characteristics above. Using Stafford Beer's (1972) formulae for error amplification and attenuation, F. Emery (1977: 91–99) has shown how the flow upwards of information from one level to the next dramatically changes between the two structures.

In both cases in Table 2.3, a manager has five people reporting to him or her, people who are truthful (T) or make sound judgements eight times out of ten. In the DP1 structure there would be, on average, only one in three occasions that the manager could say that this must be sound advice because they are unanimous. Managers, therefore, seek independent judgements to avoid collusion but the mathematics show that the more managers achieve control of subordinates, the deeper they move into error.

In the DP2 structure there would be only about three times in ten thousand that they will unanimously give wrong advice. While the assumed degree of fallibility (F) is the same in both structures, it will vary in nature. The characteristic features of communication found in DP1 structures are not found in DP2

TABLE 2.3  Error amplification and attenuation by design principle

| DP1, error amplification | DP2, error attenuation |
| --- | --- |
| $T = (1 - F)^n$ | $T = (1 - F^n)$ |
| $T = (1.0 - 0.2)^5 = 0.33$ | $T = (1.0 - (0.2)^5) = 0.9997$ |

because people have shared responsibility for coordination and control. They are also responsible for their agreed measurable outcomes that they know are aligned with the strategic goals of the organization. The symmetrical dependence of DP2 ensures cooperation rather than competition with the effect that it is in everybody's interests to provide accurate and timely feedback on mistakes. As the whole group has been involved in setting the group goals and individuals negotiate pieces of work to provide personal challenges, both the conditions for continuous learning are in place (Emery & Emery, 1974). Therefore, when errors enter a DP2 structure, they become the source of learning rather than defensive posturing.

When error rates are judged unacceptably high, quite commonly the diagnosis is that training has been inadequate and more is required. Often this training is provided on a blanket basis. While further training may indeed be required, it will not in and of itself reliably reduce error rates in the long term. That requires attention to the underlying causes. In DP2, an individual who has made a mistake will request training either by course if necessary but more frequently unless it is in a highly technical area, by change of functions to learn on the job from other more skilled persons. Therefore, the training is targeted and immediately remedial.

The class of problem called 'personality conflicts' arises from exactly the same principles and dynamics as communication problems and error rates. As errors are amplified when they enter a DP1 structure, so are personality differences. Asymmetry, egocentrism, and the 'them and us' syndrome, together with the prevalence of dependency and fight/flight, contribute to the hothouse atmosphere where even small personality differences are accentuated. Far from being a cool, impersonal task-oriented setting, bureaucratic structures are often wracked by waves of intense emotion played out as office or palace politics, clique formation and maintenance, and buck passing. In such settings, any small quirk of personality is quickly amplified and, if the predominant basic assumption is fight/flight, will fuel a 'personality conflict'.

## Summary

This brief appraisal of differences in diagnosis shows very clearly that in each case, accepting the validity of the symptom and the assumptions underlying it is doomed to result in a long-term failure of curative method. The problem presented is symptomatic of a deeper malaise, one that cannot be changed by attempting to change the people. The people are obviously just being open purposeful systems and adopting an extremely rational approach to the situation in which they find themselves, one that is not fit for purposeful systems. The assumption that the problems lie within the people or within their patterns of interaction leads directly to actions upon the people which they define in the vernacular as 'blaming the victims'. This elicits a further rational and purposeful response that does not bode well for the productivity or future of the organization.

The other major implication of this discussion is that effective organizational practice necessarily has a strong educational component. The customers are not always right and their diagnoses should not be accepted at face value. But over and above these implications is another; practitioners strongly adhere to abstract universals, the associated world hypotheses, and the assumptions that flow from them. The evidence comes a very poor second. Besides, most managers who pay the practitioners also believe in abstract universals. There is also resistance to changing the genotypical design principle which springs in part at least from educational elitism born of high valuation of abstract knowledge (Bartel & Emery, 1999).

## DESIGNING NEW ORGANIZATIONS IN AN UNPREDICTABLE ENVIRONMENT

As diagnoses must be genotypically and environmentally correct, so must the redesigns precisely meet the diagnoses. When methods are based on the primacy of communication, changing the people or incorporating assumptions of a Type III environment, which is shown by dependence on the expert role, the efficacy of these methods is usually short-lived. A study quoted by *The Economist* (2000: 61) showed that 20 per cent of organizational change projects were successful, 17 per cent showed no improvement at all, and in a whopping 63 per cent the change was only temporarily sustained. There is nothing new about this result. Apart from indicating that most methods are inadequate, this data also indicates that there is still a vast and sufficient amount of goodwill for change in organizations but, eventually, those involved discover that 'nothing has actually changed'. This is a typical comment from those who have borne the brunt of these attempts at change. If change is to be effective in the long term, it must be designed for purposeful systems living in a Type IV environment. As it would appear that the rejection of hierarchical domination is now well and truly with us, organizational structures will eventually have to be redesigned on the second design principle.

There are other implications:

1. Methods must concentrate on accelerating diffusion (Emery, F., 1969). To aid diffusion, they must incorporate practices that increase the probability of positive affect as this fuels diffusion (Emery, M., 1986; Emery & Bartel, 2000).
2. They must be genuinely participative as practitioners playing expert roles give a DP1 structure. Once genuine participation and trust are established, conceptual knowledge may be introduced. For example, the Participative Design Workshop (Emery & Emery, 1974; Emery, M., 1999) includes conceptual briefings but only after a period of comprehensive and extensive preparation.
3. Methods must be flexible rather than mechanistic in terms of fixed designs or steps in the process with fixed times. How else can we ensure that the unique circumstances of an organization are taken into account? For planning there may or may not need to be sessions dealing with changes in task environments, for example. Also, nobody can definitely know in advance where a group will flounder or shine. Process management must entail juggling times and tasks so that the group has the best possible chance of achieving a high-quality result. Working from a conceptual framework rather than a recipe provides potential for high flexibility.
4. Flexibility and sustainability demand that greater time and effort be put into participative and educative preparation before the method proper is used. This preparation period is frequently the longest part of the whole process. The better the preparation and pre-planning, the better the result. If the design principle is to be changed, attention must be paid to all the systemic changes that follow, including pay and classification systems. There should be at least an 'in principle' agreement governing the legal change from DP1 to DP2.
5. In the actual design phase, no design must be imposed. People must be able to design their own section of the organization as only they really understand it, and if they are to accept working within it, they must have psychological ownership of it (Emery & Emery, 1974). There must be guarantees that designs will not be changed arbitrarily by others. Autocratic behaviour would immediately put the project at risk.
6. Rather than the current concentration on technological systems (Purser, 1993: 217), designs should focus on the social system as, once DP2 structures come into being, employees will take responsibility for fixing or redesigning their technical systems. Giving priority to redesigning technical systems shows relatively infrequent technological innovation (Passmore et al., 1982).
7. Methods must be designed and executed with genuine collaboration, elaborated below.

## PLANNED CHANGE, PROGRAMMATIC CHANGE, AND ACTIVE ADAPTIVE CHANGE FOR DEVELOPMENT

Active adaptive change as discussed above shows that it is not planned change in the sense that it is top-down or expert-driven. It is just as clearly not programmatic in the sense that there is a planned and relatively fixed series of steps or phases to be governed by feedback mechanisms and further planned interventions if necessary, which there usually are because the change never goes to plan. Active adaptive change as pursued through the two-stage model (Emery, M., 1999) does, however, contain elements of planned and programmatic change when we use the terms in everyday language. There is a logical and psychological order to the sequence of plan followed by structural design. Similarly, there is a logical flow within the phases of the methods themselves. There are no necessary conflicts or dilemmas between planning or programming steps in the change process when some basic parameters are reconstructed.

Active adaptive change is clearly planned in Boonstra's sense of 'a conscious, deliberate, and collaborative effort to improve the operations of a human system through the utilization of scientific knowledge' (see Introduction). The first question is which scientific knowledge and from which science? The second question is, who collaborates with whom? I discuss this below.

Boonstra later gives the answer to the question of which science when he states that programmatic change 'requires the ability to predict and control developments. To be able to predict developments, an eye must be kept on relationships between cause and effect over a longer period of time.' This marks programmatic change as having its feet on the abstract universal line.

> Causal thinking has been used in science for such a long time, and in certain fields with such success, that it is almost generally considered to be the scientific thinking, although it may well be only a subvariety. It is, in any case, a firmly rooted habit, not easily changed to a basically different approach. Dealing with relations and dealing with systems involves quite different psychological processes. In causal thinking and research the task is to single out, from a multitude of data, pairs of acts between which there is a necessary connection. (Angyal, 1965: 48)

Add to this the notion that change must be planned and controlled by 'experts' or organizational authorities. 'Managers and consultants take a rational approach: they analyse the surroundings, formulate goals, develop a strategy, and then implement the change' (Boonstra, Introduction). It may be 'rational' but the assumptions it makes about others within the organization is far from according with the everyday observation that they too analyse their surroundings, formulate goals, develop strategies, and implement them. Perhaps the failure of observation is related to the fact that they often do this in ways that conflict with the demands and expectations of managers and consultants?

The very notions of expert and expert knowledge raise other dilemmas, the first of which Mao posed as the problem of 'red or expert' while the second, which is interrelated, arises directly from relevant uncertainty. The 'red or expert' dilemma is 'How does the expert make his contribution to planning without alienating people?' (Emery, F., 1977: 124). The greater the gap between the expert and the rest, the less likely they are to follow the plan. This is always the case in DP1 structures as we saw above. Relevant uncertainty leads us to ask 'How can we expect to improve our planning in the face of relatively decreasing knowledge?' (ibid.: 125). Again, we come close to a paradox: the more society changes, the more we need to be able to plan but the less we have the knowledge with which to plan. The dilemmas are interrelated in that both arise from the advent of the Type IV environment as the desire for self-determination appears to be here to stay and relevant uncertainty is still with us. But they are also interrelated because of a particular definition of 'expert knowledge'.

The expert knowledge so often used in strategic planning is derived from hypothetico-deductive science and not only is it drawn from problem-solving, it is applied as problem-solving. Problem-solving involves a known end point and needs merely to design the best means to this end. But this form of knowledge cannot devise the end point. It is abstract knowledge, knowledge abstracted from its concrete base in reality, and that is far from meeting the requirements of puzzle-solving. Only puzzle-solving (Emery, F., 1977: 126) can determine an end point and that requires extracted knowledge (Emery, F., 1980). Extracted knowledge is given by direct perception; it is ecological knowledge. Matters of ideals and values fall into this class of knowledge. No amount of up-to-date statistical data on current ideals and values as derived from methods such as survey feedback will suffice to determine an end point when there are no guarantees that the very act of surveying them has not raised expectations. Besides, if they don't like the tone of the feedback, staff might get together and change their minds about further cooperation.

There is a further problem with the science associated with planned and programmatic change as defined above. It is based on a faulty model of so-called rational decision-making. These experts 'theorize ... as if decision making was explicable in terms of only two dimensions, probable efficiency of different paths and relative value of the outcomes'. Heider (1946), Jordan (1968), and Ackoff and Emery (1972) have shown that another dimension is necessary. 'This other dimension is the probability of choice and reflects the *intrinsic* value of a course of action to the chooser (as distinct from its *extrinsic* or means-end value)' (Emery, F., 1977: 126). Again, this is available to direct observation so while the experts may claim that their approach is scientific, it is faulty science.

There is another sort of science as discussed above. It is based on accurate observation and conceptualizations adequate to the task of genuine hypothesis testing. 'An hypothesis that postulated causes lying beyond the reach of human observation must remain unverified' (Stebbing, 1948: 316). Causal thinking is replaced by systems thinking. 'In systems thinking the task is not to find direct relations between items but to find the superordinate system in which they are connected or to define their positional value within such a system' (Angyal, 1965: 48). But again the systems thinking must not be of the mechanistic, closed variety we find in GST because that does not accord with observation and evidence of the permeable boundaries of purposeful systems open to and transacting with an extended social field.

Nor does this second sort of science confine itself to deduction and induction. C.S. Peirce demonstrated in 1878 that there were three forms of logical inference and not just two, deduction and induction, as was generally supposed. The third form, which he called 'retroduction' or 'abduction', involves reasoning 'from consequent to antecedent' (Peirce, 1986). Retroduction is the only form of reasoning which contributes new ideas in science through a process of studying the facts and 'devising a theory to explain them' (4.4, Feibleman, 1946). A singular or individual occurrence consists of dynamic relations and this is what modern physics and philosophers have termed an 'event' (1.458, Feibleman, 1946: 61 footnote), the root metaphor of the world hypothesis of contextualism (Pepper, 1942). Retroduction is, therefore, the process within contextualism that produces novelty, and creativity, and contextualism is the only world hypothesis within which novelty can be conceptualized. Peirce held that it was only by this ability to arrive at 'reasonable hypotheses' that we could have advanced scientific knowledge.

> It seems incontestable that the mind of man is strongly adapted to the comprehension of the world; at least, so far as this goes, that certain conceptions, highly important for such a comprehension, naturally arise in his mind; and without such a tendency, the mind could never have had any development at all. (Peirce, 1986: 318)

Our adaptation to our planet is the basis for extracted knowledge (Emery, F., 1980) and we survived for 60,000+ years without abstract knowledge (Knudtson & Suzuki, 1992).

The science based on observable, material universals acknowledges the validity of extracted knowledge. It can distinguish the various types of knowledge, including wisdom, associated with the parameters of decision-making (Emery, M., 1999: 95–104). Therefore, it can approach planning and design flexibly, encouraging the development of the appropriate form of knowledge for the appropriate tasks and applying appropriate knowledge where required. In the face of the planning dilemmas of the Type IV environment, it acknowledges the primacy of end points over means and puzzle-solving over problem-solving. It leads to learning about the extended social field and ideal seeking. Without this scientific base it is virtually impossible to get an organizational plan which is implemented because it reflects the intrinsic value of it for those who must implement and live with it. So the parameters that need reconstructing if planned and programmatic change is to become active adaptive are the assumptions that flow from abstract universals. 'These major conceptual shifts from world hypotheses based on closed systems to contextualism have many ramifications for education, social science and its practice, not least for action research' (Emery & Emery, 1997: 139).

## ACTION RESEARCH AS AN ENABLER OF LEARNING AND CHANGE

Learning is essential to effective sustainable change. For change to be successful, employees must be motivated to implement it. If it is to be sustainable, everybody must have learnt what is involved in the change, conceptually as well as methodologically. This common-sense statement is backed by recent figures from *The Economist* (2000: 61). Four out of five of the most 'able at change' organizations quoted said that the expertise required for the change was embedded as a functional capability within the organization compared with only one out of five of the 'inept at change' organizations. The 'able' had 'institutionalized their knowledge, building it into their culture and performance assessment'. None of the 'able at change' companies said they had handed the task to consultants which a quarter of the 'inept' group had done. It is important to note here, and the above article also bears this out, that practitioners need to work with all existing levels within the organization, not just management and not just the troops. For sustainable systemic change, all levels and functional areas must be involved in the same sort of processes.

This creates a problem for some practitioners, usually consultants, who are a profession within the educated elites. Many live in a world of abstractions, pieces of disembodied 'information' and models far removed from the physical realities of most of the world's population (adapted from Lasch, 1995). They are also highly competitive and prefer to operate through *laissez-faire*, each individual consultant free to 'do their own thing'. Their culture can interfere with espoused aims of cooperation towards the common good (Emery, M., 1996). It may well be that the *laissez-faire* and competition have induced many to see their role as expert or substitute manager within an organization as it is difficult to gain higher status by other means in a highly educated and sophisticated, stratified society. While consultants continue to define their role as expert and managers accept this, it will continue to be difficult to gain acknowledgement of the need for action research that is not based on relations of hierarchical dominance.

For action research to enable learning and sustainable change, every step from the very beginning of a project through the education and preparation required for the change, to the planning and design or redesign depends on what is learnt and whether that learning fuels motivation to continue and evolve. We are not primarily discussing formal education but the extracted learning that people automatically do as they move through life with all of its changes. In particular, we are discussing that subclass called 'diffusive learning'.

The processes and principles of direct realism as medium-term adaptation, that which yields ecological or extracted learning, continue over the life span. Therefore, 'learning works because it permits the development of *effectivities* that are supported by *affordances* in a real environment' (Johnston & Turvey, 1980: 166). Affordances are properties of the environment relative to a system, the acts or behaviours permitted by objects, places, and events. They define what the environment means to a perceiver, what they can do with it, e.g. a chair affords sitting on, or for the desperate, throwing on a fire to keep warm. 'It is the affordance that is perceived' (Gibson, 1967; Michaels & Carello, 1981: 42; Reed & Jones, 1982). Affordances do not change as needs change as they are real and persistent properties. Effectivities are the potential purposeful behaviours of a perceiver, again relative to the field (Shaw & McIntyre, 1974: 307). But for people with consciousness:

> no clear boundary can be drawn between affordances and effectivities except in a specifically pragmatic sense . . . Thus learning as adaptation at the ontogenetic level is no more and no less than the simultaneous development of affordances and effectivities towards environments that

better support human purposefulness and ideal seeking. Consciousness demands that these 'goals' are also effectivities and thus *learning is the growth of the total set of actual and potential directive correlations, or contents of consciousness, towards a meaningful order.* (Emery, M., 1999: 78)

The definition above encompasses maladaptions but we can consciously choose to use our learning to create new econiches which themselves will function adaptively, affording conscious learning to those within them. And we may consciously choose to function as an affordance or resource for others. If we are motivated to do these things, we are also motivated to enter into peer relationships with others around shared purposes including that of learning. These are the characteristics required of a diffuser so we can define 'diffusive learning' 'as that learning which motivates the learner to recreate the learning environment for others either as actual or potential econiche' (Emery, M., 1999: 78). I have also shown that diffusers and lifelong learners are one and the same people.

Motivated and sustainable organizational change requires diffusive learning. If employees are not motivated to diffuse, even moderate rates of turnover will ensure that the change dies out. But common sense tells us that if they are not motivated to diffuse, the change was probably never accepted or successful in the first place.

Before we move on, it is necessary to clarify some related propositions to be found in the field:

- *Proposition 1*: There is no such thing as 'organizational learning'. 'Organizational learning' does not and cannot exist because organizations do not have nervous systems. To take seriously such a concept of 'organizational learning' is to make a nonsense of the concept of learning itself. Such usage also cannot help further development of it. The only sensible definition of a 'learning organization' is an organization 'structured in such a way that its members can learn and continue to learn within it' (Emery, M., 1993: 2). Similarly, the concept of 'organizational memory' is a dangerous myth. Many organizations have realized this when in times of rapid turnover, they discover that their 'organizational memories' have walked out the door.
- *Proposition 2*: 'My people don't learn' (statement by a manager). It is impossible to stop people learning. Human learning is a phenomenological given but our learning and behaviour as learners will differ depending on the ecosystems of which we are a part. It is currently fashionable to describe one's organization as a 'learning organization' because it has increased the training hours provided. Such training always achieves something, but the major impact of learning in DP1 is about the organization itself. It occurs at the beginning of the experience when people may learn that they really don't want to be there. From then on, negative affect frequently amplifies that learning and people put their efforts into creative ways of 'beating the system'. So they create their own conditions for continuous learning but it is not the learning that managers wish for.
- *Proposition 3*: Learning is a cognitive activity. Far from being split three ways into cognitive, affective, and conative systems, people are unitary systems and learning cannot be divorced from the total human system. It is closely tied to affects which are characterized by their urgency, generality, and abstraction. They are a free-ranging set of motivational effectivities that provide enormous amounts of information about our self-environment relationships (Tomkins, 1962).

Given the criticality of motivation and learning for effective, sustainable change, the very best possible conditions for producing both should be built into the processes to be used, right from the very first moment. As above, only DP2 structures produce continuous learning because they are variety-increasing, provide opportunities for goal setting and feedback, and attenuate errors over time. DP1 structures are variety-decreasing, do not provide those opportunities, and they amplify errors. Over time they result in the 'hatred of learning' (Bion, 1961: 86–91).

Saying that DP2 should operate from the beginning of the process indicates that a project may usefully be separated into the planning and preparation stage and usage of the method proper. While the preparation and planning stage involves discussion, negotiation, and education, DP2 can be brought into being through the nature of the relationship between the researcher and organization. This involves the nature of action research and collaboration.

## PREPARATION AND PLANNING PHASE

Action research shares with all other social science research a relationship with the researched. This may not always be acknowledged by the researcher but the researched are usually aware of its nature. There are only three basic forms of this relationship which follow from the genotypical design principles (Emery & Emery, 1997: 139–142). I am disregarding *laissez-faire* here because it is almost inconceivable that any self-respecting organization or practitioner would deliberately or knowingly enter a *laissez-faire*-based relationship with the other. Such a relationship may develop by default through poor or lack of definition of terms of reference or end point, or through drift in the process itself, but one must assume that the initiator of a change project has some definite allocation of responsibility in mind.

Let us take DP2 first because it is the simplest. Here the two parties decide on joint responsibility for their mutually agreed purposes. This is known as the *collaborative* relationship (Emery, F., 1977: 198–202).

If the first design principle (DP1) is chosen as the basis of the relationship, there is a further choice. This applies not only in the action research case but also to consultancies in general. For researcher and the researched, the responsibility may rest with either party. When it rests with the researcher, it is known as the *academic* relationship, where it is assumed, as is the case for those with a strong belief in the primacy of value of abstract knowledge, that only this 'senior' partner has special skills and knowledge. The skills here would focus on the ability to induce and deduce from the abstract knowledge gained, especially in relation to the task of identifying the universal in the particular through logical inference. That this is a special skill is a myth: we all do it (Emery, F., 1980). In action research and other practice, leaving the responsibility with the 'junior' partner is known as the *servant* relation.

In action research, this three-way choice becomes acute because the researcher has implicitly, by virtue of the fact that they are working on matters of importance to the researched, accepted the unique mission and responsibility of the social sciences, i.e. the mutual enrichment of social science and the important practical affairs of people (Emery, F., 1977: 199). Choice of design principle means choosing to see the researched and researcher as the same or different level of system, Either they are both purposeful or the researched are merely goal-seeking. By choosing the academic relationship, the action researcher has classed the researched as object in the pursuit of value-free knowledge (another myth), also denying their essential human capacities to know and to retroduce:

> But as the researched is still the same open human system, regardless of the choice of the researcher, this choice amounts to a subtle form of oppression, the same form involved in teaching the young that their experientially based theories constitute failure. The choice between design principles is the choice between relations of dominance of one person or class of people over another, or relations of non dominance. (Emery & Emery, 1997: 140)

It is rare to find the servant relation in action research although it is widespread in consultative relationships more generally where the assumption is that 'the customer is always right'. This stance denies the potential of mutual learning from the relationship. Elevating the customer to the status of omniscient being can be seen as an attempt at democracy in the relationship but amounts to no more than *laissez-faire*.

The rarity of the servant relation and the ubiquity of the academic relation in action research spring from a single source, the production and socialization of an educational elite, among which we find most social scientists and practitioners. Even action researchers who protest their advocacy of democracy and claim to practise it are often loath to give away the trappings of elite status in action. These include the right to hold closed meetings, set goals for others, unilaterally design processes for others to use or participate in, and write up reports containing *their* conclusions and recommendations.

As it is perfectly possible to achieve collaboration between 'teachers' and 'learners' in the education system, so it is perfectly possible within action research. It also achieves the same outcomes, with all parties becoming 'learners' doing mutual learning around a shared purpose. Instead of the researched (A) focusing on the researcher (B), both focus on the task (X) of achieving the purpose. This is of course the $^A X^B$ model in action (Asch, 1952; Newcomb, 1953). The learning achieved is also far richer. It increases the probability of higher system level function, of moving from purposefulness to ideal seeking, and it increases the validity of outcomes. It is 'learning for discovery, the process that centrally involves ecological learning and retroduction. It is learning for the development of creativity' (Emery & Emery, 1997: 141). With genuine collaboration within the $^A X^B$ model, openness, communication, and trust spiral towards the best possible solution for all parties.

The pragmatics of collaboration in a specific case will vary depending on people, circumstances, and task but we can outline some basic principles:

- *Principle 1*: If the researcher has accepted the joint responsibilities of social science as above, there must be a division of labour as the researched have only one set of responsibilities—to the purpose and the task of achieving it.
- *Principle 2*: Because the organization does not belong to the researcher who also does not have to live with the consequences of the change, the division of labour is usually around content and process. The researched take responsibility for all the content, the outcomes, and the implementation, while the researcher takes responsibility for designing and managing the learning environment and process within which the researched do their work. Accepting responsibility does not preclude the researcher involving at least some of those in the organization in this task, particularly the design phase. Only organizational members have first-hand ecological knowledge of that particular organization with all its idiosyncrasies. By accepting responsibility for the content and collaborating in the design work, organizational members are credited with having specialist knowledge of their own reality. Researchers also have their own specialist knowledge, usually in the design and management of such research and/or learning econiches and this too is acknowledged by the division of labour. The researcher's second responsibility of contributing to social science is usually handled by writing or publishing a report. Again, because the data belongs to the organization, the researcher can only validly write from the perspective of what was learnt in the process of designing and managing the learning environment and the implications of that for future work.

  This perspective differs from the view that the goal of participatory research 'is the improvement not of Theory, but of Practice . . . its concern is not with universal, abstract conceptual systems, but with local, timely knowledge of particular, concrete situations' (Toulmin, 1996: 221). Against this position I argue first that practice and theory are not mutually exclusive as theory should also inform practice. Effective methods flow from good theory. Second, observing and analysing a range of method designs, and the conceptual underpinnings of their approach to the management of those processes, lead to some real breakthroughs in our knowledge of people and organizational dynamics. Two cases may be mentioned, that of the relation of genotypical structure to Bion's group assumptions and the more specific case of clarifying the dual nature of the group assumption of 'pairing' (Emery, M., 1999). This knowledge came from retroductively looking back over cycles of interventions and outcomes and the patterns of relations within the open systems model. This process generates progressive hypotheses that enable both theory development about the evolving nature of the system–environment relationship and/or theory development about interventions designed to change this relationship (Gloster, 2000: 674). Gloster calls Toulmin's local action research 'ar' and that also designed to add to social science knowledge as 'AR'. They are not mutually exclusive as 'ar' is subsumed under 'AR'.

- *Principle 3*: There is nothing to prevent the researched from writing their own report from the social science perspective as well and, in fact, there is accelerating use of the Internet by non-elite researchers, diffusing their contributions to knowledge.
- *Principle 4*: In cases where the researcher has specialized knowledge in a particular field of relevant content, say, computing, the researcher may also write about the contribution of the organization to computer research through the process of the change without damaging the integrity of the collaborative relationship.

## USE OF METHOD PHASE

Methods as far as possible should have their participants organized into self-managing groups bound into a group by a genuine task. A genuine task is a piece of meaningful work with goals, clearly defined and articulated, and entirely manageable within the allotted time. Sending a group off to discuss a difficult issue does not fit this definition. Sending them off to come back with a solution to a well-defined and problematic issue does fit. All work should be reported. Ignoring a group's work is not only discourteous but clearly conveys the message that the process was a façade and paid only lip service to involvement. People are extremely sensitive to the differences between consultation, non-genuine participation and the participation that flows from DP2.

In addition, instructions should be given and limits set on the nature of the report to be given by the group. Without these specific task instructions the group does a 'shopping list' of wishes. What is required is hard, targeted work on a thoughtful and carefully considered group product that they are going to have to implement. Even less useful than the 'shopping list' approach is the case where a 'facilitator' enforces 'democracy' by rigorously going around the room and eliciting individual thoughts. This is a travesty of both small group work and participative democracy. The huge range of individual differences to be found in organizations, or anywhere, tells us that different people will take varying lengths of time to feel comfortable in a particular setting and generate the confidence to participate. Enforced 'democracy' can only intensify discomfort and reluctance to speak and the utterances hold little validity anyway as they are said for the sake of speaking. It is better to leave sufficient time to create the conditions to bring into being a group with its own unique culture, its implicit as well as explicit agreements.

With joint responsibility and such an appropriate division of labour, action researchers can more reliably generate motivation and learning to improve the human condition. They may also more co-herently and practically debate the nature of action research rather than continue to fragment the field with more hair-splitting about generic labels and genres based on abstract universals; for an example, see the special issue of *Human Relations* on action research (1993).

## CONCLUSION

Years of accumulated data and knowledge have shown that many of the tools in use in social science today do not accord with readily observable, everyday human behaviour. In particular, the assumptions made about people, drawn from abstract universals, are erroneous and account for the high failure rate of organizational interventions to achieve sustainable change. Assumptions underlie organizational diagnoses and then choice of method leading inevitably to an increasingly fragmented and fractured social science. This is unnecessary as workable alternatives based on observable material universals exist with a successful track record of change. If the majority of our tools were to conform to reality, there would certainly be more active adaptive change providing higher organizational productivity and more creative work for action researchers.

# REFERENCES

Ackoff, R.L. & Emery, F.E. (1972) *On Purposeful Systems*. Chicago: Aldine Atherton.

Alvarez, R.A. & Emery, M. (2000) From action research to system in environments: a method. *Systemic Practice and Action Research*, **13**(5), 683–703.

Angyal, A. (1941) *Foundations for a Science of Personality*. Cambridge, MA: Harvard University Press.

Angyal, A. (1965) *Neurosis and Treatment: A Holistic Theory*. Chichester: John Wiley & Sons, Ltd.

Asch, S.E. (1952) *Social Psychology*. New York: Prentice Hall.

Bartel, S. & Emery, M. (1999) Resistance to open systems theory and practice: a research note. Unpublished.

Bion, W.R. (1952) Group dynamics: a review. *International Journal of Psychoanalysis*, **33**, 235–247.

Bion, W.R. (1961) *Experiences in Groups*. London: Tavistock.

Bond, M. (2000) Father Earth. *New Scientist*, 9 September, 44–47.

Cassirer, E. (1923) *Substance and Function in Einstein's Theory of Relativity*. Chicago: Open Court.

Chein, I. (1972) *The Science of Behaviour and the Image of Man*. New York: Basic Books.

De Guerre, D.W. (2000) The codetermination of cultural change over time. *Systemic Practice and Action Research*, **13**(5), 645–663.

De Laguna, G.A. ([1927] 1963) *Speech: Its Function and Development*. Bloomington, IN: Indiana University Press.

De Paoli, D. (2000) Does time really precede existence? A reflection on Prigoginism. *21st Century*, **Spring**, 27–44.

Des Pres, T. (1976) *The Survivor*. Oxford: Oxford University Press.

*The Economist* (2000) An inside job. 15 July, 61.

*The Economist* (2001) Making the complex simple. 27 January, 79–80.

Eisler, R. (1995) *The Chalice and the Blade*. San Francisco: HarperCollins.

Emery, F. (1959) Characteristics of socio-technical systems. In F. Emery (1978), *The Emergence of a New Paradigm of Work* (pp. 38–86). Canberra: Centre for Continuing Education, Australian National University.

Emery, F. (1967) The next thirty years. *Human Relations*, **20**, 199–237. (Reprinted in *Human Relations* (1997) with postscript, **50**(8), 885–935.)

Emery, F. (1969) The historical validity of the Norwegian industrial democracy project. Tavistock Document HRC 210. In E.L. Trist & H. Murray (1993) *The Social Engagement of Social Science* (vol. II, pp. 154–258). Philadelphia, PA: University of Pennsylvania Press.

Emery, F. (1976) The jury system and participative democracy. In M. Emery (ed.) (1993) *Participative Design for Participative Democracy*. Canberra: Centre for Continuing Education, Australian National University.

Emery, F. (1977) *Futures We're In*. Revised and updated (1998). Melbourne: Fred Emery Institute. www.fredemery.com.au

Emery, F. (1978) Youth, vanguard, victims or the new Vandals? In F. Emery (ed.) *Limits to Choice* (pp. 46–59). Melbourne: Fred Emery Institute. www.fredemery.com.au

Emery, F. (1980) Educational paradigms: an epistemological revolution. In M. Emery (ed.) *Participative Design for Participative Democracy* (pp. 40–85). Canberra: Centre for Continuing Education, Australian National University.

Emery, F. (1998) *Toward Real Democracy*. Melbourne: Fred Emery Institute. www.fredemery.com.au

Emery, F. Undated notes.

Emery, F. & Emery, M. (1974) Participative design: work and community life. In M. Emery (ed.) *Participative Design for Participative Democracy* (pp. 100–122). Canberra: Centre for Continuing Education, Australian National University.

Emery, F. & Emery, M. (1976) *A Choice of Futures*. Leiden: Martinus Nijhoff.

Emery, F. & Emery, M. (1979) Project Australia: its chances. In E. Trist, F. Emery & H. Murray (eds) (1997) *The Social Engagement of Social Science* (vol. III, pp. 336–353). Philadelphia, PA: University of Pennsylvania Press.

Emery, F. & Emery, M. (1997) Toward a logic of hypotheses: everyone does research. *Concepts and Trans-formation*, **2**(2), 119–144.

Emery, F. & Thorsrud, E. (1969) *Form and Content in Industrial Democracy*. London: Tavistock.

Emery, F.E. & Trist, E.L. (1965) The causal texture of organizational environments. *Human Relations*, **18**, 21–32.

Emery, F.E. & Trist, E.L. (1972) *Towards a Social Ecology*. London: Plenum/Rosetta.

Emery, M. (1986) Toward an heuristic theory of diffusion. *Human Relations*, **39**(5), 411–432.

Emery, M. (1993) Introduction to the 1993 edition. In M. Emery (ed.) *Participative Design for Participative Democracy*. Canberra: Centre for Continuing Education, Australian National University.

Emery, M. (ed.) (1993) *Participative Design for Participative Democracy*. Canberra: Centre for Continuing Education, Australian National University.

Emery, M. (1996). The influence of culture on search conferences. *Concepts and Transformation*, **1**(2/3), 143–164.

Emery, M. (1999) *Searching: The Theory and Practice of Making Cultural Change*. Amsterdam: John Benjamins.

Emery, M. (2000a) The evolution of open systems to the 2 stage model. In M.M. Beyerlein (ed.) *Work Teams: Past, Present and Future* (pp. 85–103). Amsterdam: Kluwer Academic Publishers.

Emery, M. (2000b) The current version of Emery's open systems theory. *Systemic Practice and Action Research*, **13**(5), 623–643.

Emery, M. (2000c) The six criteria for intrinsic motivation in education systems: partial democratization of a university experience, partial success. In O.N. Baburoglu & M. Emery (eds) *Educational Futures: Shifting Paradigm of Universities and Education*. Istanbul: Sabanci Universitesi.

Emery, M. & Bartel, S. (2000) Affects, personality and the motivation to diffuse. Draft, unpublished.

Feibleman, J. (1946) *An Introduction to Peirce's Philosophy Interpreted as a System*. New York: Harper & Brothers.

Gibson, J.J. (1966) *The Senses Considered as Perceptual Systems*. Boston: Houghton Mifflin.

Gibson, J.J. (1967) New reasons for realism. *Synthese*, **17**, 162–172.

Gloster, M. (2000) Approaching action research from a socioecological perspective. *Systemic Practice and Action Research*, **13**(5), 665–682.

Gustavsen, B., Hofmaier, B., Ekman Philips, M. & Wikman, A. (1996) *Concept-Driven Development and the Organization of the Process of Change: An Evaluation of the Swedish Working Life Fund*. Amsterdam: John Benjamins.

Heider, F. (1946) Attitudes and cognitive organization. *Journal of Psychology*, **21**, 107–112.

Herzberg, F. (1987) One more time: how do you motivate employees? *Harvard Business Review*, **65**(5), 109–120.

Holman, P. & Devane, T. (eds) (1999) *The Change Handbook: Group Methods for Shaping the Future*. San Francisco: Berrett-Koehler.

Holt, E.G. (1915) *The Freudian Wish and its Place in Ethics*. New York: Holt, Rhinehart & Winston.

*Human Relations* (1993) **46**(2).

Johnston, T.D. & Turvey M.T. (1980) A sketch of an ecological metatheory for theories of learning. In G.H. Bower (ed.) *Psychology of Learning and Motivation* (vol. 14, pp. 147–205). New York: Academic Press Inc.

Jordan, N. (1968) *Themes in Speculative Psychology*. London: Tavistock.

Knudtson, P. & Suzuki, D. (1992) *The Wisdom of the Elders*. Toronto: Stoddart Publishing Co. Ltd.

Lasch, C. (1995) *The Eevolt of the Elites and the Betrayal of Democracy*. New York: W.W. Norton.

Lewin, K. (1931) The conflict between Aristotelian and Galileian modeas of thought in contemporary psychology. In K. Lewin, *A Dynamic Theory of Personality* (1935). New York and London: McGraw-Hill.

Lewin, K. (1943) Forces behind food habits and methods of change. *Bulletin of National Research Council*. National Academy of Sciences, Washington, DC, **108**, October, 35–65.

Lippitt, R. & White, R.K. (1943) The 'social' climate of children's groups. In R.G. Barker, J.S. Kounin & H.F. Wright (eds) *Child Behaviours and Development* (pp. 485–508). London: McGraw-Hill.

Maturana, H.R. & Varela, F.J. (1980) *Autopoiesis and Cognition*. Dordrecht: Reidel.

Mead, G.H. (1932) *The Philosophy of the Present*. Chicago: Open Court.

Michaels, C.F. & Carello, C. (1981) *Direct Perception*. New York: Prentice Hall.

Newcomb, T.M. (1953) An approach to the study of communicative acts. *Psychological Review*, **60**, 283–304.

Passmore, W.A., Francis, C., Haldeman, J. & Shani, A. (1982) Sociotechnical systems: a North American reflection on empirical studies of the seventies. *Human Relations*, **35**(12), 1179–1204.

Peirce, C.S. (1986) *Writings of Charles S. Peirce: A Chronological Edition* (vol. 3. Ed. E.C. Moore. Bloomington, IN: Indiana University Press.

Pepper, S.C. (1942) *World Hypotheses*. Berkeley, CA: University of California Press. Reprinted in 1970.

Purser, R.E. (1993) Opening up open systems theory: towards a socioecological understanding of organizational environments. In T. Tulku (ed.) *Mastery of Mind: Perspectives on Time, Space and Knowledge* (pp. 181–251). Dharma Publishing.

Rayner, A.D.M. (1997) *Degrees of Freedom: Living in Dynamic Boundaries*. London: Imperial College Press.

Reed, E. & Jones, R. (1982) *Reasons for Realism: Selected Essays of James J. Gibson*. Hillsdale, NJ: Lawrence Erlbaum Associates.

Sapolsky, R.M. (2000) Genetic hyping. *The Sciences*, **March/April**, 12–15.

Shaw, R. & McIntyre, M. (1974) Algoristic foundations to cognitive psychology. In W.B. Weimer & D.S. Palermo (eds) *Cognition and the Symbolic Processes* (pp. 305–362). Hillsdale, NJ: Lawrence Erlbaum Associates.

Sommerhoff, G. (1969) The abstract characteristics of living systems. In F.E. Emery (ed.) (1981) *Systems Thinking* (vol. 1, pp. 144–203).

Stebbing, L.S. (1948) *A Modern Introduction to Logic*. London: Methuen.

Thatcher, R.W. & John, E.R. (1977) *Foundations of Cognitive Processes*. Hillsdale, NJ: Lawrence Erlbaum Associates.

Tomkins, S.S. (1962) *Affect, Imagery, Consciousness*. New York: Springer.

Toulmin, S. (1996) Concluding methodological reflections. In S. Toulmin & B. Gustavsen (eds) *Beyond Theory: Changing Organizations through Participation* (pp. 203–225). Amsterdam/Philadelphia: John Benjamins.

Trist, E.L. (1985) The last time around, 1949. In E. Trist, F. Emery & H. Murray (eds) (1997) *The Social Engagement of Social Science* (vol. III, pp. 676–677). Philadelphia, PA: University of Pennsylvania Press.

Trist, E.L. & Bamforth, K.W. (1951) Social and psychological consequences of the longwall method of coal-getting. *Human Relations*, **4**(1), 3–38.

Trist, E.L. & Emery, F.E. (1960) *Report on the Barford Conference for Bristol/Siddeley, Aero-Engine Corporation, July 10–16*, Tavistock TIHR, Document No. 598. London: Tavistock.

Trist, E.L. & Murray, H. (1990, 1993) *The Social Engagement of Social Science; A Tavistock Anthology*. Vols I and II. Philadelphia, PA: University of Pennsylvania Press.

Trist, E., Emery F. & Murray, H. (eds) (1997) *The Social Engagement of Social Science* (vol. III, pp. 170–184). Philadelphia, PA: University of Pennsylvania Press.

Tuckman B.W. (1965) Developmental sequence in small groups, *Psychological Bulletin*, **63**, 384–399.

Vygotsky, L.S. (1962). *Thought and Language*. Ed. and trans. E. Hanfmann & G. Vakar. Cambridge, MA: MIT Press.

# CHAPTER 3

# Organizing Change Processes
## Cornerstones, Methods, and Strategies

**Morten Levin**
*The Norwegian University of Science and Technology, Trondheim, Norway*

There is no accepted general definition of organizational development (OD). OD as a concept sneaked its way into the vocabulary of organization behaviour and organization theory. Its precise origin is not very clear, but French et al. (1994) point to North American professionals in the early 1960s as the ones who coined the term. As a consequence of the multifaceted inheritance of OD, there is hardly any over-reaching and accepted definition. On the other hand, as the intention of this chapter is to reflect on methods and tools in OD, it is necessary to be as specific and precise in conceptualizing OD as possible.

What does it actually mean to design and organize a change process in an organization? The rhetoric we find in current textbooks is interesting. Two examples illustrate this:

> Organizational development consists of intervention techniques, theories, principles, and values that show how to take charge of planned change efforts and achieve success. (French et al., 1994: 1)

> A systemwide application of behavioral science knowledge to the planned development and reinforcement of organizational strategies, structures, and processes for improving an organization's effectiveness. (Cummings & Worley, 1993: 2)

From these quotes two issues emerge as particularly interesting. First, OD implies the application of scientific knowledge to guide change processes. Second, the change efforts are expected to be planned. Both propositions are equally difficult if the intention is to use them as the major building blocks for a discussion on methods and tools in OD. The application of scientific knowledge is problematic because it creates supremacy for academic knowledge in a context where the challenge is to create, develop, and nurture practical problem-solving (creating the new organization). The whole idea of OD is, of course, to make practices in an organization work better and it is not self-evident that academic knowledge is what will make this happen. The interplay between local practical skills and research-based knowledge can be viewed as the cornerstone for organizational transformation (Greenwood & Levin, 1998; Reason & Bradbury, 2001). Second, 'planned change' smells dangerously much like a positivistic position. Is it so that the expert OD practitioner is the one who is in charge of the planning process, or is planning of the change process a joint responsibility for the involved stakeholders? The answer will determine two quite different approaches to OD and, accordingly, it will be quite important to make the point of departure clear in order to be able to deal with issues related to change processes in organizations. It is impossible to discuss methods and tools unless this is based on a clear view of what constitutes OD.

*Dynamics of Organizational Change and Learning.* Edited by J.J. Boonstra.
© 2004 John Wiley & Sons, Ltd. ISBN 0-471-87737-9.

## FOUNDATIONS OF OD

The approach to OD taken in this chapter rests on two major foundations. The single most important feature of the change activity that is identified as OD is *participation* in the change process. This is basically a pragmatic argument identifying a set of social practices where the organizational members take an active part in shaping their own working situation. This is in contrast to a process whereby experts or power holders make decisions on what an organization should look like. This latter approach to organizational transformation is usually identified as organizational design. The other important feature of OD relates to the *type of learning processes* that will be supported. In expert-driven change processes, the learning will basically be in the hands and in the heads of the people in control of the transformation. The other option available is to create collective reflection processes involving everyone in the change process. That this learning system engages actors in collective reflection is the second prerequisite for identifying change activity as OD. Learning is conceptualized as the engine in the transformation process, where collective reflection processes create insights that feed back to new and improved organizational designs.

Participation and collective reflection can, on the surface, be interpreted as two closely interconnected factors. Participation is, on one hand, a premise for collective reflection, which again is the process by which situated knowledge relevant for the focal organization is generated. In this regard, the connection is obvious, but this is not the general condition. First, participation can take place without collective reflection. Employees in an organization can be given a say in the design of work, but this will be done on an individual basis. Levin et al. (1983) report on the major reconstruction of a chemical plant, where an external consulting firm was hired to interview all the employees in order to discover how they perceived current working conditions and identify what they expected from a future workplace. The workers participated in the process but all the learning options were reserved for the consulting firm. Collective reflection can also take place without creating a platform for involvement in the change process. A wildcat strike exemplifies this possibility. Employees will, through a shared understanding, develop an idea of what are perceived as unacceptable working conditions and join in a strike that is not in accord with accepted regulations (Lysgaard, 1961). Most often this does not lead to the process by which the workers will be involved in the change activity.

To further describe and analyse the OD process, three other factors are important. First, OD activity is expected to result in new practical solutions (a new working organization). Practical utilization (the creation of new patterns of work) is a factor that cannot be overlooked, if one intends to understand the OD process. Second, OD rests on an epistemological foundation where knowledge development is integrated into the construction process of the new organization. Third, an OD process cannot avoid raising fundamental value questions related to democracy at work. Participation and collective reflection are the two definitional cornerstones of OD, neither of which can be dealt with without paying attention to democracy at work. These relationships are illustrated in Table 3.1.

**TABLE 3.1**  Cornerstones of OD practice

|  | Democratic ideal/value | Epistemology | Practical utilization |
|---|---|---|---|
| Participation | Participatory democracy influence | Utilizing local knowledge | Implementation |
| Collective reflection | Give a voice to every participant | Generates new local insights | Shared understanding |

Table 3.1 identifies six central issues in OD. The aim is to relate democracy, epistemology, and practical use to the current definition in order to identify key features of OD processes. The discussion of these aspects presents arguments for designing OD processes.

## PARTICIPATION

Fundamentally, participation is understood as the core factor in OD. First, it is grounded in the ethical values of democracy of work (Pateman, 1970; Emery & Thorsrud, 1976). Participation is a right in itself, and in this respect it needs no further arguments to prove its relevance. The democratic ideal is nothing to vote on, it is the basis upon which our society is understood to rest. On the other hand, there is no absolute standard for what constitutes participation in organizational life. There is a wide range of operational models that grant participants different opportunities to influence the desired outcomes. Actors in different positions will have varied perceptions of what participation is, and how it should be implemented in their organization. These elements of insights will span from conceptualizing participation as an act of informing to a broad focus on the political aspects of participation (Greenberg, 1975; Levin, 1984). Participation is a democratic ideal and as such it signals a core value, but applying a participative approach in everyday organizational life is complex and multifaceted.

Participation by the involved organizational members creates an important epistemological position, as the knowledge construction process shifts to one where the members will have a voice. Knowledge generated in order to develop new organizational solutions will accordingly depend on how the members understand the current situation and what they see as desirable solutions for the future organization. This point is in stark contrast to OD strategies where external experts collect data in the organization, create an understanding of what the core problems are, and formulate recommendations how to change the organization (the OD activity). In this situation members of the organization are sidelined to passive actors delivering raw data for an expert (or experts) to construct meaning upon which further actions are based. This approach contrasts substantially with a participative take where members themselves are involved, together with OD personnel, in making sense of what has to be done to make the organization more efficient. In this latter situation, participation creates knowledge that builds on the involved actors' experiences and is distilled through a joint reflection process. This is fundamentally a constructivist epistemological situation, where participation in the OD process shapes the ground for learning, building on the sense-making activity of everyone involved (Berger & Luckman, 1966; Guba & Lincoln, 1985; Searle, 1995; Weick, 1995).

OD is expected to lead to a new way of working. The results of an OD process are only visible through identifiable new patterns of work, which, of course, is the *practical utilization* of the knowledge generated by the process. A distinction is conventionally made between the theoretical or conceptual construction of an organizational solution and its practical application. The transformation from conceptual ideas to practical operation is usually called implementation. The problems associated with this transformation are well documented in the literature. For example, the investment in information technology (hardware and software) is often argued to amount to only one-tenth of the total cost of the whole project. The biggest cost associated with the introduction of new technology is training the employees to use the new equipment. Any change process that minimizes the expenses associated with implementation is, of course, vital in order to create cost-effective organizational transformations. In participative approaches, implementation as a separate process is by definition made redundant. If employees participate in the design process, then the results do not need to be implemented, simply because implementation is integrated into the change process itself. Hence, it has no additional cost. Resources for organizational change efforts have been moved to the participation process, as implementation no longer needs attention.

## COLLECTIVE REFLECTION

The driving force in a participative change process is experimentation and learning. Organizational transformation results from participants' conscious experimentation and reflection in order to develop solutions that make the organization work better. This is the pragmatic philosophical argument for OD (Argyris et al., 1985; Greenwood & Levin, 1998). This process will be impossible unless sufficient space is created for collective reflection. Individual learning opportunities will always be available for any participant in any social context, but collective reflection identifies a situation where those involved can learn through interacting with each other. An organization is a collective enterprise where a mutual understanding of how to cooperate and of sense-making are what makes it operate. Nelson and Winter (1982) introduce routines as the shared mutual understanding of how members of an organization coordinate and cooperate in order to get the work done. These construction processes are what creates a working organization, and they emerge from people's active interaction. Any change process in an organization must take as its point of departure the collective construction of routines and meaning.

The democratic element of collective reflection is, of course, that it potentially gives a voice to every participant. This is not an automatic consequence of participation, as pseudo-participation often might be seen. 'Just let them state their meaning, but we will make the decisions' are practices that can often be seen. We do not here take into account fake or manipulative participation efforts where some power holders play games with involved actors. Even if the intention to participate is good, the results might not always lead to a process where participants have a say. Poor organization of the reflection process can, for example, give certain groups only the smallest possibility to express their opinions. Especially in situations where there are conflicting goals among the participants, the process might not lead to a mutual learning situation (Martin, 2000). One important issue in any collective reflection process is to ensure that it is based on *democratic values*.

Collective reflection creates what Schön (1983) and Argyris and Schön (1996) have identified as an 'organizational theory of action'. This 'theory of action' is shared among the members of the organization, and identifies and communicates the understanding of how the organization operates. It is both the 'organizational memory' and the conceptualizations that guide actions. The *epistemological argument* is that one way to identify an organization's theory of action is to construct collective reflection processes involving all members. Argyris and Schön (1996) envisage a process in which the outside consultant takes up an expert-dominated position to clarify the organizational theory of action. That is not what we argue for here. Our point is that only a truly collective reflection process can support the construction of the organizational theory of action. An outside consultant can, of course, play a role in this process, but this person will always have to be the facilitator and not the one who conceptualizes the organizational theory of action. On the other hand, the external adviser can play a significant role in creating space for the collective reflection process and create an appropriate learning structure. The outsiders will not only be the facilitators, but also participants in the same reflection process as the members of the organization, based on differences in roles. In this respect it constitutes a broad joint learning activity involving internal participants and external facilitators.

The practical outcome of collective reflection is obviously *shared understanding*. The meaning construction process that emerges from the social interaction in the collective learning process leads to sharing larger or smaller models of the local reality. It is a way to develop the local understanding (local theory) through the engagement in collective reflection processes. More narrowly, the collective reflection process leads to development of the organization's theory of action. The local theory of action could be interpreted as a subset of the broader shared understanding of the world. The point is that both belong to the same category of social meaning construction.

These fairly extensive initial considerations have shaped the ground for how to identify methods and tools in OD. The question would then be how to model the OD process in such a way that it builds on participation and collective reflection processes. In order to do this, the next step is to present an organizational model of an OD process. This model is called the co-generative model for OD.

## CONCEPTUALIZING THE ORGANIZATIONAL STRUCTURE OF THE OD PROCESS

Participation and collective reflection are the two cornerstones in OD as it has been presented in this chapter. One question still has to be resolved. In the literature and in the practice of OD, every so often the organizational specialist, the OD consultant, the process consultant, or other external person makes his or her way 'into' the change process. In the discussion in the previous sections the outsider has been introduced as an involved actor in the OD process. These outsiders in the change process will take on a role different from the local members or problem-owners (insiders). It is obvious that the problem-owners (insiders) are the actors facing the challenge of developing their own organization. Accordingly, they will clearly play a different role from the outside OD practitioners.

Could an OD process take place if no professional outsider is present? This is a rhetorical question, but answering it will be helpful in order to clarify the organizational structure of the OD process. A point of departure for this discussion is to make a distinction between organizational change and OD. Organizational change can be understood as a 'neutral' term identifying the simple fact that organizations do change over time. Following this line of argument, the changing organization represents the stable state while non-change is the unstable situation. Organizational transition is an integrated part of everyday activity (Levin & Klev, 2002). In much of the literature, this situation has often been identified as one of continual learning (see, for example, Senge, 1990; De Geus, 1997). In my view, this 'learning ability' is considered to be the cornerstone in organizational change. A self-sustained learning process would imply that organizational learning has become part of everyday learning. This is the highest goal for any OD process, as everyday participation in collective learning processes supports continual organizational change. In this respect, this is a 'true' participative process that clearly is in line with all the prerequisites for collective participation in OD. It reflects the highest goal of any OD process, and if an organization has this ability, OD is integrated into everyday organizational life.

Unfortunately, these self-sustained change processes are seldom identified. That is why there is a need for outside facilitators. It is apparent that this external person leading a participative change process must aim at making her- or himself redundant, as the goal is to create self-sustained learning processes. This does not imply that the outsiders should play a passive constrained role. Quite the contrary, it is important that the outsiders take on the responsibility for creating processes by which the organization's learning capability is enhanced. The vital point is that the outsider must integrate with the insiders in a joint reflection and learning process. This is the basis of the co-generative model for OD. The principal elements of this model are shown in Figure 3.1.

The main conceptualization envisaged through this model is built on a pragmatic philosophical view (Diggins, 1994). The co-generative model formulates the change process as a cycle of problem identification, experimentation, reflection, and learning. This parallels an experiential learning cycle. The concrete problem situation is what motivates experimentation aimed at finding new and better solutions that, through reflection processes, create collective and shared learning that again enhances further experimentation and learning. This experimental and experiential cycle is what shapes the ground for continual learning. The process involves outsiders as facilitators who have the skills to direct learning opportunities, and the outsiders will become partners in the local learning system. In this respect, the OD process is characterized by dual learning circles (the insiders' and the outsiders' cycles) that both interact and are separate. The outsiders experiment and learn together with the insiders, as the insiders and the outsiders both will have learning opportunities on their own. This process is called the co-generation of knowledge (Elden & Levin, 1991).

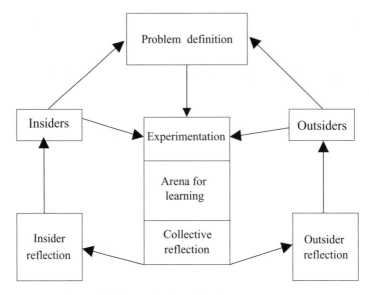

**FIGURE 3.1**   The co-generative model of organizational development

## PROBLEM DEFINITION

The co-generative model identifies a double cycle in designing an OD process. The first phase is to search for the problem focus for the OD process. This is a challenging participatory process, as that starting point has to emerge from the problem-owner's own sense-making process. One simple solution to this process is either to accept the participants' points of view and instant understanding as the point of departure, or to go for the opposite position by making the outsider's understanding the focus of the problem. In conventional survey-based OD, a social science-trained person administers a standardized questionnaire, focusing on key organizational variables, grinds out the numbers, and performs an analysis and determines what to do. This is obviously an expert-driven process, leaving little leverage for local participation and influence. Many of the current consulting practices go in the same direction, where the outside expert has a dominating position in determining the shape and focus of the OD process. One quite extreme position in this regard is reflected in Business Process Reengineering as envisaged by Hammer and Champy (1993). In this model of organizational transformation, participation is hardly mentioned or recommended. The expert has full control, and is the one who delivers the new innovative work structures. This position has gradually been modified, both through academic-oriented writing and through the practice of BPR and now points to the importance of participative change processes. At the other end of the scale, we find models where the insiders have full control over determining the focal point of the OD process. This is the case, for example, in committed participative approaches such as search conference strategies (Herbst, 1980; Emery, 1993) and in dialogue conferences (Gustavsen, 1992; Pålshaugen, 1998). Both rely on high participatory involvement where the outside facilitator usually takes on the role of a strong process leader, making little or no substantial contribution to the problem issue at all. The potential need for substantial knowledge of the actual organization, its social climate, the market, and technology is not an issue at all. The skills of the facilitator are limited to being capable of running the processes that are to lead to a participative decision on what to prioritize in the developmental process.

Our argument is that there is a middle road. It is obviously as much a waste of resources not to use the insiders' knowledge, as it is not to take advantage of the outside 'expertise'. Our position is that through creating a joint learning situation (the co-generation of knowledge), it is possible to have the best of both worlds. It is also important to remember that the backdrop is participative change strategies, and we have argued that the *laissez-faire* situation where the participants have dogmatic control over the process is as equally problematic as the power play by the outside expert. The centre road has to be a place where insiders and outsiders join in the same learning process. This puts forward demands from both parties to at least agree on a discourse ethic that creates a space for everyone's voice, to agree to consider all arguments on their substantial value, and to try to understand all involved actors' positions and interests. This ethical stand on communication processes is not automatically held by the actors involved, so quite a substantial effort has to be made to ensure that participants understand the discourse ethics and know how to practise it. Hence, this is a meta-learning process involving both insiders and outsiders that pretty much encapsulates the essence of co-generative learning.

The initial phase of a participative OD process is obviously the most difficult. Insiders and outsiders do not know each other (at least to a certain degree), their world-views are potentially very different, their mutual understanding is at a minimum, and there is probably minimal practice of open and free discourse. All these obstacles have to be overcome if a participative developmental activity is to take place. The criteria listed identifying the discourse ethics share the feature that they can only be solved (or rather developed) through mutual learning. A simple position is to point to the need of having the actors meet in a joint problem-solving process. That is why it is crucial to find a common point of departure that is meaningful both to the insiders and to the outsiders. The first negotiations must accordingly seek a problem focus that is significant for all. An old consultant's trick is to start by finding a problem that has an easy (and hopefully valued) potential solution. If these initial steps are successful in creating a common ground of practice and reflection between outsiders and insiders, the road is paved for further developmental activity. The actors would subsequently be ready for the next phase, which is the creation of a cycle of continued experimentation, reflection, and learning. In this process it is vital to merge the insights and creativity held by the insiders and by the outsiders in the co-generative discourse where everyone has a say as they bring to the table differences of opinions and skills. The co-generative discourse ethics values diversity and aims at bridging differences in the creative learning process.

## EXPERIMENTATION AND REFLECTION

The 'engine' of a co-generative model is the experimentation–learning–reflection cycle. This is in principle the same cycle that Kolb et al. (1984) have called experiential learning, and it is important to make explicit that this cycle involves both insiders and outsiders in the same learning and reflection process. Adding on to this basic cycle, two or more supplementary learning and reflection cycles will be in operation. The secondary cycles can either be planned or they can emerge spontaneously. The issue is that experiences from the core learning cycle will also invoke other peer processes, where colleagues or professional comrades meet and reflect on what has taken place in the OD process. For the outsiders, this can take place through involving colleagues in a professional discussion on the OD activity. For insiders this process will often take place through spontaneous discussions or it can be designed as planned activities.

In the introductory definition of OD we stressed the point that the aim is practical problem-solving to improve the everyday operation of the organization. Conscious and systematic experimentation is seen as the vehicle that can create workable and improved solutions. It is important to separate this conceptualization from a scientific experimental position where experimentation is controlled and carried out by the scientist and often the aim of the experimentation is not known to the participants (see, for example, the critique of Milgram's social psychological experimentation in Greenwood & Levin, 1998: 193–194). Experimentation should be understood in a pragmatic philosophical way as a way to solve a pertinent problem (as identified jointly by insiders and outsiders) through making the best attempt to develop a solution. This whole process takes place in a natural and holistic organizational setting. Experimentation is the driving force for learning and knowledge creation and should be clearly distinguished from the potentially negative connotations created by much social scientific experimentation.

Collective reflection is initiated, based on examining the results from the concrete attempts to solve a problem (experimentation). Collective reflection was introduced as the second building block (in addition to participation) of OD. The collective reflection process has to be built on judging results from the actual attempts to solve the organizational obstacles. The 'fuel' for the experimental engine is generated in the collective reflection process. Serious considerations must be paid on how to create opportunities for collective reflection. It is also important to remember that the outsiders are equal but different partners with the insiders in the same learning process, as the outsiders will have the additional responsibility of keeping the process running. In addition to being a process consultant in Schein's (1988) terms, the outsider is also a co-learner. This is in many ways a self-evident argument, but it is all too easy to overlook the fact that the process consultant is both a participant and an activist.

Collective reflection might spontaneously take place or it might be planned. In both respects it is vital in an OD process to secure the institution of collective reflection. Collective reflection is framed by the actual participants, the material context (space and time), and by the type of communication processes that is mandated. The material context and the people involved in the discourse create an arena where reflection and learning can take place. In the co-generative model for OD, conscious construction of appropriate arenas is vital. For most practical purposes, arena construction would be the responsibility of the outsider, at least in the initial phases of a developmental process. Later, the aim would be that the insiders acquire the necessary skills to take control over this process. Ability to shape appropriate arenas, given the actual situation, is the key to creating opportunities for collective reflection and learning. Reading a developmental situation, and knowing the potential learning capacities of different arenas, will be important areas of knowledge that must be in the repertoire of the outside facilitator. An arena can be anything from an informal meeting, a planned discussion between management and union people, to a departmental meeting or a structured search conference.

## STRATEGIES FOR MANAGING PARTICIPATIVE CHANGE PROCESSES

We have so far identified participative OD as a co-generative learning process involving insiders and outsiders in a collective experimentation and learning process. First, the friendly outsider, as the facilitator was coined by Greenwood and Levin (1998), emerges in the initial phase of the developmental activity as the actor responsible for the design of the process. The core design parameters are the construction of arenas for collective reflection, securing that experimentation takes place, and engaging the involved actors in reflection on the results of the experimentation. The major effort is to shape an adequate arena, given the concrete situation, both regarding who is to be involved, the problem situation, the local competence level, and the learning potential for the group enrolled in the OD process. It is evident that the outsider has the specific task of judging these different aspects in order to design an appropriate process.

What follows next is a discussion on some major alternatives available when designing fruitful reflection opportunities. These opportunities will have different characteristics and will accordingly have to be chosen, dependent on what needs to be achieved. It is beyond the limit of this chapter to deal with all the possible participative arenas, as only some select few are presented and discussed. The aim is to discuss the arenas that seem to be most convenient. In the following we discuss five major arenas for collective reflection. These arenas are: (1) search conferences; (2) dialogue conferences; (3) mutual gains bargaining; (4) conventional meetings; and (5) task forces. Search conferences and dialogue conferences are usually considered a key structure in participative approaches to OD, whereas mutual gains bargaining, meetings, and task forces are either considered to be everyday organizational events or as approaches that do not necessarily resemble OD. Therefore, it is useful to show how these activities can support participation and collective reflection. Again, the issue for the friendly outsider is to have enough knowledge to choose skilfully from potential ways of constructing learning arenas to fit the local context. The judgement of an appropriate arena must take into consideration the goals of the OD activities, the local context (the organization, the market, the technology, the politics, etc.), the actors involved, and the available resources.

## SEARCH CONFERENCE

This method emerged from the Tavistock tradition and had a fairly parallel development on two continents. In Australia, Fred and Merrelyn Emery played a central role in developing and applying search conferences in social change processes (Emery, 1993). In Europe, cooperation between Tavistock and the Norwegian Work Research Institute created experiments with search conference design (Herbst, 1980). A search conference is a staged joint planning conference where the outcome is concrete working plans initiating change activity. A search conference is usually conducted over two days and brings the participants together in a setting separate from the ordinary work context. Search conferences have been used to help organizations, schools, local communities, non-governmental organizations, etc., so a search conference can be applied in many different contexts.

  Search conferences build on the assumption that the participants can develop a joint understanding of what to do, but a search conference has limited options in situations where the participants hold conflicting points of view (Martin, 2000). There is no one accepted way of running a search conference, as we empirically can see a wide variety of approaches, even though Emery (1993) strongly argues for only one potential way. We consider a search conference as a cluster of activities that is characterized by a structured process of problem definition, development of creative alternative paths to solving the actual problem, and collective priorititizing, leading to concrete plans and activity. The whole process builds on collective interaction, leading to participative learning processes and concrete experimentation. The normal procedure for a search conference is to organize a follow-up conference to enable collective reflection on obtained results and further planning for new experimental activity. In this regard it creates a collective experiential learning cycle and is very much in line with the general structure of learning and reflection cycles in the co-generative learning model. The outsider is the facilitator who is in charge of the whole search process. This role can vary from just devoting time and energy to keeping the process running to engaging directly on substantial developmental issues. A facilitator leaning towards the co-generative model would bring to the table substantial knowledge, and will actively contribute that to the collective process.

## DIALOGUE CONFERENCES

Dialogue conferences emerged in the Scandinavian context, building on the extensive knowledge from search conferences and action research. A trademark of dialogue conferences is the focus on the discourse as a key factor in an OD activity. The intellectual influence is clearly Habermas' (1984) work on the ethics of communicative actions as a pragmatic ideal of how to equal out differences in social exchange and Wittgensteinian philosophy on language and action (Monk, 1990). The core issue in structuring a dialogue conference is to clarify a set of rules that guide the process. These rules were formulated as 13 points by Gustavsen and Engelstad (1985) and Gustavsen (1985), where the central idea is to secure the participative process characteristics, the right to participation, the right to speak, and the listeners' obligation to judge the arguments put forward. These rules guide the process and the outside facilitator usually takes on a policing role. It will be up to the participants to take the initiative and to control the process, and all potential solutions to the problem will be up to the insiders. No outside influence is generated expect for 'policing' the process. This is both a strength and a weakness of the dialogue conferences as active and substantial intervention in the process is outside the rules. A dialogue conference usually lasts about two days, and everyone relevant to a specific change activity participates, The conference takes place away from the company premises, giving some chance to avoid a situation where hierarchical positions dominate the conversation. The actual conference process is organized to enable the participants to single out key factors for change, and to envisage a process whereby the participants start working on solving these problems when they return home to their own organization.

In a situation where it is vital to give the participants as much control over their own process as possible, the dialogue conference might be a suitable solution. The downside of this approach is the potential lack of practical progress as there might be the tendency to focus too much on the process and too little on concrete experimental activity to enable a practical solution. Another weakness is the fairly passive role of the outside facilitators, as most of their duty involves keeping the process moving, with no explicit demand for substantial input to the collective reflection and learning process. The dialogue conference assumes that there is a basic line of common interest among the participants, and that no conflict will potentially derail the collective learning process. The conference will most probably stall if conflicts arise. There is no inherent mechanism to facilitate conflict resolutions in the dialogue conference.

## MUTUAL GAINS BARGAINING

Mutual gains bargaining can be traced back to the Harvard negotiation project (Fisher & Ury, 1981; Fisher & Brown, 1988). The underlying idea is to stage a learning process where the actors involved can learn about their differences and commonalities. Two concepts are vital in mutual gains bargaining. It is important to make a distinction between *positions* and *interests*. A position is a statement of a concrete choice of action whereas an interest is an identification of what an actor actually wants (the underlying interest). The difference is that a position identifies a very specific set of actions that would solve the 'problem', whereas an interest opens up a process where other possible actions might create a solution. The argument in mutual gains bargaining is that we are all too often focused on our positions and not on our interest. The core process elements are to identify the conflicting situations (the involved actors' different positions and interests) and to shape a creative process where the participants shape new actions that would potentially fulfil their interest.

Many different approaches to mutual gains bargaining can be seen. It has, for example, made some important progress in shaping the ground for cooperation between trade unions and management. In effect, mutual gains is not necessarily a participative process that leads to collective reflection, but it might easily be shaped in the format of an arena that is participative. The full potential of this mode of working has probably not been fully exploited yet.

The strength of this approach is the acknowledgement of the participants' conflicting interests as a natural fact. In mutual gains bargaining a creative process is designed where conflicting issues can be addressed and creative and workable solutions might be achieved. Neither search conferences nor dialogue conferences are particularly suitable in situations where there are explicit conflicts between participants. The outside facilitator plays an important role both in using her or his power to design a forced learning process aimed at letting the participants understand the difference between interests and positions and to support the creation of alternative solutions that attain mutual gains.

## MEETINGS

A meeting is often conceptualized as an arena that needs little attention; people do not consider clarifying the goal of the meeting nor imagine a meeting as a learning opportunity. From the perspective of OD, a meeting will always be an element in a change process that will enable or put off participative processes. A meeting is, of course, a social arena that can deliberately be designed to achieve specific goals. A meeting can contain one-way communication from the power-holders or it can encourage an open discussion involving all attendees. Meetings of different shapes and structures will always be elements of OD activities. A meeting might be an approach to inform the employees of a future development, or it might take the form of stocktaking an already running change process. In either case, there are design options. Depending on what is the expected outcome, and on what signals are transmitted to the audience, the meeting should be very consciously designed. One of the major challenges in arranging meetings in participative processes is the danger of communicating a non-participative practice, as a meeting all too often takes the form of staged one-way communication.

## TASK FORCES

A task force is a group with a fairly clear and stated goal. These goals will, in the context of OD, often be the experimental activity initiated to create a more effective organization. A task force can in itself be a mini-cosmos of a larger OD process, as it is important to create opportunities for reflection and learning within the boundaries of the group. A task force can be structured to support participation and it can be structured to give room for collective reflection. A task force is often the inner cogwheel of the larger change process and it is important to design its structure and operation in line with the general principles and values in OD. Much is written about learning and development in groups and we will not repeat that here but direct the reader to the actual literature on groups, group dynamics, teams, etc. The literature is rich and stimulating (as a starting point, see, for example, Hackman, 1990; Kolb et al., 1984).

## CHOOSING ARENAS

Choosing a suitable arena for collective reflection is an essential design criterion in OD. An arena should make it possible to create a participative collective reflection process. Hence, it is important to be able to make a conscious decision on what would be an appropriate arena, given the actual context and problems. Several questions have to be answered in order to make the right choice. This selection process can be summarized by answering three questions. Answering these questions would principally be the responsibility of all participants (insiders and outsiders), but in certain phases of the OD process the outsider would have to take on specific responsibility in shaping the answers:

1. *What concrete challenges are facing the actual organization?* It is important to make an assessment of the organization and to decide what the problem should be. The idea is to be explicit about the immediate and long-term objectives of the OD process. The answer to this question must be shared by the involved parties, but the friendly outsider might take on a special responsibility for the process leading up to an answer to this question.
2. *What type of learning would be beneficial?* Different arenas create different options for learning, and with a given focus of attention, it is important to choose an arena that would facilitate the expected learning process.
3. *How can one link learning to experimental activity?* An arena creates different opportunities for problem-solving activity. In some arenas the experimental activity emerges directly from the learning process, while other arenas only create learning possibilities and imply that action has to be organized separately. In some situations the separation of learning and action might be beneficial, while in other contexts it would be important to have a direct and strong link between learning and action.

The answers to these questions will support the information base that will enhance the judgement of the appropriate arena and subsequently create the basis for the design of the OD process. It is not automatically assumed that this should be the sole responsibility of the friendly outsider (the process consultant). Such decisions can also be the responsibility of the participants. In fact, the highest goal of the OD process is to create enough local skills so that the insiders take control of the change processes. In such a situation, the development process has created an organization that is able to continually learn and transform itself. The friendly outsider is basically the key person to facilitate a process whereby the insiders are expected to take control of their own developmental activity. This is the discussion we embark on in the next section.

## THE ROLE OF THE FRIENDLY OUTSIDER—DESIGN, MONITORING, AND MANAGING RESOURCES

The friendly outsider is a key person in the OD effort. Using the singular form of friendly outsider does not necessarily indicate that we are only talking of one person. There might be more than one friendly outsider cooperating in facilitating the same change process. In fact, we would strongly argue for the positive benefits of having more than one person involved, as it shapes a fruitful ground for outsider learning and reflection.

In the conceptualization of the OD process as co-generative learning, the friendly outsider becomes the key person in the initial phase. The friendly outsider often plays a powerful role in this phase. The outsider is the model strong actor (Bråthen, 1973) and will in most circumstances dominate the decisions on initial design. The model strength is a consequence of mediating a potentially consistent set of concepts that eventually mould the change process. In fact, co-generative learning is such a model. It is vital for the outsider to bring with him or her a professional conceptualization of organizational development as it will guide the structuring of the change activity, but a major challenge for the outsider is to make the insiders understand the premises on which the transformation activity is founded.

Before starting a change activity, it is important that the outsider develops a prior understanding of the core dimensions of the actual organization, its surroundings, and the problem. The friendly outsider has to develop a self-supported knowledge of the organization to keep his or her own integrity in the co-generative learning process. A preliminary research process is one way of creating the necessary knowledge base for the outsider to be able to make sense of the local situation. The outsider would, on her or his side, bring to the table knowledge of different types of arenas, their potentials and pitfalls, and in the actual context make a judgement on what to recommend as concrete OD activities. Such recommendations would realistically be strong in the initial phases of the project, but in a 'good' transformation process, the insiders will gradually acquire knowledge necessary to make their own decisions.

In OD design and redesign is a continual process. It lasts as long as the OD process operates. A developmental process consists of an unlimited sequence of action–reflection–new understanding–new action. In this view, design becomes a sequential and continual process that requires judgement in each sequence in order to follow an appropriate process. This mode of operation demands a monitoring function.

Monitoring will, in a sequence of learning cycles (experimentation, reflection, and learning), keep track of the developmental process. Being aware of the different elements of the change process, figuring out if problems have been solved, understanding where learning stalls, making sense of potential conflicts, and remedying adequate response are pretty much what a monitoring function should do. There is, however, one important feature of monitoring, i.e. it is always connected to a preparatory activity that will direct the developmental process to the desired goals. In a sequential design procedure, the goals will also change. For the monitoring function, this presents demands for adjustment to what is the stated goal for the developmental sequence in focus. The target for the developmental process will change and the monitoring function has to take account of this fact. Both re-design and monitoring will move in parallel.

The management of the design and monitoring function has so far been communicated as the prime responsibility of the outsider. On the other hand, I have argued strongly for a handover of responsibility for design, monitoring, and management from the outsider to the insiders. In order to fulfil this demand, one central dimension in designing a participative developmental process is to create reflection and learning that will shape the ground for the participants' increased involvement. It is not enough that the participants have a say in the day-to-day transformation process planned by the outsider, it is equally important that the insiders gradually and systematically take control over their own developmental process. This becomes, in fact, the core design, monitoring, and management principle, as it is vital to transfer skills and responsibility to the insiders.

## CONCLUSION: DON'T LOOK FOR A BLUEPRINT—MAKE YOUR OWN JUDGEMENT

I have conceptualized OD as a participative change process where participation and collective reflection are the two main building blocks. Further, I have argued for the co-generative learning process where problem-owners and outside facilitators share the reflection and learning opportunities. The major guidelines for insiders as well as for outsiders are to continually monitor the developmental process in order to judge the process and its outcomes, in order to make wise decisions on how to advance the transformative activity. This is, of course, not an activity that follows a pre-drawn blueprint. The actors involved, the local context, skills, and the resources of the outsider will create the developmental picture. Blueprinting developmental processes must be replaced by continual judgement, both from insiders as well as from outsiders.

## REFERENCES

Argyris, C., Putnam, R. & McLain Smith, L. (1985) *Action Science*. San Francisco: Jossey-Bass.

Argyris, C. & Schön, D.A. (1996) *Organizational Learning II: Theory, Method, and Practices*. New York: Addison-Wesley.

Berger, P.L. & Luckmann, T. (1966) *The Social Construction of Reality*. Harmondsworth: Penguin.

Bråthen, S. (1973) Model monopoly and communication systems: theoretical notes on democratisation. *Acta Sociologica*, **16**(2), 98–107.

Cummings, T.G. & Worley, C.G. (1993) *Organizational Development and Change* (5th edn). New York: West Publishing Company.

De Geus, A. (1997) *The Living Company Growth: Learning and Longevity in Business*. London: Nicolas Brealy.

Diggins, J.P. (1994) *The Promise of Pragmatism: Modernism and the Crisis of Knowledge and Authority*. Chicago: The University of Chicago Press.

Elden, M. & Levin, M. (1991) 'Co-generative learning: bringing participation into action research'. In W.F. Whyte (ed.) *Participatory Action Research*. Newbury Park, CA: Sage.

Emery, F. & Thorsrud, E. (1976) *Democracy at Work*. Leiden: Martinus Nijhof.

Emery, M. (1993) *Participative Design for Participative Democracy*. Canberra: Centre for Continuing Education, Australian National University.

Fisher, R. & Brown, S. (1988) *Getting Together: Building Relationships as We Negotiate*. Harmondsworth: Penguin.

Fisher, R. & Ury, W. (1981) *Getting to Yes: Negotiating Agreement Without Giving In*. Harmondsworth: Penguin.

French, W.L., Bell, C.H. & Zwaki, R.A. (1994) *Organization Development and Transformation*. Boston: Irwin.

Greenberg, E.S. (1975) The consequences of worker participation: a clarification of the theoretical literature. *Social Science Quarterly*, **65**, 191–209.

Greenwood, D.J. & Levin, M. (1998) *Introduction to Action Research: Social Research for Social Change.* Thousand Oaks, CA: Sage.

Guba, E.G. & Lincoln, Y.S. (1985) *Naturalistic Inquiry.* Newbury Park, CA: Sage.

Gustavsen, B. (1985) Work place reform and democratic dialogue. *Economic and Industrial Democracy,* **6,** 461–479.

Gustavsen, B. (1992) *Dialogue and Development.* Assen-Mastricht: Van Gorcum.

Gustavsen, B. & Engelstad, P.H. (1985) The design of conferences and the evolving role of the democratic dialogue in changing work life. *Human Relations,* **32**(9), 101–116.

Habermas, J. (1984) *The Theory of Communicative Action* (vol. 1). London: Heinemann.

Hackman, J.R. (ed.) (1990) *Groups that Work and Those that Don't.* San Francisco: Jossey-Bass

Hammer, M. & Champy, J. (1993) *Reengineering the Corporation: A Manifesto for Business Revolution.* New York: HarperCollins.

Herbst, P. (1980) Community conference design; Skjervøy, today and tomorrow. *Human Futures,* **Summer,** 1–61.

Kolb, D.A., Rubin, I.M. & McIntyre, J.M. (1984) *The Psychology of Organization and Leadership* (Orgnaisasjons og ledersespsykologi). Oslo: Universitetsforlaget.

Levin, M. (1984) Worker participation in the design of new technology. In T. Martin (ed.) *Design of Work in Automated Manufacturing Systems.* Oxford: Pergamon Press.

Levin, M. & Klev, R. (2002) *Change as Praxis: Learning and Development in Organizations* (Forandring som praksis: Læring og utvikling i organisasjonern). Bergen: Fagbokforlaget.

Levin, M., Havn, V. & Nilssen, T. (1983) *From Coverall to Jeans* (Fra kjelederess til cordbukse). Trondheim: IFIM.

Lysgaard, S. (1961) *The Workers Collective* (Arbeiderkolektivet). Oslo: Universitetsforlaget.

Martin, A.W. (2000) Search conference methodology and the politics of difference, dissertation. New York: Columbia University.

Monk, R. (1990) *Ludwig Wittgenstein: The Duty of a Genius.* Harmondsworth: Penguin.

Nelson, R.R. & Winter, S.G. (1982) *An Evolutionary Theory of Economic Change.* Cambridge, MA: Harvard University Press.

Pålshaugen, Ø. (1998) Organization development through development organization. In B. Gustavsen, T. Colbjørnsen & Ø. Pålshaugen (eds) *Development Coalitions in Working Life.* Amsterdam: John Benjamins.

Pateman, C. (1970) *Participation and Democratic Theory.* London: Cambridge University Press.

Reason, P. & Bradbury, H. (2001) *Handbook of Action Research: Participative Inquiry and Practice.* London: Sage.

Schein, E. (1988) *Process Consultation.* Reading, MA: Addison-Wesley.

Schön, D.A. (1983) Organizational learning. In G. Morgan (ed.), *Beyond Method.* Beverly Hills, CA: Sage.

Searle, J.R. (1995) *The Construction of Social Reality.* New York: The Free Press.

Senge, P.M. (1990) *The Fifth Discipline: The Art and Practice of the Learning Organization.* New York: Doubleday.

Weick, K.E. (1995) *Sensemaking in Organizations.* Thousand Oaks, CA: Sage.

# CHAPTER 4

# Art and Wisdom in Choosing Change Strategies
## A Critical Reflection

**Marc Buelens and Geert Devos**
*Vlerick Leuven Gent Management School, Ghent, Belgium*

The overall picture of change effectiveness is rather gloomy. Andrew Pettigrew rightfully observed that 'most change processes do not attract universal acclaim' (Pettigrew, 2000: 249). Efforts to implement organizational change have frequently been shown to fail (Kotter, 1995; Edmonson & Woolley, 1999). Many firms that have failed to adopt Total Quality Management (TQM) exemplify the difficulty of changing an organization (Spector & Beer, 1994; McNabb & Sepic, 1995). Research indicates that 70 per cent of business process reengineering projects have yielded limited success (Hall et al., 1993; Bashein et al., 1994). The same goes for the introduction of new technology or efforts to change corporate culture (Beer & Nohria, 2000). A study by the American Management Association showed that less than half the companies involved in repeated restructuring and downsizing achieved their expense reduction goals and less than one in four increased their productivity (Applebaum & Batt, 1993). It is obvious that not all change is effective or successful. Nevertheless, defining success or effectiveness of change strategies is a cumbersome task. 'Success can be realistically addressed only against self-proclaimed targets' (Pettigrew, 2000: 248). However, the question remains: whose targets? Different stakeholders might pursue different goals, might start from different value systems, and might give different interpretations to the same facts.

In practice, most Organizational Development (OD) consultants prefer cooperation to conflict, self-control over institutional control, and democratic and participative management to autocratic management (McKendall, 1993). Organization development could be seen as a value-driven approach where the changes and developments are successful when these values are realized.

Organizational Behaviour (OB) bestsellers emphasize that those higher benefits will not be sustainable if they are not grounded in respect for and development of the employees. Implicitly the OB approach starts from almost perfect goal congruence ('the best minute I invest is the minute I invest in people . . .') between organization and individual and bluntly ignores the political nature of change, and the diverse or even opposed interests of the parties involved.

Most economic 'bestseller' approaches, such as 'e-business', business process re-engineering, or six sigma, emphasize two stakeholders: shareholders (who will benefit from cost reduction, productivity improvement, and higher profitability) and clients (who will benefit from greater customer orientation, innovative products, and better service). Economic approaches also seem to imply a goal congruence, which is most clearly formulated in agency theory; when economically successful, the 'principal' will have more incentives at his/her disposal to successfully influence the agent (Jensen & Meckling, 1976; Eisenhardt, 1989; Spreitzer & Mishra, 1999).

*Dynamics of Organizational Change and Learning.* Edited by J.J. Boonstra.
© 2004 John Wiley & Sons, Ltd. ISBN 0-471-87737-9.

If we do not accept extensive goal congruence, we could, in the best economic tradition, consider a change management successful if at least one stakeholder is better off and the others have not suffered. This approach is rather naïve, because participants judge their outcomes in relative terms, not in an absolute sense.

To avoid an unprofitable discussion on effectiveness, we will use an approach that has proved fruitful in organization theory, namely, to look at effectiveness as the fit of the organization to its relevant environment. A reflection on the effectiveness of change is, then, a reflection on the (lack of) fit between the environment and the change, between (mis)reading the situation and the choice of a change process. We will call the overall approach of the change process a 'change strategy'. Our definition of change strategy follows Henry Mintzberg's 'pattern' approach (Mintzberg et al., 1998). A strategy is a pattern in a stream of decisions, reflecting consistency of behaviour over time. In this analysis, it is not relevant whether this pattern and the underlying choice are deliberate or not, conscious or not, pre-planned or not. Our use of the term 'change strategy' differs slightly from other approaches in the change management literature, where the term 'change strategy' is often used in the sense of 'change tactic', the sequence of different concrete steps one has to take to be successful, very often in the context of overcoming resistance.

## BASIC DIMENSIONS IN THE CHANGE ENVIRONMENT

In order to build a relevant model of the change environment, we need to choose our basic dimensions carefully. One of the major problems hindering further development of change theory is the desire to develop a general theory that can be applied to all change efforts. However, the internal and external environments of organizations can be so different that a clear understanding of the specific situation is essential to select the appropriate change strategy. Participation can be a crucial element in certain change efforts. In other cases, such as high time pressure, it might impede or obstruct the change process. The creation of a sense of urgency is vital in certain situations, and irrelevant in others.

Change processes will be described using the two basic dimensions of decision-making: facts and values (Simon, 1976). Our first dimension deals with 'values', interests, and the use of influence in order to protect values and to safeguard interests; the second dimension deals with 'facts' and the use of managerial logic in order to be economically rational.

The proposed model is a conceptual description, an essential step in further theory development. We describe the change environment in terms of two general dimensions: power distance and uncertainty. Similar dimensions can be found in management and organization theory (Mintzberg, 1979, 1983; Quinn, 1988), the study of intercultural differences (Hofstede, 1991), and the study of corporate culture (Harrison, 1972; Handy, 1978).

### CHANGE ENVIRONMENT: POWER DISTANCE

There is a large body of literature linking change to power, influence, and persuasion (Kotter & Schlesinger, 1979; Greiner & Schein, 1988; Pfeffer, 1992; Conger, 1998, 2000; Lawler, 1998). The first dimension, power distance, stems from the simple observation that all change processes are influence processes (Pettigrew, 2000). Change is inherently political. Influence supposes freedom. When freedom is absent, we talk about manipulation or coercion. In order to avoid a false dichotomy between absence of and complete freedom from, we will consider a continuum between high power distance (with relatively little freedom) and low power distance (with relatively great freedom). Therefore, our first dimension consists of high power distance versus low power distance.

A situation of high power distance can be described as a situation in which the change initiator has a much stronger power base than the target of change. This includes situations of more expert power, reference power, psychological power, and reward power (French & Raven, 1960; Pfeffer, 1981; Morgan, 1986).

## Change Environment: Uncertainty

Another extended body of literature relates change management to uncertainty (Lawrence & Lorsch, 1969; Galbraith, 1973; Nutt, 1986; London, 1987). The change process is then conceived as problem-finding and problem-solving (Schein, 1988). Therefore, our second dimension consists of high uncertainty versus low uncertainty, of information registration versus action planning. A situation of high uncertainty can generally be described as a situation of not having enough information, or lacking the framework to interpret the available information (ambiguity), having several competing or contradictory frameworks (equivocality), or having to process more information than one can manage or understand (complexity) (Zack, 1999). It requires an extensive scanning of the situation, an intensive process of information registration and framework testing, and a vigilant search process (Janis & Mann, 1977). When enough relevant information and frameworks are known and tested (a situation of low uncertainty), one has to concentrate on the 'next step', namely, action.

The second dimension stems from the inherent rational nature of all change processes. Emphasizing that all change is political (our first dimension) does not imply that change processes (at least in complex organizations) are not subject to 'norms of rationality'. Only 'permanently failing organizations' (Meyer & Zucker, 1989) can survive without a cost-benefit analysis, minimal planning, a certain logic, and a more or less systematic approach.

## Change Environment: Two Dimensions

The combination of both dimensions leads to a 2 × 2 matrix of change environment (see Table 4.1). A *high-pressure environment* is characterized by real external threats, by unexpected moves in the environment (especially by competitors). High-pressure environments are common in highly competitive sectors, in turbulent situations such as the aftermath of dramatic crises, or in pre-crisis situations. Organizations can experience a high-pressure environment when they make bold strategic moves or start new ventures in domains with strong incumbents. The organization is gambling its future and seems to be in an 'alert phase', with strong power distance as a consequence of the (perceived) strong threats. Powerful leadership is crucial to shift modes during the transition period. In addition, a vigilant search is necessary as a reaction to the high uncertainty in the environment.

An *experimental environment* is an environment where no one knows the answer. Even experience is not a relevant guide. The situation is consistently being redefined: 'People at the top will not solve our problems.' Therefore, when it becomes obvious that they are unable to solve the problems, their power base is eroded. Globalization, the introduction of new technology, and societal disrupters are causing a shift for many organizations towards experimental environments. In these environments, the organizations that flourish are described as networks, organized anarchies, or clusters. Environments are made experimental by charting new horizons, unfamiliar to all players.

A *professional environment* is an environment in which the professionals know the 'answer', under the condition that the situation is not too different from what they already know, i.e., under a condition of

**TABLE 4.1** Two dimensions of change environment

|  | Low uncertainty | High uncertainty |
|---|---|---|
| High power distance | Traditional environment | High-pressure environment |
| Low power distance | Professional environment | Experimental environment |

**TABLE 4.2**    Change tactics and their relevant environment

|                      | Low uncertainty                                                                                                | High uncertainty                                                                |
| -------------------- | -------------------------------------------------------------------------------------------------------------- | ------------------------------------------------------------------------------- |
| High power distance  | Physical force<br>Political force<br>Economic force<br>Advertising propaganda<br>Engineering<br>Rational appeal<br>Emotional appeal | Project management<br>Re-engineering<br>'Strategic change'<br>Six sigma management |
| Low power distance   | Participative management<br>Work counselling<br>Quality circles<br>Single-loop learning                         | Organization development<br>Double-loop learning                                |

low uncertainty. Environments are made 'professional' by 'pigeon holing' (Mintzberg, 1979). Change in such environments is mostly of the 'academic' type: slow, based on analysis, a high degree of participation by all professionals involved, leaving the existing small power distance untouched and only reducing uncertainty.

An environment is *traditional* when roles are clear and the future is relatively easy to predict (because it will be very similar to yesterday and today). Fixed roles define clear power distances: the role of fathers, mothers, bosses, government, etc., is well defined. Change in such an environment is mostly of the optimizing type: the kind of change that is introduced through operational research, engineering, automation, leaving the existing large power distance intact and preserving the limited uncertainty. An environment is made traditional by actively moving to 'old' environments ('delocalization'), or by imposing simplicity (government, the hidden wish behind many mergers).

A simple test of our model consists of the ease with which we can assign different well-known change tactics to our model (Olmosk, 1972; Argyris, 1982; Hammer & Champy, 1993; Harry & Schroeder, 1999; Pande et al., 2000). As can be seen in Table 4.2, this is simple and straightforward.

## FOUR BASIC STRATEGIES OF CHANGE

The four basic strategies presented here are negotiation, leadership, information registration, and action planning. These strategies are related to the basic dimensions in change environments.

### LOW POWER DISTANCE: NEGOTIATION

A situation of low power distance demands a negotiation approach. A negotiation is a decision-making process among interdependent parties who do not share identical preferences (Neale & Bazerman, 1992). Negotiation has received surprisingly little attention in the change management literature. Negotiation is often perceived as a method for dealing with resistance to change, along with education, participation, facilitation, manipulation, and coercion (Kotter & Schlesinger, 1979). Negotiation is identified as a lawyer-like transaction, where resistors are offered incentives. Hence, negotiation is often reduced to 'bargaining' (Sergeev, 1991), with a give-and-take exchange to resolve conflicting interests. However, a negotiation process is much more fundamental and encompasses all joint communication and decision processes to resolve divergence of interest and to reach a mutually satisfactory outcome (Lax & Sebenius, 1986; Putnam & Roloff, 1992; Pruitt & Carnevale, 1993). Failing to recognize the situation as 'low power distance' (and, for example, applying a 'leadership' approach) leads to what we will call a 'negotiation failure'. A negotiation failure consists of underestimating the two core elements in a negotiation process: interdependency and value differences. When change agents do not realize the interdependent nature of the change process, they will exercise power, authority, persuasion, and argumentation. When change agents do not realize the value differences, they will suppose goal congruence where relevant differences exist.

## HIGH POWER DISTANCE: LEADERSHIP

A situation of high power distance demands a leadership approach. Leadership can be defined as 'a social influence process in which the leader seeks the voluntary participation of subordinates in an effort to reach organizational goals' (Kreitner et al., 1999: 472). Leadership is the influential increment over compliance with the routine directives of the organization (Katz & Kahn, 1978).

There is a long and influential tradition in the change management literature emphasizing the close link between change and (charismatic) leadership (Kotter, 1996; Bennis, 2000; Conger, 2000). Failing to recognize the situation as 'high power distance' (and, for example, applying a 'negotiation' approach or simply ignoring the influence dimension of change) leads to a leadership failure. A complete leadership failure consists of underestimating the two core elements in a leadership process: social support and direction. When change agents do not realize the need for social support, they will use pure logic and will be blind to emotional intelligence processes such as empathy or the use of positive emotions such as hope or optimism. When change agents do not realize the need for direction and clarity, their actions will lead to higher levels of role ambiguity or role conflict.

Negotiation and leadership failures can be caused by personality (the 'autocratic dogmatic personality' will experience many negotiation failures), by cultural differences (applying participative management in a high power distance country), by misreading the situation ('I thought they were better informed'), or by a dramatic, but unnoticed, shift in the environment.

## HIGH UNCERTAINTY: INFORMATION REGISTRATION

A situation of high uncertainty demands a 'vigilant search for relevant information' (Janis & Mann, 1977; Hammond et al., 1999). Such a situation demands an information registration approach. Information registration is the first phase of rational decision-making. Failing to recognize the situation as 'registration' (and applying a 'reduction' approach) leads to a registration failure. The symptoms of poor problem recognition are well known: groupthink, 'passing the buck', and procrastination. When the 'real' problem is badly defined, this leads to the law of displacing problem definition, that is, another, readily available problem is solved. This will usually happen in situations where the problem is symbolic and in highly institutionalized environments. Registration failures can be caused by, among others, personality (the so-called dogmatic personality), high levels of stress (panic), or strong values leading to taboos.

## LOW UNCERTAINTY: ACTION PLANNING

A situation of low uncertainty demands action planning and quick decisions; it demands information reduction. The classic command-and-control management, emphasis on co-ordination, the 'decisive decision-maker', or management by objectives will all be more or less effective (depending on the acceptable power distance) in a low uncertainty environment. Situations of low uncertainty require more 'management' than 'leadership'. In those circumstances, a new job description or an improved procedure will guarantee more than 'a shared vision'. Action-planning failures can be caused by personality (a strong external locus of control), by lack of management skills such as time management, by power games, or accepting strong 'low power distance' values such as anarchism.

**TABLE 4.3**   Change strategies and their relevant environment

|              | Action planning                          | Information registration                     |
|--------------|------------------------------------------|----------------------------------------------|
| Leadership   | Command and control (traditional environment) | Project management (high-pressure environment) |
| Negotiation  | Participative approach (professional environment) | OD approach (experimental environment) |

By combining the four 'pure' strategies of change, we can describe an 'ideal type' for each quadrant (see Table 4.3). The north-west quadrant, the traditional environment, demands a 'command and control' approach, a combination of action planning and leadership. At first sight, this seems to contradict the link between (radical) change and the need for leadership (Kotter, 1996). A stable environment seems to ask only for management. However, in this context, we concentrate, by definition, on change, and even a traditional environment is confronted with change.

The north-east quadrant, the high-pressure environment, demands a 'project management' approach. Companies are not characterized by their democratic nature; personnel are not consulted before mergers or acquisitions, de-layering, re-engineering, etc. These are typical top-down processes, as are 90 per cent of the 'management by objectives' processes. A few people at the top take bold strategic moves. It demands a combination of information registration and leadership.

The south-west quadrant, or professional environment, demands a 'participative' approach. This environment is the area where highly trained professionals exercise their profession and form the operating core. They reject large power distances, but, on the other hand, they want to optimize their own profession and do not venture into radically new ground. They avoid high uncertainty environments (with the exception of highly complex problems) and essentially keep their environment predictable by pigeon-holing.

The south-east quadrant, or experimental environment, demands an OD approach: a joint process of problem definition and problem-solving, requiring empowerment and lack of censorship. Since the environment is uncertain, all participants must look for new solutions. They need a high level of autonomy to experiment and to develop new initiatives. High tolerance of mistakes, open dialogue and discussion, and team development are needed to stimulate organizational learning (Senge, 1990).

## FOUR BASIC PROCESSES OF 'CHANGE FAILURES'

In this section, we will describe the four generic change failures: leadership failure, negotiation failure, registration failure, and action-planning failure.

A leadership failure leads to a lack of orientation, vision, and inspiration (cognitive dimension). It can also lead to anxiety (emotional dimension), passive aggression, such as intense gossip, intention to leave, and organizational cynicism (behavioural dimension). The lack of social support and the increased role conflicts or role ambiguity give rise to processes normally associated with high levels of stress. We can predict that a leadership failure will lead to withdrawal.

A negotiation failure leads to a lack of accepting goal discongruence (cognitive dimension). Not being aware of value differences (mostly due to a lack of empathy) will easily lead to alienation and emotions normally associated with loss, such as anger or grief (emotional dimension). It easily leads to manipulation, flattery, coalition formation, passive aggression, and, in extreme situations, to disruptive conflicts (behavioural dimension). All things considered, we can predict that a negotiation failure will lead to what traditionally has been called 'psychological' resistance.

A registration failure leads to lack of creativity, low quality decision-making, and external attribution, such as 'the system is to blame' (cognitive dimension). It easily leads to pessimism, even despair or depression (emotional dimension), and to resignation and learned helplessness (behavioural dimension). We can predict that a registration failure will lead to 'avoidance'.

An action-planning failure leads to harsh criticism, perception of inefficiencies and of spoiling (human) resources (cognitive dimension), frustration, apathy, and feelings of unfairness (emotional dimensions). It easily leads to all kinds of 'soldiering', social loafing, or free rider behaviour (behavioural dimension). Overall, we can predict that an action-planning failure will lead to disorientation.

# FOUR SPECIFIC CHANGE FAILURES

When we look at change failures, from the point of view of the relevant situation, we can identify four specific failures.

## CHANGE FAILURES IN A PROFESSIONAL ENVIRONMENT

A professional environment requires 'negotiated', not 'imposed', planning. Negotiated can mean 'traditionally negotiated', as a result of bargaining between stakeholders with different interests, or 'participative'. Typical failures in a professional environment stem from the idea that 'one size fits all', such as applying a command and control approach to a symphony orchestra. Another example concerns a media company that starts applying budget control and aims at motivating creative people, journalists, script writers, etc., for 'the common goal'. After six months of training, threats, consultancy, attracting new MBA-ers, and endless meetings, the project is forgotten. The company, however, has lost three valuable creative researchers and reporters.

Lack of action planning occurs frequently in professional environments, making them extremely inefficient (and thus expensive), as almost all patients who have been 'clients' at hospitals can testify. The low power distance seems to dominate the low uncertainty dimension, leading to the spoiling of resources in universities, law firms, hospitals, etc., and to strong resistance to managerial approaches.

## CHANGE FAILURES IN AN EXPERIMENTAL ENVIRONMENT

An experimental environment requires a negotiation and registration strategy. The most common failure in business firms is to neglect the negotiation strategy and to apply a top-down-driven project management approach. High uncertainty is noticed and, with a kind of 'burning platform' analogy, one suspects that all participants will share a common goal. Then a single-loop learning process takes place, where a (newly) appointed leader 'shows the way'. This 'double-loop learning failure' caused havoc in companies confronted with the e-environment, where they tried to implement the transition to unknown territory with tried and true principles from project management. Less common is denial of high uncertainty, the neglect of the registration strategy, with a 'business as usual' approach. This failure can sometimes be observed in partnerships facing a dramatic shift in environment. Those partnerships are more or less well adapted to their professional environments and suddenly face high-pressure environments. Law firms, consultancy agencies, orchestras, and universities have the greatest difficulties in adapting to totally new situations.

Rather unlikely, and only possible under strong leadership, is the 'invent me the A-bomb' failure, a combination of both failures, as illustrated in the story of Los Alamos, where at the very beginning of his mission, General Groves forced top nuclear scientists to stop creative freewheeling and to start inventing on a tight time schedule. Robert Oppenheimer wrote to him at the height of the conflict: 'It is true that there are a few people here whose interests are exclusively "scientific" in the sense that they will abandon any problem that appears to be soluble' (Oppenheimer, 1944). However, scientists simply went on with their informal brainstorming sessions but concealed them from General Groves.

## CHANGE FAILURES IN A TRADITIONAL ENVIRONMENT

A traditional environment requires a leadership and action-planning strategy. Change processes based on negotiation and information registration such as OD are very often publicly announced. New managerialism, client orientation, and the introduction of new values will fundamentally change the 'traditional' organization. There seems to be an endless list of publications reporting on failures, on the tension between the rhetoric of the empowered, entrepreneurial, client-oriented 'new public manager' and the reality of even more bureaucracy (Warwick, 1975; Van Gramberg & Teicher, 2000). Organizations in traditional environments have strong built-in mechanisms to protect themselves against all adventures that could lead them into experimental environments. Disasters such as the collapse of the Barings Bank or the out-of-control situation at Chernobyl reinforce beliefs in control systems, hierarchy, enforcement of rules, etc.

The basic problem in a stable environment is that even the 'natural' processes are not applied. The most common failure is a lack of leadership. The 'quality circle disaster' in most Western companies can be seen as an illustration of a lack of leadership commitment and a clear quality strategy, and of unclear values (McNabb and Sepic, 1995).

Lack of leadership and lack of action planning (lack of management and lack of coordination) in a stable environment will lead to a loss of essential resources in political organizations, that might even become 'permanently failing' (Meyer & Zucker, 1989).

## CHANGE FAILURES IN A HIGH-PRESSURE ENVIRONMENT

A high-pressure environment requires a leadership and registration strategy. A typical failure stemming from the lack of registration is the 'reshuffling the deck chairs on the *Titanic*' failure, that is, applying an optimization strategy in a highly unequivocal situation. One does not reach consensus on the 'real problem' and apply tried and true solutions to a completely unknown situation. In many cases, executive management applies 'more of the same' in such situations, leading to 'managerial regression', namely, tighter budget control, cost cutting, and management by objectives. Another typical failure stems from the lack of leadership. Information on the dramatic shift is readily available, but management fails to react. Documented examples are the complete failure of Encyclopedia Britannica to react to the threat of Microsoft's Encarta, or the inertia at Xerox management to build on technology from their own Palo Alto research laboratory. When Xerox's top management was confronted with major breakthroughs such as the 'Graphic User Interface' or e-mail, they simply failed to grasp their relevance. Major problems seem to arise in organizations that are confronted with potential failures on both dimensions. In practice, this means that a correction in one dimension will not solve the problem, leading to an oscillation between regression on that dimension and radical shift on the other dimension. This oscillation leads to distrust, lack of even single-loop learning, and complete disorientation. For example, in the middle of an existential crisis, because stakeholders could not define its role (is this a scientific institution or a commercial firm?), a biotechnology firm opted for 'people management', such as job descriptions of all parties involved (a shift towards more planning). This project is a failure and is stopped and replaced by open debates among all stakeholders (a shift towards information registration). Many stakeholders argue for stronger leadership, a more 'businesslike' approach of managing the firm, leading to new targets, etc. A new business manager with a background in fast-moving consumer goods is appointed, but the new manager does not understand the 'academic freedom' culture of the biotechnology environment, which leads to a loss of top scientists, etc.

## CONCLUSION

Organizational change is complex and diverse. We started this chapter by pointing to the low success rate of change and have developed a contingency framework where different environments are matched with different change strategies.

In theory, there are three major reasons for change failures. First, some organizations fail to see that their environment is changing. This is a major cause of change failure in many organizations with a long history of high power distance and a low uncertainty environment. They continue to implement the change strategies that were adapted to their traditional environment, and fail to see that their environment has changed into a high-pressure or professional environment.

Second, one can apply the wrong strategies in view of the organizational environment. Those are the change failures that we have focused on in this chapter. However, even the selection of the right strategy is no guarantee of success.

Third, even the correct assessment of the environment and the selection of the correct strategy can lead to change failure. The implementation of the correct strategies can go wrong, especially when the implementation of the strategies is extremely one-sided. Leadership demands clear vision and a top-down approach, but every top-down-driven change that neglects participation in the implementation process risks overlooking local structures, relations, and knowledge that are vital for successful implementation. A vigilant search for new information in an environment that is highly uncertain must finally result in initiatives that are managed and coordinated. Otherwise, the organization will end up in complete chaos.

Eventually, it is the effective integration of the different change strategies adapted to the internal and external environment of the organization that determines the success of any change effort. The art of change management consists of applying the right mix. Academics can offer the ingredients. Only seasoned cooks can prepare the most complex dishes successfully.

## REFERENCES

Applebaum, E. & Batt, R. (1993) *The New American Workplace*. Ithaca, NY: Cornell University Press.

Argyris, C. (1982) *Reasoning, Learning and Action*. San Francisco: Jossey-Bass.

Bashein, M.L., Marcus, M.L. & Riley, P. (1994) Business Process Reengineering: preconditions for success and failure. *Informations Systems Management*, **9**, 24–31.

Beer, M. & Nohria, N. (2000) Cracking the code of change. *Harvard Business Review*, **78**(3), 133–141.

Bennis, W. (2000) Leadership of change. In M. Beer & N. Nohria (eds) *Breaking the Code of Change* (pp. 113–121). Boston: Harvard Business School Press.

Conger, J.A. (1998) The necessary art of persuasion. *Harvard Business Review*, **76**(3), 84–95.

Conger, J.A. (2000) Effective change begins at the top. In M. Beer & N. Nohria (eds) *Breaking the Code of Change* (pp. 99–112). Boston: Harvard Business School Press.

Edmonson, A.C. & Woolley, A.W. (1999) It's not the seed, it's the soil: social psychological influences on outcomes of organizational change programs. Paper presented at the annual meeting of the Academy of Management, Chicago.

Eisenhardt, K.M. (1989) Agency theory: an assessment and review. *Academy of Management Review*, **14**, 57–74.

French, J.R.P. & Raven, B. (1960) The bases of social power. In D. Cartwright & A.F. Zander (eds) *Group Dynamics* (pp. 607–623). Evanston, IL: Peterson.

Galbraith, J. (1973) *Designing Complex Organizations*. Reading, MA: Addison-Wesley.

Greiner, L.E. & Schein, V.E. (1988) *Power and Organization Development: Mobilizing Power to Implement Change*. Reading, MA: Addison-Wesley.

Hall, G., Rosenthal, J. & Wade, J. (1993) How to make reengineering really work. *Harvard Business Review*, **71**(6), 119–131.

Hammer, M. & Champy, J. (1993) *Reengineering the Corporation: A Manifesto for Business Revolution.* New York: Harper Business.

Hammond, J.S., Keeney, R.L. & Raiffa, H. (1999) *Smart Choices: A Practical Guide to Making Better Decisions.* Boston: Harvard Business School Press.

Handy, C. (1978) *Gods of Management.* London: Penguin.

Harrison, R. (1972) Understanding your organization's character. *Harvard Business Review*, **50**(2), 119–128.

Harry, M.J. & Schroeder, R. (1999) *Six Sigma.* New York: Bantam Doubleday.

Hofstede, G. (1991) *Cultures and Organizations: Software of the Mind.* New York: McGraw-Hill.

Janis, I.L. & Mann, L. (1977) *Decision Making: A Psychological Analysis of Conflict, Choice and Commitment.* New York: The Free Press.

Jensen, M. & Meckling, W. (1976) Theory of the firm: managerial behavior, agency costs, and ownership structure. *The Journal of Financial Economics*, **3**, 305–360.

Katz, D. & Kahn, R.L. (1978) *The Social Psychology of Organizations* (2nd edn). New York: John Wiley & Sons, Ltd.

Kotter, J.P. (1995) Leading change: why transformation efforts fail. *Harvard Business Review*, **73**, 59–67.

Kotter, J. (1996) *Leading Change.* Boston: Harvard Business School Press.

Kotter, J.P. & Schlesinger, L.A. (1979) Choosing strategies for change. *Harvard Business Review*, **57**, 106–117.

Kreitner, B., Kinicki, A. & Buelens, M. (1999) *Organizational Behaviour.* London: McGraw-Hill.

Lawler, E.E. (1998) *Strategies for High-Performance Organizations.* San Francisco: Jossey-Bass.

Lawrence, P.R. & Lorsch, J.W. (1969) *Developing Organizations: Diagnosis and Action.* Reading, MA: Addison-Wesley.

Lax, D.A. & Sebenius, J.K. (1986) *The Manager as Negotiatior.* New York: The Free Press.

London, M. (1987) Technological innovations: case examples and guidelines. *Personnel*, **11**, 26–38.

McKendall, M. (1993) The tyranny of change: organizational development revisited. *Journal of Business Ethics*, **13**, 93–104.

McNabb, D.E. & Sepic, F.T. (1995) Culture, climate, and total quality management: measuring readiness for change. *Public Productivity and Management Review*, **18**(4), 369–386.

Meyer, M.W. & Zucker, L.G. (1989) *Permanently Failing Organisations.* London: Sage.

Mintzberg, H. (1979) *The Structuring of Organizations.* Englewood Cliffs, NJ: Prentice Hall.

Mintzberg, H. (1983) *Power in and around Organizations.* Englewood Cliffs, NJ: Prentice Hall.

Mintzberg, H., Ahlstrand, B. & Lampel, J. (1998) *Strategy Safari: A Guided Tour through the Wilds of Strategic Management.* New York: The Free Press.

Morgan, G. (1986) *Images of Organization.* Newbury Park, CA: Sage.

Neale, M.A. & Bazerman, M.H. (1992) Negotiating rationally: the power and impact of the negotiator's frame. *Academy of Management Executive*, **6**(3), 42–51.

Nutt, P.C. (1986) Tactics of implementation. *Academy of Management Journal*, **29**(2), 230–261.

Olmosk, K.E. (1972) Seven pure strategies of change. In *The 1972 Annual Handbook for Group Facilitators* (pp. 163–172). La Jolla, CA: University Associates.

Oppenheimer, J.R. (1944) Letter from J. Robert Oppenheimer to General Leslie R. Groves. Available: www.nuclearfiles.org/docs/1944/441006-opp-goves.html

Pande, P.S., Neuman, R.P. & Cavanagh, R.R. (2000) *The Six Sigma Way.* New York: McGraw-Hill.

Pettigrew, A.M. (2000) Linking change processes to outcomes: a commentary on Ghoshal, Bartlett, and Weick. In M. Beer & N. Nohria (eds) *Breaking the Code of Change* (pp. 243–265). Boston: Harvard Business School Press.

Pfeffer, J. (1981) *Power in Organizations.* Cambridge, MA: Ballinger Publishing Company.

Pfeffer, J. (1992) *Managing with Power.* Boston: Harvard Business School Press.

Pruitt, D.G. & Carnevale, P.J. (1993) *Negotiation in Social Conflict.* Pacific Grove, CA: Brooks/Cole.

Putnam, L.L. & Roloff, M.E. (1992) Communication perspectives on negotiation. In L.L. Putnam & M.E. Roloff (eds) *Communication and Negotiation: Sage Annual Review of Communication Research* (vol. 20, pp. 1–17). London: Sage.

Quinn, R.E. (1988) *Beyond Rational Management.* San Francisco: Jossey-Bass.

Schein, E.H. (1988) *Process Consultation: Its Role in Organization Development*. Reading, MA: Addison-Wesley.

Senge, P. (1990) *The Fifth Discipline: The Art and Practice of the Learning Organization*. Garden City, NY: Doubleday.

Sergeev, V.M. (1991) Metaphors for understanding international negotiation. In V.A. Kremenyuk (ed.) *International Negotiation: Analysis, Approaches, Issues* (pp. 58–64). San Francisco: Jossey-Bass.

Simon, H.A. (1976) *Administrative Behavior* (3rd edn). New York: Macmillan.

Spector, B. & Beer, M. (1994) Beyond total quality management programmes. *Journal of Organizational Change Management*, **7**(2), 63–70.

Spreitzer, G.M. & Mishra, A.K. (1999) Giving up control without losing control. *Group and Organization Management*, **24**(2), 155–187.

Van Gramberg, B. & Teicher, J. (2000) Managerialism in local government. *International Journal of Public Sector Management*, **13**(5), 476–492.

Warwick, D.P. (1975) *A Theory of Public Bureaucracy*. Cambridge, MA: Harvard University Press.

Zack, M.H. (1999) Managing organizational ignorance. *Knowledge Directions*, **1**, 36–49.

# Designing and Organizing Organizational Change

Part II of this handbook discusses the art of designing and organizing processes of change. In this Part, an overview is given of parameters for the psychological management of change processes. Implications are discussed for initiating a change process and handling uncertainty. Also, the roles of people in changing organizations are analysed. Monitoring and feedback systems are described as part of the management of change. This Part closes with a critical reflection questioning the management of change and the assumptions that underlie problem-solving and driving forces of change.

Chapter 5 focuses on the architecture of change processes. In this chapter, Colin Carnall emphasizes the importance of reading the environment correctly, and stresses the importance of defining a suitable business model based on environmental demands, the customer value stream, and stakeholder value. He pays attention to the failures of change, raises questions about the human-centred model of Organization Development, and doubts 'one best way' of changing. Many change programmes fail because there is no integrated approach between divisions and departments. Successful change may best be achieved by focusing change efforts along the customer value chain, rather than vertically up or down the structure. According to this perspective, participation and involvement are important in change processes, but the concern for participation is a partial approach. A new theme in managing change is re-thinking organizing in terms of value-added activities focused on customers. Another neglected theme is the vital role of partnerships between groups within and outside the organization. Major changes involve implementing new organizational arrangements to deal with new conditions. This fundamental change requires and leads to learning, which is a vital component of effective change. To initiate learning, organizational restructuring and strategic change should be based on effective diagnosis and benchmarking, information and incentive systems. Change architecture is seen as that set of arrangements, systems, resources, and processes through which people are engaged in productive reasoning, aimed at creating a new future. According to Carnall, successful planned change requires an awareness of the need for change, the engagement and alignment of key stakeholders, the use of performance measures, acquisition of new skills and capabilities, mobilization commitment and resources, and using change as a learning process.

Chapter 6 deals with the following questions: what leads to the necessity of change?; in what directions do changes normally go?; why is organizational change so difficult?; and are we powerful enough to make critical changes? In this chapter, Klaus Doppler considers these questions as the core of planned change. Sensitivity to these questions makes it possible to understand the status of a change process, assess opportunities for change, and reconsider the limits of change strategies and intervention methods. The necessity of change comes from new environmental developments and market demands. Normally, planned change programmes focus on cost reduction and concentrate on strategic core competencies. The demands of the customers are key, and employees are seen as important resources. A great deal of effort is put into optimizing business processes, mergers, and dividing companies

*Dynamics of Organizational Change and Learning.* Edited by J.J. Boonstra.
© 2004 John Wiley & Sons, Ltd. ISBN 0-471-87737-9.

into relatively independent operating divisions under a general, binding strategic roof. Many of these planned change programmes fail. Explanations may be found in patterns of thinking and acting by those involved in the change process. In Doppler's view, in order to manage change successfully, it is necessary to update mental models of organizing and changing. We have to redefine concepts of leadership, organization, personnel, and planning. Other success factors include preparing the ground for change carefully, and creating awareness of the problems to be dealt with. Involvement of all those who are affected contributes to commitment for change. Clear ownership and credibility of the project and the change agents help to manage the change process effectively. According to Doppler, the use of power, conflict, and resistance to change are normal phenomena in processes of change and learning. Methods are described to deal with conflict and resistance. This chapter concludes with the use of active communication and group dynamics to finalize change projects.

In Chapter 7, Elise Walton and Michael Russell offer an extensive overview of change strategies and intervention methods for organizational change and development. Core tenets of organizational change are the involvement of those affected by change, the motivational value of meaningful work, the importance of surfacing and sharing information, the use of models to diagnose organizational functioning, and the deliberate choice of change strategies and intervention methods. The intervention methods are placed in an historical context, and examined, with the emphasis on distinguishing those interventions that have become standards in practice, and those that have not. At the organizational level, interventions are presented with a focus on the structuring of organizations, corporate governance, and clarification of roles and responsibilities. Special attention is given to cultural and large-scale systems interventions, and also to learning and information-sharing in organizational change. At the individual level and the level of human resources, interventions are described for career paths, selection, feedback and rewards, and coaching. The role of the consultant is discussed. In early writings, consultants figured prominently as the director of activity, the facilitator of feedback, and as providing counselling and direction to team members. In recent years, consultants have become more a coach, counsellor, adviser, and a specialist resource. Walton and Russell signal ongoing tensions in the field of organizational change. First, there are numerous models of change, each with their strengths and weaknesses, applicability, and irrelevance. This makes the art of choosing models and strategies more difficult than ever. Second, there is continuous tension between value sets for change, putting business needs first, and sets that serve the well-being and participation of employees. Third, even after many years of work and research, change effectiveness is still not very high. Fourth, arguments over the pace and scope of change still prevail. To handle these tensions and to develop a body of knowledge and practice for organizational change, Walton and Russell propose building a stronger sense of core beliefs and values around the intentions of change, as well as the true scope and time frame for major organizational change.

The final chapter in this Part is really reflective and critical of many concepts of organizational change. In Chapter 8, Luc Hoebeke doubts some core beliefs and basic assumptions of organizing, changing, and decision-making. He suggests a shift in perspective from the classical economic view of scarcity to an approach of choosing from abundance. This chapter provides a language in which ambiguity in an environment of abundance is articulated. The central notion is the concept of dilemma. The major legitimation for organizational change is to solve organizational problems. Hoebeke states that organizational change is not about solving problems, but is about understanding and dealing with dilemmas. A dilemma consists of two contradictory statements, each of which is defendable. Dilemmas cannot be solved. Several dilemmas are discussed: innovation vs improvement, short term vs long term, policy-making vs operations. Choosing a position between the two statements of a dilemma is an uncomfortable and difficult job, but is seen as the essential task in changing and learning. The concept of dilemmas gives a specific perspective on organized work: organizations are expressions of culture which permit us to cope with our own complexity. In coping with complexity, we are confronted with paradoxes we have to deal with. One of these central paradoxes is the tension between collaboration and competition: the dynamics of organizational change are to be found primarily in the destruction of existing relations and the creation of new ones. A second paradox is the tension between centrifugal and centripetal forces: social systems keep a certain coherence, nevertheless, forces from the environment continuously impinge upon them. Several dilemmas rising from these paradoxes are discussed in depth: money and power, science and politics, faith and ethics. The understanding of these paradoxes and dilemmas opens up new perspectives and possibilities for organizational change and learning.

# CHAPTER 5

# Change Architecture
## Designing and Organizing the Process of Change

**Colin Carnall**
*Warwick Business School, Warwick, UK*

Why do some change programmes succeed and some fail? Why can some companies achieve change quickly and some not at all? Why do more and more companies see leadership and culture as defining issues in success or failure? Why are we most concerned to establish the process of change properly? Why do changing organizations concern themselves about values and benchmarking? Is not the central issue for successful change that of 'reading' the environment right and putting in place a competitive business model? Is there not a case for saying that in many strategic changes the most important thing is to define the right business model and replicate it accurately? Are we really convinced with the 'no one best way' argument? This has it that any of a range of business models can be appropriate and therefore you should concern yourself mostly with the human-centred model.

Throughout my working career in the Business School world I have often found this dilemma. Managers are often seen as unable or unwilling to take the human-centred view seriously. Could it be that, in reality, some of this is about people arguing for the adoption of the human-centred view and not considering the 'task-centred' view seriously enough? Might there not in fact be 'one best way'—or at least only a few variants of 'one best way'? If so, getting managers to focus only on the so-called human issues is unlikely to be meaningful.

The socio-technical systems school was an early attempt to resolve this issue. It held that joint optimization was the relevant goal but then it principally focused upon work group organization as a prime work organization design innovation. Any examination of outcomes from change projects based upon this concept demonstrates that the increased flexibility arising is often a source of significantly enhanced performance. Employee satisfaction often also improves. And this leads to a further dilemma. Why do academic observers and consultants so often perceive attempts at change to be failures? Boonstra makes this very point in the Introduction to this book. In the USA by far the majority of the attempts to redesign business processes fail. The development of new strategies 'runs aground' in 75 per cent of cases. Research in the Netherlands indicates that 70 per cent or more of change programmes lead to 'insufficient results'.

And yet this perception flies in the face of the evidence surely. Industries and sectors have been transformed in recent years. We re-engineer hospitals, government itself, and the great companies of the world. Ford is very different in the year 2000 as compared with, say, the year 1960. Is anyone seriously arguing that the privatized British Telecommunications Plc of today's world has not gone through dramatic change since privatization? Or British Airways?

Pfeffer (1998) argues the case that you can 'build profits by putting people first', as does Gratton (2000). In each case these authors cite evidence which appears to show that strategic change is regularly achieved. The literature on Lean Manufacturing does much the same. However, from my own

*Dynamics of Organizational Change and Learning.* Edited by J.J. Boonstra.
© 2004 John Wiley & Sons, Ltd. ISBN 0-471-87737-9.

experience working with organizations engaged in making major change, it is clear that many executives see the process of change as problematic. It is difficult to engage stakeholders. The human-centred approach is of value but is not often used. Very little attempt is made to learn from experience, and so on.

Thus, my initial conclusion is not that major changes fail but rather that there is much to learn from success and failure in change to help us codify our knowledge and skills in this key area. Thus, to argue that changes mostly fail seems to me unacceptable from an historical perspective. In the long run, something appears to be changing! One of the reasons why a short-term view can lead us to conclude that changes often fail is that we are now experiencing significant rates of change. Rarely does the organizational context remain stable enough for us to genuinely evaluate success or failure.

As I write this chapter, I have just completed the review of an internal report from a senior executive of a global company with which I have been working. His company is concerned that they are not achieving the rate of change required of world-class companies in that sector. I was struck by part of his diagnosis which reads as follows:

> Current change methodologies are employed within functional silos and the informal way in which strategy is cascaded through various differentiated groups and departments dilutes the value of the strategy . . . [which] should be focused on understanding how the business processes deliver overall enterprise value . . . [the company] needs to develop a process for implementing strategic improvement ideas in those value streams.

This quote captures two or three 'big' ideas about change. First, that many change programmes 'fail' because they are implemented within a part of the organization—there is an absence of an integrated approach as between divisions, departments, and the like. Second, that successful change may best be achieved by focusing change efforts horizontally, i.e. along the customer value stream rather than vertically up or down the structure. This idea does not vitiate all notions of bottom-up, top-down, and cascading change programmes which you will have read about, and experienced and/or managed, but it does provide a different perspective when thinking about change.

Another 'big' idea is that of organizational learning, whether in the context of strategy, management development, organizational development, or major change. Many practitioners and consultants/researchers point to the vital role of organizational learning in a period of change. In so far as major change involves implementing new organizational arrangements to deal with new conditions (whether in external markets or internally within the organization), it is obvious that change requires and leads to learning. It requires learning if the need for change is to be accepted. It involves learning particularly because our initial attempts to resolve the change problem need to evolve with experience.

However, the circumstances within which we seek to engender change are now fundamentally different. We are each of us aware of the fundamental changes now taking place—globalization, deregulation of markets, new technology, privatization, fundamental rethinking about the nature and role of the state, and so on. Moreover, we are each of us dealing with the organizational consequences including downsizing, flattening of structures, empowerment, outsourcing, strategic focus, the 'lean' organization, acquisitions and mergers, joint ventures and strategic alliances, multi-functional teamworking, and much much more. Many now conclude that the 'mind-set' through which senior managers view the world has changed in consequence.

## CHANGING ORGANIZATIONS

Therefore, the characteristic model of the successful organization has changed. Once we sought economies of scale via horizontal and vertical integration. Eventually we discovered that these economies of scale were often illusory. Some of the 'costs' of scale were increasingly alienated and de-motivated employees but, in particular, inflexible and inwardly focused organizations. Observers concerned with these problems noted two linked points:

1. What appeared to be a growing alienation of many within modern society coalesced around attitudes to bureaucracy—whether public or private. Organizations, which could give genuine priority to delivering value to customers, would begin to break down the alienation many felt about these large bureaucracies.
2. Whatever else we could say about large, multi-level bureaucracies, it is obvious that they are expensive but much less obvious that they deliver value for money.

And so many began to seek means of encouraging flexibility and entrepreneurship. This led to a fundamental shift in our thinking about how to change organizations.

Traditionally, we have sought to change the organization within its existing boundaries. We have not sought to ask whether or not the boundaries themselves should be changed, with one exception. A change strategy adopted throughout this century is that of acquisitions and mergers. It is not our purpose here to discuss this topic. Here we merely point out that such a change strategy involves re-thinking the boundary of the organizations as pieces (companies, divisions, etc.) are added or subtracted.

This tendency to re-think the boundary of the organization has accelerated as part of the changing mind-set we refer to above and, indeed, may have caused that change in the first place. One formulation of the underlying problems has been presented by Chesbrough and Teece (1996). For them the large, integrated, and centralized organization was excellent at coordination and control and may have been good at settling conflict (these authors suggest this is so—I doubt it, albeit they may have been good at reducing the level of conflict). Conversely, in order to seek higher levels of innovation, organizations first decentralized via the multi-divisional form but faced by the continued problems, and also the inability to develop every new technology/capability internally, increasingly via joint ventures, alliances, and ultimately 'the virtual company'.

Here, however, they note something which is becoming a standard of management practice when the focus is upon the supply chain. First, a company needs to build strong ties with its suppliers in order to secure its ability to pursue innovation, improvement, and enhanced value. Second, a company needs to develop critical technologies internally if it is to secure its position on the value chain. Here we see the argument that strategic networks can be very effective as a means of acquiring particular capabilities and of creating high-powered incentives towards improvement, change, and enhanced value. Our concern here is not to evaluate the argument, but merely to emphasize the new style of thinking involved in even raising the question.

Most importantly for our present purpose we have seen a tendency to replace planned, organiza-tional change with market-induced change. Sometimes the market mechanisms are internal—and there is a long history of the development of such mechanisms—i.e. performance-related pay schemes, the emergence of strategic business units, the development of competence-based models for performance management, share option schemes, and much more. Increasingly we see the tendency to use mar-ket mechanisms to secure change. Strategic alliances, networks, outsourcing, de-regulation are all attempts to introduce or encourage market-based incentives. The idea of purchasing being separated from provision has influenced companies and governments. In the UK and elsewhere in the world, government departments have been converted to free-standing agencies. The UK Health Service has been re-organized into large-scale purchasing authorities and self-governing trusts providing hospital and other services alongside general practitioners providing primary care. Similarly, a global business, such as GlaxoWellcome, has re-configured itself from having regional sales operatives supplied by regional factories to a situation in which the sales business is free to source from the best available sup-plier. Here the certainties of allocated budgets are replaced by the pressures, disciplines, and incentives of competition.

## ECONOMIC SUCCESS AND SOCIAL CAPITAL

But is this sufficient? At the same time we all of us point to our present anxieties and uncertainties. Some argue that this is a consequence of downsizing and a consequential higher risk of unemployment. Others point to the growth in part-time employment. Critics of this kind of thinking point out that unemployment has not changed in the world's leading economies in the past 20 years, albeit the level fluctuates, inevitably. You can counter this by arguing the view that the big change is that for the first time it is middle-class employees experiencing job insecurity. They are more vocal and we are experiencing the consequences. Perhaps also the shift in organizational mind-set referred to above is relevant. Where the focus of activity is the horizontal value chain, it may be that people who once understood to whom they report must now report to more than one individual and meet multiple and sometimes even conflicting (certainly ambiguous) performance objectives.

One formulation of how to achieve economic success in the midst of these ambiguities relates to the concept of 'trust' or social capital. The most influential recent work is that of Fukuyama (1995). For him, one solution to the problem of scale lies in the emergence of networks. Networks of businesses held together by family ties, cross-ownership, long experience of joint work, etc. In particular, he points to the advantages of establishing long-term relationships between members of a network. All of this is now known to us as supply chain management. He argues that networks based upon reciprocal obligation enable scale to be achieved without the problems of size and alienation referred to above. These networks appear to have emerged in societies wherein the culture encourages high levels of trust (e.g. Japan, South Korea, Germany, Northern Italy). In 'low-trust' societies stable networks can be created via cross-ownership but will certainly be more difficult to sustain.

Increasingly, major corporations are beginning to work on the briefing of 'social capital' via value-added strategies. Here the organization is defined as a horizontal value stream supported by other activities, e.g. Marketing Development, Senior Management, Finance, etc. Each part of the organization has performance parameters defined in terms of value to its customers. Organizations use competence models and assessment, 360° feedback techniques, and the balanced scorecard as a means of putting this into effect. The objective is to identify what each activity contributes by way of value to its customers, measure that, and feed that information openly to the people involved in the activity, their customers, and senior management. Part of the role of management is to help each activity drive its performance forward in terms of these parameters. A longer-term task of senior management is to identify and access the capabilities needed for the future. There are few organizations which have developed a coherent system of the type outlined here but there are many examples (in telecommunications, financial services, health care, manufacturing, utilities) of organizations working on such approaches.

## CHANGE ARCHITECTURE

Only recently have observers begun to examine how change programmes are constructed. This may be called change architecture. And yet the principal concern of the work published so far is that of participation and involvement. This is an important but only partial approach. Nevertheless some interesting work has been published.

Thus, Emery and Purser (1996) discuss the role of 'search conferences' and Bunker and Alban (1997) look at processes for engaging the 'whole system' for rapid change. Jacobs (1994) identifies three sequential processes required to achieve strategic change, as follows:

- Building a common database.
- Discovering the future in diverse perspectives.
- Creating commitment to action plans.

The first is particularly interesting. What does it mean? Is it what many often refer to as the process of building acceptance of the need for change? No it is not. Rather, it is a process of building credible and valid measures of performance focused upon understanding how well we are doing, how we compare to competitors (benchmarking), and what else is changing in the environment. Thus, the key element of the first process is about measurement. Here balanced scorecards (Kaplan & Norton, 1996), benchmarking (Watson, 1993), and ideas such as 360° appraisal all play a part. Not least the concern is about measurement, accountability, transparency, and access to outcome measures. Value added is the key metaphor for this process. Increasingly we see a need to balance between focus on issues such as cost and scale, on the one hand, with those of product/service development, customer service enhancement, and growth.

The second and third issues require dialogue, reflection, and sharing, and therefore processes are needed to engage key stakeholders. Bruch and Sattelberger (2001), reporting on work at Lufthansa, show how processes such as strategy forums, open-space events, and learning maps utilizing data from the above but assessed and discussed from various perspectives (of internal and external stakeholders) can be used to build new 'mental models' for the business. Learning is a key issue here and this requires 'valid knowledge' and processes for reflection and dialogue. Interestingly enough, evidence is emerging about the need to combine dialogue with a focus upon action and follow-through. Thus, Norlton (1998) noted that workshop evaluations very early on show how those involved seek closure, direction and future plans, and targets—thus providing a process in which people both engage in dialogue and in creating new plans, a genuinely problem-oriented process, is vital. Much the same emerged in Greenly and Carnall (2001).

## New 'Rules for the Organizational Game'

To explore this theme further let us turn to two case examples:

---

### Case Study: Ford and the Global Car

Under the label Ford 2000, the company sought to transform itself into a global corporation deploying a new 'philosophy' of doing business. By 1993, despite being profitable, the world's second largest automotive producer had engaged on a major programme of development. Ford also recognized itself as part of a complex and intensively competitive sector, not least with issues of over-supply in various markets. The existing business philosophy emphasized producing cars in the regions where they were to be sold. Yet Ford was engaged in separate development processes in different regions of the world for what were essentially similar products. Moreover, while Ford was well positioned in the USA and Europe, it was less well placed in those areas where growth in demand was likely.

Moreover, customers are now more sophisticated, more demanding, and more aware of what is available around the world. The market is increasingly global. The company had merged its semi-autonomous regional operations into a single world-wide business. Product development was to focus globally.

Change of this type had been attempted earlier in Ford's history. The Escort development had been shared by teams in Europe and North America but differentiation resulted. Amalgamations within Europe were achieved in the late 1960s. The Escort experience led Ford to realize that a world car development needed single leadership to achieve the needed integration. Easy to say, but not easy to achieve. The Mondeo development was a further stage in the process. Led from Europe, this work was facilitated by a communications infrastructure allowing the sharing and analysis of data

---

and decision-making across borders. The communications infrastructure supported a world-wide engineering release system, a world-wide purchasing system, and a global conferencing facility. Were these infrastructure developments not as important as the concept of single leadership in enabling the company to overcome the problems of national pride and narrow perception that had limited past attempts?

In turn, the Mondeo development led Ford to learn vital lessons, in particular 'simultaneous engineering'. Achieved via 'vertically integrated teams', it contrasts with the former sequential process with its attendant possibilities for conflict between those who design and those who manufacture the product. In early 1994 a 'study team' of 27 managers from a variety of functions and countries began a 10-week programme, looking at how to learn the lessons of the past and achieve genuine globalization. It was decided to merge the existing teams in Europe and North America. Ford established five vehicle centres to take lifetime responsibility for the development of all vehicles of a given class produced and sold anywhere in the world. In addition, Ford created a single global unit for technology development. All employees with Automotive Operations have been deployed within this world-wide 'matrix'. The vehicle centre is responsible for developing and launching new vehicles and has lifetime responsibility for quality, serviceability, profitability, and overall programme management. Formerly the development team's work ended at launch.

The focus therefore now is upon *horizontal integration*. Not least of the advantages is that decisions can be made closer to the action. With the introduction of an integrated global cycle plan for product launch, major product changes are planned to be achieved in half the time. The matrix combines vertical integration with horizontal integration and raises fundamental questions about the role of senior management in devising strategy, ensuring that the needed capabilities are in place.

We point to two themes in this case study that are relevant to this book, as follows:

- Ford has begun the process of re-thinking itself as a business. Specifically, it seeks to emphasize the horizontal process of creating value for customers, not least because doing so provides opportunities to exploit economies across the horizontal value stream.
- Whether or not you deem Ford to be a 'learning organization', it is clear that Ford has learnt a number of lessons, each of which allowed it to create a new part of the 'platform' from which it now seeks to globalize.

As we shall see throughout this book, these two themes reoccur frequently when looking at leading edge practice in strategic change.

## CASE STUDY: CHANGING CHILDBIRTH

In 1993 the UK Department of Health published a report entitled *Changing Childbirth*. By the early 1980s evidence of dissatisfaction as a result of fragmented care and obstetrician-led services was apparent. Continuity of care was emerging alongside the perception that women desired choice of care and place of delivery and the right of control over their own bodies at all stages of pregnancy and birth.

While the research, evidence, and analysis underpinning and providing the context for *Changing Childbirth* is complex and not short of controversy, for our purposes the focus of the report for maternity practice is best summarized by quoting *Changing Childbirth*'s indicators of success (within five years, i.e. by 1998):

- Every woman should know one midwife who ensures continuity of her midwifery care—the named midwife.
- At least 30 per cent of women should have the midwife as their lead professional.
- At least 75 per cent of women should know the person who cares for them during their delivery.
- At least 30 per cent of women delivered in a maternity unit should be admitted under the management of the midwife.

Often measures designed to achieve these success indicators were being devised in the context of another development, Integrated Patient Care (IPC).

IPC is an example of a general re-thinking of patient care brought over from the USA in the early 1990s. It focuses upon aspects of care such as continuity of care, improved documentation, physical redesign of buildings, locating facilities close to patients, staff role reviews, etc. Sometimes known as Patient Focused Care (PFC), this philosophy places the patient at the centre, seeks active involvement of the patient, continuity of care, decentralization, multi-skilling of care staff, and streamlined documentation. Finally, a further concept is the *pathway of care* which in essence is the time sequence of events, tests, assessments, experiences, and outcomes associated with the patient's care process. If the objective is to seek high-quality 'seamless' care for individual patients across the boundaries of department, directorate, and discipline into which hospitals have been fashioned by history, then *horizontal focus* is a key issue.

At Brighton Health Care NHS Trust (a major UK hospital) these concepts have been implemented along with team midwifery within the community (Hart, 1997). Three teams of six full-time equivalent midwives based in different geographical locations aimed to provide 24-hour care for 250–350 women. The service encompassed all aspects of midwifery care including home assessment of labour and care continuity. An early evaluation concluded that team midwifery enabled Brighton to provide a more patient-centred care at the same high standard of care (avoiding a perceived risk of the team approach) with no evidence of decreased satisfaction for the women involved (there has been a very high reported satisfaction) or for midwives (again, a concern which did not appear to materialize).

The early research (see Hart, 1997) indicates significant progress towards *Changing Childbirth* success indicators. While some evidence of tension emerged between team midwives and their labour-ward colleagues, it was also clear that there were many perceived advantages. Moreover, many of the negative points emerging appeared linked to other factors, i.e. workloads in general, problems of working conditions, problems over grading within the reward arrangements. Clearly, continuity of care was seen as linked positively to job satisfaction. The general practitioners interviewed were clearly satisfied both with the service overall and with team midwifery, but this was not without perceived problems, some related to the adequacy of resourcing and GP involvement (which may lessen given continuity of team-based care?).

Interestingly enough, recommendations for further development place much emphasis upon developing relationships, partnerships, and care protocols (which define the parameters within which care professionals practise). The latter is clearly intended as a means of ensuring a clear definition of roles and thereby creating a platform for improved partnerships. Overall, the case study powerfully reinforces the horizontal focus of strategic change, applied not principally to reduce costs but rather to create improved care. That said, we do not suggest that cost effectiveness is not a key driver behind innovations of this kind, albeit given the apparently infinite demand for health care, this is probably more about securing higher volume of activity within existing budgets, i.e. about reducing cost per case. The other crucial point here is the essential role of *partnership*. Partnership between professional groups, both with the hospital and in the community, is essential and represents a complex challenge in the health-care environment for the latter part of this century.

Thus, from these two case studies we see evidence of new thinking in three areas as follows:

- re-thinking the organization in terms of a horizontal stream of value-added activities focused upon customers/clients;
- the learning organization and how to achieve that state;
- the vital role of partnerships.

Thus, it is clear that the world of major change is no longer simply a world concerned with 'resistance to change'. Indeed, I have often wondered why 'resistance to change' loomed so large in discussions about change. Many argue that people are motivated by challenging jobs, discretion, autonomy, etc. These same people also pointed to the prevalence of 'resistance to change' without posing the obvious question. Change seems likely to create the very conditions which people are supposed to find motivating. Therefore, why are we so concerned about 'resistance to change'?

It is obvious that all of this has placed greater demands on the capabilities of managers. But these changes have also transformed the nature of what some call the 'psychological contract between the employing organization and the employee'. If 'jobs for life' cannot be guaranteed, then people have to apply for their 'own' jobs on re-organization, where flattened structures mean empowerment for some but redundancy for others, and one would expect that to happen. Where organizations use early retirement or voluntary retirement as an essential part of policy and where some organizations emphasize the benefits to the organization and the employee of subcontracting, maintaining a stable core of permanent employees and a periphery of subcontractors, they are reflecting a significant change.

All of this suggests that the statement so often heard, 'the most important resource of this business is its people', is increasingly meaningful not merely as rhetoric but also in practice. If we depend more and more on fewer people and if the loyalty of those people, particularly managers, can no longer be assumed, but rather must be earned and retained, then clearly we need to be concerned about how we utilize them, develop them, and resource them and about the opportunities for rewards, promotion, and success which we provide. If changes depend upon the people who implement them, then one must be concerned to ensure that those people possess the necessary skills. If those same people are motivated by challenge and opportunity, then we must provide that as well. But if the latter will only follow if changes are successful, then the introduction of changes which our people view as being credible, as likely to succeed, becomes a paramount issue.

## LEADERSHIP IN PERIOD OF CHANGE

Why is it that people are often managed inappropriately in a period of change? There are two main reasons. Managers managing change are under pressure. This pressure undermines their own performance. Also, organizations often do not possess managers who are sufficiently skilful in handling change. Kotter (1988), for example, suggests one 'syndrome' associated with inadequate leadership, which we might similarly associate with inadequate change management. In summary, the argument is that successful organizations can carry the seeds of their own later decline, unless managers learn to be both successful and adaptable. The syndrome of ineffective leadership and change management is set out in three stages:

1. The firm is in a strong position, with little competition. It develops systems, management practices, and a culture which depend on a few capable leaders. The management style is a combination of autocratic, directive, and paternalistic.
2. The firm grows and becomes more complex. Competition increases and new technology emerges. The firm now needs strong and capable leadership but does not have enough people with these skills. Many people with good leadership potential left because of the frustrations created in stage 1. However, the firm's performance does not deteriorate dramatically. It remains well placed in its established markets. It 'lives' off its reputation.

3. Declining performance leads to a focus on short-term results. Internal tensions lead to conflict which cannot be handled constructively. Senior managers seem incapable of facing these tensions. Functional rather than corporate policies prevail. The firm lacks a coordinated strategy. This, in turn, undermines efforts to improve the quality of management.

The tensions created by declining performance create performance problems. Thus, the argument combines the success of a few key people, a period of early success, and growing organizational complexity followed by declining performance, creating pressures towards short-termism and an inward focus. All of this can lead to a lack of credibility among top management combined with a 'fear of failure' throughout the organization.

Particularly interesting is the point about 'fear of failure'; the pressures are dual in nature. On the one hand, the short-term approach, combined with a functional or departmental orientation, centralization, and autocratic management styles, creates a powerful tendency to limit risk-taking. On the other, managers moving rapidly through careers and not having to face up to their mistakes do not learn the interpersonal skills needed to do so. They find facing up to performance issues difficult. Therefore, when forced to do so by those same short-term pressures, they often do so inadequately and in a volatile, even primitive, fashion. This further reduces risk-taking, over time creating an organization within which the 'fear of failure' is very high indeed. There is a powerful 'vicious circle' in place continually reinforcing any tendency to under-perform.

Kotter (1988) identifies a number of the 'characteristics needed, to provide effective leadership', overcoming the problems identified in the syndrome outlined above. To be effective, leaders need a knowledge of industry, business functions, and the firm. Also needed are a broad range of contacts and good working relationships in the firm and the industry. Linked to this will be a good track record in a relatively broad set of activities. Kotter also refers to 'keen minds' (whatever that means), strong interpersonal skills, high integrity, seeing value in people, and a strong desire to lead.

All of this points us towards the new strategy paradigm proposed by Hamel and Prahalad (1994). For them, competing for the future means lifting our sights. Re-engineering internal processes is not enough, we must regenerate strategies. Transforming the organization is essential but the winners (such as CNN) transform their industry. Having strategic plans focuses attention internally, what is needed is a new strategic architecture. The essential point is that it may be necessary to re-engineer our processes to reduce costs and improve services but that is insufficient to gain competitive advantage because our competitors can do the same. To be successful we must create new strategies aimed at transforming our industry—whether it is food, medicine, education, entertainment, or whatever. In the modern world, renewal demands that we do more than identify how to do more, better and for less. We must also regenerate what we do.

Kay (1993) attempts to identify the origins of corporate success from distinctive structures of relationships between the corporation and employees, customers, and suppliers. Continuity and stability in these relationships allow for a flexible and cooperative response to change. At the core of his analysis lies the concept of added value. This, he argues, derives from the architecture of the firm (basically the structure of relationships referred to above), and the application of distinctive capabilities in particular markets. Continuity and stability provide for the development of organizational knowledge, i.e. of its identity, vision, distinctive capabilities, and invisible assets (Itami, 1987), the free exchange of information, and a readiness to respond quickly and flexibly to changes in the world.

In turn, the distinctive capabilities which provide the basis of competitive advantage are architecture, innovation, reputation, and strategic assets. Architecture is both internal (the corporate structure and management processes) and external (networks of relationships with suppliers and other organizations—joint ventures, strategic variances, etc). Strategic assets are the inherent advantages a corporation may possess (e.g. licences, access to scarce factors) which cannot easily be copied.

'Strategic benchmarking' has taken up a vital role in organizational diagnosis for change. This adds an important idea to the concept of diagnosis. The vital point is to compare your own organization to the world's best. Thus, we identify where we are, the reasons for our present situation, and (through benchmarking) we identify the potential for improvement and ideas for change. Benchmarking as a technique has evolved (at least in principle and concept) from first-generation benchmarking in which the focus was on benchmarking a particular product or system, through competitive benchmarking, process benchmarking, strategic benchmarking to 'global benchmarking'. Most importantly, benchmarking represents a learning technique. Essentially cognitive in orientation, it applies rational analysis based on comparisons to the process of diagnosis.

Similarly business process re-engineering has attracted wide attention and many adherents (and cynics). Admittedly more than a technique for diagnosing what needs to be changed, it nevertheless incorporates techniques for diagnosis. Most importantly, proponents of this approach conceive it as a technology for break-through or 'discontinuous leaps in performance'. The focus is upon the 'business architecture'—locations, structure, technology, and skills. Alongside the analysis of the business architecture conceived in terms of value added is risk assessment, looking at change and organizational issues. Our contention is that in techniques such as benchmarking and business process re-engineering we see a combination of the soft, organizational development approaches of the 1970s and the socio-technical systems school, but now operationalized because of the opportunities provided by new information infrastructures. Thus, diagnosis has become more thorough and broader in scope. In practice, it may be that the potential of these approaches has been under-utilized, however.

## TRANSFORMING THE ORGANIZATION

Managing major changes successfully requires us to take an organization-wide approach. Change creates stress and strain both for those who support change (through over-work, the challenge of leading change in an uncertain world, the pressure of dealing with other, often anxious people, the inherent uncertainties we all are subject to in some degree, and so on) and for those who are either indifferent, opposed to, or fearful of change.

Organizational learning is a vital component of effective change. Following the work of Quinn (see, in particular, Quinn, 1992), organizational restructuring and strategic change should be based upon effective diagnosis and benchmarking, information and incentive systems. A key point, however, in achieving strategic change amidst organizational circumstances looking less and less like traditional hierarchical structures is that 'managed incrementalism' is a strategy for change implementation explicitly designed to manage risk. However, this does not need to imply that change is slow, random, or gradual.

All of this assumes that change implementation requires the following:

- that we build an awareness of the need for change;
- that the case for changes is made convincingly and credibly;
- that the process of change is a learning process, you won't get everything right initially;
- that dramatic changes can feel chaotic and uncertain as people seek to come to terms with new skills, etc.;
- that attention must be given to broadening and mobilizing support for change, whether through task forces and project teams, through the use of incentive systems and training, through pilot schemes, and so on;
- that we should crystallize the vision and focus for the organization but not necessarily at the outset, indeed, initially the vision may be very broad; much has yet to be learned before an *emerging* strategic vision can be articulated;
- that we should focus on people and on the process of change.

Alexander (1988) provides a review of the implementation literature. He supports the Pressman and Wildavsky (1973) idea that 'Policies are continuously transformed by implementation actions that simultaneously alter resources and objectives.' Thus, strategy (or policy) and implementation interact and emerge. Alexander also notes that implementers are, or should be, concerned both with preventing failure (by avoiding the common implementation problems) and promoting success.

There are three learning modes which are of relevance to managers concerned by change, as follows:

- *Learning by doing*—this is an internal process. We learn by experimentation, by trial and error, by pilot trials.
- *Learning by use*—this is essentially learning from the external world. We learn how to improve our own product/services by gaining feedback from customers and by competitive benchmarking. Thus, we gain from customers' experience of using our products/services and through comparing ourselves with competitor organizations.
- *Learning from failure*—which speaks for itself but which, to be available to us, demands that we accept that failure will happen from time to time.

Our argument is that ideas such as transformational leadership, entrepreneurship, and the learning organization each embrace these ideas. Beyond this, we recognize that major changes are typically implemented as major programmes organized around simple themes (e.g. 'Right First Time' for total quality programmes or 'Next Steps Programme' for major programmes of culture change).

A good current example is that of 'time-based competition'. The key idea is that the way we manage time—whether in production, in new product development, in sales and distribution—represents a powerful source of competitive advantage. At the core of this idea is a strategy for change utilizing analytical techniques to explore the organization that is seeking continuous improvements to work and information flows and in the use of time. The emphasis is upon the organization doing the work itself, using its own people, empowering people at all levels to achieve change. Benchmarking is a key analytical technique used in such programmes as are techniques such as 'pilots' and 'breakthrough teams'. According to Stalk and Hout (1990), breakthrough teams should be given radical goals such as reducing time in half in order that assumptions will be challenged. Bottlenecks, breakdowns, failures, unmet customer needs, all become opportunities to learn. All of this implies radically new ways of thinking about the organization.

Finally, Argyris (1990) explains something of the constraints to achieving effective learning in organizations by pointing to the distinction between what he calls single-loop and double-loop learning. At the core of his explanation are two key points about professionals (and managers and a growing proportion of employees are professionals or quasi-professionals of one sort or another). First, the life experience of most professionals through schooling, university, and early career is characterized by success, not failure. Because they have rarely failed, they have never learned how to learn from failure. Thus, when things go wrong for them, they become defensive, screen out criticism, and put the 'blame' on others. Ironically, their ability to learn shuts down just when they need it most.

Second, Argyris takes the view that organizations assume that learning is a problem of motivation. This assumption creates the right structures of communication, rewards, and authority and account-ability designed to create motivated and committed employees—and learning and development will follow. Sadly, Argyris tells us, this is fatally flawed. People learn through how they think—through the cognitive rules or reasoning they use to design and implement their actions.

For Argyris, organizations can learn how to encourage learning, how to resolve these learning dilemmas. At the root of his solution is to find ways of constructively questioning the rationale or reasoning behind someone's actions. Argyris argues that people can be taught to reason in ways which reduce and overcome organizational defences:

> They will discover that the kind of reasoning necessary to reduce and overcome organisational defences is the same kind of 'tough reasoning' that underlies the effective use of ideas in strategy, finance, marketing, manufacturing and other management disciplines ... it depends

on collecting valid data, analysing it carefully, and constantly testing inferences drawn from the data ... Good strategists make sure that their conclusions can withstand all kinds of critical questioning.

## CHANGE ARCHITECTURE RECONSIDERED

So, ultimately, what we mean by change architecture is that set of arrangements, systems, resources, and processes through which we engage people in 'productive reasoning', focused upon creating a new future. The principles through which the various techniques (strategy forums, communication cascades, 'town meetings', 'open-space events', balanced scorecards, and much more) are designed together are as follows:

1. We seek to clarify *governance* and *accountability* for strategic change.
2. We seek to *engage* key stakeholders in appropriate ways.
3. We seek to secure *alignment* for all or at least a critical mass of key stakeholders in ways supportive of success, however defined.
4. We seek effective, credible, and accessible *performance measures* provided on a relatively *transparent* basis.
5. We need a balanced set of performance measures (i.e. covering finance, activity, quality, adaptability, markets, customer and employee satisfaction, etc.) presented on a *common platform*.
6. We seek to acquire or develop the *new skills* and *capabilities* and to mobilize *commitment* and *resources*.
7. We seek to leverage *knowledge* of relevance to the future out of the way we operate and capture the results of our use of the techniques we apply, i.e. we seek to use strategic change as a *learning process*.

## REFERENCES

Alexander, L. (1988) Successfully implementing strategic decisions. *Long Range Planning*, **181**(3), 91–97.
Argyris, C. (1990) *Overcoming Organizational Defences*. Needham Heights, MA: Allyn & Bacon.
Bruch, H.H. & Sattelberger, T. (2001) The turnaround at Lufthansa: learning from the change process, *Journal of Change Management*, **1**(1), 344–364.
Bunker, B.B. & Alban, B.T. (1997) *Large Group Interventions: Engaging the Whole System for Rapid Change*. San Francisco: Jossey-Bass.
Chesbrough, H.W. & Teece, D.J. (1996) When is virtual virtuous? Organising for innovation. *Harvard Business Review*, **January–February**, 65–74.
Department of Health (1993) *Changing Childbirth*. London: HMSO.
Emery, M. & Purser, R.E. (1996) *The Search Conference*. San Francisco: Jossey-Bass.
Fukuyama, F. (1995) *Trust: The Social Virtues and the Creation of Prosperity*. London: Hamish Hamilton.
Gratton, L. (2000) *Living Strategy*. London: Pearson Educational Ltd.
Greenly, D. & Carnall, C. (2001) Workshops as a technique in strategic change. *Journal of Change Management*, **2**(1), 33–46.
Hamel, G. & Pralahad, C.K. (1994) *Competing for the Future*. Boston: Harvard Business School Press.
Hart, A. (1997) *Team Midwifery*. Brighton: Brighton Health Care NHS Trust.
Itami, H. (1988) *Mobilizing Invisible Assets*. Boston: Harvard University Press.
Jacobs, R.W. (1994) *Real Time Strategic Change*. San Francisco: Berrett-Koehler.
Kaplan, R.S. & Norton, D.P. (1996) *The Balanced Scorecard*. Boston: Harvard Business School Press.
Kay, J. (1993) *The Foundations of Corporate Success*. Oxford: Oxford University Press.
Kotter, P. (1988) *The Leadership Factor*. New York: The Free Press.

Norlton, G. (1998) Creating the opportunity for positive change. Unpublished MBA dissertation, Henley Management College.

Pfeffer, J. (1998) *The Human Equation*. Boston: Harvard Business School Press.

Pressman, J.L. & Wildavsky, A. (1973) *Implementation*. San Francisco: University of California Press.

Quinn, J. (1992) *The Intelligent Enterprise*. New York: The Free Press.

Stalk, G. & Hout, J.M. (1990) *Competing Against Time*. New York: The Free Press.

Watson, G.H. (1993) *Strategic Bench-Marking*. New York: John Wiley & Sons, Ltd.

# CHAPTER 6

# Managing Change Successfully
## Core Questions, Issues, and Strategies

**Klaus Doppler**

*Independent Consultant, Munich, Germany*

Today, everybody swears by the necessity of change. However, when it comes to changing oneself, one prefers to let someone else go first. There must be a reason for this behaviour. Whatever we do, at the moment we do it, we find it reasonable from our own standpoint. As long as we do not understand the 'reasons' for people's actions, as long as we do not understand why things are as they are, we will not be in a position to develop strategies for change. I have been a management consultant in Europe for more than 20 years. I specialize in behavioural training for leadership and in how to manage change. Let me give you an insight into my wide store of accumulated experience, and when reading this you may compare my experience with your own which you have gained or suffered as drivers or those driven by change, in an active or in a passive role.

When we want to work on change and innovation in organizations, we must face these core questions:

1. What actually leads to the necessity of change? Do those who speak of change do so simply to make their name, or is it more than that?
2. In which direction do changes normally go? Where are the focuses, and what are the experiences? What has proved to be good and what has not?
3. If change is so urgently needed, why doesn't it come by itself? Are we helpless, do we not have suitable ideas, or are we just too lazy? What are we doing wrong? Or are there 'evil' forces, blocking changes?
4. In addition, this question: Are we truly powerful enough to make the critical changes? Isn't this claim the result of the (male) delusion—supported by the image of the manager's role—of being able to do everything one wants to do, to be able to achieve anything, even complete the 'mission impossible'?

Only on the basis of sensitivity to these questions will it be possible to understand the status of a change process, and to judge the opportunities and the limits of instruments and methods. One then can separate the wheat from the chaff, so as not to fall for the tricks of false prophets, and to distinguish between what is well meant or well intentioned and what is really professional!

## A QUESTION TO START WITH

If you ever get the opportunity to take a look at the strategy of some even average corporations and to listen to a few speeches of CEOs, you will read or hear all the keywords and buzzwords of modern management. Well, nobody knows the future, but the situation analysis in regard to the global trends

*Dynamics of Organizational Change and Learning.* Edited by J.J. Boonstra.
© 2004 John Wiley & Sons, Ltd. ISBN 0-471-87737-9.

in the industry, the assumptions made on the basis of the patterns of the recent past will all sound reasonable and very similar:

- Internet pressure for price transparency and equilibration;
- time-based competition;
- low-cost production and standardization;
- assumptions about the changing customer and consumer with increased volatility;
- new paths to market and the drivers of future change.

So one part of our initial question *why change at all?—why not proceed with business as usual?* is answered by corporations' strategy, based on the fundamental assumptions about the new environmental framework which is challenging every leader of a firm who wants to survive. The basic developments that lead to this framework can roughly be outlined by the following general factual conditions outside of our influence.

First, the developments in technology and in microelectronics, the information sciences, software technology, and telecommunications including the Internet, together with strongly decreasing prices, make it possible to channel information world-wide in practically real time, with no time delay. The results are a striking acceleration of all work processes, a radical redefining of business process and value chains, and a reduction of hierarchy. Modern information technology neutralizes one of the important functions of the middle management level, namely, to collect information, condense it, interpret it, and pass it from those above to those below in the company hierarchy, and vice versa. It therefore deprives the middle management of a very important part of its previous right to exist.

Second, the dramatic increase in mobility of people and work processes. With the global infrastructure of IT sciences, people can now control processes from any location in this world. Similarly, many work processes can be shifted to any location world-wide, typically to those locations where the job can be done at a reasonable price in the defined quality. In older times so-called bilocation was taken as a divine asset, i.e. that God is at every time at every place. Now mankind has nearly reached this state too.

Third, volatile markets which are packed continue moving. Nearly all 'necessary' products are abundant in the market. The products of almost every single corporation are not really needed. Pretty soon you could be replaced by competitors. In addition, customer groups' and customers' needs are heterogeneous, unstable, and inconsistent. The customer is disloyal in principle. He seeks his advantage wherever he can find it. The manager or organization wishing to succeed and expand in a global, crowded, and highly volatile market has to drive out competitors and be alert. There are no mourning services for those who do not survive.

Fourth, resources for entrepreneurial and social actions are limited. To invest in one area, one must conserve and save in another. So, the dominant motto of management becomes: accomplish more with less.

Fifth, everything intermingles with everything else. The consequences of this interdependency are often not noticed until much later. These consequences include a *continuously growing complexity* of the situation in which we exist and work and a *fundamental dilemma between complexity and time*. On the one hand, high complexity demands a relatively complex and thorough reaction. On the other, we are under extreme time pressure from the speed of change. Or, every change needs its time for exploring, experimenting, learning, gaining self-confidence, and for the necessary mental anchoring. But we only have a limited time. As a result, we have to learn to compensate for the missing time by creativity, innovation, and stringency. All this leads to or is summed up in the last condition.

Finally, change as a normal status. Certainly, in the past there were changes, too. But before and after such periods were long phases of stability and continuity. Today, normal life is and will be lived in constantly unstable, turbulent, and unpredictable ambiences. Change in all forms becomes more radical and increases in speed and frequency. And nothing indicates that this will alter in the near future.

The description of this landscape in which we operate, and that we cannot select or change, is certainly not complete. It is a rough sketch only. You will find quite distinctive depictions, explanations, and advice on how to deal with these developments, for example, in authors such as Paul Bate (1994), Charles Handy (1995), Francis J. Gouillart and James N. Kelly (1995), Chris Agyris and Donald A. Schön (1996), C.K. Prahalad (1998), B. Josef Pine II and James Gilmore (1999), Karsten Trebesch (2000), Karl E. Weick and Kathleen M. Sutcliffe (2001), Reinhart Nagel and Rudolf Wimmer (2002), and Peter F. Drucker (2002). The present description of the general situation and the recommendations in this chapter are mainly based on the book *Managing Corporate Change* (2000), which I wrote with my friend Christoph Lauterburg.

One thing will become clear, though: to survive the current conditions, one must draw on one's reserves! Mere modifications will not help. The models, the basic patterns of how we lead, how we plan, and how we organize, must themselves be radically questioned. The new business demand was well stated by Rudi Wimmer, an Austrian consultant: 'In these times of change only a specific kind of organization works wisely, an organization which is well prepared for surprises, and, which is able to surprise others.'

## CONTENTS OF CHANGE AND MAIN ISSUES OF LEARNING

Well, it is never true that nothing happens. On the contrary, many companies have taken the plunge, to meet the new demands and to introduce changes. So, let's turn to the topic of what the main areas of change are, what essential concepts are behind them, and how to judge the different ways and practices of change.

### ISOLATED COST-REDUCTION PROGRAMMES

Many companies concentrate solely on cost reduction, often by introducing drastic crisis-intervention measures. I do not mean here normal regular cost fitness programmes—aimed at about 10 to 20 per cent cost reduction—integrated in a holistic concept of renewal. But isolated programmes, even if they are radical, rarely bring a longer-lasting real benefit—there is more than enough proof of this. Those programmes simply indicate a lack of imagination. In the same way a person who only fasts, without changing his personal attitudes and habits towards eating, will prove the German proverb: 'He who fasts, gets fat.' Those radical crisis programmes are in many cases only 'scorched earth' policies. In the course of such ill-fated initiatives, very often a participative management, carefully built up over the years, will quickly be eradicated. Those who think the former management culture will be revitalized at the push of a button after such a crisis-intervention programme are usually mistaken. Very often the damage caused cannot be repaired. It is wise for management to link cost-reduction programmes to return-on-investment analysis. This must happen in such a way that all employees will voluntarily be involved in the programme.

If we take a close look at the various other ways of change, such as Total Quality Management (TQM), Kaizen (continuous improvement process), project-based organization, profit-centre organization, lean management, business process re-engineering, knowledge-based management, the balanced scorecard, and so on, you can discover some general trends and some underlying promising principles.

### CONCENTRATE ON STRATEGIC CORE COMPETENCIES

To meet the demands of the market, it is not enough just to get lean, to shrink or to grow, but you must also concentrate on the core competencies and power of the company. Or carefully rebuild those, when the previous ones are out of date. Best to start where you already have competence, and expand from there. It does not make sense to buy up any old company to build up a market, simply because there is enough money in the cash-box. Many famous companies drove down the road to ruin by frivolous spending. Successful firms check strategic orientation and clear out dead wood regularly.

But we have to be cautious. The upcoming new economy with its inherent new conditions may probably alter the relative importance of such traditional core business principles of the old economy, because there is a fundamental change and a completely new field of challenge with completely new possibilities for all participants in business competition, e.g. in redefining business process and value chains as we mentioned above.

## IMPORTANT RESOURCE: THE EMPLOYEE

Neither money, nor products, but the employee is the core resource of a company. In the last few years this belief has gained importance and acceptance, at least in public discussions about how a company can better register, locate, and use the knowledge of its workforce. But an executive who refers to his employees as 'human capital' as you hear now and then reveals his true motives. He sees the employee only as a certain quantifiable amount of work capacity, and not as a creative individual being, with personal demands for individual and professional development. This executive is doomed to fail as a leader.

## ORIENTING TO THE DEMANDS OF THE CLIENT

The client, identified by his or her very individual and often contradictory demands and expectations, is the yardstick of all strategic and organizational work. But that's a crucial point too: we have to abandon the idea of the client as a driver with ever constant and transparent needs. Or that there are target groups which are exactly analysable and that their consumption and buying behaviour are predictable over a long period of time. The fact is, the structure of demand is becoming much more open and volatile. However, the blessings of IT can help individualize marketing strategies, to meet the individualized structures of demand.

## OPTIMIZING BUSINESS PROCESSES

With their book *Reengineering the Corporation* (1993), Michael Hammer and James Champy made a theme marketable that has long occupied organizational experts, namely, how to adapt the organization to business processes. The general guideline is to think from the outside to the inside. This means adapting the organization sequentially to the principle of a constant process chain, with three challenges: (1) to start from the needs of the client; (2) to turn the diagnosed need into a problem-based solution; and (3) to do this with no loss of information and time, with the most efficient IT software and hardware.

The starting point is the clients' expectations. And the finishing-line is the benefit to the client. And in between, there is well-functioning teamwork in the process chain. Everyone involved in this process chain must contribute a benefit. This means that every function, every job, and every person that is part of this chain must be accountable for their contribution. All non-value-adding activities have to be challenged, including costs. Only those who contribute can be part of the process chain. Those not able to contribute must be excluded from the chain to prevent unnecessary loops. Let me expand on this with two further points.

First, non-productive elements would cause the least damage if they were just denied participation, i.e. if they did nothing at all. In this case they would merely be a cost factor. If they really become part of the programme, they understandably try to justify their participation. To boost their personal profile, they start marketing their work, and themselves. Consequently, they start tying up the capacities of those who are productive and capable of contributing to the chain, so good resources are wasted. Thus, including a non-productive area not only costs money, but also creates non-productive activities. The result: loss of time and information, and creation of anger and friction.

Second, the art of managing a process chain is above all not to split responsibilities, but to manage them as a whole.

## SEPARATING COMPANIES INTO BUSINESS UNITS OR HORIZONTAL PROCESS CHAINS

A large number of companies have grown to become large organizations, which are structured based on function. The result is that each entity, small or large, division or department, starts optimizing and perfecting only itself! This means the processes of the different business units become discordant and are unfocused. This causes unnecessary costs and unwanted side-effects. In this framework, everyone has only their own way in mind. In addition, only very few organizational units such as sales and marketing as well as service have direct contact with the market, clients, or consumers. All other units tend to organize themselves to fit their own demands. There is no holistic business process in sight. The solution: create a general binding strategic roof and divide the company under this brace into a number of small and relatively independent operating divisions. All these should have many of their employees working in direct contact with the market and clients, and these smaller entities should have more responsibility.

## MERGERS AND ALLIANCES

There is a kind of world-wide roulette going on: in the framework of globalization, all kinds of strategies and forms of mergers or joint ventures are carried out. The most common reason to enter a national or international merger is pressure from the market and from costs. This may be legitimate, at least in some cases. But one thing is already common knowledge: many corporate marriages don't succeed, or won't bring the profits that were loudly promised with words like 'synergy'. On the contrary: the time before and at the start of a merger is always a time of uncertainty and deep individual concerns. Therefore, much energy is necessary for all who are involved and affected, to gain new confidence, to be on the winning team. The most used formula for mergers of $1 + 1 = 3$ is thus a plain lie! In most cases, one is happy if in the beginning the sum adds up to 1.5. More often than not, the sum is even smaller than the starting amount, the price you have to pay if the 'psychological' and 'socio-emotional' factors are not carefully and professionally considered. The main reason for failed mergers is the power struggle between individuals and between cultures. The winner feelings of one group always cause loser feelings in the other. But most malfunctioning mergers are kept quiet for a long time. Otherwise, more than one of the famous merger architects would have to live in permanent fear of being sacked. Networks and virtual organizations in the form of alliances could be seen as an alternative to large mergers to generate the necessary flexibility and global management based on collaboration focused on process and the value-chain, without the above-mentioned ill side-effects of growth, that cannot be achieved.

## WHY SO MANY CHANGE PROJECTS GO WRONG

Looking at the sum of all those findings above, we come to a really amazing and surprising result: we know in principle *why* we have to change and meanwhile we have many consolidated experiences *how* change can be successfully carried out. On the other hand, we know as well that many change projects go wrong. What are the reasons? What's getting in the way of change?

## BASIS FOR FAILURE: ERRORS IN CONCEPT

The most intriguing result is that most 'errors' do not happen 'by accident'. They are part of the concept. Provocatively put: the mistakes are deliberate! They are the 'psychological' result of the patterns of thinking and acting by those involved. Here some examples of the most frequent mistakes and the underlying patterns of thinking we have to understand, if we want to have any chance of change at all.

One important mistake is a jump start or cold start. In a jump start, people are confronted with things they cannot understand. They are 'satisfied' with the situation they are in—or, at least, have come to terms with a given situation. They do not see the reason for change and they do not even see a chance to change the existing situation. Nobody in charge of the change has explained to them the reason for the change. Nobody has shown the purpose of the action, who benefits from the action, the meaning of the action, and what the profit for the individual is. So, passivity, anxiety, and rejection are the natural inevitable reaction. What is the benefit for the agent who is driving projects forward, but is acting with no sensitivity, disregarding the state of those who are affected and involved? Stupidity? Impudence? Brutality? What are the active agent's reasons? Remember our initial thesis: whatever we do, at the moment we are doing it, we are sure it is the right thing to do and the right way to do it. When we look at it with a psychological eye, some typical managerial problems become recognizable:

- self-induced time pressure, resulting from insufficient planning;
- looking for short-term profits instead of long-term profits;
- self-adulation;
- ignoring the wishes of others, because 'I'm the boss!';
- the anxiety of having to change one's ideas, if a discussion arises;
- the primeval fear of managers losing control if one does not constantly apply pressure.

Another mistake is not to involve those who will be affected. Wanting to manage the change as quickly as possible leads one probably to act alone or in a small group of elected supporting partners as long as possible. Solutions can be developed and finished very quickly, and left undisturbed. But the natural sense of self-esteem of the neglected, their concern about their natural desire to profile themselves, and the deep wish to participate, make them refuse to accept 'finished solutions'. 'If we did not invent it ourselves, it can't be good.' No matter if such a finished solution comes from higher ranks, other departments, or external consultants.

A third failure is to want too much at once. Change projects—for certain characters or business units—always offer the opportunity to show off. This means a quite promising approach will automatically be followed by another: project organization, team leadership, group work, a lean organization, segmenting, benchmarking (best practice), the learning organization, re-engineering, total quality management, time-based management, Kaizen, fractal organization, knowledge-based management, the balanced scorecard, or other temporarily fashionable concepts. Employees are economical with their own energy. So, one always has to remain one jump ahead for the next cliché or 'self-promoter' that will come as sure as death and taxes!

Sometimes, the solution is part of the problem. This is another reason for failure, especially when the solution stays within a basic pattern, exacerbating the problem by the very means it seeks to solve, according to Paul Watzlawick's axiom *more of the same* (Watzlawick et al., 1974). For example, a little salt in the soup may be good. More salt may be better. Still more salt, and you can throw out the soup. Or people complain about traffic congestion. To overcome congestion, more streets are built, consequently attracting even more traffic. Or employees demand appreciation by titles. The consequence is, the number of titles increases and the value of titles decreases.

Another problem is to implement isolated solutions. Implementing new ideas, or plans which are not prepared, is like building a castle on the sand. The opportunity for the success of change projects decreases with the degree of the differences between a given surrounding umbrella situation and the desired actual solution. Or in other words, compare it with a premature baby who needs an artificial 'bio-sphere', such as an oxygen tent, to have a chance of survival.

One important failure is false advertising and underestimating the credibility gap. Right at the beginning and because of tactical reasons, one is tempted to take the path of least resistance. One tries to get along by following the status quo and with half-truths. What is the sense of this strategy? In principle, it is the lack of experience and therefore the lack of belief that 'bad news', necessities, and threatening danger can release unexpected energy for self-healing. Every change takes place between polarized ideas and interests. The advantage of one party will be the disadvantage of the other. It is the spirit of the age that everyone wants or speaks of creating a 'win–win' situation. Such clichés are very often used to 'sell' undercover to the employees the following intentions of the shareholders: to introduce programmes to reduce cost, to increase productivity, to outsource departments, to increase performance, even up to requiring the employees to help in cancelling out their own jobs. It is unbelievable how much employee energy is involved in fighting those hidden strategies. Somehow, there is an unspoken alliance for resistance. Behind the scenes, highly creative methods are developed to circumvent official procedures. The result is that the energy that could move mountains for the company gets lost. It simply dissipates—consumed by resistance and slowing things down. The future is always a challenge. The degree to which people accept this challenge depends upon how much they trust their management. A word to management, it is worthwhile to do a second, parallel 'calculation': to constantly check everything we do regarding building up trust and credibility. In rough times management credibility decides the issue of winning or losing. This credibility cannot be built up 'at a moment's notice', just when the management wants and needs it.

## STARTING POINTS FOR CHANGE

As well as the errors in concept, we have to look at the deep-rooted mind-set of the people we have to deal with, when we want to understand why so many projects go wrong and to learn what we could do better. This mental starting point can be described by the following main aspects.

### NO ONE WANTS CHANGE UNTIL IT IS INEVITABLE

Many people talk about change, but if you listen closely, you will hear that they mean the other person has to change. The saying 'nobody wants to be changed except a wet baby' can even be narrowed down to 'only if the comfortable warmth of sprinkling pissing turns into inconvenient cold wetness'. Or, look at the way that a human being uses his or her resources carefully. As long as things work the way they are—fine, there is no need for change. In my early days as a consultant I was often impressed by complaints from those in the middle management and the shop floor about the top leaders. I took those complaints as a real wish for change, and a sign of energy to contribute to the change. I was badly mistaken. I had to learn that the complaints were nothing but the means of psychological relief. 'Learn to suffer without complaining' is a Christian saying. I learned to convert this axiom into 'Learn to complain without suffering.' That's the point, even when problems have been identified. The main point: I have a good explanation for the cause of the problem, and—here is the important bit—it's not me. Many people behave like a cook on a ship in distress at sea: the captain may be drunk, and the ship may therefore be in real danger: it's not my responsibility as a cook to look for a way out. So I'll go down to my kitchen to clean my equipment. If the ship sinks, at least my little world will be in good order.

### BASIC DESIRES AND DRIVING FORCES

Sigmund Freud's statement 'We are all afraid of the unknown' is still valid today. When the elemental desires of man for order and safety as well as predictability in today's tempestuous climate cannot be met, then the consequence is anxiety. And, to neutralize this anxiety, man tends to suppress it. The result is that as long as possible, we want to ignore the threatening situation and all its challenges. If we want to change something, we have to start with the ego of the individual and his or her personal benefits. This does not automatically mean money. The benefit can be calculated in different 'currencies' such as career, prestige, or personal acceptance. But benefit can also mean preventing greater damage. This is anxiety as a driving force—but carefully dosed. Anxiety in a too large a dosage may destroy all creativity and lead to a total blockage. Often curiosity and the thirst for knowledge are hailed as the sources and driving forces of change. This cannot be taken for granted. From our own childhood, we remember as children we asked questions continually and endlessly. As adults, we have the quite opposite attitude: we tend to be convinced we know many things, and we want to be right as often as possible. Not a trace of willingness to learn! Not a trace of curiosity and hunger for new wisdom any more. On the contrary, dogmatism and obstinacy are the normal starting points.

## THE DILEMMA OF EXPERIENCE

Elderly people are typically proud of the experiences they have had. And, very often, they are more than willing to tell this to the people around them, especially to young people, to enrich their view of life. This indicates how strongly we define ourselves and our identity by our past—and what an important role experiences can play in this game. But experiences do have two sides: the asset of experience is that in the future, comparable problems can be solved much more easily. But what is the value of those experiences if the reference parameters of the future are changing dramatically? Then, experiences of the past are counter-productive. It is absolutely fatal to ignore this human state as the normal starting point for our concepts of change and to betray ourselves by taking as a starting point highly motivated employees. There are highly, even self-motivated people too. But do not take it as the rule! Build your strategies of change and leadership upon normal average people—fearful, worried, timid, opportunistic, and egoistic—develop a strategy to move this normal kind of person and you will be successful! Self-motivated employees are positive surprises.

## LEARNING THROUGH UNLEARNING

As adults who define themselves through their successful past or even a rearranged past, we have a major problem relating to the future: we are driving forward with our eyes looking intently back in the rear-view mirror. What does this mean? We believe we know many things—internally, we are nearly full of experiences. For the future, we typically use the patterns of the past. Well, we must clear things to create space. To allow new things to enter our brain, we must store the old ones away. 'We must learn to forget, to un-learn,' according to Dietrich Dörner (1989). How can we achieve that while being bound by the chains of desire for safety, order, and predictability? And as Richard Sennett (1998) pointed out: an overall flexibility is not at all an unquestionable virtue.

## THE FINE ART OF MANAGING CHANGE

We know what we have to do to be prepared for change and innovation, and we know that many change projects are not successful. We have to deal with new ways and methods of commerce, production, and distribution. New systems and attitudes of customers and consumers are affecting business processes. A much higher transparency world-wide of business strategies and prices challenges our business proposition. Frequent and fast changes in the forms of corporations, alliances, mergers, de-mergers, joint ventures, and network organizations are questioning governance structures. An important question for change managers is how they can transform these environmental changes and market-demands into new possibilities for organizing. A second question is how to motivate employees and managers to the necessary outstanding performance and maximum efficiency. And, above all, because this is the situation and challenge for the competitors too, how to do this better and quicker than the competitors to have a chance to survive? Johann Wolfgang von Goethe once said: 'You only see what you know.' If we take this statement seriously, we have to find ways to involve people and supply them with the necessary knowledge. They must be enabled to see and judge the reasons for the necessity of change.

## UPDATE MENTAL MODELS

For all action-relevant aspects we have definitions in our minds, with which we explain or even create 'our world'. According to those *mental models* as Peter M. Senge described them (1990), we adjust our actions and select what comes from the 'outside'. Those patterns of interpretation are often subconscious. We 'learned' them in the course of our first education and later experiences. It is necessary to make these definitions conscious. And, to inspect them to see if they are still valid. To change them we need to raise fervent discussions, intensive dialogue, and confrontation. In an intercultural framework this is even more important because misunderstandings and misinterpretations are more likely as John Mole (1995) and Fons Trompenaars (1993) have described in many useful examples.

I will now present four examples of mental models of leadership, organization, personnel, and planning, and give new conceptions of these aspect systems.

## Leadership

The old concept of leadership we have in mind consists more or less of the following characteristics:

- Leadership is a matter of a few people, those who are at the top.
- Only the top has all the necessary knowledge and the overview of the situation.
- A manager must always know what to do.
- Leaders are heroes.
- Those in the lower ranks are well advised to adapt themselves and to follow commands.

There is a quite different new concept of leadership as, for example, Edgar Schein (2003) describes it:

- As much self-management, self-control, and self-responsibility as possible, instead of a hierarchical organization 'from above' of control and tight rules.
- New focuses of top management on strategic topics and dynamic 'target-agreements'.
- New forms of management as a service and a form of coaching and leadership that facilitates learning and constant change.
- In general, more reshaping *of* the system than operating *in* the system, or stated differently: taking care that things move, instead of moving things oneself.

## Organization

We all know the old mental model of organization:

- clear definite structures;
- split responsibilities;
- all functions exactly separate from each other;
- leading images: strong fortress, Byzantine cathedral, big tanker.

The new conception is characterized as follows:

- Organizational structures are shaped by the architectural principle that form follows function (Bauhaus) not by hierarchical principles.
- There is an unambiguous priority of the horizontal process-chain, oriented to the market and clients' benefit.
- The paradigm: flexible network and virtual organization.

## Personnel

Under the old conception, personnel are characterized as:

- a cog in a gearbox;
- reproducible elements;
- pawns in a chess game.

A new conception considers personnel as:

- an entrepreneur at work;
- a self-responsible co-creator;
- working according to the motto: make it happen.

As you would expect, today there are still enough employees who are happy not to be responsible in the sense of creative accountability. They achieve their entrepreneurship in their leisure time, at home or in clubs. The manager who prefers that kind of employee is well advised to apply the old organizational pattern of organization and leadership. But a manager who wants the entrepreneur to work in the company destroys all his opportunities, if he continues to apply the old rules.

## Planning

From the past we are used to planning procedures characterized by:

- striving for exactness and safety;
- steadiness of purpose.

The new planning implies:

- working with scenarios of different possible futures;
- thinking in moving targets;
- paradigm: sailing instead of moving on railway lines.

Only the new patterns of thinking will enable us to build an attitude and organization system that can successfully cope with the new challenges of environments and markets.

### UNFREEZING FOR CHANGE

If you want to manage a change successfully, you must prepare the ground in advance. You must to create an awareness of the problems to be dealt with right at the beginning. The necessary awareness depends on the extent of the individual's motivation and this is connected with the willingness to commit oneself. Without awareness there will be no willingness. These are the typical weaknesses in normal proceedings: one thinks everything can be reduced to simple factual logic and avoids the emotional challenges as long as possible. The stronger the individuals involved, the stronger the anxiety to handle one's own situation. This may result in not considering topics, to the point of ignoring them. To break the ice, it is not sufficient only to discuss the question of change with each individual on the basis of factual logic. Just the opposite: involvement means emotions! And so, it is a fundamental professional step in a change project to find a way that the implicated emotions become the subject of communication. The successful art of *unfreezing* as Kurt Lewin (1963) put it, or *awakening* as Noel M. Tichy (1993) described it, consists of creating unrest to deliberately upset the balance of things and to pick up people where they mentally are. As long as people are content and consider their situation unchangeable, there will be no reason for change. So, it is necessary to destabilize this balance, using scenarios about the development of a situation or project. To be able to destabilize processes, you have to get an impression of the initial mental situation. Only then can you start taking the necessary steps to sensitize people. Listen to individuals and groups carefully to clarify the following aspects.

## Awareness of the problem

- Do the people actually see or feel a problem?
- Is there any kind of pressure to change?
- If so, how widespread is this pressure?
- Did people simply come to terms with the current situation? Or, did they even find advantages for themselves in the current situation?
- Last but not least: do they talk frankly about that?

## Credibility of the project and of people planning the change

- Do people believe what the advocates of change intend?
- Is there suspicion that there is a hidden agenda?

## Energy and commitment

- How strong is the actual desire and willingness to get involved at the beginning?
- Where is the ownership? Who is actively committed to the project? Who feels responsible and will expend energy on it?

The more delicate the topics are, and the stronger the individual interests will be affected, the more time has to be invested. This is necessary to approach the 'hot' questions and to help people identify with the process. Only when you clearly recognize that people involved have woken up and are sufficiently stirred up to consider the problems can you start to realize the project. There must be sufficient energy released to give the necessary thrust before you can start.

If you want to win people over to a change process, you have to use as much effort as possible to persuade all those who are or will be affected. They must be informed about what will happen. If you ignore that factor, you cause resistance and defence tactics. Here are the essential questions to 'pick up the people, where they mentally are':

- Why do we need a change?
- Why this way and not another?
- What is our part in the project?
- What are the benefits for us?

Honesty and frankness are imperative for success, even though they require more effort than continuing with rational persuasion on a basis of a need to know.

## FIELDS OF POWERS AND RESISTANCE

These are the leading questions for successful project management:

- Who will be involved?
- Which interests do the different groups have?

- How will they react? When and how can they support the project and how could they disrupt the project?
- Who will stay 'neutral' and who will take a stand?
- Who are the official representatives, and who are the behind-the-scenes opinion leaders?
- How far will they defend the project, or how can they be won over?

If you do not describe the powers and do not see the consequences of the actions—from the start-up to the introductory phase—you risk your programme. Make one thing clear: he who disregards the 'political' dimension is working negligently. This does not call for opportunism! But it means you have to consider the different powers that will be involved over the complete period of time of the project—right from the beginning. Thinking in terms of powers is a highly important feature in a project! You must be well aware of the fact that this power does not mean simply the power of hierarchy, or anyone's position! This kind of power means it can be applied, or appear in different guises, such as an expert's knowledge, solidarization phenomena, or a power of blockage by those who are affected.

Resistance is a very normal phenomenon in the processes of learning and change. Under time pressure—actually the normal condition—resistance seems troublesome, maybe even unbearable and unacceptable. One may tend to ignore it. But that is exactly the big mistake. Whenever resistance appears, it causes one to take a break to think, and maybe to correct one's course. For a change project, it is of great importance that resistance, in whatever form, is recognized and answered in the right way. If this is not the case, the result will be delays, severe blockages, and expensive failures. To deal with resistance in a constructive and positive way is one of the essential factors in successfully managing change.

Resistance is present if decisions or measures that are seen as useful, 'logical', or even highly important encounter diffuse rejection, or if they cause doubts and strong suspicions. Resistance is commonly regarded as negative and not as a virtue. Therefore, it is usually carried out covertly. The 'symptoms' of resistance are numerous and varied: inattentiveness, sluggishness, disregard for punctuality, absence, delaying of time schedules and decisions, endless discussions about fundamental principles, etc.

If you put yourself in the position of those who are affected, the reasons for resistance are simple, and arise from different psychological roots:

- Those who are affected do not know what is going on; there is a lack of information.
- They know but they do not see the reasons for the action or its goal.
- They may very well know what is going on and even see the reasons for it, but do not believe the message or the person who delivers the message.
- They may have understood and believe what has been said, but don't want to follow because they are anxious of being unable to meet the new demands.

So resistance is a quite normal reaction to all this. If people of normal intelligence and with no behavioural distortions resist logical measures, one can conclude they do have doubts, or are afraid of the measures. In other words, one must deal not only with factual considerations or logical arguments, but also with emotions and feelings. In our culture, emotions normally are not communicated, but are hidden behind 'factual' aspects. Resistance is an important signal. It indicates where energies are blocked, energies that could be constructively unleashed. So resistance is not a disturbance but an opportunity, if it is recognized and used as such. To fight or suppress resistance is understandable, as resistance may cause unhappy feelings, but to do so is stupid, as that switches off an important signal.

There is only one reasonable and productive reaction: talk calmly with the affected persons, either individually or in small groups. Only sincere interest in the individual situation and personal opinions can build the necessary trust. This creates an atmosphere in which delicate ideas and emotions will be voiced.

It is necessary to 'probe' with special questions what the actual topic of resistance could be, for example, income, job safety, the relation to special groups or supervisors, future job qualification requirements, scope of work, or individual career issues. And it is necessary to listen carefully. Only when the main reasons for resistance are clear do the steps for action become clear too.

## CONFLICT MANAGEMENT

Along with the normality of resistance comes the normality of conflict. To cope with the phenomenon of conflicts, above all with hot emotional subjects, we need a culture of constructive dispute, where debates are hard, but reach the best possible solution, and with high esteem for all participants.

Conflicts are actually a completely normal and everyday part of human life. There is no such thing as a relationship that is permanently free of conflict. Wherever people act together, different points of view, needs, and interests collide—sometimes between individuals, sometimes between smaller groups, and sometimes also between large organizations. And when changes of some sort need to be made, conflicts are already pre-programmed because there are always some people who want to create something new, and others who want to preserve the status quo. There can never be change without conflict.

Most conflicts are resolved in everyday life in a completely undramatic way. Sometimes one person gives in, sometimes the other, and sometimes a compromise acceptable to both sides is worked out—and the next day, no one remembers that a conflict situation arose at all. From time to time, however—suddenly and unexpectedly—things take a completely different course. Dialogue develops into a dispute, which in turn becomes an argument. Emotions start to heat up: outrage and anger, hate and contempt. The opposing parties become locked in an exchange of attacks and counter-attacks. People get hurt—and before you know it, there is a war going on and the main aim is to annihilate the opponent. When it is all over, there is either a winner or a loser, or rather, there are two losers. All that is left is the damage that has been done—physically and psychologically. Recognizing conflict situations quickly and controlling them in such a way that change is possible, while at the same time damage is limited, is one of the most important things we can do.

### DYNAMICS OF CONFLICT DEVELOPMENT

If you want to repair something, you first have to understand how it works. So let us consider the most important aspects of the dynamics of conflict. An uncontrolled conflict typically has four clearly distinguishable phases:

1. *Discussion*: At the very beginning, there is always something at *issue*—the subject which, during what was a quite friendly dialogue to begin with, gave rise to differing opinions or showed that differing interests had to be asserted. Normally a perfectly everyday matter, no reason for a severe conflict to develop. Similar problems have often come up and, so far, a solution has always been found.
2. *Superimposed events*: During the discussion, a critical situation develops: one side's arguments cease to be accepted by the other. What the other side says is called into question. The other side is accused of being self-interested, behaving tactically, and therefore of being insincere. At this point, the dispute rises to the moral level. The actual issue has questions of value, relationships, and personal matters superimposed on it. Emotions come into play. Fairness and justice become the central issues. Value judgements and personal issues begin to be at stake.
3. *Escalation*: As soon as one side starts to believe that its dignity or integrity is being infringed or even that it is being lied to or abused, it reacts with anger and outrage. It thinks the gauntlet has been thrown down, and—justifiably, in its own eyes—moves onto the counter-attack. And exactly

the same happens on the other side. Communication between the partners is interrupted. Attempts are made to isolate the opposing side and injure it. Allies are sought in the vicinity. The conflict moves into the *hot* phase. What is known as *symmetrical escalation* develops. This is based on three mechanisms. First, emotions on both sides supply massive amounts of energy, with people becoming more committed than ever before. Second, events no longer take place on the basis of the logic of the issue involved; the process has escaped rational control. Third, both sides start suffering from *selective perception*. They only notice whatever confirms their own prejudices about the opposing party and systematically ignore whatever contradicts these prejudices. The effect of this is that every step taken by one side makes the other feel justified in hitting back even harder. It is no longer the original issue that is in the foreground, but the current behaviour of each side. The struggle has become self-perpetuating. Emotions now dominate the scene and questions of fairness, justice, and credibility.

4. *Hardening of attitudes*: No conflict can remain permanently in the hot phase. Sooner or later, a cooling-off period occurs—either because one side has won and imposed its own interests, or because the balance of power has created a stalemate situation that develops into a state of delicate balance. In the latter case, it is a 'cold war' that dominates the picture, and the conflict has become 'chronic'. It can go on for years. Real or perceived injustices are not forgotten, however, and the constant potential for future conflict remains—particularly under the condition of lack of communication and cooperation between the different sides.

## CONFLICT RESOLUTION

Every conflict has its own history. It is not just a sudden event, and certainly not an accidental one, it is the result of a very specific process of development. A conflict is 'learned'—and if you want to eliminate it, you have to make sure it is 'unlearned' again. An understanding of what has happened needs to be acquired, mistrust has to be broken down step by step, and trust has to gradually be built up again. The steps that led everyone astray have to be retraced for some distance before a new course for the future can be charted without the danger of a relapse.

The first and most important task is to re-establish a situation of direct communication. During the initial phase, a neutral third party may be needed to carefully monitor the interactions between the opponent parties, because there is no hope of solving the conflict if the subjective perceptions, disappointed expectations, feelings of offence and injury on each side cannot be openly articulated. It is only when this is done that the pressure of pent-up emotions can be reduced and the conflict can be led back to the level of its origin, i.e. genuine needs and interests. Both partners have to get the other side to understand the circumstances, situations, or events that caused them frustration, disappointment, or fury—and why. It is only when this is done that each party can recognize its own—intentional or unintentional—contribution to the process of conflict. This, in turn, is a precondition for ceasing to regard the other party as the only guilty one. The decisive aspect for successfully negotiating a mutually acceptable solution is that no one must be seen as a 'loser'. The solution has to take the interests of both parties into account.

## CAPACITY FOR CONFLICT

Human beings tend to lose the ability to dispute with each other. Differences of opinion stop being mentioned, open disputes are carefully avoided, and the awareness that opposing interests exist is simply repressed. The standards that apply—tacitly, of course—are the following: 'it is bad manners to be critical'; 'grown-ups never argue'; 'being emotional is a sign of immaturity'; 'conflicts are damaging'. The result: a management culture based on the so-called 'harmony model': joy, love, and pancakes. And this is precisely where the problem lies—the company's activities are placed out of the range of constant critical examination, tensions cannot be released, and the organization becomes incapable of self-renewal and becomes ossified.

If a standard has ceased to be useful, it should be changed. This is the first and most important step towards a flexible, lively, and innovative organization—developing a behavioural standard that says criticism is not 'bad manners', arguments are not 'nasty', conflict cannot be assumed to be 'bad' from the very start. A standard that says exposing differences in opinion and conflicts of interest is the precondition for mutual success; that it is not some kind of impossible 'harmony' that is needed, but a *constructive argumentation culture*—a world in which conflict is not repressed, but taken as an opportunity to discover innovative solutions by conducting disputes on the basis of partnership.

# ACTIVE COMMUNICATION

Now we come to the very core crucial aspect of managing change: only active, even offensive communication can get things going. This aims to do the following:

- to disclose ideas and interpretations (mental models), in order to check and develop them;
- to allow the exchange of judgements;
- to destabilize false contentment or resignation;
- to generate awareness of problems and release energies for change;
- to mobilize an entrenched status quo;
- to clarify the open and hidden interests in power and to negotiate them anew;
- to build up the necessary feedback culture.

## EFFECTIVE COMMUNICATION AND DIALOGUE

Communication is the vehicle and propellant for change. And, by communication, one also transmits simultaneously a very important message: the commitment to interactive leadership and partnership. Creative and competent communication arises from attention to the following basic aspects, what one might call the 'laws of communication'.

The tools, methods, and processes for building up communication are plentiful. However, the more formalized the communication, the less stimulating, vivid, or impressive it is. Therefore, if a strong impact is desired, while touching individual interests and charging emotions, the procedures must support a vivid dialogue. In practice, the more we want to avoid direct contact, or a dispute, the more necessary it probably is.

The communication researcher Paul Watzlawick originally stated this axiom—*you cannot not-communicate*—for the interaction between individuals. It can also apply to bigger organizations or social structures. Gaps in expected communication, such as silence, one-sided statements that allow no time for dispute, are all filled with interpretations. What has not been said will be interpreted according to the receiver's biases. Those messages 'filled in' by the recipient are just as powerful as those messages actually spoken.

Rapid change stimulates the need for communication without delay. Perfect, orderly communication, however, takes too long to develop and therefore usually comes too late, and so speculation always precedes planned communication, because there is no such thing as non-communication, as we just noted. Therefore, it is much better to communicate incompletely, but quickly and more frequently, than to wait in hope of communicating precisely and completely.

The more emotional a situation is, the higher the risk of selected perception. As a result, the message will not be understood as spoken and intended by the sender. Usually one understands something different more or less than what has actually been communicated by the sender. Two main factors influence selected perception: the credibility of the sender, and the personal experiences of the recipient.

Depending on the context, perspective, experiences, and evaluation of credibility, different 'truths' will be understood, or constructed. Therefore, proper communication requires careful inquiry: one can communicate successfully only if one has probed the inner state of the addressee. Only by knowing this state can communication be fine-tuned to the addressee.

If the addressee is to receive information quickly and precisely with no distortion, it must be communicated in briefly, directly throughout the organization and with the possibility of feedback. In this case, the 'cascade of hierarchy' in an official chain of command is highly disruptive. The information communicated through several steps and persons would most likely never reach the addressee unfiltered: no one wants to be seen in a bad light. So the negative aspects are removed or toned down. Even in the opposite case: the one who passes information forward is most probably tempted to ensure the message reflects positively on himself. So a scent mark is always applied. But also where direct dialogue is possible, emotional 'overlapping' and misinterpretations can arise. So in all cases, it becomes necessary to check the quality of communication, because what the addressee understands is not always what the source said. So you have to be aware of the reactions of the addressee to the message. Do the reception and the reaction of the addressee fit the original intentions? Only after checking that does one know if corrections or completions are necessary. In 1958, the cybernetics expert Norbert Wiener said, 'I do not know what I have said until I have received the answer to my message.'

Many managers avoid frank communication, as they are concerned that 'everything will be discussed'. They are afraid that employees may talk to death the basic intention or objective of a project. This anxiety is based on insecurity. If a concept has a solid foundation—which is not always the case in practice—it is rather easy to win over those who are affected. All they want is to understand the goals, background, and consequences, and be involved in decisions that affect them, so that they may be able to influence the realization.

## GROUP DYNAMICS

Managers of change make their work unnecessarily difficult, when they see themselves as the locomotive pulling a train, the only ones who can supply all the necessary driving power, so that everyone and everything depends on them. There may be two reasons for that: first, the wish to make their name, or second, deep suspicion of motivation and energy in others. The consequences for such managers are clear: personal exhaustion, sometimes to the point of exploitation. In addition, ultimately, the driving power they do provide is limited. The answer: to use more group dynamics. In a new book a team of psychologists specializing in group dynamics provide deep insight in the most significant processes of power, resistance, and group dynamics that influence projects of change (Doppler et al. 2002).

Everywhere that people work together, group dynamic fields of power exist. They develop within groups and between groups and are related to forces of mutual attraction or rivalry and rejection. There are wishes for mutual command and subjugation mixed with a drive for solidarity, the need for closeness and distance, feelings of trust and mistrust. Those fields of power are a tremendous reservoir of energy that can be used! They are present anyway, and working: either as a brake and blockage energies, or as propellants of creation and self-organization. It is increasingly accepted that teams are well able to organize and lead themselves, and fulfil their duties without hierarchical interventions. As well as the traditionally assigned work teams, we see more and more interdisciplinary work groups, quality circles, or other *ad hoc* groups, established with partial autonomy for the success of the company. In these groups, everything is discussed, including topics below the iceberg's water line, or subjects usually swept under the carpet.

Any group organization can only release its energies if the organization is carefully developed, and if there is enough care given to its maintenance and human relations. Many people riding the 'group trends' tend to overlook these points. A group is at the very beginning no more than an accumulation of individuals. This will not become a well-functioning team simply through structure or reorganization, or just by calling it a group. To transform a number of people into a team, it is necessary to have a common goal, mutual interest, and personal commitment. This does not come out of the blue. Despite that, members of the team—even with a good sense of understanding of each other—can become entangled in conflicts. Groups can lose the energy they once had. They can stall and degenerate and may become an end in themselves. Thus, in many companies there are more than a few obsolete work groups and project teams without a clear goal, leadership, or personal commitment. The social contact within the team, plus the social status as a member of the group, is often enough motivation to preserve the team. If no one ever dissolves such a team, it can carry on without real functions for months or even years.

A manager who wants productive and creative teams must invest time and effort into building the team and its maintenance. By team-oriented structure and process organization, and by dynamic systems of self-organization, one does not save expenses—one shifts them. The expenses on meaningless details and various regulations are replaced by expenses for building and maintenance. The profit: energy and self-regulation of those involved. Train carriages that were once difficult to pull and could be moved only by a locomotive now become flexible, self-driven vehicles that can couple together.

## PERSISTENCE

The big challenge is to finalize projects, not to start new ones. Without tenacity and persistence, there will be no success. If persistence to reach the set goal is accompanied by humour, based on the insight into human nature that in principle nobody wants to change until it is inevitable, then passion becomes an endless source of energy. At the end of this chapter, I want to share one more experience: discussing the leaders of the former East Germany and their hostility to reform. Mikhail Gorbachev, the last president of the former USSR, said, 'He who comes too late is punished by life.' The Polish satirist Stanislaw Lec put it the other way: 'He who is ahead of his time, must often wait for this time in very uncomfortable accommodation' (1971). In the dilemma between those two poles, we never can be sure of hitting the right time. When in doubt, I think it's better to be too early. But in general we cannot avoid one fact: changes always take longer than planned, they happen differently than expected, and everything will be tougher than hoped for. That's the normal way of things.

So let me close with a final recommendation for mentally based leadership: when you start a journey as the leader of this journey, and you know this expedition will not be easy, then the more difficult the journey is, the more necessary it will be that you do it in a quite special way: you will be a good leader only if you have reached the goal already in mental anticipation. This self-confidence will give you the needed encouragement that will attract other people to follow you, even on a difficult path.

## REFERENCES

Argyris, C. & Schön, D.A. (1996) *Organizational Learning II: Theory, Method and Practice.* Reading, MA: Addison-Wesley.
Bate, P. (1994) *Strategies for Cultural Change.* Oxford: Butterworth-Heinemann.
Doppler K. (1999) *Dialektik der Führung: Opfer und Täter.* Munich: Gerling Akademie Verlag.
Doppler, K. & Lauterburg, C. (2000) *Managing Corporate Change.* Berlin: Springer.
Doppler, K., Fuhrmann, H., Lebbe-Waschke, B. & Voigt, B. (2002) *Unternehmenswandel gegen Widerstände: Change Management mit den Menschen.* Frankfurt: Campus Verlag.
Dörner, D. (1989) *Die Logik des Mißlingens.* Hamburg: Rowohlt.
Drucker, P.F. (2002) *Managing in the Next Society.* Oxford: Butterworth-Heinemann.
Gouillart, F.J. & Kelly, J.N. (1995) *Transforming the Organization.* New York: McGraw-Hill.
Hammer, M. & Champy, J. (1993) *Reengineering the Corporation.* New York: HarperCollins.
Handy, C. (1995) *Beyond Certainty.* London: Arrow Business Books.

Lec, S. (1971) *Das große Buch der unfrisierten Gedanken*. Munich: Hanser Verlag.

Lewin, K. (1963) *Feldtheorie in den Sozialwissenschaften*. Bern: Huber.

Mole, J. (1995) *Mind Your Manners: Managing Business Cultures in Europe*. London: Nicholas Brealey Publishing.

Nagel, R. & Wimmer, R. (2002) *Systemische Strategieentwicklung: Modelle und Instrumente für Berater und Entscheider*. Stuttgart: Klett-Cotta.

Pine II, B.J. & Gilmore, J.H. (1999) *The Experience Economy*. Boston: Harvard Business School Press.

Prahalad, C.K. (1998) Managing Discontinuities: The Emerging Challenges. *Research Technology Management*, **41**(3), 14–22.

Schein, E.H. (2003) *The Role of Leadership in the Management of Organizational Transformation, Culture and Learning*. Basle: *ORGANISATIONSENTWICKLUNG*, newspaper.

Senge, P.M. (1990) *The Fifth Discipline: The Art and Practice of the Learning Organization*. New York: Doubleday.

Sennett, R. (1998) *The Corrosion of Character*. New York: W.W. Norton.

Tichy, N.M. (1993) Handbook for revolutionaries. In N.M. Tichy & S. Sherman, *Control Your Destiny or Someone Else Will*. New York: Doubleday.

Trebesch, K. (ed.) (2000) *Organisationsentwicklung: Konzepte, Strategien, Fallstudien*. Stuttgart: Klett-Cotta.

Trompenaars, F. (1993) *Riding the Waves of Culture*. London: The Economist Books.

Watzlawick, P., Weakland, J.H. & Fisch, R. (1974) *Change: Principles of Problem Formation and Problem Resolution*. New York: W.W. Norton.

Weick, K.E. & Sutcliffe, K.M. (2001) *Managing the Unexpected*. San Francisco: Jossey-Bass.

Wiener, N. et al. (1958) *Mensch und Menschmaschine*. Frankfurt: Ullstein.

CHAPTER 7

# Organizational Change
## Strategies and Interventions

### Elise Walton and Michael Russell
*Mercer Delta Consulting, New York, USA*

As a field, organizational change and development has evolved over the past 50 years. The testaments to progress in the field are too numerous to list, but a few observations stand out. The proliferation of academic journals, Academy sections, and numerous annual reviews (Beer & Walton, 1987; Porras & Silvers, 1991; Quinn & Weick, 1999) indicate the field has established itself as a domain with staying power, both in academic and organizational realms. The debates about the focus of change efforts (Beer & Nohria, 2000), the parameters of change management, and the nature of change itself (Quinn & Weick, 1999; Worren et al., 1999; Hornstein, 2001) attest to the ongoing relevance of the field. Oddly enough, the debate between theoreticians and major consulting firms about whether organization development is change management or something distinct from it underscores the growing recognition of the validity of both as mechanisms for effecting change in organizations. The emergence of purists vs pragmatists is an important milestone in the development of a field.

As companies have struggled with major changes, such as deregulation, industry restructuring, consolidation and downsizing, explosive growth, change in business models, and so on, they have reached in multiple directions for help in managing the organizational challenges they face. Now, as much as at any other time, the ability to help an organization move to a new and different pattern of functioning is important. Many of the core tenets of organizational change and development—the involvement of those affected by the change (Schein, 1999; Vogt, 1999), the motivational value of meaningful work (Vroom, 1964; Hackman & Oldham, 1980), the importance of surfacing and sharing information (Nadler, 1977), the use of models to diagnose organizational functioning (Lawrence & Lorsch, 1965; Nadler & Tushman, 1999)—are at the heart of the basic practices employed by change leaders and consultants seeking to help organizations navigate the uncertain and unforgiving environment in which they find themselves.

Before looking at strategies and interventions one can deploy, it is important to try to tease out what is actually meant by the term organizational change. It would seem to mean a process of planned change that results in a growth in capability, a seasoning, perhaps even an alignment of organization activity. From the perspective of organization development, change itself is

> a set of behavioral science-based theories, values, strategies, and techniques aimed at the planned change of the organizational work setting for the purpose of enhancing individual development and improving organizational performance, through the alteration of organizational members' 'on-the-job behaviors'. (Porras & Robertson, 1992: 723)

With these definitions in mind, this chapter reviews the developments in change management from two perspectives. First, the change and adaptation of organizational development practices—the

*Dynamics of Organizational Change and Learning.* Edited by J.J. Boonstra.
© 2004 John Wiley & Sons, Ltd. ISBN 0-471-87737-9.

interventions themselves—will be examined, with emphasis on differentiating those interventions that have distinguished themselves by becoming norms, from those that have not taken hold. Then we will provide an overview of the ongoing conceptual debates in the field of organizational change which will suggest possible directions for future research and practice.

## ORGANIZATION STRUCTURE

In the theory and practice of organizational change, attention was always paid to the importance of structure in achieving organizational goals. Initially, the concept of differentiation and integration (Lawrence & Lorsch, 1965) described the seemingly bipolar dilemma organizations face: pressures to be different based on environmental and task demands, on the one hand, and internal pressures to integrate, align, and be similar, on the other.

The tensions identified by Lawrence and Lorsch remain a core structural dilemma even today (Nadler & Tushman, 1999), and resolutions have taken many forms. Galbraith (1977) described the matrix organization as one which resolved the different needs by creating dual reporting and information flows. Thus, a company could be centralized and decentralized at the same time while still being focused and integrated. The concept is quite logical, and is the *de facto* practice in many organizations, but those living in these matrix organizations acknowledge that there is usually a dominant power. Without a dominant power, matrices often lead to lack of clear decision-making and accountability. In addition, organizations often do not need the symmetrical dual reporting proscribed by the classic matrix structure. Finally, matrices tend to be expensive.

Miles and Snow (1986) and Nohria and Eccles (1992) describe a networked organization, in which a company contracts with other companies for many of the goods, services, or processes that it would have managed internally in a traditional vertically integrated organizational structure. A networked organization is, in fact, a multiplicity of companies each doing what it does best in a shared value chain. The tension between demands for integration on one activity then another are met by a constantly changing mix of project teams. The networked organization is scalable, allowing the benefits of large size in areas like purchasing, while simultaneously allowing firms within the network to cater to niche markets best served by a smaller-scale company. Effectively, the networked organization creates the benefits of being in a large organization without requiring the building of one.

Both the matrix organization and the networked organization address needs to maintain advantages of specialization and resource minimization in order to meet various external requirements (market demands, government requirements, etc.) and obtain internal advantages (coordination advantages of project management, etc.). In this sense, each organizational form can be considered a possible reconciliation of the bipolar dilemma Lawrence and Lorsch identified above.

More recently, authors addressing the needs of global organizations have come up against the same dilemma. In a refinement of Chandler's 'structure-follows-strategy' idea, Bartlett and Ghoshal (1989) have outlined specific organization characteristics associated with specific environmental demands. For instance, a company that requires cost efficiency as a predominant performance outcome is often organized globally—which has implications for structure, decision rights, and the relationship between headquarters and local units. Alternately, a company that relies on local responsiveness has a different constellation of structure, decision rights, and headquarters–regional relationships. Bartlett and Ghoshal differentiate their case study organizations into global, multinational, international, and transnational. The transnational structure does the best to resolve the demand for local responsiveness (differentiation) and global leverage (integration).

Galbraith (2000) has posed a different solution to the differentiation–integration dilemma. Building on his earlier work, Galbraith points to environmental factors that predispose the organization toward a global design, vs factors that predispose it toward more local authority (see Figure 7.1). But equally important, he identifies certain organization activities that tend to be global (finance, research, and development) and other functions which are most frequently locally managed.

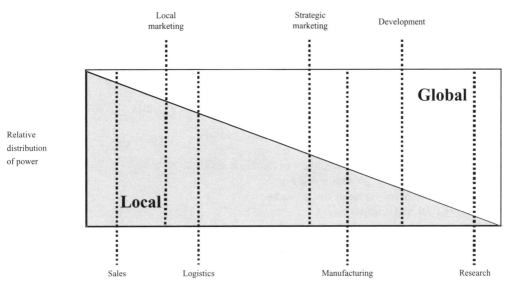

**FIGURE 7.1**   Differentiated function–geography structure

In other words, some activities are inherently a cross-organization integration effort, and others are inherently differentiated that respond to environmental demands. Many organizations have identified core staff functions as network functions such as finance and HR—those which inherently belong to a corporate network but must also serve local business needs.

Nadler and Tushman (1999) describe yet another form, which they call a 'strategic enterprise' as they have explored how focus and leverage can be obtained from asymmetrically designed functions within the organization. Similar to the old holding company concept, Nadler and Tushman build on this by identifying the unique aspects that must be corporate, and those that must be differentiated.

Effectively, Nadler and Tushman resolve the bipolar dilemma identified by Lawrence and Lorsch by redefining the internal tendency to integrate, align, and make uniform throughout the organization. In the strategic enterprise, competitive advantage comes from the ability of an organization to allow each set of businesses with a distinct value chain to organize in a manner that optimally fits its resources, markets, and delivery mechanisms. Linkage to the rest of the organization may be tight or loose, depending on the value to be gained. The goal is to derive maximum value from leveraging shared resources while keeping links to a minimum in order to maintain focus in a fragmented marketplace.

The increasing variety and complexity of these organizational forms arise from the realities of corporate life. Far from being monoliths, most large corporations are dynamic assemblies of enterprises within enterprises, frequently situated in dozens of regions. While there may be unifying structure at the highest level of global organizations, inevitably there will be powerful regional structures underneath—arguably, where many of the important decisions are made. As our knowledge of the capabilities and performance parameters of various organization structures improves, we need to build greater depth into our understanding of multiple-layered organization structures, how different functions best serve the overall organization purpose.

The understanding of structural choices has improved dramatically, with clear delineations of types made in the practitioner's world. At a high level, holding companies vs operating companies, and global vs multi-domestic organizations have all had clear design implications. Furthermore, few issues soak up more organizational energy than structure, decision rights, and authority. Conflicts over pricing ability, revenue recognition, and deal structuring—to name a few—reflect the day-to-day working out of these tensions.

# GOVERNANCE, ROLES, AND RESPONSIBILITIES

Governance has emerged as an important topic for executives. One can see its appearance in numerous corporate initiatives. Take, for instance, the Novartis 2000 Annual Report, which includes a substantial section on governance. Novartis describes governance as encompassing 'all organizational and structural elements serving directly or indirectly to protect the interests of shareholders' (Novartis, 2000). This definition can broadly encompass the following management activities:

- Determining and monitoring corporate identity and mission.
- Effectively managing trade-offs between constituencies.
- Making and executing speedy, informed, actionable decisions.
- Setting internal policies, processes, and rules.
- Managing external relationships and dependencies.
- Managing inter-unit relationships.
- Ensuring current and future executive capability.

Governance encompasses structure, but also includes key groups and councils, the flow of information and decisions, and the distribution of authority in organizations. As such, it addresses the operations of the organization at the seniormost levels, but also affects critical issues such as roles, responsibilities, decision flows, and communications. It often includes relationships with the Board of Directors as well. As such, governance draws heavily on the practice and knowledge base built in the organization development field.

In approaching the issue of governance, it is important to clarify assumptions, both about corporate strategy and the role the corporate headquarters will play in the organization. In developing the optimal structure that will enable corporate headquarters to fulfill its role, Kramer (1999) describes five requirements of good governance: clarity, economy, decision-making, a mix of stability and change, and self-renewal.

In examining the mix of stability and change that is one of the requirements of good governance, Abell (1999) points out that a CEO can combine leadership and managerial attributes as a longer-sighted 'manager of managers' or a CEO can be appointed to coordinate two top managers, each in charge of 'today' and 'tomorrow' strategies. The governance roles of Chairman, Chief Operating Officers, and even Co-COOs have received a great deal of attention over the past decade.

One of the roles of the CEO is to chair the executive team but, as Finley (2002) points out, many senior executives find it difficult to assemble then lead effective teams at the top of their organization. Despite these difficulties, well-designed teams can be key leadership instruments, allowing a flow of information between the top and the rest of the enterprise, leveraging the talents of team members, and extending the leadership of the CEO throughout the enterprise. Finley identifies a number of characteristics common to effective teams:

- The team has a single, company-wide objective.
- The team's tasks and parameters for working together are clearly defined.
- Team members each have their own voice.
- Team members perform together as a team.

The Board of Directors also has vital governance roles and responsibilities, including selection of a new CEO and audit of the organization's performance. The high-profile failure of a number of CEOs in the last few years and the spectacular collapse of Enron amid a flurry of allegations concerning weak review of its activities both illustrate the magnitude of the Board's involvement in a major enterprise. In order to be effective, a Board must perform its control and service tasks effectively and it must be able to work as a coherent group. Boards need standards and expectations that will promote high-efforts behavior among Board members. Boards must function in an environment that respects and encourages the leveraging of each member's expertise. In the absence of these elements, a Board is in danger of becoming an underutilized collection of talented and experienced but disengaged senior executives.

As the strategy and role of the CEO, the senior team, and the Board are clarified and a coherent and effective corporate center is put in place, leaders have a unique opportunity to reshape the organization from the top down. This is not limited to simply unveiling a new governance structure, but also includes reshaping the culture and principles that will enable the company to win in the marketplace and cascading them down to all levels in the organization.

Roles and responsibilities are a key element of governance, and have become a new focus of organization practice. While job descriptions are a staple element in most large organizations, the recent recognition that descriptions only go so far has led to the re-emergence of role negotiation work. Early change efforts had many role negotiation exercises and relationship clarification exercises. Senior teams are finding this type of work specifically useful in building smooth operating relationships.

## HR PROCESS INTERVENTIONS

The next group of change efforts revolves around redesigning the human resource systems to create a healthier and more productive environment. One interesting development is that of human capital research. Started by Gary Becker (1978), much has been done to understand how the elements of human resource management interact. This research looks at the human resource practices and their consequences for system performance. For instance, consider a bank troubled by high turnover among first-level supervisors. At a 40 percent churn rate, the bank will experience high replacement and training costs, as well as customer relationship costs. Based on exit interviews, the bank believed that non-competitive pay was the cause of excessive turnover. Upon an in-depth analysis of multiple HR causes, researchers found that career opportunities and lack of supervisory continuity were the actual drivers of turnover. Thus, the bank was able to address these drivers, at lower cost, and with higher effectiveness in reducing unwanted and costly turnover.

## CAREER PATHS

A career can be thought of as 'a series of experiences and events through which a person passes during a lifetime'. Individual careers develop through the goals and abilities a person brings to an organization and the work, tools, strategic aims, and environment the organization provides. Since careers are defined by experiences and events, the ongoing interaction between individuals and the organization shapes both the career and the individual's sense of self over time. Accordingly, the career paths that are made available by an employer have a significant impact on employee development, for good or ill. The key is to develop career paths that help employees develop in a way that harmonizes with company goals. Figure 7.2 illustrates ways in which elements of the environment in which the employee works can influence that employee's development.

Many employers adopt a fairly fragmented approach to career paths, reflecting specific short-term needs or objectives. The broad scope of the definition of careers advanced here reflects the reality that no one strategy can guarantee an optimal approach to building career paths that guarantee an optimal environment. Rather, change leaders should bear the impact of the environment on employee development when seeking to effect change on employee development.

One thing seems clear: career development has emerged as a powerful motivator for employee commitment (Guzzo et al., 2003). That is, an individual's ability to see a meaningful path forward and to feel like a valued member of an organization is as important as other key variables such as compensation and pay.

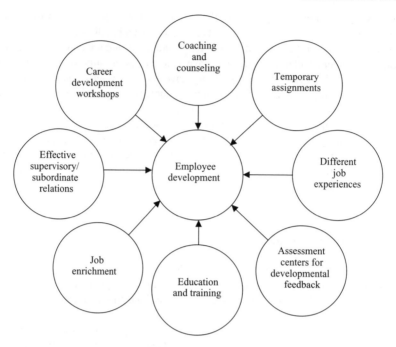

**FIGURE 7.2**   Tools for employee development

## SELECTION

Selection, as a topic, has migrated somewhat into a traditional HR area. However, most organization development authors (Hackman & Oldham, 1980; Nadler et al., 1992) note that the composition of teams, including selection of members, is vital to work design and organization effectiveness. Few articles have sought to integrate selection practices and strategies with an overall organization effectiveness approach.

Sessa and Taylor (2000) point out that inappropriate selection can be one of the most costly mistakes a company can make, regardless of whether it involves the CEO or another senior executive. They recommend two important steps that should be taken prior to even assembling a pool of candidates, to ensure an appropriate fit. First, a selection committee should be carefully chosen, bearing in mind that those who identify the successful candidate for the job are almost as important as the candidate. This committee's responsibilities and operating parameters should be completely clear at the outset. Next, get a thorough sense of what the job actually is and how success in it can be measured before the actual selection process begins—and be sure everyone on the selection committee is aligned behind this conception. It is not possible to select the optimal candidate for a job when the job itself is imperfectly understood. The job description should also harmonize with the strategy and values of the organization.

When making the selection itself, be sure to employ an approach that is disciplined, based on appropriate information (résumés, references, 360-degree feedback, etc.), and is rigorously impartial. Internal and external selection processes may differ, based on the nature of the organization and the job. Take this into account at the outset. When both internal and external candidates are being considered, it is vital not to favor—or be perceived as favoring—one class of candidates over the other.

Once the candidate is selected, the selection process itself is not over. In order to ensure success, prepare the individual for the job and the organization and prepare the organization for the individual. This involves integrating the individual into the organization's processes and culture, communicating the individual's role to the organization, and providing tools and training to ensure success on an ongoing basis. In some instances, especially where high-level positions are concerned, there may be internal contenders who are discouraged at not having secured the job. Be sure to address retention questions as they concern these individuals.

## REWARDS

Ed Lawler (1973) has argued that understanding what motivates workers is critical to thinking analytically about all behavior in organizations and making organization-design decisions. He introduced an expectancy-theory framework to explain how behavior is directed, placing substantial emphasis on job satisfaction. More recently, Lawler has focused on extrinsic rewards, from a somewhat paradoxical position: though workers can clearly be motivated by compensation, research also shows that pay for performance can cause people to stop finding intrinsic pleasure from doing work, causing them to do things only when they are paid specifically for doing them (Lawler, 1999). Accurately grading performance and consideration of alternative reward systems based on team rather than individual performance can both help address this paradox.

## CULTURE

Culture has long been a domain for change practitioners, with an early emphasis on ideal cultures and best company to work for, as well as corporate cultures best suited to specific business models or strategies (Kotter & Heskett, 1992; Schein, 1997). At the same time, many senior managers have perceived the culture issues as being hard to measure and even harder to fix. The terms 'culture' and 'climate' have also become associated in many executives' minds with initiatives that have failed to produce any noticeable change in either behavior or business performance.

Despite this criticism, many recognize the degree to which culture can make or break an enterprise. Though the wave of mergers and acquisitions continues unabated, as many as half fail to deliver the anticipated value, and it appears that unresolved cultural differences play a key role in this value loss. It is not hard to see how this can be so—in an enterprise that grows through multiple acquisitions, it becomes increasingly hard to implement overall strategies and reward systems if there are several different potentially contradictory legacy styles of working and managing in the various units of the organization.

## LARGE-SCALE SYSTEMS INTERVENTIONS

Beginning in the late 1970s, large group interventions, including structured training work, gained popularity. The search conference (Bunker & Alban, 1997; Janoff & Weisbord, 1999) was one of the earliest forms, and helped the concept gain legitimacy (Cahoon, 2000). Currently, the term 'large group intervention', and even its acronym, LGI, is recognized in most businesses. Many companies in the USA use them in the regular course of doing business. They are, however, rooted in ideas of change and involvement.

Rapid decision centers are perhaps the most common large-scale systems intervention practices being used today. These have their roots in work begun by MJThompson, a firm eventually purchased by Ernst and Young. Rapid decision centers were designed to be homes for large group interventions and had very specific physical characteristics including movable walls, room-to-room video feeds, full whiteboard walls with movable hyper-tiles, and ample supplies of toys, games, and books. The concept was to develop a creative and fluid environment that enabled large groups of people to work together.

These processes have helped resolve many intractable organization problems, particularly those that involve numerous, regionally dispersed decision-makers. In the MJThompson formula, the first day of the large group session was devoted entirely to non-specific learning and play. The environment was strewn with toys and books and consisted of movable walls and movable wall panels. Video was everywhere. After a day of small group assignments, such as team reading a book, the large group would work on a business problem with the support of video, data workers, and 'sketch hogs' (people who tracked the discussion and the board work of the groups). This process bears strong resemblance to the traditional foundations of organization development—engagement, informed group decision-making, and task-directed organization development.

The following example typifies the application of large group intervention technology. One large computer company had difficulty determining how the European sales force should be organized and compensated. Each stakeholder—the executive team, the product divisions, North American Sales and European Sales, Finance—had a different view and each had their own proposals. Solving the problem was compounded by multiple time zones and different regional agendas. Getting all of the debating parties in one room, with proper information and resource support, allowed the company to solve in three days a problem that had festered unresolved for two and a half years.

## LEARNING AND INFORMATION SHARING

One area where there has been much interesting progress is in the area of conversation, information sharing, and learning. One such thread in this stream is appreciative inquiry, a theory of organizing and a method for changing social systems (Bushe, 1995). It arose as a result of Srivastva and Cooperrider's (1987) criticism that traditional action research studies had failed to develop useful new theory. They identified both the method of action research and the implicit theory of social organization as the culprits. Most action research projects operate on the assumption that there is a stable, enduring social and psychological reality. Appreciative inquiry, however, treats social and psychological reality as a product of the moment, open to continuous reconstruction. This is consonant with the socio-rationalist view that theories and beliefs about social systems have a powerful effect on perceived social 'reality'. From this point of view, the creation of new theories of groups, organizations, and societies are a powerful aid in their change and development.

Appreciative inquiry itself is an attempt to generate a collective image of a new and better future by exploring the best of what is and has been. One begins with a grounded observation of 'the best of what is', then through vision and logic collaboratively articulates 'what might be', ensuring the consent of those in the system to 'what should be' and collectively experimenting with 'what can be'.

One observation is that communication processes still need to move more and more toward genuine engagement. For instance, Larkin and Larkin (1996) argue that senior managers—and most communication consultants—have refused to hear what frontline workers have been trying to tell them. When you need to communicate a major change, stop communicating values, communicate face-to-face, and spend most of your time, money, and effort on frontline supervisors.

Another cluster of developments is looking at the way organizations learn and make sense of the world. First, the concept of dialogue has received a great deal of attention in organizations. The concept of dialogue revolved fundamentally in getting people to speak in ways that allow learning to emerge from conversations (Kegan & Lahey, 2001).

Building on this line of thinking from Forrester was Peter Senge, who popularized ideas of systems thinking and dialogue with his book *The Fifth Discipline* (1999). This approach to understanding conversation involves helping people learn to better understand interdependency and change, and thereby deal more effectively with the forces that shape the consequences of their actions. This self-awareness is developed by a number of techniques, including simulation, an intervention which allows participants to experience first hand the systemic consequences of individual action. Senge's organization, the Society for Organizational Learning, has become an adviser and active interventionist in many organizations. Comments about the 'ladder of inference' and 'balancing advocacy and inquiry' and even 'generativity' are broadly understood in US business.

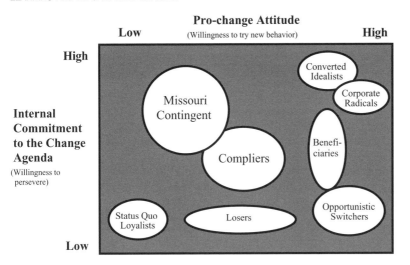

*The Status Quo Loyalists*—those who didn't want change and viewed change as a political maneuver by those who have more power.

*The Opportunistic Switchers*—those who were interested in change because it offered personal opportunity.

*The Converted Idealists*—those who believed in the change with an almost missionary zeal.

*The Missouri Contingent*—those who would support the change but took a 'show me' attitude.

*The Compilers*—those who would do what they were told, but without particular commitment or enthusiasm.

*The Corporate Radicals*—those who are concerned that change isn't going far and fast enough.

**FIGURE 7.3** Analysis of opinion groups

Senge uses the classic beer game simulation to illustrate how structure influences behavior. The beer game involves having participants take on the roles of a retailer, a wholesaler, and a brewer, each seeking to keep adequate stock on hand and each seeking to maximize profits. Participants see how the classic purchase order and inventory system used in the simulation causes first a shortage of beer in the face of an increased demand, then overproduction, and overstocking well in excess of customer desire. The first reaction of the retailer, wholesaler, and brewer is to blame the disruptions in the product flow either on demand or on the poor judgement of the other people in the supply chain. Since participants are able to see all three roles functioning within a system, however, they are able to see the degree to which the system itself, independent of the people or market forces, is able to influence behavior. In this example, the system ensures that logical decisions taken at each step actually produce an illogical result.

The concept of dialogue encourages groups to explore their different ideas and generate new, combined models from their independent models and ideas. Practices of mind mapping (Buzan & Buzan, 2000) and opinion groups build on dialogue. The differentiation of opinion groups helps manage change by identifying different implicit goals and values associated with them. For instance, an in-depth analysis of interview responses led to a set of opinion groups as described, shown in Figure 7.3. These were then used to build a strategy for enlisting leaders in the change agenda.

This breakdown helps one understand an orientation to a change in organization. By understanding different clusters of people and their views, it becomes easier to envision how to migrate views to a common place.

Ford and Ford (1995) look at how conversations work to produce change. Change agents can use conversations to generate, sustain, and complete new conversations that create an altered set of commitments. Borrowing from the field of epidemiology, he looks at how ideas 'infect' new 'hosts' and become established in an organization. Such research is promising in terms of change agents' ability to contemplate how change actually occurs.

While this may not seem like dramatic progress, it does point to the integration of organization development and human relations thinking into the everyday practice of business executives. It represents recognition that the way we talk to each other is fundamentally important, not only for interpersonal reasons, but also for effectiveness.

## TECHNOLOGY CHANGE

One fundamental change in how people work together is the rise of Internet usage. Information can be exchanged instantaneously, rendering overnight delivery the slower option (McFarland, 2001). But more important, information can be shared across firms, web pages can be used as virtual worksites, and videoconferencing allows people to share documents as well as discussion time together. Though debates rage about the real value of 'clicks' vs bricks, the reality is that the emergence of the Internet in the USA, Asia, and Europe has changed the way many firms do business.

These changes have had an important effect on work and corporate life. Information has long been acknowledged as a critical component in how people organize their work, their opinions, and their relationships. Now there is the challenge of dealing with massive amounts of real-time information.

## INDIVIDUAL INTERVENTIONS

Individual interventions have, by most measures, been an area where progress is most indisputable. That is, firms such as PDI and the Center for Creative Leadership have built sizeable businesses around individual feedback. Over time, a few common practices have emerged. Feedback should be multi-sourced—from peers, staff, managers, and often family. Feedback should be multi-dimensional, including personal feedback, paper and pencil tests, norm-based survey assessments, and so on.

The Center for Creative Leadership has a model that is perhaps the standard. They provide an offsite experience which includes feedback from recent acquaintances. Often this is coupled with tools that have been developed and have norm bases to support conclusions and directions. For instance, the Center runs in-depth management programs, which provide individual leaders with feedback from subordinates, peers, and from managers.

The importance of individual contribution and performance has been raised, particularly at the CEO level. Kotter (1999) argues that individual leadership and growth are essential. He suggests strategies for change often fail in corporations because the changes do not alter behavior. Substantive change requires leadership and Kotter makes a compelling case that the winners will be those who outgrow their rivals.

The increase of focus on the individual corresponds to a general increased focus on the leader—the CEO as savior (Welch, 2001), the CEO as failure (Charan & Colvin, 1999), or the self-promoting leader (Collins, 2001). The implicit assumption is that the CEO leadership and management style have a huge influence on the organization and its functioning. Undoubtedly this is true. But, at the other end of the organization, even supervisor training may make a difference in organizational functioning— particularly for the staff to whom that supervisor represents management.

While one can observe that the use of feedback as a personal, and organizational, development tool has increased, and that it likely improves organizational functioning of the individual and the organization around that individual, it is hard to assess the long-term impact. How much does one person's improved leadership affect the organization? How long does the change last? How long is that style effective in the face of environmental and organizational change?

One of the historic criticisms of individual interventions is that they have relatively low impact. For multiple reasons, the investment decays over time. It may be the role is not supportive of change, colleagues are not supportive of new behavior, or the new behavior is not functional in terms of real organizational demands. One interesting consideration is how to better link individual interventions with group interventions. It is hard to estimate whether companies have made progress in achieving this linkage.

This is particularly interesting in the case of CEOs. The rise of the celebrity CEO has certainly put the CEO's contribution center-stage. However, other authors point out the fallacy of resting an entire company's success on the CEO's qualities and choices.

## THE ROLE OF THE CONSULTANT

In early writings, the consultant figured prominently, as the director of activity, facilitator of feedback, providing counseling and direction to team members. In some cases, the role seemed quite akin to that of management. In fact, there can even be a blurring of the roles, even when the consultant is practicing collaborative consultation.

In recent years, the role of the consultant has become more specialized and there has been greater focus on developing managers' capacity for the type of action research that consultants usually did. At the same time, the consultant has become more of a coach, counselor, adviser, and specialist resource. The ability to plan, design, and pull off a large group intervention requires specialist skills, as well as the ability to work with groups, bring human interaction design skills to bear, and the other capabilities traditionally associated with specialists in organizational change.

## ONGOING TENSIONS IN THE FIELD

Despite many years of practice and research, there are still debates, or tensions, that define the field. Though we attempt to outline these here, we cannot claim to resolve them. In fact, the ongoing debate allows the field to grow and develop. We believe that there are four tensions which point to important directions for future research and practice.

1. *A model for change*: While we clearly have numerous models, a meta-model would be beneficial. Each model has strengths and weaknesses, applicability and irrelevance. The field can benefit from teasing these apart.
2. *A value set for change*: There continues to be tension between change management that puts employees' well-being first and change management that serves only business needs. Clearly, this is often a false dichotomy—creating an either/or situation that need not necessarily exist. However, there are often choice points in change strategy which will favor one value over the other. This is an important issue for the field.
3. *Change effectiveness*: After so many years of work and research, we may not yet have a falsifiable body of knowledge. Our theories and predictive powers are weaker than other fields which started alongside ours. What can be done to develop better predictive powers?
4. *Change magnitude*: There continue to be arguments about the pace and scope of change, and exactly what we expect organizations to adapt to in what time frame.

## WHAT IS OUR MODEL FOR CHANGE?

In Chapter 9, Quinn and Weick outline four main models of change. Specifically, they describe them as follows.

1. *Life cycle theories* which describe change in terms of natural progress: start-up, grow, harvest, terminate, and (re)start-up. Change is driven by maturation processes, and challenges reflect obvious gates as the organization (and industry) moves from one phase to another.
2. *Teleological theories* which describe change as goal-driven. Goals are envisioned as a result of dissatisfaction or ambition and drive implementation. The cycle is goal set/search/evaluate to re-set/search/evaluate, and so on. Change is generated by purpose and social consensus.
3. *Dialectical theory* sees changes as events in which circumstances emerge, and then make their opposites clear by their own existence. To put it simply, the emergence of a thesis makes it possible to see the antithesis. The thesis and antithesis resolve via a synthesis which then enables the identification of another antithesis. Change is driven by pluralism, confrontation, and conflict. There is no clear or determinate direction in this model.
4. *Evolutionary theory* sees change as an event sequence of variation, selection, retention, and variation. It has a generative mechanism of competitive selection and resource scarcity.

Each of these theories has well-known proponents, developing models, predictions, and interventions based on the components of their model.

One benefit of the emergence of these models is that the models themselves will be elaborated. That is, we will build understanding of what changes lead to what outcomes, which lead to further changes. As we build the model, we enhance our ability to predict. For instance, changes in growth rate correspond to natural organization and industry development life cycles—and the reactions correspond to life cycle predictions. Teleological theory can also explain the findings: addressing opportunities (increase in growth rate) while managing threats (decline in growth rate).

At the same time, it seems certain that these models should be woven into a meta-model. Nothing is more frustrating than trying to apply the wrong explanatory variable to a situation, or to use a wrong or insufficient model. The classic dilemma for executives, for instance, is judging whether poor business performances reflect immutable industry facts, or managerial incompetence.

And undoubtedly, we will need to be more sophisticated about the interaction between change drivers, and the direction of causality. For instance, Engdahl et al. (2000) find that the structure–strategy concept as originally posited by Chandler is in reality a two-way causal relationship and that existing organizational structure has a high potential for biasing future situation-formulation in a hyper-competitive environment. This in turn has some serious implications for the field of organization development.

## THE UNDERLYING VALUES DRIVING CHANGE PROCESSES

Organization development has at its roots a humanist and human potential philosophy. As such, it seeks to validate human contribution and worth. Not surprisingly, it comes up against some conflict with so-called hard-headed theories of economically rational behavior and good business sense. This has fomented a long-running debate among practitioners and academics about which values take precedence. Given the choice, should executives choose what is ostensibly best for employees, or best for organization effectiveness?

Michael Beer has long pursued this debate (Beer et al., 1990; Beer & Nohria, 2000) arguing that this tension needs to be re-examined. Involving people in change, and helping them shape direction and implementation, are key to creating planned change that will take place. However, when these changes are insufficient to create an economically healthy organization, then those involved in the change find themselves disillusioned and no longer interested in participating. This can create a challenge—one balancing the need for results focus and engagement and commitment.

In their recent article (2000) authors Michael Beer and Nitin Nohria describe two archetypes—or theories—of corporate transformation that may help executives crack the code of change. Theory E is change based on economic value: shareholder value is the only legitimate measure of success, and change often involves heavy use of economic incentives, lay-offs, downsizing, and restructuring. Theory O is change based on organizational capability: the goal is to build and strengthen corporate culture. Most companies focus purely on one theory or the other, or haphazardly use a mix of both. Combining E and O is directionally correct, they contend, but it requires a careful, conscious integration plan.

Beer and Nohria present the examples of two companies, Scott Paper and Champion International, that used a purely E or purely O strategy to create change with only limited levels of success in both instances. They contrast those corporate transformations with that of UK-based retailer ASDA, which has successfully embraced the paradox between the opposing theories of change and integrated E and O. The lesson from ASDA? To thrive and adapt in the new economy, companies must make sure the E and O theories of business change are in sync in their own organizations.

One might also contend that certain business-driven decisions actually destroy business value. Take the frequent practice of lay-offs: companies often find themselves in the position of having to hire back key skills—often at higher rates or consultant prices. In some cases, former employees are collecting a pension and a consultant's fee. This creates higher costs and builds in cyclicality.

Clearly, employees now more than ever believe in their right to exercise their voice—their right to have an opinion about changes and to voice that opinion. The challenge is, particularly at management levels, whose voice carries the day. Simply having an opinion does not equate to it being the right idea or an authorized opinion. Part of the dilemma of engaging people in changes is that you invariably create more opinions to deal with. In addition, high engagement processes often annoy employees who see them as cosmetic involvement.

In fact, in the real life of organizations, the human dimension and the economic dimension are rarely identified so starkly. Reactions to change may have more to do with who does what when. Consider a downsizing action determined necessary by headquarters. Usually remote locations understand and accept the need for action, but take issue with how it is conducted—usually by the corporate center's rules and with little local flexibility.

As a discipline, Organization Development has not found a simple resolution to this issue. The demand for adaptability has increased, and knowledge of how to create an adaptable organization is more valuable than ever. Yet, we have no good answers on how to tap into the goodwill and discretionary effort of employees on a sustained basis. We lack effective models for what is in the best interest of the business (lay-offs to meet quarterly earnings targets vs a longer-term approach) and what is in the best interest of employees (when to engage them and how to best utilize their time).

## FUNDAMENTALS OF MAKING CHANGE

We have many new tools—electronic and bilateral—that help us achieve a more dynamic change process. However, there is still little formulaic knowledge about how to create definitive and sustainable change, much less how to measure or evaluate real change. It would be nice to have the predictive power emerging from the field of economics. For instance, economists can predict and measure the effect of interest rate cuts, or unemployment. Organization development has little to compare. Even stranger, organization development has not really created menus of classic organizational problems. For instance, most companies struggle with the relationship between the sales force and the marketing staff. This is based on deep differences in the work to be done—the time frame of evaluation, the degree of concreteness, etc.

As some have pointed out, despite over 50 years of being a field, we have little more than rehashed concepts and simplistic ideas. We still face a fundamental challenge of creating a story which persuades line executives to sign up for organization development work as a way of managing the business.

While work within the past 10 years has become richer and more descriptive, it is still unclear whether we have built a falsifiable body of knowledge. Numerous authors (Golembiewski, 2001; Macy & Izumi,

1993; Micklethwait & Wooldridge, 1996; O'Shea & Madigan, 1997) have pointed out that we run the risk of being little more than gurus and charlatans.

Similarly, change professionals have developed multiple models, and linked up with many other change efforts. Their efforts have gone under many banners: total quality management, re-engineering, right sizing, restructuring, cultural change, and turnarounds. However, here also cumulative theory and knowledge are rare.

Other authors go further, claiming that most change efforts fail (Kotter, 2000). A few of those efforts have been very successful. A few have been utter failures. Most fall somewhere in between, with a distinct tilt toward the lower end of the scale. The lessons that can be learned will be relevant to more and more organizations as the business environment becomes increasingly competitive in the coming decade.

Leaders often feel they have, and, in fact, do have, a limited window in which to make change (Lear, 2001). A CEO, particularly a new CEO, may be on trial and need to demonstrate early success in order to build momentum for successful changes. While a complete transformation may take decades, leaders often need a meaningful transformation in shorter time frames.

Again, this is a debate which remains unresolved. One might see change as best starting with formal mechanisms—structure, rewards, selection. However, the informal aspects of organizations can still overwhelm formal mechanisms. We have few clear ways to manage, control, or even influence the informal elements of organizations.

## IS THERE TOO MUCH CHANGE?

For years, scholars and practitioners have debated whether change is speeding up. Certainly, there have been issues around change fatigue (Morgan, 2001), ill-conceived change-for-change-sake, and so forth. The question is whether there is more change today than there was in past decades, and whether the need for change management and organization development skills is more important now than in the past.

Clearly, some data, such as technology statistics (the doubling of computing power yearly, the dissemination of technology development—25 years for the telephone to reach half of the US population, and 1 year for the Internet to reach 45 percent of the US population), suggest change is becoming faster. The pacing of movies and cartoons is faster. At the same time, one can argue that a change of pastor in the local church in 1900 felt more dramatic to the community than the changes wrought by the Internet feel in 2003.

Debating the magnitude of change is probably fruitless, but there is some value in understanding the magnitude of experienced change in organizations (Morgan, 2001). Repeated changes that seem to change direction, or seem totally directionless, undoubtedly undermine an organization's ability to change. Managing the communication of change seems to be critical (Sinickas, 2001).

Business consultant William Bridges attacks an area of managing change that many not only avoid, but also do not even recognize—the human side of change. Directed at managers and employees in today's corporations, where change is necessary to revitalize and improve corporate performance, his book addresses the fact that it is people who have to carry out the change (Bridges, 1991).

## CONCLUSION

In sum, there has been substantial progress in the field of organization development—both in practice and in theory. In our view, the progress has been uneven, with growth spurts in certain areas (structure, individual feedback, large group interventions, among others), and unconsolidated progress in others (such as team dynamics). The field could benefit by finding a way to combine models of change, as well as interventions to develop a point of view on which drivers affect which outcomes, thus focusing on intervention effectiveness. Finally, we need to build a stronger sense of core beliefs and values around the intentions of change, as well as the true scope and time frame for major organizational change.

# REFERENCES

Abell, D.F. (1999) Competing today while preparing for tomorrow. *Sloan Management Review*, **Spring**, **40**(3), 73–81.

Bartlett, C. & Ghoshal, S. (1989) *Managing Across Borders*. Boston: Harvard Business School Press.

Becker, G. (1978) *The Economic Approach to Human Behavior*. Chicago: University of Chicago Press.

Beer, M., Eisenstadt, R.A. & Spector, B. (1990) *The Critical Path to Corporate Renewal*. Boston: Harvard Business School Press.

Beer, M. & Nohria, N. (2000) *Breaking the Code of Change*. Boston: Harvard Business School Press.

Beer, M. & Walton, E. (1987) Organization development. *Annual Review of Psychology*, **February**, **38**, 339–367.

Bridges, W. (1991) *Managing Transitions: Making the Most of Change*. New York: Perseus Press.

Bunker, B.B. & Alban, B.T. (1997) *Large Group Interventions*. San Francisco: Jossey-Bass.

Bushe, G.R. (1995) Advances in appreciative inquiry as an organization development intervention. *Organization Development Journal*, **13**(3), 14–22.

Buzan, T. & Buzan, B. (2000) *The Mind Map Book*. London: BBC Consumer Publishing.

Cahoon, A.R. (2000) Using the search conference technique for team socialization and strategic planning. In R.T. Golembiewksi (ed.) *Handbook of Organizational Consultation* (2nd edn). New York: Marcel Dekker.

Chandler, A. (1962) *Strategy and Structure: Chapters in the History of the American Industrial Enterprise*. Cambridge, MA: MIT Press.

Charan, R. & Colvin, G. (1999) Why CEOs fail. *Fortune*, **21 June**, **139**(12), 68 *et seq.*

Collins, J. (2001) *Good to Great: Why Some Companies Make the Leap... and Others Don't*. New York: HarperCollins.

Engdahl, R.A., Keating, R. & Aupperle, K.E. (2000) Strategy and structure: chicken or egg? (Reconsideration of Chandler's paradigm for economic success). *Organization Development Journal*, **Winter**, **18**(4), 21–33.

Finley, M. (2002) All for one, but none for all. *Across the Board*, **January/February**, **39**(1), 45–47.

Ford, J.D. & Ford, L.W. (1995) The role of conversation in producing intentional change in organizations. *Academy of Management Review*, **20**(3), 541–570.

Galbraith, J.R. (1977) *Organization Design*. Reading, MA: Addison-Wesley.

Galbraith, J.R. (2000) *Designing the Global Corporation*. San Francisco: Jossey-Bass.

Golembiewski, R.T. (2001) Six orientations for the reader: an interpretive introduction. In R. Golembiewski (ed.) *The Handbook of Organizational Consulting* (pp. 1–26). New York: Marcel Dekker.

Gunther, M. (2001) God and business. *Fortune*, **9 July**, **144**(1), 58.

Guzzo, R.A., Nalbantian, H., Kiefer, D. & Doherty, J. (2003) *Play to Your Strengths*. New York: McGraw-Hill.

Hackman, R. & Oldham, G. (1980) *Work Redesign*. Reading, MA: Addison-Wesley.

Hornstein, H. (2001) Organizational development and change management: don't throw the baby out with the bath water. *Journal of Applied Behavioral Science*, **June**, **37**(2), 223–226.

Janoff, S. & Weisbord, M. (1999) *Future Search: An Action Guide to Finding Common Ground in Organizations and Communities*. San Francisco: Berrett-Koehler.

Kegan, R. & Lahey, L.L. (2001) *How the Way We Talk Can Change the Way We Work: Seven Languages for Transformation*. San Francisco: Jossey-Bass.

Kotter, J. (1999) *Leading Change*. Boston: Harvard Business School Press.

Kotter, J.P. (2000) Leading change: why transformation efforts fail. *HBR On Point*, **February**, 13 pp.

Kotter, J.P. & Heskett, J. (1992) *Corporate Culture and Performance*. Boston: Harvard Business School Press.

Kramer, R. (1999) Organizing for global competitiveness: the Corporate Headquarters. *Design Chief Executive Digest*, **3**(2).

Larkin, T.J. & Larkin, S. (1996) Reaching and changing frontline employees. *Harvard Business Review*, **May/June**, **74**(3), 95–104.

Lawler, E. (1973, 1994) *Motivation in Work Organizations*. San Francisco: Jossey-Bass.

Lawler, E. (1999) *Rewarding Excellence: Pay Strategies for the New Economy*. San Francisco: John Wiley & Sons, Ltd.

Lawrence, P.R. and Lorsch, J.W. (1965) *Organization and Environment*. Boston: Harvard Business School Press.

Lear, R. (2001) Early warning signs. *Chief Executive*, **June**, No. 168, 12.

Macy, B.A. & Izumi, H. (1993) Organizational change, design and work innovation: a meta-analysis of 131 North American field studies—1961–1991. In R.W. Woodman & W.A. Passmore (eds) *Research in Organizational Change and Development, Volume 7*. Greenwich, CT: Jai Press.

McFarland, J. (2001) Corporate portals. *Harvard Management Communication*, letter, **June**, 4(6), 9–11.

Micklethwait, J. & Wooldridge, A. (1996) *The Witch Doctors: Making Sense of the Management Gurus*. New York: Crown Business.

Miles, R. & Snow, C. (1986) *Organizational Strategy, Structure, and Processes*. New York: McGraw-Hill.

Morgan, N. (2001) How to overcome change fatigue. *Harvard Management Update*, **July**.

Nadler, D. (1977) *Feedback and Organization Development: Using Data-Based Methods*. Reading, MA: Addison-Wesley.

Nadler, D.A., Gerstein, M.S. & Shaw, R.B. (1992) *Organizational Architecture: Designs for Changing Organizations*. San Francisco: Jossey-Bass.

Nadler, D.A. & Tushman, M.I. (1999) The organization of the future: strategic imperatives and core competencies for the 21st century. *Organizational Dynamics*, **Summer**, 45–60.

Nohria, N. & Eccles, R.G. (1992) *Networks and Organizations: Structure, Form, and Action*. Boston: Harvard Business School Press.

Novartis (2000) Novartis Annual Report 2000: Operational Review. Available at http://www.novartis.com/news/en/corporate_inter_financial.shtml.

O'Shea, J. & Madigan, C. (1997) *Dangerous Company: The Consulting Powerhouses and the Businesses They Ruin*. New York: Crown Business.

Porras, J.I. & Robertson, P.J. (1992) Organizational development: theory, practice, research. In M.D. Dunnette & L.M. Hough (eds) *Handbook of Organizational Psychology* (pp. 719–822). Palo Alto, CA: Consulting Psychologists Press.

Porras, J.I. & Silvers, R.C. (1991) Organization development and transformation. *Annual Review of Psychology*, **42**, 51–78.

Quinn, R. & Weick, K. (1999) Organization change and development. *Annual Review of Psychology*, **February, 50**, 361–386.

Schein, E. (1997) *Organization Culture and Leadership*. San Francisco: Jossey-Bass.

Schein, E. (1999) *Process Consultation Revisited: Building the Helping Relationship*. Reading, MA: Addison-Wesley.

Senge, P. (1999) *The Fifth Discipline: The Art and Science of the Learning Organization*. New York: Doubleday.

Sessa, V.I. & Taylor, J.J. (2000) *Executive Selection: Strategies for Success*. San Francisco: Jossey-Bass.

Sinickas, A. (2001) Communication is not optional. *Harvard Management Communication*, letter, **June**, 4(6), 1–3.

Srivastva, S. & Cooperrider, D. (1997) *Organizational Wisdom and Executive Courage*. Lanham, MD: Lexington Books.

Vogt, J. (1999) Consulting as empowerment: building capacity through participatory research, experiential learning and awareness. In R. Golembiewski (ed.) *Handbook of Organizational Consultation*. New York: Marcel Dekker.

Vroom, V. (1964) *Work and Motivation*. New York: John Wiley & Sons, Ltd.

Welch, J. (2001) *Jack: Straight From the Gut*. New York: Warner Books.

Worren, N., Ruddle, K. & Moore, K. (1999) From organizational development to change management: the emergence of a new profession. *Journal of Applied Behavioral Science*, **September, 35**(3), 273–286.

# CHAPTER 8

# Dilemmas and Paradoxes in Organizing Change Processes
## A Critical Reflection

**Luc Hoebeke**
*Hoebeke, Staes & Partners, Bierbeek, Belgium*

## CHOOSING AND DECISION-MAKING: DIFFERENT DYNAMICS

Decision-making is still the central tenet in organizational and management literature. It is also central to organizational change. Deciding means influencing the state of affairs with the aim of changing the natural course of affairs. With this definition I want to broaden the concept of organizational change, which too often only refers to organizational restructuring. In practice, this restructuring can be reduced to the decision to draw a new organizational chart. The conventional wisdom of what an organization is can be illustrated by Figure 8.1 (see Checkland & Holwell, 1998). An organization is a combination of people and other resources in a structure which is used to take decisions to achieve defined goals and purposes. When this image is taken seriously, decisions become the major output of 'management' and the quality of these decisions can be measured. Good decisions are assessed through their relevance in achieving the stated goals and purposes. These kinds of decisions need to be fed by the right information, by the articulation of a limited set of options, and by a rational choice of the best option, the option which has the best cost–benefit ratio. Benefit is directly related to the articulated organizational goals and purposes.

This dry skeletal image of organizational behaviour looks very strange to someone who has experienced real people struggling with real organizational issues. The majority of conflicts, choices, and negotiations consist essentially of the accommodation between the agendas, the implicit and explicit purposes and goals, of all the involved actors and stakeholders. It is really an exception when goals and purposes are understood in the same way even in small groups: in my experience, sharing a common understanding is really a miracle. Once, as is normal in an organizational setting, we are confronted with loosely coupled networks of smaller or bigger groups, with lobbying and manipulation, with the 'creation' of facts and their interpretation, with a plethora of voices, silences, and exits, the conventional wisdom of organizations breaks apart in our hands. Nevertheless, choices are still unavoidable.

I think that the major shift in perspective necessary for relevant models of decision-making in organizations has to abandon the classical economic world-view of decision-making in scarcity and approach an underdeveloped part of economic theory, choosing out of abundance. To me it is paradoxical that neo-classical economic theory only talks about decisions on the allocation of *scarce* resources by referring to the author of the *Wealth of Nations*, Adam Smith. If information is the raw material for decision-making, or for choosing, then an abundance of information is much more an issue in

*Dynamics of Organizational Change and Learning.* Edited by J.J. Boonstra.
© 2004 John Wiley & Sons, Ltd. ISBN 0-471-87737-9.

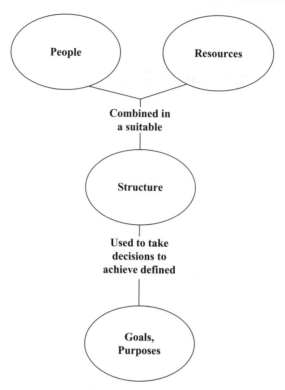

**FIGURE 8.1**  The simple model of an organization

organizations than its scarcity. And in the turbulent times in which we live, abundance of options is much more an issue than scarcity of means. Think, e.g., on the plethora of products and services which have become available in the IT world during the past five years. Choosing in abundance has quite different dynamics from decision-making in scarcity.

> When I am hiking in summer through the beautiful landscape of Provence in the South of France, decision-making when I get thirsty is rather easy, even if I am walking with other people. The slightest hint of something to drink, a small village, a green valley, the noise of running water, is sufficient to decide collectively to go towards it. If, with the same group of people, I am walking in one of the cities of Provence, where in the shadow of the trees one café follows another, the decision where to sit to have a drink becomes much more tricky. All kinds of preferences have to be agreed upon, and the functionality of thirst seems to be the least important argument to deal with the abundance of opportunities.

This simple metaphor illustrates the basic difference between decision-making in scarcity and choosing out of plenty. The classical approach to decision-making, as, e.g., described by Janis and Mann (1977), still puts strong emphasis on sharing and collecting the right data and information. Openness and the quality of the information process are the success criteria for the quality of the decision based upon them. Rightly, Janis points out, that under those circumstances, uncertainty creates the major dynamic in the process and uncertainty can be reduced when the right information becomes available. In uncertainty information helps. But uncertainty is a characteristic of scarcity of information. In abundance, ambiguity instead becomes an issue of uncertainty. The more information I have, the more difficult my choice will be. This phenomenon is called paralysis by analysis. Every supplementary report, every refined inquiry, every new scientific study adds to the ambiguity, e.g. political tergiversation over environmental issues illustrates this kind of paralysis.

In this chapter, I will try to provide a language, in which ambiguity in an environment of abundance can be articulated. A central notion of this language is the concept of *dilemma*, which I develop in the next section. Once I have clarified that notion, I will try to go into depth with three dilemmas, which in one form or another seem to contribute to choice dilemmas in all social systems. These dilemmas can be related to two fundamental paradoxes, with which we, as human beings, are confronted. As a systems theorist, looking out for invariables, and thus in a certain sense as an inveterate reductionist (the only way to deal with abundance, see Feyerabend, 1999), my claim is that trying to situate any organizational or institutional choice within the frame of these three dilemmas may help practitioners to deal with organizational issues. I will give some examples how in my practice as an organizational consultant I have made use of these dilemmas.

## FROM PROBLEMS TOWARDS DILEMMAS

One of the ways in which the scarcity model is inadvertently emphasized in an organizational context is by referring to organizational problems and problematics. Even now, the major legitimation for organizational change is to solve organizational problems. Once it is understood that dilemmas cannot be solved, the dilemma perspective could debunk much of this rationale. Organizational change, in its mainstream sense, will become less frequent. The concept of problem and problem-solving has its origins in the closed scientific and academic world, which has the freedom to choose, to define the problems to investigate and to solve, and to create the ideal setting for working: the laboratory, where all parameters are controlled so that the problem can be 'isolated'. In real life, and thus also in real organizational life, problems cannot be isolated. As one of my colleagues rightly stated: 'in organizations there are no problems, only people with problems, and stated problems are legitimate ways to express desires and wants'. Only once in my long experience as an organizational consultant have I met two directors of a blooming enterprise who declared their desire to change their organiza- tion. But on many occasions I saw how the rationale for change, although coming from a desire, was transformed into a series of imposed problems. This imposition could equally come from management as from too eager (a sign of desire) consultants. The reduction of organizational decision-making to or- ganizational problem-solving greatly impoverishes the abundance of organizational life. Furthermore, problem-solving always refers to the past, to the discovery of the causes of the problems, and the only reference to the future is that these causes have to be avoided henceforth. Many management books use past failures as their cases for helping 'managers' avoid making the same mistake in the future. Even the research in 'excellence' and in 'success' often emphasizes behaviour to be avoided to achieve it. The scientific approach necessarily builds upon the past. Choosing in abundance focuses upon the future, which is intrinsically unknown and abundant.

Srivastva and Cooperrider (1987) have stressed this point in their methodology of appreciative inquiry. Instead of approaching organizations through an inventory of problems and an inquiry into their causes, they suggest asking why the organizations are working in spite of the abundance of problems they seem to be coping with. They stress the fact that what is actually giving life to an organization, what makes it tick now, is the best guarantee for its future. In fact, it is their approach which brought me to the concept of abundance, while I was working as a business consultant in the former Yugoslavia, just before the war broke out in 1991.

In 1989 in ex-Yugoslavia everything was problematic: inflation of more than 1000 per cent a year, political and social turmoil, uncertainties of who was and who would become the owner of the enter- prises I was working for, demotivation and absenteeism (25 per cent was quite normal), you name it.

Focusing on the problems made me and my clients depressed, the 'Balkan' fatalism became an excuse for expressing this depression in inaction. The classic consultant's approach of classifying the problems, making a diagnosis, looking for causes, and eliminating these causes broke down. The only way I could start to regain effectiveness was to turn the perspective round. Couldn't we try to understand why the system was still working?: why were there still workers coming to the enterprise?; why were the machines still running?; why were clients still buying products and services and still paying for them?; how come production materials were still available and suppliers were delivering goods, etc.? Trying to discover the forces behind the (sometimes poor) life of the enterprise and trying to develop them created a completely different dynamic. Hope and faith were minimally restored, self-confidence was boosted, new opportunities emerged. In fact, choosing between new emerging alternatives became much more the issue than the discovery of the 'best' solution, the 'only' way to get out of the mess.

Once the perspective of abundance is taken, decision-making changes in nature. The environmental constraints no longer help to rationalize a decision, the environment offers itself as a series of dilemmas, which provide fields in which the 'chooser' is obliged to take a position. In abundance you cannot have it all, in scarcity you get that one thing you were looking for. Choosing in abundance always means that I am conscious of losing something. In scarcity, I have to find the 'right' solution to my problem, the best alternative, the 'winning' solution. In abundance, there is no 'best' solution which presents itself. Whatever is chosen, I will pay a price for it, because every choice forecloses other options and opportunities.

It is quite normal that in collectivities, in social systems, the discourse of scarcity, of necessity, is abused again and again: the choices are limited and the dictatorship of necessity legitimates the overruling of the individual wishes and desires. 'It is better that one man dies for the people' has always been an argument for those in power to legitimate the overruling of the individual. It is a bit strange that the man referred to normally does not belong to the power caucus.

I suggest the following criterion for assessing the quality of the leadership of any organization or institution. If the driving forces of the change to be made in an organization are referred to by the leadership as external necessities, the market, the economic situation, shareholder value, the competition, a crisis, survival, or whatever the fashion of the day, my conclusion is that there is a poor leadership. When a leader has the courage to refer to his own vision, to his self-confidence, to his dream, then the leadership shows some quality. Therefore, most of the classical approaches to business strategies only help poor leadership: the environmental parameters are the most important ones, see, e.g., Porter (1990) and René ten Bos (2000). But if desire and vision are the prime movers for choosing strategic directions, this can only work when the desires and visions of the major stakeholders of the business have been accommodated. Once one desire is legitimate, all the stakeholders can legitimate their own interests and desires. The environment loses its threatening or exploitative character (threats and opportunities) but offers a field of dilemmas in which choices have to be made.

I think that the time has come to operationalize the concept of dilemma. Technically, an articulated dilemma consists of two contradictory statements, each one of which is defendable. The short-term vs the long-term perspective, so much debated in business, is typically a dilemma. The focus on short-term results is defendable. Without them the long term cannot even be dreamt about. But also the long-term perspective is defendable, without it, organizational effort can get dispersed into all kind of interesting short-term endeavours. Good managers are torn apart by this dilemma and are obliged to choose a position between what is called the two horns of the dilemma.

Innovation vs improvement is another classical business dilemma. Continuous improvement focuses on the existing ways of working, the existing products and services, and tries to improve them incrementally. As raw material for these improvements, it uses emerging problems, customer complaints, process breakdowns, etc. Innovation is a completely different game: innovation disrupts the normal business, creates a lot of problems, changes the rules of the game. Here, also, a manager cannot have it both ways. He or she has to position him- or herself in the field of tension between both perspectives.

---

## CASE STUDY: FINANCIAL SERVICES

As an intermediary, banks have a basic dilemma in their primary process. They have a conserving function, they have to take care of the possessions of clients. On the other hand, these conservation functions can only be dealt with by taking risks, by what banks call 'commercial' activities. The professionalism of a banker consists of his or her ability to keep both perspectives in mind and to position his or her choices between both perspectives.

---

## CASE STUDY: SOCIAL AFFAIRS

In a social work department, I was confronted with the following dilemma. Customer-orientedness meant serving the people applying for unemployment or welfare subsidies. The social worker tries to help his or her clients. On the other hand, the money spent on unemployment or welfare subsidies is public money. It should not be spent without reason. Having this dilemma at the core of the profession of the social worker generated an increase in the number of lawsuits the department had to handle. Nevertheless, the department won most of these lawsuits. A new position had been established in the field of tension of the dilemma.

---

A hypothesis which I started to test, once I took the dilemma perspective, is that all institutions, all organized work has a value added to deal with societal dilemmas. Indeed, choosing a position between the two horns of a dilemma is an uncomfortable, sometimes painful, job. We try to delegate it to others. But it is exactly this difficulty which feeds the dynamic in organizations to resolve dilemmas. Dilemmas create a dynamic of splitting. Many conflicts, inefficiencies, and a lot of distrust between organizational departments are the result of this splitting. Different groups, different departments have the job of optimizing one horn of the dilemma. People in this situation mostly find themselves in a go-between situation between the two horns. Conflicts arising from dilemmas in organizations create the organizational tone, and are essential to its life. Bureaucracies are so 'dead', because all dilemmas have been organized away through splitting. When the mood of management is that conflicts should be avoided, we have the dynamics of bureaucratization in place. Many attempts at organizational change to get rid of bureaucracy are doomed to fail while the dynamics of conflict avoidance are still prevalent. Perhaps this is the main reason why, in spite of a fashionable anti-bureaucracy promoted in the management literature, bureaucracy is still the mainstream organizational form.

The division between policy-making and operations is one way to avoid the dilemma between the short and the long term. Some planners are only concerned with the short-term issues, while others focus on long-term planning. Where both meet, the real issues appear: implementing policies in existing operations is where most energy is spent and the frustrations soar. The actual tendency to appoint temporary managers for this job is one way of avoiding the real issues. As go-betweens, the temporary managers can escape in time, they do not have to live with the results of their work.

As long as innovation can be situated in the offsite R&D laboratories, it is not disturbed and it does not disturb the normal business activities. Only when innovations become part of the normal business activities does the trouble start. Vested interests start to fight against the changes of the rules of the game, which inevitably accompany innovations. Often task forces or project groups are created as go-betweens between innovation and normal business. They are the locus of the real fights to come to an accommodation in the field between the two horns of the dilemma.

---

## CASE STUDY: CREDIT CARD

Incredibly or not, this is a true experience in a credit card company. The sales people got a bonus for the number of credit cards they could sell. But the credit department got a bonus for the number of credit cards of bad payers they could get rid of. The dilemma between the sales part and the 'conserving' part had been split into two departments, which unconsciously were destroying each other's work and getting rewarded for it. The normal way in which this division is handled in banks is by the mechanism of delegating upwards. The fact that banks normally have a much higher number of 'directors' per employee than, for example, production plants can be explained by the large number of go-between tasks that these directors undertake.

---

## CASE STUDY: SOCIAL WORK DIVISION OF LABOUR

In the social work department originally there were social workers who did the intake of the clients, while others had to take the decision to grant the subsidy or not. The former could be completely client-oriented, while the latter were the guardians of the law, focusing upon the legitimate use of the taxpayers' money. The group of social workers boosted their professionalism, once they had to take on both horns of the dilemma. For a given client, one social worker did the intake, while another decided upon the attribution of the subsidy. Their roles could be reversed for another client. In the previous situation, when the division was institutionalized in the social work department, the go-betweens were the employees who had to deal with the clients after the decision was taken, those who had to implement the decision. They were the victims of angry phone calls from unsatisfied clients, they received the weight of the go-between function.

---

## CASE STUDY: PRODUCTION FACTORY

The dilemma between efficient operations of a production plant and the satisfaction of the demands (quality and delivery times) of the customers is mostly handled by the production planning department. They are the go-betweens between the sales people, who complain that the plant always produces what cannot be sold, and the production people, who complain that the sales people never can sell what they produce. Materials management and inventories are a result of the split between both perspectives. They are the go-betweens between production and sales.

Dilemmas place managers in an either–or situation, which only can be dealt with through an and–and attitude. For this reason, both sides of the dilemma must be defendable. Once the right–wrong judgement creeps into a dilemma, it loses its tension. Figure 8.2 represents the relationship between abundance and dilemmas, the two horns of abundance, which at the same time are the two horns of a dilemma, and they create the field in which a 'decision-maker' has to position him- or herself to make a choice.

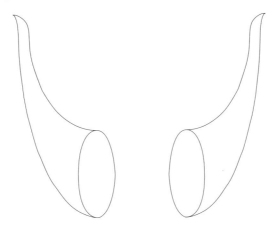

**FIGURE 8.2** Horns of a dilemma as two horns of abundance

## A PARADOXICAL VIEW OF ORGANIZED WORK

The concept of dilemmas gives a specific perspective upon organized work. In fact, human beings can survive like other animals and living systems, without the complexity of organized work. Tax systems, breweries, just-in-time logistics, stock exchanges, and you name it have intrinsically no biological survival function. They are typical expressions of human work, of human culture. Since the start of humanity, the division of labour, the division of roles between men and women, has made the human task of mere biological survival more complex. Apparently, evolution has developed in human beings a central nervous system which is much too complex for biological reasons. The way that we human beings deal with this excess of complexity (this abundance) is by creating complex ways of dealing with one another. Organizations are just as much cultural artefacts as potteries and cave paintings: they permit us to cope with our own complexity. There is no necessity for economic life: there are enough people in our real world who are able to survive on mere subsistence as autonomous beings. You can find them in the slums of all the big cities of the world: marginalized children and adults. The fact that we judge this situation as unworthy for human beings does not deny the fact that this way of survival is possible.

Organizations are not caused by necessity, they are expressions of culture, of the way human beings *like* to deal with one another. Organizing is creating desired relations and avoiding undesired ones. Biologically, organizations are superfluous. It seems, then, very strange to me that organizational survival is invoked to legitimate the language of necessity and scarcity in human affairs. Even more, that a biological law, the survival of the fittest and competitive advantage, is at the base of the actual economic ideology. Organizations are not species, their survival is irrelevant. The only biological species worthy to talk about is the human species, which cannot yet be labelled the fittest. I do not want to be wicked, but sometimes I get the impression that a glut of organizations is actually endangering the biological survival of this species. What are essentially the creations of an abundance of capabilities in the human being become a dictatorial must, which subjugates the individual.

---

### CASE STUDY: TECHNICAL UNIVERSITY OF ST PETERSBURG

In 1993 I met some students at the Technical University of St Petersburg, Russia. For 75 years of the communist regime, the government had told the people that they had to suffer and work hard so that finally paradise would arrive, if not for them, at least for their children. In the changing Soviet

Union, the same people came with an apparently new message: in order to transform the planned economy into a market economy, all Russians had to go through a painful economic shock therapy, so that at last, after this experience, they would see their dreams come true. Strangely enough, the same power caucus who gave the message in communist times was giving the new capitalist message. The fact that the core of the message had not changed, as I told the students, had escaped them. Again, the official discourse had used the terms of necessity, so that alternative ways could not be explored. A great opportunity to deal with new options, with unexplored alternatives, was foreclosed immediately by the 'new' apparatchiks.

Apparently, institutions have a great difficulty in dealing with the concept of abundance. Something essential in human beings must exist, which in fact inhibits the abundance perspective and thus avoids dilemmas and working through them. In an earlier book (Hoebeke, 1994), I tried to articulate the two basic paradoxes every human being faces:

> The paradox of I and Thou
> My existence and my self-consciousness, the development of my identity, is due only to my participation in a social context, to my being and becoming with others. What I conceive as my life as an individual is only possible as I relate to others. Even my egocentricity or egoism is the result of my relations with others, of my altruism, my relatedness.

I learned the word 'I' from my parents! Anthony Wilden in his *System and Structure* synthesizes this idea by paraphrasing Descartes' aphorism: 'I think, thus I am', by 'I speak, thus we are'.

> The paradox of the consciousness of death while alive
> The most significant experience of that relatedness comes when, in fact, relations are broken. When self-evidences are breaking down they become part of our consciousness and of our language. And the death of those who are near and dear to me, is for me the most significant breakdown of a relation. Although I cannot imagine my own death, I can experience it as an individual through the death of others, the disappearance of all their relationships.

The hypothesis I want to explore further is that human culture is a way of working through these two paradoxes. And as organizations are essentially expressions of human culture, they give form in one way or another to these paradoxes. For this reason, I stated previously that all human activity systems are built upon dilemmas. Metaphorically, one could say that at the foundation of each institution is a fault line, a locus prone to generate earthquakes. The cultural value of institutions, a much broader concept than their economic value, and surely than their price, resides in their way of dealing with this fault line, with the dilemmas stemming from the two paradoxes. Institutions are crutches, which enable us, as human beings, to mature, so that at last we are able, on our own, to deal with both human paradoxes. Institutions have a parental function after we have left our parents. In this way, I interpret the riddle of the Sphinx to Oedipus at the gates of Thebes. Before the human being can deal autonomously with the two paradoxes, he needs the two supplementary legs of organizational life. At the end of his life, he discovers that the two-legged contradiction is worked through by his discovery of a third leg: the mystery of life and death, the mystery of I and Thou reveals the 'and' between both, the third component of the two paradoxes. But let us explore how institutions help us to confront these paradoxes.

## PARADOX 1: COLLABORATION AND COMPETITION, THE PARADOX OF I AND THOU

The dilemma between competition and collaboration has its origin in the paradox of the other. My identity is socially determined by others. For this reason I am fascinated by others, they help me to discover my self. At the same time I am afraid of them, because they also signify a threat to who I am:

they can reveal things about my self, which I don't like at all. The concept of interdependency may soften this two-sided aspect of my relation with others, nevertheless I have to come to terms with this paradoxical situation.

It is clear that here again institutions and organizations are social constructs in which we try to delegate this paradox. Whatever the rationale, the dynamics of organizational change are to be found primarily in the destruction of existing relations and the creation of new ones. The clearest way in which this paradox is expressed is by the dilemma of collaboration and competition. The paradox creates still more ambiguity, because of the fact that the real basis of collaboration is the differences between the collaborating parties, while the real basis of competition is the similarities between them. Mostly, the dominant organizational discourse states exactly the contrary. Conflicts stem from the unbridgeable gap between two parties, who are too different to come to terms with one another, and the basis of collaboration is shared values, or other commonalities, which make good friends able to collaborate. Apparently the paradox of the other and I is so tricky that we are not even able to recognize the basic dynamics of it.

When business strategies are focused upon competitors, a dynamic is created where competitors begin increasingly to copy each other. A certain understanding of benchmarking and best practices creates conflicts. In the name of competition everyone starts to adopt the same behaviour. The paradox of management theories stressing success and excellence states that if everyone follows the same path, the same methods, anyone will be the best one, the real winner, the only survivor. In the name of competition, all countries start to export the same products. Where Adam Smith was pointing to the synergy between countries, where certain countries could produce different things, because of their environmental and cultural idiosyncrasies, nowadays, competition between nations means that everyone should achieve the same economic norms and standards. Europe exports cars to the Far East and America, the Far East exports cars to Europe and America, America exports cars to Europe and the Far East. The more the differences are stressed in global competition, the more equal strategies are implemented. The similarity between many mission statements and many organization charts superficially implies competitive conflict, while in fact the nature of the activities of the 'competing' enterprises may be quite different.

On the contrary, new products and services are created between parties who are very dissimilar. Suppliers and customers with quite different cultures, values, and backgrounds make succesful joint ventures, e.g. electricity companies and chemical industries start to create combined heat and electricity plants in which the waste gases of the chemical plant become the raw material for the electricity-generating plant. Interdisciplinary endeavours in R&D environments give a richer harvest of innovations than in one discipline. One sees interesting alliances between sales and distribution enterprises and transport groups, which share between them the efficiency gains of their collaboration.

In fact, similarity is a much greater threat to identity than difference. One of the ways in which individuals and social systems are denying this threat is by over-emphasizing the few remaining differences. For this reason conflicts are said to have their origin in differences. The anthropologist René Girard (1978) has made the point very clear in all his works. The fear of being eaten by the other is much greater when I am similar to him: to kill or to be killed is much more a choice between equals than between dissimilars. Ecological collaboration is the normal way in which different species find their niche and live in symbiosis. Biodiversity therefore is resilient. Competition starts in monocultures, which are much more vulnerable. Scarcity as lack of variety makes competition between the few species much more probable.

## CASE STUDY: OFFICE ENVIRONMENT

Sometimes as a consultant I am called in because of a conflict situation. Two departments cannot work together because they claim their culture, their values are too different. I remember a beautiful open plan office in which two data-entry groups were put together for efficiency reasons. The result was open war: racial differences, the nature of the work, all kinds of arguments split the groups.

When for one of the groups the temperature was too high, for the other it was too cold. Even physically, the groups started to put a wall of lockers between them, contrary to the good intentions of the office architect. In fact, the groups did slowly start to collaborate when the threat of being seen as one big group could be lessened, by stressing the differences still more. The fear in both groups of being swallowed up by the other created the trouble. Management wanted to see the two groups as one pool, and this created exactly the conditions for war between them. Once the differences were again legitimated, collaboration between the two groups became possible. Many failures of mergers and acquisitions are due to the fact that management too quickly wants to create a shared identity, a shared corporate image. This is the best way to make collaboration very difficult. The drive to make the two parties equal threatens their original identity and makes them emphasize their incompatibility.

If the fascination-distance of the other creates such strong dynamics in human beings, it is quite normal that this resonates in our institutions. In the next section we will explore three different dilemmas, which are generated by the dynamics of the two paradoxes discussed below.

## PARADOX 2: CENTRIFUGAL VS CENTRIPETAL FORCES, THE LIFE AND DEATH PARADOX

The paradox of life is that it is always in danger of dying. Henri Atlan (1979), a French biologist, defined life as existing between smoke and the diamond. Smoke is completely dependent upon the forces impinging upon it from the environment, for that reason it has no identity, no coherence. Centrifugal forces tear it apart. A diamond is perfect coherence, the atoms are completely bound with one another. It is very difficult to break the coherence of a diamond. Centripetal forces are preponderant. Living systems have a certain coherence. To an observer they maintain their identity for a certain time, until they die, until the centrifugal forces overcome the centripetal ones. But living systems have also a certain plasticity, resilience, and adaptability. As open systems, they interact with their environment, exchange material and energy, without losing their coherence. They are able to cope with a certain amount of centrifugal forces.

Social systems also are living the tension between centrifugal and centripetal forces. The environment continuously impinges upon them, people come and go, materials come and go, money comes and goes. Nevertheless they keep a certain coherence, they remain recognizable for the different stakeholders. Some of their activities are more outward-directed: dealing with their customers or other environmental stakeholders. Other activities try to keep them together, to maintain their coherence, in spite of the centrifugal forces: from uniforms to plannings, from mission and value statements to mere coercion. Many organizational dilemmas can be situated on the axis between the centrifugal and centripetal forces. The dilemma is between standardization (centripetal) and customization (centrifugal) of products and services; for example, the idea of mass customization can only become true when the products and services are strongly modularized, this means assembled from standard modules.

The dilemma is between the stress upon rules and procedures (centripetal) and the breaking of the rules to take creative initiatives (centrifugal). When everyone follows the rules, we have a form of strike and the organization stops work, it becomes a diamond. This means that breaking the rules is normal behaviour in organizations. But all anarchistic tendencies to get rid of rules and regulations also lead to stalemate. Every move, every action has to be invented anew continuously, learning cannot take place. Without rules and conventions, a social system loses its coherence, its identity.

Many meetings in organizations have no other function than to stress that the participants belong to a certain group (centripetal). For those people who think that work should be done in these meetings (centrifugal), the meeting experience can be very frustrating. For those who see the meeting as a recurrent ritual (centripetal), those who want to work are a nuisance. They don't understand how things are done here!

The tension between life and death expresses itself in social systems as the tension between belonging to the system and escaping from it. Group pressure is so strong, because being rejected by the group reminds us of the breaking of relationships, which is typical of death. In many societies exile is a harsher sentence than the death sentence. At least one is executed in a social context, the execution reinforces the social system. To be exiled is to suffer a living death! The powerful coercive forces of institutions of all kind stem, taking this paradox seriously, from our association with death, once we have been exiled from them. That these forces generate peculiar dynamics in organizations is unavoidable. Furthermore, we will try to analyse typical organizational dilemmas with this paradox as a parameter.

# INSTITUTIONAL DETERMINISM: DILEMMAS GENERATED BY THE PARADOXES

I have always wondered why it is that in organizations and institutions some dynamic patterns seem to remain much longer than the life-span of the people working in them.

---

## CASE STUDY: AUTOMOTIVE INDUSTRY

In the 1980s I did some work for the Antwerp plant of General Motors-Opel. Although the merger between the two companies was completed before the Second World War, there were still two factions in the factory. Even now, the signs at the entrance of the plant sometimes emphasize GM, at other times Opel. And this is not the only case in which I discovered remnants of previous mergers and acquisitions, even when the whole working population had changed in the meantime.

---

I think that the reader can discover on their own what I call *institutional determinisms*. Surely, those who are involved in organizational change processes are best aware of the nature of these determinisms. What sometimes is called a cultural change only is feasible when the positioning in the basic dilemmas of the organization has changed. This is a long-term process. The hypothesis, which I want to explore further, is that the resilience of these determinisms is based upon the loss of the memory of the dilemmas, which belong to the core of these institutions. And these dilemmas are forgotten, because of the unconscious repression of the two paradoxes, which I developed in the previous section. In the following paragraphs I will develop three basic dilemmas, which can be viewed as central to institutions and organizations. They are central, because nowadays the two sides of the dilemma have been organized away. Each horn is theoretically covered by specialized institutions, which apparently cannot be covered by the other horn of the dilemma. I call the dilemmas: *money and power*, *science and politics*, *faith and ethics*. The way they are dealt with in institutions constitutes what I may call their basic identity. At a time when the majority of institutions are fighting for their credibility, it seems to me that rediscovering these dilemmas and confronting them may help these institutions reaffirm their roots and increase their self-confidence. If not, they will undermine themselves in a self-regulating way and will disappear: without meaning, no institutions.

Before developing the three dilemmas separately, I think it may be useful to write something about the specific meanings I attribute to the six words used to describe them. The words I use are so ambiguous, have such an abundance of meanings, that I have to clarify my choice of them. Although it is extremely difficult for me to make the two sides of the dilemma defendable (I have my own prejudices and ideological bias), nevertheless I will try to justify all of them:

- *Money*: As a coin has two faces, money has two major functions, possession and exchange. I use the word money here only from the exchange perspective. Originally, money had only a barter function: shells in Polynesia and copper crosses in Katanga had literally only one side of the coin, their exchange value. Later on, the head of the king or emperor or the stamp of the national banks were added, to point to the owners of the money, those having the power.

- *Power*: This is the word I use to identify the other side of the coin, the side containing the head of the king or emperor, the perspective of possession and ownership. Checkland (Checkland & Scholes, 1991) has a very pragmatic way of defining the role in which this kind of power is invested: the owner is the one who can stop a human activity system. Although ideologically I have problems with the fact that people can own people, in my practice I am frequently confronted with this kind of ownership behaviour. This form of 'slavery' will always be human: it is a peculiar way to deal with the paradox of the Other. When I can decide upon his life and death, his selection and firing, his belonging to a social system, and his exile, I have the illusion that the Other is Mine. I can only tolerate people behaving in this way, but will never be able to accept their behaviour. For this reason, I don't want to deny it and take it as a defendable horn of the first dilemma. The pain and frustration coming from organizational restructurings are mainly due to the changes in the internal owner structure. When one's place in the turf is no longer determined, the turf battle can start.

- *Science*: The perspective that I take upon science is its critical position in society. Good science has always questioned the dominant ideologies of its time: in this sense the dialogues of Socrates were his specific way of expressing a scientific stance, as well as the way Copernicus and later Gallileo challenged the dominant cosmological world-view. This perspective requires the ability to be concerned with basic societal issues, but at the same time to be able to take a certain distance, a critical stance. Vickers (1995) in his *The Art of Judgment* is a marvellous exemplar of this scientific stance when he develops the concept of appreciative systems. He places appreciation and also scientific appreciation in the hermeneutic tradition, where in fact it belongs. The ideology that science provides truths *of* reality instead of truths *for* reality is fundamentally anti-scientific, because it forecloses a critical stance in relation to itself, by abusing Reality, dissociated from the one interpreting it, as the ultimate authority. Those who speak in name of the Reality are cheating themselves and others. They only can be part of Reality and cannot intrinsically put themselves outside it. Human beings are never objective subjects, they are no more than subjective objects. This statement questions fundamentally the scientific ambitions of management and organization studies in general and of the academic MBAs in particular.

- *Politics*: It may seem strange that I make an outspoken difference between power and politics, which normally are always mentioned in one breath. For me politics refer to those activities in which the ownership issues are still under debate. The owner, the executive who has the power to stop human activities, is acting beyond politics. The representative, the most typical role for the one who is involved in politics, is at the centre of important societal issues. According to Checkland (Checkland & Scholes, 1991), a representative is one who most embodies the role of actor, being able to speak in the name of other actors. Politics is the arena in which representatives of different value systems and their believers are doomed to come together and to interact. It is the arena where the ownership contracts emerge and change. Politics is a civilized way to make war. As long as politics are seen as a negative characteristic for organizations, war and destruction are on the horizon; for example, resistance to change has not to be seen as a power issue but as a political issue and dealt with politically. People have not to be convinced: conditions have to be created so that people can agree.

- *Faith*: The norms and values of someone acting out of faith are internal. There is an inner drive, which sometimes recklessly ignores the norms and values of a social system. People acting out of faith act inside out, their inner truth shapes the world they are living and acting in. For this reason it can be said that faith can move mountains. These mountains are first removed inside the one who has the faith, and then the outside mountains can be perceived in a completely different way. Strategic organizational changes which have as their rationale the fear of environmental changes show a lack of faith.

- *Ethics*: These are the norms and values which are accepted as given in a social system. They may be written explicitly or may be internalized by those belonging to the social system. They refer to the way things are done here. In this way economics belong to ethics and are not a 'scientific' discipline, e.g. the concept of intellectual ownership, with patents and licences, has only meaning in dominant Western ethics. In East Asia the concept of intellectual ownership is not even understandable. All the fuss about copies and copyright is, in my opinion, nothing more than a rearguard action of a war that has already been lost.

I hope that this first approach may enhance the understanding of the three dilemmas which will be developed in the three following sections of this chapter.

## THE DILEMMA BETWEEN POWER AND MONEY, BETWEEN THE CUSTOMS AND THE SMUGGLERS

Some years ago I discovered the seminal work of Jane Jacobs (1992), *Systems of Survival: A Dialogue upon the Moral Foundations of Commerce and Politics*. Brilliantly, she develops a view on two perspectives upon human activities. She calls them the commercial moral syndrome and the guardian moral syndrome. She helped me to discover the first dilemma, the dilemma between money and power.

Ask yourself: what is the cause of the greatest evil in this world, money or power? If you answer money, you probably belong to the customs, the guardians, if you answer power, you probably belong to the commercials, the smugglers. Here follows an over-stereotyped description of both positions of the dilemma.

We, 'the customs', are concerned about boundaries: what comes in and goes out is problematic. It distracts us from the task of keeping and saving what we possess. What we use for production and consumption are the means we have. Our possession must be safeguarded against external disturbances. We build fences and alarm systems to protect us against intruders. Our possessions keep us together, make us belong to the same group, the same family. Our uniforms are the guarantee of our mutual loyalty. We prepare ourselves for the fight against potential intruders, raiders, who envy our possessions. They want what we have: they are our competitors. When confronted with scarcity, when the exploitation of our possessions, raw materials, money, and human resources, is not enough to maintain us, then we have to increase our territory, our possessions. We prefer to do this peacefully, by colonizing territories, inhabited by primitive people. As the Greeks made it so wonderfully clear: the non-Greeks are *Barbaroi*, barbarians. Look how badly these nomads use their territory, their possessions, how they lack care. But we can civilize them, so they start to belong to us. We will educate them out of their under-development, how they can use their territory, badly defined, their raw materials, carelessly used. In the extreme case, we have to make war. Our neighbours do not know what to do with their riches, and we are hungry. This legitimates our raids and wars. We do it for our wife and kids, for our heritage and country, for our capital and cultural patrimonium.

We, 'the smugglers', are concerned about boundaries: what we cannot exchange through them is problematic. It hinders our production and consumption. What we have in plenty, in superabundance, we want to exchange with others. We have to protect our free trade against the customs, who try to hinder us with all kinds of regulations. We like to cheat them, but avoid violence as much as possible. They have better arms. We also like to cheat each other as a game, we are not too loyal to each other, but we know the rules of the game. Our competition stays inside these rules, to avoid internecine war. We don't like to be recognized, therefore we avoid uniforms and all signs which can show to which group we belong. We adapt ourselves easily to a variety of circumstances and people. We also profit from the stupid wars that the customs undertake from time to time. It permits us to trade in all kind of new products and services. We have a long tradition of trading with the indigenous people, who were civilized by the customs. Foreign products and services keep our interest and business going.

Jane Jacobs rightly uses the words 'politics' and 'commerce' to differentiate the perspective of the guardians, who fear centrifugal forces, and the commercials, who fear centripetal forces. But, as I mentioned in my introduction to the dilemmas, I should have used the word *power* instead of *politics*. Unfortunately, in our society, power and commerce have been assigned to two areas of activities. Power is reduced to the public domain while commerce is reduced to private business. The dilemma of the centrifugal–centripetal tension in society has been organized away, by assigning its horns to separate activity domains. This creates some strange incongruencies in both domains.

Governments are one of the major consumers and producers in Western economies. Politicians increasingly use the management language of private business and increasingly rely on marketing and advertising techniques to spread their messages.

Big corporations have headquarters which are pure power caucuses, where each division head guards his or her own territory against intruders and tries to widen his or her sphere of influence. All this energy is spent without any regard to the commercial aspects of the business. Economic rationalities are invoked to legitimate mergers and acquisitions. Being the biggest (the Fortune 500 as a list of honour), being top is the aim, even if these huge corporations have to exploit their customers. Free markets are invoked to build empires, oligopolies, and, if feasible, monopolies. Even more, market strategies are completely defined in terms of war, of the conquest of markets as territories. The concept of market share, one of the central tenets of marketing theory, is a pure power concept. While fortunately on a much lower level, competitors who still have a feeling for the commercial syndrome are making price agreements and other deals, at headquarters, strategic war schemes are being planned.

Apparently, the two horns of the dilemma affirm themselves in all kind of organizations and institutions. In the management literature, power has a negative connotation, while it is intrinsically linked to normal human behaviour.

The contradiction becomes even stronger in the fashionable concept of empowerment. Those who have power have to distribute it to their employees. But as we have seen, the power perspective owns the employee, and its adherents fear to share it, because of the specific way in which they deal with the paradox of the other. Ownership can only be taken, executive power is taken up by everyone who acts with or without permission. The one who gives power to the other is making him/her powerless. The abused concept of delegation of power is a justification for abusing power and ownership. Bureaucracies are nothing other than feudal systems in disguise. Loyalty and obedience, the chain of command and control in other words, are its underlying ethics, also in private business. Even clients are seen as a nuisance, as a disturbance at the boundaries of the territory. Exchange is the last thing wanted.

On the other hand, the dominant capitalistic ideology states that governments should refrain from commercial activities, while they are one of the major markets for private business. The military–industrial complex is only the tip of this iceberg, e.g. in Europe, the whole waste-disposal economy has arisen due to all kinds of environmental regulations. Waste experts in private industry are using exactly the same tactics as the military experts did 50 years ago. They lobby in such a way that the ensuing regulations lead to interesting business for them.

In my practice as a consultant, therefore, I refuse to work with the split between power and money. When working for governmental agencies, or for non-governmental ones, I try to focus upon their 'business'. In which trade are they, who are their clients and suppliers, who are their potential collaborators and competitors? Is the basic nature of their activities exchange or protection of their possessions? In what form is the exchange expressed: money, influence, goodwill, voluntary work? When working for business, I like to create settings in which the organization power can be expressed. I try to stress how essential it is that responsibility and power should go together. Choices and decisions taken by executive power should be accounted for formally and informally by those in charge. This is the way in which I try to bring back in any organization the basic dilemma between the customs and the smugglers.

---

## CASE STUDY: MULTINATIONAL

I was asked by a board of directors of a subsidiary of a multinational to facilitate a strategic process. They wanted to define the direction of the business for the next five years. I began by asking each member of the board how long he or she thought they would stay with that subsidiary. All of them said no longer than two years. For this reason I refused the assignment. They never could be the owner of their strategy.

---

A specific controversy in organization design can clarify the two horns of this dilemma: the network vs hierarchy debate. It is clear that hierarchical thinking, which stresses clearly to which layer and in which department one belongs, finds its source in the customs perspective, while networks, emphasizing horizontal relations and exchanges, find their defenders in those who have the smugglers perspective.

The refusal to deal with both horns of the dilemma leads sometimes to wonderful incongruencies. Hammer and Champy (1993), the champions of re-engineering, clearly feel much for the smugglers perspective. You have to get rid of all these useless hierarchies, only activities which add exchange value for customers have to be maintained. But, strangely enough, the ones who have to be convinced of this idea are the CEOs, those who are at the head of these hierarchies. Even to implement their concept of re-engineering in big corporations, Hammer and Champy suggest a 're-engineering tsar' at the top of a project hierarchy, containing several levels. The word 'tsar' itself, in my view, has never been used in a commercial context, only in the power one!

Trading and exchange are essentially small-scale activities, which can focus upon their relations, not with markets, but with known clients and suppliers. The smugglers perspective finds its best form in small and medium-sized organizations. However, one can find in governments as well as in big corporations many small-scale units, who in a nearly completely autonomous way, maintain satisfactory relations with well-known clients and suppliers. In fact, I state that everywhere satisfactory supplier–client relations are developed, everywhere where the smugglers perspective is dominant, we have small-scale operations. Flexibility, adaptability, inventiveness in changing circumstances can only be dealt with by groups of people who know each other by name and by face. Elsewhere (Hoebeke, 1994), I have used the concept span of relations, pointing out that the limit of persons able to know each other directly is about 700.

---

## CASE STUDY: AUTOMOTIVE INDUSTRY

One of the most efficient and effective medium-sized businesses I have worked with is the luxury coach assembler IRIZAR in Ormaeztegi in the Basque Country. It belongs to the Mondragón Cooperative Corporation and is completely organized as a horizontal organization. There is a coordinating committee of eight members and all 800 employees belong to one or more process teams, of which there are more or less 150 working at the same time. No other management function exists. Employees of suppliers and of customers also work in these teams. The whole enterprise has three financial professionals, no budgets, no control systems. The customers are the source of the autoregulation which pervades the factory. The cooperative has decided not to expand its factory. Size becomes a hindrance to maintain the 'money' focus. Instead, it has bought other plants in different countries, which have complete autonomy. There are no headquarters: if required, inter-factory teams are set up to learn from each other and to discover best practices. In this business there are also power plays going on, but the rule to deal with them is that they cannot be delegated upwards. Everyone has the responsibility to deal with his or her adversaries face to face. The many groups and the multi-membership of most of the employees create a dynamic balance of power, where group pressure is one of the major lubricants.

The power perspective wins adherents when some people take on the role of representatives. In politics representatives are elected. In power systems representatives are appointed by 'higher' powers. Power always implies that the one using it speaks in the name of others, has taken (stolen) the voices of others: a department, a constituency, mostly an aggregate of members. For this reason, power games thrive in anonymity. And for the same reason power needs a grander scale. As I prefer the smugglers perspective, it is difficult for me not to write about power without a negative connotation. I know that the customs perspective is as legitimate as the smugglers one, even more: they need each other. In a completely open world, a world which only is concerned with exchange without attention to conserve and keep what is worthwhile, a world in which one no longer knows to which group, culture, region, people one belongs, a world without boundaries, life becomes very difficult indeed. Boundaries are taken for granted for most of the activities we perform. We accept rules and regulations, and thus we accept rulers and regulators. And rules and regulations cannot be enforced if there are no guardians, who put the emphasis upon maintaining the coherence of the social fabric. This is not only the case on a societal level, but each organization has to cope with its guardians, its laws, and the enforcement of these laws.

The dilemma becomes exacerbated in the globalization ideology: all boundaries should be banished for free trade and at the same time institutional power dinosaurs are created to regulate this free trade. It is a marvellous example of institutional splitting, which certainly leads to more problems than solutions.

The problem of corruption between the two perspectives only appears when both start to mess up their function. The drive towards an economy of scale has nothing to do with increased efficiency: in fact large-scale production generates more externalized inefficiencies than small-scale production and consumption activities. But the cost of the inefficiencies of big corporations can much more easily be externalized. It is not the first time that the taxpayer has had to pay for the mismanagement of big enterprises, who politically can no longer go broke. The Savings & Loan or the Enron débâcle in the USA some years ago, the problems of the Korean and the Japanese financial systems, and the huge costs of the European Agricultural Programme are only a few examples of the inefficiencies of what are euphemistically called economies of scale. The discourse of power should never use economic concepts, real economics are for real markets, where real customers and real suppliers meet and make their deals. *The Wealth of Nations* rests upon small-scale business, as Adam Smith already knew, when he pointed to the importance of the cities in the generation of wealth.

In my practice as a consultant, I try to create platforms, in which power is legitimated, in which the various interest groups, with contradictory aims, objectives, and values, are bound to meet each other and to come to agreement on what may be called a balance of power. Democratic platforms are the natural way in which a 'smuggler' culture has expressed its way of dealing with power. Elsewhere (Hoebeke, 1997a), I have written that the challenge for the big corporations, but also for all big institutions in the coming century, will be to operationalize the democratic ideals in their own structures and systems and not to delegate democracy to the pure governmental fields. Ackoff (1994), with his circular organization, where all stakeholders are linked on each level of the hierarchy, indicates one form in which the balance of power can receive a transparent expression. Elsewhere (Hoebeke, 1997b), I have written about the difficult role of a representative and the price that one has to pay for it.

I would like to finish this section about the power and money dilemma with a quote from Jane Jacobs (1992):

> If it's true we are the only creatures with two fundamentally different ways of getting a living, it follows that to be as fully human as we can be, we should all be capable of using our two syndromes well. They belong to all of us because we are human, no other reason. They don't merely belong to this or that ordained group, as if we were social insects.

# THE DILEMMA BETWEEN SCIENCE AND POLITICS, BETWEEN THE PROPHET AND THE KING

This will probably shock a great number of scientists and practitioners alike: every scientific debate is a political one. By political, I mean that different world-views, different value systems meet each other and seek an agreement, so that acting (executive power) in a common reality becomes possible. Value-free science is a contradiction in terms: it is a trick to claim illegitimate power. It is a way to avoid all forms of responsibility by hiding behind something called Scientific Truth. The difficult dialectics between science and politics become more visible every day: the debates about global warming, about the right economics, the 'scientification' of most of the political issues is degrading science as much as politics. Let us explore a bit deeper this dilemma, by means of the prophet–king metaphor.

The *prophet* lives alone in the desert, beyond the boundaries of the kingdom. He needs this distance. He hears the concerns of the people, he belongs to the people, but nevertheless keeps his distance from them. Mostly the concerns of the people are about scarcity, hunger, other threats, plague and other epidemics, the threat from the other side of the boundaries, the threat of tyranny, the exploitative consumption of the king. The prophet feels himself connected to the people but at the same time is very critical of what is going on. In the desert, living on honey and grasshoppers, he develops a vision. He has heard the voice of the people but is confronted in the desert with another voice: what he thinks to have understood offers another perspective. He is blinded by the light outside Plato's cave and does not know what has happened to him. He mumbles, but does not find the right words. He can only go and pay a visit to the king. He knows that what he has to say is not understandable, even to himself. He has a faint hope that the king will understand him. He has a difficult path to tread. Nobody is a prophet in his own country.

The *king* lives in his palace, in the centre of his capital, in the centre of his people. This is important, because he wants to hear the voice of his people. He also hears the concerns of his people, about scarcity and hunger, and how difficult life is. But he knows that the people complain easily, often in his presence. There is no other way to express one's expectation than by stating that the king should do something about it. But the king has problems with priorities: he cannot fulfil all expectations and does not distinguish what is important from what is unimportant. Therefore, he has many counsellors, who do their best to please the king, although they do not always see what the king wants to see happen. But one does not go against the king, the king is supposed to be flattered. Until this mumbling prophet comes with his strange ideas about what is good for the people, for the kingdom, and thus also for him, the king. The prophet talks about things difficult to understand, sometimes he seems even not to understand himself. But one thing is for certain, he wants something to be done. When the king discovers that he is not able to solve the problems of his people, he starts to listen to the prophet. The prophet demands the king take up another perspective, do something out of the normal. In this way the king also starts a difficult journey.

He, who does not recognize in this parable the tension between staff and line, between R&D and other business departments, between the experts, who prepare policies and the policy-makers, between visionaries and those in charge, and nevertheless is a professional in these environments, probably fulfils the role of the counsellors in the story. They are the last ones who spot the drama going on, when boundaries are shifting, and they find themselves at once in a different world, not knowing what has happened to them. Good kings (politicians) don't like prophets (innovators), but are able to recognize them from the 'yes-minister' counsellors. When I use the word politician, I am not referring only to government, but to governance of every institution or organization. Good politicians are not afraid to take up their difficult role as representatives, as 'speakers' for their constituencies. They have the role of translating what they heard from the innovator into the language of the people and vice versa. They know that each shift in boundaries is creating a lot of problems for them and their people, but they are thankful to the innovator, who permits them to get their priorities straight. The prophet, as the specialist of scarcity, as dweller in the wilderness, is able to clarify the bounty, the abundance of tomorrow. But he cannot achieve it alone: king and prophet have to collaborate. Old truths will disappear, new rules of the game will be elaborated.

I have already mentioned the dilemma between continuous improvement and discontinuous change. The tension between both perspectives is an essential theme in all institutions and organizations. Stafford Beer (1985) in his Viable Systems Model situates this tension between what he calls System 3—the subsystem which focuses upon the here and now, upon the ongoing operations, upon the right distribution of energy, money, and information—and System 4—the subsystem which focuses upon the there and then, the environment of the system, what is beyond its boundaries and the future. System 5, that mysterious subsystem which Beer calls the Identity of the organization, is nothing other than the emerging result of the dynamic balance between System 3 and System 4. The dilemma between politics and science is illustrated by what Beer calls System 3, the operational, internally directed system, and System 4, the externally directed system. It is clear that the operational system emphasizes the centripetal forces, while the externally directed system emphasizes the centrifugal ones. Politics are centripetal, they stress the fact that one belongs to a social system, while science is centrifugal and stresses what is beyond the social system, its environment, its future.

In fact, the dynamic relation between politics and science has given me insight into what I call the dual leadership in teams and groups. It has always surprised me that in American management literature there is such a strong focus upon leadership and upon the leader, as if one leader could make all the difference. In my practice as a consultant, I started to look out for dual leadership in social systems: one embodying the 'scientific', the prophetic perspective, and the other embodying the 'political', the king's perspective. I discovered that organizational issues can be analysed by inquiring how the two perspectives interact. Moreover, as the tension between both perspectives is so difficult to handle, I discovered that in many organizations this tension has been organized away, so that they deal with each other only in informal platforms.

The introduction of project work into organizations can be looked upon as a way of restoring the interactions between the two perspectives which have been split apart organizationally. The departments, which are mostly occupied with 'analysis', 'diagnosis', 'thinking', typical staff functions, isolate the innovators. Often the professionals belonging to them have a greater loyalty to their profession and their professional development than to the organization itself, to which their department belongs. They are likely to go to conferences, on training, to professional meetings, etc. There, they find new ideas, theories, and concepts. In these departments one finds many professionals criticizing their own organization. In the 'line', they are looked upon with a certain distrust. Their schemes are seen as harbingers of trouble, problems, changing rules, and disturbing fashions. This is exactly the reason why they belong to their own departments, so that they can be kept at bay. But sometimes a 'prophet' has so much influence that the 'king' is convinced that something should be radically changed: a technology, a product or service, a policy, a strategy. The way to diffuse the tension between the actual, the operational, that which is working fine and should not be changed, and the futuristic, the fashionable, the novelty or in rare occasions real innovations, is by putting both perspectives together in project teams, task forces, or other temporary structures.

As an external consultant, whether I want it or not, I am always seen as the exponent of the 'scientific' perspective. I come from outside the organizational boundaries, and I am bound to disturb the normal ways of working. Taking seriously the concept of dual leadership, I try to connect as soon as possible with 'internal prophets' to find those places where centrifugal and centripetal forces generate the greatest force, the greatest dynamics from which the desired (never necessary) change can start. For this reason it is important to me that if a project starts, it should have a name which belongs to the system I am intervening in, and which only has meaning in the language of that system. As long as a project is labelled a 'total-quality project' or a 're-engineering project' or an 'ISO' or 'EFQM' project, it is still a foreign body. The naming has to be done by the specialists, who are unable to connect with the people. When the name of the project is owned, it is an indication that the project is owned by the 'politicians' in the system that I am asked to work for.

About 10 years ago, I started to work with large group interventions as strategic platforms in organizations or in inter-organizational contexts. The basic aim of these interventions is to bring into one room all the actors in a given work system. Meetings of 30 to 400 people during one to four days are used as organizational interventions. The way in which I design this kind of intervention is to permit the emergence of the dual leadership. The normal hierarchical structure, the crystallization of a balance of power between various kings and terrritories, is, in fact, inadequate to discover the tension between science and politics. Mostly the 'scientists' are neutralized by providing them with specialist departments and territories so that they cannot disturb the ongoing operations. What campuses and academic institutions do in society is, in fact, provide nothing else than an area for prophets, keeping them away from reality in their laboratories, and R&D departments and other specialist departments do the same in organizations. The line managers say: don't be concerned about this issue, quality, human resources, organizational development, technology asssesment, new products and services, we have some people working on it in department so and so. In fact, what they are saying is: we have well isolated and neutralized these innovators. The staff professionals complain about the conservatism of the line, about the 'resistance' to change of the 'kings', but have a good excuse not to transform their criticism into action. They are only asked to think and to produce reports. In large group interventions both perspectives are bound to meet each other as adversaries and to agree on concrete, desirable, and feasible projects, for which emergent leaders take responsibility.

In certain organizations the result of such a large group intervention has been the institutionalization of the meetings every two years, so that 'prophets' and 'kings' are bound to meet each other again and to have their fights, keeping the tension between the scientific and the political perspective. It is clear that these strategic platforms have a completely different approach from all the strategic alignment efforts, in which it is supposed that all parties should align them behind one vision, one mission, one policy, etc.

I would like to finish this section about the dilemma between science and politics by pointing out how, on a societal basis, the organizational split between both domains is creating problems and loss of credibility in the three institutions, who most visibly embody the two perspectives: government and governance bodies in large corporations; scientific bodies and the media. It is a wonder that the two institutions who claim objectivity are the media and the dominant science. But it is still more a wonder how the body politic has started to be increasingly dependent upon these two institutions. This institutional determinism can be analysed easily by means of what we have written about the normal human tendency to avoid dilemmas, to avoid the two basic paradoxes underlying all human culture: life and death, and I and the Other. Choosing to avoid dilemmas is a choice which can only be legitimated from inside out. I take a position between the two horns of the dilemma, from my own appreciative system, from my own value-system, from my own desire. This is already difficult enough as an individual, who necessarily is interdependent with others, having their values and desires. This difficulty is exacerbated for those who, formally or informally, are seen as in charge of collectivities and are accountable for the choices they make on behalf of their constituency. And the greatest responsibility is to change the rules of the game, to introduce discontinuities into these systems. Now, in modernism discontinuous change for one reason or another has become an ideological fashion: innovation and reform, change and renovation have become a must, a necessity instead of a desire, a want. This makes the role of those in charge extremely difficult and generates thus all kind of avoidance mechanisms. The media hide their responsibility behind their deontology that they only can be critical objective observers and reporters of what happens in society. The fact that 'news' is created, because of the conscious or unconscious selection of events and ideas done by the news-creators, is repressed. What is seen and communicated through the media is not reality but a well-chosen framing of reality. This selection is never value-free, because it is a selection. As long as the criteria for this selection are not under public scrutiny, as long as the values behind the selection of the 'news' are not debatable (and commercial sensationalism is as good a criterion as any other, as long as it is publicly stated), the objectivity of the media is one big lie. In the same vein, as I stated earlier, science is never value-free. The phenomena that scientists want to investigate, the choices and priorities which are made in funding sciences, are necessarily value-laden. There is nothing wrong with this, as long as the criteria for investigating certain phenomena are under public scrutiny. Hiding behind the objectivity and the value-freedom of doing science is as big a lie as the objectivity of the media. But both 'objective' stances are a welcome excuse for those, who are politically in charge, to hide their own agendas and their own desires. Institutional collusion not to declare one's own position and to avoid the accountability related to choices in abundance has emerged in our times. The dialectics between science and politics have been organized away. Fortunately, social systems show a great amount of resilience and self-regulation. Those institutions who are avoiding these dialectics are losing their credibility very quickly. The previous analysis also shows a way out of the collusion. When in each of the institutions mentioned the dialectics between politics and science are restored, and, in the case of public agencies, are made public, credibility will also be restored.

For this reason I put great effort into ways of democratizing again science and the media. By democratizing, I mean creating conditions so that the basic institutional dilemmas emerge together with the people taking up the responsibility for their choices. When it concerns real innovations, the projects coming out of these choices always have a human scale: grand reforms, grand innovations are a contradiction in terms. All the more so if, to justify them, the lie of necessity is invoked.

## THE DILEMMA BETWEEN FAITH AND ETHICS, BETWEEN DON QUIXOTE AND SANCHO PANZA

This dilemma is the trickiest one to write about, because it is strongly linked to the life and death paradox. The dominant organizational ethos is that institutions and organizations have an eternal life, in any case, they should survive the people passing through them. Eternal youth seems to be the motto which probably unconsciously pushes organizations towards early retirements, pushes out poor performers, due to illness or other reasons, pushes towards the flight into hectic action and the avoidance of reflection, is attracted to yuppies and other wise guys, and labels innovation, progress, and novelty as necessities. But the paradox cannot be avoided. The same ethos states that everything is accelerating, that product and service lifetimes are becoming shorter, that obsolescence is the biggest threat for business and government, that lagging behind is a disaster. The anxiety of finiteness creates its self-regulating context in which finiteness and obsolescence become the strategy. Mergers and alliances are made and disbanded at a great pace, ownership has become extremely volatile, companies and corporations change names as quickly as fashions change fabrics. The more the survival ideology is stressed, the quicker life disappears: from rain forests to meaningful work, from living traditions to well-established technologies.

---

### CASE STUDY: THE WORD ONSCREEN

It is evident for all those who are confronted with word processors and PCs that reports and books are the ergonomically best way to work with texts. Screens are utterly inadequate for treating texts, screens are much better for representing images. Nevertheless, the whole world has been pushed to use screens for text processing. Even though the myth of the paperless society has been with us for several years, paper use has increased enormously, just through the use of IT.

---

Management fashions come and go with great velocity. Nevertheless, I see how young managers are attracted by the old texts of Macchiavelli, of Plato's *Republic*, of the Rules of Saint Benedict, of the old Chinese strategic insights, etc. In spite of the excesses of the New Age, there is a growing interest in the old wisdom traditions from quite a variety of cultures.

It is in this context that I want to situate the dilemma of faith and ethics. The use of the figures don Quixote and his servant Sancho Panza is not only due to my personal interest in the Spanish tradition, but it illustrates, at the threshold of what historians call modern times, much of the dilemmas modernism has put on us human beings. Don Quixote has read all the old books. He is completely at ease with the epics and the ethics of the knights. All the rules of courtly love and behaviour are carved in his memory. And now that he has absorbed all this science, he can at last start to live at the end of his life. He becomes an errant knight to put his faith under test, to experience his faith. In fact, he is something of a scientist: he wants to see his hypothesis confirmed or refuted. But in some way, he is not a scientist at all: in his world there is no such word as refutation. Therefore, he needs Sancho Panza. Indeed, the first trip of don Quixote, alone on his own, nearly ended in his death. Therefore, the relatives of don Quixote, who cannot restrain this man of faith, have asked Sancho Panza to err with him. He is the one who puts on the brakes, he is the one who creates the ethics, the moral messages out of Quixote's adventures. In fact, he actualizes the lessons, which are scrutinized experimentally by don Quixote. He does not try to stop Quixote with common sense, the dominant mores. He takes the faith of Quixote seriously. He only tries to earth this faith. For this reason he finds himself regularly literally upon the earth together with don Quixote.

Men and women of faith have difficulties with themselves and create difficulties for others. They are obsessed by the dilemma of life and death. For this reason there is something self-destructive in them. Ascetism is one of their characteristics. Many of them also are murdered like Gandhi, Socrates, Jesus, or put in prison like Mandela and Martin Luther King, or even kill themselves like van Gogh. This is all extremely unethical, but paradoxically they are the foundations of new ethics.

It is clear that men and women of faith are not organization men and women. As I mentioned earlier, referring to the legend of Oedipus and the Sphinx, they are able to walk on their two legs, without the need for the organizational parental crutches. They are on their way to discover the third leg between life and death, the meaning of the copulative 'and'. Mostly they are also bad organizers. In the best cases they are able to rally people, who leave them on their own when things become serious. In a world which is over-organized, where the dominant heroes are organization men and women, where leadership and management have become organizational issues, discovering men or women of faith becomes very difficult. Nevertheless, they are the ones who are transforming the ethics of our time. They are the ones who are not shying away from the paradox of life and death. They prefer life to survival and know that only consciousness of death permits the transformation from survival to life.

There is much to do nowadays about business ethics, about the ethics of the life sciences, about the ethics of euthanasia, etc. Curious enough, ethics seem to become part of science. Value-free scientists will determine the values and their consequences for the behaviour of the future, or at the other extreme of objectivity, political correctness will be determined by polls and marketing techniques. Value-free statistics will show us the way to what is right and wrong, just and unjust. Value-free consultants preach best practices, neglecting dilemmas and focusing on problem-solving in the interest of the owners. There are many Sancho Panzas, many good-intentioned priestlike figures, who out of real concern of mankind, try to create new ethics. But they lack the don Quixotes. That is why these good intentions inevitably pave the road to hell.

In my practice, in management training and in professional development programmes, I try in the first place to confront participants with the original texts of men and women of faith. When I started myself to doubt the ethics of the dominant positivistic scientific approach, I started to read the original works of great scientists, such as Newton, Pasteur, Darwin, and Einstein. I discovered that they were not positivistic at all, they were men of faith. They expressed their inner convictions, their own approach to the mystery of life and death, in ways of observing and modelling their external environment. Inside-out and outside-in were equally important in their endeavours. They behaved very don Quixote-like and went against the dominant common-sense ethics of their times. In the same way, when I started to doubt my Judaeo-Christian faith, I could do no other than work through the original texts. For this reason I even started to learn Hebrew, and the large Judaic tradition of commenting on the Torah. And so I discovered inside me completely new ways to approach the scientific tradition I was educated in, as well as the spiritual one. In fact, I started to do the same work as don Quixote did with the epics and ethics of the knights. For this reason I like to share this experience with managers and professionals who ask themselves questions and doubt what they are doing in their profession.

A second way in which I try to organize meetings using the works of men and women of faith is by confronting participants with works of art, which come from them, works of art which deal with the mystery of life and death, in fact all Great Works, if I may use this alchemistic definition. Contemporary artists of the Great Works (and it requires a lot of effort to discover them in the huge art production) resonate in me, and resonate in my colleagues in an uneasy way. It is exactly this uneasiness which I recognize when I myself am confronted with issues of life and death, of belonging to and exile.

The whole concept of the meaning of work, which I developed in my previous book (1994), has been initiated by my study of Hebrew and by my confrontation with the works of the post-war German artist Joseph Beuys (+1986). In fact, his works allowed me to look at organizations, at the artifacts which they produce and within which they live, as expressions of the dilemmas people in them are struggling with. When in 1989 I saw in Slovenia on the shop floor a press, decorated by masses of obsolescent paper money (normal if inflation is 1000 per cent a year), I understood how the worker-artist, who made that installation, was expressing in a very difficult way the dilemma of money and power. And I saw the need to create new ethics, which were quite different from the common ones. I introduced the concept of healthy human laziness as the foundation for greater efficiency. The press was not by coincidence the only machine in the hall to have been decorated by money. How can I do more with less became the new ethics: exactly the ethics of the great avant-garde artists in the 1950s and the 1960s.

The best thing, however, which may happen is to meet, face to face, men and women of faith, don Quixotes. Fortunately I have met four of them in my lifetime, and all four have had a great influence on me. They freed my thinking and behaviour, paradoxically by pointing out the secular traditions, to which they stated they were indebted. But they were able to help me to actualize these traditions, to transform them in to actual behaviour, into actual ethics.

In fact, this chapter is one of the results of their influence. It is clear that what I wrote is far from the orthodox view, taught in MBAs and other management development activities. But my desperate faith in the gift of life can only express itself from the perspective of *money*, *science*, and *faith*. This is my bias. The only thing which I try to do consistently, the ethics I try to keep, is in spite of my bias to keep an eye on *power*, *politics*, and *ethics*.

The ethics of the art of choosing can thus be reduced to the following guidelines:

- Don't shun the abundance and its forthcoming dilemmas.
- Be aware of your own bias in these dilemmas and how they are related to your own experiences of the paradox of I and Thou and Life and Death.
- Position yourself in your bias but keep an eye on and tolerate the other horn of the dilemma.
- In this way, if you are lucky, you can discover the third component of the dilemma, the 'and' and finally the 'end'.

## REFERENCES

Ackoff, R. (1994) *The Democratic Corporation*. Oxford: Oxford University Press.

Atlan, H. (1979) *Entre le cristal et la fumée*. Paris: Editions du Seuil.

Beer, S. (1985) *Diagnosing the System for Organizations*. Chichester: John Wiley & Sons, Ltd.

Bos, R. ten (2000) *Fashion and Utopia in Management Thinking*. Amsterdam: John Benjamins.

Checkland, P. & Holwell, S. (1998) *Information, Systems and Information Systems*. Chichester: John Wiley & Sons, Ltd.

Checkland, P. & Scholes, J. (1991) *Soft Systems Methodology in Action*. Chichester: John Wiley & Sons, Ltd.

Feyerabend, P. (1999) *Conquest of Abundance*. Chicago: University of Chicago Press.

Girard, R. (1978) *Violence and the Sacred*. Baltimore, MD: Johns Hopkins University Press.

Hammer, M. & Champy, J. (1993) *Reengineering the Corporation: A Manifesto for Business Revolution*. New York: Harper Business.

Hoebeke, L. (1994) *Making Work Systems Better*. Chichester: John Wiley & Sons, Ltd.

Hoebeke, L. (1997a) Hacia la democratización de la empresa como reto del siglo XXI. In *Tendencias de Gestión en el Nuevo Milenio*. Bilbao: Cluster Conocimiento.

Hoebeke, L. (1997b). *Activar a las Personas: Actas del Symposium Internacional sobre Cooperativismo y Participación en la Gestión Empresarial*. Madrid: MCC Mondragón.

Jacobs, J. (1992) *Systems of Survival: A Dialogue on the Moral Foundations of Commerce and Politics*. London: Hodder & Stoughton.

Janis, I. & Mann, L. (1977) *Decision Making*. New York: The Free Press.

Porter, M. (1990) *The Competitive Advantage of Nations*. New York: The Free Press.

Srivastva, S. & Cooperrider, D. (1987) *Appreciative Inquiry in Organizational Life: Research in Organizational Change and Development*. vol. 1. Stanford, CT: JAI Press.

Vickers, G. (1995) *The Art of Judgment*. London: Sage.

# Organizing, Changing, and Learning in Ambiguous Contexts

In Part III of this book, strategies and interventions for organizational change are discussed in depth. A specific line of approach in this Part is initiating change in an unpredictable world with an increase in complexity and multiplicity in organizational life. Well-known approaches of change management are contrasted with more critical and topical approaches on organizing, changing, and learning. Attention is given to sense-making and management of meaning. New principles, insights, and roles for managers, consultants, and participants in changing are discussed. More light is shed on the involvement of stakeholders in the dynamics of change, and on the art of choosing the depth of interventions.

Chapter 9 by Karl Weick and Robert Quinn continues with questions raised in earlier chapters on contexts, change strategies, intervention methods, the role of change agents, and the timing of change. So far, the context of the change process is seen as important in choosing change strategies. The art of choosing change strategies and intervention methods is seen as a deliberate and sometimes difficult process of decision-making and acting. Analyses of organizational change and learning suggest a growing concern with the pace of change, understood as the characteristic rate, rhythm, or patterns of work or activities. Weick and Quinn suggest that an important emerging contrast in change processes is the distinction between episodic change and continuous change. Episodic change is contrasted with continuous change on the basis of implied metaphors of organizing, analytic frameworks, ideal organizations, intervention theories, and the roles of change agents. Episodic change follows the sequence unfreeze–rebalance–freeze, whereas continuous change follows the sequence freeze–rebalance–unfreeze. Conceptualizations of inertia are seen to underlie the choice to view change as episodic or continuous. Weick and Quinn suggest that change never starts because it never stops. Change is not seen as an on–off phenomenon, nor as a planned activity steered by top management. Processes of change are more often spiral and open-ended than linear. Therefore, it is useful if managers, practitioners, facilitators, and action-researchers focus on 'changing' rather than 'change'. A concern with 'changing' means greater appreciation that change is never completed, that its chains of causality are longer and less determined than we anticipated.

Chapter 10 continues with the debate raised in the previous chapter as Léon de Caluwé and Hans Vermaak elaborate on complexity and multiplicity in change processes. Given that more organizational change takes place unplanned than planned, and more unsuccessfully than successfully, there is reason to reflect on why change does not work. De Caluwé and Vermaak discuss several perspectives on irrationalities and why change processes are so often frustrating events. They suggest that over-reliance on rational top-down and contingency approaches can be rendered fruitless as a result of these irrationalities. After reflecting on the question of what makes change work, five prevailing paradigms about changing are explored. Each of these paradigms is associated with beliefs and assumptions, and characterized in terms of their characteristics, such as predictability, ideals, pitfalls, action strategies,

*Dynamics of Organizational Change and Learning.* Edited by J.J. Boonstra.
© 2004 John Wiley & Sons, Ltd. ISBN 0-471-87737-9.

style of change agents, and intervention methods. The presentation of this multiple approach could help participants deal with complexity in the processes of changing. The ability of change agents to take a multi-paradigmatic perspective could help to gain insight into the lack of success of planned change. Taking a multi-paradigmatic perspective permits awareness of ways of defining and solving problems, and opens up new possibilities by making conscious and collective choices for organizing and changing.

Chapter 11 focuses on the balance between the opposing perspectives of organizing and changing, and elaborates on changing as a process of co-creation. André Wierdsma states that changing and learning need collective competencies to deal with variety and complexity. For the viability of organizing, it is crucial to deal with mutual differences on the basis of action, and the ability to learn from that action in a collective context. Wierdsma distinguishes between positional and transactional organizing. The positional perspective on organizing and changing places great reliance on rationality, stability, and external control by managers and experts. From the positional doctrine, change is perceived as an implementation process with phases of problem articulation, diagnosis, defining plans for change, and care for implementation. Transactional organizing is regarded as organizing activities for the purpose of effecting transactions with stakeholders in the value chain. In this approach, organizing is seen as weaving together performance activities, maintaining relationships, and creating meaning in these relationships during interactions. In the transactional doctrine, processes of changing are related to the abilities of people to deconstruct and reconstruct meanings together, and re-order relationships and activities to take account of complexity and variety. In the processes of changing and learning, three levels are identified: rules, insights, and principles. Rules indicate how members of an organization should behave. Insights lie behind the rules and are views on organizing and changing. Principles reflect the core values and the meaning of organizing which are taken for granted. Learning processes focusing on rules, insights, and principles differ in their complexity, scope, and impact. It is assumed that learning on the level of principles has a bigger impact than learning and relinquishing of rules. In this chapter, a methodology is developed for co-creation in the processes of changing and learning on the level of insights and principles. The methodology of co-creating corresponds to the transactional perspective on organizing, changing, and learning. The starting point is that stakeholders should have the abilities to realize changes. An important demand is that stakeholders are willing to learn on the level of insights and principles. Eight principles for co-creating in change are worked out in detail. The methodology and intervention principles are illustrated with practical examples.

The final chapter in this Part offers a critical construction on organizing, changing, and learning. In Chapter 12, Dian Marie Hosking presents the duality of 'mainstream' and 'critical' approaches to organization and changing as an analytical and organizing device. New possibilities for change works theory and methodology are explored. Change is approached as multiple, ongoing, construction processes, and actors are seen as part of these reality construction processes. Producing realities are thought of as very real but, nevertheless, locally, historically, and culturally embedded. These premises invite further development of non-hierarchical ways of organizing that open up possibilities and multiple voices, rather than closing down one way of organizing and learning. Hosking starts with an overview of mainstream approaches to person–organization relations and reflects on the implications of this approach for organizational change. An alternative approach is introduced based on principles of a constructionist thought style in which organizing is seen as interactive relational processes. These interactions are processes of organizing local realities in which persons and worlds are co-constructed, maintained, and changed. These basic principles are used to reflect on constructions of changing and learning, and to develop new insights and methodologies based on relational construction processes. Several insights are discussed in depth: first, change and stability are ongoing processes. Second, change is an interactive construction process with multiple realities. Third, conventional distinctions between diagnosis and intervention are no longer helpful. Fourth, change is related to power in the sense of power to sustain multiple interdependent ways of proceeding in a state of equal relations.

Fifth, there is no resistance without force; resistance might be a locally rational response to the use of power by change agents. Sixth, knowing and influencing work together. Seventh, possibilities and positive values are appreciated and centred on changing. Finally, questioning and listening form new relations and realities. These relational premises and constructionist insights are helpful in developing a methodology in change works practices. Several methodologies are elaborated and illustrated with case studies.

# CHAPTER 9

# Organizational Change and Development
## Episodic and Continuous Changing*

**Karl Weick and Robert Quinn**
*University of Michigan Business School, Michigan, USA*

Analyses of organizational change written since the review by Porras and Silvers (1991) suggest that an important emerging contrast in change research is the distinction between change that is episodic, discontinuous, and intermittent and change that is continuous, evolving, and incremental. This contrast is sufficiently pervasive in recent work and sufficiently central in the conceptualization of change that we use it as the framework that organizes this review.

The contrast between episodic and continuous change reflects differences in the perspective of the observer. From a distance (the macrolevel of analysis), when observers examine the flow of events that constitute organizing, they see what looks like repetitive action, routine, and inertia dotted with occasional episodes of revolutionary change. But a view from closer in (the microlevel of analysis) suggests ongoing adaptation and adjustment. Although these adjustments may be small, they also tend to be frequent and continuous across units, which means they are capable of altering structure and strategy. Some observers (e.g. Orlikowski, 1996) treat these ongoing adjustments as the essence of organizational change. Others (e.g. Nadler et al., 1995) describe these ongoing adjustments as mere incremental variations on the same theme and lump them together into an epoch of convergence during which interdependencies deepen. Convergence is interrupted sporadically by epochs of divergence described by words like revolution, deep change, and transformation.

We pursue this contrast, first by a brief overview of change as a genre of analysis and then by a more detailed comparison of episodic and continuous change using a framework proposed by Dunphy (1996).

## CHANGE AS A GENRE OF ORGANIZATIONAL ANALYSIS

The basic tension that underlies many discussions of organizational change is that it would not be necessary if people had done their jobs right in the first place. Planned change is usually triggered by the failure of people to create continuously adaptive organizations (Dunphy, 1996). Thus, organizational change routinely occurs in the context of failure of some sort. A typical storyline is 'First there were losses, then there was an implementation, which led to unexpected results' (Czarniawska & Joerges, 1996: 20).

Representative descriptions of change vary with the level of analysis. At the most general level, 'change is a phenomenon of time. It is the way people talk about the event in which something appears to become, or turn into, something else, where the "something else" is seen as a result or outcome'

---

* This chapter is reprinted, with permission, from the *Annual Review of Psychology*, volume 50, © 1999 by Annual Reviews www.annualreviews.org

(Ford & Ford, 1994: 759). In reference to organizations, change involves difference 'in how an organization functions, who its members and leaders are, what form it takes, or how it allocates its resources' (Huber et al., 1993: 216). From the perspective of organizational development, change is 'a set of behavioral science-based theories, values, strategies, and techniques aimed at the planned change of the organizational work setting for the purpose of enhancing individual development and improving organizational performance, through the alteration of organizational members' on-the-job behaviors' (Porras & Robertson, 1992: 723).

The concepts used to flesh out these definitions have been surprisingly durable over the years. Lewin's (1951) three stages of change—unfreeze, change, and refreeze—continue to be a generic recipe for organizational development. As Hendry (1996) notes, 'Scratch any account of creating and managing change and the idea that change is a three-stage process which necessarily begins with a process of unfreezing will not be far below the surface. Indeed it has been said that the whole theory of change is reducible to this one idea of Kurt Lewin's' (p. 624). Lewin's assertion that 'you cannot understand a system until you try to change it' (Schein, 1996: 34) survives in Colville et al.'s (1993) irony of change: 'one rarely fully appreciates or understands a situation until after it has changed' (p. 550). Lewin's concept of resistance to change survives in O'Toole's (1995: 159–166) list of 30 causes of resistance to change and in renewed efforts to answer the question, 'Just whose view is it that is resisting change?' (Nord & Jermier, 1994). The distinction between incremental and radical change first articulated by Watzlawick et al. (1974) and Bateson (1972) as the distinction between first- and second-order change continues to guide theory construction and data collection (Bartunek, 1993; Roach & Bednar, 1997). The rhythms of change (Greiner, 1972) continue to be described as periods of convergence marked off from periods of divergence by external jolts (e.g. Bacharach et al., 1996). The continuing centrality of these established ideas may suggest a certain torpor in the intellectual life of scholars of change. We think, instead, that this centrality attests to the difficulty of finding patterns when difference is the object of study.

While work within the past 10 years has become theoretically richer and more descriptive, there is a continuing debate about whether change research is developing as a cumulative and falsifiable body of knowledge. Kahn's (1974: 487) assessment of organizational change research in the 1970s is cited by Macy and Izumi (1993: 237) as a statement that remains relevant: 'A few theoretical propositions are repeated without additional data or development; a few bits of homey advice are reiterated without proof or disproof; and a few sturdy empirical observations are quoted with reverence but without refinement of explication.' Similar sentiments are found in Woodman (1989), in Golembiewski and Boss (1992), and in the withering popular books on 'the change business' titled *The Witch Doctors* (Micklethwait & Wooldridge, 1996) and *Dangerous Company* (O'Shea & Madigan, 1997). The tone of these critiques is illustrated by the obvious pleasure the authors of *The Witch Doctors* take in their observation that 'the reason American businessmen talk about gurus is because they can't spell the word charlatan' (Micklethwait & Wooldridge, 1996: 11).

Remedies to the above problems are seen to lie in the direction of the following, all coupled with greater efforts to articulate the situated nature of organizational action (e.g. Laurila, 1997): (a) cross-organizational meta-analysis (e.g. Macy & Izumi, 1993); (b) cross-organizational interview-surveys (e.g. Huber & Glick, 1993); (c) simulations that are cross-organizational by virtue of their generality (e.g. Sastry, 1997); (d) ethnographies (e.g. Katz, 1997) and case studies (e.g. Starbuck, 1993) that are treated as prototypes; (e) reconceptualization of organizational change as institutional change (e.g. Greenwood & Hinings, 1996); and (f) cross-disciplinary borrowing (e.g. Cheng & Van de Ven, 1996). Coupled with efforts to improve the quality of evidence in change research have been parallel efforts to better understand the limitations of inquiry (e.g. Kilduff & Mehra, 1997; McKelvey, 1997). When these are combined, there appears to be simultaneous improvement of tools and scaling down of the tasks those tools must accomplish.

The sheer sprawl of the change literature is a continuing challenge to investigators who thrive on frameworks (e.g. Mintzberg & Westley, 1992). An important recent attempt to impose order on the topic of organizational change is the typology crafted by Van de Ven and Poole (1995). They induced four basic process theories of change, each characterized by a different event sequence and generative mechanism:

1. Life cycle theories have an event sequence of start-up, grow, harvest, terminate, and start-up. They have a generative mechanism of an immanent program or regulation.
2. Teleological theories have an event sequence of envision/set goals, implement goals, dissatisfaction, search/interact, and envision/set goals. They have a generative mechanism of purposeful enactment and social construction.
3. Dialectical theory has an event sequence of thesis/antithesis, conflict, synthesis, and thesis/antithesis. It has a generative mechanism of pluralism, confrontation, and conflict.
4. Evolutionary theory has an event sequence of variation, selection, retention, and variation. It has a generative mechanism of competitive selection and resource scarcity.

These four motors are classified along two dimensions: (a) the unit of change, which depicts whether the process focuses on the development of a single organizational entity (life cycle, teleological) or on interactions between two or more entities (evolution, dialectic) and (b) the mode of change, which depicts whether the sequence of change events is prescribed by deterministic laws and produces first-order change (life cycle, evolution) or whether the sequence is constructed, emerges as the process unfolds, and generates novel second-order change (dialectic, teleology).

The language of motors is useful because it alerts investigators to missing motors in change theories that aspire to comprehensiveness, it draws attention to mechanisms of interplay among motors and the necessity for balance (Van de Ven & Poole, 1995: 534), it tempts people to look for a 'fifth motor' and other hybrids, and (because the language of motors is a language of process rather than of outcome), it enables investigators to identify what is happening before it has concluded (p. 524). Because the authors propose a detailed list of conditions that must be met if a motor is to operate (Van de Ven & Poole, 1995: 525, Figure 2), they imply that when change interventions fail, there is a mismatch between the prevailing conditions and the kind of motor activated by the change intervention.

Van de Ven and Poole's review (1995) suggested that mode of change and unit of change were important partitions of the change literature. Our review suggests that tempo of change, defined as 'characteristic rate, rhythm, or pattern of work or activity' (Random House, 1987: 1954), is also a meaningful partition. We explore the contrast between episodic and continuous change by comparing the two forms on five properties that Dunphy (1996: 543) suggests are found in any comprehensive theory of change (Table 9.1). These properties are: (a) a basic metaphor of the nature of organization; (b) an analytical framework to understand the organizational change process; (c) an ideal model of an effectively functioning organization that specifies both a direction for change and values to be used in assessing the success of the change intervention (e.g. survival, growth, integrity); (d) an intervention theory that specifies when, where, and how to move the organization closer to the ideal; and (e) a definition of the role of change agent. Because we are building a composite picture using portions of work that may have been designed to answer other questions, readers should treat our placement of specific studies as evocative rather than definitive.

## EPISODIC CHANGE

The phrase 'episodic change' is used to group together organizational changes that tend to be infrequent, discontinuous, and intentional. The presumption is that episodic change occurs during periods of divergence when organizations are moving away from their equilibrium conditions. Divergence is the result of a growing misalignment between an inertial deep structure and perceived environmental demands. This form of change is labeled 'episodic' because it tends to occur in distinct periods during which shifts are precipitated by external events such as technology change or internal events such as change in key personnel.

**TABLE 9.1**  Comparison of episodic and continuous change

|  | Episodic change | Continuous change |
| --- | --- | --- |
| Metaphor of organization | Organizations are inertial and change is infrequent, discontinuous, intentional | Organizations are emergent and self-organizing, and change is constant, evolving, cumulative |
| Analytic framework | Change is an occasional interruption or divergence from equilibrium. It tends to be dramatic and it is driven externally. It is seen as a failure of the organization to adapt its deep structure to a changing environment | Change is a pattern of endless modifications in work processes and social practice. It is driven by organizational instability and alert reactions to daily contingencies. Numerous small accommodations cumulate and amplify |
|  | Perspective: macro, distant, global | Perspective: micro, close, local |
|  | Emphasis: short-run adaptation | Emphasis: long-run adaptability |
|  | Key concepts: inertia, deep structure of interrelated parts, triggering, replacement and substitution, discontinuity, revolution | Key concepts: recurrent interactions, shifting task authority, response repertoires, emergent patterns, improvisation, translation, learning |
| Ideal organization | The ideal organization is capable of continuous adaptation | The ideal organization is capable of continuous adaptation |
| Intervention theory | The necessary change is created by intention. Change is Lewinian: inertial, linear, progressive, goal-seeking, motivated by disequilibrium, and requires outsider intervention<br>1. Unfreeze: disconfirmation of expectations, learning anxiety, provision of psychological safety<br>2. Transition: cognitive restructuring, semantic redefinition, conceptual enlargement, new standards of judgment<br>3. Refreeze: create supportive social norms, make change congruent with personality | The change is a redirection of what is already under way. Change is Confucian: cyclical, processional, without an end state, equilibrium seeking, eternal<br>1. Freeze: make sequences visible and show patterns through maps, schemas, and stories<br>2. Rebalance: reinterpret, relabel, resequence the patterns to reduce blocks. Use logic of attraction<br><br>3. Unfreeze: resume improvisation, translation, and learning in ways that are more mindful |
| Role of change agent | Role: prime mover who creates change | Role: sense maker who redirects change |
|  | Process: focuses on inertia and seeks points of central leverage | Process: recognizes, makes salient, and reframes current patterns |
|  | Changes meaning systems: speaks differently, communicates alternative schema, reinterprets revolutionary triggers, influences punctuation, builds coordination and commitment | Shows how intentional change can be made at the margins. Alters meaning by new language, enriched dialogue, and new identity. Unblocks improvisation, translation, and learning |

## BASIC METAPHORS: ORGANIZING FOR EPISODIC CHANGE

The metaphor of organization implied by conceptualizations of episodic change is of a social entity that combines the following characteristics: dense, tightly coupled interdependencies among subunits; efficiency as a core value; a preoccupation with short-run adaptation rather than long-run adaptability; constraints on action in the form of the invisible hand of institutionalization; powerful norms embedded in strong subcultures; and imitation as a major motivation for change. The importance of interdependencies as a precondition for episodic change is found in discussions of alignment (e.g. Pfeffer, 1998: Ch. 4), configurations (e.g. Miller, 1990), and cultural inertia (e.g. Tushman & O'Reilly, 1996). The importance of imitation is reflected in Sevon's (1996) statement that 'every theory of organizational change must take into account the fact that leaders of organizations watch one another and adopt what they perceive as successful strategies for growth and organizational structure' (pp. 60–61).

Images of organization that are compatible with episodic change include those built around the ideas of punctuated equilibria, the edge of chaos, and second-order change. The image of an organization built around the idea of a punctuated equilibrium (Tushman & Romanelli, 1985) depicts organizations as sets of interdependencies that converge and tighten during a period of relative equilibrium, often at the expense of continued adaptation to environmental changes. As adaptation lags, effectiveness decreases, pressures for change increase, and a revolutionary period is entered. As these pressures continue to increase, they may result in an episode of fundamental change in activity patterns and personnel, which then becomes the basis for a new equilibrium period. Apple Computer illustrated a series of discontinuous changes in strategy, structure, and culture as it moved from the leadership of Steve Jobs through that of John Sculley, Michael Sprindler, Gil Amelio, and back to Jobs (Tushman & O'Reilly, 1996). Romanelli & Tushman (1994) found this pattern of discontinuous episodic change when they examined changes in the activity domains of strategy, structure, and power distribution for 25 minicomputer producers founded between 1967 and 1969. Changes in these three domains were clustered, as would be predicted from a punctuated change model, rather than dispersed, as would be predicted from a model of incremental changes that accumulate.

The image of an organization built around the idea of operating at 'the edge of chaos' (Stacey, 1995; McDaniel, 1997) depicts the organization as a set of simple elements tied together by complex relationships involving nonlinear feedback (Arthur, 1995). An important property of nonlinear systems is bounded instability or what is referred to as the edge of chaos. Here a system has developed both negative and positive feedback loops and is hence simultaneously capable of stability and instability. Behavior at the edge of chaos is paradoxical because the system moves autonomously back and forth between stability and instability. Applied to organizations, Cheng and Van de Ven (1996), for example, show that biomedical innovation processes are nonlinear systems that move episodically from stages of chaos to greater order within a larger context containing random processes. Browning et al. (1995) show how the unprecedented successful alliance called Sematech emerged from a set of small, discrete events that occurred at a point of irreversible disequilibrium when the entire US semiconductor industry was about to collapse.

The image of an organization built around the idea of second-order change in frames of reference depicts the organization as a site where shared beliefs operate in the service of coordinated action (Bougon, 1992; Langfield-Smith, 1992). These shared frames of reference may be 'bent' when first-order changes produce minor alterations in current beliefs or 'broken' when second-order changes replace one belief system with another (Dunbar et al., 1996). First-order change is illustrated by a shift of culture at British Rail from a production-led bureaucracy to a market-led bureaucracy (the firm remained a top-down bureaucracy). Second-order change is illustrated by the later culture shift at British Rail from a market-led bureaucracy to a network-partnership culture in which power was distributed rather than concentrated (Bate, 1990). Second-order change is episodic change and 'refers to changes in cognitive frameworks underlying the organization's activities, changes in the deep structure or shared schemata that generate and give meaning to these activities' (Bartunek & Moch, 1994: 24). Recently, it has been proposed that there exists a third order of change that basically questions the adequacy of schemas themselves and argues for direct exposure to the 'ground for conceptual understanding' in the form of music, painting, dance, poetry, or mystical experience. Organizational change thus gains intellectual power through alignment with aesthetics (e.g. Sandelands, 1998). Examples of third-order change are found in the work of Torbert (1994), Nielsen and Bartunek (1996), Mirvis (1997), Olson (1990), and Austin (1997).

In each of these three images, organizational action builds toward an episode of change when preexisting interdependencies, patterns of feedback, or mind-sets produce inertia.

## ANALYTIC FRAMEWORK: THE EPISODIC CHANGE PROCESS

Episodic change tends to be infrequent, slower because of its wide scope, less complete because it is seldom fully implemented, more strategic in its content, more deliberate and formal than emergent change, more disruptive because programs are replaced rather than altered, and initiated at higher levels in the organization (Mintzberg & Westley, 1992). The time interval between episodes of discontinuous change is determined by the amount of time organizations expend in other stages of organizational development. If, for example, the stages of organizational change are labeled development, stability, adaptation, struggle, and revolution (Mintzberg & Westley, 1992), then episodic change is contemplated when adaptation begins to lag. It takes provisional form as organizations struggle to confront problems and experiment with solutions, and it produces actual shifts in systems during the stage of revolution. The frequency of revolutions and episodic change depends on the time spent in the four prior stages, which varies enormously. This temporal variation in processes building up to revolution is the reason why this form of change is best described as episodic, aperiodic, infrequent.

Three important processes in this depiction of episodes are inertia, the triggering of change, and replacement. Inertia, defined as an 'inability for organizations to change as rapidly as the environment' (Pfeffer, 1997: 163), takes a variety of forms. Whether the inability is attributed to deep structure (Gersick, 1991), first-order change (Bartunek, 1993), routines (Gioia, 1992), success-induced blind spots (Miller, 1993), top management tenure (Virany et al., 1992), identity maintenance (Sevon, 1996), culture (Harrison & Carroll, 1991), complacency (Kotter, 1996), or technology (Tushman & Rosenkopf, 1992), inertia is a central feature of the analytic framework associated with episodic change. Romanelli and Tushman (1994) are representative when they argue that it takes a revolution to alter 'a system of interrelated organizational parts that is maintained by mutual dependencies among the parts and with competitive, regulatory, and technological systems outside the organization that reinforce the legitimacy of managerial choices that produced the parts' (p. 1144). Because interrelations are dense and tight, it takes larger interventions to realign them. An example of processes of inertia is Miller's research (1993, 1994) demonstrating that inertia is often the unintended consequence of successful performance. Successful organizations discard practices, people, and structures regarded as peripheral to success and grow more inattentive to signals that suggest the need for change, more insular and sluggish in adaptation, and more immoderate in their processes, tending toward extremes of risk-taking or conservatism. These changes simplify the organization, sacrifice adaptability, and increase inertia.

Although inertia creates the tension that precedes episodic change, the actual triggers of change come from at least five sources: the environment, performance, characteristics of top managers, structure, and strategy (Huber et al., 1993). Huber et al. found that all five were associated with internal and external changes, but in ways specific to the kind of change being examined (10 specific changes were measured; see Huber et al., 1993: 223). For example, consistent with Romanelli and Tushman's data, Huber et al. found that downturns in growth (a potential revolutionary period) were positively related to externally focused changes and to changes in organizational form. Interestingly, upturns in growth were also positively related to externally focused changes, a finding interpreted to suggest that 'desirable but risky changes might be held in abeyance until performance improves' (Huber et al., 1993: 230).

A final property of the analytic framework associated with episodic change is that it often assumes that change occurs through replacement (Ford & Backoff, 1988; Ford & Ford, 1994). The idea of replacement is that 'one entity sequentially takes the place of or substitutes for a second. The first identity does not become the second but is substituted for it. The change process becomes a sequence of events in which a person (a) determines or defines what currently exists (what is A), (b) determines or defines its replacement (Not-A), (c) engages in action to remove what is currently there, and (d) implants its replacement' (Ford & Ford, 1994: 773, 775). Beer et al. (1990) demonstrate that replacement of one program with another seldom works. The problem with such a logic is that it restricts change to either–or thinking. The only way to prevent A is to apply its reciprocal or a counterbalance or its opposite, which precludes the possible diagnosis that both A and not-A may be the problem. For example, authoritarian decision-making may be counterbalanced by mandating that decisions be made at lower levels (Roach & Bednar, 1997). However, this change is simply authoritarian decision-abdication, which means that authoritarian control from the top persists. As lower-level managers try harder to guess what the right decisions are (i.e. those decisions top management would have made) and err in doing so, the mandate is reaffirmed more forcefully, which worsens performance even more and creates a vicious circle. What was really intended was the creation of expectations of individual autonomy that allowed decisions to be made at the level where the expertise and information are lodged.

In conclusion, the basic analytical framework involving episodic change assumes in part that inertia is a force to contend with. When inertia builds, some trigger usually precipitates an episode of replacement. To understand episodic change is to think carefully about inertia, triggers, and replacements.

## IDEAL EPISODIC ORGANIZATIONS

There is no one 'ideal model of an effectively functioning organization' that suggests directions for episodic change and values to be used in judging the success of an episodic change intervention (e.g. survival, growth). This is so for the simple reason that episodic change is a generic description applicable across diverse organizational forms and values. There is no direct parallel in the case of episodic change for Dunphy's (1996) assertion that the ideal model of an effectively functioning sociotechnical system is 'a representative democratic community composed of semi-autonomous work groups with the ability to learn continuously through participative action research' (p. 543). If organizational change generally occurs in the context of failures to adapt, then the ideal organization is one that continuously adapts. And this holds true whether the focus is episodic or continuous change. The ideal in both cases would resemble the successful self-organizing firms that Brown and Eisenhardt (1997) found in the computer industry. Successful firms did not rely on either a purely mechanistic or purely organic process and structure. Instead, successful firms had well-defined managerial responsibilities and clear project priorities while also allowing the design processes to be highly flexible, improvising, and continuously changing. Successful firms also had richly connected communication systems, including informal and electronic grapevines, and a very high value on cross-project communication. Two important features that encouraged both episodic and continuous change were (a) semistructures poised between order and disorder with only some features being prescribed and (b) intentional links in time between present projects and future probes to reduce discontinuity and preserve direction. The authors interpret this pattern as an instance of bounded instability and argue that it may be more motivating, more attuned to sense-making in a fast-changing environment, and more flexible (as a result of capabilities for improvisation) than patterns that are pure instances of either mechanistic or organic systems.

A more generic ideal, suited for both episodic and continuous change interventions, is found in Burgelman's (1991) attempt to show how organizations adapt by a mixture of continuous strategic initiatives that are within the scope of the current strategy (induced processes) and additional episodic initiatives that are outside the current strategy (autonomous processes). An ideal model framed more in terms of management practices is Pfeffer's (1998) description of seven 'high performance management practices' that produce innovation and productivity, are difficult to copy, and lead to sustained profitability. These practices are employment security, selective hiring, self-managed teams and decentralization, extensive training, reduction of status differences, sharing of information, and high and contingent compensation.

## INTERVENTION THEORY IN EPISODIC CHANGE

Episodic change tends to be dramatic change, as Lewin made clear: 'To break open the shell of complacency and self-righteousness it is sometimes necessary to bring about deliberately an emotional stir-up' (Lewin, 1951, quoted in Marshak, 1993: 400). While strong emotions may provide 'major sources of energy for revolutionary change' (Gersick, 1991), they may also constrain cognition and performance in ways analogous to those of stress (Driskell & Salas, 1996; Barr & Huff, 1997).

Because episodic change requires both equilibrium breaking and transitioning to a newly created equilibrium, it is most closely associated with planned, intentional change. Intentional change occurs when 'a change agent deliberately and consciously sets out to establish conditions and circumstances that are different from what they are now and then accomplishes that through some set or series of actions and interventions either singularly or in collaboration with other people' (Ford & Ford, 1995: 543). And this is where Lewin comes into his own.

Lewin's ideas remain central to episodic change because they assume that inertia in the form of a quasi-stationary equilibrium is the main impediment to change (Schein, 1996). Lewin's insight was that an equilibrium would change more easily if restraining forces such as personal defenses, group norms, or organizational culture were unfrozen. Schein's (1996) work suggests that unfreezing basically involves three processes: (a) disconfirmation of expectations; (b) induction of learning anxiety if the disconfirming data are accepted as valid and relevant (we fear that 'if we admit to ourselves and others that something is wrong or imperfect, we will lose our effectiveness, our self-esteem, and maybe even our identity' (p. 29); and (c) provision of psychological safety that converts anxiety into motivation to change.

Schein's (1996) work also suggests an updated understanding of what happens after unfreezing. Change occurs through cognitive restructuring in which words are redefined to mean something other than had been assumed, concepts are interpreted more broadly, or new standards of judgment and evaluation are learned. Thus, when Lewin persuaded housewives during the Second World War to serve kidneys and liver, he cognitively redefined their standards of what was acceptable meat by means of a process that mixed together identification with positive role models, insight, and trial-and-error learning. When unfreezing occurs and people are motivated to learn something, they tend to be especially attentive to ideas that are in circulation, a mechanism discussed later as 'translation'. Refreezing that embeds the new behavior and forestalls relapse is most likely to occur when the behavior fits both the personality of the target and the relational expectations of the target's social network.

Lewin also remains relevant to episodic change because his other five assumptions about change are compatible with its analytical framework. These five assumptions (Marshak, 1993) are: (a) linear assumption (movement is from one state to another in a forward direction through time); (b) progressive assumption (movement is from a lesser state to a better state); (c) goal assumption (movement is toward a specific end state); (d) disequilibrium assumption (movement requires disequilibrium); and (e) separateness assumption (movement is planned and managed by people apart from the system). Summarized in this form, Lewin's change model resembles 'Newtonian physics where movement results from the application of a set of forces on an object' (Marshak, 1993: 412). Complexity theory is the least 'Newtonian' of the several formulations associated with episodic change, and its continued development may broaden our understanding of episodic interventions. For example, complexity theory implies that improved performance may at times be linked to the surrender of control, which is a very different image from one of attacking inertia through coercive means (e.g. Dunphy & Stace, 1988).

Newer analyses relevant to episodic change suggest how difficult it is to unfreeze patterns but also that attempts at unfreezing start earlier than was previously thought. Both conclusions are the result of microlevel research on smoking cessation and weight loss by Prochaska and his colleagues (Prochaska et al., 1992; Grimley et al., 1994). They propose that when people are exposed to change interventions, they are at one of four stages: precontemplation, contemplation, action, and maintenance. Precontemplators are unaware of any need to change, whereas contemplators are aware that there is a problem and they are thinking about change but have not yet made a commitment. People can remain in the contemplation stage for long periods, up to two years in the case of smokers. Action, the stage most change agents equate with change, is the stage in which people actually alter their behaviors. In any change intervention, few people are in the action stage. In smoking cessation programs, for example, empirical findings suggest that only 15 percent of the smokers in any given worksite are ready for action.

The important result, in the context of episodic change, is the finding that most people who reach the action stage relapse and change back to previous habits three or four times before they maintain the newer sequence. Beer et al. (1990: 50) found several false starts in renewal efforts at General Products. This suggests that change is not a linear movement through the four stages but a spiral pattern of contemplation, action, and relapse and then successive returns to contemplation, action, and relapse before entering the maintenance and then termination stages. Relapse should be more common in discrete episodic change than in cumulative continuous change because larger changes are involved. What is interesting is that 85 percent of the relapsers return to the stage of contemplation, not to the stage of precontemplation. This means that they are closer to taking action again following relapse than change agents suspected. The fact that change passes through a contemplation stage also means that people are changing before we can observe any alterations in their behavior. This suggests that interventions may have value even when no action is observed.

## ROLE OF CHANGE AGENT IN EPISODIC CHANGE

The role of the change agent in episodic change is that of prime mover who creates change. Macy and Izumi (1993: 245–250) list 60 work design changes made by prime movers in North American interventions. The steps by which people enact the role of prime mover (e.g. Kotter, 1996; Nadler, 1998) look pretty much the same. What is different in newer work is the demonstration that one can be a prime mover on a larger scale than in the past (Weisbord, 1987). Many practitioners are focusing on larger gatherings (Axelrod, 1992; Dannemiller & Jacobs, 1992) with more issues on the table for immediate action (e.g. Ashkenas & Jick, 1992), concentrated in shorter periods of time (Torbert, 1994). Large-scale change in very large groups is counterintuitive, since size and participation tend to be negatively related (e.g. Gilmore & Barnett, 1992; Pasmore & Pagans, 1992). Normally, large group settings induce stereotyping, decreased ownership of ideas, increased abstraction, and less willingness to express unique thoughts. The challenge for prime movers is to neutralize these tendencies. To do so requires that they abandon several traditional organizational development (OD) assumptions. Large-scale interventions rely less on action theory and discrepancy theory and more on systems theory; less on closely held, internal data generation and more on gathering data from the environment and sharing it widely; less on slow downward cascades and more on real-time analysis and decision-making; less on individual unit learning and more on learning about the whole organization; less on being senior management driven and more on a mixed model of being driven by both senior management and the organization; less consultant centered and more participant centered; less incremental and more fundamental in terms of the depth of change (Bunker & Alban, 1992).

There has also been an increasingly refined understanding of specific ways in which change agents can be effective prime movers. As Rorty (1989) observed, 'a talent for speaking differently, rather than for arguing well, is the chief instrument of cultural change' (p. 7). Language interventions are becoming a crucial means for agents to create change (e.g. Bate, 1990; O'Connor, 1995). Bartunek (1993) argues that to produce second-order change in a pre-existing shared schema requires a strong alternative schema, presented clearly and persistently. Barrett et al. (1995) demonstrate that changes symbolizing a successful revolution are basically interpretations that point to a new alignment of the triggers that initiated the revolutionary period.

Wilkof et al. (1995) report on their attempt to intervene in the relationships between two companies in a difficult partnership. Their initial attempts to improve cooperation focused on feeding back problems from a traditional data collection. This failed and led to the discovery that although there were technical or structural solutions available, the actors could not agree because of a vast difference in cultural lenses and diametrically opposed interpretations of meaning. The consultant, therefore, changed her strategy. She began meeting independently with the actors from each organization. In the meetings she would meet each condemnation not with data or argument but with an alternative interpretation from the cultural lens of the other company. She calls the process 'cultural consciousness raising'. The authors underscore the importance of working with actors to interpret the actions of others not as technical incompetence but as behaviors that are consistent with a particular cultural purpose, meaning, and history.

# CONTINUOUS CHANGE

The phrase 'continuous change' is used to group together organizational changes that tend to be ongoing, evolving, and cumulative. A common presumption is that change is emergent, meaning that it is 'the realization of a new pattern of organizing in the absence of explicit a priori intentions' (Orlikowski, 1996: 65). Change is described as situated and grounded in continuing updates of work processes (Brown & Duguid, 1991) and social practices (Tsoukas, 1996). Researchers focus on 'accommodations to and experiments with the everyday contingencies, breakdowns, exceptions, opportunities, and unintended consequences' (Orlikowski, 1996: 65). As these accommodations 'are repeated, shared, amplified, and sustained, they can, over time, produce perceptible and striking organizational changes' (p. 89). The distinctive quality of continuous change is the idea that small continuous adjustments, created simultaneously across units, can cumulate and create substantial change. That scenario presumes tightly coupled interdependencies. When interdependencies loosen, these same continuous adjustments, now confined to smaller units, remain important as pockets of innovation that may prove appropriate in future environments.

## BASIC METAPHORS: ORGANIZING FOR CONTINUOUS CHANGE

The metaphor of organization that is implicit in conceptualizations of continuous change is not the reciprocal of metaphors associated with episodic change. The dynamics are different, as would be expected from a shift to a more micro perspective and to the assumption that everything changes all the time (Ford & Ford, 1994). From closer in, the view of organization associated with continuous change is built around recurrent interactions as the feedstock of organizing, authority tied to tasks rather than positions, shifts in authority as tasks shift, continuing development of response repertoires, systems that are self-organizing rather than fixed, ongoing redefinition of job descriptions, mindful construction of responses in the moment rather than mindless application of past responses embedded in routines (Wheatley, 1992: 90), and acceptance of change as a constant. Although these properties may seem prescriptive rather than descriptive and better suited to describe the 'ideal organization' than the 'basic metaphor', they are straightforward outcomes when people act as if change is continuous, organizing constitutes organization, and stability is an accomplishment.

Images of organization that are compatible with continuous change include those built around the ideas of improvisation, translation, and learning. The image of organization built around improvisation is one in which variable in-puts to self-organizing groups of actors induce continuing modification of work practices and ways of relating. This image is represented by the statement that change 'is often realized through the ongoing variations which emerge frequently, even imperceptibly, in the slippages and improvisations of everyday activity' (Orlikowski, 1996: 88–89). Improvisation is said to occur when 'the time gap between these events [of planning and implementation] narrows so that in the limit, composition converges with execution. The more improvisational an act, the narrower the time gap between composing and performing, designing and producing, or planning and implementing' (Moorman & Miner, 1998a). Empirically, Moorman and Miner (1998b) found that improvisation often replaced the use of standard procedures in new product development and, in the presence of developed organizational memory, had positive effects on design effectiveness and on cost savings. Orlikowski (1996), in her study of changes in an incident tracking system, found repeated improvisation in work practices that then led to restructuring. Similar descriptions are found in Crossan et al. (1996), Brown and Eisenhardt (1997), and Weick (1993).

The image of organization built around the idea of translation is one of a setting where there is continuous adoption and editing (Sahlin-Andersson, 1996) of ideas that bypass the apparatus of planned change and have their impact through a combination of fit with purposes at hand, institutional salience, and chance. The idea that change is a continuous process of translation derives from an extended gloss (Czarniawska & Sevon, 1996) of Latour's observation that 'the spread in time and place of anything—claims, orders, artefacts, goods—is in the hands of people; each of these people may act in many different ways, letting the token drop, or modifying it, or deflecting it, or betraying it, or adding to it, or appropriating it' (Latour, 1986: 267). The controlling image is the travel of ideas and what happens when ideas are turned into new actions in new localities (Czarniawska & Joerges, 1996). Translation is not a synonym for diffusion. The differences are crucial. The impetus for the spread of ideas does not lie with the persuasiveness of the originator of the idea. Instead, the impetus comes from imitators and from their conception of the situation, their self-identity and others' identity and their analogical reasoning (Sevon, 1996). The first actor in the chain is no more important than the last; ideas do not move from more saturated to less saturated environments; it is impossible to know when the process concludes, since all ideas are in the air all the time and are implemented depending on the purpose at hand (Czarniawska & Joerges, 1996). A match between a purpose and an idea does not depend on inherent properties of the idea. Instead, it is assumed that 'most ideas can be proven to fit most problems, assuming good will, creativity, and a tendency to consensus' (p. 25). Thus, the act of translation creates the match.

The image of organization built around the idea of learning is one of a setting where work and activity are defined by repertoires of actions and knowledge and where learning itself is defined as 'a change in an organization's response repertoire' (Sitkin et al., 1998). What this adds to the understanding of continuous change is the idea that it is a range of skills and knowledge that is altered rather than a specific action, as well as the idea that a change is not just substitution but could also include strengthening existing skills. A change in repertoire is also a change in the potential for action, which means action may not be manifest at the time of learning (Pye, 1994). To specify learning in terms of a response repertoire is also to specify a mechanism by which change is retained (Moorman & Miner, 1997). Other retention-learning mechanisms discussed in the literature include organizational routines (March, 1994), know-how embedded in communities of practice (Brown & Duguid, 1991), distributed memory (Wegner, 1987), distributed information processing systems (Tsoukas, 1996), structures of collective mind (Weick & Roberts, 1993), and organizational memory (Walsh & Ungson, 1991). Summaries of recent work on organizational learning can be found in Huber (1991), Miller (1996), Easterby-Smith (1997), Mirvis (1996), and Lundberg (1989).

In each of these three images, organizations produce continuous change by means of repeated acts of improvisation involving simultaneous composition and execution, repeated acts of translation that convert ideas into useful artifacts that fit purposes at hand, or repeated acts of learning that enlarge, strengthen, or shrink the repertoire of responses.

## ANALYTIC FRAMEWORK: THE CONTINUOUS CHANGE PROCESS

The following description summarizes the analytic framework of continuous change:

> Each variation of a given form is not an abrupt or discrete event, neither is it, by itself discontinuous. Rather, through a series of ongoing and situated accommodations, adaptations, and alterations (that draw on previous variations and mediate future ones), sufficient modifications may be enacted over time that fundamental changes are achieved. There is no deliberate orchestration of change here, no technological inevitability, no dramatic discontinuity, just recurrent and reciprocal variations in practice over time. Each shift in practice creates the conditions for further breakdowns, unanticipated outcomes, and innovations, which in turn are met with more variations. Such variations are ongoing; there is no beginning or end point in this change process. (Orlikowski, 1996: 66)

Implicit in that description are several important processes, including change through ongoing variations in practice, cumulation of variations, continuity in place of dramatic discontinuity, continuous disequilibrium as variations beget variations, and no beginning or end point. What is less prominent in this description are key properties of episodic change, such as inertia, triggers, and replacement. Continuous change could be viewed as a series of fast mini-episodes of change, in which case inertia might take the form of tendencies to normalization (Vaughan, 1996) or competency traps (Levinthal & March, 1993). Triggers to change might take the form of temporal milestones (Gersick, 1989, 1994) or dissonance between beliefs and actions (Inkpen & Crossan, 1995). Replacements might take the form of substituting expert practices for practices of novices (Klein, 1998). But the more central issues in the case of continuous change are those of continuity and scale.

Issues of continuity are associated with the concept of organizational culture (Trice & Beyer, 1993). Culture is important in continuous change because it holds the multiple changes together, gives legitimacy to nonconforming actions that improve adaptation and adaptability (Kotter & Heskett, 1992), and embeds the know-how of adaptation into norms and values (O'Reilly & Chatman, 1996). Culture as the vehicle that preserves the know-how of adaptation is implied in this description: 'If we understand culture to be a stock of knowledge that has been codified into a pattern of recipes for handling situations, then very often with time and routine they become tacit and taken for granted and form the schemas which drive action' (Colville et al., 1993: 559). Culture, viewed as a stock of knowledge, serves as a scheme of expression that constrains what people do and a scheme of interpretation that constrains how the doing is evaluated. To change culture is to change climate (e.g. Schneider et al., 1996), uncover the tacit stock of knowledge by means of experiments that surface the particulars (Colville et al., 1993), or deconstruct organizational language paradigms (Bate, 1990). Although culture has been a useful vocabulary to understand stability and change, there are growing suggestions that as one moves away from treating it as a social control system, the concept may become less meaningful (Jordan, 1995).

The separate issue of scale arises because continuous changes in the form of 'situated micro-level changes that actors enact over time as they make sense of and act in the world' (Orlikowski, 1996: 91) are often judged to be too small, too much a follower strategy (Huber & Glick, 1993: 385), and even too 'unAmerican' (Hammond & Morrison, 1996: Ch. 3) to be of much importance when hyperturbulence and quantum change confront organizations (Meyer et al., 1993).

The analytical framework associated with continuous change interprets scale in a different way. The fact that the changes are micro does not mean that they are trivial (Staw, 1991; Staw & Sutton, 1993). Representative of this view is Ford and Ford's (1995) observation, 'The macrocomplexity of organizations is generated, and changes emerge through the diversity and interconnectedness of many microconversations, each of which follows relatively simple rules' (p. 560). Small changes do not stay small, as complexity theory and the second cybernetics (Maruyama, 1963) make clear. Small changes can be decisive if they occur at the edge of chaos. Furthermore, in interconnected systems, there is no such thing as a marginal change, as Colville et al. (1993) demonstrated in their study of small experiments with culture change at British Customs. Microlevel changes also provide the platform for transformational change and the means to institutionalize it. Depictions of successful revolutions, however, tend to downplay the degree to which earlier sequences of incremental changes made them possible. This oversight is serious because people tend to attribute the success of revolution to its break with the past and its vision of the future, whereas that success may actually lie in its connection with the past and its retrospective rewriting of what earlier micro-changes meant.

In conclusion, the basic analytical framework for continuous change assumes that revolutions are not necessary to shatter what basically does not exist. Episodic change is driven by inertia and the inability of organizations to keep up, while continuous change is driven by alertness and the inability of organizations to remain stable. The analytic framework for continuous change specifies that contingencies, breakdowns, opportunities, and contexts make a difference. Change is an ongoing mixture of reactive and proactive modifications, guided by purposes at hand, rather than an intermittent interruption of periods of convergence.

## IDEAL CONTINUOUS ORGANIZATIONS

The 'ideal organizations' described above in the context of episodic change serve just as well as ideals for continuous change, since those ideals incorporate capabilities for both forms of change. Thus, that discussion is compatible with the metaphors and analytical framework for continuous change.

## INTERVENTION THEORY IN CONTINUOUS CHANGE

Lewin's change model, with its assumptions of inertia, linearity, progressive development, goal seeking, disequilibrium as motivator, and outsider intervention, is relevant when it is necessary to create change. However, when change is continuous, the problem is not one of unfreezing. The problem is one of redirecting what is already under way. A different mind-set is necessary, and Marshak (1993) has suggested that one possibility derives from Confucian thought. The relevant assumptions are: (a) cyclical assumption (patterns of ebb and flow repeat themselves); (b) processional assumption (movement involves an orderly sequence through a cycle and departures cause disequilibrium); (c) journey assumption (there is no end state); (d) equilibrium assumption (interventions are to restore equilibrium and balance); (e) appropriateness assumption (correct action maintains harmony); and (f) change assumption (nothing remains the same forever).

In the face of inertia, it makes sense to view a change intervention as a sequence of unfreeze, transition, refreeze. But in the face of continuous change, a more plausible change sequence would be freeze, rebalance, unfreeze. To freeze continuous change is to make a sequence visible and to show patterns in what is happening (e.g. Argyris, 1990). To freeze is to capture sequences by means of cognitive maps (Cossette & Audet, 1992; Eden et al., 1992; Fiol & Huff, 1992), schemas (Bartunek, 1993; Tenkasi & Boland, 1993), or war stories (Boje, 1991; O'Connor, 1996). To rebalance is to reinterpret, relabel, and resequence the patterns so that they unfold with fewer blockages. To rebalance is to reframe issues as opportunities (Dutton, 1993), to reinterpret history using appreciative inquiry (e.g. Cooperrider & Srivasta, 1987; Hammond, 1996), to differentiate more boldly among 'the external world, the social world, and the world of inner subjectivity' (Thachankary, 1992: 198), or to be responsive to concerns about justice (Novelli et al., 1995). Thus, a story of intense but unproductive meetings is rewritten as a story affirming the value of 'corporateness' in an international nonprofit organization (Thachankary, 1992: 221). Finally, to unfreeze after rebalancing is to resume improvisation, translation, and learning in ways that are now more mindful of sequences, more resilient to anomalies, and more flexible in their execution.

An important new means of rebalancing continuous change is the use of a logic of attraction, which is the counterpart of the logic of replacement in episodic change. As the name implies, people change to a new position because they are attracted to it, drawn to it, inspired by it. There is a focus on moral power, the attractiveness or being state of the change agent, the freedom of the change target, and the role of choice in the transformational process. Kotter (1996) asks the question, is change something one manages or something one leads? To manage change is to tell people what to do (a logic of replacement), but to lead change is to show people how to be (a logic of attraction). R.E. Quinn (1996) argues that most top managers assume that change is something that someone with authority does to someone who does not have authority (e.g. Boss & Golembiewski, 1995). They overlook the logic of attraction and its power to pull change.

To engage this logic of attraction, leaders must first make deep changes in themselves, including self-empowerment (Spreitzer & Quinn, 1996). When deep personal change occurs, leaders then behave differently toward their direct reports, and the new behaviors in the leader attract new behaviors from followers. When leaders model personal change, organizational change is more likely to take place. A similar logic is implicit in Cohen and Tichy's (1997) recent emphasis on top managers developing a teachable point of view. Leaders who first consolidate their stories and ideas about what matters undergo personal change before organizational change is attempted. Subsequent organizational change is often more effective because it is led by more attractive leaders. Beer et al. (1990: 194–195) raise the interesting subtlety, based on their data, that inconsistency between word and action at the corporate level does not affect change effectiveness, but it does have a negative effect for leaders at the unit level. Their explanation is that inconsistency at the top is seen as necessary to cope with diverse pressures from stockholders and the board but is seen as insincerity and hypocrisy at other levels.

## ROLE OF CHANGE AGENT IN CONTINUOUS CHANGE

If continuous change is altered by freezing and rebalancing, then the role of the change agent becomes one of managing language, dialogue, and identity, as we saw above. Change agents become important for their ability to make sense (Weick, 1995) of change dynamics already under way. They recognize adaptive emergent changes, make them more salient, and reframe them (Bate, 1990). They explain current upheavals, where they are heading, what they will have produced by way of a redesign, and how further intentional changes can be made at the margins.

To redirect continuous change is to be sensitive to discourse. Schein (1993) argues that dialogue, which he defines as interaction focused on thinking processes and how they are preformed by past experience, enables groups to create a shared set of meanings and a common thinking process. 'The most basic mechanism of acquiring new information that leads to cognitive restructuring is to discover in a conversational process that the interpretation that someone else puts on a concept is different from one's own' (Schein, 1996: 31). Barrett et al. (1995) and Dixon (1997) also argue that the most powerful change interventions occur at the level of everyday conversation. J. Quinn (1996) demonstrates in the context of strategic change that good conversation is vocal, reciprocating, issues-oriented, rational, imaginative, and honest. And Ford and Ford (1995) argue that change agents produce change through various combinations of five kinds of speech acts: assertives or claims, directives or requests, commissives or promises, expressives that convey affective state, and declarations that announce a new operational reality. These speech acts occur in different combinations to constitute four different conversations: conversations of change, understanding, performance, and closure.

## CONCLUSION

Our review suggests both that change starts with failures to adapt and that change never starts because it never stops. Reconciliation of these disparate themes is a source of ongoing tension and energy in recent change research. Classic machine bureaucracies, with their reporting structures too rigid to adapt to faster-paced change, have to be unfrozen to be improved. Yet with differentiation of bureaucratic tasks comes more internal variation, more diverse views of distinctive competence, and more diverse initiatives. Thus, while some things may appear not to change, other things do. Most organizations have pockets of people somewhere who are already adjusting to the new environment. The challenge is to gain acceptance of continuous change throughout the organization so that these isolated innovations will travel and be seen as relevant to a wider range of purposes at hand.

Recent work suggests, ironically, that to understand organizational change one must first understand organizational inertia, its content, its tenacity, its interdependencies. Recent work also suggests that change is not an on–off phenomenon nor is its effectiveness contingent on the degree to which it is planned. Furthermore, the trajectory of change is more often spiral or open-ended than linear. All of these insights are more likely to be kept in play if researchers focus on 'changing' rather than 'change'. A shift in vocabulary from 'change' to 'changing' directs attention to actions of substituting one thing for another, of making one thing into another thing, or of attracting one thing to become other than it was. A concern with 'changing' means greater appreciation that change is never off, that its chains of causality are longer and less determinate than we anticipated, and that whether one's viewpoint is global or local makes a difference in the rate of change that will be observed, the inertias that will be discovered, and the size of accomplishments that will have been celebrated.

## REFERENCES

Argyris, C. (1990) *Overcoming Organizational Defenses: Facilitating Organizational Learning*. Boston: Allyn & Bacon.

Arthur, W.B. (1995) Positive feedbacks in the economy. In T. Kuran (ed.) *Increasing Returns and Path Dependence in the Economy* (pp. 1–32). Ann Arbor, MI: University of Michigan Press.

Ashkenas, R.N. & Jick, T.D. (1992) From dialogue to action in GE work-out: developmental learning in a change process. *Research in Organizational Change Development*, **6**, 267–287.

Austin, J.R. (1997) A method for facilitating controversial social change in organizations: Branch Rickey and the Brooklyn Dodgers. *Journal of Applied Behavioral Science*, **33**, 101–118.

Axelrod, D. (1992) Getting everyone involved: how one organization involved its employees, supervisors, and managers in redesigning the organization. *Journal of Applied Behavioral Science*, **28**, 499–509.

Bacharach, S.B., Bamberger, P. & Sonnenstuhl, W.J. (1996) The organizational transformation process: the micropolitics of dissonance reduction and the alignment of logics of action. *Administrative Science Quarterly*, **41**, 477–506.

Barr, P.S. & Huff, A.S. (1997) Seeing isn't believing: understanding diversity in the timing of strategic response. *Journal of Management Studies*, **34**, 337–370.

Barrett, F.J., Thomas, G.F. & Hocevar, S.P. (1995) The central role of discourse in large-scale change: a social construction perspective. *Journal of Applied Behavioral Science*, **31**, 352–372.

Bartunek, J.M. (1993) The multiple cognitions and conflicts associated with second order organizational change. In J.K. Mumighan (ed.) *Social Psychology in Organizations: Advances in Theory and Research* (pp. 322–349). Englewood Cliffs, NJ: Prentice Hall.

Bartunek, J.M. & Moch, M.K. (1994) Third-order organizational change and the western mystical tradition. *Journal of Organizational Change Management*, **7**, 24–41.

Bate, P. (1990) Using the culture concept in an organization development setting. *Journal of Applied Behavioral Science*, **26**, 83–106.

Bateson, G. (1972) *Steps to an Ecology of Mind*. New York: Ballantine.

Beer, M., Eisenstat, R.A. & Spector, B. (1990) *The Critical Path to Corporate Renewal*. Boston: Harvard Business School Press.

Boje, D. (1991) The storytelling organization: a study of story performances in an office supply firm. *Administrative Science Quarterly*, **36**, 106–126.

Boss, R.W. & Golembiewski, R.T. (1995) Do you have to start at the top? The chief executive officer's role in successful organization development efforts. *Journal of Applied Behavioral Science*, **31**, 259–277.

Bougon, M.G. (1992) Congregate cognitive maps: a unified dynamic theory of organization and strategy. *Journal of Management Studies*, **29**, 369–389.

Brown, J.S. & Duguid, P. (1991) Organizational learning and communities-of-practice: toward a unified view of working, learning, and innovation. *Organizational Science*, **2**, 40–57.

Brown, S.L. & Eisenhardt, K.M. (1997) The art of continuous change: linking complexity theory and time-paced evolution in relentlessly shifting organizations. *Administrative Science Quarterly*, **42**, 1–34.

Browning, L.D., Beyer, J.M. & Shetler, J.C. (1995) Building cooperation in a competitive industry: Sematech and the semiconductor industry. *Academy of Management Journal*, **38**, 113–151.

Bunker, B.B. & Alban, B.T. (1992) Conclusion: what makes large group interventions effective? *Applied Behavioral Science*, **28**, 579–591.

Burgelman, R.A. (1991) Intraorganizational ecology of strategy making and organizational adaptation: theory and field research. *Organizational Science*, **2**, 239–262.

Cheng, Y.T. & Van de Ven, A.H. (1996) Learning the innovation journey: order out of chaos? *Organizational Science*, **7**, 593–614.

Cohen, E. & Tichy, N. (1997) How leaders develop leaders. *Training and Development*, **51**, 58–74.

Colville, I., Dalton, K. & Tomkins, C. (1993) Developing and understanding cultural change in HM customs and excise: there is more to dancing than knowing the next steps. *Public Administration*, **71**, 549–566.

Cooperrider, D.L. & Srivasta, S. (1987) Appreciative inquiry in organizational life. In R.W. Woodman & W.A. Pasmore (eds) *Research in Organizational Change and Development* (vol. 1, pp. 129–169). Greenwich, CT: JAI Press.

Cossette, P. & Audet, M. (1992) Mapping of an idiosyncratic schema. *Journal of Management Studies*, **29**, 325–347.

Crossan, M.M., Lane, H.W., White, R.E. & Klus, L. (1996) The improvising organization; where planning meets opportunity. *Organizational Dynamics*, **24**, 20–35.

Czarniawska, B. & Joerges, B. (1996) Travels of ideas. In B. Czarniawska & G. Sevon (eds) *Translating Organizational Change* (pp. 13–48). New York: Walter de Gruyter.

Czarniawska, B. & Sevon, G. (eds) (1996) *Translating Organizational Change*. New York: Walter de Gruyter.

Dannemiller, K.D. & Jacobs, R.W. (1992) Changing the way organizations change: a revolution of common sense. *Journal of Applied Behavioral Science*, **28**, 480–498.

Dixon, N.M. (1997) The hallways of learning. *Organizational Dynamics*, **25**, 23–34.

Driskell, J.E. & Salas, E. (eds) (1996) *Stress and Human Performance*. Mahwah. NJ: Lawrence Erlbaum Associates.

Dunbar, R.L.M., Garud, R. & Raghuram, S. (1996) A frame for deframing in strategic analysis. *Journal of Management Inquiry*, **5**, 23–34.

Dunphy, D. (1996) Organizational change in corporate setting. *Human Relations*, **49**(5), 541–552.

Dunphy, D.C. & Stace, D.A. (1988) Transformational and coercive strategies for planned organizational change: beyond the OD model. *Organizational Studies*, **9**(3), 317–334.

Dutton, J.E. (1993) The making of organizational opportunities: an interpretive pathway to organizational change. *Research in Organizational Behavior*, **15**, 195–226.

Easterby-Smith, M. (1997) Disciplines of organizational learning: contributions and critiques. *Human Relations*, **50**, 1085–1113.

Eden, C., Ackerman, F. & Cropper, S. (1992) The analysis of cause maps. *Journal of Management Studies*, **29**, 309–323.

Fiol, C.M. & Huff, A.S. (1992) Maps for managers: where are we? Where do we go from here? *Journal of Management Studies*, **29**, 267–285.

Ford, J. & Backoff, R. (1988) Organizational change in and out of dualities and paradox. In R. Quinn & K. Cameron (eds) *Paradox and Transformation* (pp. 81–121). Cambridge, MA: Ballinger Press.

Ford, J.D. & Ford, L.W. (1994) Logics of identity, contradiction, and attraction in change. *Academy of Management Review*, **19**, 756–785.

Ford, J.D. & Ford, L.W. (1995) The role of conversations in producing intentional change in organizations. *Academy of Management Review*, **20**(3), 541–570.

Gersick, C.J.G. (1989) Marking time: predictable transitions in task groups. *Academy of Management Journal*, **32**, 274–309.

Gersick, C.J.G. (1991) Revolutionary change theories: a multilevel exploration of the punctuated equilibrium paradigm. *Academy of Management Review*, **16**, 10–36.

Gersick, C.J.G. (1994) Pacing strategic change: the case of a new venture. *Academy of Management Journal*, **37**, 9–45.

Gilmore, T.N. & Barnett, C. (1992) Designing the social architecture of participation in large groups to effect organizational change. *Journal of Applied Behavioral Science*, **28**, 534–548.

Gioia, D.A. (1992) Pinto fires and personal ethics: a script analysis of missed opportunities. *Journal of Business Ethics*, **11**, 379–389.

Golembiewski, R.T. & Boss, R.W. (1992) Phases of burnout in diagnosis and intervention: individual level of analysis in organization development and change. *Research in Organizational Change Development*, **6**, 115–152.

Greenwood, R. & Hinings, C.R. (1996) Understanding radical organizational change: bringing together the old and the new institutionalism. *Academy of Management Review*, **21**, 1022–1054.

Greiner, L. (1972) Evolution and revolution as organizations grow. *Harvard Business Review*, **50**(4), 37–46.

Grimley, D., Prochaska, J.O., Velicer, W.F., Blais, L.M. & DiClemente, C.C. (1994) The transtheoretical model of change. In M. Brinthaupt (ed.) *Changing the Self: Philosophies, Techniques, and Experiences* (pp. 201–227). Albany, NY: State University of NY Press.

Hammond, J. & Morrison, J. (1996) *The Stuff Americans Are Made of*. New York: Macmillan.

Hammond, S.A. (1996) *The Thin Book of Appreciative Inquiry*. Plano, TX: Kodiak Consult.

Harrison, J.R. & Carroll, G. (1991) Keeping the faith: a model of cultural transmission in formal organization. *Administrative Science Quarterly*, **36**, 552–582.

Hendry, C. (1996) Understanding and creating whole organizational change through learning theory. *Human Relations*, **49**, 621–641.

Huber, G.P. (1991) Organizational learning: an examination of the contributing processes and a review of the literatures. *Organizational Science*, **2**, 88–115.

Huber, G.P. & Glick, W.H. (eds) (1993) *Organizational Change and Redesign*. New York: Oxford University Press.

Huber, G.P., Sutcliffe, K.M., Miller, C.C. & Glick, W.H. (1993) Understanding and predicting organizational change. In G.P. Huber & W.H. Glick (eds) *Organizational Change and Redesign* (pp. 215–265). New York: Oxford University Press.

Inkpen, A.C. & Crossan, M.M. (1995) Believing is seeing: joint ventures and organization learning. *Journal of Management Studies*, **32**, 595–618.

Jordan, A.T. (1995) Managing diversity: translating anthropological insight for organization studies. *Journal of Applied Behavioral Science*, **31**, 124–140.

Kahn, R.L. (1974) Organizational development: some problems and proposals. *Journal of Applied Behavioral Science*, **10**, 485–502.

Katz, J. (1997) Ethnography's warrants. *Sociological Methods Research*, **25**, 391–423.

Kilduff, M. & Mehra, A. (1997) Postmodernism and organizational research. *Academy of Management Journal*, **22**, 453–481.

Klein, G. (1998) *Sources of Power*. Cambridge, MA: MIT Press.

Kotter, J.P. (1996) *Leading Change*. Boston: Harvard Business School Press.

Kotter, J.P. & Heskett, J.L. (1992) *Corporate Culture and Performance*. New York: The Free Press.

Langfield-Smith, K. (1992) Exploring the need for a shared cognitive map. *Journal of Management Studies*, **29**, 349–368.

Latour, B. (1986) The powers of association. In J. Law (ed.) *Power, Action, and Belief* (pp. 264–280). London: Routledge.

Laurila, J. (1997) The thin line between advanced and conventional new technology: a case study on paper industry management. *Journal of Management Studies*, **34**, 219–239.

Levinthal, D.A. & March, J.G. (1993) The myopia of learning. *Strategic Management Journal*, **14**, 95–112.

Lewin, K. (1951) *Field Theory in Social Science*. New York: Harper & Row.

Lundberg, C.C. (1989) On organizational learning: implications and opportunities for expanding organizational development. *Research in Organizational Change Development*, **3**, 61–82.

Macy, B.A. & Izumi, H. (1993) Organizational change, design, and work innovation: a meta-analysis of 131 North American field studies—1961–1991. *Research in Organizational Change Development*, **7**, 235–313.

March, J.G. (1994) *A Primer on Decision Making*. New York: The Free Press.

Marshak, R.J. (1993) Lewin meets Confucius: a review of the OD model of change. *Journal of Applied Behavioral Science*, **29**, 393–415.

Maruyama, M. (1963) The second cybernetics: deviation-amplifying mutual causal processes. *American Scientist*, **51**, 164–179.

McDaniel, R.R. Jr (1997) Strategic leadership: a view from quantum and chaos theories. *Health Care Management Review*, **Winter**, 21–37.

McKelvey, B. (1997) Quasi-natural organization science. *Organizational Science*, **8**, 352–380.

Meyer, A.D., Goes, J.B. & Brooks, O.R. (1993) Organizations reacting to hyperturbulence. In G.P. Huber & W.H. Glick (eds) *Organizational Change and Redesign* (pp. 66–111). New York: Oxford University Press.

Micklethwait, J. & Wooldridge, A. (1996) *The Witch Doctors*. New York: Times Books.

Miller, D. (1990) Organizational configurations: cohesion, changes, and prediction. *Human Relations*, **43**, 771–789.

Miller, D. (1993) The architecture of simplicity. *Academy of Management Review*, **18**, 116–138.

Miller, D. (1994) What happens after success: the perils of excellence. *Journal of Management Studies*, **31**, 325–358.

Miller, D. (1996) A preliminary typology of organizational learning: synthesizing the literature. *Journal of Management*, **22**, 485–505.

Mintzberg, H. & Westley, F. (1992) Cycles of organizational change. *Strategic Management Journal*, **13**, 39–59.

Mirvis, P.H. (1996) Historical foundations of organization learning. *Journal of Organizational Change Management*, **9**, 13–31.

Mirvis, P.H. (1997) Crossroads: 'social work' in organizations. *Organizational Science*, **8**, 192–206.

Moorman, C. & Miner, A.S. (1997) The impact of organizational memory on new product performance and creativity. *Journal of Marketing Research*, **34**, 91–106.

Moorman, C. & Miner, A.S. (1998a) Organizational improvisation and organizational memory. *Academy of Management Review*, **23(October)**, 698–723.

Moorman, C. & Miner, A.S. (1998b) The convergence of planning and execution: improvisation in new product development. *Journal of Marketing*, **61**, 1–20.

Nadler, D.A. (1998) *Champions of Change*. San Francisco: Jossey-Bass.

Nadler, D.A., Shaw, R.B. & Walton, A.E. (1995) *Discontinuous Change*. San Francisco: Jossey-Bass.

Nielsen, R.P. & Bartunek, J.M. (1996) Opening narrow routinized schemata to ethical stake holder consciousness and action. *Business & Society*, **35**, 483–519.

Nord, W.R. & Jermier, J.M. (1994) Overcoming resistance to resistance: insights from a study of the shadows. *Public Administration Quarterly*, **17**, 396–409.

Novelli, L., Bradley, L.K. & Shapiro, D.L. (1995) Effective implementation of organizational change: an organizational justice perspective. In C.L. Cooper (ed.) *Trends in Organizational Behavior* (pp. 15–37). London: John Wiley & Sons, Ltd.

O'Connor, E.S. (1995) Paradoxes of participation: textural analysis and organizational changes. *Organizational Studies*, **16**(5), 769–803.

O'Connor, E.S. (1996) Telling decisions: the role of narrative in decision making. In Z. Shapiro (ed.) *Organizational Decision Making* (pp. 304–323). New York: Cambridge University Press.

Olson, E.E. (1990) The transcendent function in organizational change. *Journal of Applied Behavioral Science*, **26**, 69–81.

O'Reilly, C.A. & Chatman, J.A. (1996) Culture as social control: corporations, cults and commitment. *Research in Organizational Behavior*, **18**, 157–200.

Orlikowski, W.J. (1996) Improvising organizational transformation overtime: a situated change perspective. *Information System Research*, **7**(1), 63–92.

O'Shea, J. & Madigan, C. (1997) *Dangerous Company*. New York: Times Books.

O'Toole, J. (1995) *Leading Change*. San Francisco: Jossey-Bass.

Pasmore, W.A. & Pagans, M.R. (1992) Participation, individual development, and organizational change: a preview and synthesis. *Journal of Management*, **18**, 375–397.

Pfeffer, J. (1997) *New Directions for Organization Theory*. New York: Oxford University Press.

Pfeffer, J. (1998) *The Human Equation*. Boston: Harvard Business School Press.

Porras, J.I. & Robertson, P.J. (1992) Organizational development: theory, practice, research. In M.D. Dunnette & L.M. Hough (eds) *Handbook of Organizational Psychology* (vol. 3, pp. 719–822). Palo Alto, CA: Consulting Psychologists Press.

Porras, J.I. & Silvers, R.C. (1991) Organization development and transformation. *Annual Review of Psychology*, **42**, 51–78.

Prochaska, J.O., DiClemente, C.C. & Norcross, J.C. (1992) In search of how people change: applications to addictive behaviors. *American Psychology*, **47**, 1102–1114.

Prochaska, J.O., DiClemente, C.C. & Norcross, J.C. (1997) In search of how people change: applications to addictive behaviors. In G. Marlatt (ed.) *Addictive Behaviors: Readings on Etiology, Prevention, and Treatment* (pp. 671–696). Washington, DC: American Psychologists Association.

Pye, A. (1994) Past, present and possibility: an integrative appreciation of learning from experience. *Management Learning*, **25**, 155–173.

Quinn, J.J. (1996) The role of 'good conversation' in strategic control. *Journal of Management Studies*, **33**, 381–394.

Quinn, R.E. (1996) *Deep Change: Discovering the Leader Within*. San Francisco: Jossey-Bass.

Random House (1987) *Random House Dictionary of The English Language* (2nd edn). New York: Random House. Unabridged.

Roach, D.W. & Bednar, D.A. (1997) The theory of logical types: a tool for understanding levels and types of change in organizations. *Human Relations*, **50**, 671–699.

Romanelli, E. & Tushman, M.L. (1994) Organizational transformation as punctuated equilibrium: an empirical test. *Academy of Management Journal*, **37**, 1141–1166.

Rorty, R. (1989) *Contingency, Irony, and Solidarity*. New York: Cambridge University Press.

Sahlin-Andersson, K. (1996) Imitating by editing success: the construction of organizational fields. In B. Czarniawska & G. Sevon (eds) *Translating Organizational Change* (pp. 69–92). New York: Walter de Gruyter.

Sandelands, L. (1998) *Feeling and Form in Social Life*. Lanham, MD: Rowman & Littlefield.

Sastry, M.A. (1997) Problems and paradoxes in a model of punctuated organizational change. *Administrative Science Quarterly*, **42**, 237–275.

Schein, E.H. (1993) On dialogue, culture, and organizational learning. *Organizational Dynamics*, **21**, 40–51.

Schein, E.H. (1996) Kurt Lewin's change theory in the field and in the classroom: notes toward a model of managed learning. *Systems Practice*, **9**, 27–47.

Schneider, B., Brief, A.P. & Guzzo, R.A. (1996) Creating a climate and culture for sustainable organizational change. *Organizational Development*, **24**, 7–19.

Sevon, G. (1996) Organizational imitation in identity transformation. In B. Czarniawska & G. Sevon (eds) *Translating Organizational Change* (pp. 49–68). New York: Walter de Gruyter.

Sitkin, S.B., Sutcliffe, K.M. & Weick, K.E. (1998) Organizational learning. In R. Dorf (ed.) *The Technology Management Handbook*. Boca Raton, FL: CRC Press.

Spreitzer, G.M. & Quinn, R.E. (1996) Empowering middle managers to be transformational leaders. *Journal of Applied Behavioral Science*, **32**(3), 237–261.

Stacey, R.D. (1995) The science of complexity: an alternative perspective for strategic change processes. *Strategic Management Journal*, **16**, 477–495.

Starbuck, W.H. (1993) Keeping a butterfly and an elephant in a house of cards: the elements of exceptional success. *Journal of Management Studies*, **30**, 885–921.

Staw, B.M. (1991) Dressing up like an organization: when psychological theories can explain organizational action. *Journal of Management*, **17**, 805–819.

Staw, B.M. & Sutton, R.I. (1993) Macro organizational psychology. In J.K. Murnighan (ed.) *Social Psychology in Organizations: Advances in Theory and Research*, (pp. 350–384). Englewood Cliffs, NJ: Prentice Hall.

Tenkasi, R.V. & Boland, R.J. (1993) Locating meaning making in organizational learning: the narrative basis of cognition. *Research in Organizational Change Development*, **7**, 77–103.

Thachankary, T. (1992) Organizations as 'texts': hermeneutics as a model for understanding organizational change. *Research in Organizational Change Development*, **6**, 197–233.

Torbert, W.R. (1994) Managerial learning, organizational learning: a potentially powerful redundancy. *Management Learning*, **25**, 57–70.

Trice, H.M. & Beyer, J.M. (1993) *The Culture of Work Organizations*. Englewood Cliffs, NJ: Prentice Hall.

Tsoukas, H. (1996) The firm as a distributed knowledge system: a constructionist approach. *Strategic Management Journal*, **17**, 11–26.

Tushman, M.L. & O'Reilly, C.A III (1996) The ambidextrous organization: managing evolutionary and revolutionary change. *California Management Review*, **38**, 1–23.

Tushman, M.L. & Romanelli, E. (1985) Organizational revolution: a metamorphosis model of convergence and reorientation. *Research in Organizational Behavior*, **7**, 171–222.

Tushman, M.L. & Rosenkopf, L. (1992) Organizational determinants of technological change: toward a sociology of technological evolution. *Research in Organizational Behavior*, **14**, 311–347.

Van de Ven, A.H. & Poole, M.S. (1995) Explaining development and change in organizations. *Academy of Management Review*, **20**(3), 510–540.

Vaughan, D. (1996) *The Challenger Launch Decision*. Chicago: University of Chicago Press.

Virany, B., Tushman, M.L. & Romanelli, E. (1992) Executive succession and organization outcomes in turbulent environments: an organization learning approach. *Organizational Science*, **3**, 72–91.

Walsh, J.P. & Ungson, G.R. (1991) Organizational memory. *Academy of Management Review*, **16**, 57–91.

Watzlawick, P., Weakland, J. & Fisch, R. (1974) *Change*. New York: W.W. Norton.

Wegner, D.M. (1987) Transactive memory: a contemporary analysis of the group mind. In B. Mullen & G.R. Goethals (eds) *Theories of Group Behavior* (pp. 185–208). New York: Springer.

Weick, K.E. (1993) Organizational redesign as improvisation. In G.P. Huber. & W.H. Glick (eds) *Organizational Change and Redesign* (pp. 346–379). New York: Oxford University Press.

Weick, K.E. (1995) *Sensemaking in Organizations*. Thousand Oaks, CA: Sage.

Weick, K.E. & Roberts, K.H. (1993) Collective mind in organizations: heedful interrelating on flight decks. *Administrative Science Quarterly*, **38**, 357–381.

Weisbord, M.R. (1987) *Productive Workplaces*. San Francisco: Jossey-Bass.

Wheatley, M.J. (1992) *Leadership and the New Science*. San Francisco: Berrett-Koehler.

Wilkof, M.V., Brown, D.W. & Selsky, J.W. (1995) When the stories are different: the influence of corporate culture mismatches on interorganizational relations. *Journal of Applied Behavioral Science*, **31**, 373–388.

Woodman, R.W. (1989) Organizational change and development: new arenas for inquiry and action. *Journal of Management*, **15**, 205–228.

# CHAPTER 10

# Thinking about Change in Different Colours

## Multiplicity in Change Processes

**Léon de Caluwé**

*Vrije Universiteit, Amsterdam and Twynstra, Management Consultants, Amersfoort,*
*The Netherlands*

**Hans Vermaak**

*Twynstra, Management Consultants, Amersfoort, The Netherlands*

Management literature has useful concepts to offer, ranging from tools such as business process redesign to concepts like the learning organization. Notwithstanding their value, each of them also have their limitations as arbitrary views of reality and solutions that have limited applicability. In that sense the literature brings value only by way of selective and capable use by change agents. It is their awareness and abilities that make change real. We are therefore inclined to advocate a balance between conceptual knowledge and reflective practitioning, the body of knowledge and learning as a guarantee for professionalism. In this chapter we summarize some insights into the field of organizational change that we have found very helpful in maintaining that balance.

Given that more organizational change takes place unplanned than planned and is more often unsuccessful than successful, we think there is justification for reflection on why change does not work. This implies making things more complex rather than simplifying them: searching for the hidden rules of the game, for informal processes, the political mechanisms in organizations, etc. In the first section of this chapter we do just that. Without going into too much detail here, we will discuss eight mini theories about irrationalities, hopefully just enough to elicit the response: 'Yes, that frustrated our change process too.' The message in this section is also that over-reliance on rational, top-down, and contingency approaches can be rendered fruitless as a result of such irrationalities.

This leads to the second section where we reflect on the question of what makes change work. For this, we explore five prevailing paradigms about change, each associated with certain beliefs and assumptions, and we characterize each in terms of their characteristics, such as predictability, ideals, pitfalls, style of change agent, and so on. These five paradigms, each typified by a colour, cover most change processes we see in real life and the theories about them in literature. The message of this section is that the existence of such multiple approaches can help organizations deal with complexity. At the same time, the fact that these approaches compete and conflict with one another can just as easily contribute to the lack of success of planned change. We propose that the ability of change agents to take a multi-paradigmatic perspective can make the difference between the two. It allows them to be aware of their own and others' ways of defining and solving problems and allows them to make more conscious and collective choices in that regard.

*Dynamics of Organizational Change and Learning.* Edited by J.J. Boonstra.
© 2004 John Wiley & Sons, Ltd. ISBN 0-471-87737-9.

# WHY CHANGE IS COMPLICATED

In this section, we describe theories and images illustrating why change is complicated. These theories and images, which we have observed in the past, have considerably widened our insight and will hopefully provide more in-depth knowledge of how change works and, more particularly, why it often does not. These are theories that are recognizable to and useful for people in our profession, and every change agent would do well to be familiar with them and take them into account. We discuss eight theories (more can be found elsewhere: de Caluwé & Vermaak, 2003a). With a degree of poetic licence, we give an outline of each theory together with one or more examples. For each of the clusters of related theories, we discuss the consequences for change processes.

In the first cluster we describe elements of Karl Weick's well-known theory regarding loosely coupled systems. We will talk about ambiguities and the loose coupling between opinions and behaviour. In the second cluster we describe the autonomy and confidence that characterize many staff members, especially in organizations of professionals, and the problems that arise in such organizations such as lack of control and the 'pocket veto'. In the third cluster we describe insights that arise from chaos theory or are related to it. The fourth and final cluster deals with socio-political mechanisms.

# ON LOOSELY COUPLED SYSTEMS

The theory of 'loose coupling' was developed by Karl Weick. He considers it applicable not only at the organizational level, with which we deal first, but also at the individual level.

## AMBIGUITIES IN ORGANIZATIONS

> Imagine that you are either the referee, coach, player or spectator at an unconventional soccer match: the field for the game is round; there are several goals scattered haphazardly around the circular field; people can enter and leave the game whenever they want to; they can throw balls in whenever they want; they can say 'that's my goal' whenever they want to, as many times as they want to, and for as many goals as they want to; the entire game takes place on a sloped field; and the game is played as if it makes sense.
>
> If you now substitute in the example above principals for referees, teachers for coaches, students for players, parents for spectators and schooling for soccer, you have an equally unconventional depiction of school organizations. The beauty of this depiction is that it captures a different set of realities within educational organizations than are caught when these same organizations are viewed through the tenets of bureaucratic theory.

The above passage is quoted from the opening lines of Karl E. Weick's (1976) article 'Educational Organizations as Loosely Coupled Systems'.

In our opinion, this passage can be broadly applied to most of the organizations we are familiar with, certainly where knowledge workers or professionals constitute the majority of the workforce. What is striking in the passage is how ambiguous many organizations are. There are a number of features that show these ambiguities:

- *Ambiguous objectives*: This is the case when an organization functions with various badly or vaguely defined, sometimes even conflicting, goals. These goals can be interpreted in a variety of ways and act as a 'cover' for a mixed bag of activities. Everyone can say 'that is my goal' whenever they want to, as often as they want to, and for as many goals as they want to. Many strategic documents and mission statements have these characteristics: they are often very ambiguous. Sometimes they camouflage disagreement (vague goals as a means of reaching compromises about differences of opinion), sometimes the words and sentences are interpreted in contrasting ways. The formal objectives might have some relationship with shop floor reality and working methods, but might equally well be entirely separated from them (loosely coupled).

- *Ambiguous technology (work processes)*: Many employees have little insight into the work processes that determine the output and value their organization produces. That causal connection between activity and value is difficult to define and to articulate. What makes good education? What factors contribute to effective medical treatment? What constitutes good consultancy? Both consensus and objective answers to these questions are hard to find. People often do things to the best of their ability and their comprehension, but such mixtures of effort and opinion do not necessarily produce tangible results. In truth, our knowledge about what works and what doesn't is limited. This explains why different teachers and doctors speak and act so differently and get away with it. What is good and what is not?
- *Ambiguous participation*: The involvement of persons or groups in any activity within an organization generally varies and thus is hard to pin down. Who participates in the decision-making about what and with what mandate? Who belongs to which group, department, or commission? Who is supposed to attend which meeting? If we work together, does that mean we take all the decisions together? If we want to increase participation, does this imply that people can sit in and listen to us, contribute ideas, have a vote, or change the whole agenda? The answers to these types of questions vary considerably depending on whom you ask, and, furthermore, the answers can vary from day to day.

In this view it is hard to see system goals that can be achieved along predictable and well-planned routes. The situation is one of ambiguity and variability, many loosely coupled elements that react to one another only slowly, infrequently, or not at all. This view is at odds with the idea of an organization as a consciously designed machine with all its parts geared to one another, with the intention of producing predictable outcomes. Weick's theory is a reaction to the systems approach where rational principles dominate (see, e.g., Knip, 1981).

## Loose Coupling between Intentions and Behavior

Loose coupling, according to Weick (1969), plays a role not only at the organizational level but also at the individual level: the way in which intentions and behaviour influence each other. There is a growing awareness that opinions and intentions have little influence on behaviour; the opposite seems to be the case. In other words, intentions and opinions are stated rationally after the event. Weick says that, consequently, behaviour and opinions at the individual level are as much uncoupled as systems are at the organizational level. Behaviour appears to function quite independently of opinions. If you ask people what the reason or motive was for their behaviour, they will construct something on the spot:

> There is a developing position in psychology which argues that intentions are a poor guide for action, intentions often follow rather than precede action, and that intentions and action are loosely coupled. Unfortunately, organizations continue to think that planning is a good thing, they spend much time on planning, and actions are assessed in terms of their fit with plans. Given a potential loose coupling between the intentions and actions of organizational members, it should come as no surprise that administrators are baffled and angered when things never happen the way they were supposed to. (Weick, 1976)

In order to clarify intentions, many organizations invest a great deal of time in developing plans. However, the theory suggests that this is a dead-end street: the coupling becomes even looser than it was. Examples of this can be found in approaches to change where people first hold numerous meetings to decide exactly what it is that needs to be changed and how the change will be tackled. The result is a mass of memos and documents but seldom an actual behaviour change. Worse still, the contents of these memos bear little relationship to how people actually work and behave.

Instead of concentrating on plans, intentions, and opinions, it is also possible to ask people to make explicit their behaviour and to reflect on it. This lays bare the implicit opinions that underlie their actions. The difference between their implicit and explicit opinions becomes clear as it reveals to scrutiny the loose coupling between behaviour and opinions. Weick regards this consciousness raising as an important exercise, the best way of creating a 'tighter coupling' between behaviour and opinions.

## IMPLICATIONS OF LOOSE COUPLING FOR CHANGE AGENTS AND CHANGE PROCESSES

Weick's observations that ambiguities increasingly occur mean that it is difficult to characterize organizations as entities that follow a univocal course and a clear rational approach. They can much better be characterized as networks of autonomous centres (sometimes right down to the level of the individual staff members) that, in their dealings with each other, are continually searching for an identity and a direction. For change agents, the loosely coupled character of organizations means that, in many cases, they cannot limit themselves to a top-down rational approach. Expanding the coupling between the parts means that the staff members must be involved in the discussions concerning objectives, in carrying out the activities, and in mastering the most important competencies.

The theory of a loose coupling between intentions and behaviour warns us not to focus such discussions on intentions, for they might then have no effect on behaviour. If one wants to influence behaviour during the change process, it is best to first make people aware of their actual behaviour and how this contributes to the problems at hand. This involves making this behaviour visible. Only then one can make explicit the underlying opinions and intentions. Others must be involved in this endeavour: it is difficult, if not impossible, to observe one's own behaviour. By making it explicit, a tighter coupling between behaviour and opinions is created. There are approaches to change or interventions that further the realization of a tighter coupling between opinions and behaviour. These are approaches in which:

- behaviour is made visible;
- there is sufficient safety for people to give and receive feedback on their behaviour;
- the people involved are committed to learning about their own behaviour;
- the skills that enable people to learn from and about each other are present.

## ON MANAGING AND BEING MANAGED

The trend of ongoing professionalization places new demands on the working methods of managers and staff, but these working methods do not develop at the same pace. We will first address the fixed set of problems that appear to arise from the conflicting orientations of professionals and managers. These problems are dealt with by a number of coping mechanisms and avoidance strategies and we will describe one of these—the pocket veto.

### AUTONOMOUS WORKERS AND HIERARCHICAL MANAGERS

(Not) managing oneself and (not) being managed is a theme that is much in evidence in professional organizations, where it can take exceptional forms. Therefore, the focus of our description is on professional organizations, but the phenomena described can be found in nearly all types of organizations.

The similarities between Erasmus, a violin maker, and a teacher include:

- both of them are learned/have learned a lot;
- both of them know best how to practise their profession;
- both decide themselves how their relationship with their clients will be;
- both identify themselves more with their profession and their fellow professionals than with the organization of which they are part;
- both learn through their own experience and shape their own professionalization.

(With thanks to M. Petri for his notions on similarities with Erasmus and (later in this section) commonalities with Ford).

In other words, they both have a high degree of autonomy in their work and their own development and in their relationship with colleagues and clients. When there are many people like this in an organization, typical phenomena will surface. We call this the professional organization. Much has been published concerning the management and changing of professionals (Van Delden, 1995; Weggeman, 1997; Vermaak, 1997). The vein is fairly sceptical. Can professionals be managed, steered, or changed? Professionals are not keen to renounce their independent and confident nature, and they behave as if they are still self-employed. Hobbies and solo performances are considered legitimate, so collectivity in products and services is usually difficult to detect. What is more, good professional quality is considered to be of overbearing importance. Correspondingly, commercial result orientation is often lacking. Another factor is that professionals do not easily agree among themselves about the current or desired quality of their work. As a rule, the opinion of someone else is valued less than their own opinion, for why should a colleague know better? The opinion of a customer or a boss is often taken even less seriously, for they are considered to have little or no professional background. Learning together and innovating prove difficult, and knowledge is regarded as personal property and remains locked in the head or in a cupboard. And so three core problems often arise:

- fragmentation as a result of everyone following their own direction;
- mediocrity because people do not learn from one another;
- lack of commitment because there is no focus on results or deadlines.

These core problems occur in most professional organizations. Professionals can hold long, emotional discussions about these problems but here, too, they act as typical freelancers: everyone has their own shrewd solution. Splendid democratic decision-making processes are often doomed when faced with the reality of 'too many cooks spoiling the broth'. 'I cannot force colleagues to do something against their will, let alone vice versa,' the professional will say. A common metaphor for this is 'the wheelbarrow full of frogs'. Pursuit of consensus can paralyse an organization, thanks to the garbage-can model of decision-making. Frustrated by the persistency of all these problems, professionals often suddenly behave like old-fashioned wage labourers: problems are laid at the manager's door.

The pharaohs, Henry Ford, and classic governmental organizations have the following in common regarding their thinking about organizations:

- the favourite way of thinking about organizations is to imagine a pyramid, with the boss at the apex;
- management's authority is legitimate and is not open to discussion;
- rationality and rational argumentation are the dominant principles in organizing;
- planning and control form the basis for steering the employees;
- employees are regarded as expendable/replaceable production resources.

According to Feltmann (1993), managers have a natural disposition to view possession and control, definition and overview, planning and evaluation as guarantees of good fortune. The news media, the shareholders, and the managers themselves refer to 'the man at the helm', 'the man pulling the strings', someone who can be held accountable for the results. Thus, it is implied that there is such a thing as actually managing and controlling an organization and that there can be one person with sufficient power to do all that. This approach has proved its worth in sectors with standardized working methods and where efficiency is prized above all else. Transportation, industry, traditional government organizations: it was here that this management wisdom evolved, a wisdom later canonized in management literature. But bureaucracy also appears to provide us with a number of inherent problems and, in the meantime, 'We have almost reached the point where the term bureaucracy is used to illustrate everything that is wrong with organizations; inflexible, not client-oriented, inhuman, ineffective, and lacking in innovative ideas' (De Leeuw, 1997).

In short, the combination of the bureaucratic manager and the autonomous professional is trouble. A boss who attempts to give strong leadership is faced with a lack of understanding. Top-down leadership is taboo; professionals are allergic to everything that even hints at the dreaded threesome of 'bureaucracy, bosses, and policies'. Professionals follow their managers' activities not only with Argus's eyes but consider it perfectly legitimate to express unsolicited criticism. They think that they are permitted to publicly discuss the incompetence of the management, but, of course, managers are forbidden to do the same about them. Furthermore, they feel that they have the right to ignore any management decision that clashes with their professional standards and, before you realize it, they try to extend their authority to cover such management matters as budgets and personnel policy. They'll show the boss how it should be done.

## POCKET VETOES

Members of staff want their autonomy to be as great as possible and to push the manager (and other professionals) out of their work domain. Here, the term *pocket veto* is instructive. This term, originating in political science, describes the right the president of the United States has to not approve a bill that has already been passed by Congress, by not signing it into law. The president can put it, metaphorically speaking, in his/her back pocket until the time for approving the bill has expired. Congress is aware of this and has no choice but to accept this prerogative.

In his book *Educational Administration and Organizational Behavior*, Mark Hanson (1996) uses the term pocket veto to describe the power teachers (professionals) have when innovations for classroom interaction are introduced from 'above'. He uses the concept pocket veto because 'its power is exerted through inaction; in other words, the teachers simply did not respond to requests or mandates for change'.

---

### CASE STUDY: POCKET VETO

Boss John sees employee Pete doing something that he does not agree with. It could have to do with the way Pete is dealing with a customer or a colleague. John finds Pete's behaviour 'unacceptable in this day and age' and asks Pete to come and have a talk with him about it.

In that discussion, John explains why this just won't do and, in turn, Pete explains why he does what he does. John then restates his point of view and Pete does the same.

The discussion is closed and both go away thinking that they have made their position perfectly clear to the other.

Two weeks later Boss John sees employee Pete doing exactly the same thing and immediately takes the initiative and arranges a new discussion. Then he explains his point of view once more, in slightly stronger language and with a little more power. Pete replies in the same vein and the atmosphere becomes frosty. Afterwards, John says to himself, 'I think he has finally gotten the message.' Pete, too, thinks that his boss has understood at last.

What happened represents only the tip of the iceberg, for below the surface lies a learning process that can be easily assimilated by the average employee.

That learning process is as follows:

1. Make sure that the boss doesn't see what you do; if he cannot observe it, he will have nothing to say about it.
2. Always agree with your boss. Humm empathically. Compliment him on his way of thinking; say, 'That's what we'll do or try', but go ahead and do just what you want to or what you think suits best your professional environment, which by now you have carefully shielded from your boss. That is the principle of saying one thing and doing another. It makes the boss believe that his staff is doing things the way he wants. He considers himself a lucky man. The staff are also happy; they carry on in their own way in their own little world.

Pocket vetoes can be found in every organization. There is likely to be a particularly high incidence of pocket vetoes where managers are convinced that their staff have exactly the same view as they themselves do. Such convictions raise alarm bells in us as consultants, whereas it is still the dream of many managers. In our view, managers should be continually aware of the presence of pocket vetoes. Pocket vetoes result from too great a recourse to hierarchy, from serious differences of opinion, or from too little discussion, respect, and acceptance. They are also often the result of staff members regarding the pocket veto as their prerogative, given how work is organized. Think of teachers who shut the classroom door, doctors who close their examining room, consultants who spend time with the client away from his home office, sales persons on the road, and so on. Many employees have the opportunity to make things invisible when it comes to certain areas of their work, and use the opportunity with zeal when the boss asks them to do something that they do not agree with.

The situation can become particularly unhealthy when lots of employees employ the pocket veto. The top then becomes completely detached from the shopfloor and two separate 'realities' arise: the reality of the apex and the reality that exists on the shopfloor. You encounter this to some extent when you join a new organization, where, after a couple of days, the booklet with the internal rules no longer seems to apply. The rules are different. Your new colleagues say: 'OK, that's what is written, but you will have to do it differently or it won't work.'

However, this can occur in various degrees, right up to the pathological. In the worst possible scenario the real communication channels are fully clogged up or are used only for irrelevant matters. A crisis or confrontation is then lurking.

## Implications of Ongoing Professionalism for Change Agents and Change Processes

Tensions in (professional) organizations are unavoidable, and change agents should be aware of this. As a result of the distribution of power and competence in these settings, by definition an arena is created where differences of opinion arise. Each professional or employee has their own ideas and is not afraid to express them. Conflict can be reduced considerably by respecting and dividing the domains of managers and staff into those they are best equipped to deal with. Allow the staff to rule over the primary process: their craft, their contact with clients, their development. In this domain the role of managers is best confined to providing support, coaching, recognition, and challenges, while insisting on accountability for the professionals' output. Conversely, managers may claim the secondary processes as their own. Professionals should not meddle here as they do not understand these processes, have no aptitude for managing them, nor do they enjoy doing that either. The managers look after the facilities, take care of support services, and consult with bodies from the surrounding environment.

What remains is a region where professionals and managers cannot leave each other alone, but need one another. Without a meeting of minds between professionals and between professionals and managers, the staff go their own way too much, which is exactly why the three core problems in this sort of organization arise: fragmentation, mediocrity, and lack of commitment. While coherence is necessary, it cannot be enforced by hierarchy or by rational arguments. The tendency to forget the human factor and to pay a lot of attention to decisions about the outcomes of change but little to the change process and implementation just creates new problems, such as a lack of support, unnecessary resistance, and so on. It is important managers or change agents realize that such forgetfulness can make them 'victims' of the pocket veto. At first, everything seems to be going well: the staff appear to be in agreement with you . . . but wait. Then the anxiety begins, you see so little of them these days . . . Any manager who thinks that all is going well in their organization because everything is ticking along quietly probably has much pocket-vetoing among the staff.

It is more fruitful to reward transparency and to be known to do so, even when what surfaces are things that you yourself do not agree with or that are, in your opinion, indisputably wrong. The staff must be encouraged to carry out their activities openly, to be open to discussion and accountable. They must be discouraged from staying out of sight, not being available to have their actions screened and discussed. In many cases it might be recommended to create horizontal groups where peers show their work, explore its quality, and are willing to learn from this and, if necessary, to adapt their ways. Examples of this type of collective learning include intervision groups, working in teams, clinics, gaming, and intercollegial review. Where learning and experimentation are allowed and supported, there is little need for pocket vetoes. As a change agent, you seek mechanisms to couple tighter what professionals think and do: their cognitions and actions; their opinions and behaviour. If there is one thing you should stay clear of during change processes, it is holding lots of meetings about the intended change. Instead, just embark on the change by acting together, exchanging experiences, reflecting together upon what works, and committing to the next step.

## ON CHAOS THINKING

Chaos thinking emphasizes a focus on the underlying patterns in an organization that determine its behaviour. These patterns come in many shapes and sizes. There are patterns that upset the dynamic balance between an organization and its environment by creating either chaos or a steady state. Oscillating patterns of behaviour emerge when organizations pursue conflicting goals, whether consciously or not. Both will be addressed here.

### DYNAMIC BALANCE

Chaos theory has many 'fathers', particularly in the sciences. One of these fathers is the theoretical physicist Bohm (1992), who reasons that we often unjustly distinguish between the thinker, the thought, and what is being thought about. Bohm sees 'everything that exists' as an explicit order, a temporary, creative swelling in a 'universal stream', which is the implicit order, for which there is no explicit description but can only be implicitly known and recognized. According to Bohm, all our knowledge and science is directed at explaining the explicit order and, in so doing, we make the mistake of not seeing our theories as representations of reality but as part of reality itself.

This explicit order is often equated with steady states, structures and systems, predictability, and controllability. Organizations are orderly constructions consisting of clear-cut elements (objects) that behave in an understandable manner. Such explicit order is in line with a mechanistic world-view that many of us are quite familiar with when growing up, and one that is still dominant in management literature, stacked as it is with quick fixes and proven remedies. In contrast, chaos theory views systems such as organizations as adaptive network or *holons* whose characteristics cannot be traced back to the characteristics of the constituent parts alone.

### HOLON

> It was biologists who first described the remarkable ability of all life to form structures with different 'layers'. Each of these systems forms a whole with regard to its parts and is at the same time part of a (bigger) whole (see Capra, 1996). Koestler (1967) coined the word holon, which represents an entity that is a whole itself and at the same time part of another whole. In his view, the world consists of trillions of holons: a whole atom is part of a whole molecule, a whole molecule is part of a whole cell, the whole cell is part of a whole organism, the whole organism is part of a (social) system. In the sense we will never see the whole; there are only whole/parts.
>
> Just like a hologram, which you can cut without losing the total image, every single holon contains an image of the bigger whole. Holons have four capabilities: the capability to act

independently as an entity, the capability to unite with other holons, the capability to transcend itself, and the 'capability' to decompose itself. (Cornelissen, 1999)

According to chaos theory, people do not focus on individual objects but rather on the relationships between these objects and the patterns that emerge from these relationships. People do not recognize reality on the basis of familiarity with objects but discern reality from observing the emerging patterns between them. In organizations, people weave these patterns into a continual cycle of sense-making. The more patterns being woven, the more dynamic the system. When an organization is extremely dynamic or in flux, then structures, systems, and strategies provide fewer footholds to a change agent than the people who create them. The borders and the identity of the organization become open and fluid: people flow through, cooperative external relationships are sometimes more important than internal ones, old and new ideas coexist, and so on.

Such an 'adaptive network' is susceptible to many forces: complexity and turbulence are considered to be the primary external forces. Dominant internal forces include both the increased autonomy and mutual dependence of the staff, and the diversity of their views about the work and their own contribution to it. The relevance of chaos theory increases as organizations are confronted with an increase in these forces. What are the consequences? Linearity decreases: a single, minor cause can have more and bigger consequences because self-reinforcing feedback loops make the organization more sensitive as a network than it was as a traditional, stable organization. The behaviour of this type of system becomes unpredictable. The best-known example of this is Lorentz's (1963) butterfly theory. To his surprise, he discovered that in his meteorological model a minute change in one of the parameters in the preliminary stage could lead to entirely different types of weather. He published his findings under the significant title, 'Could the Flapping of a Butterfly's Wings in Brazil Cause a Tornado in Texas?'

However, Lorentz also indicated something else; even the most chaotic systems, such as weather, vary within certain boundaries. They have a certain balance. This balance is not static like a marble in a glass and nor is it a periodic balance like the pendulum of a clock. It is a dynamic balance in which the speed of the development within the organization keeps roughly the same pace as the development speed of its ecosystem. If the speed of development is much faster outside the system than inside, the organization moves far from equilibrium: this may sound quite grim but the biologist Prigogine (1985) states that there is hope in this murky chaos; a type of self-organizing ability emerges that, precisely in this type of situation, is capable of creating a new order. In its functional form, this situation demonstrates the characteristics of a learning organization, where the ability of the organization to adapt to its ecosystem is greatly increased.

Loman (1998) recognizes five areas in which an organization can find itself and these are shown in Figure 10.1. The areas are specific to an organization as they are a function of the degree of the complexity and the dynamics in and around that organization:

- on the edge of control: static equilibrium;
- between the edge of control and dynamic balance;
- in dynamic balance;
- between dynamic balance and the edge of chaos;
- on the edge of chaos: out of balance.

Dynamic balance, or as Stacey (1996) calls it 'bounded instability', may sound as if it is the 'best' area. Appearances are deceiving. An out-of-balance situation, for example, can provide many opportunities for renewal. Chaos can be functional or dysfunctional. This too is specific to the *holon* in question. In environments with high-paced development, some organizations have difficulty finding the right adjustment to their dynamic surroundings.

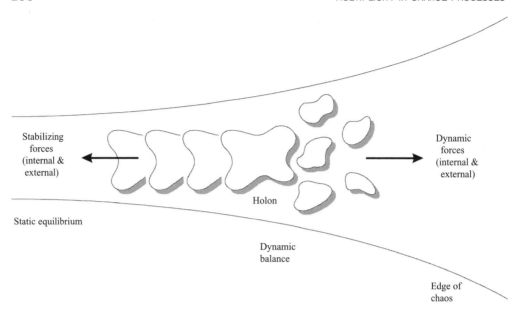

Stabilizing
forces
(internal &
external)

Dynamic
forces
(internal &
external)

Holon

Static equilibrium

Dynamic
balance

Edge of
chaos

**FIGURE 10.1**   Five areas where an organization can find itself

---

## CASE STUDY: DYSFUNCTIONAL 'STATIC EQUILIBRIUM'

Real-life example: a health care insurer that loses contact with clients and staff. Its internal organization is characterized by centralized management with corresponding 'bureaucratic layers': middle
managers who are busy maintaining the status quo. The internal organization is an archipelago of
small fiefdoms that enjoy a great degree of autonomy. The terms of employment are excellent, but
people's mobility and eagerness to learn are largely absent. There is great resistance to making a
clean sweep. It is an example of an organization that is too involved in keeping everything manageable while the environment of the financial sector undergoes dynamic changes. There is too much
emphasis on:

- internal matters, leading to navel-gazing;
- material aspects, leading to fire-fighting based on facts and figures;
- business processes, leading to 'more of the same' improvements which are too rigid to make a
  difference;
- continuity, leading to a compulsion to reach consensus and keep things together;
- problem-solving, which leads to reactive measures.

---

## CASE STUDY: DYSFUNCTIONAL OUT-OF-BALANCE SITUATION

An IT department in a bank is under great pressure from the front office to introduce all kinds of
adaptations to the IT systems. The department caves in under this pressure and all involved step up
their work tempo. Client orientation (the front office is the internal client) is, after all, the number
one priority. As a result of the enormous workload, the staff abandons the quality handbook and
the project management procedures. Mistakes start to creep in. Via various improvised adaptations

to the system and cooperation with other departments, an attempt is made to create new patterns in the applications system without these being understood by management, partly because they have not been involved in the process. The bank is confronted with an increasing and predictable operational risk. Managers come to regard the organization as a 'twilight zone'. Here, we have an organization that finds itself regularly on the edge of chaos, as if it wants to make a great leap forward in adapting itself to the dynamics of the environment. In total contrast to the previous example, in the IT department there is too much emphasis on:

- external aspects, which leads to 'overheating';
- immaterial aspects, leading to day dreaming;
- mental processes, causing unpredictability;
- evolution, with the risk of things falling apart;
- reframing, causing lots of new ideas but little being completed.

In both examples there is no dynamic balance. The health-care insurer tries to control a world where this is no longer possible. In a manner of speaking, it has fallen behind the dynamic balance. The bank IT department becomes unmanageable because it is unable to create (new) order in an uncontrollable world. It is too far ahead of the dynamic balance. We see many organizations struggling with these kind of dilemmas, and have seen that their reactions, especially when based on their own previous successes, do not guarantee successful adaptation. Making a clean sweep in the bank could result in the organization becoming more stable and their risks more controllable, something that would not be possible along traditional, bureaucratic lines. The health-care insurer can scratch the surface of the problem by providing courses in client-oriented behaviour for its personnel. Skills would improve, but this does nothing to create the kind of decentralized decision-making and self-steering that is instrumental for dealing flexibly with the turbulent environment they are in.

## STRUCTURAL TENSION AND STRUCTURAL CONFLICTS

In 1996, Fritz wrote his book *Corporate Tides*, in which he explains 'inescapable structural laws' that any organization is subject to. He states that organizations fall into two categories: they advance or they oscillate. That distinction depends on whether they take the structural laws into account in how they run their organizations. An organization that does so sees its actions crowned with success. An organization that doesn't can undertake exactly the same actions—TQM, learning conferences, breaking down the hierarchy, information system, and so on—but it will not achieve lasting success. The structural laws are an often invisible, underlying pattern that drives an organization's performance. How does it work?

> Every time we go through some major organizational change, our executive managers find 'tools' or methods to help. ABCM, reengineering, different process consultants bring in other methods—we implemented them, but then we find half way through the process the organization isn't taking them on. So then we abandon them, but later new tools are brought in. People are really up in the air about it all. (Fritz, 1996, quoting Greenidge, a manager at BC Telecom)

Oscillation is a result of 'structural conflict', people pursuing conflicting and competing goals. A posh term for this is *balance management*, and its characteristics can be found in the vision statements of many companies: it is a repository for all sorts of desirabilities but not for choices. Yet it is exactly by not making choices, by trying to please everyone, that you end up with oscillation. An example: an organization aims for both profit and expansion. First, the costs are cut, producing more profit, but then there is a reduction in growth, which is countered by more investment. As a result, the profits decrease and, once more, costs are cut. There are various types of this sort of structural conflict that bring organizations swaying from one measure to a juxtaposed one and then back again. For example:

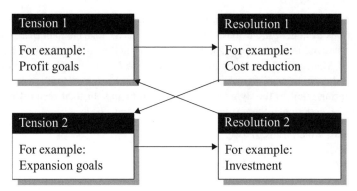

**FIGURE 10.2**  Structural conflict

- the organization wants to meet short-term demands ('quick fixes') but at the same time wants to strive towards long-term growth needs (the long haul);
- managers want to control outcomes (centralized decision-making) but, at the same time, management also wants to include and involve employees (delegation of decision-making);
- there must be entrepreneurship (decision-making) but, at the same time, risks should be avoided (avoid decisions);
- there should be growth (decentralization), but stability must be preserved (centralization).

How can you recognize a structural conflict? In a structural conflict (Figure 10.2), actions that appear to be successful in themselves make the organization even more off-balance: oscillation increases. In organizations that oscillate, success is neutralized.

Advancement works differently: there is structural tension but no structural conflict. The tension is between a desired state and the present reality. Conflict is absent as there is only *one* desire or goal, not two (or more) competing ones. Some organizations are lucky enough to have a clear hierarchy of goals and can thus advance. Some have it only on paper and their oscillating behaviour shows it to be fiction. There is only one way to stay clear of oscillation: that is to get to a situation where goals do not compete. This is not a cosmetic distinction. Sometimes this is achieved by a new overarching goal, more often by a (painful) choice to prioritize. Internet companies, for example, managed to stay out of oscillation several years back by putting growth before profit. It works if you are willing to pay the price. In structural tension the difference between goal and reality calls for action, action that is the logical consequence of structural tension. This time successful actions do not create oscillation, but bring the organization closer to its vision. Structural tension does not make life a breeze. First, it can be confrontational to be honest about both reality ('This merger does not work') and goals ('We want a smaller company'). Second, actions might still fail, but if the desire is real and persistent, obstacles are there to teach lessons and failures show us what works and what doesn't. This is in contrast to structural conflicts where setbacks are often a reason to reassess efforts or to formulate new goals or visions.

Fritz (1996) states that these laws, certainly at the organization level, are often unknown or forgotten. The organization grows, but the forces that drive it often remain undetected. An organization that fails to recognize these forces, its driving 'structure', will, he predicts, sooner or later end up oscillating.

## IMPLICATIONS FOR CHANGE AGENTS AND CHANGE PROCESSES

All theories allied to chaos thinking emphasize diagnosis: recognizing the driving force and underlying patterns and giving them meaning. What drives this organization? Why do things always end up the way they do? Taking action without a full awareness of underlying patterns leads to fight-or-flight behaviour. This statement is heartily confirmed by Fritz (1996), who predicts that any reactive course of action leads to oscillation: the incentive to fix a problem decreases with its success and thus makes the problem re-emerge at a later date. The dominant analytical, diagnostic toolkit of change agents is, however, often insufficient to detect drivers and patterns. The reason is that it is used to diagnose rational, limited areas; it focuses on facts and objects, on the organization as a closed system, and on the current situation. The desired diagnosis would have a much broader focus, for example, also on the interpretations of those involved, on interaction between people, on relationships between objects, on the interchange between the organization and its environment, and on the organization's history. One of the most important principles is that the resulting insight in 'why things are the way they are' must first be embraced, accepted, and acted upon. It is the same kind of process as in personal growth. Before you can move on to the next (life) phase, you have to take a hard look at your life up to this point, see it for what it is, and accept responsibility for it, however hard the facts may be. Crisis, from this point of view (compare a 'midlife crisis'), is a warning that you cannot carry on in the same old way. It is a call to reflect and to distance yourself from dysfunctional dreams and images. It is a time for a new start.

Another implication is that, on the basis of this insight, space must be created for new patterns. This usually requires breaking down barriers that block renewal and providing opportunities for new energy (ideas, initiatives, etc.) to manifest itself within the organization. It helps to challenge the drive and confidence of renewers; coaching and supportive leadership can further assist them to play the role of heralds and new heroes of a new organizational game. According to Loman (1998), when an organization tries to achieve a dynamic balance in a turbulent and complex environment, still more is required: raising individual self-confidence must go hand in hand with raising group consciousness. Typical interventions are examining the dominant mental maps, analysing trends and scenarios, and applying dynamic system thinking. All this should preferably be done collectively in dialogue using team settings, networks, information-rich environments, and by promoting diversity (in people, ideas, etc.). The aim is to somehow combine personal initiative and new perspectives with some kind of mutual commitment. This results in collective strategies, commitment, and choices.

Fritz is optimistic when it comes to crafting new patterns in an organization but emphasizes this final step before all others: real heartfelt choices have to be made in terms of a hierarchy of goals in order for there to be progress. This implies that common strategies have to be based on personal involvement and commitment instead of being socially desirable compromises. In this light, Loman emphasizes that any 'new order' goes beyond compromising to actually reconciling apparent opposites. He mentions, among other things, the following dichotomies:

- internal and external focus: reconciling stability with pleasing target groups;
- material and immaterial focus: reconciling matter-of-factness with experimentation and exploration;
- business processes and mental processes: reconciling efficiency with innovation;
- continuity and evolution: reconciling mutual adjustment with an optimal conflict level;
- problem-solving and reframing/breakthroughs: reconciling a drive for action with a drive for learning.

## SOCIO-POLITICAL MECHANISMS

Strong influencing mechanisms can exist in the 'invisible' world of the organization: classic action theory introduces the role of power and political processes as determining factors in organizational life, whereas the 'organizational iceberg' emphasizes that the informal organization may be stronger than the formal one and undermine it. We will address both consecutively.

### ACTION THEORY AND POWER

Action theory (Parsons, 1977, 1978) argues that people have their own interests and goals and cannot help but pursue them. In order to achieve their goals and interests, they form coalitions and power blocks (see, e.g., Cummings & Worley, 1993; Hanson, 1996). Power is used as the instrument for meetings one's interests. The seeming irrationality of a situation may disappear if statements, actions, and interactions are analysed by a change agent with an eye for the interests of members, departments, networks, or systems within the organization. This is when the action theory proves its worth: when the laws of the socio-political system come into action (see Hanson, 1996). Power is an important factor in organizations, it covers a much wider area than just the formal power of management, and can be a decisive factor in the start, the course, and the outcomes of change processes. The choice of whose definition of the environment is employed, including context and reason for change, is strongly influenced by who has the most power. The same applies to the definition of the content of the change, the appointment of an external consultant, and more. It can be extremely useful and insightful for a change agent to analyse the differences of opinion in a board of directors concerning an intended change programme and to interlink this with how power and interests are distributed in the board.

Action theory argues that each individual or group tries to hold on to or increase its influence. This can be done in various ways: by behaving unpredictably; by concealing information or distorting it; by imposing rules for the game, or, on the contrary, simply ignoring them; by forming coalitions; or by blackening somebody's reputation. Action theory sketches how individual interests and motives unavoidably lead to power blocks and conflicts. The organization as a uniform, cohesive system in no way fits into this picture.

The theory is highly relevant in professional organizations because there, by definition, power is widely distributed. Professionals possess informal power based on their knowledge, personalities, and contacts. Managers might draw on their own personality, but most of their power is generally derived from their formal hierarchic position. They are well-matched opponents, which means that conflicts flourish and victories are hard-won. An example of this is the way that medical specialists have been able to voice their criticism of hospital management for many years. In the summer of 1997, the Dutch national association of these specialists placed a full-page advertisement in the Dutch national dailies. The ad's title parodied the health warning on cigarette packets and, underneath, in small letters, was added: 'the new health bill forces us to be at the beck and call of the bookkeepers of hospitals and insurance companies. This development contravenes the principles of the Hippocratic oath and our medical ethics.' The closing sentence in the advertisement was: 'Our common sense does not allow us to understand present-day hospital policies.' We noticed that many hospital managers had an equally hard time making sense of the medical specialists. In the discussion that results from interactions such as these, one of the parties is usually a victim, and in most cases it is the manager. Looking at the consulting assignments we have carried out over the years, it appears that a change of management takes place much more often in organizations of professionals and is often instigated by conflicts between management and professionals. However, power, and the processes aimed at obtaining and guarding power, play an important part in all organizations and provide the explanation for much apparent irrationality.

## INFORMAL ORGANIZATIONS

The Hawthorne studies brought about an important revolution in the school of thought on organizations (Mayo, 1933; Roethlisberger & Dickson, 1939). These experiments aroused interest in informal group processes and inter-personal relationships: 'A happy worker is a productive worker.' Roethlisberger and Dickson conclude:

> Many of the existing patterns of human interaction are nowhere to be found in the formal organization ... Too many people assume that the organization of a company is the same as a blueprint or an organization chart while, in fact, this is never the case.

The informal organization can be seen as those processes and behaviour that are not formally planned or anticipated but that occur spontaneously as a result of people's needs. People bring their hearts and

The formal organization

Structure,
rules, procedures,
work division,
lines of reporting,
policy, goals, technology,
finance, products

The informal organization

Coalitions, psychological needs,
power, informal leadership, conflict,
moral, informal norms, sensibilities,
social codes, loyalty, friendships,
emotional feelings, perceptions,
risk-taking behaviour

**FIGURE 10.3**   The formal and the informal organization

minds to work, not just their hands. The formal organization can be regarded as the tip of the iceberg. The informal characteristics of organizations form the huge hidden mass of the iceberg, out of sight but always present and often at least as influential. Figure 10.3 illustrates these characteristics.

There are always informal activities, and these activities appear to increase if the formal organization cannot or will not meet certain needs. It is as if a 'shadow world' is formed that can both initiate and frustrate change. When the shadow world makes its presence felt, a bit more of the iceberg is revealed. Those involved often perceive this as an increase in informal activities, and because these activities are generally neither superficial nor temporary, they can cause quite a fright. Feelings, interests, loyalties, and other similarly difficult-to-control matters come out into the open. Managers start to wonder, 'What else is going on?' and suspect that it is indeed only the tip of the iceberg that has become visible.

Informal activities can help to strengthen the formal organization. For instance, difficult decisions may have been 'chewed over' in the corridors. A football tournament or a study trip can help a group of colleagues to get to know and trust one another, and the friendly atmosphere that ensues can do wonders to support much-needed cooperation in the office. However, informal activities can also hinder formal activities. A work-to-rule action by a group of secretaries can make it clear that they are no longer willing to tolerate the extra workload. Informal organization is neither good nor bad. Sometimes opposition is a valuable warning: change is necessary. If the warning is ignored, opposition can grow to destructive proportions, and then the informal organization no longer warns but undermines the formal one.

French and Bell (1984) sum up the characteristics of informal activities as the 'culture of an organization': activities that better describe the character of an organization than any set of formal activities. They claim that in many change processes these informal activities receive little or no attention during diagnosis and, because of this, what really matters is not taken into account in the change effort. Change processes then become more like a fancy lottery than a planned and professional endeavour.

## IMPLICATIONS FOR CHANGE AGENTS AND CHANGE PROCESSES

These theories emphasize how factors hidden from sight and unaddressed in the formal organization can frustrate or help a change process. The first important implication for change agents is that this world deserves to be diagnosed, but that this need not necessarily be done in great detail: French and Bell (1984) demonstrate that the informal organization is difficult to recognize fully and that gaining knowledge of this world demands much more effort and perceptive ability than understanding its formal counterpart. The diagnosis must, however, be adequate enough to identify the major opposition and support mechanisms for the change involved. Concerning action theory, it is a question of identifying sources of power, formal and informal leadership, interests, and coalitions. In the informal organization, culture aspects apply. With an economic exchange it is a matter of recognizing the unwritten rules of exchange that either strengthen or weaken the positions of the individuals in a group.

A second implication concerns the use of these insights during the change process. The change agents will have to use their insights concerning power relations and positions when assigning roles in the change process. If power plays a dominant role in the organization, they would do well to involve the most influential players in crucial decision-making processes, or to entice an influential opponent into taking responsibility as a champion of important parts of the change process or instead exclude them altogether from the process, and so on. The intention of the change agent in these kinds of organizations is to ensure that there is a sufficient power base behind the intended change. If this is not the case, they had better pack it in right away.

Change agents can approach the informal organization in two ways. They can stimulate and even initiate informal activities in support of the formal process. A weekly office cocktail hour might serve to test new ideas or sow the seeds of controversial initiatives. A night with self-made sketches, where colleagues poke harmless fun at the organization's sacred cows and each other's behaviour, can allow everyone to let off steam so that a fresher start can be made at the strategic conference the next morning. They can also try to open a discussion about dysfunctional informal activities by highlighting the goings-on of the invisible world and challenging their legitimacy. This intervention can correspond to creating a tighter coupling of opinions and behaviour: the tensions between the formal organization (intentions) and the informal real life practice (behaviour) are then out in the open. These are serious interventions that become necessary if the two worlds have grown miles apart and the taboo about discussing it has corrupted the organization.

## FOUR CLUSTERS OF THEORIES ABOUT IRRATIONALITIES

We consider the theories that we have outlined to be both applicable and relevant, irrespective of the nature of an organization or of the change process. The degree to which this is the case can, of course, vary considerably. In some situations you may encounter the pocket veto, or there may be a power struggle going on. The management may be extremely bureaucratic and have little respect for the workers. The informal organization might be at odds with the formal organization, or, conversely, none of these situations needs to occur. What a change agent needs to do is to gain a good understanding of theories and images such as these and to make use of them when diagnosing and planning a suitable approach to change.

What the theories we have outlined have in common is that they demonstrate why change is compli-cated. They emphasize the irrationality of change processes or, put more precisely, they emphasize the existence of other sorts of rationality that we might not be aware of, or familiar with in organizational life. We find this function important. The theories make us think twice about the one-sidedness of how we talk with our colleagues and clients about change.

In our opinion, the dominant way of talking about change is captured in the terms *planning* and *contingency approaches*. Both assume the rationality of change processes as if new organizational states can be predictably 'constructed'. A stereotypical example is as follows: change agents diagnose the current situation (*IST* situation) in an organization and define what it should become (*SOLL* situa-tion). To do this, they often use a checklist, e.g of organizational aspects: strategy, structure, systems, management style, culture, and personnel. The contingency approach appears in the principle that all these aspects are considered to be in a balanced and coherent relationship to one another depending on the kind of business and business environment the organization is in. Because of this, it is thought that in change processes, you cannot change one without the other. If one aspect needs to be changed, a change in the other aspects will be required. The planning approach comes in where a change process is considered to consist of placing on a time axis with neat decision moments all the activities that convert, step by step, at the same time, all the differences between the present (*IST*) and the future (*SOLL*).

This stereotype is tempting, partly due to its neatness and suggestion of control and simplicity of change processes, a desire that we recognize in ourselves as well. The theories in this chapter can be regarded as falsifications or disruptions of this stereotype: explanations of why a predictable systematic route from present to future does not (always) work. A change agent or manager can read this as bad news: there are obstacles, there is resistance. It is as if dark powers are causing disarray from a shadowy, invisible world; as if weeds and roots are causing cracks to appear in the asphalt and making the road difficult to travel.

However, this is but one side of the metaphor. In the same way that chaos is order which is not yet understood, and irrationality is a way of thinking that is not understood, each of the theories offered here also denotes positive forces; all is not negative. Resistance can also be the guardian of stability or an initiative for a different future. Ambiguities in organizations also create space for minority views and experiments. The pocket veto can help staff to survive bad management or even to achieve fantastic results in their own domain, individually or together with valued colleagues. Turning the metaphor around, it is not so much the weeds that attack the asphalt but the forces of nature that cannot be denied. Life always finds a way.

The theories give change agents food for thought and alternative viewpoints to observe and interpret organizations. The theories provide indications on how to adapt change processes to make them more effective. For instance, the very existence of loosely coupled systems implies the importance of transparency, providing feedback, and learning to understand one's own behaviour in a group setting. Such adaptations breathe new life into the change. Managing autonomous staff implies, among other things, the importance of limiting domains and providing negotiation platforms where the struggle between professionals and their collective struggle with their managers to defend their own interests can be made productive. Chaos thinking implies, among other things, the importance of discovering the driving forces behind an organization and giving them meaning, creating space for emerging champions who have a commitment to one another and to the (controversial) changes and, by so doing, create a new order. Socio-political mechanisms imply, among other things, making good use of sources of power to organize informal activities and optimizing non-formalized barter.

We are of the opinion that contingency and planned approaches can work, but we feel just as strongly that the four clusters of theories indicate that, sometimes, it is necessary to plan and implement additional interventions. There are also situations where additions will not do and a totally different approach is required. We have tried to find a spectrum of approaches that can stand up to the practice of changing organizations, views that do not nullify each other, but that can exist alongside one another. The following section contains explorations of these views.

## MULTIPLE WAYS OF THINKING ABOUT CHANGE

A search for the underlying values of the word *change* results in a whole range of meanings and different rationalities. For example, the word 'change' is used to describe the desired outcome (the aim, product, result, effect): what is finished, what has been realized or achieved. This is seen in such phrases as: 'This change is obvious', 'The building is greatly changed', 'Pete has changed a lot'. But the word 'change' is also used for the process (plan of approach, working method, route, activities); the transition from one situation to another: the change process. This can be seen in such phrases as, 'The change is still in progress', 'We are in the process of changing the building', 'Pete is changing'. The above distinction is generally common knowledge. We are used to distinguishing between the outcome and the process of change.

In addition, there is a world of difference between the underlying assumptions of the various strategies or approaches that are applied to change. As a result, the practical applications of these various strategies or approaches vary widely. Conceptual clarity is necessary to better express the various meanings of the word change for several reasons:

1. It facilitates clearer communication between the people involved. For example, communication between managers, between consultants, between academics, and between these groups. Misunderstandings and conflicts can and do arise, for instance, when change strategies are discussed in a management team between people who believe change is essentially a power game and people who believe it is a rational endeavour. Implicitness and absoluteness of their respective belief systems considerably complicate communication. A new short-hand language for this complex subject matter can increase mutual understanding and create the possibility for shared interpretations and meanings.
2. It can be used to characterize dominant paradigms in groups or organizations as a whole. In short, it could serve as a diagnostic tool for characterizing different actors involved in a change effort. Moreover, the paradigms themselves represent different views of the organization and its problems as well. Such different viewpoints help paint a more complete and complex picture of organizational life, as argued in the previous section.
3. It provides a map of possible strategies to deal with organizational issue. The idea is not that 'anything goes', e.g. a '5 to 12' situation where a company is faced with great losses is probably not best dealt with by means of patient participative planning. Thus, it is both relevant to know what kind of approaches are available as well as having some sense of indicators that facilitate a choice of which approach is more fitting is a certain situation than others.
4. It offers change agents a tool for reflection. What are your own assumptions? What is your (key) competence for bringing about change and what are your limits? In knowing the answers to such questions, change agents are more able to define the area and the limits of their expertise. Also change agents can become clearer about their preferences and rethink their own professional development.

In the next sections we will first distinguish between five meanings of the word 'change' and give colours to these meanings. Next we will elaborate on their characteristics and make a link with existing literature and schools of thought. We will apply the colours to some examples and sum up ideals and pitfalls. Finally, we will discuss the possibility of more characteristics and colours and briefly explore meta-theoretical implications.

## FIVE MEANINGS OF THE WORD 'CHANGE'

In just a couple of sentences, we want to make clear the five distinct meanings that the word 'change' can have. The five ways of thinking differ in the assumptions that they make about why and how people or things change. This is illustrated and clarified in Table 10.1. Each way of thinking has been assigned a colour. This simplifies the naming of the concept (which is further discussed later). A certain degree of logic is attached to the choice of the colours, which is also indicated below.

| A. | 'We are changing the policy.'  'Individual interests have been transformed into group interests.'  'The goal has been changed because of pressure from Pete.' |
| --- | --- |

Yellow-print thinking assumes that people change their standpoints only if their own interests are taken into account, or if you can compel them to accept certain ideas. Combining ideas or points of view

**TABLE 10.1** Assumptions behind the five ways of thinking

|              | Things/people will change if you |
| ------------ | -------------------------------- |
| Yellow-print | can unite interests of the important players<br>can compel them to accept (certain) points of view/opinions<br>can create win–win situations/can form coalitions<br>demonstrate the advantages of certain ideas (power, status, influence)<br>get everyone on the same wavelength<br>can bring people into a negotiating process |
| Blue-print   | formulate a clear result/goal beforehand<br>lay down a concrete plan with clear steps from A to B<br>monitor the steps well and adjust accordingly<br>keep everything as stable and controlled as possible<br>can reduce complexity as much as possible |
| Red-print    | stimulate people in the right way, for example, by inducements (or penalties)<br>employ advanced HRM tools for rewards, motivation, promotions, status<br>give people something in return for what they give the organization<br>manage expectations and create a good atmosphere<br>make things attractive for people |
| Green-print  | make them aware of new insights/own shortcomings<br>are able to motivate people to see new things/to learn/to be capable of<br>are able to create suitable (collective) learning situations<br>allow the learning process to be owned by the people involved and geared towards their own learning goals |
| White-print  | start from people's drives, strengths, and 'natural inclinations'<br>add meaning to what people are going though<br>are able to diagnose complexity and understand its dynamics<br>give free rein to people's energy and remove possible obstacles<br>make use of symbols and rituals |

and forming coalitions or power blocks are favoured methods in this type of change process. Change is seen as a power game or negotiation exercise aimed at feasible solutions. This way of thinking fits smoothly into change processes where complex goals or effects must be achieved and in which many people or parties are involved in mutually interdependent ways.

We call this way of thinking 'yellow-print thinking'. Yellow is the colour of power (e.g. symbols like the sun, fire) and of the type of process ('brooding and coalition formation around a fire').

> B. 'The building has been changed.'
> 'The production line has been changed to meet the specifications.'
> 'The information system has undergone radical change.'

In blue-print thinking it is assumed that people or things will change if a clearly specified result is laid down beforehand. All steps are planned down to the last detail. Control over the result, as well as the path to be taken, is kept well in check. Project management is an example of this way of thinking. It is a favourite approach in change processes where the result and the path can be well defined and predicted. Change is considered to be a rational process aimed at the best possible solution.

We call this way of thinking 'blue-print thinking'. A blueprint is the (architectural) design or plan that is drawn up beforehand and guarantees the actual outcome.

> C.   'I change the organization.'
>      'The stimuli for talent development have changed.'
>      'We have changed our way of rewarding and disciplining personnel.'

Change in this way of thinking is accomplished by stimulating people, by making things appealing to do. In this way of thinking it is important to stimulate people and to inspire them, to seduce them into acting as desired. We call this way of thinking 'red-print thinking'. Red-print thinking assumes that people and organizations will change if the right HRM (Human Resource Management) tools are employed and used correctly. In other words, people change their behaviour if they are rewarded (salary, promotion, bonus, a good evaluation) or 'penalized' (demotion, poor evaluation). Thus, a key concept is barter: the organization hands out rewards and facilities in exchange for personnel taking on responsibilities and trying their best. On top of this, however, management's care and attention are also important. The aim is a good 'fit' between what individuals want and what the organization needs.

The colour chosen here refers to the colour of blood. The human being must be influenced, tempted, seduced, and stimulated.

> D.   'I am changing Pete.'
>      'We have learned a lot, and as a result a lot has changed.'
>      'Change equals learning.'

In green-print thinking, the terms 'change' and 'learning' have very similar meanings. People change if they learn. People are motivated to discover the limits of their competences and to involve themselves in learning situations. They are provided with means of learning more effective ways of acting.

The aim is to strengthen the learning abilities of the individual and the learning within the organization. If people learn collectively, the organization learns and as a result change takes place.

The colour green is chosen because the objective is to get people's ideas to work (with their motivation and learning capacity), giving them the 'green light'. But it also refers to 'growth', as in nature.

> E.   'Pete is changing.'
>      'This change is filled with meaning.'
>      'Everything is continually changing.'

In white-print thinking, the dominant image is that everything is changing autonomously, of its own accord. *Panta rhei*: everything is in motion. Where there is energy, things change. When this is the case, 'the time is ripe'. Complexity is regarded as the enriching nature of things, not as disruptive chaos. Influencing the dynamics is a favourite approach. White-print thinking assumes that failure results where we think we can direct and manage change. It is more about understanding where opportunities lie and searching for the seeds of renewal and creativity. Sense-making plays an important role in this, as does the removal of obstacles and explicitly relying on the strength and soul of people. External stimuli are deemed of lesser importance.

The colour white reflects all colours. But more important, white denotes openness: it allows room for self-organization and evolution. The outcome remains somewhat of a surprise.

The colours are basic colours plus their 'sum': white. The word 'print' denotes the endeavours of change agents to work more or less according to some preconceived plan (compare 'planned change'), even if they consciously allow everything to run its own course, so to speak. In a certain sense, you will want to be able to forecast something about how the change is going to work out. Change agents want to maintain a causal relationship between their actions and the outcomes of the change, however different the managing and planning might look in each of the colours. We examine this more thoroughly in the following sections.

## FIVE WAYS OF THINKING ABOUT CHANGE IN MORE DETAIL

In this section, each way of thinking is discussed. We try to describe its essence, referring to existing literature. The type of change process is also described.

### YELLOW-PRINT THINKING

Yellow-print thinking is based on socio-political concepts about organizations, in which interests, conflicts, and power play important roles (see, among others, Pfeffer, 1981; Morgan, 1986; Greiner & Schein, 1988; Hanson, 1996).

Yellow-print thinking assumes that getting everyone on the same wavelength is a change in itself. Policy-making or producing a programme for action requires getting the powers that be behind it, whether it is power based on formal position or informal influence. It is thought that resistance and failure are inevitable if you do not get all or at least the most important players on board. This happens through the gathering of interests, creating a power base, and then solving contradictions or conflicts by negotiation.

Carrying out the policy or programme to successful implementation demands the careful holding together of these interests by the change agent, manoeuvring in a (possibly shifting) balance of power, resolving conflicts, and so on.

Setting goals, determining policies, and formulating programmes is done by creating (political) support, by gathering together interests, by proposing win–win situations, and by political games, power plays, and negotiating tactics. Sticking to and realizing the outcome of these processes (in terms of goals, the policies, or programmes) is a huge task because the socio-political context stays dynamic.

The 'management' of the process of policy formation and sustaining commitment demands certain political skills on the part of the change agents as well as the ability to operate in a complex area of interests. Facilitating communication, lobbying, negotiating, and third-party conflict resolution are much-used interventions. The change process can be employed within an organization or between organizations.

### Type of change process

The result of change is difficult to predict because it depends on the distribution and shifts in standpoints and influence of the most important players. What is more, for a change agent, the process is difficult to structure and plan. The creation of a 'negotiating arena' in which the interested parties are represented is a means that is often used, as is an independent authority or body as facilitator. Specific rules of the game can be agreed on. Consulting with their power bases, the interests of all representatives need to be carefully built in during the negotiation process.

The foremost consideration of the yellow-print change agent is: always bear in mind the conglomeration of interests, parties, and players.

### BLUE-PRINT THINKING

Blue-print thinking is based on the rational design and implementation of change (see, among others, Hammer & Champy, 1993; Kluytmans, 1994). Project-oriented working is a striking example of this (see, among others, Wijnen et al., 1988; Kor & Wijnen, 2000). Scientific Management (Taylor, 1913) is a classic example of blue-print thinking.

The theory behind blue-print thinking is to carefully describe and define the outcome or the result beforehand. The activities needed to achieve the result are planned according to rational arguments and expertise. There is continuous monitoring based on predetermined indicators to check whether the activities are leading to the desired result as planned. If not, adjustments are made to achieve that which has been agreed upon within the frameworks of time, money, quality, information, and organization.

The process and the result are, more or less, independent of people. Controlling (managing, planning, and monitoring progress) the change is considered feasible. Management is able to force and effect the change.

## Type of change process

The blue-print change process can be relatively short, at least in comparison with other ways of thinking. It is feasible to determine rationally and ahead of time when the change will be completed. The subject of the change (the client or project leader) and its object (the ones who undergo the change) are often different people or entities. The approach is rational (planning) and empirical (indicators). Think first (define and design) and then do (implement) is the maxim. Thinking and doing are sequential.

The foremost considerations of the blue-print changer are these: plan and organize first; use all possible expertise and do not let people's individual ideas and preferences interfere; and never lose sight of the intended result.

### RED-PRINT THINKING

Red-print thinking has its roots in the classic Hawthorn experiments (see Mayo, 1933; Roethlisberger, 1941). McGregor (1960) developed the tradition further. In recent years, 'Human Resources Management' has been a much discussed subject (see, among others, Schoemaker, 1994; Paauwe, 1995; Fruytier & Paauwe, 1996). The intention of the red-print changer is to change the soft aspects of an organization, such as management style, competencies, cooperation.

The red-print school of thought contends that people change as a result of the deployment and adequate use of a set of HRM tools such as rewards, appraisals, career paths, structures, assessments, recruitments, reorganizations, out-placements, and promotions. It has to do with the development of competencies, of talents, and of getting the best out of people—an optimal synergy between the organization and its employees. People will do something or change if they get something back (the 'barter' principle).

The outcome of the change (the result) can, according to red-print thinking, be thought out beforehand, but it cannot be fully guaranteed because it is dependent on the response of the 'victims'; the desired outcome might change somewhat as a result. Monitoring takes place, but, for both ethical and political reasons, there is a limit to how forcefully it can be adjusted along the way. Compelling change is possible to a limited extent for the same reasons.

## Type of change process

The red-print change process takes time. The subjects, the change agents, and the objects, those who are supposed to change, are different people but they do frequently interact. On the basis of intermediate results, the change agent can adjust the desired result. Management motivates and puts forward arguments for the change. They get up on a soap box, give speeches, and seduce people into embarking on a change made attractive. The HRM instruments try to make concrete what the desired behaviour is thought to be and add incentives and penalties to entice people to act accordingly.

The foremost consideration of the red-print change agent: the human factor plays an important role. People make changes happen if you guide them in the right direction and reward them for changing.

## GREEN-PRINT THINKING

Green-print thinking has its roots in action-learning theories (see, among others, Argyris & Schön, 1978; Kolb et al., 1991). It has been expanded enormously in the more recent thinking on 'learning organizations' (Senge, 1990; Swieringa & Wierdsma, 1990). Changing and learning are conceptually closely linked (see, among others, de Caluwé, 1997).

The outcome of green-print change is difficult to predict in this way of thinking because it depends, to a large degree, on the extent and the nature of what people learn, and this, in turn, depends on both their learning ability and the effectiveness of the learning environment itself. The process is characterized by setting up learning situations—preferably collective ones as these allow people to give and receive feedback as well as to experiment with more effective ways of acting. Change takes place as a result of people and organizations learning continuously. Monitoring is not meant to adjust the change in the direction of some predetermined outcome, but just to plan a follow-up that is in line with what the people involved regard as the most relevant learning goals. Compelling change is deemed counterproductive; green-print thinking is much more concerned with allowing and supporting people to take ownership of their learning.

## Type of change process

The change process takes time: you cannot force learning. It is a fluctuating process of learning and unlearning, trial and error. Subject (change agent) and object (change victims) can be different people, but there is a great deal of interaction between them. They can even switch roles; the change agent is also always learning.

The management of the change is very limited in a directive sense. Motivating, facilitating feedback, supporting experimenting with new behaviour, structuring communication, setting up interactions, giving meaning, and learning, in the broadest sense of the word, are much-used interventions. Thinking and doing are tightly coupled, not sequential (as it is in blue-print thinking).

The foremost consideration of the change agent is this: motivate people to learn with each other and from each other in order to establish continuous learning in collective settings.

## WHITE-PRINT THINKING

White-print thinking arose as a reaction to the deterministic, mechanistic, and linear world-view derived from Newton and Descartes. It is nourished by chaos thinking, network theory, and complexity theory, all of which are based on living and complex systems with limited predictability (see, among others, Bateson, 1984; Capra, 1996). Self-organization is a core concept. Stacey (1996) defines self-organization as 'The process by which people interact with one another within a system, according to their own codes of behavior, without there being an overall picture that makes clear what has to be done or how it is to be done.' The self-organization process encompasses the emergence of new structures and behavioural patterns through developmental, learning, and evolutionary processes. The system finds its own optimal dynamic balance (see, among others, Bicker Caarten, 1998).

In the white-print way of thinking, change is autonomous. 'Panta rhei: everything is in motion'; 'The route is the refuge'; and Morgan's flux metaphor (1986) are all expressions of this view. People and organizations are in a constant state of change. The inner desires and strengths of people, both individually and as groups, are the decisive factors. Outside influence, whether from a change agent or a manager, can be of only limited effect and then only if this is welcomed by the ones who are changing it.

## Type of change process

The concept of planned change is somewhat at odds with white-print thinking; planning, controlling, and managing the change are, to a great extent, irrelevant notions. Resistance is also an irrelevant concept.

It is assumed that no one can stop change from happening; it can only be aided or hindered. The opportunities to exert influence lie mainly in helping to clear obstacles and in challenging people, calling on their strengths and self-confidence. These opportunities in the relationship between the change agent and others are often spotted by these others rather than constructed by the change agent. They can request help, support, or coaching from the change agent and from each other. In a way white-print change agents catalyse the emergence of more white-print change agents.

The foremost consideration of the white-print change agent is: observe what is making things happen and change; supply meanings and perspectives, remove obstacles, get initiatives and explorations going, and empower people while giving them sufficient free rein. The belief that 'crisis provides opportunity' applies here.

Note: The above does NOT equal doing nothing or *laissez-faire*. On the contrary, it demands in-depth observation, analysis of underlying drivers, and often confronting interventions. Change agents must be capable of making sense out of complexity, often looking at historical patterns and psychological mechanisms. They will require quite a few theories about irrationalities in organizations and strong powers of observation to allow them to do so.

## SOME EXAMPLES

A few examples, shown in Table 10.2, serve to illustrate how the colours can be applied. The examples indicate, even though they are just simple exercises, how great the differences can be between the colours when it comes to aim/outcome, the change process, and the tools used. With these examples we try to show just how relevant it can be to understand the underlying concepts and ideas—the colours—behind someone's words in order to better understand each other and better communicate about change.

## IDEALS AND PITFALLS

Each colour has its own ideals; that is, what change agents dream of for the long run. But each colour also has its pitfalls: situations or conditions when the approach is no longer effective or even becomes counterproductive.

In yellow-print thinking the ideal is that people focus on common interests and strive towards collective goals. The ideal is that people want and are able to weigh different interests and achieve common ground. In a way it is a very democratic ideal. Pitfalls include lose–lose situations such as destructive power struggles. Building castles in the air (allowing a 'false' consensus) is another pitfall, severing the link between the goals, means, and efforts.

The ideal in blue-print thinking is that the future is in our hands and we can construct it. Everything is possible and controllable and can be achieved by rational planning. The pitfall is to steamroller over people and their feelings and thus create resistance rather than commitment. This can be aggravated by the inclination to pay insufficient attention to 'irrational' aspects. Impatience is another pitfall: not granting others sufficient time to come on board.

The ideal in red-print thinking is searching for the optimal 'fit' between people and 'hardware', between the goals of the organization and those of the individual. It strives to make organizations 'more beautiful' and to inspire and care for those who work there. The pitfall can lie in the lack of concrete outcomes by 'sparing the rod' and avoiding conflicts. Red-print thinkers can be addicted to

**TABLE 10.2**  Example of a workshop, a mission, and knowledge management

|  | Setting up a workshop in order to | Formulating a mission to | Introducing knowledge management by |
|---|---|---|---|
| Yellow-print thinking | reach agreement with one another about aims or policy | lay out the results of negotiations | forming heterogeneous assignment teams organizing across disciplines |
| Blue-print thinking | have a plan of approach on paper as result of the workshop | have the best strategy clearly defined (to be used in external marketing of internal monitoring) | writing handbooks developing information systems doing empirical research |
| Red-print thinking | create more involvement have a good time together | get everyone on the same wavelength give words to what brings us together/create a 'family' feeling | introducing job rotation and sabbaticals management development programmes |
| Green-print thinking | learn from one another exchange viewpoints | enable a useful exchange of views explore different possibilities together | bringing people together in such a way that they learn from one another intervision and coaching |
| White-print thinking | expand our thinking arouse creative energy stimulate creative ideas | bring about an evolutionary leap transcend apparent contradictions | taking on challenges making new things possible catalysing new communities and networks |

maintaining a good atmosphere. Also, HR systems can smother brilliant staff members as these never fit the neat competence profiles of a red-print thinker. It also ignores power in organizations, top-down as well as bottom-up.

The ideal of green-print thinking is a learning organization where learning is consciously and continuously applied. Everybody learns what they need to learn and come up with their own solutions to their own problems. The pitfall is that green-print thinkers can ignore the fact that not everybody is always willing or capable of learning. For instance, in situations that lack safety, such as power struggles or conflicts, people are not keen to participate. Also there can be a lack of 'hard' outcomes: an over-abundance of reflection can breed a lack of decisiveness and action.

In white-print thinking the ideal lies in spontaneous evolution, in 'lucky' coincidence and people taking responsibility for their own lives and learning. What is more, there is a positive attitude towards conflict and crisis. The pitfall lies in the idealization of everything magically taking care of itself. This leads to injudicious acceptance of problems. Another pitfall is fashionably using 'white' ideas without grasping white thinking's essence, e.g. managers using the concept of self-steering teams to abdicate their own responsibilities. A final pitfall is having insufficient insight into the underlying patterns of an organization to confidently know what might bring life (back) into it.

## NEW COLOURS AND NEW CHARACTERISTICS

Is this a complete overview? The colours do seem to cover most of the steady stream of experience, research, and publications that we are aware of. Nevertheless, the list is probably not complete. Recalling genocides in the Second World War, or in Rwanda or Kosovo, we realize that violence and repression are also strategies; ones of manipulating and threatening people, of infusing hate and fear. We call this type of thinking about change 'steel-print'. It characterizes methods employed in organizations as well, and that it is effective is obviously still believed by quite a few people.

Besides steel-print, there might be still another way of thinking about change. Living, travelling, and working in India, we observed that people were more inclined than we were to say 'yes' to change while also leaving action more up to circumstances like the weather, people they met, the hand of God. If God wants it, the change will happen. People work hard, but rational planning is taken much less seriously than we are accustomed to. A person is considered only a small part in the timeless game (maya) of life. This might be a way of thinking about change that is little influenced by Western beliefs in progress, and it also appears to be effective: India, the largest democracy in the world, operates under its assumptions. We think that silver may be a fitting colour for this way of thinking.

In most of our consultancy work, we do not engage in steel or silver paradigms. These are not generally considered part of the professional repertoire. What we have found since we started working with the colour-print language is that people easily attribute lots of other characteristics to the colours more than the ones mentioned here and which are summarized in Table 10.3. These are characteristics like: output criteria, diagnostic models and questions, typical sayings, glossaries, bodies of literature, ways of communications, norms and values of change agents, the meaning attached to 'resistance to change', etc. We will address these in separate publications (see, e.g., de Caluwé & Vermaak, 2003b).

## META-PARADIGMS

There is also a (meta-)paradigm behind the five-colour classification described here. The description of five ways of thinking emerges from a meta-paradigm that posits a need for distinctions in diversity and a search for professional insights and values based on these. Over the last few years several such insights have emerged (de Caluwé & Vermaak, 2003b):

1. We start to suspect that any strong colour dominance in organizations is unwanted. In order to survive in the long run, organizations seem to need qualities of all the colours. Organizations need to deal properly with power and different interests (yellow), must effectively and dependably get results and maintain organizational hygiene (blue), must take the irrational human being into account and insert care and perspective in organizational life (red), have to create spaces to learn and cooperate (green), and need to align themselves with the times they live in and the people they live with and innovate accordingly (white). The different colours have conflicting principles: that means that a balanced or sound organization has to cope with the paradoxes that result from these conflicting principles. This reinforces the need to diagnose organizations from the different coloured viewpoints in order to be aware of imbalances.

2. A foundational (colour) focus in terms of change strategy is needed, especially when problems are deeply rooted as different coloured approaches can interfere considerably with one another. For instance, trying to create a learning environment (green) while not keeping power games at bay (yellow) or down-playing the predictability of outcomes (blue) means that the learning is bound to be superficial. Each colour has its strong and weak points. The kind of organization, the issue at hand, the kind of resistance, the style of the change agents, the time pressure, and other circumstances are all factors that influence which change strategy, in terms of colour, can best make a difference. This is not to say that a change strategy has to be restricted to one colour, but it does imply that interferences between coloured actions should be taken into account when intervening in organizations. A relatively easy way of dealing with interferences is to space different colour interventions in time or have different people involved. More challenging is to maintain one constant underlying colour tenet while allowing for more superficial other coloured contributions. For instance, when restructuring a company (blue), HRM instruments can be of help in staffing the new structure. In such a case, blue will dominate and the red components help the blue restructuring

**TABLE 10.3** The five colours and their concepts

| | Yellow-print | Blue-print | Red-print | Green-print | White-print |
|---|---|---|---|---|---|
| Something changes when you | bring common interests together | think first and then act according to a plan | stimulate people in the right way | create settings for collective learning | create space for spontaneous evolution |
| in a | power game | rational process | exchange exercise | learning process | dynamic process |
| and create | a feasible solution, a win–win situation | the best solution, a brave new world | a motivating solution, the best 'fit' | a solution that people develop themselves | a solution that releases energy |
| Interventions such as | forming coalitions, changing top structures, policy-making | project management, strategic analysis, auditing | assessment and reward, social gatherings, situational leadership | training and coaching, open systems planning, gaming | open space meetings, self-steering teams, appreciative inquiry |
| by | facilitators who use their own power base | experts in the field | procedure experts who elicit involvement | facilitators who create settings for learning | personalities who use their being as instrument |
| who have | a good sense for power balances and mediation | analytical and planning skills | HRM knowledge and motivational skills | OD knowledge and feedback skills | an ability to discern and create new meanings |
| and focus on | positions and context | knowledge and results | procedures and working climate | the setting and communication | patterns and persons |
| Result is | partly unknown and shifting | described and guaranteed | outlined but not guaranteed | envisioned but not guaranteed | unpredictable on a practical level |
| safeguarded by | decision documents and power balances | benchmarking and ISO systems | HRM systems | a learning organization | self-management |
| The pitfalls lie in | dreaming and lose–lose situation | ignoring external and irrational aspects | ignoring power and smothering brilliance | excluding no one and lack of action | superficial understanding and laissez-faire |

succeed and stay a little more superficial as a result (limited to HRM instruments rather than creating a climate of care).

3. The colour of the change agent should match the change effort: incongruence frustrates change. It makes little sense to embark on a yellow endeavour with an analytical expert who strives for the best solutions (blue) rather than what is feasible given the balance of power. While change agents might be able to at least intellectually grasp that all colours are equal, when it comes down to it, most change agents have more narrowly defined beliefs/intentions and these should match their role in order for them to be believable. This is not to say that change agents can be branded in single colours and remain as they are over the years. Change agents may be able to handle different approaches to change but not to their full potential. They may change colour but take many years to do so as each colour brings with it a whole body of knowledge with many interventions, competences, diagnostic viewpoints, etc. Luckily for some colours, it is even good role modelling in change processes to profess one-sidedness, in particular, green and white. It provides space for other people's imperfections and can enhance trust and establish rapport.

4. Finally, we posit that dialogues in organizations based on a multi-paradigm perspective (such as the colours) enhances organizational vitality. 'The difficulty for change is not in the development of new ideas, but in escaping the old ideas, that determine our thinking' (Wierdsma, 2001). Seeing (too) many things through green glasses and applying green interventions will give a lot of reflection but a lack of action, results, and consensus. Moreover, organizational change is a collective effort and, more often than not, involves people with multiple perspectives on organizational life and multiple definitions of reality. Instead of narrowing participation to reach easy consensus on issues, the inclusion of multiple perspectives can create not only the kind of richness that does justice to the complexities of the social systems but also the kind of ownership that is instrumental in addressing such complexities. When problems are simple, single-minded viewpoints might suffice (e.g. building a house with a blue paradigm only). But for ambiguous problems involving people with many different backgrounds, understanding and intervening in organizations are best based on collectively taking multiple realities and corresponding paradoxes into account.

## CONCLUSION

Green and white approaches are currently favoured in words, but not in actions. Blue approaches in particular predominate as many change agents still strive for change to be effective, efficient, results-oriented, and transparent which are criteria that only blue approaches adhere the highest value too. Green approaches value learning and reflection and skill building higher, while red approaches love cohesion, improved cooperation, pride, and a good atmosphere. We think that a rise in popularity of the lesser-used paradigms, green and white, might be justified given the rise of professionalism in organizations, the speed of innovations, and the need for leadership in network organizations.

This advocacy on our part is not meant to replace one colour imbalance with another. Nor did we describe theories about why change does not work to explain irrationalities away. Both are an effort on our part to acknowledge complexity and multiplicity of organizational life as well as a way to come to grips with it. Organizations do not present a neat and orderly universe to us. Changes happen, planned and unplanned. Changes follow each other and take place concurrently. They compete with one another, but may also support each other. They happen at many levels at the same time, producing both desirable and undesirable results. Changes fail because of resistance, but resistance can also initiate change. Resistance can be a form of energy, grumbling can be an expression of vitality, and pocket vetoes can be a means of self-protection and survival. In the end, it is these dialectic tensions and complexities that may inspire change agents to keep wondering and wandering.

# REFERENCES

Argyris, C. & Schön, D.A. (1978) *Organizational Learning: A Theory of Action Perspective*. Reading, MA: Addison-Wesley.

Bateson, G. (1984) *Het verbindend patroon*. Amsterdam: Bert Bakker.

Bicker Caarten, A. (1998) *Chaos en stress: Stressoren die op kunnen treden bij spontane organisatieveranderingsprocessen bekeken vanuit de chaostheorie*, Scriptie vakgroep Arbieds- en Organisatiepsychologie. Amsterdam: Universiteit van Amsterdam.

Bohm, D. (1992) *Wholeness and the Implicate Order*. London: Ark Paperbacks.

Capra, F. (1996) *Het levensweb*. Utrecht: Kosmos-Z&K.

Cornelissen, V. (1999) Hoe til ik mezelf aan mijn schoenveters op? Doctoral thesis, University of Tilburg.

Cummings, T.G. & Worley, C.G. (1993) *Organization Development and Change*. Minneapolis, MN: West Publishing.

De Caluwé, L. (1997) *Veranderen moet je leren: een evaluatiestudie naar de opzet en effecten van een grootscheepse cultuurinterventie met behulp van een spelsimulatie*. Den Haag: Delwel; Amersfoort: Twynstra Gudde.

De Caluwé, L., Geurts, J., Buis, D. & Stoppelenburg, A. (2000) *Changing Organisations with Gaming/Simulation*. Elsevier bedrijfsinformatie bv 's-Gravenhage/Amersfoort: Twynstra Gudde.

De Caluwé, L. & Vermaak, H. (2003a) *Learning to Change: A Guide for Organizational Change Agents*. Thousand Oaks, CA: Sage.

De Caluwé, L. & Vermaak, H. (forthcoming, 2003b) *Transformational Conversations about Change*.

De Leeuw, A.C.J. (1997) Bureaucratische zegeningen. *M&O*, **1**, 92–11.

Feltmann, C.E. (1993) Help! Een manager! Waar is de professional??? *TAC*, **7/8**, 16–23.

French, W.L. & Bell, C.H. (1984) *Organizational Development: Behavioural Science Interventions for Organization Improvement* (3rd edn). Englewood Cliffs, NJ: Prentice Hall.

Fritz, R. (1996) *Corporate Tides*. San Francisco: Berrett-Koehler.

Fruytier, B. & Paauwe, J. (1996) Competentie-ontwikkeling in kennisintensieve organisaties. *M&O*, **6**, 424–529.

Greiner, L. & Schein, V. (1988) *Power and Organization Development: Mobilizing Power to Implement Change*. Reading, MA: Addison-Wesley.

Hammer, M. & Champy, J. (1993) *Reengineering the Corporation: A Manifesto for Business Revolution*. London: Nicholas Brealey.

Hanson, E.M. (1996) *Educational Administration and Organizational Behavior*. Boston: Allyn & Bacon.

Kluytmans, F. (1994) Organisatie-opvattingen door de jaren heen. In J. Gerrichhauzen, A. Kampermann & F. Kluytmans (eds) *Interventies bij organisatieverandering* (pp. 21–38). Deventer: Kluwer Bedrijfswetenschappen.

Knip, H. (1981) *Organisatiestudies in het onderwijs*. Utrecht: Drukkerij Elinkwijk.

Koestler, A. (1967) *The Ghost in the Machine*. London: Hutchinson.

Kolb, D., Rubbin, I.M. & Osland, J.S. (1991) *Organization Behaviour: An Experiential Approach*. Englewood Cliffs, NJ: Prentice Hall.

Kor, R. & Wijnen, G. (2000) *50 Checklists for Project and Programme Managers*. Aldershot/Brookfield: Gower.

Loman, J.B. (1998) *Verkenning Toepassingsmogelijkheden Chaos-Theorie*. Amersfoort: Twynstra Gudde (internal publication).

Lorentz, E.N. (1963) Deterministic non-periodic flow. *Journal of the Atmospheric Sciences*, **20**, 130–141.

Mayo, E. (1933) *The Human Problems of an Industrial Civilization*. New York: Macmillan.

McGregor, D. (1960) *The Human Side of Enterprise*. New York: McGraw-Hill.

Morgan, G. (1986) *Images of Organizations*. Beverly Hills, CA: Sage.

Paauwe, J. (1995) Kernvraagstukken op het gebied van strategische HRM in Nederland. *M&O*, **5**, 369–389.

Parsons, T. (1977) *Social Systems and the Evolution of Action Theory*. New York: The Free Press.

Parsons, T. (1978) *Action Theory and the Human Condition*. New York: The Free Press.

Pfeffer, J. (1981) *Power in Organizations*. London: Pitman.

Prigogine, I. (1985) *Orde uit chaos*. Amsterdam: Bert Bakker.

Roethlisberger, F.J. (1941) *Management and Morale*. Cambridge, MA: Harvard University Press.

Roethlisberger, F.J. & Dickson, W.J. (1939) *Management and the Worker*. Cambridge, MA: Harvard University Press.

Schoemaker, M.J.R. (1994) *Managen van mensen en prestaties: Personeelsmanagement in moderne organisaties*. Deventer: Kluwer Bedrijfswetenschappen.

Senge, P.M. (1990) *The Fifth Discipline: The Art and Practice of the Learning Organization*. New York: Doubleday/Currency.

Stacey, R.D. (1996) *Complexity and Creativity in Organizations*. San Francisco: Berrett-Koehler.

Swieringa, J. & Wierdsma, A.F.M. (1990) *Op weg naar een lerende organisatie*. Groningen: Wolters Noordhoff.

Taylor, F.W. (1913) *The Principles of Scientific Management*. New York: Harper & Row.

Van Delden, P. (1995) *Professionals: Kwaliteit van het Beroep*. Amsterdam: Contact.

Vermaak, H. (1997) Men zegt dat professionals niet te managen zijn. *Nijenrode Management Review*, **7**, 12–27.

Vermaak, H. & Weggeman, M. (1999) Conspiring fruitfully with professionals: new management roles for professional organizations. *Management Decision*, **37**(1), 29–44.

Weggeman, M. (1997) *Leidinggeven aan professionals*. Deventer: Kluwer Academic Publishers.

Weick, K.E. (1969) *The Social Psychology of Organizing*. Reading, MA: Addison-Wesley.

Weick, K.E. (1976) Educational organizations as loosely coupled systems. *Administrative Science Quarterly*, **1**, 1–19.

Wierdsma, A.F.M. (2001) *Leidinggeven aan co-creërend veranderen*. Breukelen: Nijenrode University.

Wijnen, G., Renes, W. & Storm, P. (1988) *Projectmatig werken*. Utrecht: Spectrum.

# CHAPTER 11

# Beyond Implementation
## Co-creation in Change and Development

**André Wierdsma**
*University of Nyenrode, Breukelen, The Netherlands*

One of the great problems facing company managements is the need to strike a balance between opposing perspectives. Oppositions such as centralized vs decentralized, global vs local, own core competencies vs networking: all of these demand context-specific judgements. There is a growing need for cooperation on all fronts between the different elements within the organization, as well as between different organizations, with each being expected to contribute added value. The ability to respond to customer requirements demands flexibility and cooperation at the boundaries of organizational units. This, in turn, means giving front-line entrepreneurs the scope to take decisions and be decisive (Ghoshal & Bartlett, 1997). The amount of variety and unpredictability that has to be managed is increasing.

Having the competence to deal with this variety at a decentralized level is crucial for the viability of the organization. 'Competence' is understood here as competence in the right context: the ability to convert insights and skills into actions in a specific context. Individual knowledge, skills, and attitudes must be supplemented by the competence to make variety manageable in consort with others: *collective competence*. Collective competence can be defined as the ability to deal with mutual differences on the basis of action and the ability to reflect on and learn from that action in a collective context. Competent employees are needed for this, but are not enough on their own. The key point is whether they are able to create solutions together at the interface with the customer. The viability of organizations increasingly depends on the collective competence of employees to take decisions in their own local context which are in line with the direction being pursued by the organization. This requires commitment, flexibility, and creativity. Collective competence is difficult to copy and cannot be bought.

These developments put the traditional methods of organization and change under pressure. This chapter uses the term *positional* organization to describe the traditional thinking on this issue. The first section discusses the premises on which this thinking is based as well as its ambivalence. It offers scope to broaden the organizational perspective: organizing in order to realize transactions. We describe this *transactional* organization method as an interweaving of three constituent processes: activities, relationships, and meanings. Then we look at change strategies and discuss the intensity of a change from positional to transactional organization. The third section explores the strategy of co-creation of change which ensues from the principles of transactional organization. The Method for Collective Learning (MCL) is a tool of the co-creation strategy. The construction and intervention rules of the method are illustrated. The chapter concludes with a discussion of a number of themes associated with co-creative change.

*Dynamics of Organizational Change and Learning.* Edited by J.J. Boonstra.
© 2004 John Wiley & Sons, Ltd. ISBN 0-471-87737-9.

# ORGANIZATION: FROM POSITIONS TO ACTIVITIES

## POSITIONAL ORGANIZATION: FOCUS ON POSITIONS

Traditional doctrine on organization and change places great reliance on rationality and external control by managers. Staff departments support managers in the standardization of work processes, employee starting levels, the internal norms, and the criteria for judging people by results (Mintzberg, 1979, 1989). The organization process is geared towards *reducing variety*. The organization is seen as a closed system, an entity which is separate from its environment and those connected with it (Hosking & Morley, 1991). Efforts are directed towards avoiding disruptions by perfecting the design and tightening up and refining procedures and systems. This kind of organization leads to a hierarchical ranking of people based on the degree to which they have an overview of and insight into the organization, and this, in turn, determines the differences in responsibilities and powers. Those who know a lot are at the top of the pyramid, those who know little at the bottom. This focus on ranking people is the reason for the use of the term *positional organization*.

Positional organization leads to a strong internal focus and a commitment to stability. Morgan (1986) compares these organizations to a machine, with the dedicated and loyal employees as its cogs. Employees are seen as the causers of complexity and are given few, if any, opportunities to act on their own initiative in unforeseen circumstances. The presumption is that, because of the knowledge they have built up, people in more senior positions are better able to decide how the variety in the organization's operational units should be accommodated. Not without some irony, Cherns summarizes the assumptions about employees as follows:

> People are unpredictable. If they are not stopped by the system design, they will screw things up. It would be best to eliminate them completely; but since this is not possible, we must anticipate all the eventualities and then program them into machines. (1993: 314)

These organizations are didactic because of the way that subordinate employees are approached by superior managers (Swieringa & Wierdsma, 1992).

The heart of the positional organization model is the external control and programmability of be-haviour. External control means that reality has to be made transparent through the development of a representative model which reflects the regularity of reality. Seen from this perspective, the viability of systems depends on:

- staff departments which generate sufficient knowledge of regularity to be able to achieve standard-ization;
- managers who are able to convert this regularity into concrete measures on the basis of their overview and insight;
- employees who implement these measures in a loyal and disciplined way.

Positional organization assumes that there is a consensus on the aims of the organization. The or-ganizational culture is seen as a binding force, in which the emphasis is on shared views, values, and objectives. Organization and change are regarded as two different processes. Organization is the process by which stability is achieved, while change is directed towards abandoning the familiar and achieving a desired new stability. Change management is seen as an implementation process for a new design. This is illustrated later by using the metaphor of the 'package holiday'.

What are the basic principles on which positional organization builds? And do these principles form a cohesive and consistent whole? Do they offer opportunities for developing a different organizational perspective?

## ASSUMPTIONS UNDERLYING POSITIONAL ORGANIZATION

The positional organization perspective puts a great deal of reliance on the 'ends and means' rationale, linear causality, and the ability to control behaviour externally. Great faith is put in the rational opinion of experts who have an insight into and overview of the entity to be managed. Toulmin (1990) states that this faith in rationality marks the transition from premodern to modern society. This belief in rationality and progress is sometimes regarded as the enlightened form of thinking and is one of the bastions of modernism. Modernism itself is a complex of views which have come to be taken for granted over time and on which many insights from day-to-day practice are based.

## CONTEXT-FREE KNOWLEDGE: REGULARITY

The roots of modernism lie in the idea of two worlds existing independently of each other: the objective, physical world and the world of the subjective human spirit. There is a reality to be discovered whose meaning does not depend on the observer: a truth *outside* the human being. Modernism encourages the formation of theories based on observation of facts. Observations and measurements are used to unravel facts and their mutual interrelationships, giving rise to a knowledge of regularity. This knowledge is of high quality if it is predictable, explicable, reliable, and intersubjective. The consequence of this approach is that the influence and value of the context are denied. From this perspective, knowledge gleaned from one context can be applied in another context. Ideal knowledge is independent of the social context, the time, or the observer, and can be tested against reality. It is true and valid regardless of the context: context-free regularity.

Modernism builds not only on Enlightenment thinking, but also on Romanticism (Taylor, 1985, 1991). The principles of these two cornerstones of modernism are, however, each other's opposites: they are two sides of the same coin. Enlightenment theory is founded above all on regularity, the general, the universal, and the context-free, the truth outside humankind. It is assumed that there is a natural order and that this is the norm for normality. Any deviation from that natural order is therefore abnormal. The natural order is structured hierarchically; this implies the primacy of the community, to which the individual must adapt. The 'particular' must be subordinated to the 'general'. Attention in Romanticism, by contrast, focuses on the particular, the unique, the contextual. Self-actualization, creativity, and spontaneity are not just important, but are seen as the ultimate goal of human development. Individuals use their originality, the uniqueness which sets them each apart from others. In the quest for fulfilment, individuals are asked to go in search of their own core. The emphasis in Romanticism thus lies primarily on the individual. Rather than adapting to an existing order, the challenge is for individuals to create their own opportunities. This represents a shift from adaptation and external control to creation and communicative control by individuals themselves (Cornelis, 1997).

## CREATION OF MEANING: THE PARTICULAR

Organizational theory builds, on the one hand, on the Enlightenment aspects of modernism. Checkland (1981; Checkland & Scholes, 1999) states that the Enlightenment theory applied to natural and designed systems has led to great prosperity, but when applied to social systems, it has set us on the wrong track, especially where variety increases and the future becomes less predictable. In social systems there is no meaning waiting to be discovered outside humankind; people create meaning in interaction with each other (Berger & Luckmann, 1966). Social constructionism is driven by the principle that stakeholders create meaning. Meaning is seen as the result of a process of mutual coordination. Sensory reality is meaningless until it is given meaning by human beings. Meaning is the result of coordination between stakeholders in their drive to attribute symbolic value to realities outside them (Rijsman, 1997). The stakeholders build a meaningful reality in language in interaction with each other. The meaning of an observed object therefore does not lie in the object itself, but is given substance through language and human interaction. Knowledge is thus embedded in a social context and a community.

Language and knowledge are not really subjective in the sense of specific to the individual, nor are they objective in the sense of independent of human beings. Rather, knowledge and language are *interactive*: meaning arises in language as a result of the coordination between those involved in according meaning. Language acquires meaning in the interaction process between people. This can be compared to the ritual dance in the animal kingdom, where moves made by one animal lead to movements in response by the other.

Social constructionism results in a shift in emphasis from individual to social, and from mental representation to interaction-based meaning. It is a shift from discovering the truth outside humankind to the process of meaning creation between human beings. It thus fits in with the objections to applying subject–object thinking and the separation of thought and action propounded in the Enlightenment theory.

The modern labour organization, with its professional 'knowledge workers', increasingly draws on employee qualities such as creativity and originality, in line with the idea of respect for the particular. Employee commitment and entrepreneurship are becoming increasingly important. In the (professional) services industry in particular, employees want their voice to be heard and want to make their commitment dependent on the degree to which they are treated as partners in the organization in the process of meaning creation. Organizing on the basis of commitment and decentralized decision-making by employees in contacts with clients—the 'entrepreneurial frontliners'—mean that there must be greater scope for the plurality of people and the diversity of views within organizations.

## TRANSACTIONAL ORGANIZATION: FOCUS ON TRANSACTIONS

In order to accommodate the increasing unpredictability and complexity, organizations are reappraising their structures and their views on the organization process. Departments now have to demonstrate their added value in mutual transactions on the basis of services delivered.

Transactional organization is regarded as the organization of activities for the purpose of effecting transactions in the chain of value addition. The organization of the working process is the main focus. This working process is understood to be the whole body of processes in which activities are performed, aimed at the actual creation of goods and services: external transactions, in other words. It is therefore these operational units which form the core of the organization (Beer, 1979). In order to be viable, the organization must be capable of responding to the differing demands and requirements of customers and other stakeholders with regard to products, services, and information. These stakeholders generate a great diversity of questions for organizations: external variety. This increasing external variety can only be accommodated by organizations by permitting or creating internal variety in those organizations. This is Ashby's law: 'only variety beats variety' (Beer, 1979).

The ability to make this variety manageable can be termed variety management. Variety is a measure of the complexity of a system and indicates the number of states the system can assume (Beer, 1981). The entire body of questions and problems and the complexity with which organizations are confronted are defined here using the term external variety. In order to deal with this variety, staff are given more opportunities to take decisions in their own specific circumstances. The growing input of staff to decentralized decision-making leads to a growing diversity of views, insights, and behavioural options: internal variety. A concept such as span of control then increasingly gives way to notions such as span of relations or span of support (Hoebeke, 1993).

## ORGANIZATION: AN INTERWEAVING OF THREE PROCESSES

In this approach, organization is seen as a weaving together of three processes: the performance of activities, the maintaining of relationships, and the creation of meanings. In maintaining the mutual dependences in their activities, people create a network of mutual relationships. This gives rise to meanings which are shared to a greater or lesser degree and to which those concerned refer in coordinating their activities. The meanings they develop in this way are highly context-specific.

An organization functions as a dynamic network of people connected by a network of mutually dependent activities and shared meanings. Through their actions, they generate not only the products and services, but also the organization. An organization is the context for and product of an organizational process. Transactional organization assumes processes and structures which foster both stability and dynamism. These two concepts are not mutually exclusive, but assume the presence of each other and give each other meaning.

A transactional organization process is viable if it is meaningful for both internal and external stakeholders. An organization derives its meaning for external stakeholders from the degree to which they value its products and services. Internal stakeholders expect the organization process to contribute to their own development. Transactional organization is regarded as a process in which activities, relationships, and meanings are developed, maintained, and changed in order to realize added value in products and services for external stakeholders and in order to be meaningful for the internal stakeholders.

## ORGANIZATION: AN INTERWEAVING OF ACTIVITIES

Activities are performed within the organization in order to facilitate successful transactions with external stakeholders. Where is the boundary between internal and external? System theory offers a language for analysing an organization as a body of activities within a larger series of activities; each definition of an organization can be regarded as a definition or 'cut-out' extract by an observer from a chain of activities. The activities in a business column, from raw materials supplier via goods supplier and manufacturer to client or user, form a series from which the observer makes his selection (Beer, 1979; Hoebeke, 1993). A system definition is a choice; in making that choice, a boundary is drawn and a previously undefined space is divided into a system and an environment (Herbst, 1976; Van Dongen, 1991).

An essential element in any discussion about the effectiveness of working processes is that the stakeholders should be in agreement about the definition of the system. A system definition forms part of the descriptive domain of the observer; it can be regarded as a model which facilitates human actions in the world. It thus forms part of the conceptual world, not of the real world, and one and the same reality can therefore admit several descriptions. The ability to act does not depend on representative models of reality, but on models which facilitate action *within* reality. People can lose sight of the optional nature of definitions and regard the constructed model as a representation of reality and as a given: a reification. This is reflected in statements such as: 'That isn't realistic' and 'That's just the way things are'. Within the organization as a defined system, yet other distinctions can be made. The organization is then the environment for these newly identified constituent systems. It is also a subsystem of the greater system, for example, a sector of industry. This embedding of constituent parts in bigger wholes is described using the term *recursivity* (Beer, 1979). This enables parts and wholes to be separated and their relationships with each other to be laid bare.

## ORGANIZATION: AN INTERWEAVING OF RELATIONSHIPS

People within an organization are connected by the activities they perform and are thus mutually dependent. The pyramid as a symbol of the organization is therefore a misleading image of the reality in organizations because it offers no insight into the relationships between the activities to be performed. The image which comes closer to representing the complex fabric of people and activities is the network. The people in the organization are the nodes, while the interconnections symbolize their mutual relationships. People will use their own powers and resources to pursue their own goals. The interaction gives rise to 'rules' between the 'players': 'rules and conventions by which sets of inter-locked behaviors are assembled to form social processes' (Weick, 1979: 47). This creates a degree of stability in mutual relationships. The rules reduce the uncertainty which results from other people's freedom, and thus releases energy for activity directed towards the creation of products and services.

People interact with each other mutually and simultaneously. The dynamic is undefined in the sense that none of the stakeholders can define its course unilaterally. Where people work together for some time, a pattern of interaction often develops between them. If an observer observes patterns in the way in which stakeholders accommodate the mutual interactions, this can be regarded as a pattern or 'structural coupling' (Maturana & Varela, 1980). The process is the seedbed for the interaction of which it is also the product. Rules or patterns in interaction do not determine the activity; people can always decide to ignore the rules, do something new or decide not to play. Arendt (1958) uses the term 'natality': the human capacity to do something new.

## ORGANIZATION: AN INTERWEAVING OF MEANINGS

Organization is a process in which people arrive at a definition of reality. People link these reality definitions; linked meanings condition the interaction process and are also the result of it. A meaning can undergo reification, creating the risk of losing the notion that meaning is the result of an interaction process. Meanings arise in language. However, people are limited in their ability to create meanings because words also derive their meaning from the fact that they are embedded in existing series of communications (Luhmann, 1990). The receiver of the message draws on an arsenal of concepts and texts which have a certain general level of acceptance. Communication is tied to a shared context. The interweaving of meanings overarches this and develops quite autonomously of the people who are communicating. Individuals cannot change the language independently; they can, however, help others to look at reality differently through verbal renewal (Van Twist, 1994).

## ACTING TO ACHIEVE TRANSACTIONS

Organization is a process directed towards creating added value for the ultimate transaction with the customer. In order to create products and services, many transactions are realized within the organization between departments in the primary process and support departments. Which characteristics of external transactions can the organization process take as a model? I would identify seven characteristics:

1. Transactions are the result of actions.
2. Transactions demand interaction around the boundary.
3. Transactions are the result of co-creation.
4. The receiver determines the value of a transaction.
5. Transactions are time-specific.
6. An insight into the process is necessary to improve the quality of transactions.
7. Transactions result in relationship-specific knowledge.

These characteristics can be used to sketch an outline of transactional organization. Transactional organization requires a focus on action and a continuous alternation of thinking and doing. Seen from the transactional organization perspective, the boundary acquires the function of a connection. The boundary can be seen as a membrane where interaction takes place between the members of the organization and the organization and its environment. The result and the way in which transactions are effected influence each other and are in this sense the results of a process of co-creation. In transactional organization the receiving partner is the one who must value the transaction. The appreciation of products and services arises in the receiver, usually the client. Appreciation cannot be imposed. Feedback processes and the quality of relationships are therefore crucial for viability.

## Temporary Workable Agreement (TWA)

Positional organization is based on the idea of subject–object separation and a knowable world. Everyone is pulling in the same direction; consensus is thought to be very important. This orientation carries the risk of reification and can mean that it is necessary to function for a long period in the straitjacket of the fixed allocation of meaning. Van Dongen (1996) uses the term 'continuity of consensus'. The stronger the focus on truth in an organization, the more time and energy employees will devote to achieving this consensus. Study and thinking are crucial; diagnosis is separate from action, and thought precedes action. As a result, action is postponed.

Transactional organization is aimed at coordinated action while retaining differences. It challenges the stakeholders to make an active contribution to the construction and deconstruction of the mutual agreements as a function of action. This requires a focus on TWA rather than on the truth. Temporary rather than lasting, universal truths. Workable because of the focus on the desire to make action possible in a concrete context. Agreement rather than value or principle in order to indicate that the point of departure is the uniqueness of the stakeholders and the specific circumstances of the context. The focus on transactions, on action, means that the agreement is lifted from the arena of truth and the 'continuity of differences' becomes crucial (Van Dongen et al., 1996). The question of relevance predominates: 'To what extent does any definition of reality prompt action?' Mills (1967) states that the willingness of stakeholders to act on the basis of a agreement increases if the agreement is temporary and if rules have been agreed which make it possible to rescind the agreement. This is a focus on the continuity of difference. The key is the willingness to recognize existing differences, variety, and to make them manageable for the sake of the envisaged transactions.

## Recursivity

Only a proportion of the activities carried out by people in organizations are directly related to achieving transactions with clients. Activities take place in the primary work process which result in the production of goods and services. These activities take place within the context of the rules on things such as how people within the organization work together. These rules are the result of an interaction process at an earlier moment; they coordinate the activities for the primary process. The processes of cooperation and creation of rules to make that cooperation possible are organized recursively. The cooperation rules form the bedding for the activities geared to production and service delivery. Structures and systems can be seen as 'solidified' agreements. In order to remain viable, an organization must have the competence to make—and change—these agreements.

People wishing to take part are expected to act within the framework of the implicit and explicit rules. Voogt (1990) uses the twin concepts game and play. When people play within the rules, in an ordered way, this is described as the 'game'. 'Play' involves the development of the rules for a game to be played: 'regulatory' play. The aim of play is to develop a new game. Stakeholders may conform to the game or choose to question the rules. Game and play alternate with each other. Play requires communication about the way in which mutual communication and cooperation connects stakeholders at the recursion level of the whole. People can work independently of each other, as single units, within the rules. If they wish to review these rules they have to cooperate at the level of the whole which incorporates the individual stakeholders. The level of the whole is at a higher level of recursion than the parts (see Figure 11.1).

Rules are developed in a specific context. When circumstances change, people are initially inclined to intensify the existing successful way of working. This results in a strategy of 'more of the same' (Watzlawick et al., 1970). If this proves ineffective, the stakeholders must go in search of new rules: the other. In a round of play, the solidified rules are deconstructed and then reconstructed to create new rules.

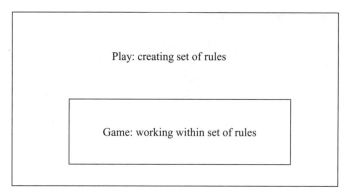

**FIGURE 11.1**   Recursivity, play and game

In a situation where there is a power differential, participation in play is impossible. This exclusion means that the less powerful stakeholders become part of a game which is shaped by the more powerful. The less powerful stakeholders lose the ability to express their own identity in the shaping of the rules. As a result, the system loses meaning for them.

Transactional organization assumes that people who are active at the level of the constituent parts have access to this dialogue at the level of the whole, where the agreements on the defined degrees of freedom are made. In addition to access, the quality of the dialogue is also important for people's willingness to contribute their views. If people begin censoring themselves in the expression of their views, dialogues at the recursion level of the whole do not fully reflect the existing variety. This has two consequences. On the one hand, there is the reduction in internal variety, possibly having an impact on the capacity to accommodate external variety. On the other, the possibility arises that stakeholders will be less able to recognize their own identity in the identity of the system. This reduces the meaningfulness of the system for them. Both developments impair the viability of the system.

## CHANGE CHANGES: FROM IMPLEMENTATION TO CO-CREATION

First, we shall look at process of change in which the implementation process is the central focus. The metaphor for this is the package tour—where everything is taken care of. Changes of this type fit in with the perspective of positional organization and the assumptions underlying it. We will then examine the intensity of change. The development of transactional organization is described as a change in which the assumptions of positional organization are questioned. Change at this level of intensity requires a process of collective learning in which existing patterns of thought and action are questioned. This means change as a process of collective learning and co-creation. The metaphor for this is the trek.

### CHANGE AS AN IMPLEMENTATION PROCESS; THE 'PACKAGE TOUR'

If change is perceived as an implementation process, the essence is the diagnosis, the correct phased plan, and care in implementation. In the diagnosis phase, an analysis is made of the best imaginable solution for a given problem. This solution is then communicated and offered for implementation to those whose position or work is affected by it. The process is often as follows. First, a steering group plus a number of working groups, supported by an authoritative consultancy, design a blueprint for the envisaged new organization: the new strategy, structure, culture, and systems. Usually this blueprint is accompanied by a staffing plan which states how many jobs will be lost due to the reorganization

(reorganization is often confused with rationalization). The blueprint is submitted for a decision to the senior managers in the organization. If they agree to the blueprint, the phased massage of the management layers begins, followed by the lower echelons. The most common reaction is to ask for more clarity, and in this phase the blueprint is therefore often fine-tuned and refined. This is followed by the 'musical chairs' phase: the restaffing of the management posts. Finally, implementation of the blueprint follows. The implementation is complete once everyone who is to stay has been reassigned, given a new job definition with associated powers, and knows to whom he or she should report. If any attention is paid to behavioural change, it takes the form of training programmes in which individual organization members learn the desired new competences. The tacit assumption is that they will then be capable of remaining 'in the groove' of the tacit collective behavioural patterns. In practice, in spite of individual intentions, people tend to fall back to the old ways of dealing with each other. This then prompts a further reorganization.

The implementation strategies are based on the assumptions of modernism: there is a meaningful reality which exists independently of the observer. This allows the observer to make a diagnosis of the situation. Based on a representative model of this situation, proposals can then be drawn up for change. Change then means implementing proposals. In a stable situation this model is able to function because reality does not change during the different phases of diagnosis, model development, and change initiatives. Where circumstances are changing, however, this approach leads to the continuous revision of plans and the postponement of action. By the time the plans have been completed, the situation has changed so much that the proposals are out of date. Stickland (1998) refers to the 'eternally failing change management machine'. This approach has no effect on the way in which people work together.

After the diagnosis phase, the implementation phase is concerned with the realization of changes in the structure or systems. The key focus of attention is on overcoming the resistance to change. In order to reduce this resistance, representatives of stakeholders may be brought in during the planning and diagnosis phase. Nevertheless, the fact remains that a relatively small group of people change the circumstances of many people; most of those involved in the change undergo it. The metaphor for this process is the 'package tour'. The change process follows a predetermined route and excursions are made which are selected by the 'tour management'. The tour management—the diagnosis team— encourages the travelling party to follow the planned activities so that the journey will be successful. Discussion about the desirability of chosen routes and excursions is interpreted as resistance.

This dominant form of change is marked by two paradoxes. First, the approach generates resistance for which it itself presumes to be the solution. Paradoxically, it is resistance which legitimizes the chosen approach. In order to make resistance manageable a structure is offered, uncertainties removed, optimum information provision ensured, and the change supported by the necessary communication and training programmes. This requires a careful diagnosis and a detailed phased plan for the realization of the envisaged goals.

The second paradox is that the structure, the strategy, or the systems are generally chosen as the starting point for the change process. However, these elements of the reality of the organization are precisely the stabilizing elements. Changing these creates additional uncertainty. Every change is ultimately directed towards the realization of a behavioural change which will enable the envisaged goals to be achieved more effectively. Implicitly, this behavioural change can only be achieved via changes in the structure or system. Every day people shape their actions on the basis of their interpretation of rules, structures, and systems. Change as implementation ignores this capacity of people within a specific context to gear their own behaviour towards the envisaged goals and to use the degrees of freedom they are permitted. With change as implementation, the process of behavioural change receives little attention because of the attention given to implementing the new structures and systems. The hope is that the structures and systems will be able to bring about the desired behavioural change. The scope for people themselves to change their behaviour within existing structures on the basis of shared insights is ignored.

## THE INTENSITY OF CHANGE

Customers are not interested in the structures or systems of organizations; they value the quality of products and services and the way these are realized: customer-friendly behaviour, a focus on service, and problem-solving ability on the part of employees in the organization. Organizing for transactions demands new conduct by employees in their dealings with each other and with the customer. Change processes are about engendering different behaviour; systems and structures can facilitate or hinder this. A change in behaviour requires learning processes by individual employees as well as imposing demands on the collective competence of employees to learn while acting *together*.

## THREE LEVELS OF CHANGE

Swieringa and Wierdsma (1992) identify three levels of change: at the level of rules, insights, and principles. These different change processes are linked to corresponding learning processes. The differences between rules, insights, and principles will be discussed first below, following which we will look at specific features of the learning processes that are needed in order to change them.

Rules, insights, and principles can be regarded as cognitive maps which people use in their actions: 'participants edit their own organizational experience into pattern of personal knowledge. A representation of that knowledge is called a *cognitive map*. A cognitive map consists of the concepts and the relations a participant uses to understand organizational situations' (Weick & Browning, 1986: 106). They are constructs for interpreting events. People use cognitive maps to recognize and create patterns with which they make variety manageable. The maps differ in the degree to which they are 'shared'. The quotation marks around 'shared' indicate that participants all accord meaning to events from their own perspective; these meanings are thus not the same for each individual. There is, however, enough overlap to make it possible to communicate about the images.

Rules in organizations indicate explicitly or implicitly how the members of the organization should behave. Often the explicit rules are laid down in job descriptions, as instructions. Norms can be regarded as implicit rules. Rules partly derive from operationalized insights on organizing, managing, and changing. The insight 'unity of management', for example, produces the rule that communication by an employee with his supervisor's superior, without the knowledge of the supervisor, is undesirable. Rules answer the 'how' questions in an organization; they indicate the bandwidth of action: what must and may be done in the organization. Underlying these rules are more or less shared insights. Insights are views about organizing, managing, and changing. Insights lie behind the rules, answering the 'why' questions. The function of insights is to explain and understand existing rules or to develop new rules. Insights are more far-reaching than rules in the sense that their scope is greater and that changing them has more far-reaching consequences. Principles are the 'natural' insights: insights which are not open to question because they speak for themselves. Principles define the identity of an organization: what an organization is or wants to be. Rules, insights, principles, and actions all impact on each other. This interrelationship is shown in Figure 11.2.

Learning processes focusing on rules, insights, and principles differ in their complexity and scope. It is assumed that the learning and relinquishing of principles have a bigger impact than the learning and relinquishing of rules: when a rule is changed, the underlying insights and principles remain unchanged. Figure 11.3 shows the relationships between the intensity of the learning processes, the domain in which learning is taking place, and the result.

## THE INTERTWINING OF RELATIONSHIPS AND MEANINGS

Transactional organization has been described as a dynamic mix of activities, relationships, and meanings. Changes in the activity system has consequences for the balance of the relational and meaning system. Changes in activities can have consequences for the relative strength of the positions of

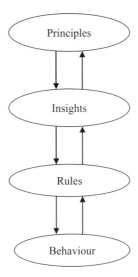

**Figure 11.2** Rules, insights, principles and behaviour

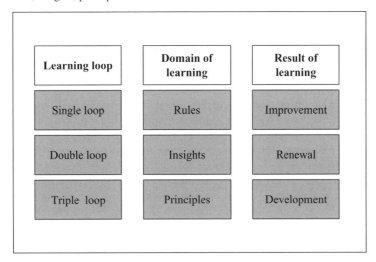

**Figure 11.3** Single, double, and triple loop learning

stakeholders. Changing balances in the relationship system influence the access to and impact on the meaning system. Organization as a process thus implies continuous changes in the interrelationship between activities, relationships, and meanings. The traditional distinction between change and organization disappears: organization means change and change initiates new organization processes.

## ACCESS TO DIALOGUES: CODIFICATION AND DIFFUSION

Access to the communication process and the method of communication differs depending on whether the learning process is focused on rules, insights, or principles. At the level of principles, the learning processes are more implicit. Access to these dialogues is reserved for the 'insiders' and barred from 'outsiders'. The meaning of a communicative message is largely determined by the shared views, values, and history of those involved in the communication process. The more familiar the context, the less the message needs to be codified. Codification refers to the degree to which the message

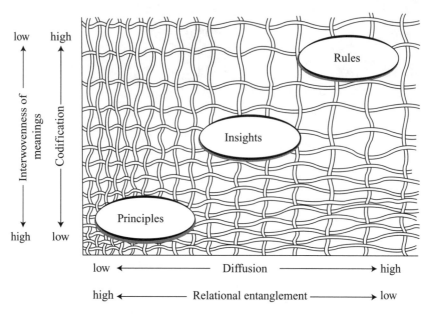

**FIGURE 11.4**  Interwovenness of relations and meanings. From Wierdsma, A.F.M. (1999) *Co-creatie van verandering*. Delft: Eburon

to be transmitted is made explicit. Principles are less codified than insights or rules. Principles are understood by stakeholders who share a history and context. It is the familiarity with each other and with the context that makes it possible to leave things implicit. The communication is therefore context-specific (Hall, 1969). Compared with insights and principles, rules are the most uniform and have the highest degree of codification. As the codification increases, the importance of a knowledge of the context declines. This makes it easier to disseminate the message. Diffusion indicates how easily and how extensively messages can be spread among people from different contexts. Not all stakeholders in an organization have an equal influence on the process of meaning creation. The degree of access to this process declines as the dialogue shifts from rules via insights to principles. Access to the dialogue about principles is reserved for those who are familiar with the context and who determine the identity of the organization. The interaction between relationships and meaning becomes more intensive as the communication becomes less codified.

## DENSITY OF NETWORKS

Metaphorically, the networks in organizations can be seen as having differing densities. Principles are characterized by a dense network of relationships and meanings. This network is difficult to change because of the limited accessibility of the dialogue and the method of communication. The density of the network is limited when it comes to rules. The network is loosely woven: the dialogue is accessible and the communication is explicit. Figure 11.4 shows the gradation in density of the networks between relationships and meanings for rules, insights, and principles.

To Summarize:

Principles are relatively difficult to change because of:

- the implicit nature of the communication;
- the limited group of people who have access to the dialogue;
- the density of the network of relationships and meanings.

Rules are easier to change because:
- the communication is codified and does not presume a shared context;
- people from different relational systems can participate in the dialogue;
- the network of relationships and meanings is 'loosely woven'.

## TRANSACTIONAL ORGANIZATION: A TRIPLE-LOOP LEARNING PROCESS

The positional and transactional organizational perspectives line up with the different views on the nature of reality and the way in which knowledge can be acquired. They differ at the level of principles. The stated differences are set against each other in Table 11.1.

Transactional organization requires that stakeholders have the willingness and the competence to deal constructively with differences in making variety manageable. The subject–object separation is abandoned. Derived separations such as separation of thought and action and of diagnosis and implementation thus lose a great deal of their relevance. Each stakeholder is both a participant and an observer in the process of organizing and changing. Meaning is created and changed in interaction.

Many change processes are directed towards the implementation of new insights without the underlying principles being questioned. The interventions and tackling of the change process are, for example, still fully in line with the old principles. The change process may, for example, be entirely focused on systems and structures, and employ consecutive diagnosis and implementation.

Many processes of change directed towards creating transactional organization behaviour—customer-orientation, decentralized decision-making, flexibility—fail because they are designed as linear reorganization processes by a limited group of experts and powerful figures who change the world for others while themselves remaining 'out of range'. This change strategy imposed from the top down is didactic and pays no attention to behavioural change, while employees are called upon to adopt learning behaviour and encouraged to be innovative and enterprising.

The credibility of change processes depends largely on the congruence between the message and the process itself (Watzlawick et al., 1970). Is the medium the message? As well as the content of change, the changers transmit their views in the method of change selected. Using the 'package tour' as a strategy for transactional organization confronts people with a dilemma. Management in reality uphold positional principles while saying that they are committed to the desirability of transactional organization. This inconsistency undermines the credibility of the change process and the intentions of the management. This leads to hesitancy in the commitment to the change process. This is then wrongly seen by the management as resistance to change, whereas in reality it is largely the result of

**TABLE 11.1** Positional and transactional organization compared

| Positional organization | Transactional organization |
|---|---|
| world which 'is' | world which 'becomes' |
| subject–object | subject–subject |
| objective knowledge—truth | context-specific knowledge—truths |
| stability | dynamism |
| positions | transactions |
| boundaries | interfaces |
| focus on constituent parts | balance between parts and whole |
| separation of thought and action | iteration of action and reflection |
| reduction of variety | maintenance of variety |
| consensus | Temporary Workable Consensus |
| separation of diagnosis and implementation | integration of diagnosis and implementation |
| change as implementation | change as co-creation |
| 'package tour' | 'trek' |

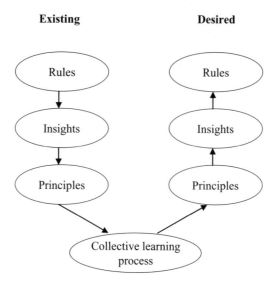

**FIGURE 11.5**   Collective learning on the level of principles

the strategy employed. If the management claims to be committed to an organization of free-thinking and learning people, it is inconsistent to treat the members of the organization during change processes as if they were unwilling to change. A didactic strategy cannot create a learning organization.

The choice of change strategy becomes crucial when seeking to make changes at the level of principles. The transition from positional to transactional organization requires a redefinition of the psychological contract between employees and the organization. Instead of adapting to the existing order, employees are asked to contribute their thoughts in the development of new possibilities. If the management is inconsistent, this makes employees even more uncertain. An important tenet for change processes at the level of principles is that credibility is related to the degree to which the change is shaped on the basis of the principles which apply to the envisaged organization (Swieringa & Wierdsma, 1992).

Moving from positional to transactional organization is a change at the highest level of learning: the level of principles. With triple-loop learning the congruence between the word and deed is essential for the credibility of the change strategy and those who define it. It is then necessary to question the underlying organizational principles. This requires a collective learning process by those mainly responsible for safeguarding the principles of the organization and who promulgate those principles in their (exemplary) behaviour. Figure 11.5 shows this by representing the transition from existing to new principles via a collective learning process.

This means that those who initiate change also form part of the change and learning process. The process of change shifts from one of implementation of solutions devised by a few for the many, to the joint creation of new possibilities: co-creation.

## CHANGE AS A COLLECTIVE LEARNING PROCESS

An organization's capacity to change is the capacity of people to deconstruct and reconstruct meanings together and to re-order relationships and activities to take account of the external variety. 'Competence' here means competence in context. This means that people, in addition to their individual competence, are also capable of linking these individual competences and converting them into action in a particular context: collective competence or collective learning.

Which processes are likely to arise in a reflection on existing principles? What criteria must a context meet in order to contribute to collective learning? To be able to answer these questions, an insight is needed into a number of processes. The following sections look at the exclusive effect of language and the occurrence of disciplining processes. The core concept is the 'zone of discomfort'.

## THE ZONE OF DISCOMFORT

Language makes communication possible between people, creates realities, and helps us to deal with reality. Reality acquires meaning in language. Language is thus both inclusive and exclusive. Language can be seen as the result of a need for order. This need may be a shared ambition or a perceived problem situation. Kooistra (1988) refers to the tension between the need for and result of order as the 'zone of discomfort' (*plek der moeite*). People construct a reality in language in conjunction with each other, in a process of interchange and negotiation: a 'regulatory result'. This is the result of social construction. Language reduces variety. To what extent does language create possibilities or obstacles for making variety in action manageable? What is needed to reinstate a sense of dynamism in realities which have become fixed in language?

The solidifying, variety-reducing features of language carry the risk that language will exclude reality and become synonymous with the truth itself: outside the existing language there is nothing. Laying bare reality in language carries the risk that the reality behind the language will be hidden. This can create a situation where language is equated to reality/truth. The reality which is generated in language confirms that language and causes that reality to coincide with the language. Language creates reality and then says, 'I didn't do it'.

## LEAVING THE ZONE OF DISCOMFORT: DISCIPLINE AND EXCLUSION

Access to the process of meaning creation is reserved for those who are credible. If an individual wishes to be seen as credible by others, his or her statements must remain within the accepted framework. Relationships and meanings are fixed through discipline. The voice of opposition is thus heard less and less. The dialogue becomes 'diluted'; the zone of discomfort is avoided. A paradigm is an example of a choice for a particular perspective. Input from outside the paradigm is then tested for its credibility using the criteria of the paradigm itself (Kuhn, 1976).

Language offers a demarcation line which is necessary in order to be able to act. In order to overcome the exclusive function of language, it is important that the process of 'inclusion and exclusion' by language is brought within the scope of thought. And collective learning means that people are able to create measures and contexts to enable them to reflect on the exclusive action of language. In this reflection new perspectives may arise which shed new light on the existing views: principles. A process of deconstruction and reconstruction presumes a willingness to question existing realities: to revisit the zone of discomfort.

## REVISITING THE ZONE OF DISCOMFORT: DIALOGUE PLATFORMS

Reflecting on the functionality of the network of relationships and meanings requires a context in which stakeholders can consider the existing patterns of thought and action. This means reflecting on the exclusive function of the existing principles at the zone of discomfort. This unavoidably brings a confrontation with the accepted self-image. Entering the zone of discomfort is therefore not just a matter of overcoming existing views, the relational dynamic will also have to be maintained. On the one hand, conditions will have to be created which make it possible for stakeholders to gain access to the dialogue, while on the other, consultation will have to be facilitated. Organization and change then become processes of co-creation.

## FROM SUBSTANTIVE QUALITY TO RELATIONAL QUALITY

When does the 'regulatory result' from a dialogue possess quality? What can be used as a criterion for quality if the 'external' reality disappears as an impartial 'third party'? The quality of a social system—relationship, group, organization, or society—can be determined on the basis of substantive agreements, views, and values shared by the stakeholders. This results in positively formulated values and views: continuity of consensus. Positional organization assumes that there is a meaningful reality outside human beings; that which corresponds most closely to reality possesses quality.

Quality within a social system can be deduced not only from the degree of consensus. The process of disciplining means that valuable views fall outside the dialogue. The quality of consensus depends partly on the quality of the interaction process underlying it. The quality of the interaction can be regarded as an independent variable which forms the context for the content: facts and values. A social system possesses quality if the stakeholders are open to another definition of reality and if others are not excluded from the underlying interaction processes. The quality of a social system lies more in the openness of the interaction than the acceptance of a substantive definition of 'the' reality. Systems which exclude stakeholders from dialogues that limit their degrees of freedom do not contribute to the development of those stakeholders and therefore lose some of their meaning for them.

The quality of social systems can be expressed as the extent to which stakeholders are challenged to make an active contribution to the construction of reality and are willing to revise that construction. This requires that the positional focus on truth be abandoned. A focus on the 'continuity of difference' implies a willingness to accept temporariness in the substantive dimension and to complement this with continuity and quality in the relational dimension. It requires the perspective of transactional organization, resulting in a willingness on the part of stakeholders to revise their views in the light of the variety to be managed. This makes it possible to change reified realities.

The core of transactional organization is a focus on temporariness and management of variety. It assumes that the meaning of a reality is the result of a process of mutual coordination. What change strategy reflects this philosophy? Which methodology can make this strategy workable? What are the dilemmas and paradoxes from which stakeholders have to choose and that they have to learn to deal with? These three questions lead us to the next section.

## CO-CREATION OF CHANGE

This section works out an alternative for the 'package tour' strategy. The metaphor is the 'trek': change as a process of co-creation. Such a process works on developing new possibilities. The principles underlying the shaping of a process of co-creation fit in with the transactional organization perspective. An indication is then given of how MCL has taken shape within the author's own experience. The construction and intervention rules of MCL are then given and illustrated with practical examples. The section concludes with a reflection on the dilemmas that arise when working with co-creation processes.

### CO-CREATION OF CHANGE: THE TREK

A development process based on co-creation is an indefinite process which, using the journey analogy, is comparable to a trek: the route and the rate of progress are developed within a bandwidth of degrees of freedom and a stated direction (Swieringa & Wierdsma, 1992). The direction is determined in consultation, following which the journey begins. Depending on specific circumstances, modifications may be made 'en route'; the phased plan develops step by step during the journey. During the 'trek', action and reflection alternate. The focus is on achieving a desired future while on the journey. The change process does not start by changing elements of the organization that are designed to give stability: structures and systems. Instead, the starting point is the stakeholders who have the ability to realize changes. In the first instance, these are the senior managers; they have a greater-than-average influence on and responsibility for the shaping of the relationships and the meanings adopted. The most important demand placed on these stakeholders is that they should show that they are also willing to learn. In the event of inconsistency between words and deeds, the organization's employees will focus on what their managers do (theory in use), not what they say (espoused theory) (Argyris & Schön, 1978).

What are the principles which form the basis for shaping the course of the 'trek'? The eight insights for designing the process of co-creation of change are as follows:

1. Activate 'actorship'.
2. Focus on connection.
3. Work on the basis of Temporary Workable Agreements.
4. Build on the past.
5. Develop the co-creation of possibilities.
6. Work backwards from the future.
7. Apply self-reference.
8. Create a shared experience.

## 1. Activate 'actorship'

If stakeholders accept that they have an active role to play in creating the context within which they function, they will recognize their influence: 'actorship'. The 'trek' relies on the willingness of stakeholders to hold each other accountable for their actorship. In a collective learning process this means that if a stakeholder does not wish to be part of the solution, he/she is part of the problem. As long as stakeholders perceive themselves as victims of circumstances which lie outside their field of influence (a reified reality), they are part of the problem. Stakeholders then become dependent on systems, structures, and other stakeholders. Often they respond to what they assume to be desired behaviour. The consequence of this may be that they blur the contact with their own views and ambitions. By disavowing their own actorship, stakeholders render themselves powerless. Since concepts such as power and powerlessness are relational, however, the picture is always complicated by the power of the powerless and the powerlessness of the powerful. Power as relative strength is a feature of relationships between players (Elias, 1975; Van Twist, 1994). The power of one player always depends on the degree to which the other recognizes and acknowledges it. Power lies within the domain of mutual negotiation.

## 2. Focus on connection

A condition for collective learning is a focus on connection: connection between actors and their own needs; connection between employees; and connection between internal and external stakeholders. Collective learning is fostered if the individuals are in contact with their own needs and ambitions. If the communication in a dialogue is truthful, a consensus is based on solid ground. There is then little or no self-censorship. In a situation where someone bases their actions on what they think others want of them, the dialogue is on shifting ground: what the stakeholder says does not reflect what he/she really thinks and feels. Increasing self-censorship is the result. Collective learning requires a focus on others. Transactional organization requires the willingness and the competence on the part of stakeholders to work together to make external variety manageable. By working to achieve a connection with external stakeholders, internal stakeholders remain open to their input.

## 3. Work on the basis of Temporary Workable Agreements

This does, however, mean that stakeholders accept responsibility for their actorship and also accept the mutual interdependency. It requires a focus on relationships between stakeholders and processes of shared meaning creation. Collective learning is then the capacity of stakeholders to utilize their actorship and create TWAs in a diversity of contexts. These consensuses are achieved in a process of social construction and are thus also changeable. Collective learning processes retain their relational and constructive quality if stakeholders are willing to work with TWAs. This means a willingness to acknowledge and work with existing differences (variety). Working with TWAs makes it easier to alternate action and reflection and to adjust principles based on the internal and external variety to be managed. This is easier if rules have been agreed to rescind a consensus. Dialogue demands a willingness on the part of stakeholders not to see their own definition of reality as the only one, and to show a mutual curiosity regarding the considerations behind the assertions of stakeholders. It is then important that stakeholders are willing to revise their existing standpoints and where necessary to reappraise their values.

## 4. Build on the past

Co-creation of change builds on the strengths generated by the viability of the organization (Beer, 1979). Remembering everything that is good offers a basis for self-confidence and ambition. This is an appreciative perspective, having an awareness of the best that there is (Cooperrider & Srivastva, 1987; Barrett & Srivastva, 1991). In a 'trek' it is important to build on these strengths. Stakeholders derive their identity from what has been achieved in the past; it forms the basis for security and self-confidence.

A second reason for starting from the past is that it offers an opportunity to see learning the present as the result of a complex creation process. In the socialization process new stakeholders learn to adapt to what is already there. A side-effect of this may be that stakeholders learn to adapt to the existing situation and that their powerlessness is unintentionally reinforced. They learn to move within boundaries which are not the result of their own learning process: they are learned rather than tested boundaries. This 'given order' has only a fraction of the wealth of meaning that it has for those who developed it: 'The originators' powerful, meaning laden world becomes translated into simple easily-memorized recipe knowledge, rules, and procedures' (Barrett & Srivastva, 1991: 238).

## 5. Develop the co-creation of possibilities

A focus on possibilities contrasts with the dominant focus on problems in the 'package tour' model. Mistakes are deviations from what is desirable. Problem-solving is repairing what was whole. 'In problem-solving it is assumed that something is broken, fragmented, not whole, and that it needs to be fixed. The function of problem-solving is . . . to help raise to its full potential the workings of the status quo' (Cooperrider & Srivastva, 1987: 153). The leap from the question of what went wrong to who made a mistake is a small one. Placing the emphasis on problems creates a danger that investigating errors leads to a defensive attitude by stakeholders. The emotion that is evoked is one of anxiety for the search for the guilty: the scapegoat mechanism.

## 6. Work backwards from the future

Future, cooperation, and mutual interdependence are concepts which fit in with the idea of a 'trek'. Willingness to act and energy ensue from a desire to achieve a shared vision of the future. Realizing this shared vision encourages stakeholders to devise opportunities to influence developments. The vision of the future can be seen as the creation of a point of attraction (Ford & Ford, 1995). In the process of co-creation, the stakeholders take stock of whether shared ambitions and images of the future can be formulated (Weisbord, 1992). Based on these ideals, they can then work backwards towards feasible action plans. While retaining 'the best that there is', they will go in search of new possibilities. The result of the change can therefore not be planned; it arises during the process of co-creation.

## 7. Apply self-reference

Stakeholders give meaning themselves to messages that are communicated to them. Meaning cannot be transferred (Maturana & Varela, 1989; Luhmann, 1990). This means that processes of change in social systems are not concerned with finding the single truth. Reality is meaningful in different ways and has multiple meanings. The ultimate meaning is created in the dialogue. It is essential that meaning creation is the result of a shared process, so that those involved in the change can give meaning themselves to the shared experience. In a process of co-creation, stakeholders have access to the process of meaning creation: constructive quality.

## 8. Create a shared experience

Transactional organization is based on the idea that meanings are created, broken down, reconstructed, and maintained in a continuous process. This happens if stakeholders reflect together on questions which concern them. Co-creation of change results in dialogues, giving rise to a process of shared experience. The stakeholders themselves create meaning on the basis of this experience; they are connected by their shared experience. Specific patterns of arguments and language use are reaffirmed in dialogues: 'Patterns of discourse reinforce the interlocking sets of assumptions that guide what members of this interpretive community select as fact and taken-for-granted common sense' (Barrett et al., 1995: 359). Stakeholders maintain and change their social reality and reinforce their social relationships through language. These relationships result in agreements, which then help to determine the relationships and the meaning creation. Co-creation of change requires a process of deconstruction and reconstruction of meanings and patterns of action. The language changes (the words, metaphors, and images used) and the network of relationships and meanings also changes. This can mean that relationship patterns alter and lead to changes in norms and values (Ford & Ford, 1995). Language and meaning are, after all, important coordination mechanisms between stakeholders.

These insights principles create a change process which builds on past performance and on the potential of the stakeholders. The future becomes binding and participation in the process of co-creation offers a shared experience. This experience offers a point of departure for the processes of meaning creation. The alternation between action and reflection which is assumed when working with TWAs keeps the process open to input from external parties and to new proposals for improvement. The construct of reality thus becomes a process of co-creation with constructive and relational quality. How can a process of co-creation be given form?

## MCL

I have built up my experience of and insights into processes of co-creation by developing and implementing large in-company customization programmes provided by a business school. MCL came about in response to a request from organizations for a method which would help with the realization of important internal change processes. In the first instance such requests are generally packaged in the form of a request for an in-company training programme. Over the years customization programmes have been developed in which the organization's own organizational questions are the carriers of the learning process. These programmes lie at the interface of management development and organizational development. MCL is a method which fits in with the metaphor of the 'trek'. It is the elaboration of a body of thought that has developed on knowledge development, learning, organizing, and change. MCL is based on the same principles as transactional organization, and, as a result, a number of accepted divisions between the thought/action, diagnosis/implementation, object/subject, and expert/non-expert disappear.

MCL provides a temporary context which offers the conditions in which stakeholders can reflect on the functionality of the existing network of relationships and meanings in relation to the external variety which has to be accommodated in the activity system. This reflection leads to a dialogue on the way in which the organization's members generate the organization, and in which the rules, insights, and principles underlying the organization process can be discussed. The method encourages the development of the competence to act on the basis of TWAs and the collective competence to safeguard the (relational and constructive) quality in their mutual interactions. MCL makes it possible for an unusual group of stakeholders to reflect in unusual circumstances on core issues concerning the organization. MCL cannot be used to sell a substantive solution, but can be used to share a problem with the participants.

The process that develops within MCL is indefinite in nature, in the sense that no stakeholders—principal, MCL facilitator nor participant—is capable of overseeing the entire interaction process and controlling it unilaterally. Participants and supervisors initiate a process of co-creation of which they then become part. The dance evolves during the dance. The creation of conditions for continuous collective learning is thus a continuous process in which the conditions continually have to be met.

While working on the substantive questions, an organization process arises in the MCL itself. MCL offers conditions for reflecting on this process. Attention can be moved from the organization process in the organization 'there and then' to the organization process within MCL 'here and now'. The way in which variety within MCL is handled then becomes a topic of reflection. The unusual conditions which MCL offers the stakeholders make it a context which encourages reflection on actions. Exploring the effectiveness of the existing orders in the light of the variety to be accommodated is the substantive task for those involved in the MCL.

## A CONTEXT FOR CO-CREATION

MCL is a temporary enlargement of the management unit of the organization as a whole. The participants enter a temporary organization: the programme as conversation space.

The core of MCL is the creation of conditions in which a facilitated dialogue can arise. It is a conversation space in which a dialogue on the core issues up to the level of principles can take place; a context in which the locus of difficulty can be entered. It offers opportunities for reflection on the existing order through the input of new actors and new meanings. The input of concepts offers opportunities to (re)order existing definitions of reality. The participants are stakeholders who represent the variety in the organization and exercise a strong influence on the identity of that organization. The patterns of interaction and the meanings which are regarded as important become evident in the dialogue. Changing the recursion level enables stakeholders to reflect on these patterns.

## MCL: CONSTRUCTION AND INTERVENTION RULES

Experience with MCL suggests that the stakeholders have to spend a significant amount of time together: at least three and a half days, and up to a week. This is necessary in order to allow situations to arise where it is possible for patterns to become visible in the 'here and now', and in which the stakeholders are willing to discuss them. There must be time to take on the confrontation with created meanings at the zone of discomfort, along with the associated hesitations and emotions. A triple-loop learning process demands the necessary conditions in terms of time, structure, and supervision. MCL is a context within which the participants are invited to exercise their actorship.

What conditions apply for this context? What are the construction rules for its creation? Which intervention rules foster a process of continuous interaction? The construction and intervention rules are aimed at:

- linking MCL and the ongoing organization process;
- the creation of a temporary dialogue space which has constructive quality;
- interventions to safeguard the relational quality of the collective learning process.

The construction and intervention rules are as follows:

1. Organize the MCL around core questions requiring attention.
2. Try to ensure that the participants represent the existing internal variety.

3. Create the means to guarantee the viability of MCL.
4. Choose a topic and working method which presuppose the commitment of the participants.
5. Choose working methods which enable variety and patterns in behaviour to be made visible.
6. Create the opportunity for changes of recursion level, so that the interplay between content and construction process can be thematized.
7. Create scope to develop new meanings.
8. Create scope to maintain the constructive quality of meanings developed within MCL.
9. Choose direct interventions towards safeguarding the relational quality of the interaction.

These construction and intervention rules are briefly discussed below and illustrated with a few practical examples.

## 1. Linking to core issues

If a strategy of 'more of the same' has proved ineffective, MCL offers opportunities for breaking the deadlock. There must be dissatisfaction with the effectiveness of the existing method of managing variety before the stakeholders are willing to enter the zone of comfort. Programmes are linked to core issues which are important for the viability of the organization. The learning process in the programme takes place on the basis of the organization's own history.

---

**CASE STUDY: GOVERNMENT ORGANIZATION 1**

A government organization is preparing for privatization, and decides to optimize the efficiency of the business process. The first request relates to supervision of a cost-cutting exercise. To ensure that adequate economies are made and prevent choices being avoided, we suggest embedding the process in a strategic orientation. In order to allow the optimization to take place at the decentralized level, a shared insight into the strategy of the organization is needed. Following consultation, the management decides on a cycle of linked workshops and conferences. Investments are made in building up an insight at the level of the whole—the strategy—so that managers can then be given the scope to come up with optimization proposals in their own specific situation. The core theme of the programme is to arrive at shared actions for optimizing the business process on the basis of a shared understanding of the strategic course of the organization. The MCL consists of 13 workshops and six conferences. The managements of the operational units prepare for this in a (partially supervised) workshop. Six strategic conferences then take place in which one or two directorates, plus heads of corporate staff departments, reflect on the strategic course. The two corporate directors are present at all six conferences. This structure is a break with the normal tradition in which these processes are run by the powerful staff departments.

---

**CASE STUDY: BUSINESS SERVICE PROVIDER 1**

Following the departure of the founder/managing director/major shareholder, the new managing director is confronted with unrest concerning the relationship between the many small business units and the large national head office. It is decided to professionalize the district managers from the line organization and a programme is requested in order to enhance the level of business insight. During the intake the request is broadened to helping resolve the stagnation in relations between the various units and the loss of striking power at decentral level. Innovation is also suffering from the deteriorating relationship between head office and the line workers. The group of participants is modified. The training programme with business-oriented modules is preceded by a collective learning process. In this programme a five-day conference is dedicated to internal cooperation, and a further five-day conference to a reappraisal of the strategy and the desired innovation. The participant group is adapted to this new structure. The management becomes part of the collective learning process.

## 2. Participants represent internal variety

Who is chosen to take part in the collective learning process? The aim is to ensure that the participant group reflects the existing internal variety of the organization as closely as possible. It is essential for the success and credibility of MCL that the consultation on the core issues is not restricted to the existing management. In order to be able to focus on the exclusive nature of existing meaning complexes, those who are excluded must have access to the dialogue in the MCL. The participation of new players means the managers in the MCL will have to make their thoughts and values explicit in order to be able to communicate with the other participants. This limits the exclusive function of language and facilitates a quest outside the boundaries of accepted meanings at the locus of difficulty.

Methodologically, limited access for stakeholders is undesirable. There are, however, practical reasons which force a certain restriction on the number of stakeholders. In order to be able to achieve sufficient depth in the interaction, the group size is limited. Seeking to make the group as heterogeneous as possible in terms of position, age, and functional background increases the variety of meanings.

---

### CASE STUDY: GOVERNMENT ORGANIZATION 2

The process of optimizing business processes in the government organization preparing for privatization initially threatens to become dominated by the large and powerful staff departments. MCL replaces a staff department-controlled protocol. Participants in the MCL are representatives of senior management, all 13 operational directorates, and a selection of staff department directors. The direct linkage of line and staff on strategic issues is a new step for the organization. In the confrontation with the operational directorates, it turns out that the prevailing ideas at group level on the strategy to be pursued are not embedded in knowledge of the market and are not in line with the abilities and wishes of the operational units.

---

### CASE STUDY: BUSINESS SERVICE PROVIDER 2

Initially the new managing director only wishes to reflect on the problem of cooperation and innovation with the commercial line managers. Following the intake for MCL, it is decided to set aside more time and to enlarge the group of existing commercial managers with the addition of representatives of the staff departments from headquarters and five newly appointed managers. In addition to the programme for the two heterogeneous groups of 20 people, six one-day workshops are organized for management. The participants reflect on core issues in both separate and combined programmes. Six weeks after the end of the programmes, management present a summary of their conclusions from the mutual dialogue. The shared diagnosis process results in complete agreement on the change proposals. The proposals harvest energy; there is no sign of resistance.

## 3. Viability of MCL as a temporary working system

To enable MCL to be viable as a temporary working system, it is important for the participants to have an insight into the effectiveness of the organization, as well as the freedom to raise this for discussion.

Processes in systems are always hedged in by restrictions imposed by the larger, enclosing system. MCL is also not immune to this. This makes a totally open learning process in MCL unrealistic. The interaction within MCL is limited by the bandwidth set by the sponsor of the collective learning process. The limitations must be indicated explicitly in the programme, to avoid a dialogue arising which cannot be coupled to the existing organization process.

MCL requires a bandwidth which enables reflection at the level of principles (triple-loop learning). The core of collective learning is that the object about which the group learns in fact consists of the principles which underlie the organization process. This demands a special contract with the sponsors so that the stated bandwidth is regarded as a TWA. This avoids MCL being inconsistent with the envisaged objective. If a reflection on principles is ruled out, the sponsor places himself outside the system and the inevitable link between subject and object is therefore broken. Sponsors are, then, not part of the solution, but part of the problem.

During the intake phase, establishing the degrees of freedom for a collective learning process is an important theme in the relationship between the sponsors and the programme facilitators. Trust and confidence often have to be won when working on the design and preparation of the programme. This trust and confidence are necessary in order to develop a learning process together with the sponsors in which the themes of their own organization are the common thread. This requires care in exploring the organizational theme, and intensive dialogue with the sponsors on the possibilities, in order to safeguard the relevance and effectiveness of the programme.

---

### CASE STUDY: BUSINESS SERVICE PROVIDER 3

During the preparation phase, which ultimately takes nine months, a new proposal is put forward based on an exploration of the questions of envisaged participants, those who report to them and those to whom they report. The programme shifts from a training programme aimed at individual learning to a reflection on the strategy and the method of mutual cooperation. It becomes a platform for the new management to sit and reflect with 40 line and staff managers on all the implicit assumptions which have arisen over time.

---

MCL requires that participants be given the opportunity to form their own opinion on the degree to which the system is able to make present and future variety manageable. The sponsor is expected to make available the necessary information for this.

---

### CASE STUDY: GOVERNMENT ORGANIZATION AND BUSINESS SERVICE PROVIDER

By way of preparation for the strategic reflection on the course of the organization, a working group of senior managers compiles a 'Book of Facts' in each programme. The aim is to obtain information which can serve as a basis for the dialogue in conferences. The Book of Facts contains all the information which is regarded as the most accurate description of the current status quo. Basic information on market trends, financial situation, staff profile, ICT investments, innovation, and development are made available. The aim is to ensure that the starting level of all participants is as equal as possible.

---

Stakeholders outside the organization are another important source of information: suppliers, partners, and customers. Customers can indicate to what extent the organization is able to respond to
the required variety. The external variety is thus given a voice and a face. The more close-knit the
networks of meaning and relationships in the organization are, the more important it is to bring in
external stakeholders. The sponsor must agree to allow customers, partners, and suppliers into the
MCL.

---

### Case Study: Business Service Provider 4

The company has a strong tradition of measuring customer satisfaction, and three loyal customers
are invited to take part in each programme. Customers suggest points for improvement and illustrate
them using concrete examples. This proves to have a twofold shock effect. In the first place, the
examples given are regarded as embarrassing by the non-marketeers among the participants. There
is a good deal of substitute embarrassment, and apologies are still being offered during the meeting.
A second effect emerges once the customers have left. There is a strong division of views within the
group. The non-marketeers and support departments are shocked by the attitude of the marketeers
to the customers; their attitude is labelled arrogant, high-handed, and condescending. The sales
and marketing people put the customer complaints into perspective. The entire day following the
customer session ends up being dominated by issues of horizontal cooperation and trust between
the departments.

---

## 4. Design working methods which presuppose actorship

MCL provides a context for change without the content of the change being defined. It offers a facilitated
and delineated space in which participants are expected to show their commitment. The boundaries
are the result of the embedding of the interaction in larger wholes. The method has relational and
constructive quality if it offers opportunities both for working within boundaries *and* for revising those
boundaries. This means that during the collective learning process the design and working methods
can themselves become the topic of discussion. MCL thus itself becomes a context within which the
transactional organization perspective can be practised.

---

### Case Study: Government Organization 3

During the preparatory workshop each operational unit directorate is familiarized with the method
to be used for the strategic orientation. The directorates prepare for the conference independently.
The conference is structured in such a way that both directorates present the results of their own
reflections at the start. The various steps in the analysis are then discussed with all present during
the conference. The confrontation of two analyses and the input of the representatives of the staff
departments create a new, undefined process. Each conference then produces a different dynamic
and different conclusions. The entire programme ultimately results in 17 project proposals.

---

The design is intended to build in increasing scope during the process for the commitment of the
participants themselves. The success of the programme grows as the participants increasingly know
and feel that they are owners of the process. This means they can influence the themes of the discussion
and its course and tempo, and that they can decide to modify the programme. The working methods
used in MCL must draw on the commitment of the participants so that they cannot place themselves

outside the process as observers. Because every behaviour has communicative value, the participants are co-creators whether they behave actively or passively. The process between the participants and the MCL facilitators is also one of co-creation.

## 5. CHOOSE METHODS THAT MAKE VISIBLE INTERNAL VARIETY AND PATTERNS IN MANAGEMENT

The working methods used in MCL are aimed at making internal variety and patterns in that variety visible and manageable.

*Making internal variety visible.* Habitual interaction patterns and solidified meanings are visible in the way the participants interact. The working methods used contribute to this if they encourage participants to state their views and values explicitly. The participants are divided into groups of differing composition, and through exercises and assignments are invited to make explicit their existing thoughts and behaviour patterns. This leads to a higher degree of codification and dissemination of implicit values and views. The result is that the knowledge can be better tested and is separated from the closed environment of the relational complexes.

---

### CASE STUDY: GOVERNMENT ORGANIZATION 4

By regularly splitting the participants into different groups, the existing variety is made visible in a way which does not emerge in the plenary sessions, where the accepted and desired meanings tend to dominate. In small groups there is scope and opportunity for participants to put forward their own views. In the reports on the findings of the subgroups, deviating views can be put forward as a voice in the subgroup without reference to any participant.

---

*Making patterns visible.* Since stakeholders in positionally organized organizations often respond to what is considered socially desirable, interaction processes in these organizations often proceed along well-defined paths. Habitual interaction patterns and solidified meanings are visible in the way participants interact. MCL offers an opportunity to recognize and evaluate these paths. The method uses scenarios, with a view to replacing 'talking about' with 'showing how'. They can take various forms: simulations, role-plays, exercises, making videos, etc.

---

### CASE STUDY: BUSINESS SERVICE PROVIDER 5

In the organizational simulation on working in a customer-oriented way, things grind almost to a complete halt after three rounds. The consultation circuit between the different management layers and the worker representatives blocks all activity on behalf of the customers. The majority of workers in the game have nothing to do and are very dissatisfied with the proceedings. One group of workers separates itself and starts its own company, promising support to two dissatisfied customers. In the follow-up discussion the participants are shocked by the way the hierarchy is automatically put beyond question, whereas it is quite evidently dysfunctional. The inability to open up for discussion the pattern that has emerged also gives rise to concern.

---

Simulations are discussed in detail afterwards. First, the time is taken to exchange experiences, and participants reflect on the patterns that have emerged. These are evaluated on the basis of how effective they have proved. The next step is to analyse the degree to which the patterns reflect the reality of the participants' own organization. The final step is a discussion of the functionality of their own cooperation patterns in the light of the demand from the external environment.

## 6. Changing the recursion level: from the theme to the pattern of cooperation

In MCL the participants reflect on the rules of the game; patterns in the existing network of relations and meanings are made visible. Whenever patterns in behaviour or thought become apparent, participants or programme facilitators can draw attention to them. Talking about variety management in the work situation alternates with reflection on the current variety management within MCL. Attention shifts from the theme on which participants are working to the construction process which underlies the patterns. This creates a learning process at a higher level of recursion: reflection on the process itself. The facilitators focus strongly on the difference between what participants say and what they do or project non-verbally. This restores the link between thought and action. The commitment and reflection on the way in which the participants jointly create a reality are the core of the collective learning process.

---

### CASE STUDY: BUSINESS SERVICE PROVIDER 6

During a discussion of the characteristics of their own culture, one of the participants presents an analysis. This prompts another participant to pull out completely from the discussion; her non-verbal actions indicate that as far as she is concerned, the entire discussion can come to an end. Because this non-verbal withdrawal has been identified as a cultural characteristic in an earlier phase, I draw attention to it. The discussion shifts from the culture 'there and then' to the current interaction pattern 'here and now'. Analysis of the series of events and making suspicions explicit facilitates a test of assumptions. Feelings experienced can now be given a voice and the atmosphere of the reflection indicates that participants are able to create a different interaction pattern. From that moment on, people no longer anticipate the 'desired' pattern; instead, the atmosphere becomes very personal. The participants decide to explore this theme in more depth and we abandon the programme for that day.

---

The essence of triple-loop learning processes is that stakeholders experience that a change in the organization requires a change in their own thinking and actions. Recognition and acknowledgement of their own contribution to the interaction processes offer an opportunity to reflect on their own way of acting. Because of the mutual interdependence, a change in their own thinking and action invites a response from others.

## 7. Create scope for developing new meanings

When reflecting on their own functioning without a new conceptual framework, there is a strong chance that the participants will continue thinking along the existing lines. The programme facilitators can offer new concepts, making possible an exchange between stakeholders in a new language which has a high degree of collective quality. New concepts also offer an opportunity to see reality differently and to shed light on other assets. This can enable participants to reframe their own behaviour.

---

### CASE STUDY: GOVERNMENT ORGANIZATION 5

A stalemate in a discussion is broken by an exercise to characterize the position of the organization *vis-à-vis* the market. The operations manager likens the organization to a gazelle. The commercial manager chooses the image of the rhinoceros. Standpoints adopted during the discussion acquire a completely different meaning now that the perceptions underlying them have become clear. The discussion shifts away from the standpoints towards those underlying perceptions.

Working with metaphors or analogies invites participants to use imagery to describe their own insights or values. It offers them a way of expressing their own insights in a different way. Metaphors and analogies are particularly powerful in situations where feelings are difficult to put into words. A well-chosen metaphor or analogy can make a concern or an ambition visible. It can also break through a habitual argumentation style within an organization, especially if there is little scope for expressing feelings and insights which are difficult to put into words.

## 8. Preserve the constructive quality of the new meanings

MCL requires that ways be found of preventing the meanings that have arisen in the process of collective learning from reifying. From the moment the participants begin working on a theme, a process of local meaning creation arises which is linked to the MCL. To obtain a useful interaction between those who have taken part in the MCL and those who are part of the regular organization process, the 'regulatory results' emerging from the MCL must have a high constructive quality. Facilities are needed to keep the meanings open for third parties who have not taken part in the process. Linking MCL to the existing organization process is important.

---

### CASE STUDY: PROFESSIONAL SERVICE PROVIDER

In a programme for a professional service provider, a working conference takes place between participants and management. The conference lasts for four sessions and is not pre-programmed. The participants invite those to whom they report, the staff directors and the Board of Management, to attend. They play host to their own management. Time is set aside in the programme for the participants to prepare the conference. They grasp this unique opportunity to set the agenda themselves with both hands. Because all decision-makers are present at this conference, it offers an opportunity to convert the ideas formed during the customized programme into decisions.

In the concluding conference a start is made on an open workshop-like structure, following which the group works towards the development of concrete projects which have to be set up in operational organizations. The directorates present each choose three projects. These projects become part of the agenda for the operating units and are monitored by the Board of Management and the operating company managements. Wide attention is devoted in the staff newsletter to this conference and the course of the projects. Within the space of two years, four different conferences have been organized by the participants in successive programmes.

---

A second conversation space has been created in the MCL where all relevant decision-makers take part in the discussion. The programme, the publicity surrounding it, and the projects that have been launched become important elements in the process of reorientation within the organization.

## 9. Safeguard the relational quality of the interaction

After designing the context and selecting the working methods to be used, the programme facilitators intervene in the interaction process in order to foster its relational quality. The facilitators attempt to keep the process of meaning creation open for all participants. Dominant behaviour dampens the willingness of other participants to contribute their own views and values.

---

## CASE STUDY: GOVERNMENT ORGANIZATION 6

During the session, one of the two participating directors of the operational units is very dominant in the discussion on setting the agenda. There is virtually no contribution from the other participants, whereas their non-verbal behaviour betrays a high level of irritation. Following an intervention by the programme supervisors, an exploration takes place of what is going on. Ultimately the dominant director turns out to be very worried about a possible merger of two operational units.

---

As soon as the facilitators have the feeling that someone is dominating the proceedings, they pay special attention to the faint signals with which participants express their displeasure about the way things are going, and then draw attention to these signals. At the higher level of recursion, consideration is given to whether the results of the discussion still enjoy sufficient support among the participants. In other words: 'Do we still have a situation with sufficient relational quality?'

## MCL: AN UNUSUAL INTERPLAY BETWEEN STAKEHOLDERS

From a transactional organization perspective, leadership lies in creating conditions which enable stakeholders to function autonomously within the agreed frameworks. Co-creation of change within MCL is a collective learning process and the result of the interaction between programme facilitators and participants. The elimination of the subject–object separation and the spread of actorship means there is no hierarchical ranking between the facilitators and the participants or between the participating managers and employees. The facilitators play a specific role and contribute specific added value.

The added value of the facilitators is found in the initiation, structuring, and facilitating of the dialogue between the participants, and the reflection on that dialogue. The facilitators create the context and intervene in order to achieve and monitor the relational and constructive quality of this process. The added value of the facilitators lies in:

- the creation of a dialogue space;
- the activation of stakeholdership;
- the creation of a safe environment;
- offering scope to experiment;
- attuning to the positive strengths and capabilities of the participants.

By asking participants to draw on their strengths, the facilitators enhance the capabilities of the participants to exercise their stakeholdership. A safe environment is created by, on the one hand, providing a structure and, on the other, protecting the 'particular' against the strength of the usual regularity. If a participant with an unusual standpoint is in danger of being suppressed, one of the facilitators will draw attention to this. This means drawing attention to the person who is dominating, the person who is allowing themselves to be suppressed, and the others who are allowing this to happen. In MCL, continuous attention is drawn to the way in which people deal with mutual variety. The facilitators seek to encourage reflection, and, where necessary, to disrupt it. Input must result in a cohesive disruption of existing processes. The facilitators aim to strengthen the individual and collective competence to create and revise organization processes. The facilitators have a role to play in the process both as facilitators and as participants.

The role of the facilitator is difficult to encapsulate in a single notion. The attitude which determines his or her functioning is also not uniform. In social systems people are constantly asked to take up positions in the no man's land between two simultaneously present forces:

- *Actor and director.* As a director, the facilitator creates the context in which the participants act. Through his or her interventions, the facilitator also becomes a player in the game. The facilitator creates and is part of that game—not like a needle in a worn-out groove, but more like a child playing with a hoop: following but also controlling.
- *Participant and observer.* Every intervention, or even the lack of intervention, is an action in the process. The facilitator's role can be described as a 'participating observer' or 'observing participant'. The facilitator is part of the process, follows the rules of the mutual game to a certain extent, but also reflects on the game itself from his or her standpoint as an observer. The facilitator continually has to strike a balance between involvement and distance.
- *Message and example.* The interventions of the facilitator are based partly on the content of what is said or done during the session. At least as important, however, is the way in which the interventions are effected. Consistency between what the facilitator says and does is of crucial importance at critical moments. The term 'professional', in the sense of distant, neutral, and expert, has to be expanded. The facilitator of a collective learning process is a committed professional with his or her own standpoint. He or she has to choose between the engaged position of a committed outsider or a reflecting insider.

Reality has two faces: thought and action, diagnosis and implementation, optimization of the existing and creation of the new, autonomy and independence, cooperation and competition. These are aspects of the same reality and not mutually exclusive concepts. Facilitators in collective learning processes within MCL, and sponsors who create the conditions for the processes of transactional organization, will constantly have to seek a position within the framework of the dilemmas: involvement vs distance, intervening vs allowing the process to develop, accelerating vs slowing down, allowing the discussion to continue vs drawing attention to the way in which the discussion is proceeding. In order to be able to make these choices in a specific context 'between the horns' of the dilemma, the professional must be securely anchored in his or her own norms and values. In addition to technical professionalism, this demands a normative professionalism from sponsors and facilitators of change processes. Normative professionalism means choosing a position on the basis of one's own norms and values. It is an extension of technical professionalism, which in this way comes within the scope of the reflection. Based on the professional's own perceptions, the tension of the insoluble dilemma can resolve itself contextually. Dilemmas which are resolved at a level of abstraction are turned into ideological choices which ignore the ambivalence and plurality of social systems. Dilemmas can only be resolved if they are contextualized, i.e. are made manageable in a specific context by means of a TWA (Wierdsma, 2001). Organization and change are thus processes of continual co-creation rather than of making a choice at a single point in time and then implementing it. The demands of employees and their growing role in the strategic self-sustainment of organizations calls for processes of co-creation of change: processes in which the members of the organization practise collective competence in dealing with differences while actually undergoing the process of change. Change takes place in concrete contexts and in a learning environment. The relational and constructive quality of internal relations eliminates the difference between diagnosis and implementation in processes of co-creation.

Change as co-creation is a 'trek', a journey in which, within agreed parameters and in a predetermined direction, stakeholders organize while changing and change while organizing.

# REFERENCES

Arendt, H. (1994) *Vita Activa*. Amsterdam: Boom. (*The Human Condition*, 1958).
Argyris, C. (1991) Teaching smart people how to learn. *Harvard Business Review*, **May–June**, 99–110.
Argyris, C. (1992) *On Organizational Learning*. Oxford: Blackwell Business.

Argyris, C. & Schön, D.A. (1978) *Organizational Learning: A Theory of Action Perspective.* Reading, MA: Addison-Wesley.

Argyris, C. & Schön, D.A. (1989) *Theory in Practice: Increasing Professional Effectiveness.* San Francisco: Jossey-Bass.

Barrett, F.J. & Srivastva, S. (1991) History as a mode of inquiry in organizational life: a role for human cosmogony. *Human Relations,* **44**(3).

Barrett, F.J. et al. (1995) The central role of discourse in large scale change. *Journal of Applied Behavioral Science,* **13**, 352–372.

Beer, S. (1979) *The Heart of Enterprise.* Chichester: John Wiley & Sons, Ltd.

Beer, S. (1981) *The Brain of the Firm.* Chichester: John Wiley & Sons, Ltd.

Berger, P.L. & Luckmann, T. (1966) *The Social Construction of Reality.* New York: Doubleday.

Burrell, G. & Morgan, G. (1979) *Sociological Paradigms and Organisational Analysis.* London: Heinemann.

Checkland, P. (1981) *Systems Thinking, Systems Practice.* Chichester: John Wiley & Sons, Ltd.

Checkland, P. & Scholes, J. (1999) *Soft Systems Methodology in Action.* Chichester: John Wiley & Sons, Ltd.

Cherns, A. (1993) Principles of socio-technical design. In E. Trist & H. Murray (eds) *The Social Engagement of Social Science* (vol. II, pp. 314–323). Philadelphia, PA: University of Pennsylvania Press.

Cohen, M.D. (1991) *Organization Science.* New York: The Institute of Management Science.

Cooperrider, D.L. & Srivastva, S. (1987) Appreciative inquiry in organizational life. *Research in Organizational Change and Development,* **1**, 129–169.

Cornelis, A. (1997) *The Logica van het gevoel.* Amsterdam: Essen.

Dixon, N.M. (1998) *Dialogue at Work.* London: Lemos & Crane.

Elias, N. (1975) *Wat is Sociologie?* Het Spectrum. *Aula* 462.

Ford, J.D. & Ford, L.W. (1995) The role of conversations in producing intentional change in organizations. *Academy of Management Review,* **20**(3), 541–570.

Gergen, K.J. (1992) Organization theory in the postmodern era. In M. Reed & M. Hughes (eds). *Rethinking Organization* (pp. 207–226). London: Sage.

Ghoshal, S. & Bartlett, C.A. (1997) *The Individualized Corporation.* New York: Harper Business.

Hall, E.T. (1969) *The Hidden Dimension.* New York: Doubleday.

Herbst, P. (1976) *Alternatives to Hierarchies.* Leiden: Martinus Nijhoff.

Hoebeke, L. (1993) *Making Work Systems Better.* Chichester: John Wiley & Sons, Ltd.

Hosking, D.M. & Morley, I.E. (1991) *A Social Psychology of Organizing.* London: Harvester Wheatsheaf.

Kooistra, J. (1988) *Denken is Bedacht.* Culemborg: Giordano Brun.

Kuhn, T.H. (1976) *De Structuur van Wetenschappelijke Revoluties.* Meppel: Boom.

Luhmann, N. (1990) *Essays on Self-Reference.* New York: Columbia University Press.

Maturana, H.R. & Varela, F.J. (1980) *Autoposiesis and Cognition.* London: D. Reidel Publishing Company.

Maturana, H.R. & Varela, F.J. (1989) *De Boom der Kennis.* Amsterdam: Contact.

Mills, T.M. (1967). *The Sociology of Small Groups.* Englewood Cliffs, NJ: Prentice Hall.

Mintzberg, H. (1979) *The Structuring of Organizations.* Englewood Cliffs, NJ: Prentice Hall.

Mintzberg, H. (1989) *Mintzberg on Management.* New York: The Free Press.

Morgan, G. (1986) *Images of Organization.* London: Sage.

Rijsman, J. (1997) Social diversity: a social psychological analysis and some implications for groups and organizations. *European Journal of Work and Organization Psychology,* **2**, 139–152.

Stickland, F. (1998) *The Dynamics of Change.* London: Routledge.

Swieringa, J. & Wierdsma, A.F.M. (1992) *Becoming a Learning Organization.* Reading, MA: Addison-Wesley.

Taylor, C. (1985) *Philosophical Papers 2: Philosophy and the Human Science.* Cambridge: Cambridge University Press.

Taylor, C. (1989) *Sources of Self: The Making of Modern Identity.* Cambridge, MA: Harvard University Press.

Taylor, C. (1991) *The Malaise of Modernity.* Don Mills, ON: Stoddart.

Toulmin, S. (1990) *Kosmopolis.* Kampen: Kok Agora.

Van Dongen, H.J. (1991) Some notions on social integration and steering. In R.J. in't Veld, C.J.A.M. Termeer, L. Schaap & M.J.W. van Twist (eds) *Autopoiesis and Configuration Theory* (pp. 47–54). Dordrecht: Kluwer.

Van Dongen, H.J., de Laat, W.A.M. & Maas, A.J.J.A. (1996) *Een kwestie van verschil*. Delft: Eburon.

Van Twist, M.J.W. (1994) *Verbale Vernieuwing*. 's-Gravenhage: VUGA.

Voogt, T. (1990) *Managen in een meervoudige context*. Delft: Eburon.

Watzlawick, P., Beavin, J.H. & Jackson, D.D. (1970) *De pragmatische aspecten van de menselijke communicatie*. Deventer: Van Loghum Slaterus.

Weick, K.E. (1979) *The Social Psychology of Organizing*. Reading, MA: Addison-Wesley.

Weick, K.E. (1995) *Sensemaking in Organizations*. Thousand Oaks, CA: Sage.

Weick, K.E. & Browning, L.D. (1986) Argument and narration in organizational communication. *Yearly Review of Management of the Journal of Management*, **12**(2), 243–259.

Weisbord, M.R. (1992) *Discovering Common Ground*. San Francisco: Berrett-Koehler.

Wierdsma, A.F.M. (1999) *Co-creatie van verandering*. Delft: Eburon.

Wierdsma, A.F.M. (2001) *Leidinggeven aan co-creërend veranderen*. Breukelen: Nyenrode University Press.

# Change Works
## A Critical Construction

**Dian Marie Hosking**
*University of Tilberg, Tilberg, The Netherlands*

In this chapter I talk about 'mainstream' and 'critical' approaches to organization—approaches that 'go together' in that each helps to define the other. I use this duality as an analytical and organizing device for the purposes of explanation and not as a truth, with better–worse or right–wrong implications. The distinction may help readers to make the jump from the better-known 'mainstream' to a 'critical' approach.

In this context I use the word 'approach' to refer to what Fleck called a 'thought style' (Fleck, 1979). A thought style is bigger than a theory but 'softer' and 'weaker' than a paradigm (Chia, 1995). My own style may be broadly described as (a) critical; (b) social constructionist; and (c) processual. I focus on ongoing processes of *organizing* (and not organization) and, in so doing, put *change* at the centre of my theorizing.

As I outline my approach I do two things. First, I reconstruct some traditional issues and practices in mainstream treatments of change and, second, I explore some new possibilities for change work theory and methodology. While I take the view that there is no such thing as a social constructionist method, critical constructionism does generate and validate some changed forms of change work (e.g., Hosking, 1999). These involve practical acceptance of (a) actors as part of—rather than apart from—reality construction processes; (b) multiple, ongoing, construction processes;[1] and (c) producing realities that can be thought of as very real but, nevertheless, local–historical–cultural rather than subjective or objective.

These premises invite further development of *non-hierarchical* ways of organizing that open up to possibilities and multiple voices[2] rather than closing down to one way, to one right view, i.e., to dominance relations. The need for this seems especially urgent in a world where 'more knowing' and 'more power over' (hierarchy) seem to produce increasing inequalities in financial wealth and economic infrastructure, destruction of landscapes and communities, pressures to mono-culturalism, and a reduced quality of experience for those whose realities are disputed, distorted, or denied. This situation seems intractable to solutions based on more of the same 'knowledge/power' nexus—solutions which rarely deliver their substantive promises (e.g., better diet, better education)—yet at the same time reproduce dominance relations.[3]

Following this overture, the first movement will (a) review mainstream approaches to person–organization relations; (b) review some of their implications for organizational change; and (c) finish

---

[1] A deliberately 'weak' concept that is meant to avoid the 'strong' claim of being a paradigm, but to convey a similar level of operation—more inclusive than theory, less bounded and totalizing than a cosmology.

[2] Here I am *not* reconstructing the common distinction between symbolic and material reality (see, for example, Rorty [1991] and Berman's [1990] discussions of the emergence of the 'Italian' heresy [Science], 'hard' and 'soft' differentiation).

[3] As additional tools and not as replacements.

*Dynamics of Organizational Change and Learning.* Edited by J.J. Boonstra.
© 2004 John Wiley & Sons, Ltd. ISBN 0-471-87737-9.

by introducing a critical alternative. The second movement overviews the premises of the present critical constructionist thought style. The third and final movement (a) uses these premises to reflect on mainstream constructions of change; (b) uses these premises to develop change work generic themes; and (c) outlines some ways of putting these themes to work.

# PERSONS ACT IN OR ON ORGANIZATIONS

Two British authors, Paul Thompson, a sociologist, and David McHugh, a psychologist, have made a broad distinction between 'mainstream' and 'critical' approaches to organizational studies (Thompson & McHugh, 1995). In the latter they included the literatures of work and organizational psychology (WOP), organization development (OD), and organizational theory (OT). I will start by reflecting on the 'logic' of this mainstream of thought.

## MAINSTREAM CONSTRUCTIONS OF RELATIONS

Much of organizational behaviour and organizational psychology has centred individuals and groups 'in organizations'. 'The' organization has been reified as the largely tacit and separate context for individual action, perceptions, satisfactions, and the like (e.g., Miner, 1980). Similarly, much of OT has focused on organizations as the seemingly separate context for individual activities, groups, and inter-group relations (e.g., Child, 1977, 1984). Both approaches are 'mainstream' in the sense that they treat individuals and organizations as if each were a singular, bounded and separate, some-one or some-thing. You could say that a 'primary distinction' (van Dongen, 1991) is made between individuals and social institutions—constructed as independent existences—as entities that exist 'in their own right', so to speak (Hosking & Morley, 1991; Thompson & McHugh, 1995). This is, of course, a very usual commonsensical distinction. In psychology it is spoken of as a dualism between 'individualistic' and 'culturalist' approaches (Allport, 1963), while in the philosophy of social science it appears as a contrast between 'individualism' and 'holism' (Hollis, 1994).

When people and/or things are separated, this has implications for how their relations are understood. The construction of sharply separated and bounded entities goes together with a 'subject–object' (S–O) discourse of relations[4] (see, for example, Harding, 1986; Reeves Sanday, 1988; Fine, 1994; Hollis, 1994; Dachler & Hosking, 1995). By 'discourse' I mean 'anything that can be "read" for meaning . . . (that) can be referred to as a text' (Burr, 1995: 51). A discourse can be thought of in terms of what it does; the S–O discourse can be said to do three things.

First, the S–O discourse constructs relationships as necessarily being between an active agent and an acted upon (passive) object. For example, organizational leaders and change agents often are discussed as active in relation to some organization which is available to be known and changed.

Second, the S–O discourse 'explains' actions, relationships, and outcomes through reference to the assumed characteristics of entities. For example, organizational leaders may be (assumed to be) characterized by vision and/or charisma which enables them to be leaders.

Third, in the S–O discourse, the entity that is explicitly positioned (by the implicit theorist/narrator[5]) as the Subject is presumed to make social realities and relationships: the Subject is the one who acts to know and to influence 'other' as a knowable and formable Object. Continuing our example, organizational leaders are often claimed to be those who can or should act in order to know their

---

[4]  Which will later be referred to as a 'subject–object' construction of relations—a 'hard differentiation'. In such relations, Self constructs 'other' as, for example, different, wrong, and opposing, or as different and 'in-between'; i.e., as unfit(ting) some 'either–or' category system. Either way, other—recalcitrant employees, rival authorities, nature—is a threat and has to be changed, usually on the basis of more (local) knowledge and 'world structuring'. Subject–object discourses are found much more widely than this. Indeed, some have said that they characterize Western ways of thinking and science since Plato (see, for example, Berman, 1981, 1990; Rorty, 1991).

[5]  I am leaving discussion of the distinctor who makes the distinction out of the story, for the moment—just as mainstream narratives do.

organization and its environment and, on the basis of their knowledge, act to (re)structure relations and thus change organizational performance.

## MAINSTREAM METHODOLOGIES OF CHANGE

Mainstream discourses of entities and relations are reflected in related constructions of organizational change and development. Two methodologies can be distinguished in which either the individual or[6] the organization are centred.

The first methodology focuses on individuals and on changing individual characteristics. Examples include human relations approaches (e.g., Guest, 1984), job enrichment, goal setting (e.g., Miner, 1980), and many OD approaches[7]—most particularly those that are directed towards developing self-awareness, building trust, and clarifying roles and roles relations (e.g., Dyer, 1984; Schein, 1987; French & Bell, 1990; see also discussions by Fineman, 1991; Hollway, 1991; Cummings & Worley, 2001).

The second methodology focuses on organizations and environments and the characteristics of each. In this case, organizational change is considered to be planned and achieved through changing organizational characteristics—such as structures and technologies—to match environmental contingencies[8] (e.g., Carnall, 1990; Evan, 1993). The Aston Studies are a well-known example in which research measures and empirical findings provide the basis for normative interventions in which the scientific researcher diagnoses the 'actual' contingent relations of a client organization, thus providing the basis for restructuring, should there be a mismatch.

Whether the methodology is directed at individuals or organizations, both assume S–O relations and both are mainstream in the sense used here. So expert social scientists, organizational leaders, consultants, change agents are implicitly or explicitly assumed to be the ones who will inquire, come to know, and then—on the basis of this knowledge—design and implement necessary changes.

## NON-CRITICAL VARIATIONS ON THE MAIN THEME

The above account is brief and ignores some variations that do not neatly differentiate person and organization. One increasingly popular 'blurring' in organization studies is found in an emphasis on sense-making (e.g., Tsoukas, 1994). However, many such approaches treat sense-making as an intra-individual cognitive activity (see Gardener, 1985). In other words, the discourses are those of 'constructivism' which, broadly speaking, presents the widely shared view that knowledge is a necessarily imperfect representation of the world as it really is (e.g., Gergen, 1985, 1999; Hosking & Bouwen, 2000). In my view, this sense-making approach is both an important variation and 'more of the same'. It is more of the same in the sense that mainstream discourses of entities and relationships can be said to remain largely unchanged.

The above mainstream discourse of sense-making makes important assumptions and points of emphasis about knowledge and reality. First, attention is directed to knowledge about the world 'in its so being', for example, inquiry is directed to what sense X has made of Y, to 'what is it' types of question, and to static characteristics and states (personhood, 'the' organization).

---

[6] As we shall see, this Aristotelian logic of either–or is founded on the Parminidean ontology embraced in what we are here calling the 'mainstream' or 'entitative' perspective (see van Dongen, 1991; Chia, 1995; Hosking, 2000).

[7] Cummings and Worley (2001) distinguish between different 'generations' of approaches to OD. They refer to the latest generation as 'social constructionist' but only discuss Appreciative Inquiry (AI) in this context. However, in my ('critical', relational constructionist) view, it is inappropriate and misleading to separate theory and method and to treat AI as 'this or that' kind of method.

[8] I have often spoken of contingency approaches elsewhere. In my view they face a serious problem of treating, for example, person and organization as separate entities and reduce person to the role of providing 'inputs' to some statistical interaction. As a result, relational processes are reduced to statistical interactions between inputs from person and inputs from context (see, for example, Hosking & Morley, 1991).

Second, conceptual language is primarily interesting for its representative function—to represent 'the world in its so being'—to represent independently existing beings such as the world, organizations, and other people. For example, words, numbers, and other kinds of symbols are viewed as standing in for (representing) some independently existing reality.

Third, rational action is assumed to be shaped in relation to pre-defined criteria 'in the world'. For example, these assumptions about knowledge and language mean that rational action (rational decision-making, organizational design, rational planning, etc.) must be grounded in inquiry that tries to know how things really are and moves (aspects of) the world (e.g., an organization) towards some better state such as a greater probability of survival, increased effectiveness and efficiency (Rorty, 1991; Gergen & Thatchenkery, 1996).

Fourth, as noted earlier, people and (parts of) 'the world' are centred as separate and independently existing entities, for example, some theorists try to make sense of organization–environment relations in as objective a manner as possible.

Fifth, theorists of sense-making continue to position themselves[9] as 'outside' their own discourse. In other words, they unreflexively and tacitly write of others as sense-makers while continuing to construct self as the (albeit imperfectly) knowing subject in S–O relation (see Steier, 1991).

## INTRODUCING CRITICAL VARIATIONS

Critical approaches can be characterized in terms of three assumptions and points of emphasis that differ from those of the mainstream. First, critical approaches assume interdependent existences. This mutualist assumption treats self and other as co-constructions—'I am because you are'.[10] So, for example, the relation between person and organization is seen as one of mutual creation: through their interactions people make organization, which in turn reflects back and influences interactions.

Second, language is given the key role of constructing social realities and, compared with mainstream approaches, representation is decentred.

Third, attention is directed to multiple, local–historical, social realities that are made in interactions or what I call relational processes.[11] This contrasts with the mainstream centring (often only tacit) of a singular and independently existing world of which persons may have objective and subjective knowledge.[12]

In my present—critical—variant of social constructionism, I view 'persons' and 'organizations', indeed, all constructed realities and relations, as produced and emergent in interaction processes. This includes the process of producing research and theory and constructing the identities of researcher and researched. I try to theorize the how of social construction and focus on action rather than on meanings as constructions 'inside the head'. My interest is in the processes of making, maintaining, and changing local realities. S–O relations are treated as possible social constructions and not as 'how things really are' or how they must be in order to produce objective knowledge.[13]

## ORGANIZING AS A RELATIONAL PROCESS

In this, the second movement, I will outline my central premises concerning 'the how' of relational construction processes. I draw upon multiple voices and literatures including, for example, the philosophy

---

[9]  Through tacit reference to discourses of the 'received view of science'—where the distinction is assumed to be 'in the world'—or made by an impartial and objective distinctor.

[10]  'The mystery of I and Thou reveals the "and" between both'; see, for example, Hoebeke, this volume.

[11]  These assumptions are part of what others have referred to as 'postmodernist' ways of thinking. See, for example, Gergen and Thatchenkery (1996).

[12]  In other words, a thought style in which ontology and epistemology are separated.

[13]  Again, it's simply that 'objective knowledge' is not part of the present discourse. I am not arguing for others to abandon talk of objective knowledge, just for a broadening of relational possibilities—including constructions of Science.

of inquiry, feminism and feminist critiques of science, the history of ideas, the sociology of knowledge, cognitive and social psychology, interactionism, cognitive and phenomenological sociologies, radical family therapy, (some) systems theories, and critical social anthropology. Two key qualities of these premises should be noted. First, they are intended to say something about the 'potentials of the phenomena that constitute the domain of inquiry'—potentials that may be very differently realized in the varying 'empirical flux of events' (Cohen, 1989: 17, emphasis in the original); in other words, they are not to be understood as substantive claims. Second, they concern 'becoming realism' rather than 'being realism' (Chia, 1995). In other words, I am talking about ongoing relational processes (a 'weak ontology') and not about entities, attributes, and discrete acts ('strong ontology'; Chia, 1995: 579). Given these qualities, it might be helpful to approach the present narrative as 'strange' rather than, for example, assuming that you already know about social constructionism and therefore know what I want to say. I will continue with a short overview of key premises before expanding them in relation to (a) issues that arise in *mainstream constructions* of change and (b) their general (and changed) implications for change work.

## PREMISES: CONSTRUCTION PROCESSES

As I have said, I regard social realities as emergent in ongoing processes. I centre coordinations or interactions in a narrative roughly similar to Weick's talk of behavioural interlocks and recurrent interactions (see Weick & Quinn, Chapter 9, this volume), and similar to Wierdsma's talk (Chapter 11, this volume) of 'transactions' as interweaving activities, relationships, and meanings. These interactions are processes of (re)organizing local realities; they are processes in which persons and worlds are co-constructed, actively maintained, and changed. But how, more narrowly, may these processes be understood? From a theoretical point of view, this requires a shift from mainstream assumptions about entities (independent existences), knowledge (knowledge that), language (representative), and rationality (grounded in 'real world' criteria). The following summarizes something of what seems required.

## ACT-SUPPLEMENT BUILDING BLOCKS

First, we must move our line of talk from entities and individual action to interaction. We need a way of talking about co-construction in interaction rather than individual acts or meanings 'inside the head'. Key to this is a shift away from language as representation to language (in the broadest possible sense of the word) as a process of coordinated actions. Coordinations might be, for example, of written and spoken texts. For example, an e-mail is sent (text) and replied to (con-text) or two people have a conversation. Equally, coordinations can be of non-verbal actions, things, and events[14]—a hand is extended (act or text) and another hand takes it and shakes it (act or con-text). These can be spoken of as 'text–context' relations (e.g., in the case of written texts) or as inter-acts. These coordinations are relational unities: an act makes no contribution to reality construction processes unless it is supplemented in some way.

With this line of argument we can see that social construction is achieved in relational processes. In sum, coordinations involve actions, objects, and artefacts available to be made relevant or irrelevant, meaningful or meaningless, good or bad, by being put into relation (e.g., Dachler & Hosking, 1995; Gergen, 1995). Related terms for discussing this relational (ontological) unit include 'joint action' (Shotter, 1993), co-action, and 'performance' (e.g., Bateson, 1993; Newman & Holzman, 1997).

---

[14] Perhaps not surprisingly, our definition is similar to definitions of 'discourse' such as that quoted from Burr earlier. However, we do not fully embrace the wider theoretical stance of 'discursive psychology' or of discursive approaches that remain unreflexive about their own social construction; see Gergen (1994) for a discussion of their qualities and relations with relational thinking; also Steier (1991).

## Multiple Coordinations

The second key point to bring out is that construction processes are made in multiple, simultaneous inter-acts, many of which are tacit. For example, the deceptively simple coordination of shaking hands relies upon reference to a great many local cultural practices. For the two hands joining to be constructed as a 'handshake' involves many simultaneous con-texts or supplements such as, for example, local greeting conventions, notions of politeness, formality, left and right, meeting and departing...All these relations need to be learned in the process of becoming a local. Imagine what it is like for a newcomer to the Netherlands trying to 'bring off' a competent local performance when greeting another person: when and whom do you kiss?, how many times?, with which cheek do you start?, what kind of relationship does this make?, and so on.

Multiplicity has another important aspect: relational processes may construct multiple realities. However, talk of multiple realities has a very different meaning from mainstream talk—where it would mean multiple subjective ('inside the head') realities in an objectively knowable world. Here it means that interactions make multiple local ontologies or local cultures. For example, plant management could coordinate with a corporate mission statement (text) on the basis of con-texts such as discourses of local and of corporate management, of previous change initiatives, of being 'messed about'. Plant management may construct the mission statement as the latest corporate management joke while, at the same time, the HRM department may be using it as the basis for team briefings and development workshops, while investors may be buying more shares in the company because they believe in the mission statement.

## Local–Social–Historical Constructions

So, our story so far is that interactions produce multiple local realities. I need to say more about what 'local' means in this context, and I need to say more about how interactions can be ongoing. First, it has to be the case that some stability is ongoing—to enable interactions to have a history. We can say that, in the course of relational processes, 'stabilized effects' (Chia, 1995: 586) are produced when actions are warranted or 'socially certified' (Hosking & Morley, 1991). These stabilized effects may be identities (e.g., plant manager), social practices (such as greeting conventions), social structures (corporate and local management relations). And, of course, it could be that some act is not supplemented and so remains unreal, or it may be supplemented—not by being socially certified but by being 'discredited' as untrue, unhelpful, immoral, and so on (Weick, 1979). This is part of what is meant by *social* construction—reality is (re)constructed when one act supplements another, when texts are put into relation and warranted or discredited.

My reference to 'local' can be further developed by returning to mainstream discourses of knowledge and 'the real world'. First, it contrasts with the mainstream discourse in which generalizable knowledge is centred. This is knowledge that remains knowledge across historical epochs and across social contexts. The present reference to 'local' is intended to situate reality constructions, in particular social–historical processes. Second, my discourse of 'local' can be contrasted with the mainstream discourse of the one reality that underlies and validates or falsifies all knowledge claims. In contrast, my present talk of 'local' is related, for example, to Rorty's talk about 'community' (Rorty, 1991) and related notions such as 'community of practice' (Lave & Wenger, 1991). However, it should be emphasized that 'local' (and community) in this sense could be as broad as, for example, 'Western', post-Enlightenment constructions, and as broad as 'Science' (the community of scientific practitioners and praxis).

Returning to an earlier example, I am soon identified as 'a buitenlander' (i.e., not local) to some community (let's call it Dutch) when I give too many or too few kisses, tangle noses, or inappropriately attempt to shake hands. Similarly, any scientific claims I might be heard to make might not be warranted by those regarded as competent judges within the scientific community if, in my fieldwork, I try to avoid the position of the knowing outsider. In other words, locals perform their particular local identity (as co-constructors of some community) when they co-act in ways that are locally warranted as 'real and good' (e.g., Weigert, 1983).[15] These ways of 'going on' in relation may seem fixed and may be (locally) taken for granted as 'how the world really is'. However, we should not forget either the essential artfulness—artificial rather than natural—of these 'stabilized effects' or the relational processes in which they are constantly made and remade.

Local processes can be said to have a *historical* quality. So acts supplement an already available act, a con-text supplements already available texts: coordinations make and remake (local) history, so to speak—in ongoing relations. For example, announcing a new mission statement might well make no sense (non-sense) unless resourced by 'pre-existing'/available discourses concerning, for example, collective working, management hierarchies, 'having all the noses pointed in the same direction' . . . Similarly, a nineteenth-century factory worker probably would not have claimed to be 'conducting participant observation' when challenged for standing around seemingly doing nothing. And had he or she done so, it seems unlikely that their claim would have been warranted!

Finally, processes can be said to both resource and constrain the future, i.e., how the process 'goes on'. Returning to the above example, accepting or rejecting someone's claim to be 'doing research' will allow the process to continue in different ways. We may say that a particular act invites a range of possible supplements but there is no local culture that I know of where 'anything goes'. Once a particular pattern of coordinations becomes 'stabilized' (e.g., greeting conventions, S–O methodologies of inquiry, and change work), then other possibilities have to be improvised and it may be harder to have them validated as relevant, 'real and good'.[16] Such difficulties are especially likely in locales where right–wrong dualisms are already in place as 'stabilized effects'.

## RELATIONAL REALITIES

Finally, we have the question of what to put in place of the displaced (but not rejected as wrong) talk of subjective and objective realities and 'the real world'. The present thought style centres reality construction processes—what we earlier called 'becoming realism'—and relational realities. The latter have been presented as co-constructions of self and other, people and worlds; self-making and world (other) making are understood as co-genetic. This means that self and other (people, material objects, events, social structures) exist as social realities only in relation (e.g., Mead, 1934; Weigert, 1983). This also means that different relations construct different realities. So, for example, who you are ('identity') varies as 'you' (a semantic place holder) interact with your boss, life partner, fellow cat lovers, etc. What the mainstream discoursed as relatively stable entity characteristics now may be seen as multiple and variable and as performed—rather than as singular and fixed, a-historic possessions. In sum, relational processes (a) are 'reality-constituting practice(s)' (Edwards & Potter, 1992: 27) that construct markets, management, hierarchy, all social realities, what is (is not), and what is good (bad); and (b) these realities are multiple, local, and performed, rather than singular and transcendent.

## SUMMARY: RELATIONAL CONSTRUCTION PROCESSES

- Relational processes construct someone and something as real and (perhaps) good.
- Entities and S–O relationships can be constructed as in mainstream narratives.

---

[15] Although it is not *necessary* to be a local to carry off a competent performance, you can participate in becoming a local, by being 'relationally responsive' to the invitation (action) of another. See, for example, Catherine Bateson's (1993) narrative of 'Joint performance across cultures: improvisation in a Persian garden'.

[16] Discourses, for example, often are theorized as resources (see, for example, Hardy et al., 2000); however, a 'both/and' view is possible once the either–or logic of a coherent and singular world is set aside.

- Processes only construct the way someone or something is here and now; other relations are always possible.
- Processes are constructed in multiple, interrelated, interactions and reference coordinations already in process.
- Interactions resource and constrain how a process unfolds.
- Relational processes are processes of self-making and world-making: self and other are co-genetic.

## RECONSTRUCTING THE MAINSTREAMS OF ORGANIZATIONAL CHANGE

These themes can be developed through a reconstruction of mainstream, change-related issues. I shall reconstruct just four: (a) stability and change as ongoing; (b) processes constructing multiple realities; (c) change as 'power over' and 'power to'; and (d) resistance presumes force. Each of these will briefly be reflected upon before introducing the final movement and the possibilities that are enabled by 'starting somewhere completely different', i.e., with critical constructionist premises in place.

### BOTH CHANGE AND STABILITY ARE ONGOING

Mainstream discourses construct organizations as relatively stable and singular entities acting in relation to a more or less turbulent environment. Given these (and related) understandings, change can only be understood as moving from one stable state to another (unfreeze–move–refreeze). The subject (change agent) attempts to achieve change by empirical–rational analysis of what is, producing knowledge 'about' (i.e., propositional knowledge of) how things are and should be, as a basis for influencing—for re-forming the other. These discourses reduce processes (in this case knowing and influencing) to input–output and feedback relations within and between entities (Hosking & Morley, 1991).

  In contrast, the critical constructionist premises outlined above centre processes and potentials. Stability is no longer taken for granted as a feature of the world 'as it really is'[17] and change is no longer considered a temporary (though increasingly common) aberration. Rather, by assuming a 'weak ontology of becoming' change (as a process) and stability (as repeated reconstructions of some local reality) are seen as ongoing and social realities now are viewed as particular, more or less temporary, local–historical achievements.

### CHANGE AS A CONSTRUCTION PROCESS CONSTRUCTING MULTIPLE REALITIES

By shifting from entities and individual acts, the locus of change shifts to interaction processes and how they co-construct, reproduce, and change social realities and relationships. This has a major implication for change work in that interactions become both the 'unit of analysis' and the locus of transformation. One radical implication is that the conventional distinction between inquiry and intervention is no longer helpful. Remember, in the present context, processes construct social realities as 'how things really are made' and not as individual, subjective (mis)constructions of how things really are.[18] The present view does not presume, for example, that the newly announced mission statement is something about which all could and should agree, barring ill will and incompetence. Agreement becomes a question of relating, social certification, discrediting . . . a matter of power—and it is to this that I now turn.

---

[17]  And, therefore, independently of any social construction process, which, of course, means that we cannot know it as it really is, independently of our ways of 'knowing'.

[18]  So, for example, talk of organizations as having 'fragmented' cultures rather than one, organization-wide, culture could be given this more radical, ontological (rather than subjective knowledge) meaning (see, for example, Joanna Martin's chapter in the *Handbook of Organization Studies* (Clegg et al., 1996)).

## Change as 'Power over' and 'Power to'

Mainstream discourses have been said to assume S–O relations and to privilege the subjects' constructions while silencing the other as object. Examples were given of knowing leaders and knowing scientists gathering information about the other (subordinates, the environment, the research objects) and then using their knowledge to influence, re-form, or change the other. Commentators have spoken of this as a relationship of 'power over', that is, as power of subject over object (e.g., Gergen, 1995).

Central to the S–O discourse are the mainstream assumptions about reality (ontology or what exists), what we can know about it (epistemology) and how we can build that knowledge (methodology). In the mainstream, knower and known are treated as if separate. Separateness warrants the scientific way of knowing—relative to other (e.g., more inclusive or participative) ways. In the mainstream construction, the world is assumed to be singular and internally consistent, knowledge is measured on a single dimension and is regarded as (more or less) right/wrong or useful. So, knowing subjects study objects to be known and use their knowledge to re-form—to construct 'power over' objects.

Many change work methodologies reproduce mainstream conceptions of S–O relations, knowledge, and methodology. Examples include the methodology of conventional action research approaches to OD.[19] In the latter case, knowing scientists reflect back their knowledge of the locals and their practices and, in so doing, also reproduce their (the scientists') discourses of science, reality, generalizable knowledge, how things usually are done elsewhere, notions of better–worse, and so on—yet these (implicit) discourses are unavailable for critical reflection. Similarly, many top-down change efforts try to impose one voice—one local reality—to get others to buy in to some shared metaphor, mission, or vision, or to 'be flexible'. Further, they often try to do so through constructing S–O ways of relating where some change agent (e.g., chief executive) knows what is necessary and tries to influence (bargain, negotiate, persuade, transform) others to 'agree' with them (e.g., Dyer, 1984; Carnall, 1990).

When considered on the basis of the present relational premises, S–O relations and 'power over' are just possible and not necessary relationship constructions. Distinctions need not be constructed (a) as binary opposites, i.e., as mutually exclusive and opposed; (b) as 'impermeable'; or as having (c) fixed boundaries. So, for example, inclusive, non-hierarchical ways of relating can be constructed in processes that treat multiple different relational realities as different but equal. This contrasts starkly with the exclusive, hierarchical world of one fixed reality (ontology) and a 'totalitarian epistemic concern for consistency' (see van Dongen, 1991). Non-hierarchical ways of relating can construct 'power to' in the sense of power to sustain multiple interdependent local ways of 'going on' in 'different but equal' relation (see Gergen, 1995; Hosking, 1995). Shortly we shall see that this is a key theme in relational change work—how to give free play to multiple local realities or 'forms of life' without imposing one form or voice on others.[20]

## There Is no Resistance without Force

Resistance to change has been receiving increasing attention as change agents have sought ways to persuade, negotiate, or in some way influence others to embrace their own (change agent's) reality constructions. The change agent is theorized[21] in relation to discourses of individual action which is rational in the sense of intentional, planned, and knowing. At the same time the object is constructed (by the subject) as resisting, known, and potentially formable (see, for example, Giddens, 1979; Hollway,

---

[19] Which may be distinguished from participative inquiry and other collaborative approaches in which everyone contributes as an expert ... attempting to avoid S–O relations (see, for example, Reason, 1994).

[20] And, as I have said, that also goes for the present thought style and its present particularities.

[21] And, of course, also the scientist-narrator who positions himself outside his narrative.

1991). The metaphor is mechanistic, for example, overcoming resistance arising from inertial forces, or organic, for example, overcoming individual defence mechanisms, or political.

Resistance is conceived of (by the subject) as something the other (as object) has or does which has to be overcome—by self as subject. This can be attempted, for example, by education or teambuilding (see, for example, O'Connor, 1995); 'social change can be accomplished only as rapidly as resistances are overcome and removed' (Jacques, 1947, in Hollway, 1991: 120). However, the present 'critical' discourses indicate that attempts to overcome resistance through more 'power over' others will repro-duce S–O relations, i.e., will reproduce the status quo rather than change it. Perhaps this is why change efforts are so often felt to be more of the same, even when the 'reality content' seems so different. I might add that, when one reality attempts to impose itself on another, resistance might well be the locally rational response. However, rather than emphasize knowledge (of how things really are) and rationality, the present (non-mainstream) view directs attention to power relations, to S–O relations as relations of 'power over', and to the possibility of non-S–O relations and 'power to'.

The next development explores some possible discourses of change work that go together with critical constructionist premises. These are first briefly outlined as 'generic themes'. These themes are then brought together in examples of possible change work practices.

## CRITICAL CONSTRUCTIONISM AND CHANGE WORK

Others have had much to say about how humans may (have) conduct(ed) their affairs without construct-ing S–O relations. Reflections of this sort have been offered both in relation to science and in relation to other 'communities of practice'. In outline, change work of this sort might include (a) opening up to possibilities rather than closing them down through problem identification, solutions, and gener-alized change programmes; and (b) constructing a community-based view of rationality grounded in 'unforced agreement' as reflected in coordinated action[22] (e.g., Rorty, 1991). Other discussions stress (c) relational processes as the location for constructing '(im)moral' (and all other) criteria. Being 'for the other'—rather than 'with'—now may be viewed as the starting point, so to speak—prior to the construction of S–O differentiation (Bauman, 1993). If so, perhaps the best that many can do to be reasonable and moral is to 'discuss any topic . . . in a way which eschews dogmatism, defensiveness, and righteous indignation' (Rorty, 1991: 37). This seems to be an argument for opening up to multiple realities—rather than imposing one local–cultural–historical reality over others.

### SOME GENERIC THEMES

I will continue by outlining some generic themes that seem important in opening up possibilities, multiple realities, 'unforced agreement', and 'power to'. The themes are relevant both to inquiry (now also viewed as intervening) and to explicitly transformative change work. In the former case, practices that may construct inclusive, different but equal relations include participative action research, co-inquiry, collaborative inquiry (e.g., Reason, 1994), and approaches to community social psychology (see, for example, McNamee, 1989; Hosking, 1999). In the case of transformative change work, relevant approaches may include, for example: Appreciative Inquiry (Cooperrider & Srivastva, 1987), narrative and re-storying approaches (Barry, 1997), working with metaphors (e.g., Barrett & Cooperrider, 1990), performative work using drama (e.g., Boal, 1992; Holzman, 1999), and dialogical work that addresses how people talk to one another (see, for example, Isaacs, 1993; Barrett et al., 1995; Anderson-Wallace et al., 2001; http://www.geocities.com/dian_marie_hosking).

---

[22] But here I am not talking about knowledge (as is Rorty) but interaction . . . and in this case 'agreement' means we can go on coordinating our actions without questioning or being questioned; we do not have to share the same story (agree) about what we are doing (see, for example, Hosking & Morley [1991]).

## Knowing and Influencing Work Together

Inquiry and change work recognize and give importance to the influence potential of all acts—asking questions, voice tone, words used, posture, including 'artefacts', interview findings, percentage summaries, diagnostic classifications. Any and all of these have the potential to contribute to the social construction of reality.[23] All acts now are seen to have the potential to change[24] how processes 'go on' and change agency is 'located' in ongoing processes and not in 'a change agent'.

## Multiple, Equal Voices

Inquiry and change work attempt to generate and work with multiplicity rather than suppress or homogenize it through the application of statistical procedures or through management drives to 'consensus'. In general terms, polyphony may be constructed in non-hierarchical ways that recognize and support difference and that construct 'power to' rather than what I earlier called power over. This may mean including everyone who has an involvement in some issue through participative change work. However, it must be stressed that the point of participation is no longer to increase the likelihood of acceptance of someone else's decision, or to increase the quality of a (consensus) solution. Rather, it is a way of including and enabling multiple local realities in a different but equal relationship.

## Possibilities and Positive Values Are Centred

The view that relational processes construct realities has major implications for all change work. For many (though not all) it means working with what is positively valued, i.e., working 'appreciatively' (Cooperrider & Srivastva, 1987) rather than reconstructing a world which is problematic, a world of deficits, failure, and blaming. The shift to possibilities invites, for example, change work that helps participants learn how better to improvise and imagine new ways of going on together (for example, 'Imagine Chicago' and other similar projects[25]). This may also mean evaluating participatively and appreciatively, building in reflexive evaluation as an ongoing quality of change work.

## Inquiry and Intervention Work Together

Since relational processes construct realities, there is no requirement (although, of course, one could) to narrate activities as either inquiry or intervention—a 'both–and' approach is enabled. So, for example, action research is developed in more participatory ways along with related methodologies such as co-inquiry and collaborative inquiry. Similarly, change work shifts from the language of intervention to the language of 'transformation' in order to capture the notion of change 'from within'. At the same time, methodologies collapse the structuring distinction between inquiry and intervention, recognizing that, for example, future searching is future making for good or ill. Attention shifts from the discourse of inquiry, for example, to careful questioning and careful listening as a way of 'doing' different but equal relations.

## Questioning and Listening as Formative of Relations and Realities

A changed role and significance are given to asking questions, to how they are asked, why, and by whom. Rather than see questioning as 'finding out' about some pre-existing reality, questioning now

---

[23] This is very different from mainstream approaches that differentiate data gathering, analysis, intervention design, and implementation. In the latter case, activities are understood *either* 'find out'/seek to know about *or* attempt to influence 'other'.

[24] Only the 'potential', as it depends on how they are supplemented and whether or not they get warranted as 'real and good'.

[25] See, for example http://imaginechicago.org.

is seen as forming, and good questions are those that help to enlarge possible worlds (see Harding, 1998) and possible ways of being in relationship. For example, Appreciative Inquiry (Cooperrider & Srivastva, 1987) gives very careful attention to the appreciative question around which the process will be based. Equally, careful attention to listening to the other is a key feature of many dialogical approaches such as the Public Conversations Project, the MIT Dialogue Project (Isaacs, 1993), and Inter-Logics' work with 'conversational architectures' (http://www.inter-logics.net). The point is to give space to the other rather than doing something to or making use of the other.

## CONSTRUCTING IN CONCEPTUAL AND NON-CONCEPTUAL PERFORMANCES

This concern with careful questioning and listening has a broader connotation when we accept that realities are constructed in performances that include, but are not confined to, conceptual language. And interactions may often construct S–O relations. Many practitioners work with how people talk with, to, and about one another and construct their wider realities and relations. Is the universe friendly? What are the prevailing metaphors—business is war or . . .? Who talks the most, interrupts, claims authority and expertise, on what basis? Other, less conceptual performances include (re)enacting local realities, for example, with the help of professional actors, or through narrative approaches in which participants learn how to re-story their lives—perhaps learning how to open up to new possible ways of 'going on' in relation (e.g., Performance of a Lifetime). Learning how to learn, getting unstuck, constructing 'power to' are central to these approaches and inclusive, performative, change work achieves a changed significance.[26]

## A DEEP ECOLOGICAL APPROACH NOW IS WARRANTED

When self and other are seen as co-constructed, care of the other is constructed as care of the (moral) self. So, for example, discourses of care no longer have to be understood in relation to 'soft' humanist narratives and opposed to a 'hard' (factual) world of, for example, economic 'realities' and relations that are (rationally) instrumentalized, secularized, and disembodied (see Hosking, 2000). In this relational thought style the question whether the universe is friendly would not seem so relevant or helpful. Rather, the question is more how can self and other relate in ways that allow and support interdependent, different but equal relations?

## CHANGE WORK PRACTICES

I shall finish with an outline of a methodology which could be discussed as critical constructionist. However, I do not wish to be understood as describing a constructionist method. The reasons are twofold. First, because all methods contribute to processes of reality construction. Second, because methods are not freestanding, rather, theory, method, and data are co-genetic.[27] For example, theory sets limits on relevant and useful methods (and vice versa), shapes how method is understood, and shapes what count as data. Many of the practices I will outline could be stripped from their present (relational-constructionist) context and claimed to be 'the same' as, for example, development practices from a humanist tradition or as might be generated on the basis of an ideology of participation. However, this would be to miss the point of the relational premises set out earlier.

---

[26] One reason it does so, and one that we have not had the space to explore, is because of the decentring of the mind–body split. Now that this is regarded as a construction—and not how things really are—some fascinating and radical possibilities arise. See, for example, Berman, 1981, 1990; Hosking, 2000.

[27] The latter is, of course, the approach of the 'received view of science', which acts 'as if' theory and data were separate, and strives to make them as separate as possible. In this way, it constructs data (the context of justification) as what's important for rejecting or accepting a hypothesis.

## NARRATIVE CHANGE WORKS

Given the present thought style all inquiry can be considered as narrative—whether reporting an experiment, a survey, or making narrative interviews. The 'inquirer' engaged in finding out is engaged in relational processes—in making self as an inquirer in relation to the other (e.g., Howard, 1991), and in relation to narratives of science, mathematics, professional practice, OD, and so on.[28]

Many approaches to inquiry explicitly use the language of story telling or narrative and these approaches have become increasingly popular in recent years (e.g., Sarbin, 1986; Calás & Smircich, 1991; Boje, 1995). Work of this sort includes narrative interviews and narrative analysis of the same, but also narrative analysis of written and spoken texts: documents, archive materials, emails, telephone calls, films, magazines. However, it should be stressed that narrative approaches include both main-stream and critical variants; here I am focusing on the latter.

As was set out earlier, critical constructionism positions texts as more or less local, embedded in multiple intertextual relations. The embedded, situated, or local-relational quality of actions/texts has two important implications.[29] First, narratives are regarded as social and not individual constructions and so, for example, interview transcripts are not treated as representations of a person's subjective knowledge. Second, the purpose of inquiry now may be thought of as being to 'articulate *local* and *practical* concerns' (Gergen & Thatchenkery, 1996, emphasis added). This means articulating mul-tiplicity, what some call 'plurivocality', and in this way giving voice to practices and possibilities that usually are muted, suppressed, or silenced. Inquiry is not to discover one truth or to reproduce a mono-logical construction of change (Dunford & Jones, 2000).

The following list summarizes the story so far:

- Story construction is a process of creating reality, in which self/story teller is clearly part of the story.
- Narratives are social constructions—not individual subjective realities.
- Narratives are situated—they are contextualized in relation to multiple local–cultural–historical acts/texts.
- Inquiry may articulate multiple narratives and relations.
- Change works with multiple realities and power relations, e.g., to facilitate ways of relating that are open to possibilities.

## NARRATIVE INTERVIEWS AS INQUIRY[30]

Explicitly narrative inquiry often proceeds through interviews that are relatively unstructured when compared, for example, with questionnaires. In other words, the interviewer leaves space for the other to tell their story in relation to some broad question such as: 'Could you tell me about—your experiences of the corporate change programme—the changes you have tried to introduce since you arrived . . .?' Part of the inquirer's intention is to get out of the way, so to speak, of what the other person wants to say (given this particular question/text), and to encourage a conversation of equals. Inquirers also will try to be as explicit as possible regarding their relevant narratives such as why they are asking the question(s) and who may do what with the texts so produced. These constructive acts become con-texts by contributing to the particular narrative that is told in the interview. So, too, do constructive acts of the interviewee who could be thought of as producing a 'twice constructed' text, so to speak:

---

[28] So, for example, psychology (Maier, 1988) and 'science' (Carrithers, 1991; Howard, 1991) can be viewed as telling particular kinds of stories (e.g., Hosking & Morley, 1991).

[29] Beware, many approaches to narrative embrace 'modernist' discourses and many are best thought of as examples of 'first order constructionism'.

[30] Narrative interviews also can be conducted where the emphasis is more on transformation. So, for example, therapists such as Milton Erickson and Frank Farelly, along with NLP practitioners, have shown how questions, body language, juxtapositions . . . may have transformative effects—even when 'the interviewee' thinks that 'the interviewer' is 'just finding out' about them.

first, by being 'relationally responsive' (McNamee & Gergen, 1999), selecting, and 'punctuating' some phenomenal stream of lived experience, and second, by reconstructing the construction in the interview (see Riessman, 1993).

## NARRATIVE ANALYSIS OF INTERVIEW TEXTS

Social construction processes continue when the text is transcribed from a tape recording and decisions are made about what to do, for example, with overlapping words, unclear words, pauses, and punctuation. Then the transcription is analysed—perhaps it is more appropriate to say reconstructed—in relation to con-texts such as those of the inquirer's own local cultures (gender, professional, ethnic), 'thought style', narratives of purpose—and, finally, the resulting narrative is reconstructed every time someone reads it.[31]

A critical constructionist thought style implies a particular approach to narrative analysis.[32] In general, it aims to preserve text–context relations, to articulate muted, suppressed, and excluded voices, and in this way to resituate dominant voices/stories, enable a 'play of differences', and open up new possible realities and relationships. Some speak of this as 'deconstruction' (Culler, 1982). It involves breaking up the seeming unities in a text (the organization, the way we do things around here), suggesting taken-for-granted dualities (management–employee, old timers and newcomers), pluralizing, de-entifying, de-naturalizing, recontextualizing, and opening up new possible local practices of power (Boje, 1995; http://web.nmsu.edu/~dboje).

Boje (2001) has given some guidelines for story deconstruction which can then resource re-storying—viewed as enabling many local cultures—and not just one hierarchy and one dominant narrative. Six interrelated tactics are proposed. These are: (a) search for dualities (the system–me; positive–negative); (b) re-interpret the hierarchy; (c) look for rebel voices and for the 'other side' of the story; (d) deny the plot; (e) find the exception; and (f) trace what is between the lines.

---

## CASE STUDY: BOJE'S (1995) ANALYSIS OF WALT DISNEY ENTERPRISES

Boje investigated the possibility that there might be stories about Walt Disney and the 'Magic Kingdom' that did not fit the (official) universalizing tale of happiness, e.g., voices of employees and former employees, historians. What were they and how were these competing voices silenced, excluded? The focus of the inquiry was on the multiple and contentious relations between stories, and on how research can become complicit in constructing one happy story over the competing voices. Boje used the Disney archives: (a) tape and video recordings of Disney leaders making speeches, giving interviews, impromptu conversations; (b) PR films; and (c) tapes of meetings. Deconstructive analysis looked at multiple variations of stories—not just positive, not just negative—assuming the 'plurivocality' of texts and showing how each version 'covered up' a great deal of ambiguity; it looked at who gets a voice, who does not (e.g., absence of screen credits for artists, removal of Roy Disney from the studio sign), and at how people and things were 'essentialized', looking at cacophony and discord rather than 'the managed harmony of the official story', showing organizational culture as fragmented and conflicted, a site of multiple meanings engaged in a constant struggle for control.

---

In the next section we can see how others have tried to put this approach to good effect in change work.

---

[31] Or, as was said earlier—every time the text/act is supplemented by another act/con-text.

[32] The term 'postmodern' is used by many writers. However, the term seems to invoke strong reactions such that a 'meeting of minds' (metaphorically speaking, of course) is made very unlikely! For this reason, I have avoided using the language of postmodernism in the main text.

## WORKING NARRATIVES, MULTIPLICITY, AND 'POWER TO'

This brings us to the point where we can clearly see one way in which inquiry and change work can be interwoven. Narratives can be worked with locally in a variety of ways that have the explicit intention of change work. So, for example, inquiry may facilitate what some call 'design conversations' (Gill, 2001) in which multiple voices/narratives are explored through dialogue.[33] Other relevant ways of working can include 'dialoguing' (e.g., Anderson-Wallace et al., 2001); generating and supporting narrative multiplicity through 'appreciative inquiry' (Cooperrider & Srivastva, 1987); working with metaphors (Barrett & Cooperrider, 1990; Barrett et al., 1995); 're-storying' (Barry, 1997), and dynamic narrative approaches to organizational learning (Abma, 2000). Work of this kind articulates differences, boundaries, and power relations, perhaps making space for generating new realities 'from within' multiple local contexts (transformation) rather than imposing a singular narrative in S–O relation.

Of course, change work that explicitly employs a narrative approach is not necessarily tied to a social constructionist thought style. The latter is usually put to work in methods that (a) help client(s) generate their own ways to go; and (b) avoid presuming a singular expertise and voice. Such approaches assume that people's lives are heavily influenced by the stories they tell about themselves; stories are empowering or disempowering, helpful or unhelpful; clients may be trapped in stories of 'problems' and 'helplessness', past failures that pathologize self, and both the change agent's and the client's stories should be listened to and reflected back to assist dissolving and re-storying.

---

### CASE STUDY: DAVID BARRY'S RE-STORYING WORK WITH ORGANIZATIONS

Some of the ways Barry works with identities and relationships can be summarized as follows. *Influence mapping*: expanding stories, giving them a more coherent and story-like nature and helping tellers to assume a more agentic role; mapping the interrelations between persons and problems over time; mapping the influence of the problem on persons (how has this problem influenced your life, organization?, perhaps making the problem less monolithic) and of persons on the problem (how s/he has influenced the problem?, giving greater sense of agency). *Problem externalization*: a storied problem is a trap: reflective listening can help to disconnect the story from the teller; reframing can loosen that particular reality and invite story teller(s) into a more open space where new possibilities (multiple realities) can be explored; making drawings (visualizations) and written portraits of the problem(s), solidifying and externalizing characters to have conversations with; sending letters about and to the characters. *Identifying unique outcomes*: finding previously untold story parts (e.g., when some competitor or context did not get the better of them) and expanding this alternative story line; (imagination, visions, social dreaming are used in other approaches). *Witnessing the performance(s)*: acknowledging and encouraging storytellers' efforts to enact a preferred story, e.g., in conversations, writing letters of reference to client.

---

Storytelling change work aims to strengthen marginalized and silenced voices by inviting their (re)telling and recording, through witnessing, through attending to someone's experience (as narrative). Such change work brings out and works with multiple voices—with multiple constructions—rather than obscuring the multiplicity in totalizing discourses, averages, third person, decontextualized accounts and other practices that aim to speak for the other. Storytelling change work analyses or in some other way starts from the assumptions, norms, metaphors, language tools, social practices that resource and constrain possibilities. Work of this kind can open up new ways of being in relation and new possible worlds.

---

[33] Dachler and Hosking used the term 'multilogue' (rather than dialogue) in order to emphasize the bringing together of multiple voices/multiple narratives.

# REFERENCES

Abma, T. (2000) Fostering learning-in-organizing through narration: questioning myths and stimulating multiplicity in two performing art schools. *European Journal of Work and Organizational Psychology*, **9**(2), 211–231.

Allport, G. (1963) *Pattern and Growth in Personality*. London: Holt, Rinehart & Winston.

Anderson-Wallace, M., Blantern, C. & Boydell, T. (2001) Advances in cross-boundary practice: inter-logics as method. *Career Development International*, **6**(7), 414–420.

Barrett, F.J. & Cooperrider, D.L. (1990) Generative metaphor intervention: a new approach for working with systems divided by conflict and caught in defensive perception. *Journal of Behavioral Science*, **26**(2), 219–239.

Barrett, F.J., Thomas, G.F. & Hocevar, S.P. (1995) The central role of discourse in large-scale change: a social construction perspective. *Journal of Applied Behavioral Science*, **31**(3), 352–372.

Barry, D. (1997) Telling changes: from narrative therapy to organizational change and development. *Journal of Organizational Change Management*, **10**(1), 30–36.

Bass, A. & Hosking, D.M. (1998) A changed approach to change. *Aston Business School Research Paper Series*, RP9808. Birmingham: Aston Business School.

Bateson, G. (1972) *Steps to an Ecology of Mind*. New York: Chandler.

Bateson, M.C. (1993) Joint performance across cultures: improvisation in a persian garden. *Text and Performance Quarterly*, **13**, 113–121.

Bauman, Z. (1993) *Postmodern Ethics*. Oxford: Blackwell.

Bennis, W. & Nanus, B. (1985) *Leaders: The Strategies for Taking Charge*. New York: Harper & Row.

Berman, M. (1981) *The Re-enchantment of the World*. Ithaca, NY: Cornell University Press.

Berman, M. (1990) *Coming to our Senses: Body and Spirit in the Hidden History of the West*. New York: Bantam Books.

Boal, A. (1992) *Games for Actors and Non-Actors*. Trans. A. Jackson. London: Routledge.

Boje, D. (1995) Stories of the storytelling organization: a postmodern analysis of Disney as 'Tamara-Land'. *Academy of Management Journal*, **38**(4), 997–1035.

Boje, D. (2001) *Narrative Methods for Organizational Communication Research*. London: Sage.

Bouwen, R. (1997) Multivoiced organizing: polyphony as a community-of-practice. In *Proceedings of Organizing in a Multi-Voiced World*. Leuven: Leuven University Press.

Bouwen, R. & Hosking, D.M. (2000) Reflections on relational readings of organizational learning. *European Journal of Work and Organizational Psychology*, **9**(2), 267–274.

Burr, V. (1995) *An Introduction to Social Constructionism*. London: Routledge.

Calás, M.B. & Smircich, L. (1991) Voicing seduction to silence leadership. *Organization Studies*, **12**(4), 567–602.

Carnall, C. (1990) *Managing Change in Organizations*. Hemel Hempstead: Prentice Hall.

Carrithers, M. (1991) Narrativity: mind-reading and making societies. In A. Whiten (ed.) *Natural Theories of Mind: Evolution, Development and Simulation of Second-order Representations* (pp. 305–319). Oxford: Blackwell.

Chia, R. (1995) From modern to postmodern organizational analysis. *Organization Studies*, **16**(4), 580–604.

Child, J. (1972) Organizational structure, environment and performance: the role of strategic choice. *Sociology*, **6**(1), 1–22.

Child, J. (1977, 1984) *Organization: A Guide to Problems and Practice*. London: Harper & Row.

Clegg, S., Hardy, C. & Nord, W. (1996) *Handbook of Organization Studies*. London: Sage.

Cohen, I. (1989) *Structuration Theory: Anthony Giddens and the Constitution of Social Life*. Basingstoke: Macmillan.

Cooper, R. & Law, J. (1995) Organization: distal and proximal views. In S. Bacharach, P. Gagliardi & B. Mundell (eds) *Studies of Organizations: The European Tradition*. Greenwich, CT: JAI Press.

Cooperrider, D. & Srivastva, S. (1987) Appreciative inquiry into organization life. *Research into Organizational Change and Development*, **1**, 129–169.

Culler, J. (1982) *On Deconstruction: Theory and Criticism after Structuralism*. Ithaca, NY: Cornell University Press.

Cummings, T. & Worley, C. (2001) *Organization Development and Change*. Cincinnati, OH: South-Western College Publishing.

Dachler, H.P. & Hosking, D.M. (1995) The primacy of relations in socially constructing organizational reality. In D.M. Hosking, H.P. Dachler & K.J. Gergen (eds) *Management and Organization: Relational Alternatives to Individualism*. Aldershot: Avebury.

Dunford, R. & Jones, D. (2000) Narrative in strategic change. *Human Relations*, **53**(9), 1207–1226.

Dyer, W.G. (1984) *Strategies for Managing Change*. Reading, MA: Addison-Wesley.

Edwards, D. & Potter, J. (1992) *Discursive Psychology*. London: Sage.

Evan, W. (1993) *Organization Theory: Research and Design*. Basingstoke: Macmillan.

Fenollosa, E. (1969) The Chinese written character as a medium for poetry. In *Ezra Pound, Instigations*. Freeport, NY: Books for Libraries Press.

Fine, M. (1994) Working the hyphens: reinventing self and other in qualitative research. In N.K. Denzin & Y.S. Lincoln (eds) *Handbook of Qualitative Research*. London: Sage.

Fineman, S. (1991) Change in organizations. In M. Smith (ed.) *Analysing Organizational Behaviour*. Basingstoke: Macmillan.

Fisch, R., Weakland, J. & Segal, L. (1982) *The Tactics of Change*. San francisco: Jossey-Bass.

Fleck, L. (1979) *Genesis and Development of a Scientific Fact*. Chicago: University of Chicago Press.

French, W. & Bell, C. (1990) *Organization Development*. Englewood Cliffs, NJ: Prentice Hall.

Gardener, H. (1985) *The Mind's New Science*, New York: Basic Books.

Garfinkel, H. (1967) *Studies in Ethnomethodology*. Englewood Cliffs, NJ: Prentice Hall.

Gergen, K.J. (1985) The social constructionist movement in modern psychology. *American Psychologist*, **40**, 266–275.

Gergen, K.J. (1994) *Realities and Relationships*. Cambridge, MA: Harvard University Press.

Gergen, K.J. (1995) Relational theory and the discourses of power. In D.M. Hosking, H.P. Dachler & K.J. Gergen (eds) *Management and Organization: Relational Alternatives to Individualism*. Aldershot: Avebury.

Gergen, K.J. (1999) *An Invitation to Social Construction*. London: Sage.

Gergen, K. & Thatchenkery, T.J. (1996) Organization science as social construction: postmodern potentials. *Journal of Applied Behavioral Science*, **32**(4), 356–377.

Giddens, A. (1979) *Central Problems in Social Theory: Action, Structure and Contradiction in Social Analysis*. Basingstoke: Macmillan.

Gill, P. (2001) Narrative inquiry: designing the processes, pathways and patterns of change. *Systems Research and Behavioural Science*, **18**, 335–344.

Guest, D. (1984) Social psychology and organizational change. In M. Gruneberg & T. Wall (eds) *Social Psychology and Organizational Behaviour*. Chichester: John Wiley & Sons, Ltd.

Harding, S. (1986) *The Science Question in Feminism*. Milton Keynes: Open University Press.

Harding, S. (1998) *Is Science Multicultural?* Bloomington, IN: Indiana University Press.

Hardy, C., Palmer, I. & Phillips, N. (2000) Discourse as a strategic resource. *Human Relations*, **53**(9), 1227–1248.

Hollis, M. (1994) *The Philosophy of Social Science*. Cambridge: Cambridge University Press.

Hollway, W. (1991) *Work Psychology and Organizational Behaviour: Managing the Individual at Work*. London: Sage.

Holzman, L. (ed.) (1999) *Performing Psychology: A Postmodern Culture of the Mind*. New York: Routledge.

Hosking, D.M. (1995) Constructing power: entitative and relational approaches. In D.M. Hosking, H.P. Dachler & K.J. Gergen (eds) *Management and Organization: Relational Alternatives to Individualism*. Aldershot: Avebury.

Hosking, D.M. (1999) Social constructions as process: some new possibilities for research and development. *Concepts and Transformation*, **4**(2), 117–132.

Hosking, D.M. (2000) Ecology in mind: mindful practices. *European Journal of Work and Organizational Psychology*, **9**(2), 147–158.

Hosking, D.M. & Bass, A. (1998) Constructing changes through relational dynamics. *Aston Business School Research Paper Series*, RP9813. Birmingham: Aston Business School.

Hosking, D.M. & Bouwen, R. (2000) Organizational learning: relational constructionist approaches. *European Journal of Work and Organizational Psychology*, **9**(2), 129–303.

Hosking, D.M. & Morley, I.E. (1991) *A Social Psychology of Organising*. London: Harvester Wheatsheaf.

Hosking, D.M., Dachler, H.P. & Gergen, K.J. (1995) *Management and Organization: Relational Alternatives to Individualism*. Aldershot: Avebury.

Howard, G.S. (1991) Culture tales: a narrative approach to thinking, cross-cultural psychology, and psychotherapy. *American Psychologist*, **46**(3), 187–197.

Isaacs, W.M. (1993) Taking flight: dialogue, collective thinking, and organizational learning. *Organizational Dynamics*, **Fall**, 24–39.

Lave, J. & Wenger, E. (1991) *Situated Learning: Legitimate Peripheral Participation*. Cambridge: Cambridge University Press.

Le Shan, L. (1974) *The Medium, the Mystic, and the Physicist*. New York: Penguin/Arkana.

Lord, R., DeVader, C. & Alliger, G. (1986) A meta-analysis of the relation between personality traits and leadership perceptions: an application of validity generalization procedures. *Journal of Applied Psychology*, **71**, 402–410.

Mair, M. (1988) Psychology as storytelling. *International Journal of Personal Construct Psychology*, **1**, 125–138.

McNamee, S. (1989) Challenging the patriarchal vision of social science: lessons from a family therapy model. In K. Carter & C. Spitzack (eds) *Doing Research on Women's Communication: Perspectives on Theory and Method*. Norwood, NJ: Ablex.

McNamee, S. & Gergen, K.J. & Associates (1999) *Relational Responsibility Resources for Sustainable Dialogue*. Thousand Oaks, CA: Sage.

Mead, G.H. (1934) *Mind, Self, and Society*. Chicago: University of Chicago Press.

Miner, J.B. (1980) *Theories of Organizational Behaviour*. Hinsdale, IL: The Dryden Press.

Newman, F. & Holzman, L. (1997) *The End of Knowing: A New Developmental Way of Knowing*. New York: Routledge.

O'Connor, E.S. (1995) Paradoxes of participation: textual analysis and organizational change. *Organization Studies*, **16**(5), 769–803.

Pearce, W.B. (1992) A 'camper's guide to constructionisms'. *Human Systems: The Journal of Systemic Consultation and Management*, **3**, 139–161.

Reason, P. (ed.) (1994) *Participation in Human Inquiry*. London: Sage.

Reeves Sanday, P. (1988) The reproduction of patriarchy in feminist anthropology. In M. McCanney Gergen (ed.) *Feminist Thought and the Structure of Knowledge*. New York: New York University Press.

Riessman, C.K. (1993) *Narrative Analysis*. Newbury Park, CA: Sage.

Rorty, R. (1991) *Objectivity, Relativism, and Truth* (vol. 1). Cambridge: Cambridge University Press.

Sampson, E.E. (1995) *Celebrating the Other*. London: Harvester Wheatsheaf.

Sarbin, T. (1986) *Narrative Psychology. The Storied Nature of Human Conduct*. New York: Praeger.

Schein, E. (1987) *Process Consultation, Vol. II: Lessons for Managers and Consultants*. Reading, MA: Addison-Wesley.

Shotter, J. (1993) *Conversational Realities*. London: Sage.

Steier, F. (ed.) (1991) *Research and Reflexivity*. London: Sage.

Thompson, P. & McHugh, D. (1995) *Work Organizations: A Critical Introduction*. Basingstoke: Macmillan.

Tsoukas, H. (1994) *New Theories in Organizational Behavior*. London: Butterworth.

Van Dongen, H. (1991) Some notions on social integration and steering. In R. in 't Veld, L. Schaap, C. Termeer & M. Van Twist (eds) *Autopoiesis and Configuration Theory: New Approaches to Societal Steering*. Dordrecht: Kluwer Academic.

Watzlawick, P. (1978) *The Language of Change*. New York: W.W. Norton.

Watzlawick, P., Weakland, J. & Fisch, R. (1974) *Change: Principles of Problem Formation and Problem Resolution*. New York: W.W. Norton.

Weick, K. (1979) *The Social Psychology of Organising* (2nd edn). Reading, MA: Addison-Wesley.

Weigert, A.J. (1983) *Social Psychology: A Sociological Approach through Interpretive Understanding*. Notre Dame, IN: University of Notre Dame Press.

Wilson, D. (1992) *A Strategy of Change: Concepts and Controversies in the Management of Change*. London: Routledge.

# Power Dynamics and Organizational Change

Part IV of this book presents new perspectives on power dynamics and resistance. Resistance is not seen as an obstruction to change, but as a reaction to the use of power by managers and change agents, and as a powerful force to enable changes and developments in human systems. This Part of the book highlights power dynamics, influence tactics, and barriers to change. After critical reflection on the traditional and managerial use of power in managing change and an analysis of the position of middle management, new experiences are presented in mobilizing energy and creativity for change and realizing involvement of middle management and employees in far-reaching change. This Part concludes with a critical and radical view of power and resistance, and opens up new perspectives on power dynamics in changing organizational arrangements.

This Part begins with a review of theories on power and influence in the processes of organizational change. In Chapter 13, Patricia Bradshaw and Jaap Boonstra explore various approaches to understanding power and change. More traditional perspectives on power and change are addressed, as well as new and emergent perspectives. Four different paradigms of power are distinguished and related to various organizational change approaches and change strategies. The paradigms are built on two dimensions. The first dimension is about manifest vs latent power. Early positivist studies of power assumed that power was latent and thus observable and that power-based conflict could be explicitly identified. An interpretative view and studies of culture and sense-making have led to an increased understanding that power also resides in more latent and unobtrusive operation of language, symbols, and myths. The second dimension is about personal vs collective power. The personal view supposes that power is best conceptualized as the ability of an actor to achieve his or her will. In the collective view, power is seen as a property of a collective. By conceptualizing these four views into paradigms of power, various strategies of organizational change are suggested. Change strategies related to the manifest–personal paradigm of power are based on the expertise of the change agent, the position power of the change agent, and on force field analyses. In the manifest–structural paradigm, a negotiation strategy is suggested. Change strategies based on the latent–cultural paradigm are democratic dialogue, symbolic modelling, and seductive strategies of change. In the latent–personal paradigm the accent is on deep learning as approach to change, overcoming resistance to change, and reflective action research. This chapter concludes with the recommendation to work with both ends of the dimensions in order for transformative change to be enabled.

In Chapter 14, Gary Yukl describes how interpersonal influence is exerted in attempts by individual leaders to initiate or facilitate organizational change. This chapter is embedded in the personal paradigms of power and change. The implications of the use of influence tactics by change agents are elaborated in the manifest–personal and the latent–personal paradigms. Yukl begins with a review of research on dyadic influence tactics, and the use of influence tactics by managers to initiate change in organizations. Ten pro-active individual influence tactics are distinguished. Consultation, collaboration, and inspirational appeals are three of the most effective tactics for influencing target commitment to support change. Rational persuasion might be helpful in convincing people that it is useful to support organizational change. Ingratiation, exchange, and apprising are moderately effective

*Dynamics of Organizational Change and Learning.* Edited by J.J. Boonstra.
© 2004 John Wiley & Sons, Ltd. ISBN 0-471-87737-9.

for influencing organizational members to support change. Personal appeals can be useful with people with whom the change agent has a friendly relationship. Pressure, coalition tactics, and legitimating tactics are very unlikely to result in commitment to change. Several limiting and facilitating conditions for initiating change are discussed. This chapter concludes with specific guidelines for using specific tactics effectively.

Chapter 15 focuses on process-oriented change management. This chapter is more embedded in the collective paradigms on power and change. Psychological explanations for resistance to change are discussed and an alternative view is presented in which a negative reaction to change is understood as a response to the change approach and the strategies of change used by change agents. In this chapter, Kilian Bennebroek Gravenhorst and Roeland in 't Veld describe four comprehensive interventions that can be used to bring different stakeholders together in processes of change. They discuss survey feedback, large group interventions, process management, and third-party interventions. Many practitioners in the field of Organization Development are familiar with these interventions. However, discussing these intervention methods in a context of power dynamics is quite new. For each intervention method, attention is given to the principles, process orientations, and conditions for success. Case examples are provided to illustrate how the intervention methods work in practice, how different stakeholders are involved, and how it contributes to the co-creation of change. The chapter concludes with the observation that process-oriented change management can deal with important limitations of programmatic change approaches and change strategies based on the exercise of power by change agents. The authors suggest that maybe we should leave the idea of opposing parties in change processes, and redefine resistance to change as a sign of commitment. This shift makes it possible to focus on what is necessary for people to work together in realizing complex changes. Implications of this line of thinking for academics, consultants, and managers who design and guide change processes in organizations are that we need to question the change strategy we choose, and reflect on our own behaviour as change managers.

In Chapter 16, Cynthia Hardy and Stewart Clegg provide an overview of different ways in which power can been understood, and relate these different understandings to theoretical insights in organizational change and the practical recommendations the literature provides for managing change. They explore two traditions in the study of power with quite different value positions. The first body of knowledge focuses on the existence of conflicting interest, and examines power as domination in the way that it serves certain interest groups. All organizational members have some creativity, discretion, and agency to use power, but some have more sources of power than others. The second tradition developed in the field of management and takes for granted the ways in which power is distributed in formal organizational structures. Organizational structures are seen as formal and legitimate arrangements of functional authority. In this view, resistance is an illegitimate, dysfunctional use of power. Much of the management literature focuses on the use of power to defeat conflict and overcome resistance. After this exploration of widespread perspectives on power and organizational change, a critical perspective is provided on power and change. From this critical perspective, an analysis is presented to see how power accommodates the traditional organizational change theory and practice. Special attention is paid to organizational structuring, decision-making, resistance to change, management of meaning, and power as an integrated system of cultural and normative assumptions. Intervention methods and communication strategies are reconsidered, and perceived as the tools of change agents to prevent resistance, and to effect changes from a unitary and pluralist point of view for managerial purposes. A new and radical view is discussed to understand power dynamics from a postmodern perspective. Based on this radical perspective, power and resistance are revisited, and recent ideas are examined in managing organizational change.

# CHAPTER 13

# Power Dynamics in Organizational Change
## A Multi-perspective Approach

**Patricia Bradshaw**
*Schulich School of Business, York University, Toronto, Canada*
**Jaap Boonstra**
*Sioo, Utrecht, and University of Amsterdam, Amsterdam, The Netherlands*

The role of power in organizational change efforts has been recognized as being important since the early 1970s and conceptual thinking about the relationship between the two has continued to evolve and been enriched by different underlying theoretical assumptions. In this chapter we review the topic and explore various different approaches to understanding power and change. The chapter is structured around a model that differentiates four different perspectives on power and is built on two polarities or dynamic tensions between manifest vs latent power and personal vs collective power. By conceptualizing four fundamentally different perspectives of power, various different approaches to organizational change are suggested. In this chapter, we address both the dominant and better-developed perspectives on power and change as well as newer and more emergent perspectives. We conclude by suggesting that transformational change in organizations can be more fully understood and enabled through the simultaneous recognition of the tensions between different perspectives on power.

Bennis was quoted in 1969 as stating that the organizational development (OD) practitioners' influence was based on their 'truth and love'. At these early stages of efforts to change organizations, using mainly group-based approaches, there was little or no reflection on the implicit power dynamics within them. The first laboratory, training, or T-groups run by Kurt Lewin out of MIT took place in 1946, and this methodology was further explored and utilized after 1947 at NTL (National Training Labs) in Bethel, Maine (Cummings & Worley, 1997). These group-based techniques formed one of the roots of organizational change approaches, and in particular of OD, and their emphasis on humanistic values was carried over to OD. By the 1970s, however, the field started to be more reflective and to more critically question this approach and the implicit values and inherent assumptions embedded within it. With this reflection came a growing recognition of the importance of power and politics in organizational change. Alderfer was a leader in this critical reflection and in 1973 he quoted Lodahl as saying 'The world was not a T-group'. Alderfer then pointed out that change approaches growing from T-groups resulted in assumptions of minimal power differentials and that this, in turn, resulted in a misunderstanding of power relations in organizational settings. Walton and Warwick, in the same year, challenged the ethics of OD and asked 'Who are its clients and what are its power implications?' (1973: 681). Nord, in 1974, used a Marxian perspective to critique the behaviour sciences and encouraged the exploration of alternative power bases for humanistically oriented change. He asked what functions change agents play in maintaining and reproducing the existing distribution of power. Similarly, Ross (1971) asked the question 'OD for whom?' He encouraged self-scrutiny while pointing out that the OD

*Dynamics of Organizational Change and Learning.* Edited by J.J. Boonstra.
© 2004 John Wiley & Sons, Ltd. ISBN 0-471-87737-9.

specialists tacitly accepted the existence of class privilege and inequality, and that democracy was not the guiding precept of the field. Based on these early critiques and challenges, there have been repeated and varied, but not always consistent, efforts to marry an understanding of power with organizational change.

In this chapter, we review these efforts to link power and change and we frame them according to four different theoretical perspectives of power that have evolved in organizational theory generally and that have concurrently come to inform thinking about organizational change (Bradshaw, 1998). There is a lot of debate concerning the definition of power (e.g. Hardy, 1985). We prefer a broad and multi-faceted definition of power and the model we are using deals with widely different assumptions and perspectives on power. The model allows us to more fully conceptualize the rich diversity of types and sources of power and ways in which power informs change efforts. Our goal is to offer a framework for understanding power dynamics and organizational change, to explore different approaches, and to introduce and relate these approaches to the other contributions to this issue.

## PERSPECTIVES ON POWER AND CHANGE

In this section, we present four perspectives on power dynamics and relate these perspectives to various organizational change approaches. These four perspectives and the change models we review are not fully comprehensive, yet they offer a good outlook on important perspectives that inform the field. Moreover, the approaches do not exclude each other but, we would argue, can be used in combinations in organizational change processes.

### POLARITIES AND TENSIONS IN STUDYING POWER DYNAMICS

We are relying on the notion of polarity to help us define four approaches to power and change. Rather than assert the dominance, legitimacy, and superiority of one idea, the notion of polarity suggests that opposites necessarily co-exist. The two polarities we would like to explore are individual power vs collective power and manifest power vs latent power.

The first tension of individual vs collective power is well articulated in the literature and informs the earliest developments in theories of organizational power (Hamilton & Woolsey Biggart, 1985; Clegg, 1990). Giddens describes two perspectives on power and says:

> One is that power is best conceptualized as the capability of an actor to achieve his or her will, even at the expense of others who might resist him—the sort of definition employed by Weber among many other authors. The second is that power should be seen as a property of the collectivity: Parson's concept of power, for instance, belongs in this latter category. (1979: 69)

This tension rests on dualisms in social theory such as between volunteerism and determinism or between individual action and structure (e.g. Burrell & Morgan, 1979; Reed, 1988). Proponents of the individual agency perspective argue that individuals have free choice to pursue and use power wilfully and towards some intended objective. This perspective deals with observable and intentionally used authority and legitimate power of agents. Personal power is required to make change happen in organizations. This view is rooted in a social psychological research tradition that investigated power bases.

On the collective side of the debate are those who say that the social structure (e.g. roles, rules, and resources) determines, or at the very least constrains, the use of power. For example, Kanter (1977) argues that structurally determined power can explain behaviours in organizations that were previously attributed to individual qualities. Others suggest that culture (e.g. values, beliefs, and assumptions) constrains individual agency (Marshall & McLean, 1985; Mills & Murgatroyd, 1991). From this

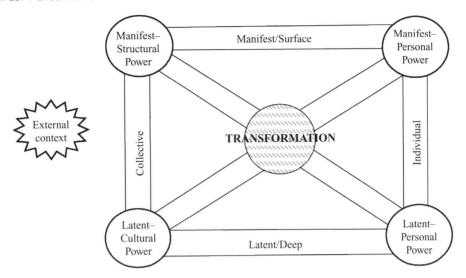

**FIGURE 13.1**   Four paradigms of power

perspective, power is a property of a social group and sources of power are shaped by the observable structures and taken-for-granted culture of the collectivity.

The second tension or polarity to inform this chapter is between surface or manifest power and latent power. Naming of this tension is more recent and is informed by the challenges to functionalist and managerially oriented approaches to organizational studies and organizational psychology. Early positivist studies of power assumed that power was latent and thus observable and that power-based conflict could be explicitly identified. An interpretative world-view and studies of culture, for example, have led to an increased understanding that power also resides in the more latent or subtle and unobtrusive operation of language, symbols, myths, and other meaning-making activities (Hardy, 1985; Bradshaw-Camball & Murray, 1991). This perspective also has its foundations in management and organization theory but its focus shifts towards the less observable and unconscious forms of power use. Central issues in this view from a managerial view are the construction of perceptions, values, and norms through management of meaning. At the level of deep structures of power, certain issues and conflicts are prevented from arising at all and the existing order of things is seen as natural and unchangeable. If power operates in an invisible or latent way, then questions of resistance and acquiescence are surfaced. Foucault (1977) and other postmodern theorists have also deepened our understanding of power and its invisibility in dominant discourses and truth claims (Knights & Morgan, 1991; Knights & Murray, 1992).

In the remainder of the chapter, we will develop four perspectives of power, which are conceptually defined by combining these two polarities. Thus, power can be conceptualized as being manifest–personal, manifest–structural, latent–personal, and latent–cultural (Figure 13.1). In the next section of the chapter, we will present each of these perspectives on power and some associated power sources, and then explore various approaches to change which emerge from each perspective.

## MANIFEST–PERSONAL POWER

This is one of the best understood and widely shared conceptions of power and is informed by the early conceptual work of scholars such as Dahl (1975), Emerson (1962), and Wrong (1968). Basically, from this perspective we say power is a force and person A has more power than B to the extent that A can get B to do something they would not otherwise do. Early social and organizational psychological research

**TABLE 13.1**   Elements of manifest–personal power

| Sources | Definitions | Strategies |
| --- | --- | --- |
| Expertise | Knowledge and skills which others see as relevant to the task accomplishment and which the individual is seen as possessing | Obtaining credentials or ongoing experiences which others respect |
| Legitimate authority | Formal position and roles which define responsibilities and appropriate scope of activity | Ensuring roles and role expectations are clear and recognized as legitimate |
| Referent | Power which comes from trust and commitment given to the individual because of his/her personal traits and characteristics | Build respect and trust through personal integrity, charisma, and group affiliation |
| Rewards/ coercion | Behaviours which reward or hurt others but which ensure compliance and buy-in | Accumulating things of value to others or punishments which can harm others |
| Association | Influence which comes from knowing powerful people | Networking and developing connections and associations |

on power focused on describing power bases of managers. From this perspective, power is viewed as the potential ability of an individual agent to influence a target within a certain system or context. As early as 1959, French and Raven created a typology of power which includes five sources of personal power, all of which are both manifest and identifiable. Table 13.1 defines the power that derives from expertise, legitimate authority, referent power, rewards and coercion, and association with other powerful people. Yukl, in Chapter 14, updates and expands this way of thinking about manifest–personal influence.

These manifest–personal power sources have been picked up in the literature on organizational change and have resulted in many attempts to mobilize this type of power to enable change in organizations. For example, Greiner and Schein (1988) contributed to the Addison-Wesley Series on OD with a book entitled *Power and Organizational Development*. They suggest that there is a need for a better integration of power and OD and that for too long they were seen as opposing and contentious approaches. They argue that there is a difference between positive and negative uses of power and call for the use of the 'high road'. In general, political tactics that arise from the use of these power sources are framed in the change literature either as dirty tricks to be avoided or as astute strategies for advancing a change effort. Despite the underlying discomfort of many with the use of manifest–personal power in organizational change, there are a number of approaches to change which draw on these power bases. Some of these are described below, two of which draw primarily on one power base (positional or expert) and the third which calls on a more broadly based political strategy.

## EXPERT POWER APPROACH TO CHANGE

A change model that fits best in the perspective of manifest–personal power is the expert or design model (Boonstra, 1997). Although every person and group in an organization has access to power bases, the process of change is often initiated, coordinated, and controlled by top management who rely on the expertise of those hired to advise them. Change agents are seen to play this important role and they use expert knowledge to assist groups in the organization with analysing and solving problems. The educational background of the change agents seems to be connected to the way problems are analysed and solved. Change agents with a background in information technology, business engineering, or business administration usually start the change process with either an information-processing rationality or an economic-technological rationality. Top management, striving for efficient service of organizational goals, employ behavioural expert knowledge in the analysis of socio-technical systems and in the design of more efficient work systems. In this situation behavioural science becomes a form of social engineering, used to assist management with the efficient implementation of the goals as defined by management.

The expert model emphasizes the design of new strategies, structures, and systems. In general, the change process starts with the designation of abstract objectives, and particular attention is given to the desired output of the organization, the formal transformation process, and the related information processes. The change process is managed as a special project, with clear-cut targets, and a restricted number of alternatives. The decision-making is highly structured and formalized. The implementation is aimed at creating acceptance for the new organization and finding solutions for different forms of resistance during the implementation. The dominant change strategy is the empirical–rational strategy (Chin & Benne, 1976). This strategy depends on knowledge as a major ingredient of power. In this view, knowledge is a legitimate source of power. The desirable direction of influence is from experts, that is, from those who know, to those who do not know through processes of dissemination of information and rational persuasion. The use of the expert model of change and the empirical–rational strategy seems suitable in a predictable and highly structured situation where the problem is known, not too complex, and a solution is within reach. The problems with the expert model of organizational change lie in an insufficient consideration of the cultural and other political impediments and the emergence of resistance to change within line management and other groups in the organization. It is argued that resistance can be prevented or averted by propagating a rational vision, by elaborately communicating about the changes, and by having line managers and other groups participate in the process of change (Boonstra, 1997). Behavioural science knowledge is used to realize compliance or commitment with the change effort. Of course, it is possible to use expert knowledge and power sources in a process of OD and bottom-up changes.

## POLITICAL/POWER APPROACH

This is an approach to change in which the change agent develops an explicitly political strategy that begins with a complete assessment of all their manifest–personal power bases. For example, Margulies and Raia (1984) argue that understanding and skilful use of political strategies in an OD intervention are critical. Bateman (1980) calls this a political/power strategy and says the change agent must align with those in power and then influence them to desire and accept the changes. To do this, a change agent must convince the powerful that the change is in their self-interest. Change agents can employ many tactics, such as increasing their referent power by expanding their social networks and having lunch or coffee with key people. Becoming an assistant or staff adviser to board members, for example, can enhance personal expert power through advice giving. Understanding personal power and developing tactics for using it, however, are not enough and constant monitoring of the political activities of others is required because this will allow the change agent to develop, adapt, and modify his/her political strategies based on carefully selected goals. A power audit, identification of targets, an inventory of tactics, adequate resources, and monitoring with a commitment of time and energy are Bateman's suggestions for implementation of a political change model.

Similarly, in 1975, Pettigrew outlined a political theory of intervention for internal change agents based on his understanding that power is a relational phenomenon. He recommends starting with an understanding of the sources of power for the consultant and exploration of the mechanisms by which such resources are controlled and used tactically within the consulting process. He argues that there are at least five interrelated, potential power sources available to an internal change agent and these include expertise, control over information, political access and sensitivity, assessed stature, and group support. While some of these fall into the manifest–structural category, Pettigrew argues that the political processes must be recognized and because of a change agent's vested interests in the change process they must be tactically utilized. A wise agent of change will manage the impressions they create in order to generate stature and will form multiplex relationships with key figures in the political network of the organization. Timing of interventions and building of credit are two of the political strategies Pettigrew identifies.

Schein (1977) goes further than Pettigrew in describing the political tactics that will build on identified power bases and these include aligning with powerful others, research, using a neutral cover, limiting communication, and withdrawing. She argues that while change agents can either play down politics or avoid them, it is better to use them to effect ends that are going to positively impact on the lives of the people in the organization.

In a similar way, Harrison (1980) argues that the positional power of a change agent is limited and it is the astute use of personal power that will allow them to accomplish the goals of the change process. Understanding of personal power allows the change agent to make choices, to feel potent and not magnify the power of others while denying their own power. He further argues that personal power is critical because positional power is not suited to the building of open, trusting, and cooperative relationships.

## PERSONAL POSITION POWER APPROACH TO CHANGE

The model of organizational change related to the perspective of position power can be described as a power (over) model of change (Bouwen, 1995). In the power-over model, the leader is an authority figure who imposes and declares organizational change and effects the changes by using legitimate position power. Position power stems from this person's formal position and implies the legitimate authority to use positive and negative sanctions such as rewards and coercion. Thus, position power mostly refers to the existing organizational hierarchy that provides management with the ability to control the behaviour of others and to change the organizational structure and processes. This use of power is observable and direct. In order to employ sanctions it is necessary to know to what extent employees perform the required actions. Therefore, management uses control systems. The power embedded in formal organizational structures and processes are directed at domination. Decision-making is based on the exclusion of employees and the one-sided realization of interests of management and shareholders. Using such power-coercive strategies enforces change (Chin & Benne, 1976; Dunphy & Stace, 1988). When management is protected by its legitimate power in a social system and is able to use economic sanctions, it can use power-coercive strategies to effect changes that they consider desirable, without much questioning on the part of those with less power. In these situations a power-coercive way of decision-making is accepted as in the nature of things and is seen as functional for the organization. The use of such an approach is common when an organization is in crisis and rapid action is needed. This strategy will result in compliance when the groups in the organization depend on each other, share a sense of urgency to take immediate action, and are not aware of alternative strategies. The limitations of this power model of change are related to the strong top-down approach. The top management of an organization initiates, leads, and controls the process. Such processes follow a linear design and have a clear starting point and desired situation. Tight planning is necessary to attain the goals of the change. Many of these design approaches fail or experience difficulties with the realization of goals (Boonstra, 1997). These problems partly arise because the power model of change allows little participation of members of the organization and disregards learning possibilities.

## MANIFEST–STRUCTURAL POWER

In this perspective on power the emphasis moves away from personal power, that is ascribed to the individual, towards an understanding of the power that rests in the position or location an interest

**TABLE 13.2** Elements of manifest–structural power

| Sources | Definitions | Strategies |
| --- | --- | --- |
| Control of scarce resources | Ability to allocate resources (information, uncertainty, money, people, etc.) among groups with competing interests | Obtain positions which are responsible for distribution and allocation of resources |
| Criticality/ relevance | Tasks which are essential in the work-flow process and which can cause the total system to break down | Obtain positions responsible for the most critical tasks or those essential to key organizational goals |
| Centrality | Tasks or positions which are in the middle of a communication network | Obtain central positions where others are dependent on you |
| Visibility | Positions which are seen by those of power and influence in the organization | Seek out tasks which have high profile |
| Coalitions | Power which comes from building support from groups with similar interests | Systematically seek support from others based on an analysis of their interests |
| Flexibility/autonomy | Positions which are characterized by discretion in decision-making, work assignment, etc. | Seek out tasks which are not routine and which contain autonomy and room for independent decision-making |

group, sub-unit, or organizational department holds in the structure of the organization. Thus, power potentially belongs to any collectivity in a particular structure regardless of their members' personal traits or characteristics (see Table 13.2). Structural factors become the major influence in understanding power relations. For example, Bacharach and Lawler (1980) identify the importance of coalitions and, using social psychological theory, argue that formal stratification of the organization constrains and facilitates the creation and collapse of coalitions between interest groups and the relational networks between groups.

From this perspective both cooperation and competition are seen to characterize relational networks of interdependent groups. On the one hand, we see that people are dependent on each other and yet, on the other, they pursue their own interests. Organizational processes are influenced both by mutual harmonization of parts of the system, and by the way power is structured and used. In organizations, the distribution of power is often characterized by stability. This stability results from a commitment to decisions concerning the realization of the business strategy, the structuring of the organization, and the distribution of power that emerged from the past (Pfeffer, 1981). The existing structure and the distribution of power are believed to be natural and unquestionable while still being largely latent and observable if appropriately assessed. In organizations, there is a balance of power between the interests of individuals and of the interdependent groups. Sometimes these interests are at odds and this can result in conflicting objectives, power games, and controversies in decision-making (Hickson et al., 1971; Pfeffer, 1994). The tension between the interest of individuals and groups is viewed as inevitable and as a normal part of the way of getting things done (Dalton, 1959; Pettigrew, 1973). This perspective on power in organizations is also known as the pluralist view (Emerson, 1962; for an overview, see Hardy & Clegg, 1996). The pluralist view is related to the exchange theory in social psychology in which the power of an actor is derived from the possibilities this actor or his or her group have of providing others with relevant resources (Kelley & Thibaut, 1978). The pluralist view maintains that groups and departments have to cooperate and that agreement between them is necessary for the functioning of the organization and to warrant its continuity. Negotiation and exchange of resources characterize the power process. Some departments have more power than others. The departmental power bases are related to what the work unit does, but the power of different departments varies among organizations and can change over time (Perrow, 1970; Pfeffer, 1994). There are three underlying dimensions that determine departmental power bases (Hickson et al., 1971). The first dimension is the ability to cope with uncertainty that influences the day-to-day operation of an organization. Departments that can cope effectively with uncertainty can increase their power and their position in negotiation processes. The second dimension is the substitutability of the department's functions and activities of the organization. Departments can prevent substitution and acquire control over scarce resources through shielding from others how the work is actually performed. The third dimension is centrality. Centrality refers to the power of a department that derives from the dependency of other departments and their significant role in the flow of work.

There are various approaches to organizational change that relate directly to this view of organizational power relations. For example, strategic redesign of the structure of the organization is often used as a way of changing the balance of power between key internal and external stakeholders and making the organization better aligned with the environment. As Tichy (1983) suggests, there is a need in these approaches to align the technical, political, and cultural systems. Pfeffer (1994) argues that organizational design is inherently a political process. The approach to change presented below is the conflict management and negotiation model.

## NEGOTIATION MODELS OF CHANGE

Conflict management and negotiation characterize the change models that draw on manifest–structural approaches to power. All interest groups play their roles in the change process, based on their position in the organization, their departmental power sources, and their own interests. In change processes, both the structure and systems of the organization and the balance of power are brought up for discussion. In the process, different coalitions will direct their attention at securing their interests, objectives, and power positions (Kanter, 1983; Steensma & Boer, 1997; Yukl et al., 2003). Resistance to change is seen as a result of the exercise of power and can be understood as a struggle to achieve power or to escape from it. The change managers focus on preventing conflict in the change process by regulating participation of the groups involved or by negotiation about the objectives of the change process and the way it is organized and managed. The dominant change strategy is the exchange strategy (Zaltman & Duncan, 1977). This strategy implies that a change agent sets the conditions for the way change is realized by providing the material or other means. Positive outcomes are for parties who accept the change. The exchange strategy appeals to the comparison of costs and benefits parties make and it stresses what will be gained by the change. Negotiations are directed at smoothing opposition, tensions, and differences in opinion between parties and the goal is to accomplish an agreement that does justice to the interest of all involved parties. In the change process, most of the negotiations are visible and parties are aware of the power processes. In the negotiations, many of the power bases described above are used to secure a good starting position and to influence the process by building good arguments, getting control of scarce resources, gaining a position of centrality, or controlling the procedures. Management usually possesses a considerable amount of structural power. It can use these power bases to win conflicts and to strengthen their position in the negotiation process. This increases the chance that their interests are realized at the expense of the interests of other parties involved in the change process. The use of an exchange strategy seems suitable in politically sensitive situations. If multiple parties with opposing interests and relatively balanced power are involved in a change process, negotiations will be needed to come to an agreement about things such as goals, the way the change is going to be implemented, and the role of the different parties in the change process. The pluralists view has been criticized because it suggests that all involved parties can defend their interests in the negotiation process. However, the power embedded in formal organizational structures and processes supports the interests of management more than those of others. Organizational structures,

**TABLE 13.3**   Elements of latent–cultural power

| Sources | Definitions | Strategies |
|---|---|---|
| Control of the agenda | Power which comes from being able to define the issues which are important and will be acted on | Direct attention and energy towards own issues which align with own group's interests; will alternatively suppress or generate conflict |
| Management of meaning | Control of the language, symbols, rituals, and values which are culturally embedded and which unconsciously determine behaviours | Use organizational procedures and events to symbolically signal which issues are important and how decisions will be made |
| Taken-for-granted rules and routines | Everyday and historically instituted processes and tasks which benefit certain groups over others but which are not questioned | Reveal (or establish) repeated processes for resource and task allocation which leave certain assumptions unexplored and unquestioned |
| Knowledge claims | The determination of what is 'seeable' and 'sayable' (known) through the construction of discourses and discursive practices | Make visible and give voice to alternative/suppressed knowledge claims and challenge the objectification of knowledge claims of the dominant groups. Rebellion, challenge, and reconstruction (or suppress them) |

rules, regulations, procedures, decision-making, and negotiation are seen as products and reflections of a struggle for control that puts management in a privileged position (Giddens, 1979; Hardy & Clegg, 1996).

Borum (1980) extends this approach to an alternative model for use in situations when power is not relatively balanced. He argues, in such a context, it is essential to first strengthen the weaker party's power bases prior to negotiations with the 'opponent' and to explicitly formalize the mechanisms for regulating the conflicts that may arise.

## LATENT–CULTURAL POWER

In the latent–cultural perspective to power it is assumed that ideas, the definitions of reality, and shared values are central features of organizing (Alvesson, 1993). Organizing is seen as a process of the creation and reproduction of shared meanings that are largely latent or unconscious (Table 13.3). In this process, shared meanings that were formed previously may be destroyed and alternative and new meanings created (Weick, 1979). Gergen (1991) addresses this social construction of reality from a psychological standpoint. Social relations are characterized by a typical structure and culture, based on rules, habits, institutions, language, communication, use of symbols, and definitions of reality which serve as a foundation.

Culture represents relative stability in an organization and is related to power because power re-lations come to be seen as natural and unquestionable. Perceptions, cognitions, and preferences of individuals and groups are shaped by culture that, in turn, prevents them from seeing alternatives. Applying an interpretative paradigm (Burrell & Morgan, 1979), we come to understand how, for ex-ample, cultural artefacts, language, rituals, and values construct meaning for organizational members and how they simultaneously work to suppress conflict, prevent issues from being identified, and con-trol, the actual agenda for decision-making and non-decision-making. In these ways, power relations become entrenched in the organization and those who can set the agenda, who manage the meaning systems and who have others believe their definitions of reality, have more power than those who do not (Smircich & Morgan, 1982; Hardy, 1985; Rosen, 1985; Alvesson, 1992; Murray & Bradshaw-Camball, 1993). Thus, power is increased to the extent that the group which defines reality has others accepting their definition in unquestioning and taken-for-granted ways. Management fulfils a special role in these unconscious power processes because it has the opportunity, more than others, to give meaning to events and in doing so management contributes to the development of norms and values in the organization. Pettigrew (1977) describes the management of meaning as a process of symbol construction and value use designed both to create legitimacy for one's own demands and to de-legitimize the demands of others. Management of meaning involves the ability to define the reality of others. Thus, managers are powerful agents who create shared meanings, ideas, values, and reality through communication and the manipulation of symbols. As Winter (1996) would suggest, power is seen as an interpretative institution and pervasively hegemonic.

From the work of more critical theorists, we can further understand the deeper aspects of latent–cultural power by reflecting on how groups come to consent to their own domination and subjugation in a passive mode characterized by lack of resistance. Lukes (1974) argues that people accept the status quo and their role in it because they view the current systems as natural and unchangeable. The role of ideological hegemony (Clegg, 1990) is important to understand as we see that existing organizational and societal structures are supported by inherently classed, gendered, and raced assumptions and values (Mills, 1992). From this perspective we can argue that organizations are, for example, inherently gendered and we unconsciously accept that the organizational systems and structures work to advantage certain groups over others. The social construction of gender then becomes objectified and is seen as being a given which is unchangeable. Other ways of constructing meaning are suppressed and silenced with resulting inequities of power. We come to see and accept the interests of the dominant group as 'objective' and as legitimate knowledge claims instead of seeing all interests as subjectively created realities embedded in multiple truth claims. A postmodern perspective helps oppressed groups attempt to reveal, expose, deconstruct, and question the ideological assumptions embedded in organizational discourses and to show how they suppress conflicts.

From this perspective, power is assumed to be take-for-granted and latent. Power is a cultural artefact that becomes entrenched in the hands of certain dominant and privileged groups. This dynamic exists to the extent that the meaning systems in which the relations of power are embedded are shared collectively by various interest groups and are reproduced through discourses, practices, and routines within organizations (Townley, 1994). While the surface–structural perspective looks at power from a more positivistic perspective, with power originating in structures and objective resources, from a latent–cultural view of power the interpretative and postmodern perspectives provide the dominant lens and underlying assumptions. Just as perspectives on latent–cultural power are informed by various theoretical views, some more critical and postmodern than others, so the literature on change and power involves a variety of approaches. Below we review democratic dialogue as an intervention into the meaning system of an organization that is still largely consistent with modernist views of power, and then explore newer and more critical approaches that are informed by postmodern theory and psychoanalytic perspectives.

As well as revealing different options for change, this view of power also calls on change agents to personally ask different questions of themselves and their role. The questions change, for example, from what should be done to improve this organization?, or how do I get the CEO on side?, to whose meaning systems will I support? (Greenfield, 1973; Bradshaw, 1990). If a change effort is seen as an intervention in the reality construction process of an organization, how does the change agent impact on these processes and towards what ends? The literature also warns change agents against losing their power by being seduced themselves into the world-view of the powerful (Burke, 1980). Marshall and McLean (1985) warn change agents against being seduced into unconsciously exemplifying the culture that they are attempting to change and thus unwittingly helping the organization stay the same. With a paradoxical intervention, they argue, the change agent can achieve radical although unpredictable change. Change agents are advised, from this perspective, to be powerful and independent enough to not be seduced into the dominant culture and subtle enough that they are not so threatening to the culture that they are expelled from the organization.

## DEMOCRATIC DIALOGUE AS A MODEL OF CHANGE

Alvesson and Deetz (2000) refer to the critical modernism of Habermas (1984) which takes the ideal of emancipation by dialogue very seriously. In this view, knowledge can counteract the realties of domination and allow for emancipation based on unrestricted freedom. This can be achieved by critical reflection and independent thought and by way of thoughtful evaluation of various viewpoints and arguments in an open dialogue (Alvesson & Willmott, 1992). In dialogue, human consciousness, cognition, and the nature and potential of communication are critical elements for a systematic improvement of the work environment. It is assumed that in dialogue and open discussions, based on good will, rational argumentation, and questioning, consensus can be reached about present and desirable states of the organization.

Organizational learning with a strong emphasis on participative design and development (Emery, 1999) and democratic dialogue (Gustavsen, 1992; Bouwen, 1995) are approaches to change that can be used in the sense that Habermas intended. Some people use these methods in a way that explicitly recognizes the latent–cultural power dynamics inherent in dialogue but others ignore power and attempt to use the methods in a power-neutral or blind fashion.

Ideally, in an organizational learning change process, the concerns of all parties are involved and appreciated through an exploration of each party's meaning systems. This strategy stresses the involvement of all organization members in programmes of change regardless of their hierarchical power. The way participants see themselves and their problems becomes the subject of a dialogue in which different perceptions and meanings are exchanged. Such a dialogue makes clear that problems are related to the definition of the situation and the underlying attitudes, values, norms, and relationships. According to this strategy, members of organizations must learn to cooperate in problem identification and the formulation of solutions, which improve organizational learning in a democratic fashion.

In the participative design and developmental approach, power differentials are minimized as members from all echelons of the organization are brought together to analyse the problems in the organization, describe their work situation, redesign the work organization, and learn from their efforts. Methods to facilitate the changes are workshops, conferences, and project groups that search for common ground to help design their own work organization (Weisbord, 1992; Emery, 1999). In the developmental approach, the organization is considered to be a source of knowledge and experience which should be optimally utilized. The organization's ability to change is enhanced by involving members of the organization in problem analysis and teaching them to gradually shape changes themselves. In the process, attention is given to the culture of the organization and the ability of the people to solve problems. Decision-making is aimed at attaining shared objectives through consultation, dialogue, and negotiation informed by power. The experience of current problems by members is established and gradual adjustments and improvements are facilitated. Much consideration is given to group dynamics. In the change process, an attempt is made to change behaviours, values, and norms, to develop shared meaning, and to enhance the change capacities and learning abilities of the organization and its members. The results of the participative design and developmental approach in realizing organizational change, redistribution of power, and the enhancement of organizational learning are seen as promising for the future (Boonstra & Vink, 1996).

The approach of democratic dialogue can also focus on networks of organizations that try to learn from each other's experiences by means of conferences. In addition, projects are often carried out simultaneously within each organization. Communication and open dialogue are the most important methods in the change process. The change agent is a facilitator with process knowledge who supports the dialogue. One of the aims of the dialogue is to realize cognitive and emotional restructuring of subjective realities (Gustavsen, 1992).

## SEDUCTIVE MODELS OF CHANGE

We would describe a second set of change models that relate to the latent–cultural view of power as a seductive model. In these approaches to change, there is a striving to achieve commitment, unquestioning adoption of the new organizational culture, and a harmonious development of new meaning. It is a form of political seduction (Calás & Smircich, 1991; Doorewaard & Brouns, 2003). This approach implies agreement by all participants with the existing structure, systems, and culture. Second, employees must identify with the demands of both the structure and the culture of an organization. Third, compliance by employees is achieved by creating seductive situations that simultaneously push less appealing situations into the background. Fourth, there is a change of perspectives that conceals negative consequences of the change and draws attention to the positive effects. The deliberate use of this strategy by managers or change agents can be seen as manipulation. In such a situation one party consciously influences the values, attitudes, and constructions of reality of other parties by using all available power bases. For example, managers can charismatically use information in such a way that some alternatives no longer seem desirable or by stressing positive outcomes and not mentioning the risks that are taken. If the use of manipulative strategies is discovered, resistance will follow. An atmosphere of distrust develops which becomes a breeding ground for conflict that can prevent parties from coming to agreement about new situations. This approach is often called transformational or charismatic leadership and not seduction, but in all cases power is accrued to the extent that others do not question the definition of reality that gets created.

This approach is related to the normative–re-educative strategy (Chin & Benne, 1976). In this strategy, patterns of action and practice are supported by socio-cultural norms and by the commitment of individuals to these norms. It is assumed that behavioural change occurs when the persons involved in a change process are brought to change their normative orientations to old behaviours and develop new ones. Changes in normative orientations involve changes in attitudes, values, significant relationships, and shared meanings. Chin and Benne argue that influencing these non-cognitive determinants of behaviour can be realized in a mutual process of persuasion within cooperative relationships. Using a seductive model to effect change seems suitable in situations where the mobilization of knowledge and experiences of employees is desired. Change is implemented gradually and the process allows participation of all involved parties. However, the methods used in the change model vary considerably and are dependent on the flow of the process. A limitation of the approach lies in the danger of manipulation by the change agent and the emergence of a paternalistic attitude towards the recipients of the change.

## SPIRITUAL/SYMBOLIC MODELS OF CHANGE

Within what we are calling the spiritual/symbolic models of change there is a recognition of the deep and pervasive operation of symbols and that often, if one takes these at the level of the psyche, they are connected to what many consider to be spiritual or sacred elements. While there is no one school of thought in this area, there are efforts by many to apply the insights that grow out of recognition of latent–cultural power. For example, there has been an acknowledgement that change agents are organizational shaman and change efforts are 'less a science than an art, and less an art than a magical, spiritual, process between those who are OD consultants and those who are clients' (Margulies, 1972: 78). This approach to change sometimes uses interventions that work at the level of the unconscious in ways that engage the myth-making processes of the organization (Boje et al., 1982) and the symbol-creating capacity of the psyche (Olson, 1990). Methods for engaging the deep meaning systems drawing on Jungian and other schools of psychology are being explored to overcome resistance to change and conflicts and to enhance understanding and integration. Olson, for example, argues that third-order change must address the unconscious and spiritual dimensions of organization. The unconscious manifests through myths or essential stories, dreams, metaphors that capture the imagination, and other underlying forces. From this view the unconscious is an irrational, creative force that often conflicts with the conscious world of objects and people. Active imagination, self-awareness, dream analysis, and other symbolic interventions facilitate integration of the two, through the activated transcendent function (Olson, 1990). Power dynamics and complexes are surfaced in these techniques and the unconscious aspects of them revealed (Bradshaw & Newell, 1993).

In a related way, Coopey (1998) suggests using radical theatre or theatre of the oppressed (Boal, 1979; Schutzman & Cohen-Cruz, 1994) to facilitate organizational learning, to challenge the knowledge claims of managers, and to overcome the 'democratic deficit' in organizations. Such interventions at the level of meaning and symbols are designed to reshape the institutional and cultural context of business and to create new local forms of politics. Coopey argues this approach is a way of moving towards a genuine learning organization, based on both trust and political action.

## CO-POWER THEORY OF CHANGE

Critical and postmodern understandings of power are still relatively new in organizational theory (Calás & Smircich, 1999) and, as a result, the implications of these theoretical perspectives for organizational change are still relatively rare. Boje and Rosile (2001) make an interesting attempt to do this by applying the theories of Follett and Clegg to reframe empowerment. Using a co-power model, in which the co-relationships between individuals and the network of systems and relations that make up the organization are the focus, they recommend organizational change agents move beyond the duality in which managers delegate, share, or donate power to workers. To do this, they suggest democratic conditions that allow people to be agents of power, and fixed meanings to come under review, so that new rules of the game can be developed. Workers' participation in governance of the firm, employees who are co-owners of production, and localized economies are all change strategies that they argue will break us out of existing and taken-for-granted relations of power. Redefining the organization's relations with its community and resistance to global transorganizational dominance are change strategies that come from the embracing of critical and postmodern perspectives on power.

## LATENT–PERSONAL POWER

Thus far we have seen that managers, change agents, and other individuals can use manifest–personal power directly, visibly, and consciously. As the polarity between manifest vs latent personal power is explored in this section, we can begin to suggest ways in which latent–personal power is being described and utilized in moving a change agenda forward in organizations. As in the section on latent–cultural power, this perspective is relatively new in organization theory and we are presenting approaches to change that are also correspondingly relatively underdeveloped.

This perspective on power has its roots in the psychoanalytic, postmodern, and feminist theories. It is not a look at how structures or cultures constrain agency but how individuals themselves come to limit themselves and to unquestioningly obey (Hamilton & Woolsey Biggart, 1985). This type of power differs conceptually from the latent–cultural power in several ways. One difference is the assumption that power is inherently diffused and shared among individuals located anywhere within a social system. This diffusion allows individuals to potentially become active agents who can deploy their power even if they are at the bottom of the hierarchy or relatively powerless (Whittington, 1992; Winter, 1996). Second, implicit in this approach to power is the recognition that power relations are often latent or even unconscious and they then become embedded in the actual psyche of the individual

**TABLE 13.4**  Elements of latent–personal power

| Sources | Definitions | Strategies |
| --- | --- | --- |
| Authentic existence | Being able to work in ways which reflect one's own truth and experience and which take into account both power/privilege and powerlessness/oppression. Ethics as critical self-awareness | Become more self-aware through reflective practice and personal growth. Acknowledge taken-for-granted advantages based on race, class, sex, sexual orientation, etc. Own both personal power and powerlessness |
| Critical consciousness | Perception of social, political, and economic contradictions and inequities. Replaces panoptic consciousness | Engage in a deep learning process which facilitates a search for political awareness (e.g. theatre of the oppressed, liberation education, feminist therapy) |
| Focused scepticism and critical detachment | An ability to stand apart from the dominant discourses, micropractices, and disciplinary mechanisms and see how they are perpetuated and carried unconsciously within ourselves | Unlearn habitualized ways of being; defamiliarization; question the conventional; overcome deference to power |
| Defiance | Use our capacity to refuse; make choices to take action against oppressive elements of reality as it is constructed | Say 'no', demonstrate agency and assert equality, refuse cooperation and compliance, veto, disobey |

(Starhawk, 1987; Bolen, 1992; Brown, 1994). Empowerment is the process of uncovering this latent power or powerlessness. According to Miller, '[power] acts on the interior of the person, through their self' (1987, quoted in Knights & Morgan, 1991: 269).

To the extent that an individual is unconsciously complicit and has internalized various mechanisms of control and obedience is the extent to which their freedom to act according to (or even to know) their own values and beliefs is constrained. From this perspective, for example, members of oppressed groups are asked to understand how they collude in maintaining the very systems that oppress them.

Alternatively, as suggested by Foucault (1977), the disciplinary mechanisms of the dominant groups and the very apparatuses of surveillance, examination, and normalization operate on us so subtly that we do not realize that we have internalized them into a type of panoptic consciousness. Such internalization of the 'gaze' renders actual mechanisms of control unnecessary. For Foucault this aspect of disciplinary power becomes 'embodied' or we carry it as individuals in our actual, physical, and 'obedient' bodies. In the face of these types of latent control mechanisms, there are a number of sources of power which can be mobilized by the individual (see Table 13.4). For example, attempting to be authentic and act in congruence with one's own values and beliefs. This involves not only honestly identifying one's powerlessness and complicity with the dominant systems but also owning one's taken-for-granted power and privilege. Peggy McIntosh (1990) defines privilege as a knapsack of taken-for-granted and unearned assets that provide special provisions that help certain individuals advance. Authentic existence requires those with power and privilege to make this explicit and then act on the consequences of this unearned advantage. Another source of deep personal power is the development of a critical consciousness that Freire (1970) defines as a perception of the social, political, and economic contradictions inherent in society. We believe that such a consciousness can replace what Foucault calls panoptic consciousness.

It is assumed that an attitude of focused scepticism and critical detachment is necessary if an individual is to have latent–personal power. Only by standing outside the dominant discourses and seeing how we have unconsciously carried them within ourselves can we unlearn these mechanisms of power. Through a process of questioning and defamiliarization, we can replace an attitude of deference to power with an ability to make autonomous choices. Often the ability to develop a detached and sceptical attitude is facilitated by exposure to other systems and styles of organizing, for example, from outside the organizations of which we are members. Whittington (1992) suggests that experiencing contradictory structural principles will allow us to move organizations in directions that are in contradiction to the dominant capitalist rules. In effect, individuals have the possibility to 'act out their roles in the light of their own autonomous cultural and ideological values' (Whittington, 1992: 701) if they can import into the organization the experiences they have with other external institutions with different beliefs, rules, values, and resources.

Many groups are experimenting with ways to help people develop a critical consciousness. For example, feminist therapists are working with women to reveal their feminist consciousness (Brown, 1994). Liberation education techniques, first used by Paulo Freire, are now being utilized in other contexts to help individuals break silences and value their own experience and voice (e.g. Starhawk, 1987). We will explore a few of these approaches to organizational change below.

## INDIVIDUAL LEARNING AND DEEP REFLECTION AS APPROACHES TO CHANGE

Quinn says he has come to believe that altering our inner world (1996: 217) can change the external world. He admits this is not a popular view and runs contrary to views of 'top-down' and 'outside in' change. His approach, he indicates, requires confidence and the ability to act on one's own values even if they are opposed to those of the system as a whole. Increasingly leadership from the 'inside out' is being advocated as a way of moving change ahead and increases in the use of personal coaches and the re-emergence of personal growth and reflection as essential managerial skills are, to us, a reflection of this shift (Schön, 1983).

Various well-known change agents model this type of 'deep reflection'. Harrison is a good example of this and in his 1995 book he describes his personal journey. He argues that the best contributions he can make are lovingly to assist others in reflection and deep learning, as opposed to scapegoating, and to help people face their shadow and speak their truth. In the Preface to the book, Block describes it as deeply political. He argues that processes such as Harrison describes will enable a genuine redistribution of power through the process of an individual's identification of their own complicity in creating the suffering around us (Block, in Harrison, 1995).

## RESISTANCE AS AN APPROACH TO CHANGE

As stated by Bennebroek Gravenhorst (Chapter 15), resistance to change is usually seen as a negative process to be overcome. People are said to be resisting the change process and their resistance must be broken down or overcome. Those who have a more emancipatory change agenda are redefining the term, however, and it is being redefined from this perspective as a way for individuals to undermine or at least distance themselves from the prevailing power structures (Collinson, 1994). Various strategies of resistance are being defined and articulated for individuals and they range from defiance to persistence. Feminist resistance (Bradshaw & Wicks, 1997) is being well articulated and women who want to make change in systems they are also a part of are being described as 'tempered radicals' (Meyerson & Scully, 1995) or as engaging in 'disorganized coaction' (Martin & Meyerson, 1998). Women who are informed by a feminist consciousness are naming injustice and are refusing to accept the subjectivities and identities defined by those in power. The essence of this approach to change is that each individual acts within their own sphere of influence and large-scale change is pursued through a series of small wins and spread by contagion (Martin & Meyerson, 1998).

## PARTICIPATORY ACTION RESEARCH

Participatory action research is an approach to change that explicitly recognizes the role of power and 'conscientization' in its interventions (Brown, 1986). Drawing on adult education principles and popular knowledge, it seeks to empower all participants in an action research project to learn as individuals through the process. Hall (1981) describes it as serving the needs and interests of the working classes who are oppressed by dis-indoctrination. This allows them to disengage from the myths imposed by the power structures and to examine deeper levels of social structure. This approach to change starts with individuals but also embraces social movements and the collective level of intervention (Gaventa & Horton, 1981).

# CONCLUSION

We have presented four perspectives on power and explored different approaches to change that emerge from each. We recognize that we have not been comprehensive in this review but we have tried to reflect the trends in thinking about power and change since the link between the two was first identified in the 1970s. Some of the approaches are well developed and tested. Others are newer and emerging as we struggle to create change in systems that are embedded in complex, latent, subtle, and fragmented power relations. We know that new approaches will continue to be developed from the margins and that the question of how to link change to power will continue to be defined. Other questions, such as how to engage the silences in organizational discourses (Morrison & Milliken, 2000) that are being dealt with through feminist and other forms of postmodern deconstruction and in textual analysis, for example, have yet to be used to inform change. Foldy and Creed (1999) argue that a postmodern approach to change is more variegated, provides a more contextual understanding of the multiple elements of change, and pays more attention to localized accounts and stories. Understanding the broader organizational change process requires attention to individual sites of struggle as well as to how individuals participate or resist, adapt or rebel and modify the change process.

Each of the perspectives on power presented in this chapter represents fundamentally different sets of assumptions or what might be called paradigms of power. There have been interesting debates in the field of organizational behaviour about the possibility of integrating fundamentally different paradigms, and we think there is a significant challenge for the field in dealing with the diversity and plurality of the insights presented here. There are various ways of dealing with multiple perspectives and Morgan (1983) suggests one of the following: supremacy, synthesis, contingency, anything goes, or dialectic. With dominance or supremacy, one perspective is used to the exclusion of others. We believe the two manifest-power approaches have dominated the field to date, to the point of excluding others. We want to suggest that this pattern of domination and exclusion needs to be challenged and that it is time to encourage more expansive thinking on the topic of power and change. Morgan suggests, in addition to supremacy, that multiple perspectives can be brought together in a contingency framework or one in which the change agent selects the best approach for the situation and draws on different assumptions about power at different times. Morgan further argues that one can be more *laissez-faire* and say anything goes or a combination of any approach in any situation without constraint can be utilized. Morgan also argues that 'there would seem to be no reason why different and contradictory knowledges of the same phenomenon should not co-exist in the nature of that phenomenon' (1983: 390). Therefore another approach is to synthesize or blend two or more approaches together and this is easier with change strategies that share the same amount of latency. For example, two approaches that draw on fundamentally positivistic assumptions about the world will be more congruent and easier to combine (e.g. manifest–personal and manifest–structural). Finally, Morgan suggests a dialectical approach and we want to suggest exploring this alternative in more depth. We have framed the chapter on two polarities and outlined the tensions between all four types of power and their related change strategies. While contradictory in fundamental ways, if a situation can be looked at first from the lens of manifest power and of latent power, in combination with the individual vs collectivist views, then rich new potential for change can emerge and be enabled. As organizational contexts become more uncertain and complex and the mechanisms of power both more entrenched and more difficult to understand, we believe a unidimensional approach has serious limitations.

We suggest that none of the approaches to change in isolation is sufficient but when taken together, and named as a part of a whole process, they may hold the keys to organizational transformation. We are also not suggesting a coordinated and systematic change process to focus simultaneously on all four types of power. But we are calling for recognition of these polarities or dialectics of power and we recommend an attempt to hold the tensions created by such a multifaceted conceptualization. Postmodern perspectives reveal how certain knowledge claims are privileged. In the field of organizational change, the manifest perspectives on power have been privileged in the dominant discourses. In this process, certain ideas, perspectives, and experiences have been silenced, denied, and oppressed. Given the difficulties of transformational change and the complexities of power, we are challenged to name and understand the multiplicity of approaches to change. If we can value and celebrate differences and nurture alternative change potentials, we are more likely to enable transformational change. If, however, we rely on one set of assumptions about change or, worse yet, suppress, deny, or devalue some perspectives, then the status quo is actually reinforced.

The problem with what we are suggesting is that tough questions must also be addressed. For example, when the latent perspectives on power are included, we must change our language and address questions of oppression, inequity, abuse, neglect, and collusion. This language is not often in the discourses of traditional literature on organizational change. Ideas from postmodernism and social constructionism offer new perspectives. When we include them, we must also ask questions such as change towards what, and towards whose ends? It is, however, naïve to assume that because we do not explicitly deal with these questions that they are not relevant and are not currently being answered in the silences. We often know whose power is currently being enhanced and we are learning how to expose silences in the dominant discourses. Once these silences are addressed, then we can also name the abuse and oppression that is being ignored. Likewise, this type of dialectical model challenges change agents to ask whose interests they are serving, what ends are served through their interventions, and how aware are they of their own internalization of existing power relations and their own unconscious privileges?

In this chapter, we have highlighted two polarities and the dynamic tensions created by simultaneously acknowledging both ends of these polarities. In conclusion, we want to re-emphasize the importance of holding both ends of the polarities in dynamic tension in order for transformative change to be enabled. For example, groups and individuals must engage in deconstruction and resistance at the deeper levels in order to reveal oppression and raise awareness. But to make meaningful change, it is also necessary to use the surface sources of power and change strategies associated with restructuring and personal action. The manifest sources of power must inform the latent and the latent inform the more manifest. Likewise, individual agency must be mobilized while simultaneously acknowledging the role of the collectivity. We can work as active agents but we also need to understand the constraints and limits imposed by the systems of which we are part. We must also understand how power is concentrated in the hands of the dominant groups and through understanding of shared oppression and privilege look at how subordinated groups can work together collectively and politically to create change. This still must be informed by an understanding of the need for the individual to resist and sustain their own critical consciousness. Oshry (1995) proposes the metaphor of a dance and how one must always dance from awareness and clarity of understanding of the systems and how they work. We are proposing this model as a way of informing and enriching our understanding as we dance towards organizational changes using all our powers. Recognizing the complexity and diversity of power sources is the first step. Embracing multiple perspectives and living in the resulting tensions are the challenges.

# REFERENCES

Alvesson, M. (1992) Leadership as social integrative action: a study of a computer consultancy company. *Organization Studies*, **13**(2), 185–209.

Alvesson, M. (1993) *Cultural Perspectives on Organizations*. New York: Cambridge University Press.

Alvesson, M. & Deetz, S. (2000) *Doing Critical Management Research*. Thousand Oaks, CA: Sage.

Alvesson, M. & Willmott, H. (1992) On the idea of emancipation in management and organization studies. *Academy of Management Review*, **17**(3), 432–464.

Bacharach, S.B. & Lawler, E.J. (1980) *Power and Politics in Organizations*. San Francisco: Jossey-Bass.

Bateman, T. (1980) Organizational change and the politics of success. *Group & Organization Studies*, **5**(2), 198–209.

Bennis, W.G. (1969) *Organization Development: Its Nature, Origins, and Prospects*. Reading, MA: Addison-Wesley.

Boal, A. (1979) *Theatre of the Oppressed*. London: Pluto Press.

Boje, D., Fedor, D. & Rowland, M. (1982) Myth making: a qualitative step in OD Interventions. *Journal of Applied Behavioral Science*, **18**(1), 17–28.

Boje, D. & Rosile, G. (2001) Where's the power in empowerment? Answers from Follett and Clegg. *Journal of Applied Behavioral Science*, **37**(1), 90–117.

Bolen, J.S. (1992) *Ring of Power: The Abandoned Child, the Authoritarian Father, and the Disempowered Feminine*. New York: HarperCollins.

Boonstra, J.J. (ed.) (1997) Barriers to organizational change and innovation. *Symposium, Proceedings of the Eighth European Congress on Work and Organisational Psychology*. 2–5 April, Verona.

Boonstra, J.J. & Vink, M.J. (1996) Technological and organizational innovation: a dilemma of fundamental change and development. *European Journal of Work and Organizational Psychology*, **5**(3), 351–376.

Borum, F. (1980) A power-strategy alternative to organization development. *Organization Studies*, **1**(2), 123–146.

Bouwen, R. (1995) Social reconstruction of power relationships in workplace conflict episodes. In J.J. Boonstra (ed.) Power dynamics and organizational change. *Symposium, Proceedings of the Seventh European Congress on Work and Organisational Psychology*. 19–22 April, Györ, Hungary.

Bradshaw, P. (1990) Organizational development and the radical humanist paradigm: exploring the implications. *Academy of Management Best Papers Proceedings*, August, 253–257.

Bradshaw, P. (1996) Women as constituent directors: re-reading current texts using a feminist-postmodernist approach. In D.J. Boje, R.P. Gephart, Jr & T.J. Thatchenkery (eds) *Postmodern Management and Organization Theory* (pp. 95–124). Thousand Oaks, CA: Sage.

Bradshaw, P. (1998) Power as dynamic tension and its tension and its implications for radical organizational change. *European Journal of Work and Organizational Psychology*, **7**(2), 121–143.

Bradshaw, P. & Newell, S. (1993) Dreams of untenured female faculty: exploring deep structures of power. *Canadian Woman Studies*, **18**(1), 123–127.

Bradshaw, P. & Wicks, D. (1997) Women in the academy: cycles of resistance and compliance. In P. Prasad, A. Mills, M. Elmes & A. Prasad (eds) *Managing the Organization Melting Pot: Dilemmas of Workplace Diversity* (pp. 199–225). Thousand Oaks, CA: Sage.

Bradshaw-Camball, P. & Murray, V.V. (1991) Illusions and other games: a trifocal view of organizational politics. *Organization Science*, **2**(4), 379–398.

Brown, L.D. (1986) Participatory research and community planning. In B. Checkoway (ed.) *Strategic Perspectives on Planning Practice* (pp. 123–137). Lexington, MA: D.C. Heath & Co.

Brown, L.S. (1994) *Subversive Dialogues: Theory in Feminist Therapy*. New York: Basic Books.

Burke, W. (1980) Is your client really involved in OD? In W. Burke & L.D. Goodstein (eds) *Trends and Issues in OD: Current Theory and Practice* (pp. 301–309). San Diego, CA: University Associates.

Burrell, G. & Morgan, G. (1979) *Sociological Paradigms and Organisational Analysis: Elements of the Sociology of Corporate Life*. London: Heinemann.

Calás, M.B. & Smircich, L. (1991) Voicing seduction to silence leadership. *Organization Studies*, **12**(4), 567–602.

Calás, M.B. & Smircich, L. (1999) Past postmodernism? Reflections and tenative directions. *Academy of Management Review*, **24**(4), 649–671.

Chin, R. & Benne, K. (1976) General strategies for effecting changes in human systems. In W. Bennis, K. Benne & R. Chin (eds) *The Planning of Change* (pp. 23–45). San Diego, CA: Holt, Rinehart & Winston.

Clegg, S.R. (1990) *Frameworks of Power*. London: Sage.

Collinson, D. (1994) Strategies of resistance: power, knowledge and subjectivity in the workplace. In J.M. Jermier, D. Knights & W. Nord (eds) *Resistance and Power in Organizations* (pp. 25–68). London: Routledge.

Coopey, J. (1998) Learning to trust and trusting to learn: a role for radical theatre. *Management Learning*, **29**(3), 365–382.

Cummings, T. & Worley, C.G. (1997) *Organization Development and Change* (6th edn). Cincinnati, OH: South-Western College Publishing.

Dahl, R.A. (1975) The concept of power. *Behavioral Science*, **2**, 201–215.

Dalton, M. (1959) *Men who Manage*. New York: John Wiley & Sons, Ltd.

Doorewaard, H. & Brouns, B. (2003) Hegemonic power proceses and team-based work. *Applied Psychology: An International Review*, **52**(1), 106–122.

Dunphy, D.C. & Stace, D.A. (1998) Transformational and coercive strategies for planned organizational change. *Organizational Studies*, **11**(1), 17–34.

Emerson, R.M. (1962) Power-dependence relations. *American Sociological Review*, **27**, 31–41.

Emery, M. (1999) *Searching: The Theory and Practice of Making Cultural Change*. Amsterdam: John Benjamins.

Foldy, E. & Creed, D. (1999) Action learning, fragmentation, and the interaction of single-, double-, and triple-loop change: a case of gay and lesbian workplace advocacy. *Journal of Applied Behavioral Science*, **35**(2), 207–227.

Foucault, M. (1977) *Discipline and Punish: The Birth of the Prison*. Trans. A. Sheridan. New York: Pantheon Books.

Freire, P. (1970) *Pedagogy of the Oppressed*. New York: The Seabury Press.

Gaventa, J. & Horton, B.D. (1981) A citizens' research project in Appalachia, USA. *Convergence*, **14**(3), 30–42.

Gergen, K. (1991) *The Saturated Self: Dilemmas of Identity in Contemporary Life*. New York: Basic Books.

Giddens, A. (1979) *Central Problems in Social Theory: Action, Structure and Contradiction in Social Analysis*. Berkeley, CA: University of California Press.

Greenfield, T. (1973) Organizations as social inventions: rethinking assumptions about change. *Journal of Applied Behavioral Science*, **9**(5), 551–574.

Greiner, L.E. & Schein, V.E. (1988) *Power and Organization Development: Mobilizing Power to Implement Change*. Reading, MA: Addison-Wesley.

Gustavsen, B. (1992) *Dialogue and Development: Theory of Communication, Action Research and the Restructuring of Working Life*. Stockholm: Swedish Centre for Working Life.

Habermas, J. (1984) *The Theory of Communication*.

Hall, E. (1981) *Beyond Culture*. New York: Anchor.

Hamilton, G.G. & Woolsey Biggart, N. (1985) Why people obey: theoretical observations on power and obedience in complex organizations. *Sociological Perspectives*, **28**(1), 3–28.

Hardy, C. (1985) The nature of unobtrusive power. *Journal of Management Studies*, **22**(4), 384–399.

Hardy, C. (1994) Underorganized interorganizational domains: the case of refugee systems. *Journal of Applied Behavioral Science*, **30**(3), 278–296.

Hardy, C. & Clegg, S.R. (1996) Some dare call it power. In S.R. Clegg, C. Hardy & W.R. Nord (eds) *Handbook of Organization Studies* (pp. 622–641). London: Sage.

Harrison, R. (1980) Personal power and influence in organization development. In W.W. Burke & L.D. Goodstein (eds) *Trends and Issues in OD: Current Theory and Practice*. San Diego, CA: University Associates.

Harrison, R. (1995) *Consultant's Journey: A Dance of Work and Spirit*. San Francisco, CA: Jossey-Bass.

Hickson, D.J., Hinings, C.R., Lee, C.A., Schneck, R.E. & Pennings, J.M. (1971) A strategic contingencies' theory of intraorganizational power. *Administrative Science Quarterly*, **16**, 216–229.

Kanter, R.M. (1977) *Men and Women of the Corporation*. New York: Basic Books.

Kanter, R.M. (1983) *The Change Masters: Innovation for Innovation Productivity in the American Corporation*. New York: University of Chicago Press.

Kelley, H.H. & Thibaut, J.W. (1978) *Interpersonal Relations: A Theory of Interdependence*. New York: John Wiley & Sons, Ltd.

Knights, D. & Morgan, G. (1991) Corporate strategy, organizations, and subjectivity: a critique. *Organization Studies*, **12**(2), 251–273.

Knights, D. & Murray, F. (1992) Politics and pain in managing information technology: a case study from insurance. *Organization Studies*, **13**(2), 211–228.

Lukes, S. (1974) *Power: A Radical View*. London: Macmillan Education Ltd.

Margulies, N. (1972) The myth and magic in OD. *Business Horizons*, **15**(4), 77–82.

Margulies, N. & Raia, A. (1984) The politics of organization development. *Training and Development Journal*, **38**(8), 20–23.

Marshall, J. & McLean, A. (1985) Exploring organization culture as a route to organizational change. In V. Hammond (ed.) *Current Research in Management*. London: Frances Pinter.

Martin, J. & Meyerson, D. (1998) Organizational culture and the denial, channelling and acknowledgement of ambiguity. In L. Pondy, R. Boland & H. Thomas (eds) *Managing Ambiguity and Change*. New York: John Wiley & Sons, Ltd.

McIntosh, P. (1990) White privilege: unpacking the invisible knapsack. *Independent School*, **Winter**, 31–36.

Meyerson, D.E. & Scully, M.A. (1995) Tempered radicalism and the politics of ambivalence change. *Organization Science*, **6**, 585–600.

Mills, A. & Murgatroyd, S. (1991) *Organizational Rules: A Framework for Understanding Organizational Action*. Bristol: Open University Press.

Mills, A.J. (1992) Organization, gender and culture. In A.J. Mills & P. Tancred (eds) *Gendering Organizational Analysis* (pp. 93–111). Newbury Park, CA: Sage.

Morgan, G. (ed.) (1983) *Beyond Method: Strategies for Social Research*. Beverly Hills, CA: Sage.

Morrison, E. & Milliken, F. (2000) Organizational silence: a barrier to change and development in a pluralistic world. *Academy of Management Review*, **25**(4), 706–725.

Murray, V.V. & Bradshaw-Camball, P. (1993) Temptations and dilemmas in the interpretive perspective on organizational politics. In G. Dlugos, W. Dorow & D. Farrell (eds) *Organizational Politics: From Conflict Suppression to Rational Conflict-Management* (pp. 51–70). Wiesbaden: Gabler.

Nord, W.R. (1974) The failure of current applied behavioral science: a Marxian perspective. *Journal of Applied Behavioral Science*, **10**(4), 557–578.

Olson, E. (1990) The transcendent function in organizational change. *Journal of Applied Behavioral Science*, **26**(1), 69–81.

Oshry, B. (1995) *Seeing Systems: Unlocking the Mysteries of Organizational Life*. San Francisco: Berrett-Koehler.

Perrow, C. (1970) Departmental power and perspective in industrial firms. In M.N. Zaid (ed.) *Power in Organizations*. Nashville, TN: Vanderbilt University Press.

Pettigrew, A. (1973) *The Politics of Organizational Decision-Making*. London. Harper & Row.

Pettigrew, A. (1975) Towards a political theory of organizational intervention. *Human Relations*, **28**(3), 191–208.

Pettigrew, A. (1977) Strategy formulation as a political process. *International Studies of Management and Organization*, **7**(2), 78–87.

Pfeffer, J. (1981) *Power in Organizations*. Cambridge, MA: Pitman.

Pfeffer, J. (1994) *Managing with Power: Politics and Influence in Organizations*. Boston: Harvard Business School Press.

Quinn, R.E. (1996) *Deep Change Discovering the Leader Within*. San Francisco: Jossey-Bass.

Reed, M.I. (1988) The problem of human agency in organization analysis. *Organization Studies*, **9**(1), 33–46.

Rosen, M. (1985) Breakfast at Spiro's: dramaturgy and dominance. *Journal of Management*, **11**(2), 31–48.

Ross, R. (1971) Comment on the two preceding articles. *Journal of Applied Behavioral Science*, **7**(5), 580–585.

Schein, V. (1977) Political strategies for implementing organizational change. *Group & Organization Studies*, **2**(1), 42–48.

Schön, D. (1983) *The Reflective Practitioner: How Professionals Think in Action*. New York: Basic Books.

Schutzman, M. & Cohen-Cruz, J. (1994) *Playing Boal: Theatre, Therapy, Activism*. London: Routledge.

Smircich, L. & Morgan, G. (1982) Leadership as the management of meaning. *Journal of Applied Behavioral Science*, **18**, 257–273.

Starhawk (1987) *Truth or Dare: Encounters with Power, Authority, and Mystery*. San Francisco: Harper.

Steensma, H.O. & Boer, G. (1997) The effectiveness of influence tactics in leadership and organizational change. In K.M. Bennebroek Gravenhorst & J.J. Boonstra (eds) *Power Dynamics and Organisational Change II. Symposium, Proceedings of the Eighth European Congress on Work and Organisational Psychology*, 2–5 April, Verona, 129–138.

Tichy, N. (1983) *Managing Strategic Change: Technical, Political, and Cultural Dynamics*. New York: Wiley-Interscience Publication.

Townley, B. (1994) *Reframing Human Resource Management: Power, Ethics and the Subject at Work*. London: Sage.

Walton, R. & Warwick, D. (1973) The ethics of organization development. *Journal of Applied Behavioral Science*, **9**(6), 681–698.

Weick, K. (1979) *The Social Psychology of Organizing* (2nd edn). Reading, MA: Addison-Wesley.

Weisbord, M.R. (1992) *Discovering Common Ground: How Future Search Conferences Bring People Together to Achieve Breakthrough Innovation, Empowerment, Shared Vision, and Collaborative Action*. San Francisco: Berrett-Koehler.

Whittington, R. (1992) Putting Giddens into action: social systems and managerial agency. *Journal of Management Studies*, **29**(6), 693–712.

Winter, S. (1996) The 'power' thing. *Virginia Law Review*, **82**(5), 721–835.

Wrong, D.H. (1968) Some problems in defining social power. *American Journal of Sociology*, **73**, 673–681.

Yukl, G., Ping Fu, P. & McDonald, R. (2003) Cross-cultural differences in perceived effectiveness of influence tactics for initiating or resisting change. *Applied Psychology: An International Review*, **52**(1), 61–82.

Zaltman, G. & Duncan, R. (1977) *Strategies for Planned Change*. New York: John Wiley & Sons, Ltd.

# CHAPTER 14

# Interactions in Organizational Change
## Using Influence Tactics to Initiate Change

**Gary Yukl**

*State University of New York, Albany, New York, USA*

In these turbulent times of globalization, technological innovation, and intense competition, change is essential for the survival and prosperity of business organizations. Leaders bear a major responsibility for advocating, initiating, and facilitating major changes in the organization. There are many opportunities to influence change. Leaders influence subordinates to implement 'top-down' change. Leaders influence bosses to approve and support a 'bottom-up' change. Leaders influence peers to join in a coalition to gain approval from higher management for a proposed change. Leaders also seek assistance from peers in implementing a change that has already been authorized by higher management.

This chapter describes how interpersonal influence is exerted in attempts by individual leaders to initiate or facilitate organizational change. The chapter begins with a description of findings in research on dyadic influence tactics. Next is a review of research on how managers use influence tactics to initiate change in organizations. Then the limiting and facilitating conditions for initiating change are discussed, followed by guidelines for using specific tactics effectively. The chapter ends with some suggestions for future research.

## DYADIC INFLUENCE TACTICS

The term 'proactive influence tactic' describes a form of observable behavior used by one person (the 'agent') to influence someone else (the 'target') to carry out a request or support a change. A number of studies have identified distinct types of proactive influence tactics (e.g., Kipnis et al., 1980; Schriesheim & Hinkin, 1990). Building on the earlier work, Yukl and his colleagues (e.g., Yukl & Falbe, 1990; Yukl & Tracey, 1992; Yukl, 2002) have identified a variety of proactive influence tactics that are relevant for influencing subordinates, peers, and superiors in large organizations. Following is a brief description of 10 tactics that appear to be distinct and relevant for most managers.

### 1. RATIONAL PERSUASION

This tactic involves the use of explanations, logical arguments, and factual evidence to show that a request or proposal is feasible and relevant for attaining task objectives. Rational persuasion is a flexible tactic that can be used for most types of requests or proposals. Strong forms of rational persuasion include a detailed explanation of the reasons why proposed change is important, and presentation of concrete evidence that it is feasible. Rational persuasion is most appropriate when the target person shares the same task objectives as the manager but disagrees about the best way to attain the objectives.

*Dynamics of Organizational Change and Learning.* Edited by J.J. Boonstra.
© 2004 John Wiley & Sons, Ltd. ISBN 0-471-87737-9.

If the agent and target person have incompatible objectives, then rational persuasion is unlikely to be successful. The effective use of rational persuasion also depends on the agent's persuasive skill, expertise about the request or proposal, and credibility with target persons.

## 2. Inspirational Appeals

This tactic involves an attempt to develop enthusiasm and commitment by arousing strong emotions and linking a request or proposal to a person's values and ideals. Some bases for ideological appeals include the desire of people to be important, to feel useful, to develop and use their skills, to accomplish something worthwhile, to perform an exceptional feat, to be a member of the best team, or to participate in an exciting effort to make things better. No tangible rewards are promised, only the prospect that the target person will feel good as a result of doing something that is noble and just, making an important contribution, performing an exceptional feat, or serving God and country. To formulate an appropriate appeal, the manager must have insight into the values, hopes, and fears of the person or group to be influenced. The effectiveness of an inspirational appeal also depends on communication skills such as the ability to use vivid imagery and metaphors, to manipulate symbols, and to employ voice and gestures to generate enthusiasm and excitement.

## 3. Consultation

With consultation the target person is invited to participate in determining how to improve a proposal or in planning how to implement a policy or change that has already been approved. In effect, consultation is one form of empowerment. The use of consultation is more likely to be effective when the agent and target person have compatible objectives (Vroom & Yetton, 1973). A target person with different objectives may decline to participate or use participation as an opportunity to resist change (e.g., slow it down, dilute it). For this reason, it is sometimes necessary to use rational persuasion or inspirational appeals in combination with consultation to bolster target commitment to the change objectives.

## 4. Exchange

This influence tactic involves the explicit or implicit offer to provide something the target person wants in return for carrying out a request or supporting a proposal. Exchange tactics are especially useful when the target person is reluctant about complying with a request because it offers no important benefits and would involve considerable effort and inconvenience. Exchange provides a way to increase the benefits enough to make it worthwhile for the target person to comply with the request. An essential condition for using this tactic is control over something the target person desires enough to justify compliance. The incentive may involve a wide range of tangible or intangible benefits (e.g., a pay increase or promotion, scarce resources, information, assistance on another task, assistance in advancing the target's career). Sometimes the incentive may be vague rather than explicit, such as a promise to return the favor in some unspecified way at a future time. An offer to exchange benefits will not be effective unless the target person perceives that the agent is able and willing to carry out the agreement.

## 5. Collaboration

This influence tactic involves an offer to provide necessary resources or assistance if the target person will carry out a request or approve a proposal. Collaboration may seem similar to exchange in that both tactics involve an offer to do something for the target person. However, there are important differences in the underlying motivational processes and facilitating conditions. Exchange involves increasing the benefits to be obtained by carrying out a request, and it is especially appropriate when the benefits of compliance would otherwise be low for the target person. Collaboration involves reducing the difficulty of carrying out a request, and it is especially appropriate when compliance would be difficult or costly for the target person. Exchange usually involves an impersonal trade of unrelated benefits, whereas collaboration usually involves a joint effort to accomplish the same task or objective.

## 6. APPRISING

With this tactic the agent explains why a request or proposal is likely to benefit the target person as an individual. One example is to explain why carrying out a request will help to advance the target person's career. Another example is to explain why a proposed change will make the target person's job easier or more interesting. Apprising may involve the use of facts and logic, but unlike rational persuasion, the benefits described are for the target person as an individual, not for the organization. Unlike exchange tactics, the benefits to be obtained by the target person are a by-product of doing what the agent requests, not something the agent will provide. Use of apprising is more likely to be successful if the agent understands the target's needs and how a request or proposal may help to satisfy them. Because the agent makes assertions about likely benefits for the target, agent credibility is required for successful use of this tactic.

## 7. COALITION TACTICS

Coalition tactics involve getting help from other people to influence the target person. The coalition partners may be peers, subordinates, superiors, or outsiders. When assistance is provided by the superior of the target person, the tactic is usually called an 'upward appeal'. Another distinct type of coalition tactic is to use a prior endorsement by other people to help influence the target person to support your proposal. To be helpful, the endorsements should come from people whom the person respects. Coalition tactics are usually used in combination with one or more of the other influence tactics. For example, the agent may bring along a supporter when meeting with the target person, and both agents may use rational persuasion to influence the target person.

## 8. PERSONAL APPEALS

A personal appeal involves asking someone to do a favor out of friendship or loyalty to the agent. This influence tactic is not feasible when the target person dislikes the agent or is indifferent about what happens to the agent. The stronger the friendship or loyalty, the more one can ask of the target person. Of course, if referent power is very strong and the request is not excessive, then a personal appeal should not be necessary to make the friendship salient to the request. Personal appeals are most likely to be used when asking for a personal favor, and the target person is more likely to be a lateral peer rather than a subordinate or boss.

## 9. INGRATIATION

Ingratiation is behavior that makes the target person feel better about the agent. Examples include giving compliments, doing unsolicited favors, behaving deferentially and respectfully, and acting especially friendly. When ingratiation is perceived to be sincere, it tends to strengthen positive regard and make a target person more willing to consider the agent's request. However, when ingratiation is used just before making a request, it is likely to be viewed as manipulative by the target person. Therefore, this tactic is less useful for an immediate influence attempt than as a longer-term strategy to improve relationships with people.

## 10. PRESSURE

Pressure tactics include threats, warnings, and assertive behavior such as repeated demands or frequent checking to see if the person has complied with a request. These tactics are sometimes successful in inducing compliance with a request, particularly if the target person is just lazy or apathetic rather than strongly opposed to it. However, pressure is unlikely to result in target commitment, and it may have serious side effects. Hard forms of pressure (e.g., threats, warnings, demands) are likely to cause resentment and undermine working relationships. Softer forms of pressure (e.g., making persistent requests, setting a specific deadline for compliance) are less likely to have adverse side effects.

## RESEARCH ON DYADIC TACTICS

A number of studies have been conducted to determine how often the various tactics are used with subordinates, peers, and bosses, and the relative effectiveness of each type of influence tactic when used alone or in different combinations. Most of this research has involved the general use of influence tactics without regard to the specific objectives of the influence attempt. It is not clear whether the results apply to the specific objective of initiating major change in an organization. Nevertheless, because the findings in this research may provide some insights about the tactics that are useful for initiating change, the major findings will be reviewed briefly in this section of the chapter.

### TACTICS AND DIRECTION OF INFLUENCE

The direction of influence involves the authority relationship between the agent and target, namely whether the target is a subordinate, lateral peer, or boss. Some tactics are easier to use in one direction than in another. Yukl and Tracey (1992) proposed that several interrelated factors determine the selection of influence tactics for a particular influence attempt. These factors include: (1) consistency with prevailing social norms and role expectations about use of the tactic in that context; (2) agent possession of an appropriate power base for use of the tactic in that context; (3) appropriateness for the objective of the influence attempt; (4) level of target resistance encountered or anticipated; and (5) costs of using the tactic in relation to likely benefits. According to Yukl and Tracey (1992), most agents are likely to select tactics that are socially acceptable, that are feasible in terms of the agent's position and personal power in relation to the target, that are not costly (in terms of time, effort, loss of resources, or alienation of the target), and that are likely to be effective for a particular objective given the anticipated level of resistance by the target.

These propositions can be used to derive hypotheses about likely directional differences in the use of each type of influence tactics. Research by Yukl and his colleagues supported most of the hypotheses (Yukl & Falbe, 1990; Yukl & Tracey, 1992; Yukl et al., 1993). Rational persuasion is a flexible tactic that is used frequently in all directions and for most types of influence attempts. This tactic is especially prominent in upward influence attempts because of the difficulty of using most other proactive tactics with bosses. Coalitions are useful for both lateral and upward influence attempts, but they are not used much with subordinates. Consultation, inspirational appeals, exchange, legitimating, personal appeals, collaboration, and apprising are used more to influence subordinates and peers than to influence bosses. Most of these directional differences have also been supported by other researchers (e.g., Kipnis et al., 1980; Erez et al., 1986; Bennebroek Gravenhorst & Boonstra, 1998); the few discrepancies may reflect differences in nationality of the managers, type of organization, and the operational definition and measurement of the influence tactics.

## EFFECTIVENESS OF INDIVIDUAL TACTICS

Several studies have examined the relative effectiveness of individual influence tactics. The studies differ with regard to the type of research method used and the types of tactics included. In survey field studies, targets or agents described how often the agent used each type of influence tactic, and researchers examined the correlation between these scores and influence effectiveness (e.g., Barry & Bateman, 1992; Yukl & Tracey, 1992). In research using influence incidents, agents or targets described an influence attempt and its outcome, then researchers coded the incident in terms of the tactics used by the agent (e.g., Schilit & Locke, 1982; Yukl et al., 1996). In field research with scenarios, managers rated the relative effectiveness of various tactics for influencing targets in several representative situations (e.g., Yukl et al., 2003). In experimental studies, one or more tactics were manipulated to examine the effect on target compliance or commitment (e.g., Barry & Shapiro, 1992; Yukl et al., 1999). Even though differences among studies make it more difficult to compare results, there appears to be considerable consistency in results for most tactics.

Consultation, collaboration, and inspirational appeals are three of the most effective tactics for influencing target commitment to carry out a request or support a proposal. Rational persuasion can also be very effective, depending on how it is used. A weak form of rational persuasion (e.g., a brief explanation, an assertion without supporting evidence) is much less effective than a stronger form of rational persuasion (e.g., a detailed proposal, elaborate documentation).

Ingratiation, exchange, and apprising are moderately effective for influencing subordinates and peers, but these tactics are difficult to use for influencing superiors. Agents have little to exchange in an upward direction, and to offer such an exchange is contrary to role expectations for a subordinate. Apprising is not feasible unless a subordinate has exclusive knowledge about likely personal benefits for a superior, which seldom occurs. Ingratiation is not very useful for proactive influence attempts in an upward direction, because this tactic is likely to be viewed as manipulative by the boss.

Personal appeals can be useful for influencing a target person with whom the agent has a somewhat friendly relationship (especially a lateral peer). However, this tactic is only relevant for certain types of requests (e.g., get assistance, get a personal favor), and the outcome is likely to be compliance rather than commitment. Personal appeals are not likely to be of much use for gaining support or approval for a major change.

Pressure and legitimating tactics are very unlikely to result in target commitment, but each of these tactics can be useful for eliciting compliance with a request that does not require initiative, dedication, and persistence by the target person. Little support was found in the research for the effectiveness of coalition tactics. The consequences of using coalitions probably depends on the influence objective and the tactics used by coalition partner(s).

Overall, some tactics tend to be more effective than others, but the outcome of any particular influence attempt is affected strongly by other factors in addition to the type of influence tactics used by the agent. Some examples include the agent's power and authority, the agent's expertise and credibility, the agent's influence skills, the relationship between agent and target (e.g., trust, friendship), and the target's perception of the request (e.g., important, legitimate, feasible). Any tactic can result in resistance if it is not used in a skillful manner, or if it is used for a request that is improper or unethical.

## EFFECTIVENESS OF TACTIC COMBINATIONS

Many influence attempts involve the use of more than one type of influence tactic. Only a few studies have examined use of tactic combinations (e.g., Case et al., 1988; Barry & Shapiro, 1992; Falbe & Yukl, 1992; Emans et al., 1999), but some tentative conclusions can be drawn from the available research.

Whether a combination of two or more tactics is better than a single tactic depends on which tactics are combined. The potency of the individual tactics is a major determinant of effectiveness for an influence attempt involving more than one tactic. For example, the effectiveness of pressure is likely to be increased by combining it with rational persuasion but not by combining it with legitimating tactics (Falbe & Yukl, 1992). The effectiveness of a tactic combination may also depend on the extent to which the component tactics are compatible with each other. Compatible tactics are easy to use together and they enhance each other's effectiveness. Rational persuasion is a flexible tactic that is usually compatible with any of the other tactics. Some other tactics are clearly incompatible. For example, pressure tactics are likely to be incompatible with personal appeals or ingratiation because they weaken feelings of friendship and loyalty. Knowing how to successfully combine different influence tactics requires considerable insight and skill.

Pressure is a tactic that has serious limitations and side effects when used alone. However, pressure may facilitate the effectiveness of an influence attempt if combined with a softer tactic. Pressure is sometimes necessary to get the target person to take the agent seriously enough to even listen to the agent's rational proposal or to participate in joint problem-solving. In a survey study of police officers in Spain, Emans et al. (1999) showed that hard tactics such as pressure and legitimating increased behavioral compliance to some extent when combined with a high level of rational persuasion and exchange, or with a high level of consultation and inspirational appeals. However, there was not a significant enhancing effect of hard tactics when the criterion variable was attitudinal change by the target person. More research is needed to clarify the complex interaction among different types of tactics.

## RESEARCH ON DYADIC TACTICS USED TO INITIATE CHANGE

Only a small number of studies have examined the use of dyadic influence tactics to initiate or facilitate change in organizations. These studies will be reviewed briefly to see what insights they provide about the tactics that are most likely to be used and their relative effectiveness.

Schein (1987) interviewed managers in the United States and Great Britain to collect descriptive incidents about influence behavior used to initiate change. The incidents were content analyzed to identify distinct tactics. These tactics were included in a checklist administered to another sample of managers, who indicated which tactics were used more often in successful than in unsuccessful influence attempts with subordinates. Tactics significantly more likely to be successful included using data to convince others (strong rational persuasion), forming coalitions, working around roadblocks (probably collaboration), focusing on target needs (probably apprising), and being persistent (pressure). Using organizational rules (legitimating) was less likely to be successful, and there was no significant difference for offering favors or monetary rewards (exchange).

Bennebroek Gravenhorst and Boonstra (1998) conducted a survey study in 14 medium-sized Dutch organizations. The sample included line managers, staff specialists, consultants, and works council members in each organization. Respondents indicated how often they used each of nine influence tactics in attempts to implement change in their organization. The tactics used most often included rational persuasion, consultation, and inspirational appeals. There were few significant differences for the four types of respondents.

Some descriptive studies have used interviews to investigate how innovations are facilitated in large organizations (e.g., Schön, 1963; Burgelman, 1983; Kanter, 1983). This research suggests that a variety of influence tactics are used by the proponents of innovations. Although the focus in this research was not on identifying effective proactive tactics, it provides indirect support for the relevance of tactics such as rational persuasion, inspirational appeals, pressure, and coalitions.

Howell and Higgins (1990) conducted a study of influence tactics used by managers who were identified as change champions. Interviews revealed that the change champions used a greater variety of influence tactics than managers not identified as change champions. The change champions used more rational persuasion, coalition, pressure, and upward appeals. The champions were also more

**TABLE 14.1** Perceived effectiveness of proactive tactics to influence a boss to support or approve a proposed change

| Influence tactic | Effectiveness |
| --- | --- |
| Rational persuasion | 4.4 |
| Inspirational appeals | 3.7 |
| Collaboration | 3.7 |
| Consultation | 3.3 |
| Apprising | 3.2 |
| Coalition | 3.0 |
| Ingratiation | 2.6 |
| Pressure | 2.2 |
| Exchange | 2.0 |
| Personal appeal | 1.8 |

*Note*: Based on ratings of tactic effectiveness on a 5-point (1–5) scale by 166 American managers.

likely to express strong conviction about ideological goals, which indicates greater use of inspirational appeals. Use of ingratiation and exchange did not differentiate between champions and non-champions.

Yukl et al. (2003) used fixed-response scenarios to determine which tactics are viewed as most effective for influencing a superior to approve a proposed change. The study included managers from China and Switzerland as well as the United States. Although cross-cultural differences were found for many of the tactics, the relative ranking of proactive influence tactics were moderately similar across countries. Table 14.1 shows the mean rating of tactic effectiveness for the American managers. The most effective tactics included rational persuasion, consultation, collaboration, inspirational appeals, and use of coalition partners. Supplementary research with open-ended versions of the scenarios suggests that a combination of different tactics is considered more effective than a single tactic.

It is difficult to draw any conclusions from this diverse set of studies. Some studies tried to identify which tactics are used most often to initiate change, and other studies assessed the relative effectiveness of specific tactics. The studies used different research methods (e.g., survey questionnaires, scenarios, critical incidents, case study), and each study included a somewhat different set of influence tactics. In general, the findings suggest that a variety of different tactics are used for influencing change, that these tactics are typically used in various combinations rather than alone, and that some tactics (or combinations) are more effective than others. The findings suggest that the most effective tactics for initiating change in organizations may be the same ones found to be effective for other types of influence objectives, namely rational persuasion, consultation, inspirational appeals, and collaboration. However, the findings also suggest that successful attempts to initiate change in organizations may include the use of some tactics that are not effective for more routine types of influence attempts (e.g., pressure, coalition, upward appeal). To confirm these preliminary insights and find more definitive answers will require further research.

## LIMITING CONDITIONS FOR INFLUENCING CHANGE

As noted earlier, the success of an attempt to initiate change depends on a number of factors in addition to influence tactics that are used. Characteristics of the agent, the target persons, and the situation can limit or enhance the effectiveness of an influence attempt. Relevant conditions for change-oriented influence attempts include ambiguity about the need for change, vested interests in avoiding change, the perceived expertise and credibility of the agent, the agent's authority, the agent's access to resources, and the agent's political power. Each condition will be described briefly in this section of the chapter.

## Ambiguity about Need for Change

It is easier to initiate major change when there is an obvious crisis and people already realize that the current strategy or practices are no longer adequate to accomplish the unit's task objectives or mission. If the organization is prosperous and conditions are only gradually worsening, it is easy to deny the need for major change. Even when people acknowledge that change will eventually be necessary, they are often inclined to put it off as long as possible. In the absence of a widespread feeling of urgency, it is difficult to overcome the forces that support continuation of the current practices. Thus, it is not surprising that creating a sense of urgency is a recommended action for change agents in theories of change management (e.g., Kotter, 1996).

## Vested Interests

It is more difficult to introduce change when there are powerful people in the organization who oppose the change because they perceive that it would have adverse consequences. Even when a change is beneficial for the organization, it is likely to have adverse consequences for some individual members, which can increase resistance. Change makes some expertise obsolete, and it requires learning new ways of doing the work. Shifts in power and status are likely, as some functions and types of expertise become less important. People who lack self-confidence and fear that they will become obsolete are likely to resist change. To convert probable opponents into converts (or at least to counter their negative influence), it is essential to identify them as early as possible and to discover the reason for their resistance.

## Perceived Expertise and Credibility

Agent expertise and credibility are relevant conditions for enhancing the effectiveness of influence attempts made by the agent. Howell and Higgins (1990) found that successful champions had more varied experience and greater previous involvement in innovations, which suggests that they had greater expertise and credibility. Agent expertise and credibility seem especially relevant for the effective use of rational persuasion. Relevant knowledge is necessary to explain why a request is important and feasible. Moreover, a rational appeal is likely to be more effective when made by someone who is perceived to have high expertise. Along with facts and logic, a rational appeal usually includes some assertions, inferences, and predictions that cannot be verified because the evidence is not available at that time. Thus, the success of the influence attempt will depend in part on whether the agent is seen as a credible and trustworthy source of opinions and inferences.

## Authority

The authority of a manager can facilitate efforts to implement changes decided at the manager's level. Clear authority to make changes provides legitimacy for directives, which is likely to result in subordinate compliance. A manager's authority is usually backed up by other aspects of position power, including control over assignments, compensation, and dismissal. This power can be used to provide pressure on anyone who fails to implement the change. A case study by Poole et al. (1989) found that implementation of major changes in a bank were influenced more by pressure tactics (demands, threats, close monitoring) than by oral and written messages explaining the need for change (rational persuasion). Of course, pressure by itself is unlikely to elicit subordinate commitment (Falbe & Yukl, 1992).

## ACCESS TO RESOURCES

To implement major change effectively usually requires access to tangible resources. Resources are needed to cover the cost of acquiring new equipment, training personnel, and paying for the performance decrement that typically occurs when people must learn to do things efficiently in a new way. The feasibility of a proposed change depends in part on the agent's access to the necessary resources. Control over resources also provides currency for trading with peers whose support and cooperation are needed to implement the change. Resources can be used to provide an incentive for people who might otherwise have little concern about the success or failure of a proposed change (Cohen & Bradford, 1991).

## POLITICAL POWER

Major change in an organization usually requires an authorizing decision by powerful executives or decision groups. Such decisions are often controversial, especially when there is considerable disagreement about the best course of action for the organization. Change agents who have political power and skill are more likely to be successful in initiating and facilitating major changes in large organizations (Pfeffer, 1981; Porter et al., 1981; Kotter, 1985). However, political power can be used to oppose as well as to support change.

Political power to influence change can take a variety of forms. It is very helpful to have sympathetic representatives in key administrative positions or on decision groups. Such representatives can increase the likelihood that a change proposal will be reviewed favorably. It is easier to influence decisions about change if the agent (or allies) can establish the criteria used to evaluate alternative proposals. The criteria can be biased in favor of the proposal offered by the agent. Exclusive access to information about costs and benefits is another source of influence. The information can be selectively disseminated to bias change decisions.

# GUIDELINES FOR USING TACTICS TO INFLUENCE CHANGE

This final section of the chapter provides specific guidelines for using six specific influence tactics to influence commitment to change. The guidelines are based on leadership theory, practitioner insights, and findings in the limited research on dyadic influence. The guidelines are made without specification of the direction of influence or other factors that may enhance or limit use of the tactic. These factors should be considered carefully when attempting to use the guidelines, because they may be more relevant for some situations than for others. Additional guidelines about influencing people in organizations and specific examples of successful influence can be found in a number of books written for practitioners (Kotter, 1985; Cohen & Bradford, 1991; Haass, 1994; Conger, 1998).

## RATIONAL PERSUASION

Rational appeals involve logical arguments and factual evidence that a request or proposed change is important for the organization and feasible for the target person. The following guidelines explain how a change agent can increase the effectiveness of rational persuasion:

- *Explain the urgent need for change.* To mobilize support for proposed changes, it is essential to explain why it is necessary and to create a sense of urgency about it. If evidence about the problem (or opportunity) can be obtained, it can be used to strengthen rational appeals about the need for change. Some examples include a summary of customer complaints each week with selective quotes from irate customers, analyses of costs involved in correcting quality problems, and data showing that the unit is falling behind competitors on key indicators of performance.

- *Explain the benefits of the proposed change.* People are more likely to support a proposed change if they understand the reason why it is necessary and important. When asked to do something unusual, people may wonder whether it is really necessary or just an impulsive whim. Explain how a proposed change will benefit the team or organization. Examples of these benefits include reduced costs, higher efficiency, more customer satisfaction, improved product quality, higher sales, and larger profits.

- *Provide evidence that the proposed change is feasible.* It is not enough for a change proposal to be relevant, it must also be seen as practical and realistic to gain the person's enthusiastic support and cooperation. The target person may exaggerate the difficulties or obstacles. If the person has doubts about the feasibility of a request or proposal, provide supporting evidence for it. Explain the underlying theoretical rationale for assuming that a proposed plan of action will lead to the desired objective. Describe a specific sequence of action steps that could be used to accomplish the objective. Cite supporting evidence from empirical research (e.g., a pilot study, a survey showing a favorable response to a proposed new product, service, or change). Describe how a similar approach was successful when used in the past. If appropriate, provide an actual demonstration for the person to observe (seeing is believing).

- *Explain why the proposal is better than competing ones.* Sometimes a change proposal is competing with other proposals for the target person's support. In this case, it is not only necessary to show that your proposal is feasible, but also to show that it is better than any of the alternatives. Point out the advantages of your proposal in comparison to the alternatives (e.g., more likely to accomplish the objective, less costly, more likely to be approved, easier to implement, less risk of undesirable side effects). Point out the weaknesses and problems with each competing proposal. Your comparison will be more credible if you also acknowledge some advantages of competing proposals rather than ignoring them altogether, especially if the person is already aware of these advantages. If feasible, cite evidence from a test of the competing proposals to show that yours is better.

- *Explain how likely problems or concerns would be handled.* All proposals and plans have weaknesses and limitations. A proposal is more likely to be accepted if you anticipate any obvious limitations and find ways to deal with them. Explain how you would avoid potential problems, overcome likely obstacles, and minimize risks. If the person expresses any unanticipated concerns about your proposal, discuss ways to deal with these concerns as well, rather than ignoring them or dismissing them as unworthy of consideration.

## INSPIRATIONAL APPEALS

An inspirational appeal is an attempt to develop enthusiasm and commitment by appealing to the person's emotions and values. The following guidelines explain how a change agent can increase the effectiveness of inspirational appeals:

- *Appeal to the person's ideals and values.* Most people aspire to be important, to feel useful, to accomplish something worthwhile, to make an important contribution, to perform an exceptional feat, to be a member of the best team, or to participate in an exciting effort to make things better. These aspirations are a good basis for inspirational appeals. For example, the task of developing a new type of software may be likened to the role of a missionary who is going to revolutionize the way computers are used in society. Some values and ideals that may be used as the basis for an inspirational appeal include liberty, freedom, justice, fairness, equality, humanitarianism, love, loyalty, excellence, truth, and progress.

- *Link the request to the person's self-image.* A proposed activity or assignment may be linked to values that are central to the target person's self-image as a professional, a member of an organization, an adherent of a particular religion, or a member of a political party. For example, most scientists have strong values about the discovery of new knowledge and its application to improve humanity; most physicians and nurses have strong values about healing people and keeping them healthy. A proposed change or activity may be described as something that will advance new knowledge, improve health care, make the organization more effective, advance the cause, serve one's god, or demonstrate patriotism to one's country.

- *Link the request to a clear and appealing vision.* Efforts to introduce major changes or innovations are more likely to be successful when they involve an appealing vision of what could be accomplished or how the future could look if the proposed activity or change is implemented successfully. The vision may be an existing one the target person is known to embrace, or one created to help gain commitment to a new project or activity. The vision should emphasize ideological values rather than tangible economic benefits (used in rational appeals to self-interest). However, it is not necessary to ignore economic benefits; they may be integrated into the overall vision of what can be accomplished as long as it is clear that they are not the primary objective.

- *Use a dramatic, expressive style of speaking.* A dramatic, expressive style of speaking often increases the effectiveness of an emotional appeal. Conviction and intensity of feeling are communicated by one's voice (e.g., tone, inflection, pause), facial expressions, gestures, and body movement. Use a strong, clear tone of voice, but vary the pace and intensity. Use pauses at appropriate times to emphasize key words, maintain interest, and arouse excitement. Maintain strong eye contact, use strong gestures, and move around to display energy and intensity of feeling. Use rhyme, rhythm, and repetition of key words or phrases to emphasize the important ideas and build strong feelings.

- *Use positive, optimistic language.* Confidence and optimism about a new project or change can be contagious. It is especially important to foster optimism when the task is very difficult and people lack self-confidence. State your personal belief in the project and your strong commitment to see it through to a successful conclusion. Use positive language that communicates you are confident a proposed project or change will be successful. For example, talk about the wonderful things that 'will' happen when a change is made, rather than what 'may' happen.

- *Use colorful, emotional language.* The ideological aspects of an inspirational appeal can be communicated more effectively with language that includes vivid imagery, metaphors, anecdotes, and stories. Metaphors and analogies are especially effective when they excite the imagination and engage the listener in trying to make sense out of them. Anecdotes and stories are more effective if they invoke symbols with deep cultural roots, such as legendary heroes, sacred figures, and historical ordeals and triumphs. However, the forms of language selected for an inspirational appeal must be relevant or they will result in confusion and distraction rather than clearly linking the proposed change to listener values and beliefs.

## CONSULTATION

Consultation increases the target person's motivation to carry out a request by allowing the person to participate in determining how it will be done. The following guidelines explain how a change agent can increase the effectiveness of consultation:

- *Ask for suggestions to improve a tentative proposal.* More participation is likely if you present a proposal as tentative and encourage people to improve it, rather than asking people to react to an elaborate plan that appears complete. People will be less inhibited about expressing concerns for a proposal that appears to be in the development stage rather than complete. The agent and target person should jointly explore ways to deal with any serious concerns or incorporate promising suggestions. A stronger version of this tactic is to ask the target person to write the initial draft of a proposal that you want him or her to support. Of course, this procedure is only feasible if the person agrees with you about the objective and has the expertise to develop a credible plan.

- *State your objective and ask how the person can help.* When you do not expect the target person to be enthusiastic about helping you accomplish an objective, it is helpful to explain why it is important (rational persuasion), then ask the person what he or she can do to help you attain it. If you have a good relationship, the target person is likely to suggest some ways to be of assistance. Show appreciation for any suggestions and explore their feasibility. Once the person has agreed to provide some assistance, it is easier to ask for additional things that build on the initial offer.

- *Involve the person in planning how to attain an objective.* In this variation of consultation, you present a general strategy, policy, or objective and ask the target person to suggest specific action steps for implementing it. If the action plan will be detailed, it is best to schedule a meeting at a later time to review the plan and reach a mutual agreement about it. This tactic is especially useful for assigning responsibilities to a subordinate to implement some aspect of a new project or change.

- *Respond to the person's concerns and suggestions.* Consultation is used mostly as a proactive influence tactic, but opportunities arise to use it also as a reactive tactic. Sometimes when asking the target person to carry out an assignment or provide assistance on a task, the person expresses concerns about it or suggestions for improving it. Whenever feasible, try to deal with the target person's concerns, even if it requires some modification of your initial plans. Ask the person for suggestions about how to deal with concerns. Good suggestions for improving an activity should be utilized whenever feasible.

## COLLABORATION

Collaboration involves offering something that will make a proposed change less costly for the target person to approve or implement. The following guidelines explain how a change agent can increase the effectiveness of collaboration:

- *Offer to help the person implement a change.* One reason for opposing a proposed change is that it will entail a substantial investment of time and effort by the target person. If the costs and difficulties for the target person can be identified in advance, you can look for ways to avoid or minimize them. When asking a peer or boss to approve a proposed change, offer to help with the implementation. When asking a peer or subordinate to support a proposed change, offer to help the person implement it.

- *Offer to provide resources needed to do the task.* Additional resources are usually needed to implement a change. As noted earlier, lack of sufficient resources to pay for the change is a major reason for opposition to it by the people who must implement it. Thus, to build support for a proposed change, offer to provide or help obtain the necessary resources.

- *Offer to help solve problems that will be created by carrying out the request.* A request is more likely to be resisted if carrying it out will cause serious new problems for the target person. Try to anticipate such problems and be prepared to offer ways to avoid them or help the person deal with them. In many cases the agent will not be aware of the problems caused by a request, but target concerns can be elicited with the skillful use of consultation and active listening by the agent.

## APPRISING

Apprising involves explanations about ways the change is likely to benefit the target person. If the target person is a member of the same organization, the focus of apprising is on potential benefits for the target person as an individual rather than on benefits for the organization. If the target person is not a member of the same organization, apprising may also involve potential benefits for constituents represented by the target person if attaining these benefits is important to the person. The following guidelines explain how a change agent can increase the effectiveness of apprising:

- *Explain how the change would help the person's career.* Explain how the proposed change will benefit the target person in terms of personal development and career advancement. Potential benefits include an opportunity to learn new skills, an opportunity to earn more money, and an opportunity to advance one's career by meeting important people, demonstrating competence, and gaining visibility.

- *Explain how the change will make the person's job easier or more enjoyable.* Another potential benefit of a proposed change is to make the person's job easier to do by reducing unnecessary tasks, solving recurring problems, providing more timely and accurate information, and removing obstacles and unnecessary controls. The change may also involve doing things that are interesting and enjoyable for the person. Explain how the change will result in these benefits for the target person.

- *Explain the benefits for an external target's constituents.* When the target person represents a different organization (e.g., client, supplier, labor union, government agency, political party) and is sincerely concerned about constituents, then it is appropriate to explain how a proposed change is likely to benefit the target person's organization or increase tangible benefits for the target person's constituents.

## COALITION TACTICS

Coalition tactics involve other people in an influence attempt, either directly or indirectly. This tactic can take a variety of forms, and guidelines are presented for using them:

- *Mention credible people who support your proposal.* One type of coalition tactic is to mention the names of others who support your proposal or request. The endorsers should be credible people whom the target person respects so that their endorsement is likely to have some influence. If you anticipate that endorsements are needed, it is best to get them before you begin the influence attempt with the target person.

- *Bring someone along to help you in an influence attempt.* Another form of coalition is to bring along somebody whom the target person respects when you make an influence attempt. This tactic is appropriate for an unusual request or proposal made to a target person who is expected to be reluctant about complying with the request or supporting the proposal. It is usually more effective to have an ally join you to actually help with an influence attempt than to merely mention the person's name as an endorser of your request or proposal. A variation of this approach is to arrange a group meeting that includes one or more target persons that you want to influence and one or more allies who are prepared to actively support your proposals.

- *Get other people to provide evidence or an endorsement.* Another coalition tactic is to enlist the aid of other people whom the target person likes and respects. The coalition partners may provide supporting evidence, or they may take a more active role and attempt to influence the target person by using influence tactics. Sometimes it is useful to have coalition partners 'soften up' the target person prior to your influence attempt. For example, when you want to suggest a change to a peer in another functional area, it is useful to have credible allies in that same function prepare the peer to be more receptive to your proposal. A coalition partner can verify you are competent and trustworthy before you attempt to influence a target person who does not know you very well. Before proposing a controversial change, it may be desirable to have someone who is influential 'set the stage' for your proposal by explaining why there is need for a change.

- *Ask for help from someone with higher authority.* An 'upward appeal' is to ask someone in higher authority to tell the target person to comply with your request. For example, if a peer is reluctant to carry out a request, you can ask the boss of the peer for assistance. Likewise, if your boss refuses to comply with a request, you can appeal to higher management. This tactic is very risky, because the target person usually views it as coercive and may resent it enough to resist, despite the increased pressure for compliance. Upward appeals should be used only as a last resort for influence attempts with a peer or boss who refuses to comply with a request that is clearly legitimate and very important to you.

## FUTURE RESEARCH

To implement a major change often requires the support and cooperation of many people in the organization as well as outsiders. Managers use a variety of influence tactics to initiate change, and some progress has been made in identifying the most useful tactics. However, the amount of research is still very limited, and only tentative conclusions can be reached.

To make further progress will require more research, and some of this research must employ stronger research methods. Moreover, it is essential in future research to take more of a systems perspective on influencing change in organizations. We will not be able to really understand how managers initiate and facilitate change without some intensive, longitudinal studies of the influence processes. In addition to specific influence tactics (used alone and in combinations), researchers should measure contextual variables that are likely to limit or facilitate an influence attempt. Finally, researchers should consider not only the proactive influence behavior of a single agent toward a single target, but also the reciprocal influence processes that invariably occur over time among the multiple parties (including other proponents and opponents) who jointly determine the success of an attempt to initiate major change in an organization.

## REFERENCES

Barry, B. & Bateman, T.S. (1992) Perceptions of influence in managerial dyads: the role of hierarchy, media, and tactics. *Human Relations*, **45**, 555–574.

Barry, B. & Shapiro, D.L. (1992) Influence tactics in combination: the interactive effects of soft versus hard tactics and rational exchange. *Journal of Applied Social Psychology*, **22**, 1429–1441.

Bennebroek Gravenhorst, K.M. & Boonstra, J.J. (1998) The use of influence tactics in constructive change processes. *European Journal of Work and Organizational Psychology*, **7**, 179–196.

Burgelman, R.A. (1983) A process model of internal corporate venturing in the diversified major firm. *Administrative Science Quarterly*, **8**, 223–244.

Case, T., Dosier, L., Murkinson, G. & Keys, B. (1988) How managers influence superiors: a study of upward influence tactics. *Leadership and Organizational Development Journal*, **9**(4), 25–31.

Cohen, A.R. & Bradford, D.L. (1991) *Influence Without Authority*. New York: John Wiley & Sons, Ltd.

Conger, J. (1998) *Winning 'em Over: The New Model for Management in the Age of Persuasion*. New York: Simon & Schuster.

Emans, B., Klaver, E., Munduate, L. & Van de Vliert, E. (1999) Constructive consequences of hard power use by leaders in organizations. Paper presented at the European Congress on Work and Organizational Psychology, May, Espoo-Helsinki, Finland.

Erez, M., Rim, Y. & Keider, I. (1986) The two sides of the tactics of influence: agent vs. target. *Journal of Occupational Psychology*, **59**, 25–39.

Fairhurst, G.T. & Saar, R.A. (1996) *The Art of Framing: Managing the Language of Leadership*. San Francisco: Jossey-Bass.

Falbe, C.M. & Yukl, G. (1992) Consequences for managers of using single influence tactics and combinations of tactics. *Academy of Management Journal*, **35**, 638–653.

Haass, R.N. (1994) *The Power to Persuade: How to be Effective in any Unruly Organization*. Boston: Houghton Mifflin.

Howell, J.M. & Higgins, C.A. (1990) Leadership behaviors, influence tactics, and career experiences of champions of technological innovation. *Leadership Quarterly*, **1**, 249–264.

Kanter, R.M. (1983) *The Change Masters*. New York: Simon & Schuster.

Kipnis, D., Schmidt, S.M. & Wilkinson, I. (1980) Intra-organizational influence tactics: explorations in getting one's way. *Journal of Applied Psychology*, **65**, 440–452.

Kotter, J.P. (1985) *Power and Influence: Beyond Formal Authority*. New York: The Free Press.

Kotter, J.P. (1996) *Leading Change*. Boston: Harvard Business School Press.

Pfeffer, J. (1981) *Power in Organizations*. Marshfield, MA: Pitman.

Poole, P.P., Gioia, D.A. & Gray, B. (1989) Influence modes, schema change, and organizational transformation. *Journal of Applied Behavioral Science*, **25**, 271–289.

Porter, L.W., Allen, R.W. & Angle, H.L. (1981) The politics of upward influence in organizations. In L.L. Cummings & B.M. Staw (eds) *Research in Organizational Behavior* (vol. 3). Greenwich, CT: JAI Press.

Roberts, E.B. (1968) A basic study of innovators: how to keep and capitalize on their talents. *Research Management*, **11**, 249–266.

Schein, V.E. (1987) Strategies used by US and UK managers in external relationships. *Best Papers Proceedings, Annual Meeting of the Academy of Management* (pp. 220–223). New Orleans, LA.

Schilit, W.K. & Locke, E.A. (1982) A study of upward influence in organizations. *Administrative Science Quarterly*, **27**, 304–316.

Schön, D.A. (1963) Champions for radical new inventions. *Harvard Business Review*, **41**, 77–86.

Schriesheim, C.A. & Hinkin, T.R. (1990) Influence tactics used by subordinates: a theoretical and empirical analysis and refinement of the Kipnis, Schmidt, and Wilkinson subscales. *Journal of Applied Psychology*, **75**, 246–257.

Vroom, V.H. & Yetton, P.W. (1973) *Leadership and Decision Making*. Pittsburgh, PA: University of Pittsburgh Press.

Yukl, G. (2002) *Leadership in Organizations* (5th edn). Upper Saddle River, NJ: Prentice Hall.

Yukl, G. & Falbe, C.M. (1990) Influence tactics in upward, downward and lateral influence attempts. *Journal of Applied Psychology*, **75**, 132–140.

Yukl, G. & Tracey, B. (1992) Consequences of influence tactics used with subordinates, peers, and the boss. *Journal of Applied Psychology*, **77**, 525–535.

Yukl, G., Falbe, C.M. & Youn, J.Y. (1993) Patterns of influence behavior for managers. *Group and Organization Management*, **18**, 5–28.

Yukl, G., Fu, P.P. & McDonald, R. (2003) Cross-cultural differences in perceived effectiveness of influence tactics for initiating or resisting change. *Applied Psychology: An International Review*, **52**, 68–82.

Yukl, G., Guinan, P.J. & Sottolano, D. (1995) Influence tactics used for different objectives with subordinates, peers, and superiors. *Group and Organization Management*, **20**, 272–296.

Yukl, G., Kim, H. & Chavez, C. (1999) Task importance, feasibility, and agent influence behavior as determinants of target commitment. *Journal of Applied Psychology*, **84**, 137–143.

Yukl, G., Kim, H. & Falbe, C.M. (1996) Antecedents of influence outcomes. *Journal of Applied Psychology*, **81**, 309–317.

# CHAPTER 15

# Power and Collaboration
## Methodologies for Working Together in Change

**Kilian Bennebroek Gravenhorst**
*University of Amsterdam, Amsterdam, The Netherlands*
**Roeland in 't Veld**
*Netherlands School of Government, the Hague, The Netherlands*

Realizing major organizational change and innovation requires a complex process. Both research and experience indicate that many change processes lead to results other than were intended, take more time than was estimated, end prematurely, and sometimes fail altogether. In the Introduction to this book, Boonstra discusses why many change programmes fail. In Chapter 4, Buelens and Devos explain that low change effectiveness is often related to the chosen change strategy. Beer et al. (1990a) found that in one-third of the cases they studied, the intensive change initiatives actually worsened the situation instead of improving it. Porras and Robertson (1983) conclude from a meta-analysis that fewer than 40 per cent of change efforts produced positive effects on the relevant dependent variables. Kanter et al. put it like this, 'Change is extraordinarily difficult, and the fact that it occurs successfully at all is something of a miracle' (1992: 370).

This would not be a problem if only a few organizations initiated a change process every so often. However, change tends to be the stable state of the contemporary organization (French & Bell, 1995; Weick & Quinn, 1999). People have to deal continuously with changes like mergers, strategic change, privatization, and redesign of business processes. Such fundamental or second-order changes (Levy & Merry, 1986) take place on multiple levels in the organization, are multi-dimensional, and involve multiple stakeholders. Realizing this kind of change requires efforts from top managers, middle managers, and employees; from production departments, sales departments, finance departments, personnel departments, and other staff units. From a power point of view, these groups have different interests and usually fulfil different positions and roles in changing organizations (Mintzberg, 1983; Kanter et al., 1992; Pfeffer, 1992).

In this chapter, we present four methodologies that allow people to interact and cooperate in changing their organizations. To have multiple stakeholders working together in realizing change requires a process-oriented and interactive approach to change. Lack of attention to the processual character of change is an important reason for problematic change and contributes to resistance by stakeholders and interest groups (Buelens & Devos, Chapter 4). We start this chapter by sketching a theoretical background for our process orientation to change, for the view on resistance we advocate, and for our way of using organization-wide change methodologies. This background enables the reader to understand the principles of the four methodologies we describe.

In the second section of this chapter, we describe four explanations for the lack of effectiveness of many change processes. We argue that thoroughly understanding the dynamic nature and

*Dynamics of Organizational Change and Learning.* Edited by J.J. Boonstra.
© 2004 John Wiley & Sons, Ltd. ISBN 0-471-87737-9.

complexity of change processes requires a focus on the interconnectedness of problems and the inclusion of different perspectives. At the end of this section, we introduce our focus on process-oriented change.

In the third section, we discuss resistance to change. A literature review results in a number of definitions of the phenomenon, its manifestations, and its causes. In psychological and management literature, resistance to change is usually described as a standard reaction resulting from a desire for stability. The general idea seems to be that organizational change causes resistance from change targets and that change agents need to overcome this resistance to change. We propose an alternative view on resistance. In this view, resistance is seen as a *response* to the change approach or to the actions of change managers that exclude relevant stakeholders. Thus, resistance can be prevented by making change a *collaborative effort* of all stakeholders.

In the fourth section, we present four methodologies that allow different stakeholders to interact and work together as *partners* in realizing change. In Wierdsma's terms (see Chapter 11), these methodologies are suitable for co-creating change. They can be used at the start of or during what he calls a journey (or 'trek') of stakeholders who fulfil an active role in shaping the future of their organization. Survey feedback, large group interventions, process management, and third-party intervention are quite well known among academics and practitioners. However, discussing these change methodologies in the context of power dynamics and organizational change is new. We introduce each methodology, show its relation to process-oriented changing, and explain why its use either prevents the build-up of resistance or how it may ameliorate conflict situations. Case studies are provided to show how the methodologies work in practice. In these examples, we focus on the collaborative nature of the change process and the way in which the methodologies stimulate interaction between and cooperation of different stakeholders. The examples illustrate the theory and can assist practitioners in making a deliberate choice of change methodology, designing it, and using it.

In the fifth section, we start with concluding remarks about the change methodologies, process-oriented changing and fundamental change, and the issue of resistance. Next, we discuss practical implications for change managers and consultants who face resistance and who plan to use the methodologies.

## WHY CHANGE IN ORGANIZATIONS PROGRESSES WITH DIFFICULTY

We distinguish four explanations for the lack of effectiveness of many change processes (see Figure 15.1). Each of these explanations is discussed in this section. The mirror image of the reasons points to an alternative way of realizing change in organizations. At the end of this section, we comment on our preference for process-oriented changing.

The first reason for the difficult progress of change processes in organizations is that both theorists and practitioners tend to focus on single issues when understanding or realizing change. In the past, many reasons have been identified that explain why change in organizations progresses with difficulty. However, these reasons are usually treated separately. Thus, people focus on either hierarchical relations, *or* organizational culture, *or* internal communication, *or* resistance from employees, thereby ignoring the complex nature of fundamental change processes. In the Introduction, Boonstra argues that obstacles during change can be understood by simultaneously addressing them as issues of policy-making and strategic management, existing organizational structures, power and politics in organizations, organizational cultures, and individual uncertainty and resistance to change. We rarely find such explanations, which focus on the interrelatedness of various aspects of an organization. In our view, paying attention to multiple causes of problems and the way they are connected helps to understand the complexity of change and offers a direction for solutions. In addition, it draws attention to the possibility that stakeholders can have different ideas about the reasons for problems (Bennebroek Gravenhorst & Boonstra, 1998).

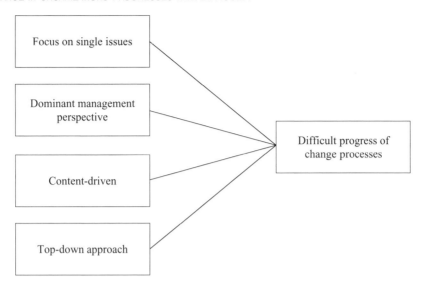

**FIGURE 15.1** Reasons for the difficult progress of fundamental change

The second reason for difficulties in change programmes is that the perspective of top managers usually dominates change processes in organizations. As change strategists they identify the need for change, create a vision of the desired outcome, decide what change is feasible, and choose who should sponsor and defend it (Kanter et al., 1992). Often, top managers hire consultants to assist them to plan and implement the change. Thus, consultants are tempted to take a similar point of view regarding the diagnosis of the situation and the direction of the change.

The third reason is that the content of the change and the solutions for problems are the focal point in many change processes. Most popular change programme like Total Quality Management and Business Process Redesign are primarily content-driven. The process of changing itself gets little attention. However, it is the actions, reactions, and interactions of the various stakeholders that produce content. Not paying attention to shaping the process, guiding it, and monitoring it creates the risk of good ideas getting lost on the way (Beer, 1988), if they are produced at all. Pettigrew (1987: 6) proposes that we pay attention to the continuous interplay of the context, the process, and the content of the change. Then we integrate the 'why', 'how', and 'what' of the change. Since attention to the process is relatively rare, we may be tempted to concentrate solely on this aspect of change. Therefore, it is important that 'process devotees' also pay attention to the reasons for change and ensure that alternative solutions are developed.

The fourth reason is that in general a top-down approach is applied. Recent case study research shows that top-down change approaches result in many barriers to change (Bennebroek Gravenhorst, 2002). Two major limitations of this approach are the dominant or central role of top managers and the strong focus on content. A change approach involving only one group has little chance of success (Kanter et al., 1992), especially if the change is complex and asks for a collaborative effort of top managers, middle managers, and employees. Beer et al. (1990b) point out that managing change requires an emphasis on process over specific content as well as the recognition that change means learning and development. The latter take time, and time is always limited in top-down quick fixes.

Process-oriented changing can deal with the four problems we outlined. Its primary focus is on the processual character of change, as the term suggests. This means that we pay specific attention to the 'how' of the change. Thus, at the outset of a change process, we ask such questions as 'How do we get from situation A to situation B?', 'How do we involve different stakeholders?', 'Which approach is suitable?', 'Which stages can we distinguish?', 'What are appropriate change methodologies?', and 'How do we monitor its course?' We prefer to discuss questions like these with relevant stakeholders in order to make the plan for change a joint product. In addition, we need to make sure that 'content' is not neglected. Thus, we prefer a broad diagnosis focusing on many issues that may be addressed in the change. This adds to the content to be dealt with in the change process. Content is produced by involving all stakeholders in the diagnosis and subsequent stages of the change. There are many ways of doing this, as will be shown later.

## RESISTANCE TO CHANGE

Resistance to change is a well-known subject in psychology and management literature. Kurt Lewin introduced the term resistance in his field theory and later work on group dynamics (Lewin, 1947). In the classical study by Coch and French (1948), resistance is connected to change in organizations. Coch and French do not provide a clear definition of the term resistance. In the section where they present their preliminary theory of resistance to change, they introduce it as primarily a motivational problem, which obstructs learning new skills required by a change (1948: 516). After analysing their initial results, they refine their theory when they describe resistance as 'a combination of an individual reaction to frustration with strong group-induced forces' (1948: 521).

Watson (1969) defines resistance as all the forces that contribute to stability in personality or in social systems. He adds that from the perspective of a consultant, these forces may seem an obstruction. Yet he continues by stating that 'From a broader and more inclusive perspective the tendencies to achieve, preserve, and to return to equilibrium are the most salutary' (1969: 488). Thus, he sees resistance to change as a natural reaction of individuals and social systems, originating from the need for a relatively stable situation.

Kotter and Schlesinger do not define resistance to change. They just state that 'one major task of managers is . . . to implement change and that entails overcoming resistance' (1979: 106). Elsewhere, they sketch a common scenario in change processes. In this scenario, a manager becomes aware of problems, initiates change, and finds that his or her initiative runs into resistance (Kotter et al., 1979: 379). For them, resistance seems to be an inevitable reaction to change.

The distinction between individual and organizational resistance is found in many contemporary management textbooks (Mullins, 1999). Mullins defines resistance as the forces against change in work organizations (1999: 824). He sees resistance as a common phenomenon, as people are naturally wary of change. After discussing sources of individual and organizational resistance, the section simply ends, as is the case in most textbooks.

We find a similar view in writings on change management (Conner, 1998). Conner states that resistance to change is a natural reaction of people to anything that significantly upsets their status quo (1998: 126). He explains that change disrupts our expectations and produces a loss of the psychological equilibrium we value. In his opinion, human inertia makes people cling to certainty and stability.

Resistance to change manifests itself in different ways. Coch and French (1948) mention grievances, turnover, low efficiency, restriction of output, and aggression against management. Watson (1969) discusses how expressions of resistance alter during a change process. In the early stage, almost everyone openly criticizes the change. In the second stage, innovators and opponents become identifiable. The third stage is marked by confrontation and conflict. In the fourth stage, innovators become powerful and opponents retreat to latent resistance. In the fifth stage, opponents become alienated from the organization. Kotter and Schlesinger (1979) mention that negative responses to change from individuals and groups can vary from passive resistance to aggressive attempts to undermine it. Mullins (1999) only mentions that resistance can take many forms. Conner (1998) distinguishes between covert and overt resistance. He does not discuss examples, but explains that it is important for managers to encourage overt expressions of resistance.

Many causes of resistance are listed in the selected publications. At the individual level, we find psychological factors such as resentment, frustration, fear, feelings of failure, and low motivation (Coch & French, 1948). Watson (1969) discusses preference for stability, habit, persistence, selective perception and retention, conservatism, tradition, self-distrust, and insecurity. Kotter and Schlesinger (1979) provide examples of what they see as the four most common reasons for resisting change: (a) people focus on their own interests and not on those of the organization as a whole; (b) misunderstanding of the change and its implications; (c) belief that the change does not make sense for the organization; and (d) low tolerance for change. Mullins (1999) discusses selective perception, habit, inconvenience or loss of freedom, economic implications, security in the past, and fear of the unknown. Conner (1998) mentions that loss of control is the most important cause of resistance.

A summary of this literature review of resistance results in the following sketch of the traditional view of the subject. Resistance is commonly considered to be the standard, and according to some authors, even a natural reaction of people to change in organizations. It is described as an almost inevitable psychological and organizational response that seems to apply to any kind of change, ranging from rather modest improvements to far-reaching change and organization transformation. Change and resistance seem to go hand in hand: change implies resistance and resistance means change is taking place. Expressions of resistance show that we are dealing with a serious issue. Aggression and turnover are reported as well as milder manifestations such as absenteeism and lower motivation. Resistance is caused by many different factors that are generally classified as individual psychological factors, on the one hand, and sometimes as organizational factors, on the other. A few authors also mention group factors. So we can distinguish between micro-, meso-, and macro-level causes of resistance. Recommendations for dealing with resistance are also provided, sometimes labelled as strategies or tactics. Before turning to these, we present an alternative way of looking at resistance.

In our view, a change approach that excludes relevant stakeholders is the major cause of resistance. This factor is not discussed in mainstream literature. In addition, the idea that resistance can be a purposeful action or reaction by change targets who require participation is not widespread either. Initially, we were surprised by the emphasis on, say, the limited change capacity of change targets. Since change management gets a lot of attention in the literature, one would expect to find more awareness of the importance of interaction between stakeholders. However, the dominance of the management perspective explains why this is not the case and that change is seen as a set of actions of change agents that lead to reactions by change targets. The standard view is that managers want to change and that employees do not. Hence, unsuccessful change is either the fault of employees, or the fault of the organizational system. We see resistance as resulting from a lack of interaction and cooperation between relevant stakeholders. More specifically, the main problem is the top-down and content-driven change approach that managers and consultants usually choose. Such an approach is logical if you believe you have to overcome resistance because other people do not want to change. We find this belief contestable and it does not match our experiences with change processes in which people cooperated successfully in realizing change.

Seeing management and employees as opposing parties is a negative effect of the dominant approach to resistance, as Dent and Goldberg (1999) explain. In addition, they argue that expecting resistance may lead to a self-fulfilling prophecy. However, we do not want to reverse the blame, and hold managers responsible for the resistance they encounter. Instead, we want to draw attention to change methodologies that aim to make change a collaborative and interactive effort instead of a struggle in which one party has to defeat another, for instance, by using power and coercion, or ineffective heavy influence tactics (Falbe & Yukl, 1992; Yukl, Chapter 14) such as pressure, legitimation, and coalition.

We encountered many instances where resistance was not a standard response to change. Bennebroek Gravenhorst et al. (2003) found that resistance to change only occurred in combination with badly designed and managed change processes. It is understandable that people do not want to put any effort into such processes. Still, in 60 of the 104 surveyed organizations involved in fundamental change processes, no resistance was found. Thus, we concluded that there was no support for the idea that

**TABLE 15.1**   Two views of resistance to change

| | Basic idea | Main cause | Evaluation | Political perspective | Solution |
|---|---|---|---|---|---|
| Traditional view | Inevitable and natural reaction to any change | Employees' insecurity and need for stability | Illegitimate behaviour directed against management | Management and employees are opposing parties | Informing and exerting pressure to comply to changes |
| Alternative view | Reaction that varies per change and can be prevented | Change approach that excludes employees from change | Understandable behaviour expressing concern for the organization and commitment | Management and employees are parties that can work together in realizing change | Making change a collaborative effort of all stakeholders |

resistance is a standard psychological reaction, or that it is caused by organizational factors such as bureaucracy, division of labour, and conservative culture. Bennebroek Gravenhorst (2002) concluded from six in-depth case studies that neither middle managers nor employees resisted change. Instead, their positive expectation of the outcome of the changes, together with their support for and commitment to the changes, were major success factors. The main focus of criticism in these cases was the top-down change approach that excludes everyone except the change agents.

In addition, if we encounter resistance, we prefer to specify the focus of this resistance. Change is too general a term. Dent and Goldberg (1999) argue that specifying the focus helps us abandon the mental model in which change implies resistance and managers must overcome it. People do not resist change *per se*. They may resist loss of their job as occurs in crises, and they may resist the negative influence of specific others as in conflict situations. Thus, in crises we need to speak of resistance to job losses, and in conflict situations we need to speak of resistance to person A or group B.

Fundamental change usually means doing things differently and better with the same people. Therefore, when we encounter resistance in such situations, we tend to believe we are dealing with resistance to a change approach that excludes relevant stakeholders. This leads to different actions from those that are logical if resistance is considered to be a result of individual conservatism or organizational inertia.

Table 15.1 summarizes the two opposing views on resistance. In the traditional view, resistance is a natural reaction to change resulting from individual and organizational forces directed at stability. At the same time resistance is seen as illegitimate behaviour, directed against management. Managers need to overcome resistance by informing people about the change and eventually pushing through what they want. An alternative view is to see resistance as a reaction to being excluded from the change process. Now, resistance is viewed as an expression of concern and an indication of bad change management. Managers can then prevent resistance by choosing a change approach that allows for cooperation and involvement of the relevant stakeholders. Such an approach contributes to commitment and true change of members of an organization instead of compliance with power (Munduate & Bennebroek Gravenhorst, 2003).

Finally, we present an overview of the recommended strategies for dealing with resistance and contrast them with process-oriented changing. Not surprisingly, most strategies are directed at managers since in the traditional view it is their job to overcome resistance. The general idea is that a sense of ownership, clear benefits, and participation reduce resistance. Kotter and Schlesinger (1979) discuss six strategies managers use for dealing with resistance (see Table 15.2). Conner (1998) proposes the following five-step strategy: (1) understand the basis mechanisms of human resistance; (2) view

**TABLE 15.2** Strategies for dealing with resistance to change

| Approach | Commonly used in situations | Advantages | Drawbacks |
|---|---|---|---|
| Education and communication | Where there is a lack of information or inaccurate information and analysis | Once persuaded, people will often help with the implementation of the change | Can be very time-consuming if lots of people are involved |
| Participation and involvement | Where the initiators do not have all the information they need to design the change, and where others have considerable power to resist | People who participate will be committed to implementing change, and any relevant information they have will be integrated into the change plan | Can be very time-consuming if participators design an inappropriate change |
| Facilitation and support | Where people are resisting because of adjustment problems | No other approach works with adjustment problems as well | Can be time-consuming, expensive, and still fail |
| Negotiation and agreement | Where someone or some group will clearly lose out in a change, and where that group has considerable power to resist | Sometimes it is a relatively easy way to avoid major resistance | Can be too expensive in many cases if it alters others to negotiate for compliance |
| Manipulation and co-optation | Where other tactics will not work, or are too expensive | It can be a relatively quick and inexpensive solution to resistance problems | Can lead to future problems if people feel manipulated |
| Explicit and implicit coercion | Where speed is essential, and the change initiators possess considerable power | It is speedy, and can overcome any kind of resistance | Can be risky if it leaves people mad at the initiators |

*Source*: Reproduced, with permission, from Kotter, J.P. and Schlesinger, L.A. (1979) Choosing strategies for change. *Harvard Business Review*, **57**, 111. Harvard Business Publishing Corporation.

resistance as a natural and inevitable reaction to change; (3) view resistance as a lack of ability or willingness; (4) encourage overt expressions of resistance; and (5) anticipate, follow, and manage its sequence of events.

Table 15.2 shows that Kotter and Schlesinger's six strategies include most of the recommendations of the other authors. In addition, they propose two hard strategies, probably because they derived their list from what they see managers do in practice. The primary reason we include this table is that it nicely illustrates the first view of managers having to overcome or break resistance to change of employees by using strategies. Surprisingly, Kotter and Schlesinger qualify the time-consuming aspect of the two pseudo-developmental strategies they mention as an important drawback. We do not share this view. Quick fixes do not lead to change (Beer et al. 1990b). Change takes time, as do efforts to truly involve different stakeholders in the process. So if a change methodology is time-consuming, we tend to believe it may well be one of the few instances where real change is actually taking place.

We wonder why the common-sense notion of making change a collaborative and interactive effort from the start is only relatively rarely practised. This approach seems logical because it makes use of the available potential in an organization and people's wish to contribute to improvement. In various situations, we experienced that such an approach prevents the build-up of resistance. Therefore, we value process-oriented changing because it allows for involvement of all the parties, facilitation of the exchange ideas and opinions, and people realizing change together. By involving all parties and having stakeholders work together, resistance is prevented because interest groups are not treated as adversaries but as partners in change. Thus, we have to design change processes in such a way that stakeholders work together, instead of against each other.

## METHODOLOGIES FOR CO-CREATING CHANGE

In this section, we present four comprehensive change methodologies that facilitate interaction between different stakeholders or interest groups in organizations. Most of these methodologies are quite well covered in contemporary organizational psychology and management literature. Practitioners, especially in the field of organization development (OD), are familiar with them. Usually, these methodologies are treated as interventions that can be used by change agents to get change targets to change or to involve them in the change process. Discussing these methodologies in the context of power dynamics and change is new. Our aim here is to explain how the four methodologies can be used to expose the viewpoints of stakeholders, to stimulate exchange of these viewpoints, to deal with differences, to initiate learning processes, and to make the change process a collective effort of all the people involved.

### SURVEY FEEDBACK

The two main elements of survey feedback are (1) systematically collecting data about the situation in an organization by using questionnaires; and (2) feeding back the data to individuals and groups at all levels of the organization (French & Bell, 1995). Contrary to the common use of surveys in organizations (Fowler, 1984), survey feedback is 'an active two-way process of information acquisition and knowledge dissemination, with the explicit purpose of serving as a basis for action by the surveyed population itself' (Kuhnert, 1993: 459). Thus, collected data form the basis of the change methodology. Then, all stakeholders work together in analysing and interpreting the meaning of these data, and they develop ideas for solutions of problems and improvement of the situation.

The degree to which survey feedback creates energy and motivates people to take action depends on the following conditions (Neff, 1965; Nadler, 1977, 1996):

- Stakeholders accept the data as valid. Although the stakeholders themselves produced the survey data, it usually takes some time before discussions focus on their meaning instead of on challenging the survey.
- They accept responsibility for the part they play in the problems that were identified. People sometimes contend that data do not apply to their team, especially when general data are reported. A sense of ownership and 'model' behaviour of team members helps to start working on interpretation and solutions.
- They commit themselves to solving the problems. When the first two conditions are met, people can focus their energy on determining the implications for their organization or team.
- The data collection itself is already a way of making change a collaborative effort. It stimulates people to think about the subjects that are addressed in the questionnaire.
- The survey is of good quality. People need to feel that the subjects it addresses are relevant and accurately measured.
- People need to know that action will be taken after the data collection. It is important that people know that powerful stakeholders take outcomes seriously and that answering the questions is not a waste of time.

Generally, the methodology consists of five steps that were initially developed by Mann (Mann, 1961; French & Bell, 1995; Cummings & Worley, 1997). In the first step, relevant stakeholders are involved in the preliminary planning of the survey feedback. In the second step, data are collected from all organization members. In the third step, data are analysed, tabulated, and prepared for feedback and client members are trained to lead the feedback meetings in the organization. In the fourth step, data are fed back to the top of the organization and then down through the hierarchy in functional teams. Mann calls this an 'interlocking chain of conferences' (1961: 609). In the fifth step, data are discussed in feedback meetings of teams where people interpret the data and make plans for improvement and change. Different steps and ways of structuring feedback meetings have been developed (Nadler, 1977). The main adaptation in the case we discuss below is that specific team results and differences between teams were not the primary focus. Instead, results were specified for the change strategists, implementers, and receivers (Kanter et al., 1992). Considerable differences were found between these groups and this was an important element during the interpretation of the findings.

---

## CASE STUDY: SURVEY FEEDBACK IN A CARE ORGANIZATION

Survey feedback is used to monitor a change process that started two years ago with a merger of two care organizations. After the merger, the first year consisted of building a new structure for the former two organizations. In the second year, the two main topics were improving the quality of the care and developing the organization. At the end of the second year, the management team got the impression that the change process was stagnating. Until then, the team had done both the strategic work and tried to realize the implementation of the changes. The department heads did not really take up their role as implementers. The CEO asked us to conduct a survey feedback. After meeting with a number of stakeholders, it was decided that a survey feedback could help to gain insight in the state of affairs in the change process, and that the results could be used to develop ideas for improvement.

The way of using survey feedback in this case dealt with the difficulties we discussed in above as follows:

1. The survey we used focused on six aspects of the organization and 10 aspects of the change process. The first part evaluated what people thought about the goals of the organization, the structure, the culture, the technology, the work, and political relations. The second part addressed the goals of the change, the role of technology in the change process, tensions, timing, information supply, creating support, the role of the management team, the role of the middle managers, the outcome expectation, and support for change (Bennebroek Gravenhorst et al., 2003). Thus, we concentrated on multiple possible problem areas.
2. The survey was administered to all members of the organization, which provided the opportunity to specify results for different groups. In this case, we specified results for the management team, department heads, and employees, rather than for teams. Thus, insight was obtained in the perspectives of the three main interest groups, who had a different position and role in the change process.
3. The methodology was explicitly chosen to monitor the progress of the change process and everyone was asked to indicate what was going well and what was not. Thus, attention was given to the processual aspect of change.
4. The survey made it possible to evaluate the change approach. Eight of the 10 subjects in the second part of the questionnaire focused on elements of the approach. Thus, the results showed what people thought of the way the change process was being conducted.
5. The survey feedback involved everyone in the interpretation of the situation and in the development of actions to address problems. By using the methodology, the management team indicated

that it took everyone seriously and that improving the change process was something to be done by working together. In addition, the last two subjects in the questionnaire measured if there was resistance to change in the first place.

The outcomes of the survey were rather dramatic (Bennebroek Gravenhorst, 2002: 289). The management team, department heads, and employees differed considerably in their evaluation of both the situation in the organization and the change process. In general, the management team thought most positively, the employees most negatively, and the department heads took an in-between view. A striking result was that more than 50 per cent of the employees negatively evaluated each aspect of the change approach. Interpretation of the general results, the differences between the groups, and the answers to the open questions in the survey led to the conclusion that the negative results were mainly an effect of the limited role that employees and, to a lesser extent, department heads had played in the change process. There was serious critique of the role of the management team and the top-down change approach. Thus, the management team concluded that its previous efforts to involve both department heads and employees in the change had failed. They used the feedback of the results as a first and immediate opportunity to do things differently.

A mixed preparation group designed a procedure for the feedback sessions in the teams. The group formulated several questions that were used to structure the sessions. One of the questions was what managers should or should not do to increase the commitment of employees. Another was how employees thought they could contribute to realizing the changes in the organization. The reports from all sessions were distributed in the organization, including a summary from the preparation group. The management team added a response. Among other things, it was explained how the team would improve communication of the change and how new ways of interaction would be sought. In addition, the CEO and other members of the management team visited all teams to discuss the situation and to exchange ideas for improvement.

A year later, the CEO answered demands for a second survey feedback. People felt that the situation had changed and that improvements had been made in the quality of the care, management, communication, working systematically, and working together. The second survey showed a substantial improvement in the situation in the care organization (cf. Bennebroek Gravenhorst, 2002: 326). Now, all aspects of the organization were evaluated positively by more than 50 per cent of each group, as were most aspects of the change process. Most notable was the increase in the positive evaluations by the employees. In addition, the differences between the groups had become much smaller. We concluded that these improvements were mainly the effect of the combined efforts of the management team, the department heads, and the employees. In the last year, these three groups had put a lot of energy into the change process and into solving the problems that were found in the first survey.

We conclude that survey feedback is a useful methodology for bringing different stakeholders together and for stimulating interaction and collaboration in change. Using surveys offers the possibility of specifying results for each interest group, showing how each group perceives difficulties. Taking differences in perspective seriously and discussing them in the feedback sessions offers opportunities for improvement. The case study showed that working together on improvement led to real results in the period of a year. Thus, survey feedback became a powerful learning tool for the organization. It created momentum: (1) by systematically examining the situation in the changing organization with all stakeholders; (2) by focusing discussions about the questions of what went well and what did not through exchanging different perspectives and interaction between groups; (3) by forming a shared idea of problems and possible solutions in the changing organization; and (4) by committing the management team, middle managers, and employees to realize improvement.

Both surveys showed that around 75 per cent of the employees had a positive expectation of the outcomes of the change, supported the change, and were committed to realizing it. The results for department heads were even more positive. Given the top-down change approach, this was a remarkable finding. One would have expected resistance to change. A closer look at the findings showed that people resisted something else. An important effect of the top-down approach was that they were excluded from the change process and that was precisely the focus of their criticism. People wanted to contribute to changes that affected the entire organization, including their work. Thus, this case study illustrates our previous point that resistance to change is not a natural reaction to any change. Instead, people are willing to change and want to be involved. This stresses the importance of choosing a change approach and methodologies that allow for this involvement.

## LARGE GROUP METHODOLOGIES

The defining feature of large group methodologies is bringing together large numbers of organization members for a two- to four-day conference or meeting (Cummings & Worley, 1997). Often, more than one hundred people participate. Conferences are organized for all members of an organization or for a representative sample, sometimes including external stakeholders such as customers and suppliers. People work together to identify and resolve organizational problems, to design new structures and ways of management, or to develop new strategic directions. Large group methodologies appear to be 'a new type of social innovation' (Bunker & Alban, 1992b: 473) that is growing fast. In Chapter 3, Levin describes the differences between a few large group methodologies and discusses the role of the facilitator in them.

Getting whole systems in the same 'room' to work together on one or more issues means a rather fundamental shift in the practice of organizational change (Bunker & Alban, 1992a). In the more traditional models of organizational change, including OD, groups work separately on relevant issues. Even in organization-wide methodologies like survey feedback, interpretation of the outcomes usually starts at the top and then cascades down the hierarchy to the teams. With large group methodologies, all organization members analyse their situation together. This is the main reason for its effect. Effective large group methodologies induce a 'paradigm shift' in participants, making people leave a conference with a different view of their organizational world (Danemiller & Jacobs, 1992). The assumption is that such events will result in a shared view of the organization and its environment. Thus, a more solid 'common ground' (Weisbord, 1992) obtained through interaction and cooperation on some sort of diagnostic assignment leads to more effective change.

A number of other conditions influence the effectiveness of large group methodologies (Bunker & Alban, 1992a: 581–585; Danemiller & Jacobs, 1992: 488–498; Weisbord, 1992: 55–70):

- Explicit links are made between an organization's past, present, and future. Analysis of the past helps people to understand the here-and-now. Next, an image is created of the future. Ending a conference with first steps and future plans ensures that the event continues in the future.
- Structure is used to manage large group dynamics. Within the larger frame, people work in all kinds of small group structures and results are subsequently communicated to the whole group. The degree to which a conference or programme is structured varies. Both the degree of specification of the outcome and the kind of large group methodology seem to influence the amount and kind of structure that is preferred.
- New forms of organizational communication take place when people from all units and levels in the organization work in mixed groups. This renders the opportunity to see across internal boundaries and to understand other perspectives.
- Full and democratic dialogue makes participants real owners of a conference and its outcomes. Effectiveness increases when people address the issues themselves rather than when they feel they are taken on a guided tour.
- Conferences help to develop a shared goal. People achieve more by pursuing a shared goal than by pursuing parallel goals.

- Conferences stimulate creativity. More specifically, the system or design of a conference increases creativeness. Whole systems learn from assorted stakeholders talking with each other without attacking other points of view or defending their own.
- Status and hierarchy are temporarily absent or become less relevant. In this different reality, people can, for instance, express critique without being sanctioned and give feedback that normally is not heard.
- Successful conferences generate enthusiasm, commitment, and the wish to take action. Conferences empower people. They see what they can manage themselves and what they need to do with others. This reduces dependency, conflict, and task avoidance.
- Conferences are fast and large groups attain high productivity. When everyone is there and sees everything happen, communication of results is not a process that needs time, it is all done in real time.

Conducting a large group event generally involves three phases (Weisbord, 1992; Cummings & Worley, 1997). In the first phase, the conference or meeting is prepared. Usually, a design team consisting of members of the organization and consultants does this. During the preliminary planning, the team discusses issues as the theme of the conference, the programme, the appropriate members to participate, and the tasks of both the team and the participants. In the second phase, the conference takes place. What happens during the conference depends largely on its purpose and on the large group methodology that is chosen. Most methodologies include developing common ground, discussing the focal issues, creating a change agenda, making plans for action, and evaluating the event. In the third phase, a follow-up on the conference takes place to secure implementation of the action plans and to measure its outcomes.

When all members of the organization participate in the conference, implementation can start directly. When a representative group participates, the follow-up starts with communicating the results, broadening commitment to the changes, and monitoring when it is time to proceed. Sometimes, the third phase is divided into short-range follow-up (first six months after the conference) and long-term follow-up (one to three years after the conference). Thus, each phase embraces a number of steps. Weisbord (1987, 1992), for example, distinguishes about 10 steps for his future search conferences and Jacobs (1994) puts 19 items on the typical agenda of a three-day real-time strategic change event.

---

## CASE STUDY: A CONFERENCE WITH AN INSURANCE COMPANY

We present a case of a conference that was attended by almost all members of an insurance company. The company was involved in a fundamental change process that simultaneously focused on a strategic repositioning to its parent company and improvement or change of almost every aspect of the organization. The general plan was to involve all members of the organization in the four stages of the change process: diagnosis, goal setting, implementation, and evaluation. Diagnosis was done with a survey feedback. Contrary to the common procedure, in this case the results were fed back to all 150 members of the organization at the same time. The CEO presented the outcomes. In addition, interpretation of the outcomes was not followed by ideas for improvement. Instead, people defined the themes that should be addressed in the goal-setting stage. This stage started with a two-day conference. During the conference, participants would set first directions for improvement. After the conference, theme groups would take up different issues and work out concrete action plans and implications.

Using a large group methodology in this case dealt with the difficulties we previously discussed in the following way:

1. It offered time for a thorough discussion of all six themes that were considered problematic in the diagnosis and to pay attention to their interrelatedness. For instance, analysing the key organization processes with mixed groups of people from all units provided insight into sources of delay and mistakes, interdependencies of teams, and inefficient procedures. Subsequently, directions for improvement were worked out for each theme.
2. Working with multiple perspectives was a central element of the conference. During the conference, people worked together in various settings with others they normally only saw in the company restaurant. Consequently, they learned about each other's work, about organizational dependencies, and about their colleagues as people.
3. The processual aspect of the change was marked by the reason for the conference. The conference formed the kick-off for the goal-setting stage in which the focus of the change process shifted from analysis to action.
4. The conference stressed the collaborative nature of the change process. Almost 90 per cent of the organization members chose to participate, even though the second day of the conference was a Saturday.
5. Resistance to change was not an issue. Everyone could contribute to the diagnosis and the conference, which resulted in a common ground for both the need for change and the direction of the changes.

The results of the conference can be described at the content and at the process levels. At the content level, the outcome of the conference was a general idea of the directions of the change for six themes: strategy, organization structure, management, technology, culture, and HRM. Organization structure was the most difficult issue, given the complicated nature of the key organization processes. Each of eight groups made flow-charts of one of the main processes, identified problems, and developed solutions. Reviewing these solutions subsequently led to three alternatives for a new organization structure. For the other five themes, the direction of change was more easily set. After the conference, a report was compiled that described the main outcomes. In addition, all flip-over sheets, wall charts, Post-its, and so on were collected. Subsequently, the report and the raw material were used by the theme groups to refine directions and to draw up action plans. Most of the theme groups needed two to four afternoon meetings to do their work.

The main process results were individual and organizational learning, a shared view of the directions of the change, and support for the directions. These directions reflected the knowledge and expertise of the entire organization. People learned about the functioning of the company by analysing processes and developing solutions to improve important issues. Furthermore, they experienced that sharing knowledge and working together lead to creative ideas. The design of the conference and the participation of almost all organization members led to a shared view of the directions for the change.

The processual aspect of the conference had been the prime focus of the preparation group. The 'why' question was answered at the outset of the change process. The answer to the 'what' question was given at the personnel meeting: during the conference, people would focus on six themes and develop directions for change. The answer to the 'who' question was simple: everyone was invited to attend. Therefore, the preparation group focused on the 'how'. It designed a programme that facilitated the exchange of ideas and learning through letting people from different teams work together in a special setting. Interestingly, carefully paying attention to process resulted in high-quality content. For instance, the mixed groups produced a detailed mapping of the main organization processes and a challenging but realistic profile for managers in the future organization. The conference integrated the knowledge of all organization members and elicited available creativity. The quality of the content and the success of the process were acknowledged by the management team. It declared that the conference report and other results formed the official directions for the change to be further worked out by the theme groups.

This case study demonstrates that large group methodology is a useful method for bringing different stakeholders together. Many authors stress that this is a core element of the methodology (Bunker & Alban, 1992a; Weisbord, 1992; Jacobs, 1994). In this case, people diagnosed their organization together and discussed the outcomes during a personnel meeting. The conference amplified the cooperation in the change process. The case study portrays one way of working with a conference. Here, almost every member of the organization participated. Thus, the focus was on internal stakeholders, developing together the direction for fundamental change of their organization. Important effects were: (1) a shared vision on the state of affairs; (2) strong support for the future organization; (3) individual and organizational learning; (4) enthusiasm for action; and (5) high-quality content. The authors cited in this subsection report similar effects.

People enthusiastically engaged in interacting on the directions for the change. This is illustrated by the participation of 90 per cent of the organization members at the conference and the positive remarks people made about the event. Four months later, when the new units and teams started, a survey showed that 100 per cent of the middle managers and over 80 per cent of the employees supported the change (Bennebroek Gravenhorst, 2002: 360). This is not to say that the change process progressed without any difficulty. The most important issue was the new organization structure. A number of people questioned the structure that was chosen by the management team. The team made its decision after reviewing three alternatives including their pros and cons, which were developed by the theme groups. We do not feel that the term resistance to change is suitable to describe the situation of a group of people who would have chosen another alternative. Still, people were involved in the development of the three alternatives and supported the procedure that the management team should make an informed choice in this matter. Other than this, no tension occurred during the process of collaborative development of the organization. We believe this was mainly due to the change approach that allowed all stakeholders to contribute in each of the phases of the process.

## PROCESS MANAGEMENT

In general, process management refers to all kinds of interventions and activities that focus on structuring processes of change in organizations. De Bruijn et al. (1998, 2002) developed a form of process management that regulates decision-making processes in the case of (1) complex problems, which (2) need to be solved by a network of actors, and (3) are dynamic in nature. Their approach is based on available theories on decision-making in networks (Marin & Mayntz, 1991), the tension between individual and collective rationality (Wildavsky, 1980), and process design (in 't Veld et al., 1992). This methodology applies to situations where there is no objective solution available that will more or less spontaneously be accepted by all parties involved.

The different perspectives of the various stakeholders in a network make it difficult to set off with a shared vision of the problem. Different actors need each other to solve problems but at the same time they pursue their own interests (Boonstra & Bennebroek Gravenhorst, 1998). Thus, a shared vision needs to be developed along the way. The garbage can metaphor (Cohen et al., 1972; March, 1981) illustrates how stakeholders arbitrarily dump their problems and solutions during a decision-making process. Process management seeks to regulate the activities of stakeholders in such a way that they start to work on defining problems at the same time, then develop different options in interaction, and finally choose one or more solutions (De Bruijn et al., 1998, 2002).

The tension between individual preferences and collective rationality is demonstrated in the classical 'prisoners dilemma' (Luce & Raiffa, 1957). In this dilemma, cooperation between both prisoners would result in shared benefits for each party. Competition results in losses for both. However, if party A cooperates and party B competes, B maximizes his benefits and A obtains the worst outcome. The trick is that neither party knows what the other will do. Process management can aggregate and weigh individual preferences, but not by making a single collective solution according to the majority rule. The application of a decision rule is not enough to guarantee the quality of a collective decision. In addition, the freedom of choice of the parties involved needs to be taken into account, as well as the equality of parties, equal chances for alternatives, mutual control over the decision, the majority of votes, and preferences of a minority (De Bruijn et al., 1998: 35). There is no general method of decision-making that satisfactorily deals with these issues (March, 1981). Individual and collective rationality cannot be brought together. Process management aims at organizing communication and argumentation in order to produce consensus or consent. It structures collective decision-making in such a way that the process itself is acceptable for the parties, as are the solutions.

Process design guides the decision-making process and creates a collective rationality through integrations of different perspectives and different preferences (De Bruijn et al., 1998). A process manager works in unique situations for which standard solutions are not available, as does Schön's (1983) reflective practitioner. He or she continuously monitors whether problem definitions, options, and solutions are attractive for the involved stakeholders. Process rationality also implies that the process manager acknowledges the rules of the game (Scott-Morgan, 1994). New decisions may interfere with the existing rules of the game in an organization. Therefore, it is important that stakeholders and other members of the organization investigate these rules together. Thus, while developing solutions it is possible to anticipate on interference with existing rules. Process design needs to create support among stakeholders and should involve organization members in the development of ideas for change. In short, process design focuses on the *process* of problem identification, decision-making, and change, instead of on the *content*. Thus, a process manager fulfils the role of a decision-shaper rather than a decision-maker (Galbraith, 1995: 157).

The general principle of process management is that an acceptable, authoritative decision can only be developed if all relevant stakeholders are involved in all phases of the process, from problem definition to choosing a solution. Both the process manager and the stakeholders should pay attention to the key elements of process design: openness, protection of core values, speed, and substance (De Bruijn et al., 2002: 45–56). Openness refers to the opportunity for stakeholders to contribute to the decision-making. Protection of core values refers to guarding parties to act against their own central interests. Speed refers to measures that are taken to move forward and come to a decision. Substance refers to close attention for the quality of the alternative proposals that are developed and for the final decision. For each of these key elements, De Bruijn et al. (1998) distinguish conditions for success:

- Openness of decision-making is achieved through the inclusion of all relevant parties in the decision-making process, agreements about the procedures for developing content during the process, and transparency of the process and the process management.
- The core values of stakeholders in the decision-making process are protected by the possibility of postponing commitments to a decision to a later moment in the process, the protection of the principal interests of each party, exit rules to prevent parties from feeling they are led into a trap, and loosely coupled partial decisions and final decisions in order to secure flexibility and to create several opportunities for exercising influence.
- Speed of the decision-making process is obtained through creating opportunities for profit and incentives for cooperative behaviour, participation of powerful representatives for the relevant parties, actively utilizing the field in which the stakeholders operate, developing the authority and reputation of the decision-making process to prevent external criticism, using the situation after the decision as an incentive for stakeholders to behave cooperatively, and preventing conflicts among key players.
- Substance or the quality of the content of the decision is guarded by distinguishing between the roles of content experts and stakeholders without separating them and developing a variety of options before selecting a final solution.

## CASE STUDY: PROCESS MANAGEMENT AND DECISION-MAKING IN THE AIR TRAFFIC SECTOR

In the case study we present, process management is used for the debate about the utility and necessity of expanding the Dutch air traffic sector. One of the five European main ports for air traffic is situated in the densely populated western part of the Netherlands. When an Israeli Boeing crashed a couple of years ago on an apartment building in Amsterdam, many voices arose to close down Schiphol airport or to move it to another location. At the same time, Schiphol demanded expansion to sustain its position as a main port. The environmental movement uttered bitter complaints about noise and safety. In 1998, the government initiated a large debate on the future infrastructure of air traffic in the Netherlands. Here, we see that the strategic opportunities of one organization, Schiphol airport, are strongly influenced by numerous other organizations and public bodies. Schiphol's desire to grow has significant effects on society and therefore it was subjected to public debate. After the opportunities for growth became clarified in this debate with external parties and through political decision-making, the airport could move on with the necessary internal changes. We focus on the way process management structured the public debate because it shows how the methodology brought very different parties, diverging interests, and opinions together. This setting involves a network of organizations.

Using process management in this case dealt with the difficulties we discussed before in the following way:

1. The debate started with investigating perspectives on the economic and societal importance of air traffic. Thus, multiple definitions of the problem were collected. In order to prevent polarization at the outset, the process did not start with focusing on solutions such as the fiercely debated options for airport locations.
2. Involving all relevant stakeholders is a central principle of the methodology. Here, this meant that the insights of, for instance, the environmental movement and related organizations were taken into account as seriously as those of the economic stakeholders.
3. Process management explicitly focuses on designing the decision-making process. It is required that the process design allows participants to develop the content by interaction, consultation, and negotiation.
4. All parties are involved in thinking about the process as well as in developing content. A process manager may propose a design, yet stakeholders need to agree with the procedures. Here, each subsequent phase was discussed quite intensely with all stakeholders as well as in parliament.
5. An important reason to involve all relevant stakeholders is that this helps to prevent resistance. In addition, a special committee was formed to overview the decision-making process from an independent point of view and to advise on further steps to be taken. The committee published its insights immediately after each meeting.

The results of the methodology become apparent in its three stages. At first, alternative options on the future development of air traffic and airports in the Netherlands were discussed by hundreds of organizations and public bodies. In this phase, relative consensus was reached on a target of moderate growth. During the second phase, the debate concentrated on the most adequate future size and place of Dutch airports. Again, various alternative options were developed. Expansion of Schiphol at its current location was considered. The idea of building a new airport in the North Sea and some locations in areas of reclaimed land were subjected to equally serious deliberation. The idea of an airport in the North Sea, for instance, was not developed by public authorities but by private consortia. Regional authorities brought forward other proposals for future airports. This process took care of the selection of feasible options. In the third phase, two years later,

moderate expansion of Schiphol was agreed upon. The study of an airport in the sea is continued as a potential long-term option. In the end, an issue that had divided Dutch society before
the debate started was solved in a satisfactory manner after a well-managed communication and
argumentation process. The environmental movement, the main economic actors, and the public
bodies accepted the outcomes of the process. The final political decision was taken in a quiet atmosphere.

This case study shows that process management can effectively bring different stakeholders together in a
decision-making process about an important societal issue involving representatives from organizations
and public bodies with different perspectives and interests. Acceptance of the outcome is created by
paying careful attention to the design of the decision-making process. At the outset, parties agree on
the fairness of the process. Thus, their first focus lies on the process that will be used to investigate a
problem and develop solutions. If they agree on this, stakeholders start producing content themselves.
Alternatively, if the decision-making process were to start with presenting three solutions, it is unlikely
that a choice would ever be made. Chances are high that conflict would arise over the content of these
solutions.

Resistance to the decision for moderate growth of the airport was not a big issue. Naturally, given
the large number of stakeholders, different interest, and perspectives, it was highly improbable that
the parties would develop a solution to satisfy everyone. However, if we take two parties that strongly
opposed each other in the beginning, we see the benefits of process management and its potential
to prevent strong resistance and the exclusion of relevant stakeholders. At first, it seemed that the
environmental movement and the economic actors could not be brought together. The former focused
on issues as noise, nearby inhabitants, and pollution. The latter focused on issues as growth of the
airport to keep its international position as a main port and employment. However, the design of the
process stimulated interaction, and the exchange of viewpoints and arguments. In addition, both parties
learned to appreciate the complexity of the situation and the fact that satisfying many stakeholders
would be impossible by choosing an extreme position. Recognition of the fairness of the process and
input of all parties resulted in support for the final output of the process.

## THIRD-PARTY INTERVENTION

Third-party intervention aims to resolve conflict and tension in organizations. The two defining characteristics of third-party intervention are that (1) an external party is asked to intervene in (2) a conflict
situation or a potential conflict situation between two or more parties (Walton, 1987). The external
party often is a consultant or a manager. It is important that this third party is external to the conflict,
that it takes an objective position, and that it has no preference for a specific solution. The conflicting
parties can be individuals, teams, and other kinds of groups within an organization.

In the previous subsections, we have discussed methodologies that prevent conflict and tension
through interaction, exchange of ideas, and cooperation. However, conflict and tension are part of
organizational reality. Since opposing interests of stakeholders is a main cause of conflict (Fisher &
Ury, 1981; Bisno, 1988), we feel that it is relevant to pay attention to a family of methodologies
that can help to bring them together. These methodologies are useful when we are confronted with
disturbed relationships in the initial stages of a change process that need to be resolved before such
methodologies as survey feedback, large group methodologies, and process management can start.
Alternatively, conflicts can occur during change processes when the flow of events takes a negative
turn. Thus, in this last subsection, we focus on methodologies that aim to change harmful situations.
Besides, the scope of most interventions by a third party is smaller than the previously discussed
organization-wide methodologies. Even though conflicts often affect an entire organization, dealing
with conflicts generally starts at the interpersonal or intergroup level.

We need to assert that conflicts are not necessarily negative. Conflict can be functional and productive (Tjosvold, 1993) and enhance motivation and innovation (Cummings & Worley, 1997). Here, we focus on the negative and dysfunctional side of conflict. To understand conflict, we need to look at both content and process. If we look at content, we focus on the issue that the conflict is about. A major distinction is between substantive and emotional conflict (Walton, 1987). Substantive issues involve disagreement over, for instance, strategy, management systems, distribution of tasks, or work organization. Emotional conflict involves negative feelings between parties such as anger, distrust, or resentment. Mastenbroek (1993: 123) calls these two kinds of conflict instrumental and social-emotional conflicts. In addition, he distinguishes negotiation conflicts and power-dependency conflicts (1993: 124). Negotiation conflicts involve tensions arising from the allocation of scarce resources such as budget, personnel, and equipment. Power-dependency conflicts involve rivalries within the organization or within groups, which are aimed at safeguarding or strengthening one's strategic position.

If we look at process, we focus on how conflicts evolve. Walton states that conflicts are cyclical and that 'the cycles may be either escalating, de-escalating, or maintaining of the level of conflict' (1987: 65). Conflicts are only manifest part of the time. Certain events make the conflict salient, lead to conflict-relevant behaviour, and then the conflict disappears from the foreground before the cycle repeats itself. Thus, conflict consists of a sequence of events and 'conflict behavior is . . . influenced by both preceding events and the anticipation of future events' (Prein, 1984: 86). A typical cycle of feelings that accompany conflicts is: disagreement, confusion, blaming, alienation, hostility, stronger misunderstanding, stronger disagreement, anger, and so on (Conner, 1998). Fisher states 'conflict appears inherently open to certain self-aggravating mechanisms which foster escalation' (1972: 89). If parties try to work out solutions in such a situation, we often see this: one party presents an idea, the other party attacks it, the presenters defend it, they launch a counter-attack, and the other party defends itself against the counter-attack.

A third party can help to break such cycles. Here, we focus on integrative solutions that ask for both parties to work together in solving their conflicts. Walton states that this is 'the most obvious and straightforward [approach], although it is often the most difficult to achieve' (1987: 81–82). Prein (1987) investigated to what extent internal and external consultants apply the main strategies presented in the literature. He concludes that consultation and mediation are the two main strategies used for conflict intervention. Third-party consultation (Fisher, 1983) means that the external party focuses on the process of conflict solving and is non-directive regarding content. For this, process expertise and referent power are used. The primary goal is to improve the relations between the parties in such a way that they can continue working on the conflict themselves. Third-party mediation (Moore, 1996) means that the external party focuses on the content of the conflict. For this, he uses content expertise and information power. The primary goal is to settle the issue, if necessary by exerting pressure and insisting on a compromise (see Table 15.3).

Many interventions are available to a third party. Prein (1984) argues that the appropriateness of an intervention depends on the type of conflict and the context in which it occurs. Some well-known methodologies for dealing with conflict and tension are: constructive dialogue for interpersonal conflict

**TABLE 15.3**  Main third-party intervention strategies

|              | Consultant's influence      | Power base                          | Primary goal                                  |
|--------------|-----------------------------|-------------------------------------|-----------------------------------------------|
| Consultation | Directive about procedures  | Process-expertise<br>Referent power | Improved relations between<br>conflict parties |
| Mediation    | Directive about content     | Content-expertise<br>Information power | Settlement of issues                        |

*Note:* Adapted from Prein, H. (1987). 'Strategies for third party intervention'. *Human Relations*, **40**, 699–720.

(Walton, 1987), a 10-step procedure for resolving intergroup conflict (Blake et al., 1964), confrontation meetings for management (Beckhard, 1969), principled negotiations (Fisher, 1990), and coordinative behaviour or integrative agreements for negotiation (Pruitt, 1981). They follow a similar stepwise plan in the conflict-solving process. At the outset, the goal of the intervention is discussed with the conflicting parties and they are invited to clarify the situation. The search for a solution is characterized by interaction and communication between the parties, efforts to enhance understanding and exchange of perspectives, and the exploration of a higher goal or common goal. Recognition of the interests of the parties and their perspectives is a central element of the process. Most interventions end with action planning, implementation, and follow-up.

The following conditions influence the effectiveness of intervening in conflict situations by a third party (Walton, 1987: 83–99; Mastenbroek, 1993: 128–133):

- The conflict parties need to accept the third party and they need to express a positive motivation to solve the conflict.
- The network of conflicting parties needs to be structured.
- The conflicting parties need to be kept somewhat in equilibrium. When asymmetrical power relations develop during the intervention, this will probably lead to the defeat of one party.
- The third party needs to maintain an optimal level of conflict intensity. Low conflict intensity can lead to resignation. High conflict intensity can lead to escalation or parties exiting the process.
- The third party needs to align his or her interventions with the kind of conflict between the parties.
- The third party needs to secure synchronization of the efforts of the conflict parties. The initiatives to solve the conflict and investment in the process should be in concert between the conflict parties.
- The third party needs to stimulate synthesis by sequentially alternating between differentiation and integration of conflict issues.
- Conditions favouring openness in dialogue need to be created and communication needs to be reliable. The conflict parties should be able to express their ideas and feelings and the third party has to make certain that they understand each other well.
- The third party should be guided by the criteria of directivity, attainability, urgency, and movement when choosing interventions.
- Time, money, and energy need to be invested in dealing with a complex issue as conflicts.

## CASE STUDY: THIRD-PARTY INTERVENTION IN A DUTCH MINISTRY

The case study we present here is set in a directorate of a Dutch ministry. A new Directorate Head was recently appointed to lead the directorate to a situation where its four main departments would be more sensitive to developments in society and the demands of the public, would work more efficiently, and effectively carry out the ministry's policy. She felt this asked for a fundamental change process in which involvement of all civil servants of her directorate was needed. In one of the initial conversations about this process, she mentioned a conflict situation that involved the General Support Services and the Technical Support Services. When we asked for more detail, she explained that she had not yet met the teams herself but that everyone in the directorate knew about the conflict. It seemed that the conflict originated as an interpersonal conflict between two members of the teams, then it spread within the teams as other members developed hostile feelings towards the other team, next it became an intergroup conflict, and in the end it resulted in a nasty situation that affected the entire directorate. The conflict escalated frequently. When this happened, the team members barely did their job. Mail was neither delivered nor sent, reproduction work got delayed, meeting rooms were not equipped, and so on. Everyone in the directorate had an opinion about the situation, the causes, the effects, and why the previous Head did nothing about it.

We proposed investigating the situation to see if action could be taken. After interviewing five members of each team we reported our findings to the Head. In our opinion, the conflict situation did not directly threaten the change process that was going to be initiated because of the limited role the services teams would have in that process. Still, we felt that the teams and the directorate would benefit if the conflict could be settled. In addition, from a human perspective, the conflict was a tragedy. It started three years ago, it escalated at least once a month, people were tense, stressed, sickness absence was close to 20 per cent, and so on. The managers of both teams were incapable of doing something about it, as were the team members themselves. We discussed a few scenarios to approach the situation and then the Head asked us to make a plan and to discuss it with the teams.

In each team, we proposed third-party intervention and explained how it worked. Both teams recognized that the conflict existed and that they had been unable to solve it. In addition, each of the team members individually expressed his or her wish for a solution, a commitment to finding it, and a positive opinion about the procedure that we proposed. The intervention consisted of a number of steps. We started with bringing the teams together for a diagnosis of the situation. People wrote on Post-it notes what they felt was wrong and put those notes on either the 'feelings wall' or the 'work wall'. Thus, they distinguished between the emotional and work-related aspects of the conflict. We briefly worked on getting control over the emotional issues. This did not work because it made people re-experience the past. Thus, it was decided to focus on the substantive issues and on the future because that was where people expected to find a solution. During this process, the teams worked on assignments such as interdependency exercises, appreciation and concerns exercises, and responsibility chartings (French & Bell, 1995).

The way third-party intervention was used in this case dealt with the difficulties we discussed before in the following manner:

1. In diagnosing their situation people distinguished between the emotional and the substantial aspects of the conflict. This introduced a new point of view. Before, emotions reigned over the situation. Now, people found that their substantive differences were relatively easy to deal with, progress was made, the goals of the teams came into focus, and people started to see how their work was important for the directorate.
2. During the intervention, different perspectives on the conflict and possible solutions were discussed. Previously, only the perspectives of the people that most strongly influenced the conflict were seen. These 'instigators' were taken aback when they learned to what extent everyone was affected by the situation.
3. The intervention focused on the processual aspect of conflict resolution. Careful attention was paid to developing a procedure that gradually brought the teams together and helped them to define a shared goal.
4. We felt that imposing a solution would not have led to acceptance and could not have been defended, bearing in mind the neglect of the previous Head. Instead, we started by asserting that the new Head took the situation seriously, that she felt that a solution needed to be found, and that she offered the teams the assistance of a third party to improve the situation by working together.
5. Resistance to change was not an issue here. Instead, people felt that change was urgent but they were unable to realize it by themselves. The fact that everyone was involved in finding a solution was an important success factor. Imposing one would definitely have led to resistance to the new Head from both services teams. The departments may have perceived it as strong and effective leadership, but at the same time it would not have been consistent with the approach of the change process in the ministry.

The initial result was that the conflict came under control. Solving the conflict was not possible in the 12 sessions that took place. Later, we heard from members of both teams that the control over the conflict limited expressions of hostility and emotional responses. In addition, the way of working together in the sessions had led to respect for each other, insight into the other's perspective, and a few cautious attempts at conciliation. A focus on the future and on the tasks of the teams stimulated a positive atmosphere. The turning point came when the managers of the teams launched the idea to do a survey about the quality of the services the teams provided. Somebody else proposed to make one survey for both teams. Next, the teams made an inventory of all their services and asked the departments to fill it in. Subsequently, they discussed the outcomes in a combined meeting of both teams, processed the sometimes strong criticism, and decided what they needed to do to improve. Unexpectedly, somebody sketched the hypothetical situation of merging the teams so that they could provide quicker and better services. Both teams thought about the idea for two weeks, a week later it was discussed with the Directorate Head, and the next month the new General and Technical Services started. It has recently done its third annual quality survey and found that results were again more positive than the year before.

We conclude that third-party intervention can help to bring different stakeholders together. This is not really surprising because that is exactly the purpose of this family of interventions. So let us turn to the question of how this was done. In the case study, we aimed for an integrative solution to the conflict. Our ambition was to make both teams satisfied with the result of the intervention. An alternative was to have the Secretary satisfied. As Head of the ministry, he was informed about the conflict and the intervention. He suggested outsourcing as a cheaper and more efficient option. In our option, the third party invested 75 hours and together the team members spent 861 hours of working time. The return on this investment is that 24 people did not lose their jobs and that the directorate has a highly committed services team that works very well.

In this case study, we encountered a form of resistance. We found that especially in the first weeks of the intervention, the teams progressed slowly and people were stuck in their situation. Still, this could not be called resistance to change. Instead, people showed resistance against members of the other team and sometimes even against members of their own team because they were in league with the 'enemy'. At the same time, our initial conversations showed that people longed for change, some even desperately, because of the strain the situation put on them. Sharing emotions between the teams did not work well. It refreshed old memories and contributed to the resistance against the other team. We also found resistance against the former Head. Here, the resistance did not focus on his actions, but on the lack thereof. He neglected signals and requests for help that were made in the past. There was mild resistance against the lack of action of the team manager. People also blamed him for not doing anything, but in discussions they recognized his efforts and saw that he could not stop their fights. Fortunately, they were able to do so themselves.

## CONCLUSION

The main aim of this chapter was to show how fundamental change can be realized when organization members work together in the change process. We discussed four methodologies that bring different stakeholders together and make change a collaborative effort of all parties involved. Each of these methodologies is primarily process-oriented. Instead of focusing on the content of change, they focus on structuring the change process in such a way that stakeholders can work together in producing their own content. As a result, the content is based on the expertise of the parties that combine their knowledge and skills. Due to participation in the process of creating solutions for the issues that are at stake, there is no need to create acceptance of new ideas, proposals, or directions of change. People produce solutions themselves, which contributes to the quality of the outcomes and to commitment to their implementation.

We showed that process-oriented changing can deal with some important limitations of programmatic top-down change approaches. However, process-oriented change does not lead to positive results without effort. The discussion of the basics of the four change methodologies and the case studies demonstrated that these methodologies require an investment in process design, specialist skills of consultants and managers, and time and energy of relevant stakeholders. Thus, choosing to use these methodologies may seem more intense and expensive than the more common approaches in which a few experts design solutions that subsequently need to be implemented by others. For some situations this can be a cheaper, faster, and more efficient approach. In a context of fundamental change, it is not. Such changes require the involvement of all stakeholders, interaction, exchange of perspectives, learning, and development. In these kinds of situations, it is relevant and worthwhile to invest in organization-wide change methodologies that allow for co-creation of change. Results from our cases and from other research discussed in the previous section suggest that such an approach leads to support and enthusiasm for change processes that people consider themselves to be the owners of.

The idea of ownership is a central issue in our discussion of resistance to change. In the traditional view of resistance to change, managers need to overcome resistance to *their* change process. Employees presumably resist change because they have a natural preference for stability and fear the unknown. Thus, managers and employees are seen as opposing parties. In the alternative view we proposed, employees resist change because they are generally being excluded from change processes. Top-down and planned change efforts make change the exclusive domain of higher management. Employees that are merely recipients of change do not resist the change itself, they resist the way the change process is organized and managed. Thus, dealing with resistance does not ask for reducing uncertainty through information or using formal and coercive power to implement change. Instead, it asks for making change a collaborative effort of all stakeholders. Thus, resistance is prevented by choosing a change approach that allows managers, employees, and other stakeholders to work together as partners in a change process.

As a final thought, we would like to take this idea one step further and propose a more contemporary view on how people respond to change. We assume that people can enjoy changing and improving their organization, given the condition that they are involved. Resistance may be an old-fashioned concept that applied to stable organizations where change was unusual. Nowadays, people are used to the idea that change is the steady state of organizations. In addition, change is a constant factor of our non-working life. We adapt effortlessly to new situations, learn, grow, and develop as persons. We raise children, become older, and move to another city without much difficulty. We travel around the world, explore other cultures, and adapt to customs we are not familiar with. So why should we have difficulty with changing the organization where we work? As long as we can participate and contribute to improvement and change, it can be fun. We should leave the idea of opposing parties in organizations and focus on what is necessary for people to work together in realizing complex change in their organization.

A first implication of this line of thinking is that if we are confronted with resistance, we need to question the change approach or our conduct as change managers. The general tendency is to question the capabilities for change of the resisting party. We prefer to start looking at how the process is designed and if people are excluded from the change. In addition, we investigate our own behaviour and that of managers to see if this explains the resistance. As we argued before, it also helps to be specific about the focus of resistance. The term change is too broad. In fundamental change processes, people usually resist the change approach, or the conduct of change managers. In crises, resistance can be focused on loss of job, but that is not the kind of change we have been discussing here.

A second implication is that we have to think about the profile of change managers. Process-oriented change management requires specific skills and expertise. In design approaches, a manager or consultant needs content expertise to develop solutions for the problem he or she is asked to solve. Process-oriented changing requires expertise in working with groups, facilitating learning processes, process attention, social sensitivity, structuring meetings, structuring and facilitating data collection by organization members, helping them analyse and interpret outcomes, and stimulating taking action.

In addition, we pointed out that content should not be neglected. The manager or consultant does not produce content. Instead, he or she ensures that others provide high-quality content, by asking them to develop alternatives so that a conscious and deliberate choice can be made. Thus, if we consider both implications, a new way of dealing with resistance can emerge.

## REFERENCES

Beckhard, R. (1969) *Organization Development: Strategies and Models*. Reading, MA: Addison-Wesley.

Beer, M. (1988) The critical path to change: keys to success and failure in six companies. In R.H. Kilmann & T.C. Joyce & Associates (eds) *Corporate Transformation: Revitalizing Organizations for a Competitive World* (pp. 17–45). San Francisco: Jossey-Bass.

Beer, M., Eisenstat, R.A. & Spector, B. (1990a) *The Critical Path to Corporate Renewal*. Boston: Harvard Business School Press.

Beer, M., Eisenstat, R.A. & Spector, B. (1990b) Why change programs don't produce change. *Harvard Business Review*, **68**, 158–166.

Bennebroek Gravenhorst, K.M. (2002) *Sterke staaltjes van samenwerking: Survey-feedback voor het aanpakken van belemmeringen bij organisatieverandering* (Strong cases of cooperation: survey feedback for working on barriers to organizational change). Deventer: Kluwer Academic Press.

Bennebroek Gravenhorst, K.M. & Boonstra, J.J. (1998) The use of influence tactics in constructive change processes. *European Journal of Work and Organizational Psychology*, **7**, 179–196.

Bennebroek Gravenhorst, K.M., Werkman, R.A. & Boonstra, J.J. (2003) The change capacity of organizations: general assessment and five configurations. *Applied Psychology: An International Review*, **52**, 83–105.

Bisno, H. (1988) *Managing Conflict*. Newbury Park, CA: Sage.

Blake, R.R., Shepard, H.A. & Mouton, J.S. (1964) *Managing Intergroup Conflict in Industry*. Houston, TX: Gulf.

Boonstra, J.J. & Bennebroek Gravenhorst, K.M. (1998) Power dynamics and organizational change: a comparison of perspectives. *European Journal of Work and Organizational Psychology*, **7**, 97–120.

Bunker, B. & Alban, B.T. (1992a) Conclusion: what makes large group interventions effective. *Journal of Applied Behavioral Science*, **28**, 597–591.

Bunker, B. & Alban, B.T. (1992b) Editors' introduction: the large group intervention—a new social innovation? *Journal of Applied Behavioral Science*, **28**, 473–479.

Coch, L. & French, J.R.P. Jr (1948) Overcoming resistance to change. *Human Relations*, **1**, 512–532.

Cohen, M.D., March, J.G. & Olsen, J.P. (1972) A garbage can model of organizational choice. *Administrative Science Quarterly*, **17**, 1–25.

Conner, D.R. (1998) *Managing at the Speed of Change: How Resilient Managers Succeed and Prosper Where Others Fail*. Chichester: John Wiley & Sons, Ltd.

Cummings, T.G. & Worley, C.G. (1997) *Organization Change and Development* (6th edn). Cincinnati, OH: South-Western College Publishing.

Danemiller, K.D. & Jacobs, R.W. (1992) Changing the way organizations change: a revolution of common sense. *Journal of Applied Behavioral Science*, **28**, 480–498.

De Bruijn, J.A., Ten Heuvelhof, E.F. & in 't Veld, R.J. (1998) *Procesmanagement: Over procesontwerp en besluitvorming* (Process Management: On Process Design and Decision-making). Schoonhoven: Academic Service.

De Bruijn, J.A., Ten Heuvelhof, E.F. & in 't Veld, R.J. (2002) *Process Management. Why Project Management Fails in Complex Decision Making Processes*. Dordrecht: Kluwer Academic Press.

Dent, E.B. & Goldberg, S.G. (1999) Challenging 'resistance to change'. *Journal of Applied Behavioral Science*, **35**, 25–41.

Falbe, C.M. & Yukl, G. (1992) Consequences for managers of using single influence tactics and combinations of tactics. *Academy of Management Journal*, **35**, 638–652.

Fisher, R.J. (1972) Third party consultation: a method for the study and resolution of conflict. *Journal of Conflict Resolution*, **16**, 67–94.

Fisher, R.J. (1983) Third party consultation as a method of intergroup conflict resolution: a review of studies. *Journal of Conflict Resolution*, **27**, 301–334.

Fisher, R.J. (1990) *The Social Psychology of Intergroup and International Conflict*. New York: Springer-Verlag.

Fisher, R. & Ury, W. (1981) *Getting to Yes: Negotiating Agreement Without Giving in*. London: Hutchinson.

Fowler, F.J. (1984) *Survey Research Methods*. Beverly Hills, CA: Sage.

French, W.L. & Bell, C.H. (1995) *Organization Development: Behavioral Science Interventions for Organization Improvement* (5th edn). Englewood Cliffs, NJ: Prentice Hall.

Galbraith, J.R. (1995) *Designing Organizations: An Executive Briefing on Strategy, Structure, and Process*. San Francisco: Jossey-Bass.

In 't Veld, R.J., De Bruijn, J.A. & Ten Heuvelhof, E.F. (1992) *Processtandaard voor de uitvoering van de milieu- en markt-economische analyses zoals vastgelegd in het Convenant Verpakkingen* (Process standard for performing environmental and market economical analyses following the Packaging Covenant). Rotterdam: Erasmus Universiteit Rotterdam.

Jacobs, R.W. (1994) *Real Time Strategic Change: How to Involve an Entire Organization in Fast and Far-reaching Change*. San Francisco: Berrett-Koehler.

Kanter, R.M., Stein, B.A. & Jick, T.D. (1992) *The Challenge of Organizational Change*. New York: The Free Press.

Kotter, J.P. & Schlesinger, L.A. (1979) Choosing strategies for change. *Harvard Business Review*, **57**, 106–114.

Kotter, J.P., Schlesinger, L.A. & Sathe, V. (1979) *Organization: Text, Cases, and Readings on the Management of Organizational Design and Change*. Homewood, IL: Irwin.

Kuhnert, K.W. (1993) Survey/feedback as art and science. In R.T. Golembiewski (ed.) *Handbook of Organizational Consultation* (pp. 459–465). New York: Marcel Dekker.

Levy, A. & Merry, U. (1986) *Organizational Transformation: Approaches, Strategies, Theories*. New York: Praeger.

Lewin, K. (1947) Frontiers in group dynamics: concept, method and reality in social science; social equilibria and social change. *Human Relations*, **1**, 5–41.

Luce, R.D. & Raiffa, H. (1957) *Games and Decisions: Introduction and Critical Survey*. New York: John Wiley & Sons, Ltd.

Mann, F.C. (1961) Studying and creating change. In W.G. Bennis, K.D. Benne & R. Chin (eds) *The Planning of Change* (pp. 605–615). London: Holt, Rinehart & Winston.

March, J.G. (1981) Decisions in organizations and theories of choice. In A.H. van de Ven & W.F. Joyce (eds) *Perspectives on Organization Design and Behavior* (pp. 205–244). New York: John Wiley & Sons, Ltd.

Marin, B. & Mayntz, R. (1991) *Policy Networks: Empirical Evidence and Theoretical Considerations*. Frankfurt am Main: Campus.

Mastenbroek, W.F.G. (1993) *Conflict Management and Organization Development* (expanded edn). Chichester: John Wiley & Sons, Ltd.

Mintzberg, H. (1983) *Power in and around Organizations*. Englewood Cliffs, NJ: Prentice Hall.

Moore, C.W. (1996) *The Mediation Process: Practical Strategies for Resolving Conflict* (2nd edn). San Francisco: Jossey-Bass.

Mullins, L.J. (1999) *Management and Organisational Behaviour* (5th edn). London: Financial Times/Prentice Hall.

Munduate, L. & Bennebroek Gravenhorst, K.M. (2003) Introduction to the special issue on power dynamics and organizational change. *Applied Psychology: An International Review*, **52**, 1–13.

Nadler, D. (1977) *Feedback and Organization Development: Using Data-based Methods*. Reading, MA: Addison-Wesley.

Nadler, D. (1996) Setting expectations and reporting results: conversations with top management. In A.I. Kraut (ed.) *Organizational Surveys: Tools for Assessment and Change* (pp. 177–203). San Francisco: Jossey-Bass.

Neff, F.W. (1965) Survey research: a tool for problem diagnosis and improvement in organizations. In A.W. Gouldner & S.M. Miller (eds) *Applied Sociology: Opportunities and Problems* (pp. 23–38). New York: The Free Press.

Pettigrew, A.M. (1987) Researching strategic change. In A.M. Pettigrew (ed.) *The Management of Strategic Change* (pp. 1–13). Oxford: Blackwell.

Pfeffer, J. (1992) *Managing with Power: Politics and Influence in Organizations*. Boston: Harvard Business School Press.

Porras, J.I. & Robertson, P.J. (1983) Organization development: theory, practice, and research. In M.D. Dunette & L.M. Hough (eds) *The Handbook of Industrial and Organizational Psychology* (vol. 3, pp. 719–822). Palo Alto, CA: Consulting Psychologists Press.

Prein, H. (1984) A contingency approach for conflict intervention. *Group and Organization Studies*, **9**, 81–102.

Prein, H. (1987) Strategies for third party intervention. *Human Relations*, **40**, 699–719.

Pruitt, D.G. (1981) *Negotiation Behavior*. New York: Academic Press.

Schön, D.A. (1983) *The Reflective Practitioner: How Professionals Think in Action*. New York: Basic Books.

Scott-Morgan, P. (1994) *The Unwritten Rules of the Game: Master Them, Shatter them, and Break through the Barriers to Organizational Change*. New York: McGraw-Hill.

Tjosvold, D. (1993) *Learning to Manage Conflict: Getting People to Work Together Productively*. New York: Lexington.

Walton, R.E. (1987) *Managing Conflict: Interpersonal Dialogue and Third-party Roles* (2nd edn). Reading, MA: Addison-Wesley.

Watson, G. (1969) Resistance to change. In W.G. Bennis, K.D. Benne & R. Chin (eds) *The Planning of Change* (2nd edn, pp. 488–498). New York: Holt, Rinehart & Winston.

Weick, K.E. & Quinn, R.E. (1999) Organizational change and development. *Annual Review of Psychology*, **50**, 361–386.

Weisbord, M.R. (1987) *Productive Workplaces: Organizing and Managing for Dignity, Meaning, and Community*. San Francisco: Jossey-Bass.

Weisbord, M.R. (1992) *Discovering Common Ground: How Future Search Conferences Bring People Together to Achieve Breakthrough Innovation, Empowerment, Shared Vision, and Collaborative Action*. San Francisco: Berrett-Koehler.

Wildavsky, A. (1980) *The Art and Craft of Policy Analysis*. London: Macmillan.

# CHAPTER 16

# Power and Change
## A Critical Reflection

**Cynthia Hardy**
*University of Melbourne, Australia*
**Stewart Clegg**
*University of Technology Sydney, Sydney, Australia*

Power has typically been seen as the ability to get others to do what you want them to, if necessary, against their will (Weber, 1978). In the context of change, the use of power—by management—seems both logical and inevitable given the high risk of failure attributed to employee resistance noted in the opening chapter. If employees do not want to change, then managers must use power—the ability to make them change despite their disinclination—against their resistance. Yet behind this apparently straightforward understanding of the role of power and this 'no nonsense' approach to organizational change, lies a series of important struggles, not just about different conceptualizations of power, but also about the interplay between critical and managerial thought; and between academic and practitioner discourses.

The aim of this chapter, therefore, is to provide an overview of the different ways in which power has been understood and to relate these different understandings to the literature in organizational change and the practical recommendations it provides for managing change. The first section explores the historical development of two traditions in the study of power: the broader heritage of Marx and Weber and the early management work on power. The second section then elaborates two diverging views and their underlying assumptions: critical theory, which draws and builds on the Marxian/Weberian heritage; and the more recent work in management which, for the most part, has adopted a very different conceptualization. The third section provides an analysis of the traditional organizational change literature to see how it accommodates these divergent assumptions. The fourth section focuses on the insights provided by Foucault, which have radically changed our understanding of power. The fifth section examines some of the more recent ideas in managing organizational change in the light of these insights.

## EARLY STUDIES OF POWER

This section examines some of the key work that provided the foundations for the current work on power and politics in organizations. Broadly speaking, the impetus came from two, quite different directions. One tradition stems from the work of Marx and Weber. Obviously, with such a parentage, this body of work has focused on the existence of conflicting interests and has examined power as domination. As a result, it has addressed how power becomes embedded in organizational structures in a way that serves certain, but not all, interest groups. The second tradition developed more centrally

*Dynamics of Organizational Change and Learning.* Edited by J.J. Boonstra.
© 2004 John Wiley & Sons, Ltd. ISBN 0-471-87737-9.

within the field of management. Less interested in how power might be used to dominate and to serve specific interests, this body of work takes for granted the ways in which power is distributed in formal, hierarchical organizational structures and, instead, examines how groups acquire and wield power that has not been granted to them under official bureaucratic arrangements.

## POWER AND INTERESTS

One approach to the way in which power is structured into organization design has derived from work on class structures (see Clegg & Dunkerley, 1980: 463–482, for a discussion of the key literature). In as much as conceptions of interests depict the arena of organizational life in terms of the leitmotif of 'class' and its social relations, they will be attuned to the general conditions of economic domination and subordination in organizations, as theorists of the left from Marx onwards have defined them (see, for instance, Carchedi, 1987: 100, for an identification of these conditions).

Marx (1976) argued that class interests are structurally predetermined, irrespective of other bases of identity. They follow from relations of production: these define classes through their ownership and control of the means of production or through the absence of that ownership and control. While relations concerning production, property, ownership, and control are inscribed as the key social relations of capitalist modernity (Clegg & Dunkerley, 1980; Clegg et al., 1986), few scholars would be restricted to this deterministic view today. Indeed, not long after Marx's death, others, especially Max Weber, who was the first sociologist to render Marx's view more complex by considering relations *in* production as well as relations *of* production, questioned the dichotomous representation.

While Weber acknowledged that power was derived from owning and controlling the means of production, he argued that it was not reducible exclusively to these dichotomous categories of ownership and non-ownership, as proposed by Marx. From Weber's perspective, power also derived from the knowledge of operations as much as from ownership. Organizations could be differentiated in terms of people's ability to control the methods of production, as these are embedded in diverse occupational identities and technical relations at work. It is from these relations that the subjective life-world of the organization grows. In this way, Weber emphasized the forms of identification and representation that organizational members actually made use of, rather than simply assume that their view of the world was merely a 'false' consciousness if it did not correspond to the Marxist theorists' view of the world.

In the view of Marx and much subsequent theory, there is little room for discretion or opportunity for strategic agency other than through collective class-based action. Economic conditions regulate the context in which labour is sold and capital raised and, at the outset, two classes are defined: those who possess capital and those who do not. The latter have creative, differentially trained, and disciplined capacities, but the fact that they are obliged to offer these on the labour market in order to be employed renders them, necessarily, as sellers, rather than buyers, of labour power and thus as members of the working class. From Weber's perspective, all organizational members, in principle, have some creativity, discretion, and agency to use power (although some more than others). Once their labour is sold to bureaucratic organizations (Clegg, 1990), employees have the opportunity to use their capacities creatively in 'certain social relationships or carry out forms of social action within the order governing the organization' (Weber, 1978: 217). So, by factoring in the differential possibilities for creativity, it becomes clear that organizational members have some control over their disposition to exercise power, both to challenge and reproduce the formal organization structure in which differential powers are vested, legitimated, and reproduced. Thus organizational 'structures of dominancy' do not depend solely on economic power for their foundation and maintenance (Weber, 1978: 942).

In this way, labour power represents a capacity embodied in a person who retains discretion over the application of that capacity. From the employer's point of view, the employee represents a capacity to labour that must be realized. Standing in the way of realization is the embodiment of potential power in the capacities of the people hired, who may be more or less willing to work as subjects ruled by managerial discretion and control. Always, because of embodiment, the people hired as labour will retain an ultimate discretion over what they do and how they do it. Consequently, a potential source of resistance resides in this irreducible embodiment of labour power.

The gap between the capacity to labour and its effective realization implies power and the organization of control. The depiction of this gap is the mainstay of some Marxian traditions of analysis, particularly of alienation (Mézáros, 1970; Schacht, 1971; Gamble & Walton, 1972; Geyer & Schweitzer, 1981). Management is forever seeking new strategies and tactics through which to deflect discretion. The most effective and economical are thought to be those that substitute self-discipline for the discipline of an external manager. Less effective but historically more prolific, however, have been the attempts of organizations to close the discretionary gap through the use of rule systems, the mainstay of Weberian analyses of organizations as bureaucracies. Such rule systems seek to regulate meaning to control relations in organizations through the structure of formal organization design. Thus, a hierarchy is prescribed within which legitimate power is circumscribed.

In summary, this founding research focused on the way in which power derived from owning and controlling the means of production, a power that was reinforced by organizational rules and structures. Weber's work provided more room for strategic manoeuvre than Marxian views: workers had options and possibilities to challenge the power that controlled them. Although, as we shall see, these options proved to be far from easy to exercise due to more sophisticated strategies on the part of dominant groups.

## POWER AND HIERARCHY

As the section above demonstrates, power in organizations necessarily concerns the hierarchical structure of offices and their relation to each other. Particularly (but not exclusively) the field of management has tended to label such power as 'legitimate' power. One consequence of the widespread, if implicit, acceptance of the hierarchical nature of power has been that social scientists have rarely felt it necessary to explain why it is that power should be hierarchical. In other words, in this stream of research, the power embedded in the hierarchy has been viewed as 'normal' and 'inevitable' following from the formal design of the organization. As such, it has been largely excluded from many analyses, which have instead focused on 'illegitimate' power: power exercised outside formal hierarchical structures and the channels that they sanction.

One of the earliest management studies of such power was that of Thompson (1956), who researched two USAF Bomber wings. The work of the USAF personnel was characterized by highly developed technical requirements in the operational sphere, for both aircrew and ground crew. While the aircrew possessed greater formal authority than the ground crew, the latter were in a highly central position within the workflow of the USAF base, relevant to the more autonomous aircrew. The aircrew depended upon the ground crew for their survival and safety, which conferred a degree of power on the latter not derived from the formal design of the base relations. Thompson attributed the power of the ground crew to their technical competency *vis-à-vis* the flight security of the planes and the strategic position it accorded them because of the centrality of concerns for the aircrew's safety.

Other writers confirmed Thompson's (1956) view that it was the technical design of tasks and their interdependencies that best explain the operational distribution of power, rather than the formal prescriptions of the organization design. Dubin (1957: 62), for example, noted how some tasks are more essential to the functional interdependence of a system than others, and the way in which some of these may be exclusive to a specific party. Mechanic (1962) built on this argument, extending it to all organizations, saying that such technical knowledge generally might be a base for organization power. In this way, researchers began to differentiate between formally prescribed power and 'actual' power, which was also regarded as illegitimate.

'[Researchers] have seldom regarded actual power...[but] have stressed the rational aspects of organization to the neglect of unauthorized or illegitimate power' (Thompson, 1956: 290). Other researchers were to echo this distinction as they followed in Thompson's footsteps. Bennis et al. (1958: 144) made a distinction between 'formal' and 'informal' organization. In the formal organization there resides 'authority', a potential to influence based on position, while in the informal organization there exists power, 'the actual ability of influence based on a number of factors including, of course, organizational position'.

Also important was Crozier's (1964) study of maintenance workers in a French state-owned tobacco monopoly whose job was to fix machine breakdowns referred to them by production workers. The maintenance workers were marginal in the formal representation of the organization design compared to the production workers, who were at the technical core of the organization and central to the workflow-centred bureaucracy that characterized the organization. In practice, however, the story was very different. The production workers were paid on a piece-rate system in a bureaucracy designed on scientific management principles. Most workers were effectively 'de-skilled': the bureaucracy was a highly formal, highly prescribed organization and there was little that was not planned and regulated, except for the propensity of the machines to break down, and thus diminish the bonus that the production workers could earn. Hence, to maintain their earnings the production workers needed the machines to function, which made them extraordinarily dependent on the maintenance workers. Without their expertise, breakdowns could not be rectified or bonus rates protected. Consequently, the maintenance workers had a high degree of power over the other workers in the bureaucracy because they controlled the remaining source of uncertainty.

Management and the production workers were aware of this situation and had attempted to remedy the situation through preventative maintenance. But manuals disappeared and sabotage sometimes occurred. The maintenance workers were indefatigable in defence of their relative autonomy, privilege, and power. Through a skilled capacity, the result of their technical knowledge, they could render the uncertain certain. The price of restoring normalcy was a degree of autonomy and relative power, enjoyed and defended by the maintenance workers, well in excess of that formally designed for them.

Crozier's (1964) study was a landmark. He had taken an under-explicated concept—power—and had attached it to the central concept of the emergent theory of the firm—uncertainty. A central feature of organizations as conceptualized in the 'behavioural theory of the firm' (Cyert & March, 1963) was that they attempted to behave as if they were systems. Yet, they did so in an uncertain environment. The ability to control that uncertainty thus represented a potential source of power.

After Crozier (1964) and Thompson (1956), the field developed rapidly. A theory emerged, called the 'strategic contingencies theory of intra-organizational power' (Hickson et al., 1971), which built on these ideas. At the core was the idea that power was related to uncertainty, or at least to its control. More formal survey methods were used, instead of grounded research, in which departmental managers presented a series of hypothetical scenarios for evaluation. In this way, the functionally specific personnel who used esoteric technical knowledge to control uncertainty and thus increase their power relative to the formally designed hierarchy were identified.

The change in methodology helped produce a formal functionalist model. The organization was conceptualized as comprising four functional sub-systems or sub-units. The sub-units were inter-dependent, but some were more or less dependent, and produced more or less uncertainty for others. What connected them in the model was the major task element of the organization, which was conceptualized as 'coping with uncertainty'. The theory ascribed the balance of power between the sub-units to imbalances in how these interdependent sub-units coped with this uncertainty. Thus, the system of sub-units was opened up to environmental inputs, which were a source of uncertainty. Sub-units were characterized as more or less specialized and differentiated by the functional division of labour, and were related by an essential need to reduce uncertainty and achieve organizational goals: 'to use differential power to function within the system rather than to destroy it' (Hickson et al., 1971: 217).

According to this model, power is defined in terms of 'strategic contingency'. Strategically contingent sub-units are the most powerful, because they are the least dependent on other sub-units and can cope with the greatest systemic uncertainty, given that the sub-unit is central to the organization system and not easily substitutable. The theory assumes that the sub-units are unitary and cohesive in nature whereas, in fact, they are more likely to be hierarchical, with a more or less problematic culture of consent or dissent. To be unitary, some internal mechanisms of power must exist to allow such a representation to flourish, silence conflicting voices, and over-rule different conceptions of interests, attachments, strategies, and meanings. The theory assumes that management definitions prevail but research suggests it is not always the case (Collinson, 1994). Nor can we assume that management itself will necessarily be a unitary or cohesive category. For it to speak with one voice usually means that other voices have been marginalized or silenced. In other words, the strategic contingencies theory provides very little about these aspects of power because it does not challenge existing patterns of legitimacy.

Similar to the strategic contingencies view of power, in terms of theoretical approach, is the resource dependency view (Pfeffer & Salancik, 1974; Salancik & Pfeffer, 1974; Pfeffer, 1992). It derives from the social psychological literature that Emerson (1962) developed and which was implicit in Mechanic's (1962) study of the power of lower-level participants. Sources of power include information, uncertainty, expertise, credibility, position, access, and contacts with higher echelon members and the control of money, rewards, sanctions, etc. (e.g., Crozier, 1964; French & Raven, 1968; Pettigrew, 1973; Benfari et al., 1986). Such lists of resources are infinite, however, since different phenomena become resources in different contexts. Without a total theory of contexts, which is impossible, one can never achieve closure on what the bases of power are. They might be anything, under the appropriate circumstances.

Possessing scare resources is not enough in itself, however, to confer power. Actors have to be aware of their contextual pertinence and control and use them accordingly (Pettigrew, 1973). This process of mobilizing power is known as politics (Pettigrew, 1973; Hickson et al., 1986), a term whose negative connotations have helped to reinforce the managerial view that power used outside formal authoritative arrangements was illegitimate and dysfunctional. It was the dichotomous nature of power and authority that created the theoretical space for the contingency and dependency approaches. The concept of power was thus reserved primarily for exercises of discretion by organization members, which were not sanctioned by their position in the formal structure. Such exercises are premised on an illegitimate or informal use of resources; while the legitimate system of authority, on the other hand, is taken for granted and rendered non-problematic.

In summary, the comparison of this early work on power reveals two diverging streams of research. The former, developed and sustained by the work of Marx and Weber, adopted a critical look at the processes whereby power was legitimated in the form of organizational structures. For these researchers, power was domination, and actions taken to challenge it constituted resistance to domination (see Barbalet, 1985). The work that was more directly located in management tended to view power quite differently: existing organizational arrangements were not structures of domination but formal, legitimate, functional authority. Power was effectively resistance, but of an illegitimate, dysfunctional kind. In other words, in studying 'power', the early work speaks to different phenomena, and from quite different value positions. The Marxist/Weberian tradition equated power with the structures by which certain interests were dominated; while the management theorists defined power as those actions that fell outside the legitimated structures, and threatened organizational goals.

## THE EMERGENCE OF CRITICAL AND MANAGERIAL TRADITIONS

Subsequent work in both these areas was designed to enhance and extend these foundational ideas. In so doing, it served to widen the gulf that had already grown between the two approaches, as researchers directed their work principally at their own constituencies, rather than at trying to bridge the gulf between them. In this section, we examine the different paths that these two approaches took: an interest in domination and how consent was manufactured; and an interest in the use of power to defeat conflict.

## STRATEGIES OF DOMINATION: MANUFACTURING CONSENT

The various constituent parts of the critical literature began to probe the means of domination in more detail. The heritage left by Weber provided a theoretical basis for reflecting on resistance by subordinate groups. But, if resistance was to be expected, why did subordinate groups so often consent to their own subjugation? Equally puzzling was the prevalence of passivity, which was so much more marked than revolutionary fervour. Marx had predicted that individual acts of resistance to exploitation would meld into a revolutionary challenge to existing power structures by the proletariat, those who peopled the base of most large, complex organizations. Yet, such dreams of a proletarian class-consciousness had failed to materialize.

One writer who addressed this issue, through a somewhat circuitous route, was Steven Lukes (1974). He traced the developments in the study of power made in the political sciences. Early studies had typically focused exclusively on the decision-making process (e.g., Dahl, 1957, 1961; Polsby, 1963; Wolfinger, 1971). Researchers analysed key decisions that seemed likely to illustrate the power relations prevailing in a particular community. The object was to determine who made these decisions. If the same groups were responsible for most decisions, as some researchers had suggested, elite rule characterized the community. The researchers found, in contrast, that different groups prevailed in decision-making. Such a community was termed pluralist, and it was hypothesized that America as a whole could be considered to be a pluralist society. People who did not participate in a specific arena could be considered to be happy with their lot and to gain their satisfaction from participation in other areas of life.

Some writers began to question the pluralist assumptions that decision-making processes were accessible, and that non-participation reflected satisfaction with the political system. The civil rights movement and the backlash to the Vietnam War prompted doubts about the 'permeability' of the US political system (Parry & Morriss, 1975). The pluralists were criticized for their failure to recognize that interests and grievances might remain inarticulate, unarticulated, and outside the decision-making arena especially when access to formal decision-making arenas was not equally available to all members. Consequently, researchers began to conclude that conflict might well exist even if it was not directly observable (e.g., Gaventa, 1980; Saunders, 1980). Studies started to examine how full-and-equal participation was constrained. For example, Schattschneider (1960: 105) argued non-participation might be due to:

> the suppression of options and alternatives that reflect the needs of the non participants. It is not necessarily true that people with the greatest needs participate in politics most actively— whoever decides what the game is about also decides who gets in the game.

Building on this insight, Bachrach and Baratz (1962, 1963, 1970) developed the concept of a second face of power—a process whereby issues could be excluded from decision-making, confining the agenda to 'safe' questions. A variety of barriers are available to the more powerful groups to prevent subordinates from fully participating in the decision-making process through the invocation of procedures and political routines. The use of these mechanisms has been termed non-decision-making, because it allows the more powerful actors to determine outcomes from behind the scenes. This work highlights the fact that power is not exercised solely in the taking of key decisions, and that visible decision-makers are not necessarily the most powerful.

Lukes (1974) argued, however, that Bachrach and Baratz's model did not go far enough because it continued to assume that some form of conflict was necessary to stimulate the use of non-decision-making power. 'Their focus was very much upon "issues" about which "decisions" were made, albeit "non-decisions"' (Ranson et al., 1980: 8). Lukes maintained, however, that power could be used to prevent conflict by shaping people's perceptions, cognitions, and preferences to the extent that:

> they accept their role in the existing order of things, either because they can see or imagine no alternative to it, or because they view it as natural and unchangeable, or because they value it as divinely ordained and beneficial. (Lukes, 1974: 24)

The study of power could not, according to Lukes, be confined to observable conflict, the outcomes of decisions, or even suppressed issues. It must also consider the question of political quiescence: why grievances do not exist; why demands are not made; and why conflict does not arise. Such inaction may also be the result of power: we can be 'duped, hoodwinked, coerced, cajoled or manipulated into political inactivity' (Saunders, 1980: 22). It was this use of power that helped to sustain the dominance of elite groups and reduced the ability of subordinate interests to employ the discretionary power they possessed. '[P]ower is most effective and insidious in its consequences when issues do not arise at all, when actors remain unaware of their sectional claims, that is, power is most effective when it is unnecessary' (Ranson et al., 1980: 8).

In this third dimension, Lukes focused attention on the societal and class mechanisms that perpetuated the status quo. They relate to Gramsci's concept of ideological hegemony (Clegg, 1989a)—where 'a structure of power relations is fully legitimized by an integrated system of cultural and normative assumptions' (Hyman & Brough, 1975: 199). According to this view, the ability to define reality is used by dominant classes to support and justify their material domination, thus preventing challenges to their position.

Another stream of research on this issue came from labour process theory (e.g., Braverman, 1974; Burawoy, 1979; Edwards, 1979), who examined the day-to-day minutiae of power and resistance, built around the 'games' that characterize the rhythms of organizational life (Burawoy, 1979). Studies (e.g., Edwards, 1979) also examined the historical patterns that structure the overall context of power, from simple, direct control premised on surveillance; through technical control based on the dominance of the employee by the machine, and particularly the assembly line; to fully fledged bureaucratic control—Weber's rule by rules. This tradition focuses on the dialectics of power and resistance in relation to phenomena such as gender, technology, ethnicity, managerial work, and other aspects of the structuration of work and its organizational context (Knights & Willmot, 1985, 1989; Knights & Morgan, 1991; Knights & Murray, 1992; Kerfoot & Knights, 1993).

The notion of 'organizational outflanking' (Mann, 1986: 7) provides another answer to the question of why the dominated so frequently consent to their subordination. Outflanking works against certain groups in two related ways: either because they do not know enough to resist; or they know rather too much concerning the futility of such action. The first concerns the absence of knowledgeable resources on the part of the outflanked. Frequently those who are relatively powerless remain so because they are ignorant of the ways of power: ignorant, that is, of matters of strategy such as assessing the resources of the antagonist, of routine procedures, rules, agenda setting, access, informal conduits as well as formal protocols, the style and substance of power. It is not that they do not know the rules of the game so much as that they do not recognize the game itself. Here, resistance remains an isolated occurrence, easily surmounted and overcome. The second concerns precisely what the organizationally outflanked may know only too well: that the costs of resistance outweigh the chances of success or the benefits of succeeding. The necessity of dull compulsion in order to earn one's living, the nature of busy work, arduous exertion, and ceaseless activity as routinely deadening, compulsory, and invariable—such techniques of power may easily discipline the blithest of theoretically free spirits.

## STRATEGIES OF MANAGEMENT: DEFEATING CONFLICT

The management literature took a different approach—instead of concerning itself with the use of power to prevent conflict, it focused almost exclusively on the use of power to defeat conflict. Definitions explicitly linked power to situations of conflict that arise when actors try to preserve their vested interests (e.g., Pettigrew, 1973, 1985; MacMillan, 1978; Pfeffer, 1981a, 1992; Narayanan & Fahey, 1982; Gray & Ariss, 1985; Schwenk, 1989).

> From the definition of power, it is clear that political activity is activity that is undertaken to overcome some resistance or opposition. Without opposition or contest within the organization, there is neither the need nor the expectation that one would observe political activity. (Pfeffer, 1981a: 7)

Such definitions evoke the idea of a 'fair fight' where one group (usually senior management) is forced to use power to overcome the opposition of another (perhaps intransigent unions or dissident employees). It is a view reinforced by the definition of politics in terms of illegitimacy: a common definition of politics in the management literature is the unsanctioned or illegitimate use of power to achieve unsanctioned or illegitimate ends (e.g., Mintzberg, 1983, 1984; see also Mayes & Allen, 1977; Gandz & Murray, 1980; Enz, 1988). It clearly implies that this use of power is dysfunctional and aimed at thwarting initiatives intended to benefit the organization for the sake of self-interest. Distilled to its essence, politics refers to behaviour that is 'informal, ostensibly parochial, typically divisive, and above all, in the technical sense, illegitimate—sanctioned neither by formal authority, accepted ideology, nor certified expertise (though it may exploit any one of those)' (Mintzberg, 1983: 172). Thus power was equated with illegitimate, dysfunctional, self-interested behaviour, which raised an interesting question concerning what happens when there is no conflict: does power simply cease to exist or does it turn into something else? If so, what does it become? According to this work, only 'bad guys' use power—and discredited with the term 'political'—the 'good guys' use something else, although the literature is not clear on exactly what.

Good guy/bad guy views are also problematic in so far as they ignore the question of: in whose eyes is power deemed illegitimate, unsanctioned, or dysfunctional? Legitimacy is usually defined in terms of the 'organization', when writers really mean organizational elites: that is, senior management. Thus managerial interests are equated with organizational needs and the possibility that managers, like any other group, might seek to serve their own vested interests is largely ignored (Watson, 1982). But organizational structures and systems are not neutral or apolitical—they are structurally sedimented phenomena. There is a history of struggles already embedded in the organization. The organization is a collective life-world in which traces of the past are vested, recur, shift, and take on new meanings. In Weber's terms, organizations already incorporate a 'structure of dominancy' in their functioning: authority, structure, ideology, culture, and expertise are invariably saturated and imbued with power.

The management tradition has, however, taken the structures of power vested in formal organization design very much for granted. The focus is on the exercise of power within a given structure of dominancy (Perrow, 1979). Such an approach focuses only on surface politics and misrepresents the balance of power. It attributes far too much power to subordinate groups who are chastised for using it; while the hidden ways in which senior managers use power behind the scenes to further their position by shaping legitimacy, values, technology, and information are conveniently excluded from analysis. This narrow definition (see Frost, 1987) also obscures the true workings of power and depoliticizes organizational life (Clegg, 1989a). It paints an ideologically conservative picture that implicitly advocates the status quo and hides the processes whereby organizational elites maintain their dominance (Alvesson, 1984) as mechanisms of domination such as leadership, culture, and structure are treated as neutral, inevitable, or objective and, hence, unproblematic (Clegg, 1989a, 1989b; see also Ranson et al., 1980; Deetz, 1985; Knights & Willmott, 1992; Willmott, 1993).

Some management researchers did start to question these assumptions as they became interested in power as legitimation (Astley & Sachdeva, 1984). Political scientists had long recognized the advantages of creating legitimacy for existing institutions, thereby avoiding the necessity of using more coercive, visible forms of power (Lipset, 1959; Schaar, 1969; Roelofs, 1976; Rothschild, 1979). Legitimacy can also be created for individual actions, thus reducing the chances of opposition to them. Edelman (1964, 1971, 1977) pointed out that power is mobilized, not just to achieve physical outcomes, but also to give those outcomes meanings—to legitimize and justify them. Political actors use language, symbols, and ideologies to placate or arouse the public. In the manner described by Lukes' (1974) third dimension of power, the process of legitimation prevents opposition from arising:

> Political analysis must then proceed on two levels simultaneously. It must examine how political actions get some groups the tangible things they want from government and at the same time it must explore what these same actions mean to the mass public and how it is placated or aroused by them. In Himmelstrand's terms, political actions are both instrumental and expressive. (Edelman, 1964: 12)

One writer who attempted to draw legitimation processes into the management fold was Pettigrew (1977). His work on the management of meaning explicitly addressed how power was used to create legitimacy:

> Politics concerns the creation of legitimacy for certain ideas, values and demands—not just action performed as a result of previously acquired legitimacy. The management of meaning refers to a process of symbol construction and value use designed both to create legitimacy for one's own demands and to 'de-legitimize' the demands of others. (Pettigrew, 1977: 85)

This work acknowledges that political actors do not always define success in terms of winning in the face of confrontation where, as others have pointed out, there must always be a risk of losing, but in terms of their ability to section off spheres of influence where their domination is perceived as legitimate and thus unchallenged (Ranson et al., 1980; Frost, 1988). In this way, power is mobilized to influence behaviour indirectly by giving outcomes and decisions certain meanings; by legitimizing and justifying them.

Pfeffer (1981a, 1981b) considered a similar use of power when he distinguished sentiment (attitudinal) from substantive (behavioural) outcomes of power. The latter depend largely on resource dependency considerations, while the former refer to the way that people feel about the outcomes and are mainly influenced by the symbolic aspects of power, such as the use of political language, symbols, and rituals. Pfeffer (1981a) argued that there is only a weak relationship between symbolic power and substantive outcomes: that symbolic power is only used *post hoc* to legitimize outcomes already achieved by resource dependencies. In this way, Pfeffer stops short of acknowledging that power can be used to prevent conflict and opposition. There is, however, an inconsistency in Pfeffer's arguments: if symbolic power is effective enough to 'quiet' opposition *ex post*, why not use it *ex ante* to prevent opposition from arising in the first place? The only factor preventing Pfeffer from reaching this conclusion is his refusal to acknowledge the existence of power in situations other than those characterized by conflict and opposition (Pfeffer, 1981a: 7).

Despite the work of these writers and others (e.g., Clegg, 1975; Gaventa, 1980; Ranson et al., 1980; Hardy, 1985), the management 'school' remained distant from the more critical work on domination. The majority of management writers continued to focus on dependency and to define power in terms of conflict and illegitimacy (e.g., Mayes & Allen, 1977; MacMillan, 1978; Gandz & Murray, 1980; Narayanan & Fahey, 1982; Mintzberg, 1983; Gray & Ariss, 1985; Pettigrew, 1985; Enz, 1988; Schwenk, 1989; Pfeffer, 1992). Pfeffer's (1981a) prevarication is, in fact, indicative of the entire field. The idea of managers conceptualizing power in a more critical way threatens to open up a can of worms for a perspective grounded in managerialism. Rather than delve into the power hidden in and mobilized through apparently neutral structures, cultures, and technologies, the vast majority of researchers preferred to continue to view these constructs as apolitical management tools.

# POWER AND CHANGE: RELUCTANT INCREMENTALISM?

The previous two sections document the emergence of two approaches, with diverging trajectories, to the study of power—the critical and the managerial, which by the mid-1980s appear firmly established. In this section, we explore how these two conceptualizations of power relate to work on organizational change. As Bradshaw and Boonstra note in Chapter 13, the role of power in organizational change efforts was recognized in the early 1970s. What have been its assumptions regarding the nature of power and how have they changed?

We would argue that the change literature has been—and still is—firmly fixated on the idea that power is exercised only in the face of conflict. It fact, this assumption is embedded in the obsession of both practitioners and academics with resistance. In Chapter 15 (Table 15.1), Bennebroek Gravenhorst and in 't Veld show how, in traditionally, resistance is seen as an inevitable and natural reaction to organizational change. Estimates suggest that around three-quarters of change programmes fail because of some form of resistance, whether in the USA, the UK, or Europe (see the Introduction). The reasons are complex but many change theorists attribute the blame to the way in which employees experience a loss of self-control, autonomy, status, and benefits (Morris & Raben, 1995) either because of the change or because of the way the change is handled (Spiker & Lesser, 1995).

In this regard, organizational change theorists do subscribe to one assumption of the critical theorists, that is: power and resistance, although substantively different, are intertwined. Without the possibility of resistance there is no need for power. Or, to be more accurate, if there is resistance (on the part of the employees), there is justification for the use of power (on the part of managers). Despite this similarity, the conceptualization of resistance in the organizational change literature is not the one associated with the critical tradition: this is not resistance to domination, but resistance of a dysfunctional kind driven by employees' need for security. When critical theorists differentiate resistance and power to signify 'qualitatively different contributions to the outcome of power relations made by those who exercise power over others, on the one hand, and those subject to that power, on the other' (Barbalet, 1985: 545), they juxtapose resistance against domination and in so doing legitimate resistance. Organizational change theorists, on the other hand, juxtapose resistance against rationality—management's 'rational' approach to change is 'threatened' by resistance in the form of illegitimate behaviour that is directed against it—and in so doing legitimate the use of power by managers. The result, as we shall see, has been the grafting of power strategies on to the 'truth and love' of the original T-groups and the common sense of the rational manager.

For example, the humanist, rational traditional has pushed effective communication to the forefront of change strategies: most change models refer to the importance of communicating change as a means of avoiding resistance, with various suggestions for developing an effective communications strategy (Klein, 1996). The potential for communication glitches are considerable. Ford and Ford (1995) identify a number of communication breakdowns, e.g., conversations may take place with the wrong people, i.e., individuals who are not in a position to take action relating to change; there may be a lack of clarity in communicating what the change is, where it is headed, and what expectations are associated with it; even when there is agreement about the need for change, there may be a lack of understanding about what needs to be done and who has responsibility for specific actions; and expectations or deadlines are not always adequately communicated, leading to problems with implementing change. However, by engaging in the right kind of conversations, managers can overcome these problems.

Other writers have highlighted the need for the right kind of talk (Marshak, 1993). Use of the imagery of building, growing, or nurturing for incremental, developmental change; and phrases such as 'leaving the old behind', 'taking the best route', and 'avoiding obstacles and dead ends', will help implement transitional change, which entails moving from the existing situation to an improved one; transformational change needs terms like 'recreating ourselves', 're-inventing', and 'waking-up'. Use the wrong words to communicate a particular type of change, and you will run into problems as you send a mixed message and add confusion to the change process. Other writers relate the type of talk to the underlying value structure of the organization (e.g., Kabanoff et al., 1995). Elite organizations need to communicate change in a top-down manner; meritocratic organizations emphasize the constructive role of employees in change; collegial organizations are more apt to convey positive images of change including employee involvement and benefits. This research indicates that communication strategies that fail to appreciate the change context will run into problems (Palmer & Hardy, 2000).

In other words, communicate the change properly and employees will see the light: change is beneficial and, once everyone understands that, change programmes can progress uninterruptedly. In this way, humanist and rational views are both based on a unitary view of organizations where common goals bind employees and managers to the organization (Fox, 1973). In the unhappy event that employees remain unconvinced of the benefits of change, which must surely attach to managerial prerogative, managers can resort to the pluralist model of organizations and use 'power and conflict to force movement through the process by overcoming resistance and encouraging the driving forces of change' (French & Delahaye, 1996: 22). However, in both informing employees and exerting pressure on them (Bennebroek Gravenhorst & in 't Veld: Chapter 15, Table 15.1), organizational change managers sit astride a rather uneasy and conflicting set of assumptions: the pluralist perspective of management and employees as opposing parties jostles against the unitarist view of management and employees as united by common goals (Fox, 1973). Similarly, the change strategies advocated by Kotter and Schlesinger (1979) in Chapter 15, Table 15.2 (Bennebroek Gravenhorst & in 't Veld), range from education, participation, and facilitation—all associated with a unitary view of management— to negotiation, manipulation, coercion, which are associated with a pluralist framework. Nor have things changed much: Chapter 14 by Yukl suggests a combination of rational persuasion, consultation, collaboration, and apprising on the unitary side vs coalitions, ingratiation, pressure, and exchange, on the side of pluralism. The uneasy jostling still exists.

What is new to Yukl's list, perhaps, is the use of inspirational appeals for change. This strategy is undoubtedly influenced by the work on charismatic power and transformational leadership that emerged in the 1980s and 1990s, which assumes (usually implicitly) that power is used responsibly to achieve organizational objectives, even though much of what we know about charismatic power comes from studying such leaders as Hitler and Mussolini (Hardy & Clegg, 1996). We would also argue that this type of strategy represents a management of meaning: change is linked to a person's values through 'ideological appeals' wherein 'no tangible rewards are promised, only the prospect that the target person will feel good as a result' through invocation and use of vivid imagery, metaphors, symbols (Yukl, Chapter 14) in a manner reminiscent of Lukes' third dimensional use of power.

In this way, communication strategies make the transition from revealing the truth to managing meaning. Now, it would seem, organizational change theorists have the complete portfolio of strategies— having bolted the pluralist on to the unitary model, they can manage those situations when humanism and rationality fail to do the job. The radical model has been appropriated (although not necessarily knowingly) for managerial use in circumventing the inconvenience of resistance. The reluctance in the change literature to deal with power in the context of change has been overcome through the way in which it has been incrementally incorporated into strategies for change.

## THE END OF SOVEREIGNTY

Neither the critical nor the managerial conceptualization of power described above remained fixed. In fact, important changes were about to occur as the work of postmodern thinking started to infiltrate organization and management theory. In particular, the arrival of Foucault on the power scene posed a fundamental challenge by sounding the death-knell of sovereignty. The idea that power could be exercised strategically and successfully against intended targets was deeply embedded in the views of critical and management theorists alike. In disposing of sovereignty, Foucault's work transformed the study of power through the way it introduced the idea of disciplinary power, de-centred the subject, and laid the foundations for new notions of resistance (see, for example, Deetz, 1992a, 1992b; Alvesson & Deetz, 1996; Hardy & Leiba-O'Sullivan, 1998; Mumby, 2001).

## POWER AND DISCIPLINE

Foucault's (1977) understanding of 'disciplinary practices' led to an interest in the 'micro-techniques' of power. Unlike Weber's rule systems, these techniques are not ordinarily thought of in terms of the causal concept of power (the notion of someone getting someone else to do something that they would not otherwise do). Instead, they represent ways in which both individual and collectively organized bodies become socially inscribed and normalized through routine aspects of organizations—much closer to Weber's emphasis on the importance of discipline in phenomena such as Taylorism than his more theoretical accounts of power as a social action. Through discipline, power is embedded in the fibre and fabric of everyday life. At the core of Foucault's work were practices of 'surveillance', which may be more or less mediated by instrumentation. Historically, the tendency is for a greater instrumentation to develop as surveillance moves from a literal supervisory gaze to more complex forms of observation, reckoning, and comparison. Surveillance, whether personal, technical, bureaucratic, or legal, ranges through forms of supervision, routinization, formalization, mechanization, legislation, and design that seek to effect increasing control of employee behaviour, dispositions, and embodiment. Surveillance is not only accomplished through direct control. It may happen as a result of cultural practices of moral endorsement, enablement, and persuasion, or as a result of more formalized technical knowledge, such as the computer monitoring of keyboard output or low cost drug-testing systems.

The effectiveness of disciplinary power in the nineteenth century was linked to the emergence of new techniques of discipline appropriate for more impersonal, large-scale settings in which the *Gemeinschaft* conditions whereby each person knew their place no longer prevailed (Foucault, 1977; Bauman, 1982). Previous localized, moral regulation, premised on the transparency of the person to the gaze of the community, was no longer viable. So, new forms of state institution emerged in which new forms of control were adopted, and later copied by the factory masters. However, as Foucault was at pains to point out, no grand plan caused these institutions to adopt similar forms of disciplinary technique. Rather, people copied what was already available, creating their own world in isomorphic likeness of key features they already knew. Disciplinary techniques had been readily available in the monastic milieu of religious vocation, the military, institutional forms of schooling, poor houses, etc., and their effectiveness had been established during the past two centuries. These relations of meaning and membership were reproduced and dispersed as the basis for social integration in other organizations in a manner not unlike that described as institutional innovation (Meyer & Rowan, 1977; DiMaggio & Powell, 1983).

At a more general level, the 'disciplinary gaze' of surveillance shaped the development of disciplines of knowledge in the nineteenth century in such areas as branches of social welfare, statistics, and administration (Foucault, 1977). Organizationally, the twentieth-century development of the personnel function under the 'human relations' guidance of Mayo (1975) may be seen to have had a similar tutelary role (see Clegg, 1979; Ray, 1986). Such mechanisms are often local, diverse, and uncoordinated. They form no grand strategy. Yet, abstract properties of people, goods, and services can be produced that are measurable, gradeable, and assessable in an overall anonymous strategy of discipline. In this way, Foucault challenged sovereign notions of power: power was no longer a deterministic resource, able to be conveniently manipulated by legitimate managers against recalcitrant, illegitimate resistance by lower orders. Instead, all actors operated within an existing structure of dominancy—a prevailing web of power relations—from which the prospects of escape were limited for dominant and subordinate groups alike.

## POWER AND IDENTITY

The work of Foucault and other postmodern theorists has also been important in challenging previous conceptions of identities, showing:

> the contemporary vanity of humankind in placing the 'individual', a relatively recent and culturally specific category, at the centre of the social, psychological, economic, and moral universe. The subject, decentred, relative, is acknowledged not as a stable constellation of essential characteristics, but as a socially constituted, socially recognized, category of analysis. For example, no necessarily essential attributes characterize 'men' or 'women'. Instead the subjectivity of those labelled as such is culturally and historically variable and specific. (Clegg & Hardy, 1996: 3)

Not surprisingly, Foucauldian insights have played an important role in the work on gender. Early contributions (e.g., Kanter, 1975, 1977; Wolff, 1977; Gutek & Cohen, 1982) had already noted the way in which women were systematically subjected to power inside organizations in ways that were inseparable from their broader social role.

By the 1970s, scholars were increasingly aware of not only the gender blindness of organizations but also of organization studies itself (see Mills & Tancred, 1992, for a brief overview). Major texts were reassessed in terms of how their contribution to the literature was often premised on unspoken assumptions about gender or unobserved and unremarked sampling decisions or anomalies, in gender terms (Acker & Van Houton, 1974; Brown, 1979). For example, Crozier's (1964) maintenance workers were all men while the production workers were all women. As Hearn and Parkin (1983) were to demonstrate, this blindness was symptomatic of the field as a whole, not any specific paradigm within it.

A peculiar irony attaches to this, as Pringle (1989) was to develop. Gender and sexuality are extremely pervasive aspects of organizational life. In major occupational areas, such as secretaries and receptionists, for example, organizational identity is defined through gender and the projection of forms of emotionality, and, indeed, sexuality, implicated in it. The mediation of, and resistance to, the routine rule enactments of organizations are inextricably tied in with gender since behaviour is defined not only as organizationally appropriate or inappropriate, but its appropriateness is characterized in gendered terms. Neatness, smartness, demureness take on gendered dimensions (Mills, 1988, 1989; Mills & Murgatroyd, 1991). Rather than challenging these taken-for-granted assumptions, the gender bias inherent in the study of organization has helped to preserve the status quo. How else could the vantage point and privileges of white, usually Anglo-Saxon, normally American, males have been taken for granted for so long (Calás & Smircich, 1992)?

Functionality attaches to dominant ideologies: presumably that is why they dominate (Abercrombie et al., 1980). Repression is not necessarily an objective or a prerequisite, but often simply a by-product of an ideology that maximizes the organization's ability to act. Masculinist ideology has long been dominant in the majority of organizations. Certain male identities constituted in socially and economically privileged contexts routinely will be more strategically contingent for organizational decision-making, and for access to and success in hierarchically arranged careers (Heath, 1981). However, organizations do not produce actions that are masculinist, so much as masculinism produces organizations that take masculinist action. Often they do this without anyone even being explicitly aware of it. In such a case the decisions that characterize organizational action will be a result, not a cause, of ideology. Organizations may be the arenas in which gender politics play out, and, as such, suitable places for treatment through anti-discriminatory policies. But, such 'solutions' may address only the symptoms and not the causes of deep-seated gender politics. Attacking their organizational expression may suppress these symptoms but it is unlikely to cure the body politic, behind which there is a history of living and being in a gendered world that is tacit, taken for granted, and constitutive of the very sense of that everyday life-world.

People's identities are not tied up only in their gender or sexuality, any more than in the type of labour power that they sell to an organization. People in organizations are signifiers of meaning. As such, they are subject to regimes of specific organizational signification and discipline, usually simultaneously. Identities premised on the salience of extra-organizational issues such as ethnicity, gender, class, age, and other phenomena, provide a means of resistance to these organizational significations and discipline, by providing resources with which to limit the discretion of organizational action. Who may do what, how, where, when, and in which ways are customarily and, sometimes, legally specific identities, which are prescribed or proscribed for certain forms of practice. Embodied identities will only be salient in as much as they are socially recognized and organizationally consequent. Consequently, forms of embodiment such as age, gender, sexuality, ethnicity, religiosity, and handicap are particularly recognizable as bases that serve to locate practices for stratifying organization members, as evidenced by their being the precise target of various anti-discrimination laws.

Accordingly organizations are structures of patriarchal domination, ethnic domination, age domination, and so on. Such matters are clearly contingent: most organizations may be structures of class, gender, or ethnic dominancy but not all necessarily will be. Too much hinges on other aspects of organization identity left unconsidered. In specific organizational contexts, for example, the general conditions of economic or class domination may not necessarily be the focus of resistance or struggle. More specific loci of domination may be organizationally salient; after all, divisions of labour are embodied, gendered, departmentalized, hierarchized, spatially separated, and so on. As a result, organizations are locales in which negotiation, contestation, and struggle between organizationally divided and linked agencies are a routine occurrence.

Divisions of labour are both the object and outcome of struggle. All divisions of labour within any employing organization are necessarily constituted within the context of various contracts and conditions of employment. Hence the employment relationship of economic domination and subordination is the underlying sediment over which other organization practices are stratified and overlaid, often in quite complex ways. This complexity of organizational locales renders them subject to multivalent powers rather than monadic sites of total control: contested terrains rather than total institutions. It is these struggles of power and resistance that those approaches influenced by Foucault seem best able to appreciate, because they are not predisposed to know in advance who the victorious and vanquished *dramatis personae* should be. Rather, the emphasis is on the play of meaning, signification, and action through which all organization actors seek to script, direct, and position all others.

## POWER AND RESISTANCE REVISITED

Resistance may be defined as the 'efficacious influence of those subordinate to power' (Barbalet, 1985: 542). Given that any member of a complex organization is only one relay in a complex flow of authority up, down, and across organization hierarchies, resistance will always be incipient. Ideally, according to management, connections between these relays should not confront resistance; there should be no 'problem' of obedience. Rarely, if ever, is this the case, as organization researchers have long known because of the complexity and contingency of human agency. Instead, resistance is pervasive as organizational actors use their discretion. It is the ability to exercise discretion—to have chosen this rather than that course of action—which characterizes power, both on the part of power holders, those who are its subjects, and on the part of those who are its objects.

Important implications flow from the relationship between power, resistance, and discretion. Power will always be inscribed within contextual 'rules of the game', which both enable and constrain action (Clegg, 1975). Such rules can never be free of surplus or ambiguous meaning: they can never provide for their own interpretation. Issues of interpretation are always implicated in the processes whereby agencies make reference to and signify rules (Garfinkel, 1967; Wittgenstein, 1968; Clegg, 1975; Barnes, 1986). 'Ruling' is thus an activity: it is accomplished by some agency as a constitutive sense-making process whereby attempts are made to fix meaning. Both rules and games necessarily tend to be the subject of contested interpretation and, although some players may have the advantage of also being the referee, there is always discretion, and therein lies the possibility of resistance.

Thus, there is the central paradox of power: the power of an agency is increased in principle by that agency delegating authority; the delegation of authority can only proceed by rules; rules necessarily entail discretion; and discretion potentially empowers delegates. From this arises the tacit and taken-for-granted basis of organizationally negotiated order, and, on occasion, its fragility and instability, as has been so well observed by Strauss (1978). Matters must be rendered routine and predictable if negotiation is to remain an unusual and out of the ordinary state of affairs. Thus, freedom of discretion requires disciplining if it is to be a reliable relay. In this way, power is implicated in authority and constituted by rules; rules embody discretion and provide opportunities for resistance; and, so, their interpretation must be disciplined, if new powers are not to be produced and existing powers transformed.

Given the inherent indexicality of rule use, things will never be wholly stable even though they may appear so historically (Laclau & Mouffe, 1985). Resistance to discipline is thus irremediable because of the power/rule constitution as a nexus of meaning and interpretation, which is always open to being re-fixed. So, although the term 'organization' implies stabilization of control—of corporate and differential membership categories across space and across time—this control is never total. Indeed, it is often the contradictions in the evolution of regimes of control that explain their development (Clegg & Dunkerley, 1980). Resistance and power thus comprise a system of power relations in which the possibilities of, and tensions between, both domination and liberation inevitably exist (Sawicki, 1991: 98). Politics is a struggle both to achieve and escape from power (Wrong, 1979; Hindess, 1982; Barbalet, 1985; Clegg, 1994). Such a view involves a reconceptualization from the duality of power (domination) or resistance (liberation) that had existed in sociological literature (e.g., Giddens, 1979, 1982). It challenges the views of sovereign power which, at their furthest reach, embraced the fiction of supreme 'super-agency' while denying authentic sovereignty to others: an overarching 'A' imposing its will on the many 'B's. Concepts of the ruling class, ruling state, and ruling culture or ideology overwhelmed the consciousness of subjects, thereby creating false consciousness (and explaining the absence of the realization of Marx's revolutionary predictions). In this way, writers like Lukes (1974) accepted the problematic of 'hegemony' (Gramsci, 1971) or 'dominant ideology' (Abercrombie et al., 1980) and presumed to know, unproblematically, what the real interests of the oppressed really were.

The recognition that the space and ambiguity in which resistance is fostered do not lead to a transformation of prevailing power relations, that resistance only reinforces those power relations, is the sobering implication of the Foucauldian-influenced tradition (Clegg, 1979; Knights & Willmott, 1989; Knights & Morgan, 1991). The death of the sovereign subject also killed originating sources of action: none were to inhabit the post-structural world since the pervasiveness of power relations makes them difficult to resist. Prevailing discourses are experienced as fact, which makes alternatives difficult to conceive of, let alone enact. In addition, the production of identity confers a positive experience on individuals (Knights & Willmott, 1989). It transforms 'individuals into subjects who secure their sense of what it is to be worthy and competent human beings' (Knights & Morgan, 1991: 269). Consequently, resistance has a price to pay—the positive effects of power, as experienced in the individual's sense of him or herself, have to be repudiated as part of any emancipatory process. A critical questioning of one's beliefs may 'estrange the individual from the tradition that has formed his or her subjectivity' (Alvesson & Willmott, 1992: 447).

Another limitation on resistance came from Foucault's attack on modernist assumptions that with knowledge comes 'truth'. Foucault regarded the concept of ideology—which helped to explain why individuals did not act on their 'real' interests—as a 'falsehood' whose relational opposition to 'truth' can never be too far away. By demonstrating how the 'truths' and 'falsehoods' of particular discourses had been constituted historically, Foucault showed that language cannot mask anything; it simply represents possibilities. No assumption of reality exists as anything more than its representation in language and, consequently, no situation is ever free from power. With knowledge only comes more power:

> [T]ruth isn't the reward of free spirits, the child of protracted solitude, nor the privilege of those who have succeeded in liberating themselves. Truth is a thing of this world: it is produced only by virtue of multiple forms of constraint. And it induces regular effects of power. Each society has its regime of truth, its 'general' politics of truth: that is, the type of discourse which it accepts and makes function as true; the mechanisms and instances which enable one to distinguish true and false statements, the means by which each is sanctioned; and the techniques and procedures accorded value in the acquisition of truth; the status of those who are charged with saying what counts as true. (Foucault, 1980: 131)

The idea that power/knowledge could not be decoupled meant that salvation was not to be found in privileged understandings and attempts to discover a 'genuine' order. Thus, the modernist idea that demystifying processes and structures of domination would help the subjugated to escape from them and set up new structures that were free from power was shaken to its roots:

> No longer a disinterested observer, acutely aware of the social and historical positioning of all subjects and the particular intellectual frameworks through which they are rendered visible, the researcher can only produce knowledge already embedded in the power of those very frameworks. No privileged position exists from which analysis might arbitrate. (Clegg & Hardy, 1996: 3)

Claims to know the real interests of any group, other than through the techniques of representation used to assert them, could not survive this re-conceptualization of power. Accordingly, critical writers started to view their phenomenon of choice afresh and to consider the implications for resistance.

The result was a theoretical struggle between those who contended that Foucault's work was compatible with the idea of resistance (e.g., Smart, 1985, 1986, 1990; Sawicki, 1991; Alvesson & Willmott, 1992; Knights & Vurdubakis, 1994) and those who argued that his work was antithetical to notions of liberation and emancipation (e.g., Hoy, 1986; Said, 1986; Walzer, 1986; White, 1986; Ashley, 1990; Ackroyd & Thompson, 1999). Emerging from this debate came a more nuanced view of resistance. Wrestling with not only with Foucauldian pessimism, but also the 'advent of corporate cultural manipulation, electronic surveillance and self-managing teams', critical depictions of workplace resistance seemed to 'herald the demise of worker opposition' as studies showed 'totalizing portrayals of new management controls' (Fleming & Sewell, 2002: 858). Some blamed Foucault for writing resistance out of the story (Ackroyd & Thompson, 1999). Others used Foucault to reconceptualize resistance in governmental terms: if management practice targeted 'the hearts and minds of workers' (Fleming & Spicer, 2002) to produce 'engineered selves' (Kunda, 1992), 'designer selves' (Casey, 1995), and 'enterprising selves' (du Gay, 1996), then definitions of resistance needed to be less conspicuous, less organized, and more subtle (Fleming & Spicer, 2002). Accordingly, recent studies have included more mundane, micro, individualist, and localized forms of resistance (e.g., Tretheway, 1997; Murphy, 1998; Ackroyd & Thompson, 1999; Knights & McCabe, 2000; Ezzamel et al., 2001; Fleming & Sewell, 2002; Fleming & Spicer, 2003).

## POWER AND CHANGE: SELECTIVE SUBVERSION?

Our earlier analysis shows that change management initially dealt with critical developments in the conceptualization of power by ignoring them and clinging to unitary assumptions. When practice did not prove consistent with these assumptions, change management then appropriated critical insights. Thus, when employees refused to conform to the unitary view, managers abandoned the original humanist principles and adopted the power tactics worthy of any self-respecting pluralist; when conflict proved inconvenient, the instrumental aspects of the management of meaning were incorporated into change management strategies. In this way, change management subverted critical goals of emancipation by selectively employing strategies for managerial purposes. This is not to say that this was necessarily a conscious or deliberate move. In fact, it is more likely to have been an emergent strategy—as ideas from critical theory started to seep out into the wider academic and practitioner arena, ideas that were useful were adopted in a de-contextualized fashion that stripped usage from underlying assumptions and resulted in the uneasy jostling of unitary and pluralist approaches.

Similar moves seem to be occurring in the case of Foucault's insights. At first glance, Foucauldian conceptualizations of power pose problems for organizational change: if sovereignty is dead, how can managers use power to bring about change? Notwithstanding this potential difficulty, these ideas are infiltrating change management (Grant et al., 2002), as indicated by Table 13.4 in Chapter 13 by Bradshaw and Boonstra, which talks of 'deep personal power' as defined by authentic existence (self-awareness through reflection), critical consciousness (deep learning and political awareness), scepticism (questioning), and defiance (disobedience). What can we detect from these as yet undeveloped strategies for change management?

We would argue that these strategies simply ignore the inconvenient aspects of Foucault's work, while colonizing those that offer potential for change management. Thus, the inability to pull the strings of power, associated with a view of power that 'is never localized here or there, never in anybody's hands, never appropriated as a commodity or piece of wealth' (Foucault, 1980: 98), is reinterpreted as a system of power that is 'inherently diffused and shared among individuals' that allows individuals 'to become potentially active agents' (Bradshaw & Boonstra, Chapter 13). The net is appropriated; the problem of strategic agency is ignored. Similarly, to counter the disciplinary gaze, individuals are exhorted to be 'authentic' by 'acting in congruence with one's own values and beliefs' and to stand 'outside dominant discourses'. Foucault's gaze is acknowledged; his disavowals of the authentic self and the possibility of standing outside discourse are rejected.

In reinterpreting Foucault for managerial purposes, change programmes home in on one aspect of Foucauldian-inspired work in particular—the notion of identity. If power is productive of identity, then identity becomes a target of change programmes—it is no longer enough for employees to believe that change is good; now they must *feel* it. The very emotions of the employee are at stake, which must now be made consistent with and supportive of change programmes (e.g., French & Delahaye, 1996; Vince & Broussine, 1996). The hearts and souls of employees are to be won over to the change effort. Perhaps that is what explains the selectivity and the subversion of the change literature—never quite able to discard the loving memory of its T-group history, the change management literature would like everyone to be on board, committed to what can only be the common good. And, if that is not possible, then power can be used to try to keep the hearts and minds of employees on track.

## CONCLUSION

We conclude with the acknowledgement that organizational change inevitably involves power: those who fulfil change agency roles in organizations, as well as those who wish to sabotage or resist others involved in such roles, must steer their strategies through the use of power. Proponents and opponents of change alike have to be good players in the game of power and good game players will be those who can creatively improvise around political themes, using governmental tactics such as image building and releasing selective information; those who can scapegoat opponents or create alliances to encircle them, networking with significant others and compromising them when necessary; those who can be ruthless strategists as the occasion demands, manipulating rules when needs be. Such skills need to be deployed in a context of specific organizational features, stakeholders, and political entrepreneurship, all of which must be mastered on the basis of formal and tacit warrants for power, produced through accounts that create reputations and identities as they seek to achieve outcomes.

Additionally, players in the game of organizational change need to be able to ask questions about the ways in which to characterize their power games. Are they ethically acceptable? Are they warranted in terms deemed contextually reasonable? Can they account for them plausibly? What will be the consequences for those whose identities are involved? What aspects of whose identity will be weakened, strengthened, or unchanged? These players must address the appropriate *degree* of politics deployed; the acceptability of the political means engaged, and the extent to which they can create an appearance of legitimacy of the political goals for which they strive (Buchanan & Badham, 1999). To manage change is to be politically competent. Those change agents who are not politically skilled will fail but their failure will not discredit the need for change so much as merely strengthen the governmental resolve to get it right next time. Perversely, much of the organizational change management literature will only assist their failure, because of its lack of pragmatism about power.

## REFERENCES

Abercrombie, N., Hill, S. & Turner, B.S. (1980) *The Dominant Ideology Thesis*. London: Allen and Unwin.

Acker, J. & Van Houton, D. (1974) Differential recruitment and control: the sex structuring of organizations. *Administrative Science Quarterly*, **119**(2), 152–163.

Ackroyd, S. & Thompson, P. (1999) *Organizational Misbehaviour*. London: Sage.

Alvesson, M. (1984) Questioning rationality and ideology: on critical organization theory. *International Studies of Management and Organizations*, **14**(1), 61–79.

Alvesson, M. & Deetz, S. (1996) Critical theory and postmodernism approaches to organizational studies. In S.R. Clegg, C. Hardy & W.R. Nord (eds) *Handbook of Organizational Studies* (pp. 191–217). London: Sage.

Alvesson, M. & Willmott, H. (1992) On the idea of emancipation in management and organization studies. *Academy of Management Review*, **17**(3), 432–464.

Ashley, D. (1990) Habermas and the completion of the 'project of modernity'. In B.S. Turner (ed.) *Theories of Modernity and Post Modernity* (pp. 88–107). London: Sage.

Astley, W.G. & Sachdeva, P.S. (1984) Structural sources of intraorganizational power: a theoretical synthesis. *Academy of Management Review*, **9**(1), 104–113.

Bachrach, P. & Baratz, M.S. (1962) The two faces of power. *American Political Science Review*, **56**, 947–952.

Bachrach, P. & Baratz, M.S. (1963) Decisions and nondecisions: an analytical framework. *American Political Science Review*, **57**, 641–651.

Bachrach, P. & Baratz, M.S. (1970) *Power and Poverty*. London: Oxford University Press.

Barbalet, J.M. (1985) Power and resistance. *British Journal of Sociology*, **36**(4), 531–548.

Barnes, B. (1986) On authority and its relationship to power. In J. Law (ed.) *Power, Action and Belief: A New Sociology of Knowledge?* (pp. 180–195). London: Routledge.

Bauman, Z. (1982) *Memories of Class: The Pre-History and After-Life of Class*. London: Routledge.

Benfari, R.C., Wilkinson, H.E. & Orth, C.D. (1986) The effective use of power. *Business Horizons*, **29**(3), 12–16.

Bennis, W.G., Berkowitz, N., Affinito, M. & Malone, M. (1958) Authority, power and the ability to influence. *Human Relations*, **11**(2), 143–156.

Braverman, H. (1974) *Labor and Monopoly Capital*. New York: Monthly Review Press.

Brown, L.K. (1979) Women and business management. *Signs: Journal of Women in Culture and Society*, **5**, 266–287.

Buchanan, D. & Badham, R. (1999) *Power, Politics, and Organizational Change: Winning the Turf Game*. London: Sage.

Burawoy, M. (1979) *Manufacturing Consent*. Chicago: Chicago University Press.

Calás, M.B. & Smircich, L. (1992) Using the 'F' word: feminist theories and the social consequences of organizational research. In A. Mills & P. Tancred (eds) *Gendering Organization Analysis* (pp. 222–234). London: Sage.

Carchedi, G. (1987) *Class Analysis and Social Research*. Oxford: Blackwell.

Casey, C. (1995) *Work, Self and Society: After Industrialism*. London: Sage.

Clegg, S.R. (1975) *Power, Rule and Domination*. London: Routledge.

Clegg, S.R. (1979) *The Theory of Power and Organization*. London: Routledge.

Clegg, S.R. (1989a) *Frameworks of Power*. London: Sage.

Clegg, S.R. (1989b) Radical revisions: power, discipline and organizations. *Organization Studies*, **10**(1), 97–115.

Clegg, S.R. (1990) *Modern Organizations: Organization Studies for the Postmodern World*. London: Sage.

Clegg, S.R. (1994) Power relations and the constitution of the resistant subject. In J.M. Jermier, W.R Nord & D. Knights (eds) *Resistance and Power in Organizations: Agency, Subjectivity and the Labour Process* (pp. 274–325). London: Routledge.

Clegg, S.R. & Dunkerley, D. (1980) *Organization, Class and Control*. London: Routledge.

Clegg, S. & Hardy, C. (1996) Introduction. In S. Clegg, C. Hardy & W. Nord (eds) *Handbook of Organization Studies* (pp. 1–28). London: Sage.

Clegg, S.R., Boreham, P. & Dow, G. (1986) *Class, Politics and the Economy*. London: Routledge.

Collinson, D. (1994) Strategies as resistance: power, knowledge and subjectivity. In J.M. Jermier, W.R Nord & D. Knights (eds) *Resistance and Power in Organizations: Agency, Subjectivity and the Labour Process* (pp. 25–68). London: Routledge.

Crozier, M. (1964) *The Bureaucratic Phenomenon*. Chicago: University of Chicago Press.

Cyert, R.M. & March, J.G. (1963) *A Behavioral Theory of the Firm*. Englewood Cliffs, NJ: Prentice Hall.

Dahl, R. (1957) The concept of power. *Behavioral Science*, **20**, 201–215.

Dahl, R. (1961) *Who Governs: Democracy and Power in an American City*. New Haven, CT: Yale University Press.

Deetz, S. (1985) Critical-cultural research: new sensibilities and old realities. *Journal of Management*, **11**(2), 121–136.

Deetz, S. (1992a) *Democracy in an Age of Corporate Colonization: Developments in Communication and the Politics of Everyday Life*. Albany, NY: State University of New York.

Deetz, S. (1992b) Disciplinary power in the modern corporation. In M. Alvesson & H. Willmott (eds) *Critical Management Studies* (pp. 21–45). London: Sage.

DiMaggio, P.J. & Powell, W.W. (1983) The iron cage revisited: institutional isomorphism and collective rationality in organizational fields. *American Sociological Review*, **48**, 147–160.

Dubin, R. (1957) Power and union–management relations. *Administrative Science Quarterly*, **2**, 60–81.

du Gay, P. (1996) *Consumption and Identity at Work*. London: Sage.

Edelman, M. (1964) *The Symbolic Uses of Politics*. Champaign, IL: University of Illinois Press.

Edelman, M. (1971) *Politics as Symbolic Action*. Chicago: Markham.

Edelman, M. (1977) *Political Language*. London: Academic Press.

Edwards, R. (1979) *Contested Terrain*. New York: Basic Books.

Emerson, R.M. (1962) Power-dependence relations. *American Sociological Review*, **27**(1), 31–41.

Enz, C.A. (1988) The role of value congruity in intraorganizational power. *Administrative Science Quarterly*, **33**, 284–304.

Ezzamel, M., Willmott, H. & Worthington, F. (2001) Power, control and resistance in the factory that time forgot. *Journal of Management Studies*, **38**(8), 1053–1079.

Fiol, M. (2002) Capitalizing on paradox: the role of language in transforming organizational identities. *Organization Science*, **13**(6), 653–666.

Fleming, P. & Sewell, G. (2002) Looking for the Good Soldier, Svejk: alternative modalities of resistance in the contemporary workplace. *Sociology*, **36**(4), 857–873.

Fleming, P. & Spicer, A. (2002) Workers playtime? Unravelling the paradox of covert resistance in the contemporary workplace. In S. Clegg (ed.) *Paradoxical New Directions in Management and Organization Theory* (pp. 65–85). Amsterdam: John Benjamins.

Fleming, P. & Spicer, A. (2003) Working at a cynical distance: implications for subjectivity, power and resistance. *Organization*, **10**(1), 157–179.

Ford, J.D. & Ford, L.W. (1995) The role of conversations in producing intentional change in organizations. *Academy of Management Review*, **20**(3), 541–570.

Forester, J. (1989) *Planning in the Face of Power*. Berkeley, CA: University of California Press.

Foucault, M. (1977) *Discipline and Punish: The Birth of the Prison*. Harmondsworth: Penguin.

Foucault, M. (1980) *Power/Knowledge: Selected Interviews and Other Writings 1972–1977*. Brighton: Harvester Press.

Fox, A. (1973) Industrial relations: a social critique of pluralist ideology. In J. Child (ed.) *Man and Organization*. London: Allen and Unwin.

French, E. & Delahaye, B. (1996) Individual change transition: moving in circles can be good for you. *Leadership and Organization Development Journal*, **17**(7), 22–32.

French, J.R.P. & Raven, B. (1968) The bases of social power. In D. Cartwright & A. Zander (eds) *Group Dynamics*. New York: Harper & Row.

Frost, P.J. (1987) Power, politics and influence. In F.M. Tablin, L.L. Putnam, K.H. Roberts & L.W. Porter (eds) *Handbook of Organizational Communications: An Interdisciplinary Perspective*. London: Sage.

Frost, P.J. (1988) The role of organizational power and politics in human resource management. In G.R. Ferris & K.M. Rowland (eds) *International Human Resources Management*. Greenwich, CT: JAI Press.

Gamble, A. & Walton, P. (1972) *From Alienation to Surplus Value*. London: Croom Helm.

Gandz, J. & Murray, V.V. (1980) The experience of workplace politics. *Academy of Management Journal*, **23**(2), 237–251.

Garfinkel, H. (1967) *Studies in Ethnomethodology*. Englewood Cliffs, NJ: Prentice Hall.

Gaventa, J. (1980) *Power and Powerlessness: Quiescence and Rebellion in an Appalachian Valley*. Oxford: Clarendon Press.

Geyer, R.F. & Schweitzer, D. (1981) *Alienation: Problems of Meaning, Theory and Method*. London: Routledge.

Giddens, A. (1979) *Central Problems in Social Theory*. London: Macmillan.

Giddens, A. (1982) A reply to my critics. *Theory, Culture and Society*, **1**(2), 107–113.

Gramsci, A. (1971) *Selections from the Prison Notebooks*. London: Lawrence and Wishart.

Grant, D., Wailes, N., Michelson, G., Brewer, A. & Hall, R. (eds) (2002) Special issue: rethinking organizational change. *Strategic Change*, **11**(5).

Gray, B. & Ariss, S.S. (1985) Politics and strategic change across organizational life cycles. *Academy of Management Review*, **10**(4), 707–723.

Gutek, B.A. & Cohen, A. (1982) Sex ratios, sex role spillover, and sex at work: a comparison of men's and women's experiences. *Human Relations*, **40**(2), 97–115.

Hardy, C. (1985) The nature of unobtrusive power. *Journal of Management Studies*, **22**(4), 384–399.

Hardy, C. & Clegg, S. (1996) Some dare call it power. In S. Clegg, C. Hardy & W. Nord (eds) *Handbook of Organization Studies* (pp. 621–641). London: Sage.

Hardy, C. & Leiba-O'Sullivan, S. (1998) The power behind empowerment: implications for research and practice. *Human Relations*, **51**(4), 451–483.

Hearn, J. & Parkin, P.W. (1983) Gender and organizations: a selective review and a critique of a neglected area. *Organization Studies*, **4**(3), 219–242.

Heath, A. (1981) *Social Mobility*. Glasgow: Collins.

Henderson, A.M. & Parsons, T. (eds) (1947) *Max Weber: The Theory of Social and Economic Organization*. New York: Oxford University Press.

Hickson, D.J., Butler, R.J., Cray, D., Mallory, G.R. & Wilson, D.C. (1986) *Top Decisions: Strategic Decision-Making in Organizations*. San Francisco: Jossey-Bass.

Hickson, D.J., Hinings, C.A., Lee, R., Schneck, E. & Pennings, J.M. (1971) A strategic contingencies theory of intraorganizational power. *Administrative Science Quarterly*, **16**(2), 216–229.

Hindess, B. (1982) Power, interests and the outcomes of struggles. *Sociology*, **16**(4), 498–511.

Hoy, D.C. (ed.) (1986) *Foucault: A Critical Reader*. Oxford: Blackwell.

Hyman, R. & Brough, I. (1975) *Social Values and Industrial Relations*. Oxford: Blackwell.

Kabanoff, B., Waldersee, R. & Cohen, M. (1995) Espoused values and organizational change themes. *Academy of Management Journal*, **38**(4), 1075–1104.

Kanter, R.M. (1975) Women in organizations: sex roles, group dynamics, and change strategies. In A. Sargent (ed.) *Beyond Sex Roles*. St Paul, MN: West.

Kanter, R.M. (1977) *Men and Women of the Corporation*. New York: Basic Books.

Kerfoot, D. & Knights, D. (1993) Management, masculinity and manipulation: from paternalism to corporate strategy in financial services in Britain. *Journal of Management Studies*, **30**(4), 659–677.

Klein, S.M. (1996) A management communication strategy for change. *Journal of Organizational Change Management*, **9**(2), 32–46.

Knights, D. & Collinson, D. (1987) Disciplining the shop floor: a comparison of the disciplinary effects of managerial psychology and financial accounting. *Accounting, Organizations and Society*, 457–477.

Knights, D. & McCabe, D. (2000) Ain't misbehaving? Opportunities for resistance under new forms of 'quality' management. *Sociology*, **34**(3), 421–436.

Knights, D. & Morgan, G. (1991) Strategic discourse and subjectivity: towards a critical analysis of corporate strategy in organisations. *Organization Studies*, **12**(3), 251–273.

Knights, D. & Murray, F. (1992) Politics and pain in managing information technology: a case study from insurance. *Organization Studies*, **13**(2), 211–228.

Knights, D. & Willmott, H. (1985) Power and identity in theory and practice. *Sociological Review*, **33**(1), 22–46.

Knights, D. & Willmott, H. (1989) Power and subjectivity at work: from degradation to subjugation in social relations. *Sociology*, **23**(4), 535–558.

Knights, D. & Willmott, H. (1992) Conceputalizing leadership processes: a study of senior managers in a financial services company. *Journal of Management Studies*, **29**(6), 761–782.

Knights, D. & Vurdubakis, T. (1994) 'Power, resistance and all that' in resistance and power. In J.M. Jermier, W.R. Nord & D. Knights (eds) *Organizations: Agency, Subjectivity and the Labour Process*. London: Routledge.

Kotter, J.P. & Schlesinger, L.A. (1979) Choosing strategies for change. *Harvard Business Review*, **57**, 106–114.

Kunda, G. (1992) *Engineering Culture: Control and Commitment in a High-Tech Corporation*. Philadelphia, PA: Temple University Press.

Laclau, E. & Mouffe, C. (1985) *Hegemony and Socialist Strategy*. London: Verso.

Lipset, S.M. (1959) Some social requisites of democracy: economic development and political legitimacy. *American Political Science Review*, **53**, 69–105.

Lukes, S. (1974) *Power: A Radical View*. London: Macmillan.

MacMillan, I.C. (1978) *Strategy Formulation: Political Concepts*. St Paul, MN: West.

Mann, M. (1986) *The Sources of Social Power*, Vol. 1: *A History of Power from the Beginning to A.D. 1760*. Cambridge: Cambridge University Press.

Marshak, R.J. (1993) Managing the metaphors of change. *Organizational Dynamics*, **22**(1), 44–56.

Marx, K. (1976) *Capital*. Harmondsworth: Penguin.

Mayes, B.T. & Allen, R.W. (1977) Toward a definition of organizational politics. *Academy of Management Review*, **2**, 674–678.

Mayo, E. (1975) *The Social Problems of an Industrial Civilization*. London: Routledge.

Mechanic, D. (1962) Sources of power of lower participants in complex organizations. *Administrative Science Quarterly*, **7**(3), 349–364.

Meyer, J.W. & Rowan, B. (1977) Institutionalized organizations: formal structure as myth and ceremony. *American Journal of Sociology*, **83**(2), 340–363.

Mézáros, I. (1970) *Marx's Theory of Alienation*. London: Merlin.

Mills, A.J. (1988) Organization, gender and culture. *Organization Studies*, **9**(3), 351–369.

Mills, A.J. (1989) Gender, sexuality and organization theory. In J. Hearn, D.L. Sheppard, P. Tancred-Smith & G. Burrell (eds) *The Sexuality of Organizations* (pp. 29–44). London: Sage.

Mills, A.J. & Murgatroyd, S.J. (1991) *Organizational Rules: A Framework for Understanding Organizations*. Milton Keynes: Open University Press.

Mills, A. & Tancred, P. (1992) *Gendering Organization Analysis*. London: Sage.

Mintzberg, H. (1983) Power in and around organizations. Englewood Cliffs, NJ: Prentice Hall.

Mintzberg, H. (1984) Power and organizational life cycles. *Academy of Management Review*, **9**(2), 207–224.

Morris, K.F. & Raben, C.S. (1995) The fundamentals of change management. In D.A. Nadler, R.B. Shaw, A.E. Walton & Associates (eds) *Discontinuous Change: Leading Organizational Transformation* (pp. 47–65). San Francisco: Jossey-Bass.

Mumby, D. (2001) Power and politics. In F. Jablin & L.L. Putnam (eds) *The New Handbook of Organizational Communication* (pp. 585–623). Thousand Oaks, CA: Sage.

Murphy, A.G. (1998) Hidden transcripts of flight attendant resistance. *Management Communication Quarterly*, **11**, 499–535.

Narayanan, V.K. & Fahey, L. (1982) The micro-politics of strategy formulation. *Academy of Management Review*, **7**(1), 25–34.

Palmer, I. & Hardy, C. (2000) *Thinking about Management*. London: Sage.

Parry, G. & Morriss, P. (1975) When is a decision not a decision? In L. Crewe (ed.) *British Political Sociology Yearbook* (vol. 1). London: Croom Helm.

Perrow, C. (1979) *Complex Organizations: A Critical Essay* (2nd edn). Glenview, IL: Scott, Foresman.

Pettigrew, A.M. (1973) *The Politics of Organizational Decision Making*. London: Tavistock.

Pettigrew, A.M. (1977) Strategy formulation as a political process. *International Studies of Management and Organizations*, **7**(2), 78–87.

Pettigrew, A.M. (1985) *The Awakening Giant: Continuity and Change in Imperial Chemical Industries*. Oxford: Blackwell.

Pfeffer, J. (1981a) *Power in Organizations*. Marshfield, MA: Pitman.

Pfeffer, J. (1981b) Management as symbolic action. In L.L. Cummings & B.M. Staw (eds) *Research in Organizational Behavior* (vol. 3, pp. 1–52). Greenwich, CT: JAI Press.

Pfeffer, J. (1992) Understanding power in organizations. *California Management Review*, **35**, 29–50.

Pfeffer, J. & Salancik, G. (1974) Organizational decision making as a political process. *Administrative Science Quarterly*, **19**, 135–151.

Polsby, N.W. (1963) *Community Power and Political Theory*. New Haven, CT: Yale University Press.

Pringle, R. (1989) Bureaucracy, rationality, and sexuality: the case of secretaries. In J.D. Hearn, D.L. Sheppard, P. Tancred-Sherriff & G. Burrell (eds) *The Sexuality of Organizations*. London: Sage.

Ranson, S., Hinings, R. & Greenwood, R. (1980) The structuring of organizational structure. *Administrative Science Quarterly*, **25**(1), 1–14.

Ray, C. (1986) Social innovation at work: the humanization of workers in twentieth century America. PhD thesis. University of California, Santa Cruz.

Roelofs, H.M. (1976) *Ideology and Myth in American Politics*. Boston: Little, Brown.

Romano, C. (1995) Managing change, diversity and emotions. *Management Review*, **84**(7), 6–7.

Rothschild, J. (1979) Political legitimacy in contemporary Europe. In B. Denitch (ed.) *Legitimation of Regimes*. Beverly Hills, CA: Sage.

Said, E.W. (1986) Foucault and the imagination of power. In D.C. Hoy (ed.) *Foucault: A Critical Reader* (pp. 149–155). Oxford: Blackwell.

Salancik, G. & Pfeffer, J. (1974) The bases and use of power in organizational decision making. *Administrative Science Quarterly*, **19**, 453–473.

Saunders, P. (1980) *Urban Politics: A Sociological Interpretation*. Harmondsworth: Penguin.

Sawicki, J. (1991) *Disciplining Foucault*. London: Routledge.

Schaar, J.H. (1969) Legitimacy in the modern state. In P. Green & S. Levinson (eds) *Power and Community*. New York: Pantheon.

Schacht, R. (1971) *Alienation*. London: Allen and Unwin.

Schattschneider, E.F. (1960) *The Semi-Sovereign People*. New York: Holt, Rinehart & Winston.

Schwenk, C.R. (1989) Linking cognitive, organizational and political factors in explaining strategic change. *Journal of Management Studies*, **26**(2), 177–188.

Smart, B. (1985) *Michel Foucault*. London: Tavistock.

Smart, B. (1986) The politics of truth and the problem of hegemony. In D.C. Hoy (ed.) *Foucault: A Critical Reader* (pp. 157–173). Oxford: Blackwell.

Smart, B. (1990) *Theories of Modernity and Post Modernity*. Ed. B.S. Turner. London: Sage.

Smircich, L. (1983) Concepts of culture and organizational analysis. *Administrative Science Quarterly*, **28**, 339–358.

Spiker, B.K. & Lesser, E. (1995) 'We have met the Enemy'. *Journal of Business Strategy*, **16**(2), 17–21.

Strauss, A. (1978) *Negotiations*. San Francisco: Jossey-Bass.

Thompson, J.D. (1956) Authority and power in identical organizations. *American Journal of Sociology*, **62**, 290–301.

Tretheway, A. (1997) Resistance, identity and empowerment: a postmodern feminist analysis of clients in a human service organization. *Communication Monographs*, **64**, 281–301.

Tsoukas, H. & Chia, R. (2002) On organizational becoming: rethinking organizational change. *Organization Science*, **13**(6), 567–582.

Vince, R. & Broussine, M. (1996) Paradox, defense and attachment: accessing and working with emotions and relations underlying organizational change. *Organization Studies*, **17**(1), 1–21.

Walzer, M. (1986) The politics of Michel Foucault. In D.C. Hoy (ed.) *Foucault: A Critical Reader* (pp. 51–68). Oxford: Blackwell.

Watson, T.J. (1982) Group ideologies and organizational change. *Journal of Management Studies*, **19**(3), 259–275.

Weber, M. (1978) *Economy and Society: An Outline of Interpretive Sociology* (2 vols). Eds G. Roth & C. Wittich. Berkeley, CA: University of California Press.

White, S.K. (1986) Foucault's challenge to critical theory. *American Political Science Review*, **80**(2), 419–432.

Willmott, H. (1993) Strength is ignorance: slavery is freedom: managing culture in modern organizations. *Journal of Management Studies*, **30**(4), 515–552.

Wittgenstein L. (1968) *Philosophical Investigations*. Trans. G.E.M. Anscombe. Oxford: Blackwell.

Wolff, J. (1977) Women in organizations. In S. Clegg & D. Dunkerley (eds) *Critical Issues in Organizations* (pp. 7–20). London: Routledge.

Wolfinger, R.E. (1971) Nondecisions and the study of local politics. *American Political Science Review*, **65**, 1063–1080.

Wrong, D. (1979) *Power: Its Forms, Bases and Uses*. Oxford: Blackwell.

# Learning and Developing for Sustainable Change

Part V of this book focuses on learning and developing for sustainable change and innovation. A review of theories on learning is presented to understand perspectives on individual and organizational learning, and the dynamics of learning processes. The implications of these theoretical insights mean a departure from general training programmes and adoption of lifetime learning by experience, reflection, and doing. Methods are presented for assessing learning conditions in processes of change. This Part concludes with a discussion of the relationships between patterns of learning, organizational forms, and societal institutions. This discussion offers a useful framework for analysing directions of organizational change and learning dynamics related to change. This Part helps understand why developing learning organizations is difficult and it offers ideas on how learning processes facilitate organizational change.

In Chapter 17, Alfons Sauquet raises the question why learning in organizations became so popular with academics and practitioners, and why the issue of learning has entered the stage of management theories so quickly. One reason may be the efforts to bridge the gap between planned change and organization development. Managers, practitioners, and academics encounter each other in proposing ways of turning organizations into learning arenas to achieve competitive advantage. Another reason that has fuelled interest in learning has to do with the rise of status that knowledge has gained in contemporary society, and the increase of knowledge workers. Knowledge became part of the market economy and knowledge workers were those who create value and have to be managed. A third reason for the expanding field of learning theories came from the possibilities the field offers to academics. A final reason may be found in the management discourse where learning theories offer good opportunities to introduce new normative frames of control from the perspective of learning. Sauquet continues with an overview of learning theories. He revises the basic understanding of learning theories, groups them in different schools of thought, and confronts perspectives of theories and models. First, the grammar of behaviourism is elaborated. Based on ideas of classical conditioning, this school pays attention to training programmes to develop practical skills and basic competencies. Second, the cognitive school is described with great emphasis on information and information processing. In this school, learning is basically understood as properly connecting thoughts, actions, and outcomes. Third, the school of pragmatism is presented. This school has been influential in building concepts such as learning from experience. Learning is associated with purposeful action and is geared to making sense out of a confusing or problematic situation. The fourth school of thought is about situated learning and opens up the possibility of developing a social version of learning by involving the dynamics of participation in groups and learning communities. Based on this broad perspective on learning, several dilemmas are proposed with respect to speech, learning, and knowledge. This presentation of different perspectives on learning facilitates a critical approach of learning in organizations and offers reflections on the restrictions and opportunities embedded in the different perspectives and practices.

*Dynamics of Organizational Change and Learning.* Edited by J.J. Boonstra.
© 2004 John Wiley & Sons, Ltd. ISBN 0-471-87737-9.

In Chapter 18, Chris Argyris builds on Chapter 17 by questioning the effectiveness of producing transformational learning and change in organizations. Ideas from the cognitive and pragmatic school are used to understand why there is a mismatch between the intentions to produce change and what actually happens when change is planned and executed by change agents and change managers. According to Argyris, all actions are produced through designs-in-use, and mostly people hold by these designs-in-use even when they produce errors in the world of practice. The designs-in-use are sub-routines based on theories-in-use. The theories-in-use are seen as master programmes held by individuals to design their actions. He proposes a distinction between Model I and Model II theories-in-use. Model I tells individuals to advocate their positions, evaluations, and attributions in a way that inhibits questioning and testing them with the use of independent logic. The consequences of Model I strategies are likely to be defensiveness and misunderstanding. The governing values of Method II theories-in-use are valid information, free and informed choice, and monitoring the implementation of choice in order to detect and correct error. Usually, Method II theories-in-use are espoused theories. The challenge for individuals is to transform their espoused theories into theories-in-use by learning new sets of skills and governing values, with the emphasis on productive reasoning and testing of claims. Double-loop learning focuses on detecting and correcting errors in the theories-in-use underlying the designs-in-use. Argyris offers methods and descriptions of change programmes that include double-loop learning and redesigning actions-in-use. He proposes criteria for success in diagnosing and changing at the level of the individual, the group, and the organization as a whole. This theory of action and learning provides an important contribution to the effective implementation of managerial functions based on productive reasoning, and offers perspectives and methods which facilitate transformational leadership, change, and learning.

Chapter 19 focuses on a methodology for change and learning in organizations based on the pragmatic and situational schools of thought. Gerhard Smid and Ronald Beckett start this chapter by playing with some concepts on innovation, change, and learning. Innovation is seen as a form of sustainable change because it refers to explorative processes, tangible new outcomes, and embedded organizational change. Innovation processes themselves may be seen as collective iterative learning by doing, experimenting, exploring, and combining multiple initiatives. Any change is only seen as sustained when it is embodied in the workforce and embedded in long-lasting relations between the people in the company and the company and its suppliers and customers. Smid and Beckett describe the experiences of two companies pursuing innovation and learning as a source of competitive advantage. They observe that learning about new things supports the process of innovation, and that introducing an innovative new product or practice requires learning new things to support it. Learning is considered to be an aspect of everyday life and is embedded in work contexts. Innovative learning is based on the fundamental idea that learning processes are iterative, cyclical, and the learners are active, playing, and exploring. Innovation depends on the learning capacity of the organization and can be facilitated by appropriate support structures for learning. These support structures can be built from components such as the physical learning environment, the linguistic learning environment, the social learning environment, and the future context associated with learning. Designing an appropriate and effective space for learning and innovation needs dedicated consideration of these components. Creating organizational value through learning requires more than quick fixes, it requires the enhancement of various learning cycles. In a setting of innovation and sustainable change, deep learning is required with processes of conceptualization, reflection, and criticism. A method of cooperative learning is proposed where academics, practitioners, and managers work together in designing learning spaces. In these learning spaces, a balance is realized between experimenting, reflecting, conceptualizing, and criticism on practices, theories, and methods, and on the assumptions behind the processes of learning.

The final chapter in this Part on learning in organizations broadens the scope on organizational learning and opens up new possibilities by using a pluralistic epistemological perspective. In Chapter 20, Alice Lam proposes a conceptual framework for understanding interdependent relationships between patterns of learning, organizational forms, and societal institutions. She argues that patterns of learning and knowledge configurations of companies cannot be separated from specific organizational forms and institutions. A large part of human knowledge is subjective and tacit. The transfer of this kind of personal intuitive knowledge requires social interaction and the development of shared understanding. The knowledge of the company is socially embedded and rooted in coordination mechanisms and organizational routines. External societal institutions interact with internal organizational structures and processes and form networks of mutual understanding. Lam distinguishes between explicit and tacit knowledge and between individual and collective knowledge. These two dimensions give rise to four categories of knowledge. Embrained knowledge is dependent on individual conceptual skills, based on rational understanding, and learned by formal education. This form of knowledge is connected to professional bureaucracies and related to a professional community. Embodied knowledge is action-oriented, context-specific, based on problem-solving experience, and learned by experience. This kind of knowledge is connected to adhocracies and related to an occupational community. Encoded knowledge is shared in organizations through rules, procedures, and formal information systems. This knowledge is visible in bureaucracies and related to a bureaucratic form of learning and career hierarchies. Embedded knowledge is a collective form of knowledge residing in organizational routines and shared norms. It is relation-specific and learned in social interaction. This kind of knowledge corresponds to J-form organizations and dynamic learning in organizational communities. The perspective proposed by Lam offers a useful framework for analysing directions of organizational change and the learning dynamics related to organizational change. This perspective helps to understand why developing learning organizations are difficult processes, and offers ideas on how learning processes may facilitate radical organizational change.

# CHAPTER 17

# Learning in Organizations
## Schools of Thought and Current Challenges

**Alfons Sauquet**
*Esade Business School, Barcelona, Spain*

In this chapter I plan to address three issues which link learning to organizations. First, there is the matter of why learning has blossomed and occupied the organizational centre stage. Second, we need to understand why it is that the field is becoming more fragmented as theories and models have proliferated in this expanding field, and the embedded limitations due to the different theoretical sources used. Finally, I will advance a couple of dilemmas which the existing literature has so far overlooked, despite the fact that they touch on very basic issues and hence need to be thoroughly understood.

## THE BLOSSOMING OF LEARNING IN ORGANIZATIONAL DISCOURSE

Although psychology has developed learning theories since the early days of the discipline, these theories only entered the organizational discourse relatively recently. Although relevant work was produced in the 1950s (Revans, 1982) and the 1960s (Cangelosi & Dill, 1965) it was only with the publication of a seminal work by Argyris and Schön (1978) that a fully fledged theorization of the meaning and consequences of learning within the organization took shape. Argyris and Schön have since continued developing the ideas they advanced in 1978 (Schön, 1983; Argyris et al., 1985; Argyris & Schön, 1996), and other researchers made significant contributions during the 1980s (Hedberg, 1981; Shrivastva, 1983; Fiol & Lyles, 1985; Levitt & March, 1988). However, it is in the past decade that the link between learning and organizations has really become widely recognized. As an example, Crossan and Guatto (1996) reported that in 1993 alone, as much literature appeared on the field of learning organizations as had appeared in the whole of the 1980s.

Three kinds of reasons can be advanced to explain the pervasive interest in learning in organizations: (1) competitive advantage and organizational development; (2) the relationship between knowledge and learning; and (3) the dynamics of institutionalization in the field.

### COMPETITIVE ADVANTAGE AND ORGANIZATION DEVELOPMENT

Propositions which relate to learning within organizations and competitive advantage (De Geus, 1988; Stata, 1989) are most appealing in turbulent times when guidance provided by traditional long-term planning strategies appears more questionable (Mintzberg, 1994). As haste has become a feature of contemporary society (Virilio, 1977), it might appear that internal readiness to confront environmental changes is a better strategy than carefully determining goals and resources well in advance since the latter approach tends to distract one from emerging opportunities. If this is the case, organizations

*Dynamics of Organizational Change and Learning.* Edited by J.J. Boonstra.
© 2004 John Wiley & Sons, Ltd. ISBN 0-471-87737-9.

which are quicker to notice environmental change and realize that there is a link between action and consequences would seem to be better prepared to cope with the changes of the twenty-first century.

Developing organizations that are able to learn has thus captivated the interest of academics as it seems a natural response for management in times of rapid change that require constant innovation. A similar argument was put forward in the field of adult learning by Knowles (1980) and Houle (1980) who advanced the concept of andragogy and life-long learning to underscore the need for a better understanding of adult learning in the light of increasingly changing societal demands.

There has been a constant and devoted effort towards reaching this goal of developing learning organizations and it has thus become a legitimate goal to pursue. Probably helped by the TQM movement which paved the way for internal organization scrutiny and capturing the interest of classical OD proponents (Burke, 1993), learning organizations have become a point of encounter between managers and academics who proposed ways of turning organizations into learning arenas (Garratt, 1987; Senge, 1990; Pedler et al., 1991; Watkins & Marsick, 1993). Despite the differences between the proponents of learning organizations, they share a common interest in acting throughout the organization with the purpose of fine-tuning their practices in order to become an organization that learns continually. To do so, they take the organization as a whole as the unit for intervention in which different layers and processes must be simultaneously considered if the organization is to turn into a learning one. Change within this perspective is yet more multifaceted since it is conceived as the flow of steps necessary to turn a classical organization into a learning one as defined by a previous model or blueprint (Pedler et al., 1991). Thus, at the individual level, it may involve work on mental models (Senge, 1990), broad human resource development policies (Pedler, et al., 1991), an organizational culture that does not punish experimentation (Pedler et al., 1991; Watkins & Marsick, 1993), or cherishing teamwork under specific orientation (Senge, 1990).

## RELATIONSHIP BETWEEN KNOWLEDGE AND LEARNING

The second thing that has fuelled interest in learning has to do with the new status that knowledge and learning have gained in contemporary society (Drucker, 1994). Knowledge workers have increased in numbers and relative weight in the past decades and the trend is likely to continue. Barley and Orr (1997) have shown that in the USA, professional and technical occupational categories now outweigh operatives/labourers and craft and kind. They argue that work has become technified and by technification they mean the increasing ability to intervene in the world of objects through symbols.

In a short history of the concept of knowledge, Jenssen (2001) noted how knowledge production has been displaced from its original settings. Universities and research laboratories had, for centuries, been the locus of knowledge. Production researchers and knowledge producers were actors who operated on the fringe of the production system in which the dominant actors were workers and capitalists. Access to knowledge was reserved to those custodians and its use was access-free through payment (e.g. patents). The same functional separation became present in organizations as R&D departments were displaced from the organization's core activity. Learning organizations can be thus read as the acknowledgement that strict functional divisions are to be dissolved, particularly as this concerns the displacement of the knowledge and learning activities from the classical production functions. In this vein, holographic metaphors are more suggestive descriptions of organizational forms as they capture the intertwined nature of long-held dichotomies such as thinking and acting, researching and learning, developing and producing.

However, as the economy is reconceptualized as a knowledge economy, knowledge production ceases to be a prerequisite for a market economy. Rather, knowledge becomes a part of the market economy and the knowledge worker becomes a person who creates value rather than a person who enables others to create values. In the knowledge economy, the knowledge worker does not merely use knowledge in his or her activities but acquires it as and when the knowledge production takes place. The argument boils down to blurring the classical distinction between knowledge acquisition and knowledge production as well as the differences between learning and research, where knowledge is also acquired in the act of its production and where research ceases to be an autonomous activity separated from practice. All in all, classical positivistic–empiricist epistemologies might well be giving way to more pragmatic understandings of knowledge and learning. This pragmatic turn was partly advanced by Argyris et al. (1985) as they conceptualized action science as an organizational learning tool, a science of interpersonal communication which attempted to frame the practitioners' intersubjectivity by use of practices and procedures which were already commonly present in scientific communities, thus facilitating the learning processes.

I will explore the relationship between knowledge and learning in more detail at the end of the chapter when discussing arguments and facts concerning learning.

## THE DYNAMICS OF INSTITUTIONALIZATION

I feel that a third reason for interest in learning in organizations relates to the possibilities the concept offers academics. On the one hand, it is broad enough to attract the interest of multiple disciplines. As Dodgson (1993) noted, academics from fields as diverse as economics, innovation theory, general management, or organization theory find it relevant to refer to and include learning in organizations in their developments. On the other hand, learning has a broad analytical value as it allows one to simultaneously consider different levels of analysis, such as the individual and the organizational. Some efforts have been made to look for specific connections between them (e.g. Kim, 1993; Crossan et al., 1999). Finally, moving learning theories to organizational centre stage offers an image of management that avoids traditional planning and control models (Miner & Mezias, 1996). Indeed, the encompassing quality of organizational learning is such that there is scarcely an academic who would not feel at home with some version of learning in organizations.

Barley and Kunda (1992) have analysed managerial discourse to find that management concepts alternate throughout time between rational and normative frames of control. Thus, after a period in which rational approaches dominate management language (e.g. scientific management), more normative discourses take the stage (e.g. human relations), to be in turn reframed with a new rationalistic impetus (e.g. systems theory). According to this pendulum movement, after going through a period when organizations were approached from a cultural stance, learning theory might offer a good opportunity to replace an unfashionable concept or combine it with something new.

Learning concepts applied to organizations are normatively driven either explicitly through the diffusion of ideal models of LO (e.g. Pedler; Marsick and Watkins; Senge) or implicitly in the discourse of OL which ultimately links the kind of arguments advanced at the beginning of this chapter with the unquestionable usefulness of learning in organizations.

Finally, all the previous reasons converge in the institutionalization of a field (Gherardi, 1999). This is so by creating the very phenomenon of interest through the action of consultants who diffuse the concept and use it in their exchanges with companies, and eventually through the action of companies that publicly endorse practices conducive to learning within the organizations and attribute to those different degrees of success. Then concepts which had acquired legitimacy in the scientific community are applied by consultants and in turn diffused by organizations so that the phenomenon has its existence proved.

## REVISITING LEARNING ORIGINS: SCHOOLS OF THOUGHT

However promising the subject may seem, the academic contributions to the field of learning are extremely diverse. Some attempts are regularly made to map the learning field (Huber, 1991; Dodgson, 1993; Tsang, 1997; Easterby-Smith & Araujo, 1999) and provide some clarity on what to expect from such a promising concept. However, I contend that most learning theories applied to management are developed as mid-range theories based upon assumptions or conceptual developments which are not necessarily compatible among them. I further contend that this is central to understanding the possibilities and limitations they each offer to organizations. I believe that unless we are fully aware of our intellectual debts, it will be difficult to escape the perils of devising an over-promising horizon and, in consequence, we may be running the risk of creating confusion and disappointment. In the next pages, I plan to revise the basic understanding of learning theories and group them within different schools of thought.

## THE GRAMMAR OF BEHAVIOURISM

Classical conditioning has had an enormous influence on learning. Its main tenet is that of association. Organisms learn by associating certain responses to certain stimuli. Generalization of responses and discrimination of stimuli are mechanisms by which what is learned can be refined or applied in response to different stimuli or in different contexts.

According to behaviourism, association mechanisms are universal. In other words, all organisms fundamentally learn in similar ways, so that there are no essential differences in the way human beings and animals acquire new behaviours. Thus, within the same species, there are no fundamental differences between organisms. Behaviours can be studied as though they were connected by syntactical rules. Complex behaviours can thus be broken down into simple units. Additionally, stimuli are to be considered in terms of the possibility for connections regardless of the stimulus content. They are all equivalent. Consequences of this programme are the extreme passivity under which human beings learn, the absence of consideration of internal mental states, and the tremendous emphasis on ambientalism.

Despite its shortcomings, behaviourism has been more influential than we are ready to admit and its influence has been persistent. Simon (1972) coins the expression 'long glaciation' to evaluate the influence and persistence of this school of thought. It was not until the second half of the 1950s that an alternative programme began to be developed with the goal of studying meaning (Bruner, 1990). What was later called the cognitive revolution aimed to focus on the internal processes of human beings who had so far been conspicuously disregarded by the behaviourists. In addition to the alternative research programme within behaviourism, there were indications that some fundamental assumptions of the theory needed revision. This was particularly evident when it was advanced that neutrality of stimuli was not the case for animals and it was shown that stimuli association was not arbitrary but that animals had 'preferences' (García & Koelling, 1966).

Although in its crude form one would not expect to see many examples of pure associative learning in organizations, whenever we encounter behavioural practices which are routinely developed regardless of their present usefulness, we may well ask ourselves if they are not products of crude association-ism with certain environmental cues persistently producing a particular, often meaningless, behaviour.

Elting Morrison (1977) provides a striking example of this when coastal artillery crews in Britain were the object of time and motion studies in order to improve efficiency during the Second World War. Filmed material revealed that in some particular cases two soldiers loaded their guns, then turned their backs to the weapons and waited motionless for several seconds. Not that the movement was time-consuming but it seemed clearly meaningless for there was nothing that pair of soldiers did except stand and wait a couple of seconds for the gun to be shot, after which they began moving again. Most intriguing was that, when asked, the soldiers could not provide a single reason for their behaviour. It was, so it seemed, a meaningless routine. It was not until the material was shown to an expert that the explanation came about. After watching the film, the expert, a veteran colonel from the Boer War, immediately got the point. 'Ah!' he said. 'They're holding the horses!' The example is illustrative enough for the purpose of underscoring that behaviours learned as sheer drill may survive over time regardless of the fact that their initial purpose is no longer valid (Schein, 1993a).

Behaviourism has had some influence on models that touch on learning and organizations. Popular concepts such as unlearning (Nystrom & Starbuck, 1984) are probably to be partly located within this tradition. Insofar as learning is understood as a connection between action and outcomes, and the bond is reinforced through practice, it becomes easier to understand terms such as competency traps. Also learning can be understood as mere variation (Weick, 1991), a view that has support in basic connectionism. It goes without saying that the learner's role within this school of thought is clearly a minor one. Learning strategies deriving from this school of thought focus on student development through training programmes which aim to impart pre-established practical skills and basic competencies. In any case, the frontier between learning and change is conceived as a fuzzy one, given that behavioural change is the central aim of training programmes and the only indication that learning has taken place.

## COGNITIVE SCHOOL

What has been termed as the cognitive revolution (Gardner, 1985) was an attempt to bring the mind back to the human sciences. Indeed, it was an attempt to replace the objectivism that had dominated psychology. Bruner (1990) has argued that although the initial goal was to study meaning, the movement soon focused its efforts on information and information processing. Indeed, information processing was conceived as the nucleus of mental activity. The strong version of the programme asserted that the mind could be understood as though it were a computer (Lieber, 1991). Thus, cognition could be conceived as logical systems of processing information exclusively constituted by formal processes. The human mind was then conceived as following syntactical rules with no attention being paid to semantics (Shanon & Weaver, 1964). Information processing requires clear specific rules that, as in a computer programme, dictate what operations the programme should put into operation.

Information processing provides a constructivist understanding of human beings. Inasmuch as there is a mind that directs operations—top-down—it determines the way in which information will be processed and how representations will be built.

The strong point of the cognitive revolution is that it drew attention to such mental entities as attentional filters, limitations on information processing, long-term memory, and so on. However, it failed to provide an adequate theory of mind. Searle (1984) noted that any theory of mind would have to provide an adequate explanation of consciousness, intentionality of mental states, subjectivity of mental states, and the existence of mental causality. As far as intentionality is concerned, information processing deals with means, ends, goals, and the like. However, information-processing systems do not have purposes or intentions other than that the satisfaction of certain conditions triggers the search for certain goals. Thus, the explanation of intention falls perilously close to that of behaviourism. While the explanation for action resided there in pairs of S–'R, in information processing it turns to pairs of condition–action (Pozo, 1989).

Although the cognitive school has been very influential in fuelling concepts and helping frame models of organizational learning, it lacks a proper theory of learning (Pozo, 1989; Spender, 1999). Again, Searle (1984) stressed that the Chinese room story reveals a difference between executing and understanding. In the story a human being is inside a room surrounded by piles of Chinese ideograms. He has very specific and unambiguous instructions about how to proceed and thus when a sign of type A is brought into the room he must send out a sign of type B, and so on. The point is that even if the individual proceeds accurately (that is, executes a task), he does not understand it because meaning is absent from the programme. Brown and Duguid (2000) give a similar example. A typographer at Oxford University Press stopped his work and claimed that the bilingual classical book he was working on had a translation error. Since the book was in Greek, he was interrogated about his knowledge of

Greek, to which he answered that his knowledge of classical Greek was none but he was sure that there was a mistake. His claim was based on the fact that in all his experience of working with classical Greek texts he had never seen that X pair of signs were followed by Y pair of signs. Needless to say, the typographer's claim was correct.

Bruner (1996) takes the point a little further when he reminds us that meaning/making are inseparable from context and that computational devices cannot cope with the variety of contexts within which words acquire their meaning.

In a variety of ways the cognitive school has been the most influential for the field of learning in organizations. First, the overall perspective is widely concerned with the limitative aspects of human cognition. This is far from surprising, provided that computer science runs parallel to the cognitive impulse.

Learning, basically understood as properly connecting thoughts, actions, and outcomes, is hampered by the possibility of establishing wrong connections due to improper interpretations of environmental cues (March & Olsen, 1976). Cognitivism focuses the attention on the fact that cognitive resources are limited. Once the learner is qualified as fallible due to cognitive limitations (e.g. bounded rationality), an effort must be made to keep high levels of alertness because experiences may be interpreted improperly and thus have no learning value (Feldman, 1986). Thus, individual judgement might be systematically biased under certain conditions (Tversky & Kahneman, 1974) and because it constrains the interpretation range, problem framing may implicitly orient decision-making and determine the degree of commitment (Staw, 1976). All in all, cognitive theories underscore the need for better understanding of mental models and wise use of limited cognitive resources.

Reality within this stream of thought is taken as a given but it is individually constructed in the interaction of mental models with the data fed back after action. The cognitive school is in a sense indebted to Descartes and Kant in that it assumes that reality can be apprehended, provided that a refined tool for reflection is used. As long as we are aware of our cognitive limitations, we will be better equipped to critically analyse the results of our cognitions.

Proper management of cognitive resources is also called for. Within this school of thought, forgetting is not only a matter of getting rid of a dysfunctional association (as behaviourism would contend) but of liberating cognitive space for further use. The cognitive understanding of forgetting would be nicely illustrated by a short story by J.L. Borges in which the main character has the 'gift' of an ever-increasing memory. His expanding memory capability is in perpetual activation so that a casual glance at a tree during a routine stroll activates all mnemonic processes to the extent that the whole history of the tree unfolds before the character in full detail. The growth of every branch, and every leaf can be traced back to its origins, to its changing shape, and all changing shades of colour are imaginary, set between the character's eyes. As this gift becomes more highly developed, life becomes increasingly difficult and in his final days the hapless character is locked in a dark room and kept in bed in a vain attempt to deprive him of stimuli. That forgetting is a human capability was already advanced by a philosopher concerned with moral renewal (Nietzsche, 1967) but, from a cognitive science point of view, forgetting is a prerequisite for any variation. Since cognitive capabilities are limited, liberating cognitive resources is necessary if a different cognitive programming is to be tested.

Within the cognitive theoretical framework there is an obvious division between thought and action. Although the relationship between them is conceptualized in different ways, the more classical rational understanding of the relation between thought and action gives beliefs a sequential pre-eminence. Thus, within organizations role constraints limit action possibilities and create internal incoherence in individuals (March & Olsen, 1976) as they cannot act on their beliefs. In turn, at the organizational level, it is considered that part of the very activity of organizing involves limiting discretionality (Weick & Westley, 1996) and the limited resources available are to be devoted to regular operations which give expected outputs (March & Olsen, 1991): well-designed and executed programmes (e.g. organizing) guarantee the necessary flow of activities. Needless to say that changing this activity programme requires a full revision of the programme as such, a moment of reflection that may well be conceptualized as organizational re-engineering.

Some authors (Weick, 1979; Mayrhofer, 1996) would give action pre-eminence. Thus, cognition would be *ex post facto* produced as a rationalization of activity that would be triggered by environmental cues or by more or less unpurposeful changes (Weick, 1993).

This school of thought helps us understand the different types of knowledge available. Since knowledge is what should direct the programmes, it is important that it is formalized so that it can be more widely spread and further used. The distinction advanced by Anderson (1983) between declarative and procedural memory illustrates this point. Declarative formal knowledge is introduced in a programme. As individuals practise the procedure, the formal sequence becomes progressively substituted by sequences that do not activate formal declarative procedures. In a sense, the declarative knowledge is internalized and made operational in practice. Intuition is thus 'analysis frozen into habit' (Simon, 1987).

Back and forth movements between formal and non-formal forms of knowledge shape the basis for innovating (Nonaka & Takeuchi, 1994). Though they make ample use of the concept of tacit knowledge (Polanyi, 1966) to illustrate the difference between formal and non-formal knowledge, they make a different use of what Polanyi originally conceived. For him tacit knowledge is a different sort of knowledge (not a variant of explicit knowledge). Thus, taking tacit knowledge into serious consideration is less a matter of communication ('we know more than we can tell') or a matter of access ('we know more than we know we know') (Spender, 1998) than a matter of acknowledging that there is no translation between them. For tacit knowledge is not mere knowledge of acquaintance (James, 1950) waiting to be translated into a superior breed of formal abstraction, but a different kind of knowledge which does not accept translation. Indeed, when it is decomposed, knowledge of the tacit sort comes closer to absurdity. A story by Cortazar serves to illustrate the problematic nature of the attempt of formalizing tacit knowledge. As he describes a human being attempting to formalize the steps needed to climb a flight of stairs, it becomes quite clear that the computer-like attempt is bound to fail as the limitations of the human being in analysing the problem formally render no positive results.

The cognitive school has been very influential in the field of learning in organizations though paradoxically it lacks a theory of it (Spender, 1998). This is most apparent when organizational learning is described (Huber, 1991). Learning is subsumed under knowledge acquisition and emphasis is placed on knowledge dissemination. In that view, knowledge is treated basically as a commodity that circulates throughout the organization as information does. The vocabulary of problems is thus that of overload, capacities, noise application, and the like. The separation between thought and action allows for this de-contextualized understanding of knowledge. Knowledge is thus treated as a commodity that can be transferred from place to place. In consequence, knowledge can be managed like any other resource of the organization. Not surprisingly, knowledge management activities end up being close to refined forms of information management systems.

But this dualism serves practice very badly. Indeed, by way of analysing what he termed 'intelligent practice', Ryle (1949) was able to show that there is a logical error in supposing that for efficient practice to occur, there is always a precedent of intelligent thought. This reasoning, which is at the very core of the understanding of learning from the cognitive perspective, implies that careful thought precedes action but, as Ryle notes, for thought to be intelligent, it should be preceded by a planning activity, activity which itself is susceptible to preparation. Falling into an infinite regression is the most likely result of careful analysis of intelligent practice. Ryle's point is then clear, namely, intelligent practice is action of a specific kind. Rather than considering intelligent action as the consequence of intelligent precedent, intelligence is embedded in practice.

Exploration and exploitation have been widely used concepts (March & Olsen, 1991). Associated with exploratory practices is the search for new organizational routines and the discovery of new approaches to technologies, business processes, or outputs. Exploration is associated with an increase in internal variety. The fundamental dilemma in which an organization is caught is that of producing the optimal amount of internal variance (McGrath, 2001), for if internal variance is too low, the organization tends to ossification, and if it is too high, there may be no capitalization on discovery. Thus, the role of management is to provide some sort of balance. For instance, while autonomy (i.e. decoupling projects and the company's current operations) favours increased variance, goal-directed projects tend to decrease variance since outcomes can be contrasted in the light of goals and thus judged accordingly, thereby narrowing the field of search, increasing the probability of discounting disconfirming data, and creating a field for internal competition.

In sum, the influence of the cognitive school in the field of learning in organizations has broadened the more limited perspective behaviourism implies. Attention has been given to the cognitive processes and particularly to the inherent limitations of human beings. As a consequence, fundamental trade-offs such as exploration and exploitation are better understood and can be handled. Also, its focus on information has been of tremendous use in connecting organizing with information flows. However, its basic approach to mind life as an information system does not allow consideration of different types of knowledge nor a development of a better understanding of purposes and meanings. Also, it presents an indistinct consideration of the relationship between thought and action, and the dynamics of learning are clearly and insufficiently unexplored. To understand action, we need to start by revisiting the work of pragmatism, a philosophical trend (*pragma* in Greek) that puts action at the very core of its programme.

The cognitive approach presents problems insofar as we lack a proper learning theory. Learning is close to adaptation as it involves the replacement of current schemas by new ones. However, cognitive schemas are persistent in framing problems (Dearborn & Simon, 1958) and stubbornly resist conflicting information (Staw, 1976)—in such circumstances unlearning can present serious difficulties (Hedberg, 1981). Thus, learning comes close to mere variation (Weick, 1991) or there is the explicit call for outsiders to engage in exploratory practices (March & Olsen, 1991). In any case, we are left with a paradox since this school of thought (which has been very influential in advancing the field of learning) is problematic when we discuss learning. In practice, this may explain why the enormous interest in the advance of information systems and their possibilities for promoting learning in organizations has been replaced by a more moderate attitude.

## PRAGMATISM

American pragmatism is initially concerned with overcoming the separation between subject and object. To avoid that separation, they focus on action, for in activity the boundaries between subject and object are less problematic and relevant. Current versions of pragmatism (Rorty, 1996) are more concerned with underscoring claims towards non-authoritative discourses than with the problem of subjectivity.

With reference to learning, pragmatism has offered a great deal of theorizing which has been equally influential in building concepts such as learning from experience (Kolb, 1984). Most works build on the work of John Dewey, who theorized the inquiry process and the nature of experience. In his view, human beings learn as they try to solve problematic situations. Otherwise it is habit that governs action (Dewey, 1938). When individuals are faced with unexpected situations, they experience a state of confusion that has to be reduced by turning the confusing situation into a problem. Problematizing means setting limits to the situation. To do this, they resort to previous knowledge and to their purpose. This first step results in a problem frame that serves to direct further inquiry. Inquiry takes the form of hypothesis elaboration on the elements involved in the problem. Once the hypothesis has been set, human beings act to correct the situation: the situation is changed as a result of action. Dewey's theory underscores the relevance of developing a frame for future action. This frame is not a pure cognitive act but a combination of available knowledge and individual purpose. The process is a basic individual one but it takes place in a social context and affects social organization. In his view, language plays the role of a mediator—the tool of tools—by which individuals develop internal dialogues as they relate externally. Dewey's theory of learning is very close to a Popperian understanding of how problems are solved (Popper, 1997). Error in Dewey's conceptual framework takes on a different meaning than that usually associated with blind trial. Rather than a lost opportunity, error is simply a probe that enhances our learning and changes our understanding of the situation. As learning from experience is not a detached, more or less abstract, activity but one which involves individual reflection and undergoing an experience, learning is assumed to be oriented towards betterment.

Dewey's work has a number of important features which are worth underscoring. First, his coupling of learning with experience and the role given to reflection has helped shed light on how professionals actually do their work in practice (Schön, 1983, 1987). Second, learning is associated with purposeful action and is oriented to making meaning out of a confusing or problematic situation. Thus, learning is not restricted to a cognitive activity but should be understood as a wilful effort that encompasses the whole person as well as connecting past and future.

From Dewey's work we can deduce that, except in limited cases, learning cannot take place independently of experience. Consequently, the effects of training or the development of knowledge repositories are to be relativized as triggers of organizational learning. Finally, mere variation, as suggested by cognitive science, is a route which might be void of meaning for individuals. Despite its value for organizational adaptation, it basically focuses on changing organizational routines or sheer innovation but adds little qualitative value.

Dewey's work, on the other hand, mostly focused on the individual. His work is based upon a liberal conception of society and the collective dimension of action is scarcely discussed. Indeed, his understanding of language as the tool of tools (Dewey, 1925) sets a limit on how he envisions the relationship of the individual and society. A better understanding of social context comes from the ideas of Vygotsky (1978), who, from the outset, undertook the task of elucidating individual learning processes in specific socio-historical contexts. Indeed, it is surprising that the schools of thought reviewed so far add so little in terms of discussing the role of the social context for learning. This is even more paradoxical for interest in learning is associated with organizations. However, as Cook and Yanow (1993) suggest, most theories are concerned with how individuals learn in organizations. This is probably the case for the basic assumptions of behaviourism, cognitive psychology—even in its more constructivist version—and pragmatism takes on an understanding of human beings in which social interaction is not a constitutive process.

However, pragmatism has had a considerable influence on learning concepts applied to organizations. Kolb's experiential learning cycle is a good example of it. According to Kolb (1984), learning takes place in a succession of moments which combine reflection and action with data stemming from actual experience and concepts that emerge from existing theories. Thus, the learner facing a surprising experience makes observations in which data are collected to be contrasted with or related to previous knowledge or concepts. This inductive step is followed by a moment when the learner frames the problem in a new way, guiding future action which, in turn, results in a new experience. This cycle is repeated until the learner finds a satisfactory solution. Learning is thus tied to an experience. This model, which is indebted to Dewey's description on the thinking process (Dewey, 1910), has influenced training programmes, which have made an attempt to move beyond conceptual transmission by introducing some kind of experience upon which participants are called to reflect. However, these kinds of programmes find that participants fail in many cases to transfer the learning to the workplace. This failure may be due to a number of factors but it is interesting to note that the original point made by Dewey (1938) underscored that for learning to take place; the problem (i.e. the quality of the experience) should not be vicarious or simply contain similarities but rather have full meaning for the participants. In other words, experiential learning would take place if the experience were a real one. It is precisely this objection which has been addressed through action learning programmes in which participants confront actual problems in small groups with the double goal of solving them and learning at the same time.

In action learning, individuals learn to build up common frames out of the diversity of perspectives—anchored in unique combinations of concepts and previous experience—which each individual brings to the group. In addition, individuals learn how to explore the differences and the content issues as well as to link the whole process with the development of relationships among the actors.

The knowledge generated by the process is highly contextual as it is problem-driven but it can touch upon aspects which were not recognized in the initial framing of the problem. This process is both centred on the learner and on the problem and there is no previous content definition of what learning means for the learner. Accordingly, the role of external agents is closer to that of a facilitator than to that of a formal teacher.

The pragmatic school of thought enjoys wide influence. The work of Argyris and Schön is clearly to be included in this tradition insofar as they understand learning processes as problem-centred. Additionally, the work of Schön on how professionals actually work and learn is very much influenced by Dewey's work in at least two respects. First, because from his descriptions of how professionals work, he understands that they proceed in repeated circles of reflection and action. Second, because he introduces the professionals' values and intentions as drivers of the whole process. Thus, the definition of a situation as problematic is less of a technical or abstract matter and more related to the existing gap between professional aims and what is actually being produced.

## SITUATED LEARNING

In his last book, Gustave Flaubert started off with a tale of two adult Parisians, Bouvard and Pecuchet, who, thanks to an unexpected inheritance, left their dull jobs as civil servants and decided to embark on an agricultural adventure in some rural corner of France. Like all lovers of encyclopaedias, they dived into all conceivable sources in order to acquire the knowledge they would need to realize their dream of cultivating farmland in accordance with established scientific principles. The story describes the trials and tribulations of these two modern heroes. To their nonsensical actions, their failed sowing, or animals that were not the least bit interested in reproduction, was added a permanent disenchantment with the rural population for miles around. The unfinished tale leaves us with the two friends fruitlessly engaged in a study of new and better sources of information. To every obstacle they respond with more energetic studies and the most detailed reading of the most relevant sources. The example serves to introduce the last of the schools of thought by way of describing two characters who, in tune with the assumptions of the Enlightenment, adhere to a formal way of learning and fail to realize the intricacies involved in actual practice as well as the contextual importance of the different kinds of knowledge necessary for farming in nineteenth-century France. The approach that situates learning in specific contexts and the exploration of the consequences of this approach is indebted to the work of Vygotsky.

The work of Vygotsky (1978) has been fundamental in opening up the possibility of developing a social version of learning. On the one hand, he assigns language a substantially different role than the one conceived by Dewey. If, for Dewey, language was the refined tool which allowed for internal dialogue and external communication, for Vygotsky, language is a tool that is inward-directed and changes the individual (Vygotsky, 1978). Symbolic activity is thus not only oriented towards transforming the environment but towards transforming the individual. In learning activity this has a durable effect both on the environment and the individual. Indeed, the connection between the individual and the environment is not merely dialogic but constitutive of psychological processes. No learning can take place in isolation.

Vygotsky's work gives us the chance to consider learning from a perspective in which social considerations play a special role. Thanks to his work, it is not only possible to understand that there is no such thing as abstract learning disconnected from the social context but that the very social context determines the way ideas and concepts as well as learning content and horizons are incorporated.

Moreover, learning does not leave the subject of learning intact. Instead, his or her very capacities are changed.

The fundamental role that Vygotsky assigns to context and its social nature has guided a series of works which show how the application of knowledge is closely linked to the setting or context of application. For example, Lave (1988) has described how simple mathematical calculations are performed depending on the content, and the normative mechanisms of calculus are not observed in their application. In contrast, when learning takes place in a social context, this determines both the content and the forms of learning. Thus, Lave and Wenger (1991) affirm that learning is not a matter of acquiring a more or less abstract body of knowledge, but that it must be approached as a process which involves acquiring an identity within a specific community of practice. Thus, learning a trade or a task not only involves acquiring certain given knowledge but also involves the dynamics of participation in a group. These dynamics of participation, which these authors conceptualize as 'legitimate peripheral participation', is what enables the individual to simultaneously acquire knowledge and a place in the community. In this sense, learning is less a matter of content than a matter of being. It is a process by which the individual learns how to perform—as a professional—and uses the language and performs the tasks defined by his or her particular professional group. Thus, *learning how* comes close to *learning to be* (Bruner, 1986).

Nevertheless, introducing social factors into the learning environment can be understood as complementing the intra-individual theory typical of cognitivism by including the social context in its analyses. The 'cognition plus view', as Lave (1993) put it, is a position that enjoys a remarkable acceptance. The working model of Argyris and Schön (1978) is a good illustration. Let us recall that double-loop learning takes place when the basic assumptions are examined by the participants in a problem situation and the examination is performed by reformulating the social context so that any impediments to the exchange of ideas, data, or opinions are minimized. The social context—e.g. the organizational culture—is then put between parentheses to the extent to which it is dysfunctional in examining practice. As mentioned earlier, the aim is to transpose the model from a scientific community to an organizational environment, a transposition which, aside from the idealism it involves, can only take place in practice through an external intervention (Edmondson & Moingeon, 1998) so that its continuity over time is always seriously hampered. These operations are possible only by understanding the social facet as context and not as a constituent of cognitive action. The formalist conception of context, understood as a precursor of an activity, thought, or learning, tends to produce a conception of knowledge creation as a process of abstraction. Ultimately, knowledge creation is understood as progressively moving away from engagement in the world (Lave, 1993) and, as Bruner points out poignantly, science can go so far as to take no interest in application and practice as it 'disclaims in principle any explanatory value at all where the particular is concerned' (1986: 13). A more modest but relevant conclusion is that the discussion concerning the limitations of such understanding of context enlightens us on the reported difficulties involved in transferring knowledge or establishing best practices. For knowledge and best practices develop in specific contexts and are tied to people behaving in specific social arrangements.

On the contrary, understanding context can be taken as having a constitutional function, helping us to understand the role of expectations in the learning process. For example, Säljö and Wyndham's (1993) study revealed that simple cognitive actions such as calculating the correct amount of stamps to put on a letter were dependent on the context and the actors' (students') expectations of the best way to resolve a problem. Indeed, the students not only demonstrated the appropriate means of solving the problem but they also constructed broad contexts in terms of the type of solution accepted as rational. Thus, the result was that calculations varied depending on the teacher and the class in which the students were confronted with the task. Maths and humanities students tackled the problem in a way which was consistent with their expectations of what they thought their respective teachers wanted from them. Not only were the expectations of the two groups radically different, but so too were the solutions they came up with.

If knowledge cannot be separated and form an inert and stable 'objective' realm, we should then think about knowledge creation with an eye on institutions (e.g. schools), so that what is learned is not considered independent and unaffected by the circumstances in which it is learnt. Taking into consideration the particulars is of capital importance inasmuch as it admits the possibility of a critical reflection on knowledge creation in organizations and on learning.

The situated learning perspective attempts to describe the learning processes interwoven with practice in context. From this standpoint we gain a better understanding of the relationship between learning and identity building and the role communities play in it. We also are better equipped to understand some of the current problems concerning knowledge dissemination beyond a general appeal regarding the importance of people. More importantly, the perspective helps us to undertake a more critical reading on learning coming close to the question formulated by Shotter in terms of knowing as the possibility ingrained in identity (1993) or in more Vygotskian terms, underscoring the importance of *others* in constructing our identity and knowledge. In addition, the perspective binds our interests to the careful analysis of verbal interaction since learning processes are understood in connection with our relationship to others.

## SPEECH, LEARNING, AND KNOWLEDGE

Although the sociology of scientific knowledge has provided enough instances of the problems involved in knowledge creation and justification, when it comes to organizations, learning or knowledge creation is likely to be treated in a more naïve way as though little has been learned from the scientific community *modus operandi*.

Organizations can be studied from different standpoints, whether they are mechanical, organic, or symbolic ones. Such perspectives can help us gain a richer understanding of them, however, all organizations exhibit functionality to a greater or lesser extent. In other words, they have to pass the test of efficiency and efficacy at some point. Indeed, knowledge creation and learning organizations are popular to the extent that they seem to provide solid grounds for thriving. To forget this is naïve. To assert that knowledge production is no longer restricted to specific institutions—e.g. universities—is not to state that universities and profit organizations are interchangeable but that organizations should be concerned about learning and knowledge and that this concern is legitimate in achieving their goals.

However, knowledge creation is a complicated matter for scientists since it touches on traditions and vested interests and involves more uncertainty than lay people recognize. Professionals in organizations need to recognize that learning and knowledge are fraught with problems.

Learning processes are dependent on contexts, be they hallways (Dixon, 1997) or enablers (Von Krogh et al., 2000). They are predicated on conversations among individuals. When thinking of learning, or creating knowledge, verbal exchanges are crucial vehicles for sharing experiences, ideas, or previous knowledge. They are advanced in public arenas such as teams, communities, and the like. In all cases, free speech is a basic precondition if learning is to take place.

This fact has not gone unrecognized and empirical research focusing on teams that learn have underscored the importance of creating the appropriate conditions for advancing individual thoughts (Kasl et al., 1997), an atmosphere tolerant of mistakes (Edmondson, 1996), or devising a content appropriate for enhancing productive dialogue (Isaacs, 1993). In a sense, these works undertake the task of upgrading the well-known lessons from the group dynamics tradition and fit it into the purpose of learning and knowledge creation. They logically tend to identify the appropriate conditions for exchange and discussion that result in learning and knowledge creation. In turn, these conditions can be applied to the organization as a whole and thus be linked to an organizational culture that favours dialogue (Schein, 1993b) or, alternatively scaling down its focus of attention, on productive conflict management (Deutsch, 1973; Tjosvold, 1991).

Nevertheless, this focus on conditions tends to miss the intricacies involved in speech. On the one hand, there is little mention of the fact that individual utterances may be made with the purpose of persuasion. Thus, those individuals, consciously or not, use specific rhetorical devices in their address to audiences that go well beyond competence in communication techniques. These devices are necessary because individuals seldom produce irrefutable proof in their utterances but rather enter an argumentative arena in which claims are far from self-evident and ideas or experiences are framed and advanced through forms which leave ample room for interpretation and reconstruction such as narratives (Bruner, 1986; Orr, 1990). That is the nature of professional argument as opposed to demonstration.

Perelman (1982) noted the main difference between argumentation and a demonstration is that in the former case the status of axioms are not self-evident, thus argumentation is concerned with gaining adherence to sets of theses presented to an audience. Classic Aristotelian rhetoric tells us that a discourse consists of different parts involving the presentation of the individual in terms of credibility—ethos—the content matter or the informative part—logos—and the impact on the audience—pathos. Rhetorical devices such as enthymemes, which are frequently used in public addresses, have an impact by arousing the audience's commitment. Also, advancing individual cases, examples, or models that shape presentation of the content matter are ways of supporting arguments which can be presented as relevant examples, aiming to provide sufficient empirical foundation for the case being advanced. The point to be made here is that in the interaction involved in the knowledge creation process, there is more at work than simply advancing one's ideas for the purpose of sharing them in an atmosphere of mutual respect. Rather, the ideas advanced have to comply with rhetorical requirements to be 'heard' by specific communities.

To speak about rhetoric still evokes mixed feelings. On the one hand, Western thought is still imbued with the Socratic non-rhetorical claim. On the other, the realm of rhetoric entered a historical decline as there was an increasing trust in 'evidence'—personal in the case of Protestantism; rational for Cartesians or tangible for empiricists—which rendered the logic of argumentation useless. As in logic, there was no need for debate among logicians, for a demonstration that follows the appropriate rules is either true or false and does not require public debate. The stature gained by different forms of evidence was matched by a declining interest in rhetoric. Currently, this self-evident kind of demonstration is at best rare. As Perelman notes, 'all who believe in the existence of reasonable choice, preceded by deliberation or discussion where different solutions confront each other cannot avoid a theory of argumentation' (1982: 9). Thus, it is important to determine and analyse not only the conditions for entering debate but also how argumentation actually unfolds in specific groups or micro-communities in relation to learning and knowledge creation. In addition to relating claims and arguments in terms of their rhetorical structure and the interests of their producers, it is equally important to acknowledge that specific accounts provide better or worse support for the facts they present. That is, they have different degrees of facticity depending on how accounts are associated with specific categories of speakers. The question, as Potter notes, is not merely to recognize the vested interest of any speaker in relation to the account but the sophisticated ways by which 'people themselves undermine descriptions through invoking interests and how, in turn, they design descriptions to attend to such undermining' (1996: 123). Additionally, the proximity of the speaker to the account has also an influence on how the account is perceived. Simple forms of introducing a subject, such as 'It is said . . .', draw a line between the speaker and someone represented—the principal in Goffman's terms (1981), allowing the speaker to present a neutral face. The question is to recognize that there are complex ways of developing an account and to make it more credible—to construct their facticity—to an audience. In addition, these ways are to some extent contingent on the organizations or communities involved. These resources are very much dependent on professional worlds and in this vein it is likely that tensions arise among different sorts of professionals and between organizations and professionals. For example, experts in information systems have developed a language within which there are specific ways of arguing or accounting or documenting a fact which are very likely to strike a different register than those of other professionals.

The fact that, except for a very few scholars (e.g. Argyris et al., 1985; Donnellon, 1996), there does not seem to be much interest in exploring the linguistic aspects involved in learning may be due to the fact that the majority of models are embedded in a more or less Popperian view. Let us recall that, according to Popper, the scientific community is committed to the process of problem-solving and, as he stated, unlike other species 'the scientist does not die with the hypothesis' (1997). The implication being that discarding hypotheses is a relatively simple matter that can be solved in rational debate. This has distracted our attention from the debate itself. This is so because complicated debate was explicitly to be expected only when the discussion concerned values (Popper, 1994), but as long as this was not the scientists' case—nor that of individuals in organizations—rational argumentation would, in the end, suffice.

However, as this rational debate has been analysed, it is clearly less simple than Popper was ready to admit. Scientific debate is constructed according to certain forms and rules which point to the use of rhetoric (Nelson et al., 1987) for arguments to be constructed and accepted in specific communities of scientists. Accordingly, we should expect specific forms of argumentation depending on the community of practice involved. This remains a little-explored area which should not be relegated if we are to understand learning processes. This is particularly so regarding knowledge dissemination but it also concerns knowledge creation.

Argumentation should not be separated from the knowledge creation process. Indeed, when talking about knowledge we imply some kind of previous justification. For example, Von Krogh et al. (2000) understand knowledge as *justified true belief*, thus the question of justification regarding truth, first, is not a matter of data, or of confirming or ruling out evidence, but of the criteria set up and used to establish the confirmation procedures and, second, how these criteria are legitimized. Bonet and colleagues (2003) underscore this fact by recalling that Aristotelian physics was not to be considered less truthful than Galilean physics if the criteria used to evaluate it were the ones developed by Aristotle. Thus, argumentative procedures are to be studied in organizations as long as we are concerned with how persuasion takes place involving content matters as well as the criteria set up to evaluate or justify a belief. Criteria set up to evaluate arguments are, in turn, a construction of communities and in this sense they require an institutional reading as well as some mention on how power is articulated through them.

I started this chapter with the explicit goal of advancing a set of reasons to help understand the phenomenon of the interest in learning within and between organizations. As a result, it appears that different stakeholders see a confluence of sets of interests which has made the field blossom. Second, I planned to put forward an intellectual map of the field by explicitly addressing the basic schools of thought. As with any other map, it contains over-simplifications for the sake of clarity. My contention is that every school of thought sheds some light on different sets of problems and that they all have some pragmatic use, provided that we are all aware of the limitations involved in each of them. For example, the current accounts of disappointment in organizations, which have forged ahead with hasty investments in information systems and the reported difficulties in knowledge transfer, have stimulated a more cautious interpretation of the supposed benchmarking processes and a less euphoric approach to knowledge management. The problems here can be better understood as limitations which are partly inherent in the cognitivist standpoint. Finally, I advance a discussion on a neglected area of study, that of persuasion, to end up considering the importance of argumentation. A preliminary conclusion is that for each community of practice, there must be, first, a consideration of the specifics involved in each of them for the purpose of sharing knowledge (Brown & Duguid, 2000) and, second, the development of a critical reading of learning in organizations which are less anchored in politics (Coopey, 1994) and more oriented to revealing the restrictions and opportunities embedded in institutionalized practices (Engeström, 1993; Lam, 2000).

# REFERENCES

Anderson, J.R. (1983) *The Architecture of Recognition*. Cambridge, MA: Harvard University Press.

Argyris, C. & Schön, D.A. (1978) *Organizational Learning*. Reading, MA: Addison-Wesley.

Argyris, C. & Schön, D.A. (1996) *Organizational Learning II*. Reading, MA: Addison-Wesley.

Argyris, C., Putnam, R. & Smith, D.M. (1985) *Action Science*. San Francisco: Jossey-Bass.

Barley, S.R. & Kunda, G. (1992) Design and devotion: surges of rational and normative ideologies of control in managerial discourse. *Administrative Science Quarterly*, **37**, 363–399.

Barley, S. & Orr, J. (1997) The neglected workforce. In S. Barley & J. Orr (eds) *Between Craft and Science*. Ithaca, NY: Cornell University Press.

Bonet, E., Sauquet, A. & Bou, E. (2003) *Truth and Judgement: Socratic Dialogue and Organizational Learning*. Esade Working Paper 168. Barcelona: Esade.

Brown, J.S. and Duguid, P. (1991) Organizational learning and communities-of-practice: toward a unified view of working, learning and innovation. *Organizational Science*, **2**(1), 47–57.

Brown, J.S. & Duguid, P. (2000) *The Social Life of Information*. Boston: Harvard Business School Press.

Bruner, J.S. (1986) *Actual Minds, Possible Worlds*. Cambridge, MA: Harvard University Press.

Bruner, J.S. (1990) *Acts of Meaning*. Cambridge, MA: Harvard University Press.

Bruner, J.S. (1996) *The Culture of Education*. Cambridge, MA: Harvard University Press.

Burke, W.W. (1993) *Organizational Development: A Process of Learning and Changing*. Reading, MA: Addison-Wesley.

Cangelossi, V. & Dill, W.R. (1965) Organizational learning: observations toward a theory. *Administrative Science Quarterly*, **10**, 175–203.

Cook, S.D.N. & Yanow, D. (1993) Culture and organizational learning. *Journal of Management Inquiry*, **2**(4), 373–390.

Coopey, J. (1994) The learning organization: power politics and ideology. *Management Learning*, **26**(2), 193–214.

Crossan, M. & Guatto, T. (1996) Organizational learning research profile. *Journal of Organizational Change Management*, **9**(1), 107–112.

Crossan, M.M., Lane, H.W. & White, R.E. (1999) An organizational learning framework: from intuition to institution. *Academy of Management Review*, **24**(3), 522–537.

Dearborn, D.C. & Simon, H.A. (1958) Selective perception: a note on the departmental identification of executives. *Sociometry*, **21**, 140–144.

De Geus, A. (1988) Planning as learning. *Harvard Business Review*, **March–April**, 70–74.

Deutsch, M. (1973) *The Resolution of Conflict*. New Haven, CT: Yale University Press.

Dewey, J. (1910) *How We Think*. Amherst, NY: Prometheus.

Dewey, J. (1925) *Experience and Nature*. New York: Dover Publications.

Dewey, J. (1938) *Experience and Education*. New York: Collier Books.

Dewey, J. (1954) *The Public and its Problems*. Chicago: Swallow Press.

Dixon, N.M. (1997) The hallways of learning. *Organizational Dynamics*, **Spring**, 23–34.

Dodgson, M. (1993) Organizational learning: a review of some literatures. *Organization Studies*, **14**(3), 375–394.

Donnellon, A. (1996) *Team Talk: The Power of Language in Team Dynamics*. Cambridge, MA: Harvard Business School Press.

Drucker, P.F. (1994) The age of social transformation. *The Atlantic Monthly*, **November**, 54–90.

Easterby-Smith, M. & Araujo, L. (1999) Organizational learning: current debates and opportunities. In M. Easterby-Smith & L. Araujo (eds) *Organizational Learning*. London: Sage.

Edmondson, A.C. (1996) Learning from mistakes is easier said than done: group and organizational influences on the detection and correction of human error. *Journal of Applied Behavioral Science*, **32**(1), 5–28.

Edmondson, A.C. & Moingeon, B. (1998) From organizational learning to the learning organization. *Management Learning*, **29**, 5–20.

Engëstrom, Y. (1993) Developmental studies of work as a testbench of activity theory: the case of primary care medical practice. In S. Chaiklin & J. Lave (eds) *Understanding Practice: Perspectives on Activity and Context*. Cambridge: Cambridge University Press.

Feldman, J. (1986) On the difficulty of learning from experience. In H.P. Sims & D. Gioia (eds) *The Thinking Organization: Dynamics of Organizational Social Cognition*. San Francisco: Jossey-Bass.

Fiol, M.C. & Lyles, M.A. (1985) Organizational learning. *Academy of Management Review*, **10** (4), 803–813.

García, J. & Koelling, R.A. (1966) Relation of cue to consequence in avoidance learning. *Psychonomic Science*, **4**, 123–124.

Gardner, H. (1985) *The Mind's New Science: A History of the Cognitive Revolution*. New York: Basic Books.

Garratt, B. (1987) *The Learning Organization*. Worcester: Gower.

Gherardi, S. (1999) Learning as problem driven or learning in the face of mystery? *Organization Studies*, **20**(1), 101–124.

Goffman, E. (1981) *Forms of Talk*. Oxford: Blackwell.

Hedberg, B. (1981) How organizations learn and unlearn. In P.C. Nystrom & W. Starbuck (eds) *Handbook of Organizational Design*. Oxford: Oxford University Press.

Houle, C.O. (1980) *Continuing Learning in the Professions*. San Francisco: Jossey-Bass.

Huber, G.P. (1991) Organizational learning: the contributing processes and the literatures. *Organization Science*, **2**(1), 88–115.

Isaacs, W.N. (1993) Taking flight: dialogue, collective thinking, and organizational learning. *Organizational Dynamics*, **Fall**, 24–39.

James, W. (1950) *The Principles of Psychology*. New York: Dover Publications.

Jenssen, H.S. (2001) A history of the concept of knowledge. Paper presented in the European Doctoral Programme on Knowledge Management, Copenhagen Business School.

Kasl, E., Marsick, V.J. & Dechant, K. (1997) Teams as learners: a research-based model of team learning. *Journal of Applied Behavioral Science*, **33**(2), 227–246.

Kim, D.H. (1993) The link between individual and organizational learning. *Sloan Management Review*, **Fall**, 37–50.

Knowles, M.S. (1980) *The Modern Practice of Adult Education*. Chicago: Association Press.

Kolb, D.A. (1984) *Experiential Learning*. Englewood Cliffs, NJ: Prentice Hall.

Lam, A. (2000) Tacit knowledge, organizational learning and societal institutions: an integrated framework. *Organization Studies*, **21**(3), 487–513.

Lave, J. (1988) *Cognition in Practice*. Cambridge: Cambridge University Press.

Lave, J. (1993) The practice of learning. In S. Chaiklin & J. Lave (eds) *Understanding Practice: Perspectives on Activity and Context*. Cambridge: Cambridge University Press.

Lave, J. & Wenger, E. (1991) *Situated Learning: Legitimate Peripheral Participation*. Cambridge: Cambridge University Press.

Levitt, B. & March, J.G. (1988) Organizational learning. *Annual Review of Sociology*, **14**, 319–340.

Lieber, S. (1991) *An Invitation to Cognitive Science*. Cambridge, MA: Blackwell.

March, J.G. & Olsen, J.P. (1976) *Ambiguity and Choice in Organizations*. Bergen: Universitatsforlaget.

March, J.G. & Olsen, J.P. (1991) Exploration and exploitation in organizational learning. *Organization Science*, **2**, 71–87.

Mayrhofer, W. (1996) Warning: flexibility can damage your organizational health. Paper presented at the First International Conference on The European Challenge to Work Flexibility. Barcelona: Esade.

McGrath, R.G. (2001) Exploratory learning, innovative capacity and managerial oversight. *Academy of Management Journal*, **14**, 118–131.

Miner, A. & Mezias, S. (1996) Ugly-duckling no more: past and futures of organizational learning research. *Organization Science*, **7**(1), 88–99.

Mintzberg, H. (1994) *The Rise and Fall of Strategic Planning*. New York: Prentice Hall.

Morrison, E. (1977) *Men, Machines and Modern Times*. Cambidge, MA: MIT Press.

Nelson, J.S., Megill, A. & McCloskey, D.N. (1987) Rhetoric of inquiry. In J.S. Nelson, A. Megill & D.N. McClosey (eds) *The Rhetoric of the Human Sciences: Language and Argument in Scholarship and Public Affairs*. Madison, WI: University of Wisconsin Press.

Nietzsche, F. (1967) *On the Genealogy of Morals*. Trans. by W. Kaufman & R.J. Hollingdale. In *On the Genealogy of Morals and Ecce Homo*. New York: Random House.

Nonaka, I. & Takeuchi, H. (1994) *The Knowledge Creating Company*. Cambridge, MA: Harvard University Press.

Nystrom, P.C. & Starbuck, W. (1984) To avoid organizational crisis, unlearn. *Organizational Dynamics*, **12**(4), 53–76.

Orr, J.E. (1990) Sharing knowledge, celebrating identity: community memory in a service culture. In D. Middleton & D. Edwards (eds) *Collective Remembering*. London: Sage.

Pedler, M., Burgoyne, J. & Boydell, T. (1991) *The Learning Company*. London: McGraw-Hill.

Perelman, C. (1982) *The Realm of Rhetoric*. Notre Dame, IN: University of Notre Dame Press.

Polanyi, M. (1966) *The Tacit Dimension*. London: Routledge.

Popper, K. (1994) *The Myth of the Framework*. London: Routledge.

Popper, K. (1997) *Toute Vie est une Résolution des Problèmes*. Paris: Actes Sud.

Potter, J. (1996) *Representing Reality: Discourse, Rhetoric and Social Construction*. London: Sage.

Pozo, J.I. (1989) *Teorías Cognitivas del Aprendizaje*. Madrid: Morata.

Revans, R. (1982) *The Origins and Growth of Action Learning*. Bromley: Chartwell-Bratt.

Rorty, R. (1996) Pragmatism and religion. The Girona Lectures. Unpublished Manuscript. Girona: University of Girona.

Ryle, G. (1949) *The Concept of Mind*. London: Hutchinson.

Säljö, R. & Wyndham, J. (1993) Solving everyday problems in the formal setting: an empirical study of the school as the context for thought. In S. Chaitklin & J. Lave (eds) *Understanding Practice: Perspectives on Activity and Context*. Cambridge: Cambridge University Press.

Schein, E.H. (1993a) How organizations can learn faster: the challenge of entering the green room. *Sloan Management Review*, **34**(2), 85–92.

Schein, E.H. (1993b) On dialogue, culture, and organizational learning. *Organizational Dynamics*, **Fall**, 40–51.

Schön, D.A. (1983) *The Reflective Practitioner*. New York: Basic Books.

Schön, D.A (1987) *Educating the Reflective Practitioner*. San Francisco: Jossey-Bass.

Searle, J. (1984) *Minds, Brains and Science*. Cambridge, MA: Harvard University Press.

Senge, P. (1990) *The Fifth Discipline*. New York: Doubleday.

Shanon, C.E. & Weaver, W. (1964) *The Mathematical Theory of Communication*. Urbana, IL: The University of Illinois Press.

Shotter, J. (1993) *Cultural Politics of Everyday Life*. Milton Keynes: Open University Press.

Shrivastava, P. (1983) A typology of organizational learning systems. *Journal of Management Studies*, **20**(1), 7–28.

Simon, H. (1972) *Human Problem Solving*. Englewood Cliffs, NJ: Prentice Hall.

Simon, H. (1987) Making management decision: the role of intuition and emotion. *Academy of Management Executive*, **1**, 57–64.

Spender, J.C. (1998) The dynamics of individual and organizational knowledge. In C. Eden & J.C. Spender (eds) *Managerial and Organizational Cognition: Theory Methods and Research*. London: Sage.

Starbuck, W.H. & Mezias, J.M. (1996) Opening Pandora's box: studying the accuracy of managers' perceptions. *Journal of Organizational Behavior*, **17**(2), 99–107.

Stata, R. (1989) Organizational learning: the key to management innovation. *Sloan Management Review*, **30**, 63–74.

Staw, B.M. (1976) Knee-deep in the ig muddy: a study of escalating commitment to a chosen course of action. *Organizational Behavior and Human Performance*, **16**, 27–44.

Tjosvold, D. (1991) *The Conflict-Positive Organization*. Reading, MA: Addison-Wesley.

Tsang, E. (1997) Organizational learning and the learning organization: a dichotomy between descriptive and prescriptive research. *Human Relations*, **50**(1), 73–89.

Tversky, A. & Kahneman, D. (1974) Judgement under uncertainty: heuristics and biases. *Science*, **185**, 1124–1131.

Virilio, P. (1977) *Vitesse et Politique*. Paris: Galilée.

Von Krogh, G., Ichijo, K. & Nonaka, I. (2000) *Enabling Knowledge Creation*. Oxford: Oxford University Press.

Vygotsky, L.S. (1978) *Mind in Society*. Cambridge, MA: Harvard University Press.

Watkins, K.E. & Marsick, V.J. (1993) *Sculpting the Learning Organization*. San Francisco: Jossey-Bass.

Weick, K.E. (1979) *The Social Psychology of Organizing*. New York: Random House.

Weick, K.E. (1991) The nontraditional quality of organizational learning. *Organization Science*, **2**, 116–124.

Weick, K.E. (1993) The collapse of sensemaking in organizations: the Mann Gulch disaster. *Administrative Science Quarterly*, **38**, 628–652.

Weick, K.E. & Roberts, K.H. (1993) Collective mind in organization: heedful interrelating on flight decks. *Administrative Science Quarterly*, **38**, 357–381.

Weick, K.E. & Westley, F. (1996) Organizational learning: affirming an oxymoron. In S.R. Clegg, C. Hardy & W.R. Nord (eds) *Handbook of Organization Studies*. London: Sage.

# CHAPTER 18

# Double-loop Learning and Organizational Change

## Facilitating Transformational Change

**Chris Argyris**

*Harvard University, Cambridge, MA, USA*

Recently, there has been an emphasis on leadership and learning that is intended to change existing ideas about organizations as well as changing the status quo. A key word is 'transformational' where learning and leading are focused on underlying changes in the routines that dominate managing organizations of all types.

Yet, reviews of research suggest that 70 percent of such programs are failures (Boonstra, in press). Heller, Pucu, Strauss, and Wilpert (1988) in a worldwide review conclude that those programs that succeed deal with relatively routine issues where the status quo is not challenged and Argyris (2000) is in agreement with both of these findings. Barker (1999) reports similar findings in an in-depth study of teamwork. The conclusion is that there is a large-scale mismatch between the intentions to produce transformational learning and change and what actually happens. The mismatches between intentions and actuality are, in effect, illustrations of error:

Question I: Why do similar errors occur in such large numbers, in different organizations, in different cultures even, and when planned and executed by change professionals supported by line executives?

Question II: Since these studies represent efforts which have been going on for at least a decade, why is it that so little learning occurs to detect and correct the errors?

The answers many give to such questions as these is that transformational change and learning are very difficult to implement; they take a long time to bear fruition; they require behavior and practices that often threaten the status quo; and they are about complicated problems that have many variables. The answers make sense but they are incomplete. As a result of a review of the literature that I recently completed, I found that the current theorizing and practice about dealing with producing such learning and change bypass these issues and bypass the bypasses (Argyris, 2000).

Question III: How come these issues are systematically bypassed and the bypass is bypassed?

In order to answer these questions, I believe we must dig deeper into the meaning of error and the theories of action that produce the errors and encourage bypassing them. Actionable knowledge specifies the actions required to effectively implement the intentions of the actors. Effective implementation occurs when (a) a match is produced between intended and actual outcomes; (b) in such a way that the outcomes persevere; and (c) without harming the present level of problem-solving effectiveness.

*Dynamics of Organizational Change and Learning.* Edited by J.J. Boonstra.
© 2004 John Wiley & Sons, Ltd. ISBN 0-471-87737-9.

# MIND/BRAIN AND A PERSPECTIVE ABOUT ERROR

As I understand some of the recent findings about the mind/brain (M/B), they suggest the following:

1. Behavior is produced by using the M/B. The executive function of the M/B is the vehicle through which the actions are produced. By executive function I do not mean some centralized or hierarchical control point, I mean processes of implementation. These processes may exist in one part of the M/B or in many parts. In order for the executive function to produce action, it has designs for action that are warehoused in, and retrievable from, M/B in an on-line manner. There are two types of designs. They are designs-for-action and designs that are actually used by the executive function to produce the actions. I call these the designs-in-use.
2. Designs-in-action specify the intended consequences and the sequence of behaviors that are necessary to produce these actions. In order to be retrieved and used in an on-line manner, these designs are programmed. It is practice that produces the skills that, in turn, creates the ruthless program.
3. The designs-in-use are *causal* specifications of what actions are required in order to produce the intended consequences. The feature of causality is key and is inferred from observation of the actual behavior.
4. Errors are mismatches between intended and actual consequences.
5. If errors are inferred from the observed behavior, and if the observed behavior is produced by designs-in-use in the executive function, then it is not possible for human beings to knowingly produce errors. This is true because a produced action is always consistent with the design-in-use and thus it is a match and not a mismatch.

But, I have just claimed that all actions are produced through the designs-in-use stored in the executive function. How come human beings hold designs-in-use that produce errors in the world of practice?

One way to begin to solve the puzzle is to ask where the designs-in-use come from. The answer is that they are produced by the skills developed by human beings. But, how do we explain that human beings develop skills that produce designs-in-use that, in turn, create the puzzle, namely, that the actions are skilled (or else they could not be designs-in-use) yet they produce counter-productive consequences?

A theory that will help us to solve the puzzles must be a theory where the executive function plays a central role. Such a theory must be about action. The theory must specify how to enhance effective action and reduce ineffective action. Effective action occurs when (a) a match is produced between intended and actual outcome; (b) in such a way that the outcomes persevere; and (c) without harming the present level of problem-solving effectiveness.

The theory must produce propositions that are generalizable and testable. The same theory must be usable in a concrete situation or context. If a theory of action is to be user-friendly, it cannot have one set of propositions for the 'many' and another for the 'one'. The theory must deal with thoughts and reasoning used to plan or invent actions as well as how to implement the inventions effectively. The theory must specify how to test the validity of the invention and the effectiveness of the implementation. The tests should especially focus upon disconfirmation. Such tests can then be used to correct the theory and any future action.

Such a theory must be usable to describe how human beings, groups, intergroups, and organizations behave. Since the theory is about effective and ineffective actions, it will be normative because the basis for such actions are values and norms that are constructed by the actors. Since the theory makes claims about enhancing effective action and reducing ineffective action, it will also be prescriptive. It should inform us about the skills required for effective action as well as the educational experiences where the ideas and the skills can be learned.

One theory that seeks to fulfill these criteria is called a theory of action (Argyris, 1982, 1990, 1993, 2000; Argyris & Schön, 1996).

## A THEORY OF ACTION

Human beings hold two types of theories of action. There is the one that they espouse, which is usually expressed in the form of stated beliefs and values. Then there is the theory that they actually use; this can only be inferred from observing their actions, that is, their actual behavior.

Theory-in-use is a master program held by individuals to design their actions and to implement the design. Designs-in-use are subroutines. They are derivable from, and consistent with, the Model I master program.

To date, most human beings studied have the same theory-in-use. There is diversity in espoused theories, but not in theories-in-use. A model of the theory-in-use (that we call Model I) follows (see Figure 18.1). Model I theory-in-use is the design we found throughout the world. It has four governing values. They are: (a) achieve your intended purpose; (b) maximize winning and minimize losing; (c) suppress negative feelings; and (d) behave according to what you consider rational.

The most prevalent action strategies that arise from Model I are the following: (a) advocate your position; (b) evaluate the thoughts and actions of others (and your own thoughts and actions); and (c) attribute causes for whatever you are trying to understand (Argyris, 1982, 1990, 1993; Argyris & Schön, 1996).

These actions must be performed in such a way that satisfies the actors' governing values—that is, they achieve at least their minimum acceptable level of being in control, winning, or bringing about any other result. In other words, Model I tells individuals to craft their positions, evaluations, and attributions in ways that inhibit inquiries into and tests of them with the use of independent logic. The consequences of these Model I strategies are likely to be defensiveness, misunderstanding, and self-fulfilling and self-sealing processes (Argyris, 1982).

Model I theory-in-use requires defensive reasoning which means that: individuals keep their premises and inferences tacit, lest they lose control. They create tests of their claims that are self-serving and self-sealing. The likelihood of misunderstanding and mistrust increases. The use of defensive reasoning prohibits questioning the defensive reasoning. We now have self-fueling processes that maintain the status quo, inhibit genuine learning, and reinforce the deception.

Human beings learn their theories-in-use early in life, and therefore the actions that they produce are highly skilled. Little conscious attention is paid to producing skilled actions; indeed, conscious attention could inhibit producing them effectively. This leads to unawareness of what we are doing when we act skillfully. The unawareness due to skill and the unawareness caused by our unilaterally controlling theories-in-use produce a deeper unawareness; namely, we become unaware of the programs

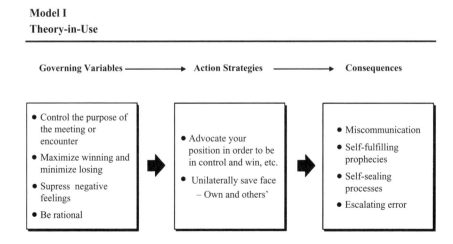

**Model I**
**Theory-in-Use**

Governing Variables ———————▶ Action Strategies ———————▶ Consequences

- Control the purpose of the meeting or encounter
- Maximize winning and minimize losing
- Supress negative feelings
- Be rational

- Advocate your position in order to be in control and win, etc.
- Unilaterally save face – Own and others'

- Miscommunication
- Self-fulfilling prophecies
- Self-sealing processes
- Escalating error

**FIGURE 18.1**   Model I: theory-in-use

in our heads that keep us unaware. The results are skilled unawareness and skilled incompetence. For example, when individuals have to say something negative to others (e.g., 'Your performance is poor'), they often ease in, in order not to upset the other. Two of the most frequent easing-in actions that we observe are (a) non-directive questioning and (b) face-saving approaches. In order for these to work, the individuals must cover up that they are acting as they are, in order not to upset the other. In order for a cover-up to work, the cover-up itself must be covered up.

When organizational worlds become dominated by these consequences, human beings become cynical about changing the self-fueling counter-productive process. Not surprisingly, they learn to distance themselves from taking responsibility, and suppressing negative feelings, especially those associated with embarrassment or threat. Individuals use behavioral strategies consistent with these governing values. For example, they advocate their views, making evaluations and attributions in such a way as to ensure their being in control, winning, and suppressing negative feelings.

In short, individuals learn theories-in-use that are consistent with producing unilateral control. It is true that organizations are hierarchical and based on unilateral control. It is equally true that individuals are even more so. Place individuals in organizations whose structures are designed to be more egalitarian, and individuals will eventually make them more unilateral and authoritarian.

Why is this so? Because Model I governing values and behavioral strategies will produce hierarchies and coordination practices (in groups, intergroups, and organizations) that are characterized by unilateral, top-down control.

In this connection, I have tried to show that the fundamental bases for pyramidal hierarchy and Model I theory-in-use is probably the limited capacity of the human mind as an information processor. The argument leads to predictions, for example, that capitalist and socialist countries will not vary in the use of unilateral control and Model I theories-in-use. The same should be true for unions, churches, schools, and voluntary organizations (Argyris, 1978).

## ORGANIZATIONAL DEFENSIVE ROUTINES

Organizational defensive routines are any action, policy, or practice that prevents organizational partici-pants from experiencing embarrassment or threat and, at the same time, prevents them from discovering the causes of the embarrassment or threat. Organizational defensive routines, like Model I theories-in-use, inhibit genuine learning and overprotect the individuals and the organization (Argyris, 1990).

There is a fundamental logic underlying all organizational defensive routines. It can be illustrated by one of the most frequently observed defenses, namely, sending mixed messages, such as, 'Mary, you run the department, but check with Bill', or 'John, be innovative but be careful'. The logic is: (a) send a message that is inconsistent; (b) act as if it is not inconsistent; (c) make steps (a) and (b) undiscussable; and (d) make the undiscussability undiscussable.

Organizational defensive routines are caused by a circular, self-reinforcing process in which indi-viduals' Model I theories-in-use produce individual strategies of bypass and cover-up, which result in organizational bypass and cover-up, which reinforce the individuals' theories-in-use. The explana-tion of organizational defensive routines is therefore individual *and* organizational. This means that it should not be possible to change organizational routines without changing individual routines, and vice versa. Any attempts at doing so should lead to failure or, at best, temporary success.

To help individuals recognize their skillful Model I incompetence and unawareness, the intervener introduces Model II theories-in-use (see Figure 18.2). Model II theories are, at the outset, espoused theories. The challenge is to help individuals transform their espoused theories into theories-in-use by learning a 'new' set of skills and a 'new' set of governing values. Because many individuals espouse Model II values and skills, these traits are not totally new to them. However, the empirical fact to date is that very few individuals can routinely act on their espoused values, yet they are often unaware of this limitation.

**Model II**
**Theory-in-Use**

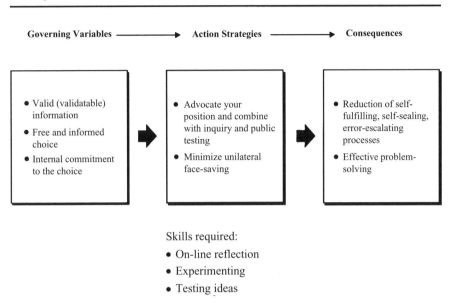

FIGURE 18.2   Model II: theory-in-use

The governing values of Model II are valid information, informed choice, and vigilant monitoring of the implementation of the choice in order to detect and correct error. As in the case of Model I, the three most prominent behaviors are advocate, evaluate, and attribute. However, unlike Model I behaviors, Model II behaviors are crafted into action strategies that openly illustrate how the actors reached their evaluations or attributions, and how they crafted them to encourage inquiry and testing by others. Productive reasoning is required to produce such consequences. Productive reasoning means that the premises are explicit, the inferences from the premises are also made explicit, and finally conclusions are crafted in ways that can be tested by logic that is independent of the actor. Unlike the defensive reasoning, the logic used is not self-referential. As a consequence, defensive routines that are anti-learning are minimized, and genuine learning is facilitated. Embarrassment and threat are not bypassed and covered up; they are engaged (Argyris, 1982; Argyris & Schön, 1996). In summary, we have human beings using Model I that creates organizational defensive routines which feedback to reinforce Model I actions. The result is an ultra stable state that inhibits learning, especially double-loop learning.

Double-loop learning focuses on detecting and correcting errors in the designs of the master programs that underlie the routines. When this is the case, the attention is focused on changing the governing of the values, policies, and master programs that produced the routines in question in the first place. Double-loop learning is at the heart of the distinction, often made in the literature, between doing something right and doing the right thing.

## DESIRED ORGANIZATIONAL CHANGES

Over the past several decades much has been written about what is the right thing. In a recent review of the literature, the objectives have been defined as moving away from features of the status quo to moving toward new features and new characteristics. The reasons for this movement are, we are told, to make organizations more flexible, agile, adaptive and, at the same time, make their performance more efficient and effective (Argyris, 2000). These features are especially important in environments that are turbulent and more global. Examples of these features include the following:

| *Move away from* | *Move forward* |
|---|---|
| Mechanistic hierarchies | Organic, flatter structures |
| Top-down leadership | Participative leadership |
| External commitment | Internal commitment |
| Emphasis on stability | Emphasis upon continuous change |
| Loyalty to power | Loyalty to valid information and competence |

Model I theories-in-use and organizational defensive routines are root causes of the features described in the left-hand column. Model II theories-in-use and organizational routines that sanction and reward double-loop learning are root causes of the features described in the right-hand column.

If our theory of double-loop learning is correct, then the transformational changes required to create the features in the right-hand column will require learning Model II theories-in-use and effective organizational dialectic, that results in double-loop learning (Argyris & Schön, 1996). This will not be easy because individuals' sense of competence and confidence in that competence are presently tied to Model I and to the existence of organizational defensive routines that reinforce Model I. Moreover, individuals exhibit skilled incompetence, skilled unawareness, and defensive reasoning, all of which focus attention on not changing the status quo.

Before I turn to a description of the change processes intended to produce double-loop learning, I should like to pause for a moment to identify our recent research on how to strengthen double-loop learning by the integration of what is typically called the 'hard stuff' (e.g., accounting, finance, marketing, and strategy) with the 'soft stuff' (e.g., human side of organization).

First, the advances in cognitive science and neuro-science suggest, as mentioned above, the human mind implements action by designs (theories-in-use) that are programmed (Simon, 1969; Abelson, 1981; Lord & Kernan, 1987). This is true for the technical as well as the human features. Human behavior such as being imprecise is produced by precisely programmed designs. The same is true for actions such as ambivalence, uncertainty, rambling, and emotionality.

Second, Model II productive reasoning is consistent with the productive reasoning used to develop such managerial disciplines as accounting, finance, marketing, and strategy. Thus, there is a deep basis for the integration of both. This integration can occur at least at two levels. The human-side 'stuff' can be used to help implement the technical stuff more effectively. For example, management agrees that the result of cost drivers is correct. They agree on the forecasts of the savings that will be produced. Yet, they do not implement the recommendations largely because of the existence of powerful organizational defensive routines (Argyris & Kaplan, 1994).

A second level of integration is to enlarge the technical theory so that it includes the human perspectives as part of its inner intellectual structure. For example, Jensen (1998) has integrated into his theory of finance the concept of pain avoidance which deals with individual and organizational defensive routines.

The claim being made here is that integration is more likely to be achieved if the change programs include features of double-loop learning at the individual and organizational levels.

## DOUBLE-LOOP LEARNING CHANGE PROGRAMS

Because of limitations of space, I am able to provide only a cursory description of change programs that include a heavy focus on double-loop learning (for details, see Argyris, 1982, 1986, 1990, 1993, 2000; Argyris & Schön, 1974, 1996). I therefore will summarize some of the features of such intervention activities intended to produce double-loop learning in organizations.

## DESIGN OF RESEARCH-INTERVENTION ACTIVITIES FOR DOUBLE-LOOP LEARNING

There are design rules that follow from the theoretical framework described above that can be used to design the research and the intervention activities:

1. Discover the degree to which the clients' theories-in-use are consistent with Model I.
2. Discover the degree to which the clients use defensive reasoning whenever they deal with embarrassing or threatening issues.
3. Discover the designs (rules) the clients have in their heads that keep them unaware of the discrepancies among their espoused values, their actions, and their theories-in-use.
4. Surface and make explicit the rules that 'must' be in their heads if they maintain there is a connection between their designs for action and the actions themselves.
5. View any bewilderment or frustration that results as further directly observable data that can be used to test the validity of what is being learned.
6. Produce opportunities to practice Model II ways of crafting actions that will reduce counterproductive consequences.

In principle, the kind of research of which I write can begin with identifying either the theories-in-use or the organizational defensive routines. It does not matter which, because one will necessarily lead you to the other. I usually make the choice on the basis of which of the two is most likely to generate the participants' internal commitment to the research and to the eventual intervention. Some questions that I use to make these determinations are published in Argyris (1970).

## THE LEFT- AND RIGHT-HAND COLUMN-CASE METHOD

We often use a case study instrument to discover theories-in-use and organizational defensive routines. The case method described next is one of several instruments used in our action science research (Argyris et al., 1985). The key features of all the research methods and this case method in particular are:

1. It produces relatively directly observable data such as conversation. Such data are the actual productions of action, and therefore can become the basis for inferring theories-in-use.
2. It produces data in ways that make clear the actors' responsibility for the meanings produced. When used properly, the respondents cannot make the research instrument causally responsible for the data that they produced (e.g., 'I didn't really mean that'; or 'I didn't understand the meaning of that term').
3. It produces data about the respondents' causal theories, especially those that are tacit because they are taken for granted.
4. It provides opportunities for the respondents to change their responses without hindering the validity of the inferences being made. Indeed, the actions regarding 'changing their minds' should also provide data about their causal reasoning processes. It provides opportunities to change their actions as well as the actions of groups, intergroups, and organizations over which they have some influence. It provides such knowledge in ways that are economical and do not harm the respondents or the context in which they are working.

The directions for writing a case are given to each individual. The directions request:

1. In one paragraph, describe a key organizational problem as you see it.
2. Assume you could talk to whomever you wish in order to begin to solve the problem. Describe, in a paragraph or so, the strategy that you would use in this meeting.
3. Next, divide your page into two columns. On the right-hand side write how you would begin the meeting—what you would actually say. Then write what you believe the other(s) would say. Then

write your response to their response. Continue writing this scenario for two or so double-spaced typewritten pages.

4. In the left-hand column, write any idea or feeling that you would have that you would not communicate for whatever reason.

In short, the case includes:

- a statement of the problem;
- the intended strategy to begin to solve the problem;
- the actual conversation that did or would occur as envisioned by the writer;
- the information that the writer would not communicate for whatever reason.

Some of the results can be illustrated by reference to a CEO and his executive group. The executives reported that they became highly involved in writing the cases. Some said that the very writing of the case was an eye-opener. Moreover, once the cases were distributed to each member, the reactions were jocular. The members were enjoying them, as these comments demonstrate:

> That's just like . . .
>
> Great, . . . does this all the time.
>
> Oh, there's a familiar one.
>
> All salesmen and no listeners.
>
> Oh, my God, this is us.

## CASES AS AN INTERVENTION TOOL

What is the advantage of using the cases? The cases, crafted and written by the executives themselves, become vivid examples of 'skilled incompetence', see Table 18.1. They illustrate the skill with which each executive tried not to upset the other.

And the skill used to persuade them to change their position. They also illustrate the incompetence component because the results, by their own analysis, were to upset the others and make it less likely that their views would prevail.

The cases are also very important learning devices. It is difficult for anyone to slow down the behavior that they produce in milliseconds during a real meeting in order to reflect on it and change it. The danger is that others will grab the airtime and run with it. Moreover, it is difficult for the human mind to pay attention to the interpersonal actions and to the substantive issues at the same time.

The dialogue continues with each person stating his views candidly but not being influenced by what the other says. To give you a flavor of what happened, here are some further left-hand column comments:

> He's doing a great job supporting his people. I better be careful.
>
> This guy is really not listening.
>
> I wonder if he's influenceable.
>
> This is beginning to piss me off.
>
> There he goes getting defensive. I better back off and wait for another day.

**TABLE 18.1**  A collage from several cases

| Thoughts and feelings not communicated | Actual conversation |
| --- | --- |
| He's not going to like this topic, but we had to discuss it. I doubt that he will take a company perspective, but I should be positive | I: Hi, Bill. I appreciate the opportunity to talk with you about this problem of customer service vs product. I am sure that both of us want to resolve it in the best interests of the company<br>Bill: I'm always glad to talk about it, as you well know |
| I better go slow. Let me ease in | I: There are an increasing number of situations where our clients are asking for customer service and rejecting the off-the-shelf products. My fear is that your salespeople will play an increasingly peripheral role in the future<br>Bill: I don't understand. Tell me more |
| Like hell, you don't understand. I wish there was a way I could be more gentle | I: Bill, I am sure you are aware of the changes (and explains)<br>Bill: No, I do not see it that way. It's my salespeople that are the key to the future |
| There he goes, thinking as a salesman and not as a corporate officer | I: Well, let's explore that a bit ... |

## Reflection on the cases

In analyzing their left-hand columns, the executives found that each side blamed the other side for the difficulties, and they used the same reasons. For example, each side said about the other side:

> You do not really understand the issues.

> If you insist on your position, you will harm the morale that I have built.

> Don't hand me that line. You know what I am talking about.

> Why don't you take off your blinders and wear a company hat?

> It upsets me when I think of how they think.

> I'm really trying hard, but I'm beginning to feel this is hopeless.

These results illustrate once more the features of skilled incompetence. It requires skill to craft the cases with the intention not to upset others while trying to change their minds. Yet, as we have seen, the skilled behavior used in the cases had the opposite effect. The others in the case became upset and dug in their heels about changing their minds.

## Redesigning their actions

The next step is to begin to redesign their actions. The executives turned to their cases. Each executive selected an episode that he wished to redesign so that it would not have the negative consequences. As an aid in their redesign, the executives were given some handouts that described Model II set of behaviors. The first thing they realized was that they would have to slow things down. They could not produce a new conversation in the milliseconds as they were accustomed. This troubled them a bit, because they were impatient to learn. They kept reminding themselves that learning new skills does require that they slow down.

**TABLE 18.2**  Model I and II social virtues

| Model I social services | Model II social services |
| --- | --- |
| *Caring, help, and support* | |
| Give approval and praise to other people. Tell others what you believe will make them feel good about themselves. Reduce their feelings of hurt by telling them how much you care and, if possible, agree with them that the others acted improperly | Increase the others' ability to confront their own ideas, to create a window into their own mind, and to face their unsurfaced assumptions, biases, and fears by acting in these ways toward other people |
| *Respect for others* | |
| Defer to other people and do not confront their reasoning or actions | Attribute to other people a high capacity for self-reflection and self-examination without becoming so upset that they lose their effectiveness and their sense of self-responsibility and choice. Keep testing this attribution (openly) |
| *Strength* | |
| Advocate your position in order to win. Hold your own position in the face of advocacy. Feeling vulnerable is a sign of weakness | Advocate your position and combine it with inquiry and self-reflection. Feeling vulnerable while encouraging inquiry is a sign of strength |
| *Honesty* | |
| Tell other people no lies or tell others all you think and feel | Encourage yourself and other people to say what they know, yet fear to say. Minimize what would otherwise be subject to distortion and a cover-up of the distortion |
| *Integrity* | |
| Stick to your principles, values, and beliefs | Advocate your principles, values, and beliefs in a way that invites inquiry into them and encourages other people to do the same |

One technique they used was that each individual crafted, by himself, a new conversation to help the writer of the episode. After talking for five or so minutes, the individuals shared their designs with each other. In the process of discussing these, they learned much about how to redesign their words. However, the designers also learned much as they discovered the gaps in their suggestions and the ways in which they made them.

Practice is important for several reasons. First, it is through practice that new designs-in-use are created and stored in the M/B. Often the practice is about crafting dialogue that advocates, evaluates, and attributes in ways that encourages inquiry and robust (disconfirming) testing.

There is a second reason for practice. As human beings strive to craft Model II dialogue, they begin to realize that Model II dialogue is not the opposite of Model I dialogue. What they learn is that the very meaning of social virtues change. For example, Table 18.2 illustrates some differences between Model I and II social virtues.

Most people require as much practice to learn Model II as is required to play a not-so-decent game of tennis. However, the practice does not need to occur all at once; it can occur in actual business meetings where people set aside some time to make it possible to reflect on their actions and correct them. An outside facilitator could help them examine and redesign their actions, just as a tennis coach might do. But, as in the case of a good tennis coach, the facilitator should be replaced by the group. He or she might be brought in for periodic boosters or to help when the problem is of a degree of difficulty and intensity not experienced before.

## Examples of Consequences of Change Programs

There are several consequences of this type of change program. First, the executives begin to experience each other as more supportive and constructive. People still work very hard during meetings, but their conversation begins to become additive—it flows to conclusions that they all can own and implement. Crises begin to be reduced. Soon, the behavioral change leads to new values, and then to new structures and policies to mirror the new values.

This, in turn, leads to more effective problem-solving and decision-making. In the case of this group, they were able to define the questions related to strategy, to conduct their own inquiries, to have staff people conduct some relevant research, and to have three individuals organize it into a presentation that was ultimately approved and owned by the top group. The top group also built in a process of involving their immediate reports so that they too could develop a sense of ownership, thereby increasing the probability that all involved will work at making it successful. In a recent study (Argyris, 1993) of what is now an 11-year program, the key to change is practice and use of Model II theory-in-use, plus productive reasoning in solving major difficult problems. This means that the participants select key meetings in which to continue their learning. These meetings cannot be scheduled in a lockstep fashion.

It also means that the change program that began at the top is spread to the next levels, as the competence of those above them becomes persistent. This has led not only to changes in the internal management of the firm (which is a managerial consulting firm), but to the development of new services for their clients.

One might ask whether interventions go wrong and, if so, are the errors corrected. I hope that my previous description illustrates that the participants are made continually responsible for their participation in the program. One of their main responsibilities is to monitor their actions so that, if errors occur, they are corrected. Moreover, they are free to stop a program at any time they deem necessary. To date, no program has been stopped. However, there is variance in the degree of enthusiasm individuals may have for managing through the use of Model II. In a few instances where these differences occur, it would violate the governing values of Model II for one subgroup to require the others to act consistently with Model II. What is required is that the doubters be open about their doubts and that they do not use their power to prevent further dialogue, especially by subordinates or peers.

## Basic Criteria for Success in Diagnosing and Changing at any Level of the Organization

There are four criteria that we found central to design diagnostic instruments and interventions in organizations. They are:

1. The ultimate criterion for success should not be change in behavior or attitudes. We must get at the causes of behavior and attitudes. The criterion should be changes in defensive reasoning and the theories-in-use that produce skilled unawareness and skilled incompetence and the resulting organizational defensive routines.
2. The changes just described should unambiguously lead to reductions in the self-fulfilling counter-productive activities, at all levels of the organization.
3. It is not possible to achieve criteria 1 and 2 without focusing on the actual behavior of the participants. The trouble with the old criteria is that they began and ended with behaviors. The new criteria begin with behavior in order to get a window onto the mental maps and type of reasoning that the individuals use and the organizational culture that they create.
4. The success of programs is not assessed by measuring insight gained or learning reported by the participants. Individuals often report high scores on insight and learning, yet have not changed their defensive reasoning, their theories-in-use, their skilled unawareness and incompetence, and the organizational defensive routines.

Most experimental learning, at its best, helps individuals change their behavior without changing their defensive reasoning or their theory-in-use. They accomplish this primarily by helping individuals behave in the opposite manner than they presently display. If they dominate, they learn to become more passive. If they talk most of the time, they learn to listen more. Being passive or listening more is not a change to a new theory-in-use; it occurs by suppressing the old one. Such changes usually wash out the moment the individual is bewildered, threatened, or feels betrayed.

Most large corporations expose their executives to various kinds of leadership programs where the fundamental criterion is to present knowledge in an interesting manner, in a way that leads to action, and in a way that is not disquieting to the audience. For example, recently I participated in a one-week program on leadership attended by the top 40 executives of one of America's largest corporations. The presenter, one of the most sought-after speakers, talked about the difference between managing and leading. He advised the top executives to focus more on being leaders and less on being managers. He used cases, videotapes, simulations, and skillful questioning. He generated a great deal of interaction and enthusiasm. The presentation was rated as one of the best.

The next day, I met with the CEO and his immediate advisers. They discussed how to become more effective. As the discussion began to get into the undiscussables, the dialogue became cautious—individuals spoke abstractly. They cautioned about changes that were too dramatic and quick. Soon, the group members produced a remarkable example of managing these issues rather than leading. No one appeared to realize the inconsistency they were creating (or, if they did, they were not saying). A month later I had a chance to meet the presenter. We got into a discussion about education for leadership. I then told him the story I just related here. It did not surprise him. After all, he asked, how much can one accomplish in a few hours? How much can one examine senior managers' inconsistencies without getting in trouble? After all, aren't the most effective change attempts incremental? The argument that he was making to defend his own practice was consistent with managing and not leading in his practice.

## CONCLUSION

The dominant mode for designing organizations is the pyramidal structure that is based upon top-down leadership and coordination that are characterized by unilateral control. This mode is operationalized by creating routines that prescribe acceptable behavior and performance (Follett, 1924; Fayol, 1949; Simon, 1969; Nelson & Winter, 1982).

These features, in turn, are implemented by human beings using Model I theories-in-use that are also theories of unilateral control. Model I theories-in-use, in turn, lead to organizational defensive routines that reinforce Model I theories-in-use and the unilateral control features of routines. The result is an ultra stable state that maintains the status quo. Changes are typically designed to remain within the dictates of the stable state. These changes are produced by single-loop learning.

There are, at least, two important limitations to the status quo. First, the underlying reasons for the routines can become obsolete. The second is that, as societies mature in social–political–economic dimensions, the traditional theories of management become obsolete. For example, they no longer produce the learning, flexibility, and vigilance required in a global world.

Double-loop learning is required to bring about the new effective performance and to manage it in such a way that the changes persist. This requires that individuals learn Model II theory-in-use with its emphasis on productive reasoning and robust testing of claims.

Such a perspective provides an important bridge to the effective implementation of managerial functions such as accounting (Argyris & Kaplan, 1994), finance (Jensen, 1998), and strategy (Argyris, 1986). This is the case because the intellectual structure of these disciplines used productive reasoning. The effective implementation of these disciplines, especially when it requires confronting the status quo, is facilitated by Model II theory-in-use and Model II organizational dialectic.

# REFERENCES

Abelson, R.P. (1981) Psychological states of the script concept. *American Psychologist*, **36**, 715–729.

Argyris, C. (1970) *Intervention Theory and Method*. Reading, MA: Addison-Wesley.

Argyris, C. (1978) Is capitalism the culprit? *Organizational Dynamics*, **Spring**, 21–37.

Argyris, C. (1980) Skilled incompetence. *Harvard Business Review*, **64**(5), 74–79.

Argyris, C. (1982) *Reasoning, Learning, and Action*. San Francisco: Jossey-Bass.

Argyris, C. (1986) *Strategy, Change and Defensive Routines*. Marshfield, MA: Putnam Publishing.

Argyris, C. (1990) *Overcoming Organizational Defenses*. Needham Heights, MA: Allyn & Bacon.

Argyris, C. (1993) *Knowledge for Action*. San Francisco: Jossey-Bass.

Argyris, C. (1996) Unrecognized defenses of scholars: impact on theory and research. *Organization Science*, **7**(1), 79–87.

Argyris, C. (2000) *Flawed Advice and the Management Trap*. New York: Oxford University Press.

Argyris, C. & Kaplan, R.S. (1994) Implementing new knowledge: the case of activity based costing. *Accounting Horizons*, **8**(3), 83–105.

Argyris, C. & Schön, D. (1974) *Theory in Practice*. San Francisco: Jossey-Bass.

Argyris, C. & Schön, D. (1996) *Organizational Learning II*. Reading, MA: Addison-Wesley.

Argyris, C., Putnam, R. & Smith, D. (1985) *Action Science*. San Francisco: Jossey-Bass.

Barker, J.R. (1999) *The Discipline of Teamwork: Participation and Concertine Control*. Thousand Oaks, CA: Sage.

Boonstra, J.J. (in press) *Redesign, Development and Organizational Learning*.

Cohen, M.D. & Sproull (1991) Organizational learning. *Organization Science*, **2**(1), (entire issue).

Fayol, H. (1949) *General and Industrial Management*. New York: Pitman.

Follett, M.P. (1924) *Creative Experience*. New York: Longmans.

Haire, M., Ghiselli, E.E. & Porter, Z.W. (1966) *Managerial Thinking: An International Study*. New York: John Wiley and Sons, Ltd.

Heller, R., Pucu, E., Strauss, G. & Wilpert, B. (1998) *Organizational Participation: Myth and Reality*. Oxford: Oxford University Press.

Jensen, M. (1998) *Foundations of Organizational Strategy*. Cambridge, MA: Harvard University Press.

Levitt, B. & March, J.G. (1988) Organizational learning. *Annual Review of Sociology*, **14**, 319–340.

Lord, R.G. & Kernan, M.C. (1987) Scripts as determinants of purposeful behavior in organization. *Academy of Management Review*, **12**, 265–277.

McGregor, D. (1960) *The Human Side of Enterprise*. New York: McGraw-Hill.

Nelson, R.R. & Winter, S.G. (1982) *An Evolutionary Theory of Economic Change*. Cambridge, MA: Harvard University Press.

Payne, R.L. (2000) Eupsychian management and the millennium. *Journal of Managerial Psychology*, **15**(3), 219–226.

Pfeffer, J. (1998) *The Human Equation: Building Profits by Putting People to Work*. Boston: Harvard Business School Press.

Simon, H.A. (1969) *The Science of the Artificial*. Cambridge, MA: MIT Press.

# CHAPTER 19

# Learning and Sustainable Change
## Designing Learning Spaces

**Gerhard Smid**
*Sioo, Utrecht, The Netherlands*
**Ronald Beckett**
*The Reinvention Network, Liverpool, NSW, Australia*

We, a Dutch and an Australian practitioner, met once in Sydney at a conference. We discovered a shared interest in a situational approach to innovation, change, and learning, and a shared aversion to the use of rigid standardized behavioural training and pre-packaged knowledge transfer, typical examples of the patterns of thought that guarantee that change programmes do not produce change (Beer et al., 1990). We started to cooperate to develop an approach to learning in the context of innovation and change that would really contribute to achieving an outcome. We wanted to develop a radically non-pedagogical approach of support for learning. Our enterprise might be seen as an attempt to create a construction language for professional activity within the pragmatic and situational schools of thought as described in Chapter 17. Our attempt is not unique. With some admiration we regard the scholarly but sociological work of Wenger (1998). We feel, however, that his design language does not adequately reflect the position of a practitioner. The same applies to the work of Hite (1999). Of course, we have learned from them, for example, Hite's criticism of common approaches such as Instructional Systems Development, OD, and Human Performance Technology endorsed our more intuitive critical view on the dominant discourse on learning and learning support.

We felt we had to do the job ourselves, so we organized a virtual reflective space in order to create transferable concepts. We exchanged information on our work and tried to understand differences. The apparent similarities and the contrasts made us reflect on our tacit assumptions that are sometimes related to differences in the national business systems we work in. This careful practice has produced a valuable and instructive exchange for us as professionals. We tested our results at some conferences (Beckett & Smid, 2001; Smid & Beckett, 2001) and compared them with other work we had done (Smid, 2001).

We now invite you to join this reflective space. We present here some outcomes of our exchange. In the first section, we outline some views on change, innovation, learning, and learning support, concepts that helped us in our conversation. We then describe two cases. The first case study tells how one of us, an innovation manager in an aircraft company, created a learning system to steer the company down the path of change and cooperated with universities. The second case study tells how an educational designer and a consultant supported a professional service firm in transition in the area of occupational health and safety. Based on these cases, we discuss some essential attributes of learning support. We present some principles for the design of learning support for adults in the context of sustainable change and innovation and suggest better learning outcomes can be achieved by combining the strengths of industry and academia.

*Dynamics of Organizational Change and Learning*. Edited by J.J. Boonstra.
© 2004 John Wiley & Sons, Ltd. ISBN 0-471-87737-9.

# TWO SITUATIONS ...

Australia
A bright sunny day in the Australian summer, December 2000. I walk through the premises of my company, the Hawker de Havilland factory in Sydney. A couple of minutes ago we left the main office, where we met and had a look at the old models of Hawker de Havilland, like the Tiger Moth and the Vampire Jet Trainer. This Dutchman seems to be really interested. We enter the central hall, and I show him the large oven where we bake the aerostructures made out of layers of carbonfibre. I tell him about the interconnectedness of the technical innovations we started 20 years ago and the principles we use in our organizational design and practice, our migration from straight construct to design and construct; from internal self-sufficiency to outsourcing, strategic alliances and collaborative research, adopting technologies earlier in their life cycle, multi-skilling individuals to make better business decisions, and to stimulate innovation.

The Netherlands
A day in March 2001. It is 12.25 hrs. I am in a conference resort with a group of professionals from the Dutch Social Security. They have the task of developing new work methods for their company, a large social security organization, a typical professional bureaucracy. As facilitators we have complete support from the corporate level, we have no problems with the budget, and we have the freedom to experiment with the support we deliver. We contracted an action learning programme with 14 professionals. These professionals formed four groups, formulated ideas, tested them, contacted their CEO to make the contract, made a project plan, etc. But—they seem to take no action at all. As supporting staff, we try to understand what is happening here. What are the forces that push them back into their daily routines, what should we do to help them to think and work out-of-the-box?

# INNOVATION AND CHANGE

While change may not lead to innovation (for example, simply making an existing business process more efficient), innovation is a good word for sustainable change: it refers to explorative processes, tangible new outcomes, and embedded organizational change. There are various kinds of innovations. We constructed a typology based on the work of Whitley (2000: 871) and Van Dongen et al. (1996). It consists of five types.

The first three types of innovation stay mainly within existing patterns of products, production processes, and organization. They stay 'within the box'. A *parametric innovation* is a small variation on known practice, as a reaction, for example, to a client's need. In fact, one modifies an existing process or product. The knowledge that is involved is mainly tacit, industry-specific, and simple, except for the case when coordination of the production and supply chain change is needed. A *developmental innovation* is proactive, not reactive. Here, one pursues new product qualities for existing and new customers, improved technology, and improved use of knowledge. The knowledge that is involved is not new but tacit, the improvement of skills is most important. The production processes and the organization are changed only marginally. In an *adaptive innovation*, new generic products are developed, existing routines are optimized. Here, existing competencies and capabilities are better exploited, the focus is on incremental innovation of technology. The knowledge involved is of a low complexity.

The two other types are 'out-of-the-box'. In some situations an organization migrates to a quite different business or market. Here, not only process or products change, often new methods, new definitions, and cooperation with new actors are developed. In the case of *strategic innovations* one develops new product qualities, gets new customers, new kinds of applications, new markets or niches. This kind of change is technologically discontinuous, with 'architectural aspects'. These innovations

**TABLE 19.1** A typology of innovation processes

| Type | What stops | What continues | New |
|---|---|---|---|
| Parametric | Nothing | Everything | Minimal change to produce new product or service |
| Developmental | Nothing except things that do not work any longer | Everything | New product, same process, and organizational frame |
| Adaptive | Sub-optimalization, stop under-utilization | Optimalization existing routines; better utilization of competencies, incremental innovation of technology | New generic products |
| Strategic | Existing technology (is technologically discontinuous, with 'architectural aspects') | Same market. Same organizational competencies | New users, new process, and product qualities. New methods, new definitions, and new actors |
| Transformative | Nearly all existing activities (markets, products, processes, organizational infrastructure) | No existing activities | New markets, new products, new processes, new technology, new organizing process |

have strong effects on processes and organization, but are often based on existing organizational competencies.

In some change processes, the organization has an unknown destination, a *terra incognita*. Here, change is more like trekking (as opposed to travelling towards a known destination). Sometimes one has to sink the ship or use a scorched earth policy: existing competencies and capabilities are destroyed. These are *transformative innovations*. Here, one builds a 'new industry' and generates completely new needs. The knowledge involved is very varied, cognitive and organizational, and dynamic.

We summarize these various types of innovation in a matrix, shown in Table 19.1. This indicates for each type what kind of activity stops, what kind of activity is continued, and what new activities are established.

The literature often concentrates on the fourth and fifth type of innovations. Why? Because one expects the most competitive advantage and societal progress here, even when one has to destroy existing competencies. This exclusive interest may be regarded as restrictive. In fact, this is an effect of the tacit reproduction of the US context in a lot of literature. In the innovative business system of the 'responsive corporatism' typical of the Netherlands (see Unger, 2000), the overall innovation processes are taken step by step, are incremental, and often are not radical at all. They seem to be composed of many small events of a parametric, developmental, and/or adaptive nature, often built on the development of the competencies of the workforce. In a chain of events, discontinuities occur suddenly, and are often not understood as such (Hillis, 2002). We only understand this when we look at this chain from the 'innovation domain' (Hoebeke, 1994: 39), i.e. within a time frame of two to 10 years. Here, each 'small' innovation might appear as a potential part of a 'large' one, as a part of an implicit or enfolded order that is unfolding, which might be a migration or even a transformation process. The issue here is that comparing the base year with that 10 years later may well lead to a pronouncement of strategic or transformational innovation, but such a view in isolation will mask the real underlying processes that resulted in the outcome observed.

When we want to think about or support innovation processes, we often have to switch explicitly from day-to-day concerns to this other longer time frame, to estimate the potential strategic or trans-formational meaning of a minor event such as a change in a market, a product or service, a process, the technology, and/or the organizing process. The essence is often in the detail (and so is the devil)! And when we want to support innovation, we have, of course, to think about the market, the prod-ucts or services, the technological issues, the work processes, and the organizing processes. Thinking about learning is also essential, because this forces us to think about people and the development of their knowledge, their attitudes and behaviours or competencies that complement the technologies and processes. Any change is only sustained when it is embodied in the workforce and embedded in the long-lasting relations between the people in the company and between the company and its suppliers and customers.

And we have to consider the relation between organizational type and the possibilities of organiza-tional learning. Each organizational type is a specific 'ba', i.e. a shared space for emerging relationships of a cognitive and/or social nature (Nonaka & Konno, 1998). Each type functions as a specific habitat for its people, forms their habitus and their habits, and conditions, in general, the learning within the organization. One might say, the possibilities for innovative organizational and individual learning are locked in the organizational model (see Chapter 20).

## LEARNING

As we saw in Chapter 17, there are quite different schools of thought on learning. In practice, mainstream thinking considers learning as knowledge acquisition or the acquisition of new behaviour.

---

### THE DOMINANT DISCOURSE ON LEARNING

In the dominant discourse on learning (that stresses the acquisition of new behaviour or new cog-nitions), learning and non-learning are seen as mutually exclusive periods in work and/or life. Learning seems to be an attribute of a period between two periods of non-learning. When an exist-ing quasi-stationary situation (non-learning) becomes more dynamic (unfreeze), then a movement follows and the new quasi-stationary situation of non-learning is installed (refreeze). In this dis-course, normally no learning seems to occur within an organization, the learning is external, in a space outside the ongoing business. There one internalizes new knowledge. This discourse on learning tends not to consider daily internal and external practice as a source for learning. One enters the organization as 'learned' persons, one starts working, sometimes leaving to internalize a bit extra and enter again. We can observe this sequential pattern of alternating working and learn-ing in rule-based work systems, or exit economies like the UK, the USA, and Australia (Dobbin & Boychuk, 1999). In such a pattern, learning appears as 'costs', as expenditures to be avoided. In so-called 'voice economies', work and learning are much more intertwined, and this is more reflected in their discourse on learning.

---

More recently, learning has been considered to be an aspect of everyday life. Adults learn in their jobs due to, for example, new ways of organizing work (Arthur & Rousseau, 1996) such as project work (Tough, 1971; Price, 1997; Lundin & Midler, 1998), growing variation in their tasks and increasing job control (Karasek & Theorell, 1989), hybridization of their work roles (Causer & Jones, 1996), starting a new job in another firm (Ibarra, 1999), or they learn to understand new developments or to work with a new tool.

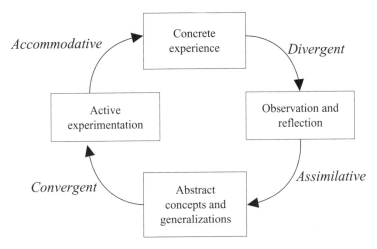

**FIGURE 19.1** The Lewinian experiental learning model and the Kolbian learning styles (1984)

Many authors describe 'learning cycles', or present some kind of model made up of linked learning process steps. We are both inspired by the cyclic model of experiential learning that originates from Lewin (1951) and forms one of the sources of the popular model of Kolb (1984). The model, in the form of a continuous cycle, is shown in Figure 19.1.

Experience with this model highlights that individual adult learners seem to have a preference for a particular aspect of learning (e.g. active experimentation or formation of concepts) and often stick to that habit. Often, individuals do not go through the entire cycle. They do not fully exploit a learning opportunity, with, as a result, incomplete outcomes, as Jarvis (1987) showed. He found that there were a number of different potential outcomes arising from exposure to a learning opportunity, such as:

- No learning may take place: the opportunity may not be understood, it may conflict with individual values, or it may be perceived as simply reinforcing current knowledge.
- Non-reflective learning may take place: a skill may be enhanced, or some information may be committed to memory.
- Reflective learning may take place: resulting in a changed person, or changed personal practices.

Kolb developed a very useful instrument that helps identify these preferences in individuals, the Learning Styles Inventory (LSI). And, as Kolb (1984) shows, the concept also delivers prescriptions for the design of a supportive learning environment. People who have an accommodative learning preference need a different learning environment from people with an assimilative preference. Incomplete learning may stem from a learning environment that does not match the dominant learning style of the learner.

The Finnish psychologist Engeström (1995) sees learning as a practical and mental activity. Like Kolb, Engeström thinks learning follows cyclic or spiral patterns. Learning starts with motivation, arising from a conflict or friction between a practical problem for which the learner's former conceptions or tools are not sufficient. The next step is orientation, where the learner forms a first model which helps him or her to see and select essential points of concern and link them together, followed by internalization, where the new model is transformed into the learner's already existing internal model. Now follows the phase of externalization where the learner applies his or her new model in practice, and then, in the phase of critique, evaluates whether the model has validity and is useful. In the phase of control, the learner analyses his or her performance as a learner. Learning is, according

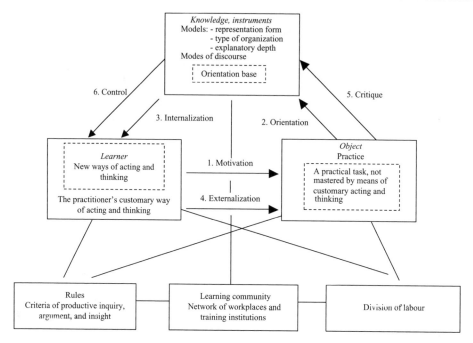

**FIGURE 19.2** A full-blown model of investigative learning
*Source*: Engeström, 1995: 42

to Engeström, a process not only within the individual, but also embedded in larger entities. Many elements of the process are embedded in the environment of the learner, such as the practical problem situation, models for the phase of orientation, models for other ways of thinking, new tasks, etc. (see Figure 19.2).

In fact, learning is a spiral process of criticism (1, 5, 6—questioning, contradicting, debating), a context of discovery (2, 3), and a context of application (4) embedded in the community where the learner participates, in the rules in the context and in the ruling division of labour.

Like Jarvis, Engeström points to various forms of learning, but offers more distinctions. *First-order learning* is passive internalization of pre-given culture. The learner focuses on copying readily available correct behaviour in the context, only peripherally conscious or not at all. First-order learning has two forms: learning by conditioning (the learner learns by reward and punishment to react in a certain manner), and learning by imitating (the learner appropriates a certain behavioural model by imitating an example). In both cases, the learning cycle is not completed.

In *second-order learning*, the focus is on finding out how correct solutions can be produced when the context does not provide anything to copy. This is trial-and-error learning. Another form of second order learning is problem solving by experimentation or *investigative learning*. Here the learner pauses in order to reflect upon the problem and formulates a hypothetical explanation of the principles behind successful solutions. The learner tests the hypothesis and modifies it according to the results.

In *third-order learning*, the learner questions the validity of tasks and problems posed by the context and begins to transform the context itself. In such learning processes, internalization of given culture recedes into the background while externalization of novel cultural practices gains priority. Engeström mentions here *expansive learning*, when a community of practice begins to analyse and transform itself. Such expansive learning is no longer limited to pre-defined contents and tasks. Rather, it is a long-term process of redefining the objects, tools, and social structures.

**TABLE 19.2** Five types of learning according to Engeström (1995)

| Kind of learning | Explanation | Type |
|---|---|---|
| Conditioning | Learning by reward and punishment to react in a certain manner, passive internalization of pre-given culture, peripherally conscious or not at all so | surface-level, first-order |
| Imitation | Copying readily available correct behaviour in context, peripherally conscious or not at all so | surface-level, first-order |
| Trial and error | Finding out how correct solutions can be produced even when they are not readily available in context for copying | surface-level, second-order |
| Investigative | Reflect upon problem, hypothetical explanation of the principles behind successful solutions. Test of hypothesis and modification according to results | deep-level, second-order |
| Expansive | Not limited to pre-defined contents and tasks, questioning validity of tasks and problems posed by context, transform the context itself, not limited to pre-defined contents and tasks, externalization of novel cultural practices gains priority | deep-level, third-order |

It is important to realize the qualitative leap that separates investigative and expansive learning from the other types. This leap might be characterized as transition from surface-level to deep-level learning, a distinction Engeström takes following Marton et al. (1984). In Table 19.2, we summarize these distinctions.

Engeström also provides us with important notions for thinking about support: the concepts of the 'zone of proximal development', and the concept of 'scaffold', both taken from Vygotsky (1978). He defines the zone of proximal development at an individual level as 'the distance between the performance the student is capable of on his or her own, and the performance he or she can attain in collaboration with a more knowledgeable or skilled colleague' (Engeström, 1995: 128). The student is seen as active, but with a colleague who functions as 'a scaffold', he or she can make more progress. In general, the 'scaffold' is an 'extra' element in the context. The idea of a scaffold is derived from the world of building construction. A scaffold is, for example, used in the building of an arch: stones are aligned along a wooden scaffold until they support each other and the scaffold can be removed (Nooteboom, 2000: 122). Other forms of the 'scaffold' are more modern temporary structures of reusable modules made out of metal, assembled to suit the operating environment. These are typical temporary 'extras' that will be removed. 'Scaffolding' helps create an invitation to a learner to make a perceived risky step with improved or accelerated development as a result. The literature tells us that it is essential that the invitation is perceived by the learner as within his or her reach. An invitation that does not fit is perceived either as too close or as 'distal', i.e. out of reach. A scaffold serves to manage the perception and performance of learners and its presence and quality help determine the kind of learning that might occur. When a scaffold is absent or inadequate, only first-order learning is likely, or no learning will occur at all.

According to this concept, the direction of the development of the individual learner is co-determined by the pre-existing social and competency structure delivered by the more experienced colleague; learning at the individual level seems to be always either within the box or from box to box, and not towards an unknown field. This differs from collective learning. Engeström uses these ideas also to analyse collective learning and collective zones of proximal development. According to him, such a zone is 'at the level of a whole community of practice . . . a contested area between the traditional practice and alternative future directions' (1995: 128). In any community or system, there are tensions and inner contradictions that produce alternative directions: any collective activity system, is a disturbance-producing system (Blackler et al., 1999).

## LEARNING AND CHANGE

In all innovation processes, the people who are involved learn and unlearn. They stop doing some things, go on with others, start doing new things, change their habits, develop new attitudes, behave in new ways, produce new interactions and new meanings, start to work with new tools, accept new rules, etc. It is seductive to think learning/unlearning only happens during formal change or innovation processes. This fallacy is produced by the dominant discourse on learning.

The concepts of learning that we are inspired by consider daily practice not only as sources for learning, but as learning itself. The Kolb model is a generalization of problem-solving behaviour, and the situational learning approach stresses participation in social, productive, and expansive activity. These concepts turn the spotlight on developmental dynamics in daily practice, on the micro-processes that relate to emergent innovation. One type of learning may lead to another, and several types of learning are parallel aspects of the activities within a community of practice where people help each other learn via rapid incremental processes. What is happening or needed in a particular situation will depend on the nature of the innovation sought (e.g. relating to new technologies or new supply chains), and on the current competencies of the organization (e.g. its current culture and facilities for experimentation). Here, we are starting to understand some situation-specific considerations. But, one thing is certain: even simple innovations (e.g. parametric) might need deep learning in one way or another!

## INNOVATION, LEARNING, AND SUPPORT

In thinking about learning, and considering processes to support it, education or training using existing course-work is a common response. This seems to be applied in nearly all settings. It is a powerful device to reduce complexity; it legitimizes certain things to do and legitimizes for people things that are uncommon (that have to do with the remaking of sense, the redefinition of the self, the role and/or the task); and it has the promise of coming to an end (and there will be peace again)! The use of this device is risky because of its tendency to ignore the operational context itself as a source for learning. In fact, it hinders contact with the specificity of the context.

How can we put it differently? Not by refusing to use existing course-work, but rather by building towards a radically non-pedagogical approach of support for learning. Brown and Duguid (1996) distinguish the 'teaching curriculum' from the 'learning curriculum'. This distinction is closely related to distinct concepts of the meaning of knowledge, experience, and learning. Jean Lave describes the distinction thus:

> The difference may be at heart a very deep epistemological one, between a view of knowledge as a collection of real entities, located in heads, and of learning as a process of internalising them, versus a view of knowing and learning as engagement in changing processes of human activity. In the latter case knowledge becomes a complex and problematic concept, whereas in the former it is learning that is problematic. (Lave, 1993: 12)

In the 'teaching curriculum', support means: present knowledge and (eventually) facilitate internalization. In the 'learning curriculum', support might mean: be keen on the conflict between the new activity and the existing thinking, enhance development by invitations for the individual and collective production of new models, by broker contacts, etc.

This non-pedagogical view must be combined with more classical forms of support in order to stimulate change and innovation. We can express the variety of support within the Kolb learning cycle from Figure 19.1. In this model, the point of departure is the activity in the real world. Here, people experiment, get conditioned, imitate, etc. Through interaction with each other's mental maps, they develop knowledge and rules of thumb and these are used again and again. Under certain conditions, provided by a third party, the normal practical and mental activity develops at a deeper level and this might lead to the development of new individual and collective competencies that enable new innovative practices. Reflection in action, through lessons learned in practice, is the norm. A better process of reflection and generalization is obtained through interaction with an external partner, such as a university. In the academic forum, support is provided by a third party focused on the learning process, not necessarily on the content. We consider that interaction with the academic partner creates transferable competencies, whereas the interaction with industry creates repetitive skill and collective competencies.

We consider that the concept of 'scaffolding' is very important to conceptualize the issue of delivery of support. A 'scaffold' might be a metaphor for any element in the environment of the 'learner' that supports him or her in an adequate way (i.e. within their reach, matched to their learning style, matched to their position in the learning cycle), so as to enable them to explore activities in a certain direction. The provision of support means that we might produce all kinds of little scaffolds for explorative activity, for experimentation or expansion, for imitation (such as provision of persons as role models), or to juggle with knowledge. Here, we must never forget that an organization in itself is also a scaffold, by its implicit learning opportunities and constraints. When we want to support learning in a certain direction, several scaffolds are in use already. An 'extra scaffold' has to compete with these or has to be a complement to be of added value.

## PRACTICES

With these concepts in mind, we were able to discuss our quite different practices. We selected two case studies for this chapter, because they have a history of eight to 10 years, and both contain the issue of supporting individual and collective learning and its alignment with innovation and change. The first case study describes a migration from a construction firm towards a 'design' centre and a learning programme for the engineers in order to prepare them for participation in the ongoing change process. The second case describes the migration from a standard occupational health and safety company towards a modern consulting firm in work, health, and organization and the various elements of support for the professionals. The choice of these case studies reflects the growing importance of networks in industry and the professional services industry and the related issues of innovation, organizational change, and learning.

---

### CASE STUDY: FROM A CONSTRUCTION COMPANY TOWARDS A DESIGN CENTRE

This Australian aerospace company has been in existence since 1927. The company had 1350 employees in 2000 and is regarded as large in Australia (though small as a global player). It has facilities in Sydney and Melbourne. Throughout its history it has changed its market positioning and core competencies a number of times. It had been primarily a licensed builder of military aircraft for the Australian market and a minor subcontractor for components. In the early 1990s, it became a global supplier of aircraft structural components. Globalization of the industry had started decades before. Military aircraft markets were shrinking and commercial aircraft markets were growing (albeit with some ups and downs). This company redefined itself in the business-to-business chain and used customer intimacy as a competitive strategy.

In this context, the management took a number of decisions that would require the acquisition of some enhanced competencies by the personnel. It decided to operate as a large version of a small niche company, rather than as a small version of a large, broadly skilled aerospace company, in order to operate with a flatter organization structure. This required more staff multi-skilling, and sought to effect business decisions further down in the organization. To discriminate itself in the marketplace, and access further value-adding activities, the company began to design the components it would build, using a concurrent engineering philosophy (whereas, in the past, this design work had been done by its customers) and using new materials (carbonfibres instead of metals). Outsourcing, strategic alliances and collaborative research with universities and government laboratories were undertaken to access a broader range of competencies. The company also wanted to try to adopt relevant new product technologies earlier in their development life cycle, and access the diverse inputs of its various collaborations to try to innovate. In this long-term strategic change initiative, the company started to cooperate with universities to obtain a programme with a mixture of MBA and Technology Management subjects. The change process was not always smooth. There were conflicts related to the turbulent environment within the company: changing several things in parallel and increasingly more complex customer demands produced tensions. People who resisted were lucky: the business was growing at the time, so no one was forced to leave, but some people were given new job assignments.

The champion of the change process was an executive management committee of about 10 people, including the CEO who undertook strategic planning reviews twice a year to examine what the company could do better in its current operations, and where it needed to be positioned for the future. The owners of the company had an executive development programme running across all of the businesses that they owned. One programme was for CEOs. It focused on strategic management and strategic change, and the aerospace company CEO took part in that course. The other was a senior management development course focused on business unit management in a global business environment, and two members of the executive committee took part in that course. The participating managers were already committed to change, but these courses improved their understanding of it.

The cooperation with a university started with a post-graduate learning programme, primarily for its engineers in Sydney. The main considerations that stimulated this investment were:

- Competitiveness would be dependent on an ability to innovate, which was associated with learning new things. Lifelong learning had to be a company norm.
- People needed to better understand how their technical and operational decisions would impact on business outcomes, as some decision-making was being devolved from the executive management. Everyone needed to be a 'business manager'.
- The company had decided to use new technology earlier in its life cycle, which would change the approach to technology management. The company had to be able to introduce more complex technology faster.

Swinburne University of Technology in Melbourne, 1000 km away, was thought to have developed such a good approach by modifying MBA subjects to suit entrepreneurial enterprises. A pilot programme was run with senior management, which gave the programme some prestige within the workforce. As the lecturers had to travel some distance, an intensive two-day block delivery on site was the norm to make the economics sensible. The whole programme was compressed from a semester length to about six weeks. The extensive subject readings were distributed between the participants to read on behalf of the cohort, and to comment on the relevance of their assigned reference to the company. Small teams of three or four were assigned study tasks relevant to a company issue and utilizing the course module theory. Both individual and group assignments were formally presented to the whole cohort for critical review.

Subsequently, the programme was expanded in conjunction with the University of Western Sydney (UWS), accessing their technology management modules, and in some cases creating completely new modules as no single existing programme from one university provided the profile of competencies being sought. This university also agreed to handle formal accreditation opportunities arising from the course-work, as the company had undertaken to provide nationally recognized training for its employees where possible, as requested by the unions. The kind of format used in the pilot programme was also applied to all subsequent programmes.

In the pilot programme, two cohort groups were set up, and participants were nominated by the company. This practice of nomination was difficult to sustain. The volume of business in the company increased, making time access difficult, and requiring some of the potential participants to train other new staff. Some of the pilot programme participants did not like the university-style delivery and assessment work, even though individuals did not have to participate in the formal assessment process if they did not want to. Some managers did not want to participate with subordinate staff, nor be subjected to critical questioning. So voluntary participation became the norm, with the suggestion that there could be career development opportunities for those people who demonstrated initiative. This resulted in participants from management, the factory, and from office backgrounds in one cohort. Even though most of the students had worked with the company for many years, they had not necessarily met each other before. Many of the participants were experienced in industry, but some had not been to university at all. A particular cohort commonly had a significant multi-national element, generally reflecting the community in Sydney. This provided more variety within the group and, as a peripheral benefit, helped participants learn more about other parts of the company. Altogether, about 100 employees completed at least one module, and about 20 have graduated or will graduate with a Master of Technology Management award from UWS.

The teachers encountered some resistance from students who had substantial work experience who challenged some of the theoretical ideas and models being presented, which for some teachers was a shock. Subsequent debate on these challenges improved class understanding of the subject, and, after a while, the teachers changed their teaching style and enjoyed it more than traditional teaching. Student assignments for each course module involved studying how some aspect of company operations might be improved. This required students to enunciate their concerns, then suggest how these concerns might be addressed, which deflated any negativism a student might have.

The people who attended the courses did learn a new 'language'. Some of this related to the jargon of a particular course, for example, marketing jargon or finance jargon. But because most of the course-work assignment tasks were completed in a small team arrangement, people learned to rapidly establish collaboration arrangements, even though they may not have worked together before. This had an unexpected benefit in normal business—if any of these people were brought together for a company project, they rapidly got on with the job with minimal supervision.

Questionnaire and interview surveys were conducted to assess progress about 18 months after the pilot programme had started, and again about four years into the programme. The attitude to learning had clearly changed over the period. In the first survey, many participants suggested that they would not have started such learning if the company had not set it up and paid for it. In the second survey, many students expressed interest in continuing to learn at their own expense and in their own time.

Management perception of the programme varied. It was clear that significant time and money were being put into the university programme, but it was not clear if these resources would deliver better value if they were to be applied elsewhere. What direct benefits could be demonstrated from the course-work? Would the people involved stay with the company? Was an elite group developing within the company? There were some who saw direct benefits, others saw lost employee time.

Some middle managers were defensive: they resisted going on courses themselves, citing lack of time as a reason; and they were not happy with some of their staff being off the job when they were behind schedule. Some classified the activity as training, which in their view should have been delivered only to the extent needed for current business activities.

Of course, it was anticipated that investment in learning would be reflected in beneficial action. But the pathways were not simple. Action means change. If this improved the efficiency of the learners in their current activities, this was readily accepted. However, if the student introduced some kind of innovation (e.g. in the work process) and wanted to change things, this was not always readily accepted. Issues of interaction with the rest of the organization, consistency with its current norms, and consistency with the desired future direction of the organization arose. A survey indicated that a student and their supervisor/manager sometimes collaborated to influence and use what was learned to introduce beneficial, incremental change in their part of the organization. In other instances, the very specific scope of the student's current job, and the focus of their supervisor/manager towards only doing that efficiently, severely restricted opportunities to introduce change. In this latter situation in particular, some students withdrew and focused only on the personal value of their learning, for example, in enhancing their status with professional peers, or in enhancing their résumé.

But where interactive processes between learning and change were established, the company observed direct benefits. Where functional competencies and process competencies improved inputs, conditions, or mechanisms that facilitate innovation, progress that supported the long-term strategic innovation sought by the company could be observed. The outcomes for the participants and the company may best be summarized by the following comment, made in an evaluation by a participant:

> In presentations to & discussions with [the company's] customers & suppliers the background information gained on project management & people interactions was invaluable in allowing me to confidently & usually successfully steer the conclusion on various issues toward an outcome beneficial to (the company). I believe the improved level of confidence, self-assurance, people and presentation skills gained from the course was partly responsible for [the company] winning the [XX] project due to me being able to present a more professional style and outlook to the customer during negotiations.

## Case Study: From OHS towards Consulting in Work and Organization

This case study relates to a variety of support activities delivered within a company that provides services in the area of occupational health and safety, as one aspect of a long-term strategic change initiative. The company had operated since 1946 in Doetinchem, in the east of the Netherlands. In 1994, it was a company of 70–80 people. The majority (>80 per cent) of the professionals were physicians or paramedics, only two persons had expertise in organizational or psychological issues. The company was a regional player, but also a leading member of a nationwide network of OHS companies, with an outstanding reputation. Some 'enlightened' entrepreneurs governed the company. A member contribution to the mutual company was paid in advance, and when less money was spent than expected, it was paid back to the members: a matter of trust. In its history, the organization was mainly a not-for-profit facilitating body with some secretaries to support the physicians, who performed the surgery and associated research. Many of these physicians had obtained PhDs. In the 1980s, technical professions such as toxicologists, safety experts, and paramedics, but also social workers, were also hired. The occupational physicians set up a system of teamworking, with each team managed by an occupational physician. In the early 1990s, a new director moved in. He faced a complex situation. Since 1994, all Dutch companies have been obliged by law to cooperate with an OHS company, as a reflection of the severe problems faced by workers in the workplace, such as work-related stress. Many new OHS companies were founded, and competition grew. The occupational physicians were still in power, but their authority was fading. In fact, they seriously lacked the management skills and systems needed to run the growing company and to lead the expanding variety of professions.

The CEO estimated that the company had to develop towards some kind of a management consulting firm. He changed relations with the customers, and reformed the governance structure. The contribution system was abandoned, and a common tender and billing system was introduced. He invested in the development of new non-technical and non-medical services such as organizational diagnosis, socio-technical redesign, coaching, and occupational therapy, and he hired new kinds of experts. He thought all the professionals urgently needed training in consulting skills. He wanted to buy an in-company version of a standard course in consulting practice from an inter-university centre for postgraduate education in organization studies and change management. However, this Centre, a network of management consultants, academics, and learning technologists, refused to deliver such a course.

The CEO was surprised, but understood the reasons for the refusal and formed a team consisting of an independent consultant/trainer and two professionals from the Centre. He let them investigate the need for training. The team interviewed the CEO, middle managers, their assistants, coordinators, various professionals, and secretaries. It was not a normal assessment of training needs and training necessity. The focus in the interviews was the perception of the various actors of the role of the professionals (and the company) towards clients, to other colleagues, of the management, of the history, the purpose and the strategy of the firm. Why? The team noticed quite early that the situation was not a proper context for an investment through straight training. The interviews showed some important 'facts': some medical professionals did not seem to be interested in the client firms at all, nor in the future the CEO had in mind. Their focus was entirely on their surgery with individual workers. Some were only interested in their own position and income, some were openly uncooperative. However, other professionals criticized them and shared the ambitions of the CEO; others ended up crying about the work culture in the interviews. It seemed to be a social jungle, where the occupational physicians tried to rule and to impose their business definition by any means.

The team's conclusion, in short, was that the company was halfway towards a fragmentation process. The external strategy was *ad hoc* and reactive. The company was losing its position in the market and slipping slowly towards a market segment with standardized low-level service at too low a price level. The internal structure was unclear, tasks and roles were ambiguous. There had been attempts to coordinate by standardization, using procedural control. The communication process was a mess. Inside the company, all kinds of strategies were used to defend positions or gain power. Many professionals also had exit strategies; they invested a lot of time in their professional education that they needed for their personal accreditation, which increased their personal market value. This all resulted in a low level of psychological safety. Further, cooperation in processes for clients was weakly developed. In summary, the organization presented a highly political culture.

The CEO was rather shocked by this conclusion. It was clear that any training to prepare the professionals for a consulting practice would be a senseless investment. The team presented the findings to the management team. They got the message: 'This is the mess you have made', and they were shocked by this picture in the external mirror. In the following phase of contracting, the CEO and the management team had to underline the diagnosis before the next step could be made. The CEO then commissioned a team consisting of the consultant and one member of the Centre (an educational designer) to help him with the change process and to organize interventions. These two did three intense workshops with nearly half of the personnel (from all management levels and presenting a good representation of all professional categories) within one month. As a preparation, all participants were invited to reflect individually on their actual practice, their ambitions, and their individual and collective future. These reflections were inputs for the conferences to create a shared vision for the future practice. We quote from the personal report of the educational designer:

> We have just started the first conference. The CEO opens. He talks about his aim to de-
> velop the company into a really innovative service firm in the areas of occupational health,
> employee benefits, management consulting, etc. In small groups the participants discuss
> some issues from their essays: 'What do I learn in this company?, what do we learn?' They
> present their findings, in an emotional atmosphere. Some participants (medical profession-
> als) start to cry and shout how awful it is to work in this company. Other participants and,
> especially, one of the managers ignore these outbursts by starting to talk about something
> else or just attack the crying people by calling them 'emotional' and 'non-businesslike'.
> The consultant counters these ignoring and offending behaviours directly. He explains to
> everyone some principles of NLP. He shows the strategies and tactics some people use (like
> mismatching by 'chunking up' or 'chunking down', the use of container words, making
> the context unclear). Each time one of the professionals shows this kind of behaviour, the
> consultant pauses for feedback . . . . He introduces rules for feedback, and for the first time
> these colleagues correct each other's misbehaviour. The consultant introduces a lot of new
> concepts of the marketing of services. The group of participants then defined a new mission
> (and this is certainly not a common mission statement for a management consulting firm):
> 'We work with organizations that are committed to the continuity of the competencies of
> the people and of the enterprise, by improving this relation. We provide understanding and
> perspectives, and guarantee the negotiated performances. We work in a way that our clients
> experience as added value and based upon recognition of each other's qualities and coupling
> of strengths.' The participants made a living version of this vision and formed a 'tableau'.
> Later on, they negotiated new habits and constructed a rulebook for the company, with a
> clear description of the formal organization.

After these conferences, the managers organized separate dissemination meetings with the other
staff. The CEO formed a change factory to monitor and direct the process of change with the slogan
'towards a new style of professionalism'. The implementation of the outcome of the negotiations on
responsibilities and authorities started. The motto was: first things first. Priority was given to acquiring new clients, renewing existing contracts, improving the financial structure by learning to budget,
the acquisition of new premises, and being the first to acquire ISO accreditation. One professional,
an organization expert and manager, left. He still wanted to build a management consulting practice
outside the OHS practice. This direction conflicted with the new mission statement (the group result)
that implied migration of the whole company to a new business. His departure was used to introduce
self-steering teams with clearly defined team roles. A new front office for the SME sector was built.

In the period 1995–2000, the company grew and merged with some smaller OHS companies in the
region. The CEO started to employ work and organization consultants. Two partners in the network
of the Centre took key managerial and professional responsibilities in the OHS company, while other
players in the network were hired by the CEO to help with mergers, team development, learning on
the job, etc. Individual managers and key professionals participated in various generic professional
development programmes on 'Work and Organization', 'Change Management', 'Basics of Management Consultancy' offered by the Centre. In these programmes, the participants have to create an
innovative project together with clients. Such a project was supported by the Centre through meetings with other participants and experienced consultants and/or trainers and/or teachers to work on
critical aspects of the projects. The CEO participated in a learning programme from another provider.
Occupational physicians continued their participation in the normal course-work for their professional registration. The aim of being an innovating consulting firm in Occupational Health and Safety
and to continue the leading role in the Dutch network of OHS firms became a reality to a certain
extent. The CEO is a manager (in 2001) of 800 people. The 'new' business is now about 10 per cent
of the turnover with 80 professionals. But classical medical and technical services still dominate.

# REFLECTION ON THE CASES

Both companies show attempts to innovate in the long term. They migrate towards partly unknown 'worlds', i.e. transformative innovation. The aerospace company sees itself as a designer and manufacturer of aerostructures in a close relationship with the users, the OHS company sees itself as health work and organization consultants providing services that are developed in close cooperation with its clients. Both consider themselves as a part of a chain. The change not only included the products or services, but also the technology, the work process, and the organization process.

In both cases, the support that was delivered showed considerable variation: support for experiments in the daily work, support for the development of new routines for work such as collaboration skills, possibilities for broader contacts, and the formation of networks through the whole company, access to knowledge and information thought to be relevant for the development of new practices.

Of course, the cases differ. They operate in entirely different contexts, work with entirely different technology and people, the one producing products and the other services. The most striking differences might be found in the inner state of the companies and its consequences. The aerospace company seems to be a rather well managed-for-profit company, proactive, aware of its zones of proximal development, future-oriented, changing its strategies in time. The management knew how to deal with the universities, and these had to modify their habits. The OHS company had a fragmented focus. The ambitions of the CEO conflicted with the developmental direction of the dominant group of professionals. This was not a creative tension. The CEO tried to get out of this situation by a purchase strategy. The academic partner refused to respond with instant delivery. Instead, both parties created a partnership together with the independent consultant. And this consultant played an important role in the (clinical) interventions that were necessary to dismantle the habits (such as the ignoring and offending behaviours) that served to keep the occupational physicians in power and to build a shared vision of the future.

What also strikes us is the issue of the relation between the companies and the knowledge institutes. We saw different possible definitions of the relation between two organizations: 'purchaser–provider of product/service' developing into tailor-made course-work in the first case, and 'investor in innovation/ partner in investment' in the second. The conditions for a proper relationship were seen in the flexibility of the higher-education institutions. In the first case, the government invited universities and polytechnics to be more flexible and to cooperate with industry. Institutions like Swinburne and UWS got the message and started deep and effective partnerships, which they call industry-based learning (National Report, 1993). In the second case, the partner is an independent not-for-profit body, a joint venture of universities with a great deal of freedom. Both institutions did not play assume the 'ivory tower' perspective, and did more than just providing competent teaching and challenging ideas. The first case suggests that this was not initially done on purpose, some serendipity occurred. Because Swinburne is more than 1000 km away from Sydney, this university changed its habits. Instead of a series of lectures during a semester, the mode of two-day workshop on site was used, to reduce the travelling costs of the lecturers. Freed from the constraints of a fixed weekly time slot, lecturers were able to design interactive exercises requiring extended delivery sessions, or fully utilize seminar discussions to extend students' understanding of the course material. Ready access to the company's workplace enabled the immediate implementation of textbook exercises (e.g. workplace safety audits). It also led to the design of assessment tasks that not only tested the students' understanding of theoretical concepts, but also provided solutions that were valuable to the company. Through this flexibility, the delivery mode changed. Voluntary participation became the norm. Instead of constructing a cohort by pre-selection, the student body in one cohort consisted of people from the factory and from the offices, from many nationalities, providing more variety within the group. The new delivery mode also implied a lot of work in small teams. This improved the collaboration competencies of the participants. They worked with company employees they had not met before, enhancing their overall knowledge of company operations, and creating an environment for future cooperative working.

# PROVIDING EXTENDED SPACES FOR LEARNING

We can learn from these two cases when we stop seeing them as examples of formal education in the context of industry. Seen from another angle, we can redefine them as stories of creating a shared extra space for emerging relationships of a cognitive and/or social nature. The cases show that various activities can extend the existing space within a focus company in order to make innovation happen. From this perspective, we redefine the how-to-support-learning issue as the issue of how to create a cooperative relationship between two companies and create or design extended spaces for learning, that enable emerging relationships of a social and cognitive nature to make innovation happen in the focus company. In this formulation, we recognize an important proposition as formulated by Etienne Wenger (1998: 234): no community can fully design the learning of another, no community can fully design its own learning. Or it takes two to tango. It is our view that a combination of industry and academic practices would offer more complete learning than either can in isolation. Designs that enhance self-organizing processes and are likely to stimulate innovation comply with four criteria: (1) requisite variety; (2) redundancy of functions; (3) minimal critical specification; and (4) double-loop learning (Kuipers, 1989). We stress here the criterion of 'minimal critical specification': the extended space must not prescribe more for the learners than is strictly necessary. Learning spaces must have minimal normalization, must be flexible and transparent, and be inviting. Such spaces must not have restrictive borders or walls. Temporary structures like 'scaffolds' will do.

Anything can function as a scaffold; a scaffold is not necessarily a teacher, a programme, or any other formal entity designed for support. Any specific event within the environment of the learners can function as an element of a scaffold, whether it was placed there on purpose or not. Common role definitions like 'teacher' must be completed with others. We think the role of facilitator is very important, provided that it is not exclusively focused on the process. This role might enhance participation by issuing invitations, brokering contacts, monitoring the development of the new activities and its outcomes, but also by intervening in order to remove blockages that result from behaviours that are not directed towards the zone of proximal development, but backwards.

# DESIGN OF LEARNING SUPPORT

When we (as actors of a focus firm and a support firm) want to extend the space for learning for emerging social and cognitive relations and provide support for learning or scaffolding in a certain direction related to the zones of proximal development, we must determine the following:

- the developmental frame;
- the inner state of the focus organization;
- the inner state of the support organization.

Based on that, we can then determine:

- what kind of relation is needed between two cooperating organizations;
- what kind of 'extra space' would be of added value.

We will briefly discuss these issues with some information drawn from the cases.

## 1. DETERMINE THE DEVELOPMENTAL FRAME

The first issue is the developmental frame: one has to estimate the zones of proximal development. Into what world is the innovation process or migration of the organization aimed? Towards a known world? Can the future situation be very well defined? Or do the innovations take the organization into an unknown world? In that case, will it be possible to define the new company as a part of a chain? Who will be clients? Who will be partners in the chain? Is it possible to define the change, not only of the products or services, but also of the technology, the work process, and the organization process? What will be the essential new task of the people? To be competitive in unpredictable markets, to cooperate in a new way and to contribute to changes in work, in routines, in organization? And what is the main friction or conflict?

- *Case one*: The zones of proximal development were: continue as an independent producer of air-planes, continue as a producer of components, or innovate as a producer of composite components into a co-designer. The third was chosen, a radical turn from production based on designs made by others.
- *Case two*: The zones of proximal development were: keep the system running as it is with some improvements, migrate to a known but other world (become a consulting firm), or migrate towards an unknown world, a consulting firm for health work and organization. The third was chosen; this conflicted with the reactive process and the dominance of the physicians.

## 2. Assess the Inner State of the Focus Organization

Support must be a complement. When we want to build extended spaces, we must know what is going on in the focus organization. Is the organization a rather well-managed company, pro-active and future-oriented, aware of its zones of proximal development, changing its strategies in time? Does the management know how to deal with other players in a chain? Or is the inner state of a different nature? Where are the tensions? Whose innovative ambitions conflict with the direction of others? Is this a creative tension?

What kind of learning is common in such organizations? What kind of learning is enhanced by the organizational model? Is some kind of experimentation or exploration common, or is the company mainly directed towards the mode of exploitation? Can we detect practices and behaviours that might hinder the exploration of zones of development and hinder the development of deep learning? Are there some scaffolds in use, such as management development programmes, mentoring, individual participation in professional training programmes?

- *Case one*: The level of learning was adequate in relation to the existing practice: building aircraft under licence and producing components to specifications provided by external partners. The range of learning normally would go as far as investigative learning. Existing scaffolds consisted of man-agement development programmes, supporting the search for market chances. On the shopfloor a practice of mentoring was frequently used, which is not uncommon in such technical manufacturing companies; mentoring supports the transfer of common practice.
- *Case two*: The OHS firm was slipping downward. Through its members, one of the professions aimed to continue their domination within the company and their business definition; to hinder the exploration of other zones of development; and to hinder the development of deep learning. Combined with the general trait of professional bureaucracies that mainly allow narrow learning, this produces very little deep learning. The main learning was conditioning and imitation; trial-and-error learning was discouraged. Existing scaffolds did exist, to the extent that individual professionals participated in medical professional training programmes. This supports the transfer of common practice.

## 3. Consider the Inner State of the Support Organization

Flexibility within the support organization is essential. Is one prepared to produce tailor-made support activities? The educational institutions have to deliver more than just providing competent teaching and contesting ideas. Often one has to experiment during the process of delivery.

- *Case one*: Instead of series of lectures during a semester, the mode of a two-day workshop on site was used. Instead of lectures in a fixed weekly time slot, interactive exercises requiring extended delivery sessions were used.
- *Case two*: This shows that even activities that one might consider not to be educative at all might be needed, like creating a shared vision in the focus firm and its expression in a living tableau, coaching of the CEO, experiments with new services of physicians.

## 4. DEFINE A RELATION WITH ANOTHER ORGANIZATION OR COMMUNITY

A negotiated relationship is crucial. In both cases, the focus companies wanted to cooperate with an external party, in both cases a higher-education institution. Both parties negotiated the nature of the relationship *ex ante* or by experimenting in a pilot.

- *Case one*: The definition of the relation unintentionally changed (from provider of commodities to tailor-made educational opportunities) and this was facilitated by calling the first activities a pilot.
- *Case two*: The issue of the definition of the relation has been addressed in an early stage, and was raised again a couple of times during the cooperation process. Cooperation with a partner that has serious internal tensions (the conflict between the ambitions of the CEO and the dominant practice) requires specific attention to the relation.

## 5. DETERMINE THE BASIC IDEA OF THE 'EXTRA SPACE'

It is important to have a leading idea about the extra space. This is important for communication within the focus and the support company, but also to steer the design process.

- *Case one*: The chosen direction makes it clear that a significant number of employees have to develop from technicians into more interacting and commercial people. Here, an extra space consisting of course-work near the shopfloor seemed to be the best option with invitations to elicit investigative learning.
- *Case two*: The choice made it clear that the internal organization needed improvement and quite a number of employees had to develop towards other external and internal roles. Here, the extra space needs first some interventions to address the problem of low-level learning. The three conferences tried to create some level of reflexivity by giving the professionals a mirror on the ongoing processes. In the conferences, the group participants also formulated a new mission, as a precondition for expansive learning and the creation of new business.

## DESIGNING EXTENDED LEARNING SPACE

When the developmental frame can be defined, the learning level is sufficiently related to the innovation one wants to pursue, the partners decide that they will cooperate, and the relation can be established, and then an extended space and its scaffolds can be designed. One might use here five aspects: (1) the physical; (2) the social; (3) the linguistic; (4) a focus on the future; and (5) the management within the space. These aspects contain issues from a list as described by Knowles (1984), but reorganized and completed with the aspect of content (the linguistic) and time; the list also contains the elements mentioned by Nonaka and Konno (1998).

## 1. PHYSICAL ASPECTS

Learning processes are fostered or hindered by what can be seen and heard, how people can move, what they can smell or taste. Brick and mortar, furniture, symbols, and so on strongly determine the kind of relations that can come to fruition. This aspect must be assessed in terms of its potential: there should be no incongruence between the physical and the other aspects. A key issue is always: do we accept the present physical environment (e.g. on-site), or do we extend and vary this aspect and locate the 'learners' temporarily in another building, a conference centre, a museum, a hotel, a ship or take the learners to another organization, etc.? For some kinds of learning, computer technology can be used to support and stimulate personal interaction with the learning environment.

- *Case one*: The course-work was done on the premises of the aerospace company. Being on-site minimized logistics problems for the students, provided ready access to case material for their assignments, and, for many of them, provided a familiar environment in which to take an unfamiliar journey (post-graduate university work). In addition, small work crises that required the student in the workplace could be accommodated, generally during breaks in the course. In many cases, however, there was still more scope for involving workplace colleagues in between formal lecture periods.
- *Case two*: The conferences were held in a conference centre located just outside the region of the OHS company, with a very large hall to work in with this large group. The group could use many small rooms for discussions. Altogether it had an atmosphere of 'work'. The later activities were on-site, in a large meeting room, by tradition 'the' meeting room of the medical professionals, with a large painting of the founding father of the company on the wall. The programmes for the individual professionals were in standard conference centres.

## 2. THE SOCIAL ASPECT

We often give a learning space a social character; it consists then of possibilities to contact new people in various possible roles and patterns of relations. Of course, these people form a social structure, and this structure can be designed. It is common practice to form small groups, because in small groups people can learn better. Such an automatic response is not wise. The choice of group size depends primarily on strategy: the way people are invited to cooperate must be congruent with the future mode of the cooperation processes. When people want to work as individuals, an obligation to form a group is not congruent. When all members of a company are involved, why work in a small group? A small group with its cohesion has a small learning potential if there is minimal challenging of views and interpersonal risk-taking (Admonson, 1999). If the group moves away from the primary task, this will lead to high transaction costs, long learning times, irritation, and low returns (Sinclair, 1992). On the other hand, if a sense of teamwork and competition between small groups are encouraged, utilizing temporary small teams may be beneficial.

The choice of size depends also on the present ability of the participants to manage communication and power relations. As the number of participants and their heterogeneity increase, process losses through communication difficulties may arise. These may hinder the learning. Those difficulties can be limited by promoting an atmosphere of sympathy and cooperation. Safety in the space is important. Participants in a learning space might negotiate a minimal code of conduct that provides this safety. But such a minimal code does not have to lead towards group cohesion. It is like the safety code on a construction site. Power games must be prevented, because—according to Scholl (1992)—any growth in knowledge is hindered by the exercise of power for the sake of gaining power.

Extra people can be scaffolds as well. They might be text providers, but also provide tacit knowledge, entrance to other cognitive and/or social networks, be a living behavioural model, or encourage processes of exploration and discovery. They must not have a too dominant role, because then imitation is encouraged. Their actions and texts are, of course, hard to 'design' but might be influenced by joint prior preparation, or by limiting their field of action, for instance, by surrounding their contribution with outcomes of participants' learning projects that cannot be ignored. So they must align their own activity.

A small number of formal presentations by, e.g., teachers will do. An interactive atmosphere is to be encouraged, both in formal and informal meetings. Control over whether the participants apply the knowledge in the appropriate way is not congruent with innovation. In innovation processes people work often on ill-defined, so-called 'messy' problems. Quality is primarily measured here in terms of its possible added value in the innovation process; control over suitable application is related to work on well-defined problems.

- *Case one*: The composition of the cohorts first was done by selection, later the composition was left to individual choice. This improved the variety. Each cohort had significant diversity in many ways, and individual, small team, and group learning elements were all utilized, but always in the spirit of group learning (e.g. individuals reviewing reference material on behalf of the group). The small team membership was changed for each course module. The dynamics of the course timetable—covering material in a short time with distractions in between—simulated the work environment, and course participants had to rely on each other to complete assignments, even though they recognized that some inputs were imperfect. Peer pressure seemed to elicit both support and extra effort. Having some external participants later in the programme broadened the view of the subjects being presented. Changes seen on the shopfloor arising directly from course project work were generally parametric innovations, but they did involve others in addition to the course participants.
- *Case two*: The group was composed by the CEO and it was a sufficient mirror of the company as a whole. Much time was invested in building safety in the group; although most people knew each other already, some participants showed ignoring and offending behaviour that hindered communication and learning. The consultants sometimes needed to intervene at a deep level to eliminate these destructive patterns, to establish safety. During the process, in the subsequent conferences the group felt invited to make those patterns explicit when they occurred again.

## 3. THE LINGUISTIC ASPECTS

Often scaffolds seem to be built of linguistic elements alone. New (chains of) words seem to be essential in the production of new activities and new interaction. A proper scaffold must be rich in the linguistic aspect; otherwise the learning opportunity may not be properly considered and may be rejected (Jarvis, 1987). Designers can construct the linguistic aspect of the scaffold by selecting the new words, from texts such as books and articles. They are then providers and interpreters of texts, like teachers. However, advanced learners need scaffolds that support them in identifying and selecting information, and in avoiding meaningless combinations. So instead of providing lots of selected texts, we suggest it is better to provide rules for text exploration. Designers have to be careful about natural language and jargon. If people have difficulty in understanding what is presented or its significance, learning will be inhibited.

- *Case one*: Working in familiar surroundings with at least some people they knew encouraged students to seek clarification of new language from the teacher or classmates, and to challenge some of the material presented that seemed inconsistent with their experiential learning. This encouraged critical questioning and dialogue. (It was a shock for some lecturers initially if they had previously taught undergraduates, but, in the end, they enjoyed this practice.) This critical questioning was not always taken beyond the classroom, however, leading to a language mismatch between some participants and their workplace colleagues.
- *Case two*: The consultant and the professional of the Centre selected for the three conferences some essentials on marketing of services, service development, and negotiating skills, introducing these as 'relevant and important', using their reputation as an experienced management consultant and management scholar. Each concept was turned into practice right away.

## 4. THE FUTURE

It is essential to bring in a future focus, i.e. work with the learners to create a collective vision on their individual and collective zones of proximal development. The future must be made imaginable by anticipating future activities in the work roles of the learners and then define competencies one has to develop by backtracking. It is essential that the learners create their own images of future in a facilitated dialogue between learners and their stakeholders such as sponsors, managers, and clients. In this dialogue, one has to explore what the learners and/or their company will be doing in a couple of years, and together produce ideas about future performance in the workplace, because that is the level most people will recognize. Change that does not produce imaginables will not touch or inspire the individual and encourage collective maps of the learners, nor will it create conflict or friction.

- *Case one*: The whole programme was seen as supporting a vision of the future capabilities needed by the aerospace company, based on its changed market positioning and operational style. The assignments chosen were, as far as possible, related to how to do something new or better in the company in the future. Where the organization provided appropriate support, this provided immediately measurable benefit. Where that element of the platform was missing, full value was not obtained from the assignment work, i.e. there was individual learning, but little organizational change. The competencies acquired positioned the company to better implement other change initiatives.
- *Case two*: The consultants invited the participants to write essays, reflect on their own professional future, and compare this to their present practice. For some of them this was a strong confrontation of their own personal and professional ideals with their 'messy' practice. This friction we used as the base for the construction process of the new mission statement. The participants did this in a large group meeting together and then this was anchored in a 'tableau'. They defined for themselves some preconditions (organizational, relational, training) required to perform according to such a mission.

## 5. STIMULATING LEARNING WITHIN THE EXTRA SPACE

Design of a learning space is intended to stimulate action as a result of learning. The space must be an invitation in general, but the process of learning still needs some complementary action, and we observe that learning support practice is also situation-dependent, conditional on what has to be learned and how. The nature of what is to be learned: is it something specific (such as learning to carry out a new task), or something general (such as improved understanding of financial management)?; and the nature of how it is to be learned: is it by relatively autonomous individual or collective action (such as self-paced e-learning), or by interaction with and interdependency on others (such as in sports coaching)? These all combine to give four generic modes: specific/autonomous, general/autonomous, specific/interdependent, and general/interdependent. Roles such as 'teacher', 'facilitator', 'trainer', 'mentor', 'coach', 'workshop leader', 'role model', 'interventionist', or even 'clinician', with methods such as creativity development, design methods, on-the-job support in experiments, decision support, conflict management, learning to give and receive feedback, futuring, and, of course, lectures and assignments may be needed to support learning in these modes.

One of these modes, its associated roles, and its methods may be the norm in a particular organization, and if other modes are the most appropriate in supporting change and acquiring new competencies, there may be tensions or even barriers created by the 'rules' of the company that inhibit expansive learning. These tensions and barriers must be removed by intervention if necessary.

- *Case one*: The trade unions wanted the learning to be formally accredited. This contained the risk that university teaching would be the norm. By two-party negotiation the first pilots functioned as a lab to develop the proper level of contingency (situation-dependency): a good fit of roles and methods facilitated experiments on the shopfloor to improve various aspects of work. And, as the case shows, the participants acquired a collective competency to collaborate in projects with external partners. The UWS agreed to handle the accreditation; here also government policy played a positive role.

- *Case two*: The CEO initially wanted an in-company version of a standard course in consulting practice. The CEO was persuaded that this was not a wise strategy for investment in his case. The diagnosis showed that a whole variety of interventions and learning activities was needed, far more than standard course-work. The management of the learning was a joint activity of the consultants and the CEO and some managers, in the change factory.

## CHECKING THE SPACE

A design process is iterative. When various aspects are covered properly, we have to look at outcomes from the resulting space as a whole. Here, some performance measurement criteria we have mentioned play a role in addition to the kind of activities that are sought from the participants: the four criteria of Kuipers (1989) for self-regulation: (1) requisite variety; (2) redundancy of functions; (3) minimal critical specification; and (4) double-loop learning and the invitations must all be within the reach of the learners, and the space as such must fit to the various learning styles.

- *Case one*: A variety of course topics giving different views of the world were available to programme participants. However, the development directions of many of the participants in the operational environment were restricted by a need to focus on efficiency in current operations. From this point of view, it could be said that the requisite variety was restricted. Redundancy of functions was provided by the participant's opportunity to learn in a variety of ways: with the help of mentor, with the help of colleagues, through critical questioning, through reference texts, and working on the shopfloor. Minimal critical specification was achieved through the choice of project work offered with each programme subject. Double-loop learning, defined for this purpose as exploring unexpected learning directions, was evidenced by the changed attitudes to learning, enhanced collaboration skills, and broader views of the company that were additional to the course-work subject matter.
- *Case two*: The criteria: requisite variety: the team of consultants had sufficient possibilities to cover the variety of aspects of the process: to eliminate the patterns that produce stagnation, support the definition of a new mission, new propositions, and new roles. Their actions were continuously legitimized by the CEO. Redundancy of functions consisted of the various meetings in syndicates. Here, the participants could discuss issues without the presence of the consultants and the CEO. Minimal critical specification occurred as follows: the consultants attacked certain patterns, showed perspectives on new practices, but the participants decide themselves on the content. Once in, they were not allowed to leave the conference. The criterion of double-loop learning was covered by organizing planning sessions with the CEO, and with the change team. Here, the learning activities of the participants were varied. They had to reflect, to write, to experiment, and to negotiate. They certainly received new cognitive input. Because the participants came from all over the company, a lot of new contacts emerged, especially between members of various teams who were in different departments. New cognitive patterns emerged, e.g. reflected in new mission statement and the rule book that they produced.

## CONCLUSION

This chapter presents a construction language for professional activity within the pragmatic and situational schools of thought as described in Chapter 17. Why this attempt? As indicated in the Introduction, many patterns and schools of thought show that change programmes do not produce change. In the last 25 years, the pragmatic and situational schools of thought have started to produce interesting knowledge products. In Engeström's terms, they certainly provided an orientation basis but at a high level of abstraction. In our view, the related design language is too general, and does not reflect the position of a practitioner well enough to be of practical value. That is why in this chapter we played with some concepts on innovation and change, learning and support, and with reports from practice.

We have discussed the experiences of two companies pursuing innovation as a source of competitive advantage. We have observed that learning about new things may support the process of innovation, and that introducing an innovative new product or practice will require learning new things to support it. We see that the approach to innovation needed to achieve company goals may be incremental or radical. From this point of view, we see innovation, change, and learning mixed in ways that are very situation-dependent. In addition, we have observed that a particular company may be starting its journey of change with a unique repertoire of competencies, practices, and norms, introducing additional situation-dependency. There will be a gap between where a company is today and where it needs to be in the future. People may not be able to bridge this gap in one step, so a series of steps may have to be designed. The size of each step depends on the learning capacity of the organization, but we observe that larger steps can be taken if appropriately designed support structures are put in place. While these support structures will be situation-dependent, we suggest that they can be built from components that we define as: the physical learning environment; the linguistic learning environment; the social learning environment; and the future context associated with the learning, all assembled to provide appropriate learning support for each learning step. To use a building construction analogy—identify the gap to be bridged and design temporary scaffolding assembled from components to help bridge that gap.

Our representation is intended to aid you as a reader in your process of orientation, and this is the step that precedes internalization and externalization as the learning model of Engeström suggests. We offer a language that might be useful in a variety of circumstances. We do not claim to cover all issues such as the design of a learning organization or the design of support to organizational learning or group learning. This is a restricted construction language with a grammar we derived from the pragmatic and situational school of thinking. But this reflection certainly does not recommend any action in any specific situation, such as an algorithm or a ready-to-use check-list might do. This is simply because we do not believe that such a type of orientation bases will have enough quality to support the work of the professional or managerial practitioner. On the contrary, it will prevent them from getting in contact with the context, because such a basis suggests that the construction of a learning space and the design of support might be simple and a matter of a quick fix.

Creating organizational value through learning and change requires more than quick fixes; it requires the enhancement of various complete learning cycles. In a turbulent setting often associated with change and innovation, deep learning is required with processes of conceptualization, reflection, and criticism. From our practical experience, we observe that the latter processes are more strongly embedded in academia than in industry, where the favoured learning processes are experimenting and doing. This leads us to promote cooperative learning that builds on both of these respective strengths. Both of the case studies we have presented describe some form of academia–industry interaction that was either designed, or evolved in such a way that a good blend of support activities was achieved. However, effective collaboration was not obtained without some conflict. Academic delivery and assessment practices had to be modified, and the industry participants had to provide significant resources. We observe that without a willingness by the collaborators to embrace change in these ways, the collaboration would have been ineffective.

And as a final remark: the flexibility of the support organization must be tested over and over again. Educational organizations always are inclined to stick to their old habits. This is reinforced by the dominant discourse on learning with its dominance of the first two schools of thought on learning and its institutionalization. Do the educationalists control the 'tug to teach' and give room to the 'yearn to learn' (Ballou et al., 1999)? Do they have access to a variety of role definitions, methods, and techniques to deliver scaffolds at the various moments of the learning cycles? Do they experiment often enough to develop and maintain the design competencies that are required to build an effective learning space? And how do they experiment? Do they take risks? Do they accept tensions, frictions, and conflicts? Do they go through full learning cycles? This is important, because even in educational organizations that act as support organizations for innovation, deep learning in their own practice is not natural!

## REFERENCES

Admonson, A. (1999) Psychological safety and learning behavior in work teams. *Administrative Science Quarterly*, **44**, 350–383.

Arthur, M. & Rousseau, D. (1996) *The Boundaryless Career: A New Employment Principle for a New Organizational Era*. New York: Oxford University Press.

Ballou, R., Bowers, D., Boyatzis, R. & Kolb, D. (1999) Fellowship in lifelong learning: an executive development program for advanced professionals. *Journal of Management Education*, **23**(4), 338–356.

Beckett, R.C. & Smid, G. (2001) Methods and tools for the design of learning support for adults in the context of sustainable change and innovation. In *Proceedings of the Asia-Pacific Researchers in Organisation Studies (APROS) conference*. 'Organisation theory in transition: transitional societies; transitional theories', 3–5 December, Hong Kong.

Beer, M., Eisenstat, R.A. & Spector, B. (1990) Why change programs don't produce change. *Harvard Business Review*, **68**, 158–166.

Blackler, F.H.M., Crump, N. & McDonalds, S. (1999) Managing experts and competing through innovation: an activity theoretical analysis. *Organization*, **6**(1), 5–31.

Brown, J.S. & Duguid, P. (1996) Stolen knowledge. In H. McLellan (ed.) *Situational Learning Perspectives*. Englewood Cliffs, NJ: Educational Technology Publications.

Causer, G. & Jones, C. (1996) One of them or one of us? The ambiguities of the professional as manager. In R. Fincham (ed.) *New Relationships in the Organized Professions* (pp. 91–112). Aldershot: Avebury.

Dobbin, F. & Boychuk, T. (1999) National employment systems and job autonomy: why job autonomy is high in the nordic countries and low in the United States, Canada and Australia. *Organization Studies* **20**(2), 257–293.

Engeström, Y. (1995) *Training for Change: New Approach to Instruction and Learning in Working Life*. Geneva: ILO.

Hillis, D. (2002) Stumbling into brilliance: true breakthroughs are almost always unexpected. *Harvard Business Review*, **80**(8), 152.

Hite, J. Jr (1999) *Learning in Chaos: Improving Human Performance in Today's Fast-Changing Volatile Organizations*. Houston, TX: Gulf Publishing Company.

Hoebeke, L. (1994) *Making Work Systems Better: A Practitioner's Reflections*. Chichester: John Wiley & Sons, Ltd.

Ibarra, H. (1999) Provisional selves: experimenting with image and identity in professional adaptation. *Administration Science Quarterly*, **44**, 764–791.

Jarvis, P. (1987) *Adult Learning in the Social Context*. New York: Croom Helm.

Karasek, R. & Theorell, T. (1989) *Healthy Work: Stress, Productivity and the Reconstruction of Working Life*. New York: Basic Books.

Knowles, M. (1984) *Andragogy in Action*. San Francisco: Jossey-Bass.

Kolb, D.A. (1984) *Experimental Learning*. New Jersey: Prentice Hall.

Kuipers, H. (1989) Zelforganisatie als ontwerpprincipe. Inaugural address. Eindhoven: Technical University Eindhoven.

Lave, J. (1993) The practice of learning. In S. Chaiklin & J. Lave (eds), *Understanding Practice: Some Perspectives on Activity and Context*. New York: Cambridge University Press.

Lewin, K. (1951) *Field Theory in Social Sciences*. New York: Harper & Row.

Lundin, R. & Midler, A. (1998) *Projects as Arenas for Renewal and Learning Processes*. Boston: Kluwer.

Marton, F., Hounsell, D. & Entwistle, N. (eds) (1984) *The Experiences of Learning*. Edinburgh: Scottish Academic Press.

National Report (1993) *National Report on Australia's Higher Education Sector*. Canberra: Australian Government Publishing Service.

Nonaka, I. & Konno, N. (1998) The concept of 'ba': building a foundation for knowledge creation. *California Management Review*, **40**(3), 40–54.

Nooteboom, B. (2000) *Learning and Innovation in Organizations and Economies*. New York: Oxford University Press.

Price, M. (1997) *Patterns of change and learning in the practices of selected Oklahoma architects*. www.telepath.com/mprice

Scholl, W. (1992) The social production of knowledge. In M. Von Cranach, W. Doise & G. Mugny (eds) *Social Representations and the Social Bases of Knowledge*. Lewiston, NY: Hogrefe & Huber.

Sinclair, A. (1992) The tyranny of a team ideology. *Organisation Studies*, **13**(4), 611–626.

Smid, G. (2001) *Professionals Opleiden. Over het ontwerpen van competentiegericht vervolgonderwijs voor hoger opgeleiden*. Schoonhoven: Academic Service.

Smid, G. & Beckett, R.C. (2001) Co-operation in learning for innovation: aspects of the design of co-operation between companies and educational providers in the context of sustainable change. Paper presented at the EGOS colloqium, Lyon. July.

Tough, A. (1971) *The Adults Learning Project: A Fresh Approach to Theory and Practice in Adult Learning*. Ontario: The Ontario Institute for Studies in Education.

Unger, B. (2000) Innovation systems and innovative performance: voice systems. *Organization Studies*, **21**(5), 941–969.

Van Dongen, H.J., de Laat, W.A.M & Maas, A.J.J.A. (1996) *Een kwestie van verschil: conflicthantering en onderhandeling in een configuratieve integratietheorie*. Delft: Eburon.

Vygotsky, L.S. (1978) *Mind in Society: The Development of Higher Psychological Processes*. Cambridge, MA: Harvard University Press.

Wenger, E. (1998) *Communities of Practice: Learning, Meaning and Identity*. Cambridge: Cambridge University Press.

Whitley, R. (2000) The institutional structuring of innovation strategies: business systems, firm types and patterns of technical change in different market economies. *Organization Studies*, **21**(5), 855–886.

# CHAPTER 20

# Knowledge, Learning, and Organizational Embeddedness

## A Critical Reflection

**Alice Lam**

*Brunel University, West London, UK*

Much of the literature on organizational learning points to the importance of social interaction, context, and trust for learning and knowledge creation (Brown & Duguid, 1991, 1998; Lave & Wenger, 1991; Nonaka, 1994; Nonaka & Takeuchi, 1995; Wenger, 1998). This builds on Polanyi's (1962, 1966) idea that a large part of human knowledge is subjective and tacit, and cannot be easily codified and transmitted independent of the knowing subject. The transfer of this kind of personal, intuitive knowledge requires social interaction and the development of shared understanding. The idea that shared social context and common understanding facilitate the transfer of tacit knowledge and learning also constitutes a basic assumption in recent thinking in the knowledge-based theory of the firm (Kogut & Zander, 1992, 1996; Spender, 1996a, 1996b; Tsoukas, 1996). The knowledge-based view argues that all firms are in essence knowledge-creating organizations because they have the ability continuously to generate and synthesize collective organizational knowledge. This gives firms an advantage to create types of knowledge and innovative capability that cannot be generated in a marketplace of individuals. Many organizational and management researchers regard the firm as a critical source of social context through which a great deal of collective learning and knowledge creation takes place. Nonaka and Takeuchi (1995) talk about the 'knowledge creating company'. Argyris and Schön (1978) suggest that an organization is, at its root, a cognitive enterprise that learns and develops knowledge.

All organizations can learn and create knowledge; but their learning patterns and types of knowledge generated may vary. This chapter argues that there is an interactive relationship between dominant knowledge types, patterns of learning, and organizational structural forms. Further, the extent to which tacit knowledge constitutes the knowledge base of the firm, and how it is formed and used, are powerfully shaped by the broader institutional context (Boisot, 1995a, 1995b; Lam, 1996, 1997, 2000). The knowledge of the firm is socially embedded. It is rooted in firms' coordination mechanisms and organizational routines which, in turn, are heavily influenced by societal institutions. The aim of this chapter is to develop a typological framework, at the cognitive, organizational, and societal levels, to explain the links between knowledge types, organizational forms, and societal institutions. It shows how these three levels interact to shape the learning and innovative capabilities of firms. It focuses on the role of tacit knowledge and how firms located in different institutional context might differ in their capability in mobilizing it.

The framework developed here builds on and integrates the following three major strands of literature. First, the theory of knowledge and organizational learning, most notably, the work of Polanyi (1962, 1966), Spender (1996a, 1996b), and Nonaka (1994), which seeks to understand the nature of knowledge

*Dynamics of Organizational Change and Learning.* Edited by J.J. Boonstra.
© 2004 John Wiley & Sons, Ltd. ISBN 0-471-87737-9.

and organizational learning from a pluralistic epistemological perspective. It distinguishes between explicit and tacit knowledge and argues that the interaction between these two modes of knowing is vital for the creation of new knowledge. Their emphasis on tacit knowing as the origin of human knowledge directs our attention to the social and interactive nature of learning. Second, the chapter also draws upon the theoretical insights of the resource- or knowledge-based theory of the firm. Following Penrose (1959), the knowledge-based theory sees the firm as a body of knowledge residing in its structures of coordination, which, in turn, defines the social context for cooperation, communication, and learning (Kogut & Zander, 1992, 1996). At the heart of this theory is the idea that the primary role of the firm and the essence of organizational capability are the integration and creation of knowledge (Grant, 1996; Spender, 1996a; Tsoukas, 1996). Differences in the organizing principles of firms thus reflect their differing knowledge base and learning capabilities. And, finally, the perspective adopted in this chapter follows the 'societal' approach in industrial sociology, and builds on the theoretical foundations of the literature on the 'national systems of innovation'. The 'societal' approach demonstrates how external societal institutions interact with internal organizational structures and processes to generate societally distinctive organizational forms (Maurice et al., 1986; Maurice, 1995). Literature on 'national innovation systems', most notably, the work of Freeman (1987, 1995), Lundvall (1992), and Nelson (1993), seeks to understand the link between national institutions, primarily at the macro-level, and the innovative performance of firms and economies. Lundvall's work is particularly relevant in highlighting the 'specificity' and 'interconnectedness' of societal institutions bearing on learning and innovation.

This chapter represents the first attempt to integrate the above three intellectual developments to build a systematic conceptual framework to explain how knowledge, organizational forms, and societal institutions interact to shape learning and innovation. The concept of 'social embeddedness', as used by Granovetter (1985), refers to how behaviour and institutions are affected by networks of social relations. At the *cognitive level*, the notion of social embeddedness underlines the 'tacit' nature of human knowledge and the dynamic relationship between individual and collective learning. At the *organizational level*, it focuses on how the organizing principles of the firm shape the social structure of coordination, the behavioural routines and work roles of organizational members within which the knowledge of the firm is embedded. At the *societal level*, it draws attention to the way societal institutions shape organizational routines and coordination rules. This chapter focuses on the education and training system, and types of labour markets and careers, as the key societal institutions shaping work organization and the knowledge base of the firm. The typology presented below seeks to integrate the different levels of analysis into a coherent framework.

## KNOWLEDGE WITHIN THE FIRM: CHARACTERISTICS AND TYPES

The knowledge of the firm can be analysed along two dimensions: the epistemological and ontological (Nonaka & Takeuchi, 1995). The former concerns the modes of expression of knowledge, namely, Polanyi's distinction between explicit and tacit knowledge. The latter relates to the locus of knowledge which can reside at the individual or collective levels.

### THE EPISTEMOLOGICAL DIMENSION: EXPLICIT VS TACIT KNOWLEDGE

Human knowledge exists in different forms; it can be articulated explicitly or manifested implicitly (tacit). Polanyi (1962) argues that a large part of human knowledge is tacit. This is particularly true of operational skills and know-how acquired through practical experience. Knowledge of this type is action-oriented and has a personal quality that makes it difficult to formalize or communicate. Unlike explicit knowledge which can be formulated, abstracted, and transferred across time and space independent of the knowing subjects, the transfer of tacit knowledge requires close interaction and the build-up of shared understanding and trust among them. The main methods for the acquisition and accumulation of these two knowledge forms also differ. Explicit knowledge can be generated through logical deduction and acquired by formal study. Tacit knowledge, in contrast, can be acquired only through practical experience in the relevant context, i.e. 'learning-by-doing'. Although it is possible to distinguish between explicit and tacit knowledge conceptually, they are not separate and discrete in practice. Nonaka and Takeuchi (1995) argue that new knowledge is generated through the dynamic interaction and combination of these two types. However, firms differ in their ability to foster such interaction, and the relative importance and status of the two types may also vary. More importantly, the creation of new knowledge in itself will necessarily involve the use and generation of tacit knowledge. Polanyi (1962) sees the origin of all human knowledge in individual intuition. The learning and innovative capability of an organization is thus critically dependent on its capacity to mobilize tacit knowledge and foster its interaction with explicit knowledge.

## THE ONTOLOGICAL DIMENSION: THE INDIVIDUAL VS COLLECTIVE

Knowledge within the firm can reside at the level of the individual, or be shared among members of the organization. Individual knowledge is a repertoire of knowledge 'owned' by the individual, which can be applied independently to specific types of tasks or problems. It is also transferable, moving with the person, giving rise to potential problems of retention and accumulation. In contrast, collective knowledge refers to the ways in which knowledge is distributed and shared among members of the organization. It is the accumulated knowledge of the organization stored in its rules, procedures, routines, and shared norms which guide the problem-solving activities and patterns of interaction among its members. It can either be a 'stock' of knowledge stored as hard data or represent knowledge in a state of 'flow' emerging from interaction. Collective knowledge can be more, or less, than the sum of the individuals' knowledge, depending on the mechanisms that translate individual into collective knowledge (Glynn, 1996: 1093–1094).

## FOUR TYPES OF KNOWLEDGE

The explicit–tacit and individual–collective dimensions of knowledge give rise to four categories of knowledge: 'embrained', 'embodied', 'encoded', and 'embedded' knowledge (Figure 20.1). These conceptual distinctions were first suggested by Collins (1993) to explain the psychological and behavioural

Ontological dimension

| Epistemological dimension | | Individual | Collective |
|---|---|---|---|
| | Explicit | Embrained knowledge | Encoded knowledge |
| | Tacit | Embodied knowledge | Embedded knowledge |

FIGURE 20.1 Cognitive level: knowledge types

aspects of knowledge. Blackler (1995) adapts them to describe the different 'images' of knowledge within organizations. The typology presented here integrates the cognitive and organizational dimensions.

- *Embrained knowledge* (individual and explicit) is dependent on the individual's conceptual skills and cognitive abilities. It is formal, abstract, or theoretical knowledge. It is typically learnt through reading books and in formal education. Scientific knowledge, which focuses on the rational 'understanding' and 'knowing' of universal principles and laws of nature, belongs to this category. Embrained knowledge enjoys a privileged social status within Western culture.
- *Embodied knowledge* (individual and tacit) is action-oriented; it is the practical, individual types of knowledge on which Polanyi focused. It is learnt through experience and in training based on apprenticeship relations. Embodied knowledge is also context-specific; it is 'particular knowledge' which becomes relevant 'in light of the practical problem solving experience' (Barley, 1996). Its generation cannot be separate from application.
- *Encoded knowledge* (collective and explicit) is shared within organizations through written rules and procedures, and formal information systems. It is formed in making explicit as much as possible of tacit knowledge. This is well illustrated by the principles of Scientific Management which attempt to codify worker experiences and skills into objective scientific knowledge. Encoded knowledge is inevitably simplified and selective, for it fails to capture and preserve the tacit skills and judgement of individuals.
- *Embedded knowledge* (collective and tacit) is the collective form of knowledge residing in organizational routines and shared norms. It is the Durkhemian type of tacit knowledge based on shared beliefs and understanding within an organization which makes effective communication possible. It is rooted in an organization's 'communities-of-practice', a concept used by Brown and Duguid (1991) to denote the socially constructed and interactive nature of learning. Embedded knowledge is relation-specific, contextual, and dispersed. It is an emergent form of knowledge capable of supporting complex patterns of interaction in the absence of written rules.

## KNOWLEDGE TYPES AND ORGANIZATIONAL FORMS: FOUR CONTRASTING MODELS OF ORGANIZATIONAL LEARNING

All organizations potentially contain a mixture of knowledge types, but their relative importance differs. Organizations may be dominated by one type of knowledge rather than another. To each of the knowledge forms there corresponds an ideal type organization. Drawing upon Mintzberg's (1979) classic typology of organizational forms and the work of Aoki (1988), and Nonaka and Takeuchi (1995) on the 'Japanese model', the analysis below distinguishes four ideal typical organizational forms, using two dimensions: the degree of standardization of knowledge and work; and the dominant knowledge agent (individual or organization) (see Figure 20.2). These different organizational configurations vary in their ability to mobilize tacit knowledge, resulting in different dynamics of learning and innovation.

### 'PROFESSIONAL BUREAUCRACY' AND 'EMBRAINED KNOWLEDGE'

A professional bureaucracy, dominated by 'embrained knowledge', refers to a hierarchical complex organization where individual experts are highly specialized and where they operate within narrowly defined fields of knowledge. Coordination is achieved primarily by the standardization of knowledge and skills through the individual's formal education and training. The formal knowledge constitutes an important basis of internal work rules, job boundaries, and status. Although the professional bureaucracy accords a high degree of autonomy to individual professionals, its structure is primarily

Knowledge agent

(Autonomy and control)

Standardization
of knowledge
and work                                    Individual                          Organization

| | Individual | Organization |
|---|---|---|
| High | Professional bureaucracy<br><br>(narrow learning) | Machine bureaucracy<br><br>(superficial learning) |
| Low | Operating adhocracy<br><br>(dynamic learning) | J-form organization<br><br>(cumulative learning) |

**FIGURE 20.2**   Organizational level: learning patterns

'bureaucratic': coordination is achieved 'by design and by standards that pre-determine what is to be done' (Mintzberg, 1979: 351). The source of standardization originates outside the organization. The external education institutions and professional bodies play an important role in defining the standards and boundaries of the knowledge in use.

The individual professionals are the key knowledge agents of professional bureaucracy. They are the 'authorized experts' whose formal training and professional affiliations give them a source of authority and a repertoire of knowledge ready to apply. Problem-solving involves application of an existing body of abstract knowledge in a logical and consistent way. This inevitably restricts the use of tacit knowledge and judgemental skills in dealing with uncertainty in problem-solving. As noted by Starbuck (1992), formal expert knowledge often entails 'perceptual filters'. Professional experts have a tendency to interpret specific situations in terms of general concepts and place new problems in old categories. Mintzberg (1979) uses the term 'pigeonholing' to describe how, in a professional bureaucracy, the uncertainty in problem-solving is being contained in the jobs of single 'experts', and circumscribed within the boundary of conventional specialization. This allows the organization to uncouple the various specialist tasks and assign them to autonomous individuals, leading to a high degree of individual and functional specialization.

The knowledge structure of a professional bureaucracy is individualistic, functionally segmented, and hierarchical. Individual experts have a high degree of autonomy and discretion in the application and acquisition of knowledge within their own specialist areas, but the sharing and dissemination of such knowledge across functional boundaries are limited. The lack of a shared perspective and the formal demarcation of job boundaries inhibit the transfer of non-routine tacit knowledge in day-to-day work. Moreover, the power and status of the 'authorized experts' inhibits interaction and sharing of knowledge with the 'non-experts'. The problem of coordination in a professional bureaucracy translates itself into problems of innovation (Mintzberg, 1979: 375).

The learning focus of a professional bureaucracy tends to be narrow and constrained within the boundary of formal specialist knowledge. Tacit knowledge is circumscribed and contained; it plays a limited role in a professional bureaucracy. A professional bureaucracy can deal only with limited innovation and will get into serious difficulty when faced with radical change in the environment.

## 'MACHINE BUREAUCRACY' AND 'ENCODED KNOWLEDGE'

A machine bureaucracy depends heavily on 'encoded knowledge'. The key organizing principles are specialization, standardization, and control. This is an organizational form designed to achieve efficiency and stability, and is well suited for mass production in a stable environment. It may be said to be the ideal type of Fordist production where principles of Taylorist management are predominating. Coordination of operating tasks is achieved via standardization of work process, sharp division of labour, and close supervision. The organization displays a continuous effort to formalize operating skills and experience into objective knowledge through codification. The objective is to reduce and eliminate uncertainty in the operating tasks, or to put it in Mintzberg's words: 'the sealing off of the operating core from disruptive environmental influences' (Mintzberg, 1979: 315).

The knowledge agents of a machine bureaucracy are not the individuals directly engaged in operations, but the formal managerial hierarchy responsible for formulating the written rules, procedures, and performance standards. There is a clear dichotomy between the 'execution' and 'conception' of knowledge. The rules and procedures store the operating knowledge of the organization. The managers are the key agents responsible for translating individual knowledge into rules and procedures and for filtering information up and down the organizational hierarchy. Knowledge within the machine bureaucracy is highly fragmented and only becomes integrated at the top of the hierarchy. The organization relies heavily on management information systems for knowledge aggregation. It is a structural form in which the organization's dependence on the individual's knowledge is minimized. By forming the rules and standards for operation and by centralizing knowledge through the formal hierarchy, the organizational structure and the management information system become knowledge itself (Bonora & Revang, 1993). The whole organization operates on the basis of 'encoded knowledge'. A large part of tacit knowledge is naturally lost in the translation and aggregation process.

The knowledge structure of a machine bureaucracy is collective, functionally segmented, and hierarchical. The organization seeks to minimize the role of tacit knowledge; it operates on a partial, incomplete, and impoverished knowledge base. It learns by 'correction' through performance monitoring. It can only accumulate new knowledge through a slow process of formalization and institutionalization. It is a structure designed to deal with routine problems but is unable to cope with novelty or change.

## 'OPERATING ADHOCRACY' AND 'EMBODIED KNOWLEDGE'

This is a highly organic form of organization with little standardization of knowledge or work process. It relies not only on the formal knowledge of its members, but draws its capability from the diverse know-how and practical problem-solving skills embodied in the individual experts. The administrative function is fused with the operating task, giving the individual experts a high degree of autonomy and discretion in their work. The operating adhocracy has a strong capacity for generating tacit knowledge through experimentation and interactive problem-solving.

Coordination in the operating adhocracy is achieved via direct interaction and mutual adjustment among the individual experts operating in market-based project teams. Organizations engaged in providing non-standard, creative, and problem-solving services directly to the clients, such as professional partnerships, software engineering firms, and management consultancies, are typical examples. In these organizations, formal professional knowledge may play only a limited role; a large part of the problem-solving activities has very little to do with the application of narrow standardized expertise and more to do with the experience and capacity to adapt to new situations. Hence, the importance of 'embodied skills' and 'know-how competencies'. Starbuck's (1992) concept of 'knowledge-intensive firms', which emphasizes the significance of 'esoteric expertise' over commonplace standardized knowledge, illustrates the idiosyncratic nature of the knowledge base underlying an operating adhocracy. Sveiby's and Lloyd's (1987) idea of 'know-how companies' in which technical and managerial expertise are integrated suggests the broad-based and varied nature of the knowledge required for creative problem-solving in such organizations.

The knowledge structure of an operating adhocracy is individualistic but collaborative. The individual experts deployed in market-based project teams are the key knowledge agents. Learning occurs as experts of diverse backgrounds jointly solve shared problems. Unlike in the professional bureaucracy, learning is not confined within the boundary of conventional specialization; it is broad-based and draws upon the diverse experiences and know-how of different experts. Quinn (1992) stresses the importance of 'inter-dependent professionalism' in an operating adhocracy. Learning occurs on multiple levels as shifting teams of experts regroup in line with market-based problems. The individual's performance is assessed in terms of market outcomes; the ultimate judges of their expertise are their clients, and not the professional bodies (Starbuck, 1992). Hence, a strong incentive to engage in 'extended occupational learning', and the accumulation of tacit skills beyond the pursuit of formal knowledge.

The knowledge base of an operating adhocracy is diverse, varied, and 'organic'. A large part of the knowledge in use is organic, i.e. tacit knowledge generated through interaction, trial-and-error, and experimentation. It is an organization capable of divergent thinking, innovation, and creative problem-solving.

Operating adhocracies are fluid and fast-moving organizations. The speed of learning and unlearning is critical for their survival in a complex and dynamic environment. This, however, creates potential problems in knowledge accumulation. The frequent restructuring and shifting of individuals between project teams mean that tacit knowledge may not be fully and adequately articulated before an individual moves on. Another related problem is knowledge retention. The organization's competence is embodied in its members' market-based know-how and skills which are potentially transferable. This makes the organization vulnerable to the loss of its competencies to potential competitors. Starbuck (1992: 725), for instance, talks about the 'porous boundaries' of the 'knowledge-intensive firms' and points out that these organizations often find it hard to keep unique expertise exclusive. The operating adhocracy is the most innovative and yet least stable form of organization.

## 'J-FORM' ORGANIZATION AND 'EMBEDDED KNOWLEDGE'

An organization which derives its capability from knowledge that is 'embedded' in its operating routines, team relationships, and shared culture can be described as a 'J-form' organization. The term 'J-form' is used because its archetypical features are best illustrated by the 'Japanese type' of organization, such as Nonaka's and Takeuchi's (1995) 'knowledge creating companies', and Aoki's (1986, 1988) model of the 'J-form'. The J-form organization combines the stability and efficiency of a bureaucracy with the flexibility and team dynamics of an adhocracy. It allows an organic, non-hierarchical team structure to operate in parallel with its formal hierarchical managerial structure. These two structural layers are 'glued' together by a strong corporate culture, which constitute the third layer—the knowledge base of the organization. Coordination is achieved via horizontal coordination and mutual adjustment. This is reinforced by shared values embedded in the organizational culture. Nonaka and Takeuchi (1995) use the term 'hypertext organization', an analogy borrowed from computer science, to illustrate the dynamic interaction between the different layers of the organization and the freedom of the members to switch among the different contexts. They argue that the dynamic interaction among the different contexts facilitates the interaction between tacit and explicit knowledge, which ultimately determines the capability of the organization to create new knowledge.

The key knowledge agent in the J-form organization is neither the autonomous individual expert nor the controlling managerial hierarchy, but the semi-autonomous project team, comprising members from different functions. The cross-functional team integrates and synthesizes knowledge across different areas of expertise and serves as a bridge between the individual and the organization. It is at the level of the team, positioning at the intersection of horizontal and vertical flows of knowledge, where the greatest intensity of interaction, learning, and knowledge diffusion take place within the J-form organization. Similar to the operating adhocracy, a great deal of the learning occurs through shared work experiences and joint problem-solving.

However, unlike the operating adhocracy where the temporary nature of the project team inhibits the transfer of the knowledge generated beyond the level of the team, the J-form organization is capable of diffusing the knowledge widely throughout the entire organization. This occurs as members rotate across functional units and as they return from their temporary assignments to their formal positions. The formal structure in the J-form organization constitutes an important integrating mechanism. It captures the tacit knowledge generated and stores it at the level of the organization for future use. While the operating team is the focal point for the acquisition and generation of knowledge, the dissemination of knowledge in the J-form organization is organization-wide. Knowledge stored in the formal hierarchy constitutes only a small part of the knowledge base of the J-form organization. A large part of the knowledge in use is stored organically in the operating routines, and networks of human relations.

The J-form organization is adaptive and innovative. It is marked by a tremendous capacity to generate, diffuse, and accumulate tacit knowledge continuously through 'learning-by-doing' and interaction. New knowledge is generated through fusion, synthesis, and combination of the existing knowledge base. It has a unique capability to generate innovation continuously and incrementally. However, learning in the J-form organization is also potentially conservative. Its stable social structure and shared knowledge base can reduce the capabilities of the organization to learn from individual deviance and the discovery of contrary experience (Dodgson, 1993: 383; Levinthal & March, 1993: 108). The J-form organization may find it difficult to innovate radically.

## THE INSTITUTIONAL FRAMEWORK: LEARNING AND ORGANIZATIONAL EMBEDDEDNESS

Organizations are socially constituted and their knowledge configurations reflect this. The relative dominance of the different knowledge types, and the ability of an organization to harness tacit knowledge as a source of learning, are powerfully influenced by the broader societal and institutional factors. The 'societal' approach, for example, demonstrates an interactive relationship between patterns of work organization and the education and training system, and types of labour markets and careers. Maurice et al. (1986), in their comparative studies of organizational structures in France, Britain, and Germany, emphasize how the different ways and degrees to which workers are qualified and promoted shape the patterns of coordination and work organization in the three countries. They speak about the degree of 'professionality' with which tasks are accomplished by different categories of the workforce. By this they mean the relative importance of formal knowledge vs mastery of practical (tacit) skills, and the formal recognition of qualifications. Their study underlines the importance of education and training as a key institutional factor shaping the knowledge configurations and patterns of social interaction within firms.

The role of the formal education and qualification system in defining the knowledge and competence criteria within organizations is closely related to the nature of labour market organization: the extent to which organization of skills and careers are governed by markets or firms. This broad distinction draws attention to the major differences between an occupation-based labour market (OLM) and a firm-based internal labour market (ILM) (Marsden, 1986). Generally speaking, an OLM implies a higher degree of market control over skills and competence criteria and hence a stronger tendency towards formalization and codification of knowledge across firms. In contrast, an ILM allows a greater degree of individual firm control over the definition of expertise, leading to a lower level of standardization of expertise around formal knowledge.

The education and labour market dimensions are inextricably linked and there is an institutional logic defining their specific configurations (see Figure 20.3). This section examines how these institutional

Labour markets (careers and mobility)

|  | OLM (Market) | ILM (Firm) |
|---|---|---|
| Education and training (degree of formalization and academic bias) | | |
| High | Professional model | Bureaucratic model |
| Low | Occupational community model | Organizational community model |

**FIGURE 20.3**  Societal level: education and labour markets

configurations interact with organizational structures and processes to generate different types of knowledge, patterns of learning, and innovation.

## EDUCATION AND TRAINING SYSTEMS: 'NARROW ELITISM' VS 'BROAD-BASED EGALITARIANISM'

On the education and training dimension, national systems can vary according to the relative importance they attach to different types of knowledge (e.g. formal academic knowledge vs practical skills), and the distribution of competence among the entire workforce. A narrow and elitist system is characterized by the dominance of formal academic knowledge and a highly uneven two-tier distribution of competence: a well-developed higher-education system for the elite while the majority of the workforce is poorly trained. For example, the system in the UK and the USA can be described as 'elitist'. It displays a strong bias towards academic education and attaches little social status and economic credibility to practical skills which acts as a disincentive for investment in this area. As a result, there is a widespread lack of formal intermediate skills and qualifications among the general workforce in these two countries (Buechtemann & Verdier, 1998). Such a system creates a bias in the use of human capital and labour market polarization. It is associated with a bureaucratic form of work organization. The wide disparity in the educational backgrounds and skill levels between the different categories of the workforce generates knowledge discontinuities and social distance within firms. It reinforces the domination of formal knowledge over tacit skills.

In contrast, a broad-based education and training system recognizes the value of both academic education and vocational training. It is characterized by a widespread and rigorous general and vocational education for a wide spectrum of the workforce. Such a system is more conducive to a decentralized mode of work organization. A more even distribution of competence among the workforce provides a better basis for interactive learning and the cultivation of tacit knowledge as a source of organizational capability. The cases of Germany and Japan are illustrative (Koike, 1995; Soskice, 1997). The systems in these countries accord relatively high social status to 'practical experience', and recognize it as a source of competence and qualification. This encourages investment in vocational training which has resulted in a good supply of intermediate skills. This enables firms to organize work in a more cooperative and decentralized manner, conducive to the transmission and mobilization of tacit knowledge.

## Labour Markets and Careers: Occupational and Internal Labour Markets

Labour markets and the nature of employment relationship influence the knowledge base and learning capabilities of the firm in three main ways. First, these determine the extent to which expertise is developed outside or within the firm, and hence the relative importance of formal education and training institutions *vis-à-vis* employers in defining the knowledge base of the firm. Second, they determine career mobility and incentives for individual workers and the capability of the firm in acquiring and accumulating different types of knowledge. And third, they shape the individual's career and social identity and define the boundaries of learning.

## Occupational Labour Market (OLM)

An occupational labour market (OLM) offers a relatively high scope for job mobility. Knowledge and learning are embedded in an inter-firm career. A large part of the knowledge and skills required is developed outside the firm, or within the firm but according to inter-firm occupational standards. Formal education and training play a much greater role in generating directly relevant occupational competence, and hence exert a direct influence on the knowledge base of firms. The type of qualifications generated can be highly task-specific based on standardized, advanced 'packaging' of knowledge and skills (e.g. craft-oriented training or professional education). Alternatively, it can be a broad-based general education providing the 'meta-competences' that can be adapted and applied across a wide variety of work settings and tasks (Nordhaug, 1993). The former approach assumes that the task environment is relatively stable and the knowledge required can be codified and pre-packaged in initial training programmes. The latter, in contrast, rests on the notion that the task environment is uncertain and the knowledge required is fluid and emergent. It cannot be easily bundled into occupations or codified in advance, and hence requires a broad-based initial qualification to enable individuals to pursue a more varied and flexible approach to continuous learning.

In an OLM, knowledge and skills are owned by and embodied in the individuals; they are personal properties for career advancement. The transparency and transferability of the knowledge acquired are of paramount importance for inter-firm career mobility. Such career mobility relies on effective signals: dependable information about the type and quality of skills and knowledge that individuals have. This can be based either on public certification (institutional signals), or peer group recognition (information signals). The former approach works well provided that the knowledge and skills required can be easily identified and codified, i.e. bundled into specific occupations with a distinctive set of tasks or problems to which these skills and knowledge are applied (Tolbert, 1996: 336–337). In situations where the tasks are highly fluid and unpredictable, and the knowledge used constitutes a large tacit component, institutional signals become insufficient and unreliable. This is because tacit skills cannot be easily codified; they can only be revealed through practice and work performance. Their transfer will have to rely heavily on social and professional networks based on shared industrial or occupational norms. In other words, the efficient transfer and accumulation of tacit knowledge in an OLM require the support of a 'containing social structure', for example, the formation of a community-based OLM based on localised firm networks and industry clusters (DeFillippi & Arthur, 1996; Saxenian, 1996). Social networks facilitate the 'marketability' of cumulative personal tacit skills.

Learning within an OLM tends to be person-centred and market-oriented. It is rooted in the individual's professional and career strategy, and characterized by a greater degree of autonomy and latitude in the boundary and domains of learning. Learning may occur not only within the confines of the firm and the groups and networks attached to the firm, but also within the individual's professional and social networks which extend beyond the firm (Bird, 1996). This can potentially enlarge the knowledge base of the firm. Moreover, firms operating in an OLM can add variety and diversity to their knowledge base through external recruitment. The greater degree of mobility in the labour market allows firms closely to align their knowledge base with shifting market requirements and technological changes.

## INTERNAL LABOUR MARKET (ILM)

Internal labour markets are characterized by long-term stable employment with a single employer and career progression through a series of interconnected jobs within a hierarchy. Knowledge and learning are embedded in an intra-firm career; a large part of the knowledge and work-related skills is generated through firm-specific on-the-job training (OJT). Formal knowledge acquired through education serves only as an entry qualification and provides the basis upon which work-related skills are built within the firm. The nature of the work organization and careers determines the quality and boundaries of learning through OJT.

Where jobs are narrowly defined and careers are organized around hierarchies of jobs with tiered boundaries based on formal entry qualifications as in the case of a machine bureaucracy, OJT will tend to be narrow and job-specific, and the opportunities for career progression based on OJT will be limited. Narrow OJT reduces the variety of the individual's experience and hence limits the scope for creative thinking and the generation of tacit knowledge (Nonaka, 1994: 21). The containment of learning within a single job prevents the creation of common understanding and knowledge integration. Moreover, the association of formal knowledge with higher positions implies that tacit skills accumulated through practical experience will be under-valued and not recognized as a basis for promotion. The incentives for individuals to accumulate such knowledge are weakened and the organization fails to exploit the potential of 'learning-by-doing'. An ILM based on narrow job specialization and a career structure characterized by clear tier boundaries generates a fragmented and hierarchical knowledge base.

In contrast, an ILM can also be organized around broadly defined jobs and a continuous career hierarchy based on a common ranking system (e.g. the case of Japan). Progression to upper-level positions is achieved, in this case, through accumulation of a wide range of skills and organizational experience. Formal knowledge plays only a limited role in defining competence criteria and entry to senior positions; the key emphasis is on the long-term accumulation of firm-specific skills and practical experience. OJT is broad-based and linked systemically with career progression. Broad-based OJT increases the variety of experience and facilitates the generation of tacit knowledge. Job rotation also serves an important socialization function and helps to reduce social distance between different categories of the workforce. The close integration of OJT with career progression also gives individuals a strong incentive to accumulate knowledge through practical experience. The career hierarchy becomes a device for tacit knowledge creation and learning.

Learning within an ILM tends to be organizational-oriented and self-reinforcing. It evolves along the internal requirement of the firm, and is rooted in a firm-based career and organizational identity. The stability of personnel within an ILM facilitates the retention and accumulation of knowledge. Organizational memory becomes an important source of learning (Huber, 1991: 105). It allows firms to exploit its knowledge base on a continuous basis, linking their past and present activities and extend to future possibilities (Hamel & Heene, 1994). Firms may display a strong capacity in incremental innovation and focus on developing a distinctive core competence (Prahalad & Hamel, 1990; Leonard-Barton, 1992). The career structures that encourage social identification, however, may also reduce the firm's capability to learn from individual deviance and inhibits the insertion of radical skills.

## FOUR CONTRASTING 'SOCIETAL' MODELS OF ORGANIZING KNOWLEDGE AND LEARNING

The interaction between education and labour market institutions gives rise to four contrasting institutional configurations underpinning the different organizational forms and knowledge types discussed earlier. These institutional configurations can be taken to represent different 'societal' models of organizing knowledge and learning: the 'professional', 'bureaucratic', 'occupational community', and 'organizational community' models (see Figures 20.3 and 20.4). Their effects on the learning and innovative capabilities of firms are mediated through the different organizational forms. The term

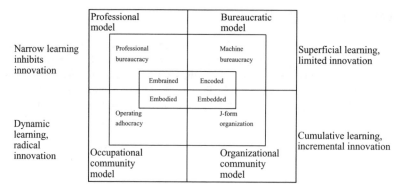

**FIGURE 20.4**   Knowledge, organizations, and institutions: three inter-locking levels

'societal' requires some qualification. It is used in a broad sense to point out the effect of institutional environments on ways of organizing knowledge and learning, rather than simply to emphasize national distinctiveness. The institutional environment may exist at the societal, regional, or sector levels. Although dominant models may exist in countries, it is also possible to find a variety or mixture of models in the same country. The four contrasting 'societal' models described below are archetypes, not country 'averages'.

## THE PROFESSIONAL MODEL

The professional model is characterized by a narrow, elitist education based on a high degree of formalization of knowledge. It is rooted in an open labour market based on a high level of occupational codification and specialization. The system is geared to the generation of explicit knowledge and favours an individual approach to learning; the incentives and social structure required for the diffusion and accumulation of tacit knowledge are relatively weak. The professional model gives rise to the dominance of the 'professional bureaucracy' and 'embrained knowledge' within firms. It prevails in countries where the notion of 'professionalism' is deeply rooted in the fabric of societal institutions, such as Britain and the USA. The professional model generates a narrow approach to learning and inhibits innovation.

## THE BUREAUCRATIC MODEL

The bureaucratic model shares many common characteristics with the professional model on the formal education and training dimension. However, it is rooted in an ILM organized around narrowly defined jobs and a tiered career hierarchy. These institutional features underpin the 'machine bureaucracy' dominated by 'encoded knowledge'. Crozier's (1964) portrayal of the French type of organization epitomizes this category. The bureaucratic model seeks to control and eliminate tacit knowledge. It generates a superficial approach to learning and has little capacity to innovate.

## THE OCCUPATIONAL COMMUNITY MODEL

The occupational community model is rooted in a region-based OLM surrounding a cluster of interdependent occupations and firms. It is characterized by a high rate of inter-firm mobility which fosters the development of social networks and transmission of knowledge. It provides an institutional framework and social infrastructure for tacit learning to emerge. The occupational community is an institutional prerequisite for fostering and sustaining the innovative capability of the 'operating adhocracy'. In a 'boundaryless' open labour market, the operating adhocracy will be under pressure to bureaucratize because of the difficulties in accumulating and transferring tacit knowledge. The tacit knowledge-creating capability of the operating adhocracy can only be sustained if it operates as a member of a localized firm network. An archetypical example is Silicon Valley where a fluid OLM is embedded in a rich fabric of regional and professional networks (Rogers & Larsen, 1984). Such networks of social relationships provide the 'social capital' and 'information signals' needed to ensure the efficient transfer of tacit knowledge in an inter-firm career framework (Saxenian, 1996: 36). The shared industry-specific values within the regional community ensure that tacit knowledge will not be wasted when one changes employers, and thus gives the individual a positive incentive to engage in tacit 'know-how' learning (DeFillipi & Arthur, 1996: 123). The occupational community also fosters the 'know-who' network that supports high rates of job mobility. Tacit knowledge is made visible through social reputation in a community-based OLM.

A community-based OLM creates a stable social structure within an open labour market. The inter-firm career mobility and social networks provide multiple learning opportunities which amplify the learning and innovative capability of the firm. Learning is not confined within the boundaries of individual firms; it draws on the knowledge base of the community as a whole. The community's social and technical networks operate as a kind of superorganization, through which individuals and firms, in shifting combinations, engage in 'experimentation, entrepreneurship, and interactive learning' (Saxenian, 1996: 30).

## THE ORGANIZATIONAL COMMUNITY MODEL

The organizational community model is characterized by a broad-based education system and an ILM based on broadly defined jobs and a continuous career hierarchy. It favours the J-form organization typically found in Japan. The organizational community model generates a decentralized and cooperative approach to problem-solving. It facilitates the transmission and accumulation of tacit knowledge through collective learning within a stable career hierarchy. It has a unique capability to generate innovation continuously and incrementally. Learning within the organizational community, however, is bounded within the firm-based ILM. This generates conservatism and inhibits radical innovation.

## TWO ALTERNATIVE MODELS OF LEARNING AND INNOVATION

The above four contrasting 'societal' models illustrate the logic of institutionalized variation in the organization of knowledge and patterns of learning. The key factor that differentiates their learning capability is their ability to create organizational relationships for harnessing tacit knowledge. The analysis suggests that both the 'occupational' and 'organizational community models' are favourable to this. However, the different labour market structures generate some significant differences in their learning and innovation patterns.

The occupational community supports the operating adhocracy, and the organizational community supports the J-form organization. Individuals enjoy a much greater degree of autonomy in the operating adhocracy; their careers and social identity are rooted in the wider occupational community. In contrast, the J-form organization emphasizes the close integration of the individuals into the organizational community. These differences are reflected in their dominant knowledge types and learning patterns. The operating adhocracy derives its capability from the knowledge and skills embodied in the individual experts. It is a 'knowledge-intensive', market-based organization focusing on the strategic advantage of continuous change, adaptation, and entrepreneurship. In contrast, the J-form organization draws its capability from the collective knowledge 'embedded' in the organization's routines and shared values.

It adopts a firm-centred approach to learning. It is a 'knowledge-distributing' organization, depending on the collective competence of its members. It derives its competitive strength from the cultivation of firm-specific core competence. The contrasting strategies adopted by the two models generate different types of organizational capabilities and innovation patterns. The occupational community model facilitates the diffusion of tacit knowledge within a broader boundary and varied contexts. It encourages experimentation and entrepreneurial behaviour and has the potential to achieve radical innovation. The organizational community model, however, allows the accumulation of tacit knowledge within the boundary of the firm. It has the capacity to enhance its knowledge base through internalization and absorption. It is geared to incremental innovation.

Despite these differences, the two models share an important common feature: the role of tacit knowledge in generating learning and innovation within 'communities-of-practice' (Brown & Duguid, 1991), albeit on a different scale. They suggest that learning and innovation cannot be separated from social interaction and practical experience, both of which are vital processes for tacit knowledge creation.

## CONCLUSION

This chapter has suggested a conceptual framework for understanding the interdependent relationships between patterns of learning, organizational forms, and societal institutions. It argues that knowledge configurations of firms and patterns of learning cannot be separated from specific organizational forms and institutions. Although the recent literature has stressed the importance of tacit knowledge in organizational learning and innovation, it has ignored the role of societal institutions in shaping this. Much of the literature in organizational learning has tended to focus on learning and knowledge-creation processes within organizations to the exclusion of their institutional contexts. In contrast, research on national innovation systems (Lundvall, 1992; Nelson, 1993), and more recently, the 'varieties of capitalism' literature (e.g. Whitley, 1999), emphasize the importance of macro-level societal institutions in shaping the learning and innovative capabilities of firms. However, this strand of research has not given adequate attention to patterns of learning and knowledge creation at the micro-level. The framework developed in this chapter provides a bridge between these two contrasting strands of analysis to arrive at a more comprehensive understanding of the nature of organizational learning.

The four-fold typology developed in the chapter illustrates the logic of institutionalized variation in patterns of learning and knowledge creation. Such typologies are useful, in so far as one does not treat them as descriptive models for making unqualified generalizations about specific countries. While specific societal modes of organizing knowledge and learning do exist, societies do not usually fall unambiguously into one of the four types. Putting aside the 'societal specificity' debate, a fruitful line of inquiry would be to explore how such institutionalized variation may enable, or constrain, firms and countries to create different organizational forms needed to generate the types of learning and innovation associated with different technologies or industrial sectors.

The typology also provides a useful framework for analysing the direction of organizational change in terms of moving from one archetype to another. Much of the current debate about developing learning organizations concerns the move away from bureaucratic models towards either the 'J-form' organization or 'operating adhocracy'. Given the 'social embeddedness of organizations', one would expect such radical organizational change—that is, movement from one archetype to another—to be rare. However, radical organizational change does occur and learning plays an important part in facilitating such a change process. An important area for future research would be to arrive at a better understanding of how the intra-organizational dynamics of learning and knowledge creation interact with the institutional context to bring about radical shifts in organizational models.

# REFERENCES

Aoki, M. (1986) Horizontal vs. vertical information structure of the firm. *American Economic Review*, **December**, 971–983.

Aoki, M. (1988) *Information, Incentives and Bargaining in the Japanese Economy*. Cambridge: Cambridge University Press.

Argyris, C. & Schön, D. (1978) *Organizational Learning: A Theory of Action Perspective*. Reading, MA: Addison-Wesley.

Barley, S.R. (1996) Technicians in the workplace: ethnographic evidence for bringing work into organization studies. *Administrative Science Quarterly*, **41**(3), 404–441.

Bird, A. (1996) Careers as repositories of knowledge: considerations for boundaryless careers. In M.B. Arthur & D.M. Rousseau (eds) *The Boundaryless Career: A New Employment Principle for a New Organizational Era* (pp. 150–168). New York: Oxford University Press.

Blackler, F. (1995) Knowledge, knowledge work and organizations: an overview and interpretation. *Organization Studies*, **16**(6), 1021–1046.

Boisot, M.H. (1995a) *Information Space: A Framework for Learning in Organizations, Institutions and Culture*. London and New York: Routledge.

Boisot, M.H. (1995b) Is your firm a creative destroyer? Competitive learning and knowledge shows in the technological strategies of firms. *Research Policy*, **24**, 489–506.

Bonora, E.A. & Revang, O. (1993) A framework for analyzing the storage and protection of knowledge in organizations. In P. Lorange, B. Chakravarthy, J. Roos & A. Van de Ven (eds) *Implementing Strategic Processes: Change, Learning and Co-operation* (pp. 190–213). Oxford: Blackwell.

Brown, J.S. & Duguid, P. (1991) Organizational learning and communities of practice: towards a unified view of working, learning and innovation. *Organization Science*, **2**(1), 40–57.

Brown, J.S. & Duguid, P. (1998) Organizing knowledge. *California Management Review*, **40**(3), 90–111.

Buechtemann, C.F. & Verdier, E. (1998) Education and training regimes: macro-institutional evidence. *Revue d'économie politique*, **108**(3), 291–320.

Collins, H.M. (1993) The structure of knowledge. *Social Research*, **60**(1), 95–116.

Crozier, M. (1964) *The Bureaucratic Phenomenon*. Chicago: University of Chicago Press.

DeFillippi, R.J. & Arthur, M.B. (1996) Boundaryless contexts and careers: a competency-based perspective. In M.B. Arthur & D.M. Rousseau (eds) *The Boundaryless Career: A New Employment Principle for a New Organizational Era* (pp. 116–131). New York: Oxford University Press.

Dodgson, M. (1993) Organizational learning: a review of some literatures. *Organization Studies*, **14**(3), 375–394.

Eliasson, G. (1996) *Firm Objectives, Controls and Organization*. Dordrecht: Kluwer Academic Publishers.

Finegold, D. & Soskice, D. (1988) The failure of training in Britain: analysis and prescription. *Oxford Review of Economic Policy*, **4**(3), 21–53.

Foray, D. & Lundvall, B.A. (1996) The knowledge-based economy: from the economics of knowledge to the learning economy. In *Employment and Growth in the Knowledge-Based Economy*. Paris: OECD.

Freeman, C. (1987) *Technology and Economic Performance: Lessons from Japan*. London: Pinter Publishers.

Freeman, C. (1995) The national system of innovation in historical perspective. *Cambridge Journal of Economics*, **19**, 5–24.

Glynn, M.A. (1996) Innovative genius: a framework for relating individual and organizational intelligence to innovation. *Academy of Management Review*, **21**(4), 1081–1111.

Granovetter, M. (1985) Economic action and social structure: the problem of embeddedness. *American Journal of Sociology*, **91**(3), 481–510.

Grant, R.M. (1996) Toward a knowledge-based theory of the firm. *Strategic Management Journal*, **17**, 109–122.

Hamel, G. & Heene, A. (1994) *Competence-Based Competition*. Chichester: John Wiley & Sons, Ltd.

Hedlund, G. (1993) Models of knowledge management in the West and Japan. In P. Lorange et al. (eds) *Implementing Strategic Processes: Change, Learning and Co-operation* (pp. 117–144). Oxford: Blackwell.

Hedlund, G. (1994) A model of knowledge management and the N-form corporation. *Strategic Management Journal*, **15**, 73–90.

Huber, G.P. (1991) Organizational learning: the contributing processes and the literatures. *Organization Science*, **2**(1), 89–115.

Karnoe, P. (1996) The social process of competence building. *International Journal of Technology Management*. Special Publication on Unlearning and Learning, **11**(7–8), 770–789.

Kogut, B. & Zander, U. (1992) Knowledge of the firm, combinative capabilities, and the replication of technology. *Organization Science*, **3**(3), 383–397.

Kogut, B. & Zander, U. (1996) What firms do? Coordination, identity and learning. *Organization Science*, **7**(5), 502–518.

Koike, K. (1986) *Gendai no jinzai keisei* (Contemporary skills formation). Kyoto: Minerubiya.

Koike, K. (1995) *The Economics of Work in Japan*. Tokyo: LTCB International Library Foundation.

Lam, A. (1996) Engineers, management and work organization: a comparative analysis of engineers' work roles in British and Japanese electronics firms. *Journal of Management Studies*, **33**(2), 183–212.

Lam, A. (1997) Embedded firms, embedded knowledge: problems of collaboration and knowledge transfer in global cooperative ventures. *Organization Studies*, **18**(6), 973–996.

Lam, A. (2000) Tacit knowledge, organizational learning, societal institutions: an integrated framework. *Organization Studies*, **21**(3), 487–513.

Lave, J. & Wenger, E. (1991) *Peripheral Legitimated Learning*. Cambridge: Cambridge University Press.

Leonard-Barton, D. (1992) Core capabilities and core rigidities: a paradox in managing new product development. *Strategic Management Journal*, **13**, 111–125.

Levinthal, D.A. & March, J.G. (1993) The myopia of learning. *Strategic Management Journal*, **14**, 95–112.

Lundvall, B.-A. (1992) *National Systems of Innovation: Towards a Theory of Innovation and Interactive Learning*. London: Pinter Publishers.

Marsden, D. (1986) *The End of Economic Man*. New York: St Martin's Press.

Maurice, M. (1995) The social foundations of technical innovation: engineers and the division of labour in France and Japan. In W. Littek & T. Charles (eds) *The New Division of Labour: Emerging Forms of Work Organization in International Perspectives* (pp. 317–347). New York: Walter de Gruyter.

Maurice, M., Sellier, F. & Silvestre, J.-J. (1986) *The Social Foundations of Industrial Power: A Comparison of France and Germany*. Cambridge, MA: MIT Press.

Maurice, M., Sorge, A. & Warner, M. (1980) Societal difference in organizing manufacturing units: a comparison of France, West Germany and Great Britain. *Organization Studies*, **1**(1), 59–86.

Mintzberg, H. (1979) *The Structure of Organizations*. Englewood Cliffs, NJ: Prentice Hall.

Nelson, R.R. (1993) *National Innovation Systems: A Comparative Analysis*. Oxford: Oxford University Press.

Nelson R.R. & Winter, S.G. (1982) *An Evolutionary Theory of Economic Change*. Cambridge, MA: The Belknap Press of Harvard University Press.

Nonaka, I. (1994) A dynamic theory of organizational knowledge creation. *Organization Science*, **5**, 14–37.

Nonaka, I. & Takeuchi, H. (1995) *The Knowledge Creating Company*. New York: Oxford University Press.

Nordhaug, O. (1993) *Human Capital in Organizations: Competence, Training and Learning*. Oslo: Scandinavian University Press.

Penrose, E.T. (1959) *The Theory of the Growth of the Firm*. New York: John Wiley & Sons, Ltd.

Polanyi, M. (1962) *Personal Knowledge: Towards a Post-Critical Philosophy*. New York: Harper Torchbooks.

Polanyi, M. (1966) *The Tacit Dimension*. New York: Anchor Day Books.

Prahalad, C.K. & Hamel, G. (1990) The core competence of the corporation. *Harvard Business Review*, **May/June**, 79–91.

Prais, S. (1993) *Productivity, Education and Training: Britain and Other Countries Compared*. London: National Institute of Economic and Social Research.

Quinn, J.B. (1992) *Intelligent Enterprise: A Knowledge and Service Based Paradigm for Industry*. New York: The Free Press.

Reich, R. (1992) *The Work of Nations*. New York: Vintage Press.

Rogers, E.M. & Larsen, J.K. (1984) *Silicon Valley Fever: Growth of High-Technology Culture*. London: Allen and Unwin.

Saxenian, A. (1996) Beyond boundaries: open labour markets and learning in the Silicon Valley. In M.B. Arthur & D.M. Rousseau (eds) *The Boundaryless Career: A New Employment Principle for a New Organizational Era* (pp. 23–39). New York: Oxford University Press.

Sorge, A. (1991) Strategic fit and the societal effect: interpreting cross-national comparisons of technology, organization and human resources. *Organization Studies*, **12**(2), 161–190.

Sorge, A. & Warner, M. (1986) *Comparative Factory Organization: An Anglo-German Comparison of Management and Manpower in Manufacturing*. Aldershot: Gower.

Soskice, D. (1997) German technology policy, innovation, and national institutional frameworks. *Industry and Innovation*, **4**, 75–96.

Spender, J.C. (1996a) Making knowledge the basis of a dynamic theory of the firm. *Strategic Management Journal*, **17** (Winter Special Issue), 45–62.

Spender, J.C. (1996b) Organizational knowledge, learning and memory: three concepts in search of a theory. *Journal of Organizational Change Management*, **9**(1), 63–78.

Starbuck, W.H. (1992) Learning by knowledge-intensive firms. *Journal of Management Studies*, **29**(6), 713–740.

Sveiby, K. & Lloyd, T. (1987) *Managing Knowhow: Add Value by Valuing Creativity*. London: Bloomsbury.

Tolbert, P.S. (1996) Occupations, organizations, and boundaryless careers. In M.B. Arthur & D.M. Rousseau (eds) *The Boundaryless Career: A New Employment Principle for a New Organizational Era* (pp. 331–349). New York: Oxford University Press.

Tsoukas, H. (1996) The firm as a distributed knowledge system: a constructionist approach. *Strategic Management Journal*, **17** (Winter Special issue), 11–25.

Wenger, E. (1998). *Communities of Practice: Learning, Meaning, and Identity*. Cambridge: Cambridge University Press.

Whitley, R. (1999) *Divergent Capitalism: The Social Structuring and Change of Business Systems*. Oxford: Oxford University Press.

Winter, S.G. (1987) Knowledge and competence as strategic assets. In D.J. Teece (ed.) *The Competitive Challenge: Strategies for Industrial Innovation and Renewal* (pp. 159–184). Cambridge, MA: Ballinger.

# Conclusion
## Some Reflections and Perspectives on Organizing, Changing, and Learning

### Jaap Boonstra
*Sioo, Utrecht, and University of Amsterdam, Amsterdam, The Netherlands*

This final chapter reflects on theories, methodologies, and practices which have been presented in this book on the dynamics of organizational change and learning. In the Introduction to this book it was stated that almost three-quarters of all change efforts fail to achieve the intended result. The authors of this book wish to contribute to achieving better results in changing organizations. We want to understand the dynamics of organizational change and learning, untangle the mysteries of change processes, and we would like to share our knowledge, experience, and reflections. This book offers no clear set of 'rules of thumb' or 'best ways' to change organizations effectively. Together we present theoretical insights, implications, methods, and critical reflections. We strongly believe that the presentation of divergent perspectives in this book may be useful in developing new knowledge and new perspectives. By doing so, we hope to encourage practitioners, scholars, and scientists to reflect on their own practices and theories, to elaborate on their own fascinations, and to develop and explain their own methodologies.

This chapter starts with reflections on the dynamics of organizational change and learning. It compares multiple perspectives on change and learning, and explores tensions between the perspectives. The second section summarizes change methods presented in this book, and links them to assumptions and values in organizational change. The third section focuses on specific issues in organizational change and learning. This chapter concludes with opportunities and questions the dynamics of organizational change and learning.

## DYNAMICS IN ORGANIZATIONAL CHANGE AND LEARNING

There is no consensus on a workable set of principles in organizational change and learning. Theories and practices of change and learning are rooted in deeply held assumptions and values. This means that it is useful to make the values that underlie different approaches to change and learning explicit and the subject of discussion.

### Multiple Perspectives on Changing and Organizing

The first Part of this book focuses on Organization Development (OD). Several definitions of OD have been presented, but there seems to be no accepted general definition, although some distinctions are recognizable (see the chapters in Part I).

- Basic values in organizing are a strong belief in human potential, participation in the workplace, and interpersonal relationships based on trust and openness.
- Basic values for change are employee participation in the change process, and learning through feedback and collective reflection by all actors.
- Human beings are seen as being inherently good, creative, and searching for new experiences to develop their potential.
- Human beings are open, purposeful people who use conversation in preparation for concerted action and constructing realities.
- Organizations are seen as purposeful, social, and technical systems in interaction with each other.
- Organizations are seen as open systems in interaction with their environment.
- Change is aimed at enabling organizations to be effective in their relations with their environment, and to contribute to the quality of work life.
- Change is treated not as discrete events, but as a process with phases and logical flows.
- Change practices and interventions are based on the application of behavioural science.
- Change practices rely on knowledge about individuals and their relationships in organizations, the division and coordination of labour, and organizational strategies.
- Learning is a collective, ongoing, and cognitive activity of all participants in change and is fuelled by experimentation in and reflection on practices and methodologies.
- Knowledge of organizing and changing is gained through the collaboration between practitioners and researchers in change processes, and through action research using local knowledge.

A key issue for OD is to integrate the interests and needs of individuals with the collective interest of organizations. OD consultants prefer cooperation to conflict, self-control to institutional control, and participative leadership to autocratic management (see also Buelens & Devos, Chapter 4).

Part II centres on planned change. The focus of planned change is on realizing competitive advantage and stakeholders' value. Basic values of planned change are less pronounced; nevertheless, some distinction can be made (see the chapters in Part II).

- A basic value in organizing is the need for organizations to adjust to environmental changes and market demands by implementing new organizational arrangements based on the customer value stream.
- A basic value for change is an integrated approach steered by management which pays attention to business strategy, corporate structure, management processes, technology, and social capital.
- Human beings are seen as the social capital of the organization with skills and capabilities to perform objectives and contribute to the value stream.
- Human beings are motivated by challenging jobs, and are willing to change when they see advantages for themselves.
- Organizing is a primary business process in terms of a horizontal stream of value-added activities focused on customers and clients.
- When organizing, the boundaries between the organization and the environment are blurred, due to external networks with suppliers and customers, and strategic alliances with competitors.
- Change is induced by market demands and changing environments, and is aimed at achieving performance measures in order to realize competitive advantage.
- Change takes an organization-wide approach and attention must be given to broadening and mobilizing support for change by bringing the key stakeholders into line.
- Change practices and interventions are based on economic reasoning to create credible measures of performance, and on behavioural science to realize commitment to change.
- Change practices rely on knowledge about competitive advantage, the structuring of organizations, and developing new skills and capabilities of human resources.
- Learning is primarily a process of change managers reflecting on change experiments, and on the failures and successes of earlier change efforts.
- Knowledge of organizing and changing is obtained by the way in which we operate and capture the results of the use of applied techniques.

**TABLE 21.1** Planned change and OD

| Planned change (Theory E) | OD (Theory O) |
| --- | --- |
| Organizations as adaptive systems to market demands | Organizations as purposeful socio-technical system |
| Human beings as social capital to perform objectives | Human beings as creative and collaborative people |
| Employees motivated by personal advantage | Employees motivated by developing human potential |
| Managers using position power in steering changes | Managers using personal power in mutual collaboration |
| Consultants as knowledge-driven experts | Consultants as process-driven facilitators |
| Organization life as source of shortcomings | Organization life as source of experience |
| Focus on economic measures of performance | Focus on improvement of effectiveness and working life |
| New design of business processes | Improvements based on the existing organization |
| Top-down steering of change process | Utilization of knowledge and insight of personnel |
| Solution-oriented based on value chain | Problem-oriented based on working experiences |
| Episodic change with stable end situation | Continuous improvement |
| Single linear change process | Iterative change process |
| Techno-economical process rationality | Socio-political process rationality |
| Strict norms and planning in change process | Regard for ability to change in emergent change process |
| Start with abstract business models | Start with concrete working experiences |
| Emphasis on expert knowledge | Application of operational knowledge |
| Separation of design and implementation of changes | Smooth transition between phases in change |
| Learning as reflection by change managers | Learning as a collective and ongoing activity |
| Knowledge development by using techniques | Knowledge development by action research |

A key issue for planned or market-induced change is to achieve competitive advantage in a competitive world by organizing work processes around the value chain, developing the skills of human resources, and realizing commitment to change by bringing key stakeholders in line. The values of planned change are rooted in organizational behaviour and economic approaches (see also Buelens & Devos, Chapter 4). Organizational behaviour scholars emphasize that change will not be sustainable if it is not embedded in the development of human resources. The economic approach focuses on shareholders and customers as the most relevant stakeholders, and implies goal congruence in effective, credible, and accessible performance measures presented on a common platform.

It seems that two dramatically different approaches to organizational change are being employed, guided by very different assumptions on organizing, changing, and learning. This observation was also made by Beer and Nohria (2000). They refer to these approaches as Theory E and Theory O (see also Walton & Russell, Chapter 7). The purpose of Theory E is to create economic value. Its focus is on formal structure and systems. It is driven top-down with extensive help from consultants and financial incentives. Change is planned and programmatic (see also Ghoshal & Bartlett, 2000; Jensen, 2000). Theory E is comparable with the design approach described in the Introduction to this book. The purpose of Theory O is the joint optimization of social and technical systems, and the simultaneous development of organizational effectiveness and the quality of working life. It is based on collaboration in the change process of managers and employees facilitated by consultants. Change is emergent, less planned, and programmatic (see also Senge, 2000; Weick, 2000). Theory O is comparable with the development approach contained in the Introduction. The practices and theories in use for both approaches are summarized in Table 21.1.

The question that arises concerns the possibility of using the tension between Theories E and O in organizational change and learning, and minimizing their negative consequences. Mixing the approaches without being aware of the inherent tension between them leads to tensions in the change process itself as well as to negative outcomes for the transparency of the change process and negative results for commitment of those participating in change.

Beer and Nohria (2000) plead for the integration of the theories and approaches to change. They suggest two possibilities. The first possibility is sequencing change strategies, starting with Theory E followed by Theory O. Theory E focuses on rapid, dramatic, and painful changes that may be required to increase economic value, which cannot be achieved through a long-term Theory O strategy. Theory O strategy focuses on building new trust and commitment and the development of human competencies. Switching strategies seems to be difficult because change managers are unable to alter their style and thinking, and find it difficult to change employee opinion that they are ruthless and cannot be trusted. The second possibility is to integrate both theories and keep the tension between the two approaches. This requires simultaneous and equal emphasis on optimizing shareholder value, developing organizational capabilities, and improving the quality of working life. A synthesis requires that change managers mobilize energy for performance improvement, but also that they enable managers throughout the organization to lead a process of innovation and change, and invite employees to participate in the change process.

Another possibility, suggested in the Introduction, is to choose a change strategy based on contingency factors. Planned change seems suitable when the problem is known, not too complex, and a solution is within reach. The approach is mandatory when the organization is in crisis and quick action is required. Planned change also seems more appropriate when no reasonable degree of consensus about the nature of the proposed change can be reached or a sizeable reduction in personnel is expected. OD appears to be more suitable in the case of complex issues for which no evident solution is at hand. OD is preferable when gradual and incremental improvements and innovations can be effected, and value is placed on enhancing the organization's ability to innovate. Marc Buelens and Geert Devos elaborate on this contingency position in this book (Chapter 4). They argue that one of the major problems obstructing the further development of change theories is the desire to develop a general theory that can be applied to all change efforts. In their view, a clear understanding of the specific situation and complexity of organizing and changing is essential when selecting an appropriate change strategy.

## OD, PLANNED CHANGE, AND CONTINUOUS CHANGING

Reflecting on the assumptions of OD and planned change we see fundamental differences in basic values pertaining to organization, human beings, organizational change, and learning. The differences between change practices are quite clear. Nevertheless, there are similarities as well. Both approaches see organizations as an entity, and more or less as a combination of people and resources to be optimized in a structure which is used to take decisions to achieve defined purposes. Both distinguish between organization and environment, agree on the need for adaptation to environmental developments, distinguish between persons and organizations, focus on the organization of work processes and organizational strategy, and distinguish between change agents and employees.

There are other perspectives on organizing, changing, and learning. Luc Hoebeke (Chapter 8) gives another view of organizing when he describes how he, as a practitioner and scientist, was confronted with loosely coupled networks of smaller or bigger groups, with lobbying and manipulation, with the creation of 'facts', with many interpretations and realities, with a plethora of voices, silences, and exits. It seems there is no such thing as an organization as an entity. People working together and relating to each other create processes of organizing, relating, and sense-making. This perspective corresponds with the view of Léon de Caluwé and Hans Vermaak (Chapter 10) when they describe organizations as loosely coupled systems and networks of autonomous centres that interrelate in performing activities and are continually searching for identity in an ambiguous world. André Wierdsma (Chapter 11) calls

**TABLE 21.2**  Continuous changing and constructing realities

| Continuous changing and constructing realities (Theory C) |
| --- |
| Organizing and changing is an ongoing process of inter-activities, sense-making, and self-making |
| Human beings construct organizing and changing as social realities by multiple interaction and sense-making |
| Employees, organizational leaders, and consultants interact and work together in a non-hierarchical manner |
| Changing and organizing are processes of endless modifications in work processes and social realities |
| Changing and organizing are rooted in multiple realities to facilitate ways of relating that are open to new possibilities |
| Changing and organizing become continuous and interrelated processes in which all participants are involved |
| Focus on agreements and modifications based on interweaving activities, interrelations, and sense-making |
| Involvement of all stakeholders as participants in a joint interaction process of creating new realities |
| Searching for new possibilities in a continuous process of transformation and learning |
| Continuous changing with no end state; accumulation of endless small agreements |
| Cyclical process of changing and equilibrium seeking between stability and change: freeze–rebalance–unfreeze–freeze |
| Social constructionist rationality in which relations and realities are constructed as real in their consequences |
| An ongoing process of improvising, sense-making, and agreeing |
| Concrete inter-activities in multiple, local–historical, and social realities |
| Changing is a collaborative approach in which everyone contributes as an expert |
| Inquiring, intervening, and changing stay joined |
| Learning and knowledge development as process of interaction, reflection, and sense-making by all participants |

this transactional organization in which the performance of activities, maintenance of relationships, and creation of meaning are interwoven. From these perspectives, organizations are seen as cultural artifacts where people make choices in dealing with complexities and with each other. By making choices they create a subjective reality. The contribution of Dian Marie Hosking (Chapter 12) gives a critical perspective on organizing, changing, and learning. She distances herself from organization theory and organization psychology that separate the organization from people as a context for individual activities, satisfactions, and inter-group relations. In her view, the relation between person and organization is seen as one of mutual creation: through their interactions people construct an organization as a social reality, which in turn reflects and influences interactions. Language plays a key role in constructing these social realities. To understand processes of organizing and changing, attention is paid to multiple, local–historical, and social realities that are constructed in relational processes and through interaction. These interactions are processes in which realities are constructed, actively maintained, and changed.

When organizing, changing, and learning are seen as interactive processes in which people construct their relationships, activities, and meanings, the basic assumptions and methodologies of organizational change are constructed in a new way (see the chapters in Part III). This way of looking at organizing and changing might be helpful in understanding the tensions between OD and planned change; it provides ways to understand our own bias in dilemmas of organizing and changing, and helps to choose a position between the two sides of these dilemmas. Perhaps it is useful to construct this perspective as Theory C (see Table 21.2).

Changing becomes a continuous process of constructing and reconstructing realities. To illustrate this process of continuous changing, Karl Weick and Robert Quinn (Chapter 9) turn Lewin's three-stage change model of unfreeze–change–refreeze around in an equilibrium-seeking cycle of freeze–rebalance–unfreeze–freeze (see also Cummings, Chapter 1). This cycle is constructed and emerges as the change process unfolds. Freezing makes patterns visible through narratives, metaphors, causal loop diagrams, cognitive maps, and schemes. Rebalancing is a process of reinterpretation, re-labelling, and re-sequencing patterns to reduce blocks and to open new possibilities for interaction and sense-making. Unfreezing resumes improvisation, translation, and learning in ways that are more mindful.

Changing is a continuous activity at local levels where people interact and make sense of their own social reality. On this local level, histories, narratives, practices, and multiple realities may be voiced and contribute to small-scale changes. These small-scale changes can be decisive if they occur at the edge of chaos or in a context of rebalancing and unfreezing. In their chapter, Léon de Caluwé and Hans Vermaak (Chapter 10) relate to chaos theory to understand how large systems become innovative and adaptive systems. Small changes can have large consequences because of self-reinforcing feedback loops and relations in a social network. In interconnected systems, small changes emerge through the diversity and interconnectedness of many micro-conversations (Ford & Ford, 1995). Micro-level changes provide a platform and a context for transformational change at the macro-level.

Continuous changing is a collaborative approach in which everyone contributes as an expert (see Emery, Chapter 2; Levin, Chapter 3; Hosking, Chapter 12). This means that everyone is included who has an involvement in change issues, enabling multiple local realities in different but equal relations. Of course, several roles can be played in this process of interaction, and in attempts to understand how things are really going on here. In processes of interaction, to understand social realities and construct new multiple realities, organizational leaders, employees, consultants, and change agents contribute different knowledge and experiences. Organizational leaders may introduce the voice of shareholders, present their perspectives of global developments, and express their concern about continuity. Employees may express how things are really going on, explain processes of inertia, share their experiences with customers, competitors, and market developments, and express their relationship with colleagues and managers. Consultants and change agents may share their experience with changing and organizing, contribute to reframing current patterns, introduce new language, unblock improvisations, facilitate dialogues, and open up new possibilities. These ways of relating that are not based on hierarchy or expertise make space for sustaining multiple interdependent ways of organizing and changing, and give free play to multiple local realities. Continuous changing is focused on interweaving activities, interrelations, and sense-making. Working with what is valued as being positive invites participants to learn better how to improvise and stimulate the exchange of experiences. Small-scale innovations spread naturally and contribute to large-scale change. Creating new possibilities strengthens a holistic vision of social reality and allows scope for intuiting, improvising, imagination, and the desire for better futures.

Inquiring and intervening stay joined in a continuous process of transformation and reconstruction. Inquiring may articulate multiple narratives and relations, and it supports searching for patterns of inertia, understanding multiple relationships, exploring new ways of carrying on together, and experimenting with new ways of organizing and changing. In this sense, inquiring is a process of deconstructing and constructing social realities and an ongoing process of intervening.

Continuous changing is connected to learning as a collective process. Changing and learning on the level of principles mean that people reorder relationships and activities, and deconstruct and reconstruct meanings together (see Wierdsma, Chapter 11). Learning is seen as a change in routines, response repertoires, and basic assumptions about social realities and interrelations. A range of skills, rules, insights, principles, and knowledge is altered in an interactive process of relating, acting, reflecting, interpreting, and sense-making.

## TEACHING, LEARNING, AND INTERACTIVE LEARNING

This book presents several perspectives on organizational learning. These perspectives are related to the paradigms on organizing and changing as discussed in this book and reflected upon in this chapter. Several authors distinguish between first-, second-, and third-order learning (see the Introduction; Cummings, Chapter 1; Wierdsma, Chapter 11; Smid & Beckett, Chapter 19).

First-order or single-loop learning focuses on changing rules, practices, and competencies. It is a passive internalization of an existing culture in which the learner copies correct behaviour that is readily available in an organizational context. Learning is knowledge acquisition and the application of the rules of action based on an acquired store of knowledge and experience. The acquisition and improvement of skills and competencies are important.

First-order learning is related to the grammar of behaviourism and the cognitive school of thought (see Sauquet, Chapter 17). It corresponds to Model I theories-in-use as described by Chris Argyris (Chapter 18) and the ideas of positional organization presented by André Wierdsma (Chapter 11). This type of learning is congruent with a design principle which Merrelyn Emery calls redundancy of parts, according to which people are seen as parts and human resources (Chapter 2). First-order learning is based on explicit knowledge and connected to embrained and encoded knowledge as described by Alice Lam in her critical reflection (Chapter 20).

First-order learning takes the form of learning by conditioning, learning by imitation, or learning by teaching. Training programmes are provided to impart skills and basic competencies or to change human behaviour. This kind of learning is often visible as a specific phase in planned change programmes which teach employees new competencies, helping them to operate in new contexts. The learners are seen as objects and as human capital, and teachers are the ones who know.

Second-order or double-loop learning focuses on changing rules and insights. It is an active adaptation in finding out how correct solutions can be produced when the context does not provide for copying existing rules of action and known solutions no longer work.

Second-order learning is related to the cognitive school of thought and to pragmatism (see Sauquet, Chapter 17). In the cognitive school, learning is understood to be the proper connection between values, thoughts, actions, and outcomes. Knowledge can be transformed and managed as any other resource, and new routines and insights can be shared with others. It corresponds to Model II theories-in-use (see Argyris, Chapter 18), the design principle of redundancy of functions (see Emery, Chapter 2), and ideas of transactional organization (see Wierdsma, Chapter 11). Second-order learning is connected to embodied knowledge which focuses on practical and individual types of knowledge that is developed through experience and reflection (see Lam, Chapter 20). These perspectives on organization and learning influence learning programmes which have attempted to move beyond conceptual transmission through teaching. Learning is associated with purposeful action and it is close to adaptation as it involves replacing current values and insights by new ones. The learning process is basically individual but it takes place in a social context and affects social organization through the exchange of new insights.

One form of second-order learning based on the cognitive school is problem-solving through experimentation and the exchange of successful practices through the use of knowledge systems. The pragmatic school of thought on learning proposes action learning programmes in which participants confront actual problems in small learning groups with the purpose of solving them and learning at the same time (see also Revans, 1998). Individuals learn to explore different perspectives on problems and issues, and to link their exploration to the development of the organization, their relationships with others, and to reflection on their own insights and assumptions. Experimental learning and action learning are often visible in OD practices. Learners play and explore in a purposeful action to develop their own individual competencies and the competencies of the organization to cope with environmental changes. The role of consultants and trainers is beyond teaching and closer to facilitating learning processes on individual and organizational levels.

Third-order or deutero learning is initiated by interactions in organizational networks and reflections on principles of organizing and changing. Learners question the validity of activities, relationships, and meanings posed by context and interactions. During organizing, changing, and learning, contexts and principles are inquired, deconstructed, and reconstructed. Existing cognitive maps and competencies are destroyed and new competences, activities, relations, and meanings emerge in a process of acting, reflecting, and relating. Knowing and learning exist as engaging with others in a context of organizing and changing.

Third-order learning is connected with some insights of the cognitive and the pragmatic schools of thought on learning, and with principles of situated learning (see Sauquet, Chapter 17). It is related to transformational organization (Wierdsma, Chapter 11), perspectives on organizing as relational construction processes (Hosking, Chapter 12), and to principles of interactive learning presented in the Introduction. The cognitive and pragmatic schools help in our understanding of how cognition and action are interrelated in a process of enactment and how people make sense in confusing and ambiguous contexts (see also Weick, 2001). The school of situated learning suggests that language and symbolic activities may transform principles of organizing and changing. Learning is an interactive process of people acting within social contexts. The social context forms a ground in which ideas, acts, and relations as well as learning contents and learning possibilities are constructed. In this sense, Alice Lam talks about organizational embeddedness of knowledge and learning which shapes and inhibits the learning and transformational capabilities of organizational communities (Chapter 20). The dynamics of participation in organizing, changing, and learning enables participants to acquire knowledge in an interactive process with other participants (see Emery, Chapter 2, and Levin, Chapter 3). Third-order learning is related to embedded knowledge, which is based on shared beliefs and understandings and rooted in communities of practice (see Lam, Chapter 20).

Third-order learning implies that meanings are constructed socially in interaction with others, and in dialogue that makes room for multiple voices and multiple social realities. In these interactive processes people try to make complexities and ambiguities clear by constructing a shared meaning to issues and new possibilities. By exchanging meanings, arguments, and ideas, participants mutually influence each other's perspectives, insights, and principles, which may construct new sets of values on organizing, changing, and learning. In third-order learning, people learn how to learn. This perspective points to the importance of social interaction, contexts, trust for learning, and development of knowledge. Knowledge is seen as being subjective and tacit, not easily codified, and difficult to transmit independent of the subject (see Lam, Chapter 20). This kind of learning and development of knowledge contributes to the accumulation of knowledge on identity formation, community building, and working principles in social realities. Learners, members of organizational communities, and people creating and holding social contexts are subjects in processes of self-making and world-making.

## DYNAMICS OF ORGANIZATIONAL CHANGE AND LEARNING

Undoubtedly, theories and practices of organizational change and learning have become more elaborate, complex, and dynamic during the past decades. At the same time, people in organizations experience many changes in their professional life which are not helpful or successful. In many organizations change projects succeed each other, while the results of these change efforts are dubious. What are the reasons for the dynamics in the world of management and organization? How can we understand the increased interest in questioning existing theories and practices on organizational change and learning?

Of course, the dynamics in organizational change and learning could be explained because of an environment which seems less predictable, more turbulent, and more dynamic. The boundaries between organizations and their surroundings are becoming vaguer as a result of globalization, developments in communication technology, changes in distribution channels, growth in knowledge and exchange of knowledge, building of strategic alliances and networks, increasing interdependence between public and private sectors, and growing concern for good governance. Furthermore, market demands seem to be higher than ever with economic instability, more demands from shareholders, increased competition, and time-based competition.

The dynamics in organizational change and learning may be understood from the internal complexity of organizations. This complexity grew because of the expansion of organizations, the availability of new technologies, more attention for the customer chain, the diversity in cultural background of employees, increased alienation or increased structural tensions, conflicts, and political mechanisms.

The external and internal world of management and organization seem to be less structured, more dynamic, and more ambiguous. But I do not see this as a satisfactory explanation why tensions arise in theories and practices of organizational change and learning. The explanations so far distinguish between organization and environment, and see organizations as an entity separated from change managers. The reasoning goes outside in from the environment to the organization. The reasoning does not take the choices and principles of scholars and practitioners in organizational change and learning into account. It does not reflect on ways in which we construct dynamics in change and learning by ourselves.

To understand the dynamics of organizational change and learning, it is worthwhile to reflect on our own practices and thinking as scholars and practitioners in organizing, changing, and learning. The construction of our own framework has momentous implications for our actions and the choices we make. In my view, the dynamics we experience in theories and practices lie not in the changing environment or changing organizations, but in the conceptual frameworks and assumptions we ourselves use in organizing, changing, and learning. These assumptions lie behind the choice of frameworks, change strategies, and methods. To understand the dynamics of change and learning that we experience, it is useful to examine the ideas and assumptions that lie behind our practices. What does it mean to opt for a specific change approach? What are the implications of this choice? The distinctions we made between planned change (Theory E), OD (Theory O), and continuous changing (Theory C) may be helpful in understanding difficulties we experience in organizing, changing, and learning, and in constructing new realities and possibilities for organizational change and learning.

Perhaps the theory and practice of planned change underestimates value differences, creativity of people, how problem definition and problem-solving are interrelated, and principles of second-order learning. This may result in resistance and avoidance, superficial change, and management based on control and intervention. The theory and practices of OD may underestimate the importance of conflict, institutional control, and how values are embedded in autocratic management and positional organization, resulting in inertia during changing and learning, and failure in reaching sustainable changes. And perhaps theories and practices of continuous changing underestimate economic drives, power and politics, the dominant influence of traditional management practices, and difficulties in the diffusion of knowledge. Does this distinction in theories and practices mean that there is a need to develop an integrated perspective on how to manage change effectively and that we have to break the code of change (Beer & Nohria, 2000)? I don't think so. To avoid an unproductive discussion on effectiveness, and to avoid attempts to smooth over epistemological differences, I argue in favour of making clear differences between approaches that fundamentally differ in underlying values and principles. This can be helpful for scholars and practitioners to reflect on their own assumptions, fascinations, preferences, and values, and to position themselves in the dynamic field of organizing, changing, and learning. The reality of organizing, changing, and learning is a multiple reality full of tensions, conflicts, and dynamics, and we are well advised to use these dynamics in our professional learning and the development of knowledge.

Theories are conceptual narratives with underlying assumptions that provide us with views of the essence of reality, how we can understand reality, and how we can build knowledge to understand and change realities. Every theory has value as well as limitations as arbitrary views of reality. All theories provide us with methodologies that are applicable in specific contexts and of no use in other contexts. Therefore, a deliberate and conscious choice of change methodologies by consultants and change managers needs an extensive body of knowledge, reflection-in-action, and reflecting on the way in which we learn and develop knowledge. Debates between the different approaches and their working principles could attribute to our knowledge and the diffusion of knowledge as well as to the development of new theories on organizational change and learning. We ourselves created the dynamics of organizational change and learning by constructing theories, principles, methodologies, and practices, and by applying them in social realities of organizational life. These dynamics, which we create as practitioners and scholars, open up new perspectives in professional dialogues with all participants active in organizing, changing, and learning.

# INTERVENTIONS AND CHANGE WORK PRACTICES

Many interventions and change works are described in this book, although we do not provide a complete overview. This section gives a comprehensive overview and a reflection on the change methods presented in this book. There are many overviews of intervention methods and several ways to arrange them (e.g., Tichy, 1983; French & Bell, 1998; Schein, 1998; Block, 1999; Cummings & Worley, 2001; de Caluwé & Vermaak, 2002; Kubr, 2003). The arrangement here is on the primary pretext to act, and on a rough fit with assumptions and thought worlds of organizing and changing. The conceptual framework and the aim of the method place limits on relevant and useful methods, shape how methods are understood, and shape how methods are carried out (see Figure 21.1).

## Business Performance

Several methods are proposed to improve business performance. Colin Carnall (Chapter 5) stresses the importance of 'reading' the environment correctly and putting a competitive business model in place. Future searches may contribute to rapid change by building a common data base, discovering the future in diverse perspectives, and creating commitment to action plans (see also Weisbord, 1992; Jacobs, 1994). Colin Carnall advocates that these searches are a process of building credibility and valid measures of performance focused on understanding how well we are doing, and how we compare to competitors. He proposes balanced scorecards, analyses of strengths, weaknesses, opportunities, and threats (SWOT analyses) and the method of benchmarking to collected solid and reliable data

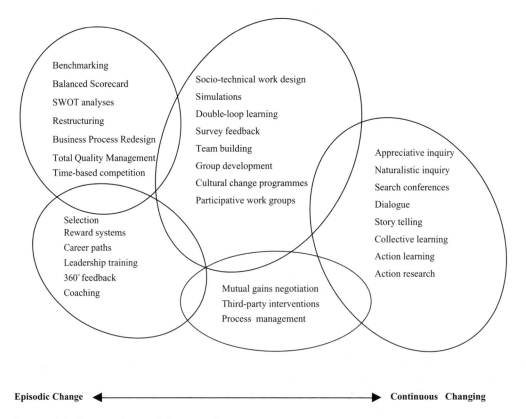

**FIGURE 21.1**  Interventions and change works

on market demands and environmental changes, and to contribute to measurement, accountability, transparency, and access to outcome measures. Benchmarking focuses on a comparison of one's own organization with the best competitors in the world and pays attention to products, product systems, business strategies, and business processes. A project for Business Process Redesign may start from these diagnoses for a breakthrough change and irregular leaps in performance (see Carnall, Chapter 5).

The term 'business process re-engineering' (BPR) is often used when redesigning business strategy, information technology, and organizational processes (Hammer & Champy, 1993). In essence, BPR is a fundamental rearrangement of business processes enabling information technology to realize reduction of costs, increase of profitability, and an enhancement of performance in quality, service, and speed.

Other major change programmes, such as Total Quality Management and time-based competition, may contribute to major changes to improve business performance (see Carnall, Chapter 5). Applications of these major change programmes are widespread in industry and the service sector; nevertheless, their contribution to sustainable performance improvement could be doubted.

The methods for improving business performance are related to the assumptions of planned change. The change manager is a purposeful subject in the role of powerful agent or expert. The organization and employees are objects and the ones who undergo the change.

## STRUCTURING ORGANIZATIONS

Restructuring of organizations could be used to improve business performance, profitability, and competitive advantage. Business Process Redesign is an example. This book proposes other design principles and methods for structuring organizations (see Walton & Russell, Chapter 7). Organizing can be seen as balancing between the dilemma of differentiation and integration. Pressures for differentiation stem from a differentiated environment and market demands, while the need for coordination creates internal pressures for integration. Several organizational structures are suggested for better alignment with their strategy and environment. Thomas Cummings (Chapter 1) refers to borderless organizations and virtual organizations, and Elise Walton and Michael Russell (Chapter 7) refer to matrix organizations, networked organizations, and the strategic enterprise. These suggestions for organizational designs are based on organization theory and the design principles seem to be related to planned change.

Open systems theory recommends organizational design methods based on socio-technical work design (see Emery, Chapter 2). The aim of socio-technical work design is to improve organizational effectiveness, improve the quality of working life, and level power. In contemporary socio-technique, attention is paid to the relation between corporate strategy, organizational structure, the nature of the transformation process, the technology, and the work design. Socio-technical work design is definitely rooted in OD. Participation of workers is a principle and based on values of autonomy, self-regulation, and democracy. Besides this, there is the insight that participation of workers is necessary for creative design. Change agents and workers are participants in this method, who bring in different knowledge and experience. The methods for redesign could be applied in various ways depending on whether assumptions and values for change are rooted in planned change or in OD.

## EMPLOYEE MOTIVATION

Improving employee satisfaction and motivation is suggested in order to contribute to increased flexibility of the organization and business performance (see Carnall, Chapter 5). Many interventions to increase motivation are based on human resources management, and work organization.

Human resources management is traditionally associated with the personnel function in organizations. Based on motivation theories, it is assumed that reward systems can play a powerful role in promoting performance (see Walton & Russell, Chapter 7). This led to interventions aimed at making rewards more contingent on performance. One popular method is the implementation of gain sharing (see Cummings, Chapter 1). In gain sharing, employees are paid a bonus based on measurable gains in performance above some baseline standards. The underlying belief is that people are motivated by external rewards and do things for which they are rewarded. Other human resource interventions are selection and career paths (see Walton & Russell, Chapter 7). One classic idea pertaining to selection is to put the right person in the right place, assessing skills and competencies needed for a specific job. Another idea is that the composition of teams, including the selection of members, is vital to group performance and organizational effectiveness. The introduction of career paths is aimed at developing employee goals, abilities, and skills to fit with the organizational strategy and market demands. It is supposed that career paths may increase the employee's ability to see a meaningful path forward and to feel a valued member of an organization. Interventions based on human resource management fit with the assumptions of planned change. The change manager is an active subject and a behavioural expert, and the employees are objects to be motivated by career paths and other forms of rewards.

OD assumes that new forms of work make work more motivating and fulfilling by improving the quality of one's professional life. Practices in OD of job enrichment and job enlargement resulted in work designs that enhance both productivity and employee satisfaction. The design principles are based on redundancy of functions and expanding jobs horizontally and vertically. The assumption is that improving employee motivation through work redesign may contribute to improved organization performance and reduces absenteeism and turnover (see Cummings, Chapter 1, and Emery, Chapter 2).

## LEADERSHIP AND CULTURE

The development of leadership is paid a lot of attention in behavioural science interventions. Theoretical perspectives on managerial traits and skills lead to a huge training industry for teaching individual managers how to become an effective leader (see Walton & Russell, Chapter 7). Coaching can help in individual learning and development. Individual feedback may help to understand the effects of one's own behaviour on others. Individual feedback can take many forms, such as personal feedback, norm-based assessments, surveys, 360° feedback, or even pencil tests (see Walton & Russell, Chapter 7). The use of personal feedback as a personal development tool is widespread, although it is hard to assess the long-term impact on behavioural and organizational change. The effectiveness of training programmes for managers is debatable. Therefore, other forms of learning are proposed, such as game simulation. Game simulation is an intervention which allows participants to experience first hand the systemic consequences of individual action and how structures influence behaviour (see Walton & Russell, Chapter 7).

Survey feedback is a classic intervention method and has become a major component of company-wide interventions based on OD. It involves systematically collecting survey data about the organization and feeding the data back to members at all levels of the organization so that they can discover sources of problems and devise relevant solutions (see Cummings, Chapter 1). Kilian Bennebroek Gravenhorst and Roeland in 't Veld (Chapter 15) consider survey feedback to be an active process of information acquisition and knowledge dissemination, with the explicit purpose of serving as a basis for action for all organizational members.

Culture has long been a domain for change practitioners. Scholars have prescribed corporate cultures best suited to specific business models and strategies (see Walton & Russell, Chapter 7). Implementation methods based on this idea of 'best cultural fit' are mainly in the form of large-scale training and communication programmes. Based on the values of OD, cultural change is a comprehensive intervention method which combines various intervention methods. In general, the first step is to assess the organizational culture by using survey feedback or by bringing groups together to identify espoused values and underlying assumptions. Various artifacts, theories-of-action, and designs-of-action are investigated. As this process proceeds, the facilitator begins to push for some of the underlying assumptions by noting areas of consistency and inconsistency between espoused theories, actions-in-use, and artifacts. The next step is to identify cultural assumptions that will aid in getting to shared goals, and cultural assumptions that hinder goals being achieved. After this reflective diagnosis, an action plan is developed to determine what steps might be appropriate. The execution of the action plan is monitored by the members themselves with the help of the facilitator. Members of the organization are fully involved in owning both the diagnoses and the interventions (see also Schein, 1992).

The behavioural science interventions described above are rooted in assumptions of OD. The change agent is subject, takes a role as facilitator, and strives for involvement of other actors as participant.

In this book, Chris Argyris (Chapter 18) raises the question as to why so little learning occurs on individual and organizational levels. He believes that we must dig deeper into theories-of-action. The challenge for the intervener is to help individuals transform their espoused theories into theories-in-use by learning new sets of skills and new governing values. This whole process is the essence of double-loop learning. In double-loop learning attention is focused on changing the governing values and master programmes that produced the routines in question. Interventions to facilitate double-loop learning are researching the theory-in-use and the action designs of the client, the use of case studies to get at the theories-in-use and the organizational defensive routines, and the use of cases as an intervention tool in reflecting and redesigning actions (see Argyris, Chapter 18; see also Argyris, 1990).

## GROUP DYNAMICS, CONFLICT, AND PROCESS MANAGEMENT

Group dynamics have a long history in the theory and practice of OD. The earliest intervention methods based on OD principles focused on improving social processes in organizations. Team development is still a robust intervention method. Klaus Doppler (Chapter 6) states that to transform a group into a well-functioning team, it is necessary to create a common goal, mutual interests, and personal commitment.

In teams and organizations, the emergence of conflict is normal. Whenever people work together, different points of view, needs, and interests collide between individuals, in groups, or between groups. Klaus Doppler provides a method for conflict management (Chapter 6). In his view, an understanding of what has happened must be acquired, mistrust has to be broken down step by step, and trust has to be built up again. One important task is to re-establish a situation of direct communication. A neutral third party may be needed to monitor the interactions between parties and to facilitate conflict resolution. In communication, parties can learn about their differences and commonalities. Morten Levin (Chapter 3) describes a method for mutual gains bargaining. The core process elements are making a distinction between positions and interests, identifying conflicting situations, acknowledging the participants' conflicting interests as a natural fact, and designing a creative process in which conflict situations can be addressed, interests are made clear, and participants create new actions that would potentially fulfil their interests. The principles, method, and practice of conflict resolution are meticulously described by Kilan Bennebroek Gravenhorst and Roeland in 't Veld (Chapter 15).

Workshops and task forces are widely used in organizational change (see Levin, Chapter 3). Workshops are used to enable participative processes. Task forces may be used to support a participative change process and give room for collective interaction in line with the general values of OD.

Process management is an intervention method that regulates dynamic decision-making processes in cases of complex problems which need to be solved by a network of actors (see Bennebroek Gravenhorst & in 't Veld, Chapter 15). This intervention applies to situations in which no objective solution is available and tensions exist between the interests of the different parties. It involves different actors who need each other to solve problems while at the same time they pursue their own interests. The general principle is that an acceptable decision can only be developed if all the relevant stakeholders are involved in all the phases of the process, from problem definition to deciding on a solution. Design principles necessary are openness, protection of the core values of stakeholders, continuity and speed, and substance and quality in the solution.

Group dynamics, conflict resolution, and process management are mainly related to the assumptions of OD. The change agent is the facilitator and subject and collaborates with the other agents as subjects in a pluralist world.

## INQUIRING, DIALOGUE, AND NARRATIVE

The view of continuous changing tells us that organizing, changing, and learning are ongoing processes of human interaction and communicating. This is congruent with the idea of appreciative inquiry. Appreciative inquiry is a theory of organizing and changing and a method for changing socially constructed realities (see Walton & Russell, Chapter 7). Working appreciatively means working with what is positively valued and appreciated by people in social realities (see Hosking, Chapter 12). The shift to possibilities, rather than problems, invites participants to learn how better to improvise, and helps participants imagine new ways of proceeding together. In general, the interaction process starts with grounded observation of the 'best of what is'. Through vision, participants jointly articulate 'what might be', ensuring the consent of participants to 'what should be'. Then, experimenting starts with 'what can be' (see Walton & Russell, Chapter 7, and also Cooperrider & Srivastva, 1987). A nice example of appreciative inquiry is described by Luc Hoebeke (Chapter 8).

Searching for new ways and new futures can be stimulated by bringing participants together in a conference, usually for more than one day. A search conference is a joint visioning and planning conference of which the outcome is concrete working plans initiating change activities (see Levin, Chapter 3). The idea is that participants can construct visions of a desired future and a joint understanding of what to do. Guiding principles for designing and facilitating conferences are provided by Kilian Bennebroek Gravenhorst and Roeland in 't Veld (Chapter 15).

Appreciative inquiry and search conferences are related to the theory and method of dialogue. Dialogue encourages people to explore their interactions, their different ideas about reality, and to generate new interactions and ideas by constructing new realities from their interactions and dialogue. A design principle in dialogue is to clarify a set of rules that guides the process and secures participation (see also Gustavsen, 1992). An outside facilitator usually takes on the policing role, while participants take initiatives and control the process. One specific dialogue approach is focused on networks of organizations that try to learn from each other's experiments. Based on shared experiences, and mutual definition of problems or desirable states, experiments are carried out simultaneously within each organization.

Narrative change works have become increasingly popular in recent years. The idea is to work with how people talk with, to, and about one another and construct their wider realities and relations. Narrative inquiry often proceeds through open interviews. The interviewer encourages a conversation of equals by being relationally responsive and leaving room for the other to tell his or her story. Analysing the narratives is an act of deconstruction of the story by searching for dualities, denying the plot, finding the exception, tracing what is between the lines, and other cognitive activities (see Hosking, Chapter 12). Several stories can be brought together for deconstruction by multi-voicing, and reconstructing by making new stories and opening up new possibilities.

## LEARNING AND RESEARCHING IN ACTION

Continuous changing cannot be separated from learning. Second- and third-order learning are related to continuous changing and constructing realties. In this book, two methodologies for organizational learning are elaborated. Gerhard Smid and Ronald Beckett (Chapter 19) explain design principles to create an extended space for learning that enables emerging relationships and creates innovations. A method for collective learning is provided by André Wierdsma (Chapter 11). The method provides a temporary context which offers conditions in which stakeholders can reflect on their relationships, activities, and meanings. This reflection supports dialogue on how the organization of work is constructed, and in which the rules, insights, and principles underlying organizing, changing, and learning can be discussed. Both methods for collective learning are connected to the tradition of action learning. Action learning sees organizing and changing as a continuous learning and transformation process (see Cummings, Chapter 1). Action learning involves interrelated actions that comprise an iterative learning process in which participants learn to reflect on their values in changing, organizing, and learning. Double-loop learning is possible when actors learn how to confront value inconsistencies and conflicts and modify values accordingly. Action learning may involve deutero learning or third-order learning when participants start learning how to learn.

Action research can serve as a methodology for action, changing, and learning. Principles for action research are a collaborative relationship between researchers and actors. Researchers become actors and actors become researchers. They have a mutual responsibility for exploring, interacting, experimenting, and enriching knowledge. Accepting this mutual responsibility does not imply that the parties do not have specific responsibilities and contributions. Researchers have their own specialist knowledge, usually in social science, and in designing and facilitating processes of action research and action learning. Actors have first-hand ecological knowledge of their own social reality and the interaction patterns in which they are involved. In action research, the action researcher may add value by sharing his or her specialist knowledge of organizing and changing, while organizational members are credited with having specialist knowledge of the social reality of organizing and changing in their local contexts. Collaboration means equality in an inter-subjective relationship and working in mutual agreement with the activities in the progression of researching and learning (see Cummings, Chapter 1; Emery, Chapter 2). In the Introduction, a methodology of reflective action research is proposed in which participants act, reflect on their actions, and pay attention to the way in which they learn and generate knowledge.

## ISSUES IN ORGANIZATIONAL CHANGE AND LEARNING

In the previous section, different theories on organizational change and learning were presented based on multiple perspectives presented in this book. This reflective overview may be helpful in reflecting on one's own theories-in-use and choosing and developing one's own methodologies. This section reflects on some issues in organizational change and learning that are discussed in various parts of this book. These issues seem to be main themes and offer possibilities for the development of practices and the construction of knowledge.

### FAILURES AND SUCCESS

There are many explanations for failures in organizational change. The strategic management perspective looks for the cause of failures in problems with implementation, lack of sufficient support, or technical and political factors that hinder the implementation of the strategic policy by those implementing it. The structural perspective suggests that technologies in place and the division of labour are the main reasons for difficulties in realizing effective change. The view of power and politics attributes the failures in organizational change to existing power relationships and agents defending their interests and positions. The cultural perspective seeks the reasons for barriers to change in rules, habits, institutional arrangements, and values within the organization limiting the ability of people to develop alternative behaviours and interaction patterns. The psychological perspective attributes problems encountered in change processes primarily to lack of employee motivation and people's desire for certainty, security, and stability (see also the Introduction). These perspectives seek obstacles for change in the existing organization and the behaviour of people in this organization. Many intervention methods are suggested to overcome these barriers, i.e., interactive policy development, redesigning business processes, breaking politics by using legitimate power, broad cultural training programmes, game simulations, conference methods, large group interventions, reduction of uncertainty through teaching, and good communication concerning the change. Reflecting on these explanations and interventions, we can see how a distinction is made between the organization, people, and the change managers. Aspects of the organization and people in the organization are seen as things that have to be changed as objectives by change managers as knowing subjects. Failures are not explained by the change process itself, the choice of frameworks, the choice of change strategies, the assumptions and behaviour of change agents, and the interactions of people involved in change.

There are also many explanations for failures that reflect on the change process itself. Attention is given to a perspective based on change management practices, a perspective rooted in values and basic assumptions, and an interactive perspective.

The change management perspective proposes that ineffective change management stems from the fact that the environment, the organization, and the change strategy that is chosen do not fit. Marc Buelens and Geert Devos (Chapter 4) present some generic failures in change management, i.e., failing to see that the environment of the organization is changing, choosing and applying an ineffective change strategy, and a one-sided implementation of change strategies. Furthermore, they call for attention to a lack of vision for change, a lack of accepting goal disconguence and value differences, a lack of creativity and poor decision-making, and a lack of understanding the change strategy and the progression of change. The failure of not reading the environment correctly is supported by Colin Carnall (Chapter 5). Other failures he proposes are a one-sided, human behaviourist approach to change, ineffective leadership of change managers, the absence of an integrated approach, and the implementation of change in only one part of the organization. Klaus Doppler (Chapter 6) adds several failures connected to the change manager's actions, namely, lack of clarity as to the reason and purpose for change, top-down steering and control of change managers, not involving those who will be affected, too many change projects at once without a clear necessity, no thought for vested interests, insufficient communication as to the purpose of change, and the continuation in change projects. Kilian Bennebroek Gravenhorst and Roeland in 't Veld (Chapter 15) state that obstacles in change should be understood as being a response to a chosen change strategy by change managers. Change strategies often focus on single issues and on implementing solutions as identified and formulated by change strategists and top managers. In their view, change processes are underestimated or neglected too often.

The perspective focusing on assumptions about change managers suggests that managers use a traditional, positional, or episodic view of organizing and changing. These assumptions influence the purposes of change and how the change processes are managed. Merrelyn Emery (Chapter 2) believes the traditional view of organizing is reflected in the use of a closed system framework, an organizational design principle based on redundancy of parts, and a lack of interaction between subject and object. Klaus Doppler (Chapter 6) refers to old concepts of leaders as heroes, organizations as clear structures with division of functions, personnel as reproducible objects, and planning as a procedure to ensure accountability and steadiness of purpose. André Wierdsma (Chapter 11) explains how the model of positional organization focuses on external control and programmable behaviour with functional and cognitive barriers between managers, professionals in staff departments, and employees. Positional organization assumes that there is consensus on the aims of the organization, that organizational culture is a binding force, and that hierarchal structures contribute to control and clear responsibilities. In these organizations, there is a strong internal focus on stability and change is seen as an episodic implementation process for a new design.

The interaction perspective considers organizing and changing as an ongoing process of interaction, sense-making, and self-making. Failures of organizing, changing, and learning have to be sought in these processes of interaction and sense-making. During interaction and sense-making actors have a certain amount of freedom to interact. At the same time, interaction and sense-making are restricted

**TABLE 21.3** Success factors in organizational change

| Success factors in organizational change |
| --- |

*Principles:*
There is no one best way in organizing and changing
Human beings are motivated by meaningful work
Organization is a process of interaction
Participation of stakeholders in changing contributes to involvement and engagement
Learning is an ongoing process of reflecting and interacting
Knowledge construction is an ongoing process in which every member has a voice

*Insights:*
Concentrate on accelerating diffusion and incorporate practices with positive effect
Realize genuine participation of all people and actors involved in organizing and changing
Design and execute methods with genuine collaboration in active and adapted change
Opt for flexibility rather than mechanistic order in terms of fixed designs or steps
First, concentrate on design of social systems, and, second, on adaptation of technological systems
Create a joint and reflective learning process for all participants involved in organizing and changing
Continually monitor change processes to reflect on the process and the outcomes in order to make
    conscious decisions on how to advance
Deliberate the involvement of outsiders and external stakeholders in organizing and changing
Give strict attention to the horizontal work processes oriented towards clients and customers
Ensure active, multi-sided communication and dialogue

by institutionalized contexts and assumptions that are taken for granted and, as such, are embedded in existing distinctions, technologies, and routines that were constructed in earlier interactions (see also Lam, Chapter 20). It is not unusual that open interactions and dialogue about principles of organization and changing never start because of the dominant values based on positional organizing and Model I reasoning (see Argyris, Chapter 18). Defensive routines may develop during interaction processes in organizing and changing. These routines prevent people from experiencing embarrassment and, at the same time, prevent them from discovering the causes of embarrassment. As a result, there is a growing misunderstanding and mistrust which, in turn, inhibit interacting, changing, and learning. If interactions about these principles do start, people could create contexts at the edge of chaos and may no longer be able to find a new balance in organizing and changing. As a result, conflicts may arise which cannot be overcome, interaction stops, and the process of organizing and changing comes to an end.

Practitioners and scholars looking for failures in organizing and changing may reflect on the different explanations provided above, and ask themselves: 'What did I do wrong, that the other person is behaving so oddly, and that changing and learning are blocked?'

Success in organizational change and learning depends on the purposes or the perceived outcomes of organizing and changing. Assessing success is difficult because different actors might pursue different purposes, start from different value systems, and might give different and conflicting interpretations to the same events and outcomes. Therefore, I choose to reflect on principles, insights, and methods that may contribute to success. Based on the contributions and descriptions in this book, success factors can be identified that contribute to successful organizational change and learning. This is not an easy task, given the different approaches to change. Some success factors we can agree on, others are conflicting. Success factors in this book that we agreed on are listed in Table 21.3. The insights and use of methods are embedded in the values underlying the change approaches described in the previous section. This means that the methods can be applied in very different ways depending on the epistemological framework chosen. The epistemological frameworks contribute to different perspectives and practices in organizational change and learning. Grounded in these differences, there appear to be debates on success factors in organizing and changing.

One ambiguous issue is the importance of taking horizontal work processes and the customer value stream as a point of departure for organizing and changing. From the perspective of planned change and Theory E, this statement is quite obvious. But, from the perspective of OD and continuous changing, there are also reasons to consider this insight carefully. Scholars in OD see the workplace and self-steering groups as the most important units in designing and changing organizations, and these units are related to horizontal work processes. Scholars and practitioners in continuous changing refer to activity systems, work systems, or communities of practice as groups in which interaction, sense-making, and organizing are most profound. This means that groups in the value stream are the most obvious points of action. Besides this, focusing on the value stream proves opportunities for relating the world of customers, suppliers, and competitors with organizing, changing, and learning.

Reflecting on the chapters, in this book we can see opposing views regarding success factors. These opposing views correspond to the values behind the change approaches as discussed earlier. From the perspective of planned change, success factors are:

- Create problem awareness and awareness of the need for change.
- Build a system of credible and valid measurements of performance aimed at understanding how well we are doing as compared to competitors.
- Opt for an organization-wide approach and implement change in the whole organization.
- Get people and departments in the organization in line with the objectives and directions for change.
- Broaden and mobilize support for change, raise commitment and resources.

From the perspective of continuous changing, these insights are doubtful because they suppose an active change agent as the subject who manages other people as object. Second, measurements of performance assume that there is an objective reality that can be measured; the questions are, whose performance criteria are to be measured? and whose purposes are to be ignored? Third, the aim of alignment and commitment ignores differences and conflict, while the expression of differences is perceived as being a contribution to changing and learning from the perspective of continuous changing. Again, it appears that the application of insights and methods is rooted in the values of change approaches.

## POWER AND EMPOWERMENT

For many years, little attention has been paid to the issue of power in theory and the practice of organizational change and learning. And even today, publications on the power issues lag far behind in numbers as compared to publications of empowerment, change strategies, and interventions. OD used to be blamed for the neglect of power and politics (see Bradshaw & Boonstra, Chapter 13) and planned change was criticized because of the implicit use of power by managers and change agents (see Hardy & Clegg, Chapter 16). In Part IV, we turn our attention to power in processes of organizing and changing. Patricia Bradshaw and Jaap Boonstra (Chapter 13) present four perspectives of power from a dynamic view, based on tensions between personal vs collective power, and manifest vs latent power. The four perspectives are related to perspectives on organizational change and change strategies.

The paradigm of personal–manifest power states that power is a force that can be attributed to a person as the potential ability of an agent to influence others. The potential power is grounded in sources of power that can be attributed to specific persons or groups. Cynthia Hardy and Stewart Clegg (Chapter 16) refer to power as domination when only the legitimate position of management is taken into account. This paradigm can be seen in coercive and expert approaches to change. It presumes an active subject using power over other persons (see Hosking, Chapter 12). Power can be used to define objectives for change, control the change process, design new structures with expertise, break through vested interests, align people to change, and realize commitment. This paradigm is especially related to the perspective of planned change whereby top management initiates and steers the change process. This perspective becomes more interactive when attention is given to interpersonal power and the use of power by people or groups in interaction. The chapter by Gary Yukl (Chapter 14) is one example of this interactive perspective.

The paradigm of structural–manifest power attributes power to positions of specific groups in the structure of the organization or to relational networks. In the view of Cynthia Hardy and Stewart Clegg, this kind of power is derived from owning and controlling the means of production and is reinforced by organizational rules, procedures, and structures (see Chapter 16). In many organizations, the distribution of power is characterized by stability. Sometimes this stability is disrupted by conflicting interests and controversies in decision-making. However, some variants of OD are also related when attention is focused on collaboration and solving conflicts, on structural change to realize empowerment, or on alignment of technical, structural, cultural, and political systems.

The paradigm of personal–latent power raises the question of how individuals come to limit themselves in behaving, relating, changing, and learning. Cynthia Hardy and Stewart Clegg pass on disciplinary practices and the formation of dominant ideologies restricting people to develop their identities and activities (Chapter 16). On the other hand, the question is raised as to how individuals can become active agents in empowerment. Based on this paradigm, one can understand how one's own values and beliefs constrain acting and interacting by latent control mechanisms in contexts which are embedded in dominant discourses and internalized by people. The idea of Model I reasoning presented by Chris Argyris (Chapter 18) is partly related to this perspective. This paradigm could be recognized in the perspective of individual learning and deep reflection as approach to change.

The paradigm of cultural–latent power assumes that organizing is a process of interaction and sense-making, creating social realities that are reflected in values, principles, rules, institutions, and dominant discourses. The use of power could be prevented by shaping people's assumptions and values (see also Hardy & Clegg, Chapter 16). This paradigm is connected to OD efforts that strive to achieve commitment, adaptation of a new organizational culture, and a harmonious development of new meaning. In general, these efforts take the existing power relations for granted. When the existing power relations and assumptions of those participating in change are taken into account, the perspective of continuous changing emerges, giving space to dialogue, interaction, deconstructing and reconstructing, organizing, and changing. Non-hierarchical ways of relating can construct power to sustain multiple independent, local ways of proceeding in different but equal relations and can give free play to multiple local realities (see Hosking, Chapter 12). Many of the ideas on changing in Part III and learning in Part V are related to this paradigm, although the issue of power is not always discussed explicitly.

This reflection on power teaches us that organizing and changing inevitably involve power. Ignoring power games may result in excluding voices, ignoring identities, avoiding conflict, denying ambiguity, neglecting the rules of the game, overlooking the roles of different players, and closing space for changing and learning. This may result in conforming existing order and putting aside possibilities for transformational change.

## RESISTANCE AND COMMITMENT

Contrary to the limited awareness of power relations, resistance has been given a lot of attention in theory and practice of organizational change. This seems strange from the perspective that there is no resistance without force (see Hosking, Chapter 12), and from the view that resistance and power comprise a system of power relations in which both domination and liberation are possible (see Hardy & Clegg, Chapter 16).

In their contribution, Kilian Bennebroek Gravenhorst and Roeland in 't Veld give an overview of perceptions on resistance to change (Chapter 15). The traditional perception in management literature states that resistance is illegitimate, dysfunctional, and self-interested behaviour that has to be beaten.

This reasoning implies that if there is resistance, there is a justification for the use of power on the part of managers. In mainstream change literature, resistance is seen as an inevitable and natural behavioural reaction to organizational change. This behaviour has been explained by individual psychological factors such as fear, low motivation, preference for stability, self-distrust, and insecurity. Another more political explanation for resistance is found in the behaviour of people defending their own interests. Resistance may also be perceived as a misunderstanding of the change and its implications, or employees doubting the objectives or feasibility of the change. From this perspective, resistance is seen as an expression of concern that has to be taken seriously. In these explanations, resistance is attributed to people as objects for change, and resistance is seen as a barrier that has to be recognized and responded to in the right way by change agents as purposeful subjects. One of these right ways is to show a sincere interest in the individual situation and personal opinions, and to build trust and an atmosphere in which fragile ideas and emotions can be voiced. Another possibility is active communication between change managers and the people affected to get things in motion as required (see Doppler, Chapter 6).

From an OD approach, resistance is allocated more to ongoing social processes in organizations creating driving and restraining forces that affect change (see Cummings, Chapter 1). The backgrounds for resistance are existing work habits and routines, cultural values developing over time, group thinking in teams, decision-making in organizational strategies, and the application and use of technologies. Driving and restraining forces shape how social processes evolve over time creating a quasi-stationary equilibrium. To change organizations, driving and restraining forces must first be identified. The strengths of these opposing forces can then be decreased or increased to achieve desired change. The underlying assumption is that effective change strategies face less resistance when restraining forces are reduced and driving forces are promoted. If the assumption is made that people are open to purposeful systems that have the potential to look for the ideal, sufficient conditions for motivated actions lie with the people and their interactions with others. Motivation to change can be increased by changing the nature of their interactions and transactions between subject and object (see also Emery, Chapter 2).

Another interactive view on resistance is put forward by Kilian Bennebroek Gravenhorst and Roeland in 't Veld (Chapter 15). They state that change approaches that exclude relevant stakeholders are the main reason for resistance. Resistance is not seen here as an entity of a person or a group, but as a purposeful action of an actor in reaction to an action of another actor. Their explanation of resistance is sought in the traditional top-down management of change processes, and in the exclusion of relevant stakeholders. Resistance is now an indication of bad change management and managers can prevent resistance by choosing a change approach that allows for cooperation and involvement of relevant stakeholders. Interventions to support this change strategy are survey feedback, conference methods, process management, and third-party interventions. This interactive perspective on resistance and commitment is supported by Gary Yukl (Chapter 14). He shows that the use of consultation, collaboration, and inspiration is effective in realizing commitment, while pressure by means of threats and rewards, and legitimating the need and approach for change, are likely to result in compliance or resistance.

The interactive perspective on resistance is revisited by Cynthia Hardy and Stewart Clegg (Chapter 16). They make clear that the strategy of involving different stakeholders is close to a unitary view of management to give meaning to ambiguous situations by giving attention to different points of view, facilitating interactions, consulting people in defining problems and directions for improvement, and inspire people to contribute to change and collaborate in organizing and changing. Undoubtedly, an interactive change strategy and many of the suggested interventions result in commitment for transitional or second-order change, although their contribution to transformational or third-order change is uncertain. This reflection on resistance makes it clear that the underlying values and assumptions on human beings, power, organization, and change shape our ideas about the reasons for resistance and affect the choice of interventions or acts of people involved. The questions remain as to whether we want to bring the content, the rules, and the players of the game under discussion, and to what extent we consider change strategies and interventions to be ethically acceptable.

## PERSUASION AND COMMUNICATING

Many chapters in this book pay attention to communication processes, but the approaches differ. Is communication the vehicle and propellant for change? Is it close to persuasion? Could communication be used by change agents to generate and sustain new conversations that contribute to shared visions and commitment? Is communicating a necessary condition for people to act socially? Or is communicating equivalent to organizing, changing, and learning?

Those who use a conceptual framework of planned change make distinctions between communication, organization, change, and people. To overcome problems in the structure of the organization it is important to have proper communication skills. Communication is helpful in spreading information, coordinating activities, and reducing conflicts in the organization. Proper communication in change programmes reduces uncertainties by informing people, introduces other courses of action by instructing, or contributes to successful change by enlightening and through empowerment. Many 'laws of good communication' are proposed, i.e., communication must be reciprocal, consistent, complete, authentic, based on data and shared goals, and repeated many times. The communicator needs to be credible, aware of the inner state of the addressee, and open to feedback (see Doppler, Chapter 6; Walton & Russell, Chapter 7). These ideas come close to persuasion. The change agent and communicator may use several influences or communication tactics in interaction with others, such as rational persuasion, inspirational appeals, consultation, and apprising. Gary Yukl (Chapter 14) provides guidelines on how to use these communication tactics to influence commitment in change. He discards pressure and legitimating as tactics which are not very successful in realizing commitment for change. Merrelyn Emery (Chapter 2) makes it clear that in organizations based on the design principle of redundancy of parts, relations are not symmetrical and lack the reciprocity of sender and receiver. In these organizations, there is an absence of discussion, a predominance of orders and instruction, and an autocratic style of management with persuasion, pressure, and legitimating as the main communication principles. Cynthia Hardy and Stewart Clegg (Chapter 16) discuss this perspective on communication and change in rational and unitary views on organizing, and criticize the idea that the application of communication strategies by change managers avoids resistance and stimulates change because the underlying value structure of the organization and its members is not changed.

OD scholars and practitioners emphasize participation, dialogue, collective reflection, and knowledge construction as critical processes of organizing and changing. Participation and dialogue create knowledge that is built on the experience of the actors involved, and is distilled through their reflection process (see Emery, Chapter 2; Levin, Chapter 3). Communication is reciprocal and almost equivalent to OD. In search conferences and dialogue conferences people develop a joint understanding of 'what is going on', 'what to do', and 'how to proceed'. The developmental process builds on collective interaction and communication leading to participative learning and experimentation. In these conferences, everybody has a voice and the obligation to judge arguments that are put forward (see also Gustavsen, 1992; Emery, 1999). In participative design workshops, conferences, and large group interventions, new forms of communicating take place when people from different hierarchical levels and units work together in mixed groups, diagnosing the existing situation and developing new futures (see Bennebroek Gravenhorst & in 't Veld, Chapter 15). The communication itself creates change in organizational arrangements and communication patterns, and opens up new possibilities for communicating and organizing. Cynthia Hardy and Stewart Clegg (Chapter 16) relate this perspective of communication to a humanist and unitary view of organizations in which common goals bind people to the organization, and caution us that this kind of communication may result in seductive change strategies and manipulation.

From the conceptual framework of continuous changing, communication constructs meanings which emerge from social interacting in ongoing processes of organizing, and changing. Communicating, organizing, and changing are interrelated. In organizing and changing, meanings that were formed previously may be destroyed and alternative and new meanings may be created. In transactional organizations people perform activities, form relations, create meaning, and construct social realities.

Meanings arise in language. Language is embedded in communities and becomes an interpretative framework for giving meaning to activities (see also Wierdsma, Chapter 11). The use of language in communication constructs social realities, and at the same time language is deconstructed and reconstructed in organizing and changing. Change works enable multiple-voicing, not to increase the likelihood of acceptance or the quality of solutions, but to include multiple local realities, to imagine new ways of going on together, and to construct new realities in organizing and changing (see Hosking, Chapter 12). In this way of thinking, communicating is organizing, changing, and learning.

## ROLES OF CHANGE MANAGERS AND CONSULTANTS

Change managers and consultants can take on different roles in organizational change and learning, namely, powerful change agent, expert, process manager, facilitator, friendly outsider, or active participant.

The role of powerful change agent refers to the existing organizational hierarchy that gives managers the ability to control the organization and the behaviour of others, and to change the organizational structure and processes. This role may be fulfilled by organizational leaders who feel responsible for effective change or by consultants who operate as interim managers. The powerful change agent sets the goals, imposes and declares organizational change, and leads and controls the change programme by using legitimate position power. This power stems from the formal position of the change agent and implies the use of positive and negative sanctions such as rewards, support, coercion, warnings, and threats. In order to employ sanctions, it is necessary to know how the change programme is proceeding and to what extent employees perform the required actions. Therefore, feedback and control systems are widely used. Other power bases could be used besides legitimate power, such as inspiring people and arousing enthusiasm by appealing to aspirations, using relationships to establish coalitions, using knowledge and information to persuade others, apprising others why change is beneficial for them, and legitimating the change by pleading scarcity and threats from the environment (see Yukl, Chapter 14). This role of the powerful and active change agent is related to positional organization (see Wierdsma, Chapter 11) and connects with what Patricia Bradshaw and Jaap Boonstra (Chapter 13) call manifest–personal and manifest–structural power. The approach to change is based on personal–position power. It fits with episodic change in which the role of the change agents is that of prime mover who creates change (see Weick & Quinn, Chapter 9).

The role of expert is connected to particular abilities, skills, and expertise of the change agent. These change agents use expert knowledge to assist groups in the organization in analysing and solving problems. The experts use their analytical and planning skills, and focus on knowledge and results (see de Caluwé & Vermaak, Chapter 10). This role can be carried out by professional staff members or external consultants who take on a role as adviser to management or as project leader. The change manager as organizational expert contributes to change through expertise in specific fields, such as information technology, business strategy, work processes, business design, or employee motivation. Business consultants usually start the change process by business and information analyses based on an economic technological rationality. The change manager as behavioural expert contributes to change by assisting managers with an efficient implementation operation mostly within the perspective and goals as defined by managers. Behavioural knowledge is now used to realize compliance with or commitment to the implementation of changes. In this situation, behavioural science and practice become a form of social engineering. The role of expert is related to manifest–personal power, and an expert-power approach to change (see Bradshaw & Boonstra, Chapter 13). This role is linked to blue-print thinking (see de Caluwé & Vermaak, Chapter 10), and fits in with episodic change in which experts, in collaboration with management, are prime movers and subjects of change.

Process managers depart from a pluralist perspective on organizational change. This view maintains that groups and departments are dependent on each other but on the other hand pursue their own interests (see Hardy & Clegg, Chapter 16). The change model is characterized by conflict management and negotiation and connects with surface–structural power relations (see Bradshaw & Boonstra,

Chapter 13). Process managers focus on preventing conflict in the change process by regulating the participation of groups involved by structuring the decision-making process, facilitating negotiations on the objectives of change and the way the change process is organized and managed. Negotiations are directed at smoothing opposition, tensions, and differences in opinion between parties. The objective is to accomplish agreement that does justice to the interests of all parties involved (see also Bennebroek Gravenhorst & in 't Veld, Chapter 15). The freedom of choice of parties involved needs to be taken into account, as well as the equality of parties, equal changes for alternatives, mutual control over decision-making, the majority of votes, and the preferences of minorities. Managing the process of policy formation and creating support demand certain political skills of the process manager, as well as the ability to operate in complex arenas of interest. Léon de Caluwé and Hans Vermaak relate this role to yellow-print thinking (see Chapter 10).

Facilitating can be conducted in many ways. It can be based in the application of behavioural knowledge and take on a form of management by seduction (see Bradshaw & Boonstra, Chapter 13). In this case, the facilitator is a purposeful subject in change and helps the organization and the employees by striving for commitment, harmonious development of new meaning, and adoption of new attitudes, organizational constellations, and cultural values. Change is implemented gradually and the process allows the participation of all people involved. In the red-print school of thought, the facilitator is there to change soft aspects of an organization, such as management style, competences, and cooperation (see de Caluwé & Vermaak, Chapter 10). This school of thought is focused on motivating the human factor and developing human competencies and talents by applying human resources management techniques and by teaching and training. This facilitating method verges upon episodic change because the change activities carried out by the facilitator stop when new human resources techniques are implemented or culture learning programmes come to an end. In the green-print school of thought, facilitators focus on setting up learning environments. The facilitator supports the development of continuous learning in collective settings and participates in action learning settings and co-creation for change and development (see also Wierdsma, Chapter 11). The contribution of the facilitator lies in the creation and continual monitoring of conditions to facilitate continuous learning processes. The facilitator is the friendly outsider as described by Morten Levin (Chapter 3). Morten Levin states that it is vital for the outsider to introduce a professional conceptualization of the principles of OD as it guides the structuring of change activities, makes the mutual roles of all people involved clear, and helps insiders understand the premises on which transformation is founded. In this kind of facilitating, action research could be used to generate a collective knowledge base, and to shape new relations and interactions. These new relation patterns may support the development of new activities, behaviours, values, and norms. This may help enhance the change and learning abilities of the organization and its members. The role of the facilitator as a friendly outsider is rooted in the paradigm of cultural–latent power (see Bradshaw & Boonstra, Chapter 13). This role of friendly outsider could be associated with continuous changing because the development and learning process is an unlimited sequence of action, reflection on action, mutual understanding, and new action.

The active participant in processes of changing and learning plays a specific role by sharing his or her experience and knowledge of changing and learning in a process of self-organization. The active participant becomes director, actor, and participating observer. The director creates a context in which the participants interact and, by doing this, becomes a player in the game. The participating observer is part of the process, follows the rules of the mutual game, and reflects on the game. The active participant is a friendly outsider and insider at the same time and balances between involvement and distance. The added value of the active participant lies in creating space for dialogue, activating stakeholders, building safe environments, offering scope to experiment, and appreciating positive strengths and capabilities of participants in interacting and self-organizing (see Wierdsma, Chapter 11). The importance of dialogue in changing and learning is underlined by Schein (1994). Genuine dialogue provides possibilities for exchanging ideas and cross-influencing attitudes and opinions of each other in a process of interacting. Such a process allows the development of new interaction patterns, multiple but shared sets of norms and values, and shared knowledge and language to understand events that occur in the change process. The role of active participant in changing and learning is connected to white-print thinking (see de Caluwé & Vermaak, Chapter 10). Activities in this white-print thinking are observing what it is that makes things happen and changing, recognizing, and removing obstacles, clearing perspectives, supplying meanings, getting initiatives started, recognizing emergent activities, and making space for exploring and experimenting. These activities are related to continuous changing (see Weick & Quinn, Chapter 9).

## DELIBERATE AND CONSCIOUS ACTION

Based on the theories and practices presented in this book, several issues were described, and roles of change agents were distinguished. In practice, it is difficult to draw a sharp distinction between the roles of change agents. Some roles seem quite akin to management, like the powerful change agent, the process manager, or the project manager. Management literature includes behavioural expertise in change management. Theories and practices in organizational change take up an important position in MBA courses and training programmes for managers. This means that behavioural knowledge is included in the body of knowledge of management, and managers now perform activities that consultants usually used to perform (see also Walton & Russell, Chapter 7). The roles of consultants are not strictly defined either. Consultants may become temporary managers, interim managers, or project managers with delegated legitimate power and a clear position in the hierarchy. The role distinction between managers and consultants may blur when consultants practise collaborative consultation. The autonomy and credibility of consultants may come under pressure when they adopt unquestioningly the problem definitions and goal orientation of top management. Many experiences and techniques in organizational change have been standardized in models, products, and prescriptive rules. Applying these models, products, and rules turns the consultancy firm into a service factory and the applying consultant into a service provider who uses instruments, rather than an actor in changing and learning who uses methods by design. In any case, in practice, change agents and consultants will overlap several roles. What is the benefit of distinguishing the roles as described above? The first reason is that it may help to define one's own roles in change works. The second reason is that it provides the possibility of combining roles more consciously and deliberately. But most importantly, it creates a reflective framework for looking at and choosing one's own position in the epistemology and methodology of organizational change and learning.

Questions that arise are: What is my position in relation to top management? What is my relationship with different actors? Do I see change as an episodic change programme or as continuous changing and learning? What knowledge and added value do I have to offer? Do I work with standardized models and do I see change as an organized tour, or is changing similar to hiking, searching, and discovering? What does organization mean? How do I define people in change? How do I view power and resistance? What does communication mean to me? Who is subject and who is object in change, or are we all purposeful subjects in changing and learning? The answers to these questions reflect assumptions, and these assumptions lie behind the choice of conceptual framework and change strategies, intervention methods, and change works that ensue from that choice. Virtually every intervention method and all change works could be applied in many ways, depending on thought worlds and assumptions. Examining one's own assumptions enables one to enter into the practice of intervention methods and change works without making intervention rules and tools to convert an object, but creating a professional and personal change methodology.

## QUESTIONS AND POSSIBILITIES IN ORGANIZATIONAL CHANGE AND LEARNING

The multiple perspectives presented in this book help to reflect on change works and may prove helpful in understanding complexity and dynamics in organizational change and learning. Such multiple

**TABLE 21.4** Professional questions in organizational change and learning

| Professional questions in organizational change and learning |
| --- |
| Why am I working in organizational change and learning? |
| To what purpose am I working on changing and learning? |
| How do I perceive human beings and define people in change? |
| What are my assumptions as to organization, change, and learning? |
| What kind of paradoxes and dilemmas do I experience in change works and how do I work with them? |
| What is my definition of failure and success in organizational change? |
| What is my own theoretical framework and what does it mean to me and others I am working with? |
| When is change episodic for me and others and when is it more continuous? |
| How do I relate myself to the different thought worlds of changing? |
| What are the principles that guide my choices and actions? |
| Who is subject and who is object in my change works, or are we all purposeful subjects? |
| What is my position in relation to top management? |
| What are my relations with people involved in changing and learning? |
| How do I work with participation in changing and learning? |
| What are my preferences regarding roles for change managers and consultants? |
| How do I view power and resistance in organizing and changing? |
| What is the power I have and will use myself, and what are the ethical values that guide my choices? |
| What does interaction and communication mean for me in organizing, changing, and learning? |
| Why do I choose some intervention methods more often than others? |
| How do I choose specific intervention methods and change works? |
| What are my assumptions as to the efficacy of specific interventions in context? |
| What knowledge and added value to professionalism do I have to offer? |
| Why should I contribute to the development of knowledge in organizing, changing, and learning? |
| How could I contribute to sharing insights and knowledge with participants, practitioners, and scholars? |

perspectives provide new possibilities in organizing and changing, and can be helpful in choosing a position from among multiple paradigms and dilemmas of organizing, changing, and learning. This final section begins with reflections on professional, epistemological, and research questions. This chapter concludes with possibilities for change works in organizing, changing, and learning.

## PROFESSIONAL QUESTIONS

Professionals in organizing, changing, and learning work in fields full of paradoxes, thought worlds, and arenas of actors with multiple ideas of what is going on. Hence, it is important to be able to make conscious decisions in these paradoxes, thought worlds, and arenas in order to contribute to organizational change and learning, and to create a participative collective reflection process. This conscious and informed decision-making may help to develop and explain one's own methodologies in interaction with others. Mixing change approaches without being aware of the inherent tension between them leads to tensions and less transparency in change processes themselves. It is useful to make the values underlying the professional choices explicit and a subject of discussion in order to be accountable to participants and other professionals and to contribute to collective learning.

The conceptual distinctions we made between planned change (Theory E), OD (Theory O), and continuous changing (Theory C) invite one to reflect on one's own assumptions and points of departure. They may help in choosing a position and constructing one's own frameworks for action and interaction. Reflective questions for professionals in organizational change and learning are summarized in Table 21.4.

Reflecting on these questions may help in the search for one's own professional assumptions, principles, and insights. Answers to these questions reflect assumptions, and these assumptions underlie choices of conceptual frameworks, change strategies, intervention methods, and change works ensuing

**TABLE 21.5** Some research issues in organizing, changing, and learning

Some research issues in organizing, changing, and learning

Basic assumptions of planned change, the background for the dominant logic of this change approach in management and business schools, and the way this approach is related to the design principle of redundancy of parts and Model I reasoning.

Institutional embeddedness of business schools and consultancy firms, and the meaning of this embeddedness on espoused theories and theories-in-use in organizing, changing, and learning.

Relationship between organizational and institutional embeddedness, management education, action learning, action science, and practices of organizational change and learning.

The working principles in practices of OD and the development of new insights, methods, and principles to contribute to organizational change and learning.

The underlying principles and the dynamics in choosing change strategies with respect to contexts, assumptions, perceived problems, ambitions, and people involved in interaction.

Tensions, energies, interactions, and dynamics in continuous changing, and inertia in continuous changing from dynamic systems theory, chaos theory, and social constructionism.

Investigating failures and successes in organizational change and learning, and searching the principles and change approaches behind the effectiveness of change efforts.

Working principles in intervention methods and change works and their efficacy in organizational change and learning.

Roles taken by change managers and consultants, the process of choosing roles, and the interactions and dynamics that flow from these choices.

Paradoxes and dilemmas in organizational change and learning, and the art of choosing and holding balance in these dilemmas.

Dynamics of the dilemma between faith and ethics in organizing, and the meaning of this dilemma for change managers, practitioners, scholars, and scientists.

Dynamics of power and politics in organizational change and learning, and the willingness to exchange power positions and come to dialogue in order to create new possibilities for organizing, changing, and learning.

Sources and dynamics of defence mechanisms in organizational change and learning from a multidisciplinary perspective, and the development of methods of visualizing, vocalizing, and overcoming these defences.

Principles for designing learning support for people in contexts of continuous changing, and reflection on the efficacy of these design principles.

Ways in which people learn and act in ambiguous and conflicting situations by collective reflection on contexts, their actions, and their assumptions concerning social reality.

Principles and dynamics in processes of constructing, deconstructing, and reconstructing during interaction between people in organizing, changing, and learning

Development of communities of practice and their role in developing and sharing knowledge in organizing, changing, and learning.

Possibilities of bringing principles and basic assumptions of organizational change and learning into dialogue in theory and practice, and of finding new ways to work with multiple perspectives in development of practices, theories, and meta-theories.

---

from that choice. Interacting with others on these assumptions, principles and insights may result in second- and third-order learning, and in positive contributions to our professional knowledge.

## RESEARCH QUESTIONS

This book gives an idea of dynamics in organizational change and learning. It elaborates on various theoretical perspectives, practical implications, methods, and critical reflections. It reflects on basic assumptions and values in changing and learning which guide our actions as practitioners. Many new questions emerge from the chapters in this book. Some issues could be given dedicated attention in research activities and knowledge development during processes of organizing, changing, and learning. A proposal for some research issues is made in Table 21.5.

## POSSIBILITIES IN CHANGE WORKS AND KNOWLEDGE DEVELOPMENT

The social reality of organizing, changing, and learning is rather dynamic. It is a world of people inter-acting, practising, experimenting, and exploring. How can we get to know this social reality and develop new insights and knowledge? Possibilities for developments in the field of organizational change and learning have been presented in this book by academics, practitioners, scholars, and consultants. Based on the chapters in this book, this final chapter provides many possibilities for personal reflections, research activities, and knowledge development. Three more issues are added. First, new arrange-ments emerging between organizations require further development of inter-organizational analyses and change works. Collaboration between organizations provides possibilities for inter-organizational learning in organizing and changing. Collaboration often depends on trusting relationships. This raises the question as to how trust can be conceptualized and created as a communicative sense-making process. Another question might be how inter-organizational relationships affect the change of insti-tutional fields, and how strategies of power are involved in these changes (see also Hardy & Clegg, 1996). Second, the perspective on language and communicating in organizational change and learning provides possibilities for change works with narratives, metaphors, story-telling, dialoguing, sense-making, and identity formation. This is still an under-developed field which seems to be very promising in a world in which people interact with each other to make sense out of ambiguous contexts. Conver-sation is inter-subjective, shared, and embedded within local practices. Therefore, postmodern theories and insights through social constructionism may be helpful in jointly developing new knowledge and practices in change works. Third, the development of new methodologies in action research reveals an emergent interactive social reality and a participative world-view (see also Reason & Bradbury, 2001). This raises questions concerning epistemologies of the various action research methodologies in practice, such as participative inquiry, appreciative inquiry, collaborative inquiry, democratic dia-logue, and other large group processes, narratives, and critical change works. Related questions are how to integrate knowledge and action, and how to present new insights and knowledge which are grounded locally.

By sharing insights and knowledge, the authors of this book have provided a multiple perspective and given a topical representation of theories, implications, methods, and critical reflections. Together we have tried to give a better insight into dynamics of organizing, changing, and learning. We provided possibilities for collaborative action between practitioners, academics, and participants in organiza-tional change and learning. By doing this we opened up possibilities for practitioners, scholars, and scientists to reflect on their own assumptions and theories-in-use, and we invite you to develop your own methodologies and make your own contributions to organizing, changing, and learning.

## REFERENCES

Argyris, C. (1990) *Overcoming Organizational Defences: Facilitating Organizational Learning*. Boston: Allyn & Bacon.

Beer, M. & Nohria, N. (2000) Resolving the tension between Theories E and O of change. In M. Beer & N. Nohria (eds) *Breaking the Code of Change* (pp. 1–33). Boston: Harvard Business School Press.

Beer, M. & Walton, A.E. (1987) Organization change and development. *Annual Review of Psychology*, **38**, 339–367.

Block, P. (1999) *Flawless Consulting: A Guide to Getting your Experience Used* (2nd edn). San Francisco: Jossey-Bass.

Boonstra, J.J. & Gravenhorst, K.M. (1998) Power dynamics and organizational change: a comparison of perspectives. *European Journal of Work and Organizational Psychology*, **7**(2), 97–102.

Boonstra, J.J. & Vink, M.J. (1996) Technological and organizational innovation: a dilemma of fundamental change and participation. *European Journal of Work and Organizational Psychology*, **5**(3), 351–376.

Cooperrider, D. & Srivastva, S. (1987) Appreciative inquiry into organizational life. *Research into Organizational Change and Development*, **1**, 129–169.

Cummings, T.G. & Worley, C.G. (2001) *Organization Development and Change* (7th edn). Cincinnati, OH: South-Western College Publishing.

De Caluwé, L. & Vermaak, H. (2002) *Learning to Change: A Guide for the Organizational Change Agent*. Thousand Oaks, CA: Sage.

Emery, M. (1999) *Searching: The Theory and Practice of Making Cultural Change*. Amsterdam: John Benjamins.

Ford, J.D. & Ford, L.W. (1995) The role of conversations in producing intentional change in organizations. *Academy of Management Review*, **19**, 756–785.

French, W.L. & Bell, C.H. (1998) *Organization Development: Behavioural Science Interventions for Organizational Improvement* (6th edn). Englewood Cliffs, NJ: Prentice Hall.

Ghoshal, S. & Bartlett, C.A. (2000) Rebuilding behavioural context: a blueprint for corporate renewal. In M. Beer & N. Nohria (eds) *Breaking the Code of Change* (pp. 195–221). Boston: Harvard Business School Press.

Gustavsen, B. (1992) *Dialogue and Development: Theory of Communication, Action Research and the Restructuring of Working Life*. Assen: Van Gorcum.

Hammer, M. & Champy, J. (1993) *Reengineering the Corporation: A Manifesto for Business Revolution*. New York: Harper & Row.

Hardy, C. & Clegg, S. (1996) Some dare call it power. In S. Clegg, C. Hardy & W. Nord (eds) *Handbook of Organization Studies* (pp. 621–641). London: Sage.

Harrison, B.D. & Pratt, M.D. (1993) Reengineering business processes. *Planning Review*, **9**(2), 53–61.

Jacobs, R.W. (1994) *Real Time Strategic Change: How to Involve an Entire Organization in Fast and Far-reaching Change*. San Francisco: Berrett-Koehler.

Jensen, M.C. (2000) Value maximization and the corporate objective function. In M. Beer & N. Nohria (eds) *Breaking the Code of Change* (pp. 37–57). Boston: Harvard Business School Press.

Katzenbach, J.R. & Smiths, D.K. (1993) *The Wisdom of Teams: Creating the High Performance Organization*. Boston: Harvard Business School Press.

Kottler, J.P. (1988) *The Leadership Factor*. New York: The Free Press.

Kottler, J.P. (1996) *Leading Change*. Boston: Harvard Business School Press.

Kubr, M. (2003) *Management Consulting: A Guide to the Profession* (4th edn). Geneva: International Labour Office.

Mohrman, S.A. & Cummings, T.G. (1989) *Self-Designing Organizations: Learning how to Create High Performance*. Reading, MA: Addison-Wesley.

Reason, P. & Bradbury, H. (2001) *Handbook of Action Research*. London: Sage.

Revans, R. (1998) *The ABC of Action Learning*. London: Lemos & Crane.

Schein, E.H. (1992) *Organizational Culture and Leadership* (2nd edn). San Francisco: Jossey-Bass.

Schein, E.H. (1994) On dialogue, culture, and organizational learning. *Organizational Dynamics*, **22**, 40–51.

Schein, E.H. (1998) *Process Consultation Revisited: Building the Helping Relationship*. Reading, MA: Addison-Wesley.

Senge, P.M. (1990) *The Fifth Discipline: The Art and Practice of the Learning Organization*. New York: Doubleday/Currency.

Senge, P.M. (2000) The puzzles and paradoxes of how living companies create wealth: why single-value objective functions are not enough. In M. Beer & N. Nohria (eds) *Breaking the Code of Change* (pp. 54–81). Boston: Harvard Business School Press.

Tichy, N.M. (1983) *Managing Strategic Change: Technical, Political and Cultural Dynamics*. Chichester: John Wiley & Sons, Ltd.

Weick, K.E. (2000) Emergent change as a universal in organizations. In M. Beer & N. Nohria (eds) *Breaking the Code of Change* (pp. 223–241). Boston: Harvard Business School Press.

Weick, K.E. (2001). *Making Sense of the Organization*. Oxford: Blackwell.

Weisbord, M.R. (1992) *Discovering Common Ground: How Future Search Conferences Bring People Together to Achieve Breakthrough, Innovation, Empowerment, Shared Vision and Collaborative Action*. San Francisco: Berrett-Koehler.

# Index